ISBN: 0-9769118-0-9

The type in this book is the property of
St Athanasius Press and except for brief
excerpts, may not be reproduced in whole
or in part without permission in writing
from the publisher.

Printed and Bound in the United States of America.

Published by:
St Athanasius Press
133 Slazing Rd
Potosi, WI 53820
1-800-230-1025
http://www.stathanasiuspress.com

Distributed by:
Mel Waller
St Joan of Arc Books
133 Slazing Rd
Potosi, WI 53820
1-800-230-1025
Wallmell@aol.com
http://www.stjoanofarcbooks.com
Our online bookstore specializing in pre-1964
used and new Catholic books or reprints thereof.

Check out our other titles on last page of book!

THE HISTORY OF HERESIES,

AND

THEIR REFUTATION;

OR,

THE TRIUMPH OF THE CHURCH.

TRANSLATED FROM THE ITALIAN OF

ST. ALPHONSUS M. LIGUORI.

BY THE RIGHT REV. DR. MULLOCK,

Bishop of Newfoundland.

SECOND EDITION.

DUBLIN:
PUBLISHED BY JAMES DUFFY,
7, WELLINGTON-QUAY.
1857.

Dublin:
PRINTED BY J. M. O'TOOLE,
13, Hawkins'-street

TRANSLATOR'S PREFACE.

THE ardent wish manifested by the Faithful for an acquaintance with the valuable writings of ST. LIGUORI, induced me to undertake the Translation of his History of Heresies, one of his greatest works. The Holy Author was induced to write this work, to meet the numbers of infidel publications with which Europe was deluged in the latter half of the last century. Men's minds were then totally unsettled; dazzled by the glare of a false philosophy, they turned away from the light of the Gospel. The heart of the Saint was filled with sorrow, and he laboured to avert the scourge he saw impending over the unfaithful people. He implored the Ministers of his Sovereign to put the laws in force, preventing the introduction of irreligious publications into the Kingdom of Naples; and he published this work, among others, to prove, as he says, that the Holy Catholic Church is the only true one—the Mistress of Truth—the Church, founded by Jesus Christ himself, which would last till the end of time, notwithstanding the persecutions of the infidel, and the rebellion of her own heretical children. He dedicates the book to the Marquis Tanucci, the Prime Minister of the Kingdom, whom he praises for his zeal for religion, and his vigorous execution of the laws against the venders of infidel publications. He brings down the History from the days of the Apostles to his own time, concluding with the refutation of the Heresies of Father Berruyer. I have added a Supplementary Chapter, giving a succinct account of the Heretics and Fanatics of the last eighty years. It was, at first, my intention to make it more diffuse; but, then, I considered that it would be out of proportion with the remainder of the work. This book may be safely consulted as a work of reference: the Author constantly quotes his authorities; and the student of Ecclesiastical History can at once compare his statements with the sources from which he draws. In the latter portion of the work, and especially in that portion of it the most interesting to us, the History of the English Reformation, the student may perceive some slight variations between the original text and my translation. I have collated the work with the writings of modern historians—the English portion, especially, with Hume and Lingard—and wherever I have seen the statements of the Holy Author not borne out by the authority of our own historians, I have considered it more prudent to state the facts, as they really took place; for our own writers must naturally be supposed to be better acquainted with our history, than the foreign authorities quoted by the Saint. The reader will also find the circumstances, and the names of the actors, when I considered it necessary, frequently given more in detail than in the original.

In the style, I have endeavoured, as closely as the genius of our language would allow, to keep to the original. ST. ALPHONSUS never sought for ornament; a clear, lucid statement of facts is what he aimed at; there is nothing inflated in his writings; he wrote for the people; and that is the principal reason, I imagine, why not only his Devotional works, but his Historical and Theological writings, also, have been in such request: but, while he wrote for the people, we are not to imagine that he did not also please the learned. His mind was richly stored with various knowledge; he was one of the first Jurists of his day; his Theological science elicited the express approbation of the greatest Theologian of his age—Benedict XIV.; he was not only a perfect master of his own beautiful language, but profoundly read in both Greek and Latin literature also, and a long life constantly employed in studies, chiefly ecclesiastical, qualified him, above any man of his time, to become an Ecclesiastical Historian, which no one should attempt unless he be a general—I might almost say a universal, scholar: so much for the Historical portion of the work.

In the Second Part, the Refutation of Heresies, the Holy Author comprises, in a small space, a vast amount of Theological information; in fact, there is no Heresy which cannot be refuted from it. Not alone are the usual Heresies, which we have daily to combat—such as those opposed to the Real Presence, the Authority of the Church, the doctrine of Justification, clearly and diffusely refuted, but those abstruse heretical opinions concerning Grace, Free Will, the Procession of the Holy Ghost, the Mystery of the Incarnation, and the two Natures of Christ, and soforth, are also clearly and copiously confuted; the intricacies of Pelagianism, Calvinism, and Jansenism, are unravelled, and the true Doctrine of the Church triumphantly vindicated. The reader will find, in general, the quotations from the Fathers in the original, but those unacquainted with Latin will easily learn their sentiments from the text. The Scripture quotations are from the Douay version.

Every Theologian will be aware of the difficulty of giving scholastic terms in an English dress. In the language of the Schools, the most abstract ideas, which would require a sentence to explain them in our tongue, are most appropriately expressed by a single word ; all the Romance languages, daughters of the Latin, have very nearly the same facility; but our Northern tongue has not, I imagine, flexibility enough for the purpose. I have, however, endeavoured, as far as I could, to preserve the very terms of the original, knowing how easy it is to give a heteredox sense to a passage, by even the most trivial deviation from the very expression of the writer. The Theological Student will thus, I hope, find the work a compact Manual of Polemic Theology ; the Catholic who, while he firmly believes all that the Church teaches, wishes to be able to give an account of the faith that is in him, will here find it explained and defended; while those not of the "fold," but for whom we ardently pray, that they may hear the voice of the "one Shepherd," may see, by its attentive perusal, that they inhabit a house "built upon the sand," and not the house "on the rock." They will behold the mighty tree of Faith, sprung from the grain of mustard-seed planted by our Redeemer, always flourishing, always extending, neither uprooted by the storms of persecution, nor withered by the sun of worldly prosperity. Nay more, the very persecution the Church of God has suffered, and is daily enduring, only extends it more and more; the Faithful, persecuted in "one city," fly elsewhere, bearing with them the treasure of Faith, and communicating it to those among whom they settle, as the seeds of fertility are frequently borne on the wings of the tempest to the remote desert, which would otherwise be cursed with perpetual barrenness. The persecution of the Church in Ireland, for example, "has turned the desert into fruitfulness," in America, in Australia, in England itself, and the grey mouldering ruins of our fanes on the hill sides are compensated for by the Cathedral Churches across the ocean. The reader will see Heresy in every age, from the days of the Apostles themselves down to our own time, rising up, and vanishing after a while, but the Church of God is always the same, her Chief Pastors speaking with the same authority, and teaching the same doctrine to the trembling Neophites in the Catacombs, and to the Cæsars on the throne of the world. Empires are broken into fragments and perish—nations die away, and are only known to the historian—languages spoken by millions disappear—everything that is man's work dies like man; heresies, like the rest, have their rise, their progress, their decay, but Faith alone is eternal and unchangeable, " yesterday, to-day, and the same for ever."

CONTENTS.

WITH REFERENCES TO THE MARGINAL NUMBERS IN EACH CHAPTER

PAGE.

CHAPTER I.

Heresies of the First Century, ... 33

    1. Simon Magus. 2. Menander. 3. Cerinthus. 4. Ebion. 5. Saturninus and Basilides. 6. The Nicholites.

CHAPTER II.

Heresies of the Second Century, ... 37

    1. Corpocrates. 2. Valentine. 3. Epiphanes. 4. Prodicus. 5. Tatian. 6. Severus. 7. Cerdonius. 8. Marcion. 9. Apelles. 10. Montanus. 11. Cataphrigians, Artotirites, Peputians, Ascodrogites, Pattalorinchites. 12. Bardesanes. 13. Theodotus the Currier, Artemon, and Theodotus Argentarius. 14. Hermogenes.

CHAPTER III.

Heresies of the Third Century, ... 42

    1. Praxeas. 2. Sabellius. 3. Paul of Samosata. 4. Manes. 5. Tertullian. 6. Origen. 7. Novatus and Novatian. 8. Nepos—The Angelicals and the Apostolicals.

CHAPTER IV.

Heresies of the Fourth Century, ... 50

ARTICLE I.—Schism and Heresy of the Donatists.

    1, 2. Schism. 3. Heresy. 4, 5. Confutation of St. Augustin. Circumcellionists. Conference commanded by Honorius. 7. Death of St. Marcellinus, and Council of Carthage.

ARTICLE II.—The Arian Heresy, ... 55

§ I.—Progress of Arius, and his Condemnation by the Council of Nice.

    8. Origin of Arius. 9. His Errors and Supporters. 10. Synod of Bythinia. 11. Synod of Osius in Alexandria. 12. General Council of Nice. 13. Condemnation of Arius. 14-16. Profession of Faith. 17. Exile of Eusebius of Nicomedia, and insidious Letter of Eusebius of Cesarea. 18. Banishment of Arius. 19. Decree for the Meletians. 20. Decree for the Quartodecimans. 21. Canons. 22. End of the Council.

CONTENTS.

§ II.—Occurrences up to the Death of Constantine, . . . 64

23. St. Athanasius is made Bishop of Alexandria; Eusebius is recalled; St. Eustasius exiled, and Arius again taken into Favour. 24. Council of Tyre. 25. St. Athanasius accused and exiled. 26. Arius banished from Alexandria. 27. His Perjury and horrible Death. 28. Constantine's Baptism and Death; Division of the Empire.

§ III.—The Emperor Constantius persecutes the Catholics, . . 71

30. Eusebius of Nicomedia is translated to the See of Constantinople; Synods in Alexandria and Antioch. 31. Council of Sardis. 32. Council of Arles. 33. Council of Milan and Exile of Liberius. 34. Exile of Osius. 35. Fall of Osius. 36. Fall of Liberius. 37. First Formula of Sirmium. 38. Second Formula of Sirmium. 39. Third Formula of Sirmium. 40. Liberius signs the Formula, &c. 41, 42. He signs the First Formula. 43. Return of Liberius to Rome, and Death of Felix. 44. Division among the Arians. 45-48. Council of Rimini. 49. Death of Constantius. 50. The Empire descends to Julian. The Schism of Lucifer.

§ IV.—Persecution of Valens, of Genseric, of Hunneric, and other Arian Kings, ... 83

51. Julian is made Emperor, and dies. 52. Jovian Emperor; his Death. 53. Valentinian and Valens Emperors. 54. Death of Liberius. 55, 56. Valens puts eighty Ecclesiastics to Death—his other Cruelties. 57. Lucius persecutes the Solitaries. 58. Dreadful Death of Valens. 59-61. Persecution of Genseric. 62-64. Persecution of Hunneric. 65. Persecution of Theodoric. 67, 68. Persecution of Leovigild.

ARTICLE III. 95

69-74. Heresy of Macedonius. 75-77. Of Apollinares. 78. Of Elvidius. 79. Of Aetius. 80, 81. The Messalians. 82. The Priscillianists. 83. Jovinians. 84. Other Heretics. 85. Of Audæus, in particular.

CHAPTER V.

Heresies of the Fifth Century, ... 104

ARTICLE I.—The Heresies of Elvidius, Jovinianus, and Vigilantius.

1. Heresy of Elvidius. 2. Errors of Jovinian. 3. Adverse Opinions of Basnage refuted. 4. Vigilantius and his Errors.

ARTICLE II.—On the Heresy of Pelagius, ... 109

5. Origin of the Heresy of Pelagius. 6. His Errors and Subterfuges. 7. Celestius and his Condemnation. 8. Perversity of Pelagius. 9. Council of Diospolis. 10, 11. He is condemned by St. Innocent, Pope. 12. Again condemned by Sozymus. 13. Julian, a Follower of Pelagius. 14. Semi-Pelagians. 15. Predestination. 16-19. Godeschalcus.

ARTICLE III.—The Nestorian Heresy, ... 119

20. Errors of Nestorius, and his Elevation to the Episcopacy. 21. He approves of the Errors preached by his Priest, Anastasius; his Cruelty. 22. He is contradicted, and other Acts of Cruelty. 23. St. Cyril's Letter to him, and his Answer. 24. The Catholics separate from him. 25. Letters to St. Celestine,

and his Answer. 26. He is admonished; Anathemas of St. Cyril. 27. The Sentence of the Pope is intimated to him. 28. He is cited to the Council. 29. He is condemned. 30. The Sentence of the Council is intimated to him. 31. Cabal of John of Antioch. 32. Confirmation of the Council by the Legates, in the Name of the Pope. 33. The Pelagians are condemned. 34. Disagreeable Affair with the Emperor Theodosius. 35. Theodosius approves of the Condemnation of Nestorius, and sends him into Banishment, where he dies. 36. Laws against the Nestorians. 37. Efforts of the Nestorians. 38. The same Subject continued. 39. It is condemned as heretical to assert that Jesus Christ is the adopted Son of God. 40-43. Answer to Basnage, who has unjustly undertaken the Defence of Nestorius.

ARTICLE IV.—The Heresy of Eutyches, ... 136

§ 1.—The Synod of St. Flavian.—The Council or Cabal of Ephesus, called the "Latrocinium," or Council of Robbers.

44. Beginning of Eutyches; he is accused by Eusebius of Dorileum. 45. St. Flavian receives the Charge. 46. Synod of St. Flavian. 47. Confession of Eutyches in the Synod. 48. Sentence of the Synod against Eutyches. 49. Complaints of Eutyches. 50. Eutyches writes to St. Peter Chrysologus, and to St. Leo. 51. Character of Dioscorus. 52, 53. Cabal at Ephesus. 54. St. Flavian is deposed, and Eusebius of Dorileum. 55. The Errors of Theodore of Mopsuestia. 56. Death of St. Flavian. 57. Character of Theodoret. 58, 59. Writings of Theodoret against St. Cyril; Defence of Theodoret. 60. Dioscorus excommunicates St. Leo. 61. Theodosius approved the Council or Cabal, and dies. 62. Reign of St. Pulcheria and Marcian.

§ II.—The Council of Chalcedon, ... 150

62. A Council is assembled in Chalcedon, under the Emperor Marcian, and the Pope St. Leo. 63. The Cause of Dioscorus is tried in the first Session. 64. He is condemned. 65. Articles of Faith defined in Opposition to the Eutychian Heresy, according to the Letter of St. Leo. 66. Privileges granted by the Council to the Patriarch of Constantinople. 67. Refused by St. Leo. 68. Eutyches and Dioscorus die in their Obstinacy. 69. Theodosius, Head of the Eutychians in Jerusalem. 70. His Cruelty. 71. Death of St. Pulcheria and of Marcian. 72. Timothy Eleurus intruded into the See of Alexandria. 73. Martyrdom of St. Proterius, the true Bishop. 74. Leo succeeds Marcian in the Empire. 75. Eleurus is expelled from the See of Alexandria, and Timothy Salofacialus is elected. 76. Zeno is made Emperor; he puts Basiliscus to Death; Eleurus commits Suicide. 77. St. Simon Stilites. 78. His happy Death. 79. Peter the Stammerer intruded into the See of Alexandria.

§ III.—The Henoticon of the Emperor Zeno, ... 163

80. The Emperor Zeno publishes his Henoticon. 81. Mongos anathematizes Pope St. Leo and the Council of Chalcedon. 82. Peter the Fuller intrusted with the See of Antioch. 83. Adventures and Death of the Fuller. 84. Acacius, Patriarch of Constantinople, dies excommunicated.

CHAPTER VI.

Heresies of the Sixth Century, ... 166

ARTICLE I —Of the Acephali, and the different Sects they split into.

1. Regulation made by the new Emperor Anastasius, to the great Detriment of the Church. 2. Anastasius persecutes the Catholics; his awful Death 3. The Acephali, and their Chief, Severus. 4. The Sect of the

Jacobites. 5. The Agnoites. 6. The Tritheists. 7. The Corruptibilists. 8. The Incorruptibilists. 9. Justinian falls into this Error. 10. Good and bad Actions of the Emperor. 11, 12. The Acemetic Monks; their Obstinacy.

ARTICLE II.—The Three Chapters, ... 174

13. The Condemnation of the Three Chapters of Theodore, Ibas, and Theodoret. 14, 15. Defended by Vigilius. 16. Answer to the Objection of a Heretic who asserts that one Council contradicts another.

CHAPTER VII.

The Heresies of the Seventh Century, ... 177

ARTICLE I.—Of Mahometanism.

1. Birth of Mahomet, and Beginning of his false Religion. 2. The Alcoran filled with Blasphemy and Nonsense.

ARTICLE II.—Heresy of the Monothelites, ... 179

4. Commencement of the Monothelites; their Chiefs, Sergius and Cyrus. 5. Opposed by Sophronius. 6. Letter of Sergius to Pope Honorius, and his Answer. 7. Defence of Honorius. 8. Honorius erred, but did not fall into any Error against Faith. 9. The Ecthesis of Heraclius afterwards condemned by Pope John IV. 10. The Type of the Emperor Constans. 11. Condemnation of Paul and Pyrrhus. 12. Dispute of St. Maximus with Pyrrhus. 13. Cruelty of Constans; his violent Death. 14. Condemnation of the Monothelites in the Sixth Council. 15. Honorius condemned in that Council, not for Heresy, but for his Negligence in repressing Heresy.

CHAPTER VIII.

Heresies of the Eighth Century, ... 188

The Heresy of the Iconoclasts.

1. Beginning of the Iconoclasts. 2, 3. St. Germanus opposes the Emperor Leo. 4. He resigns the See of Constantinople. 5. Anastasius is put in his Place; Resistance of the Women. 6. Cruelty of Leo. 7. Leo endeavours to put the Pope to Death; Opposition of the Romans. 8. Letter of the Pope. 9. A Council is held in Rome in Support of the Sacred Images, but Leo continues his Persecution. 10. His Hand is miraculously restored to St. John of Damascus. 11. Leo dies, and is succeeded by Constantine Copronymus, a greater Persecutor; Death of the impious Patriarch Anastasius. 12. Council held by Constantine. 13. Martyrs in Honour of the Images. 14. Other tyrannical Acts of Constantine, and his horrible Death. 15. Leo IV. succeeds to the Empire, and is succeeded by his Son, Constantine. 16. The Empress Irene, in her Son's Name, demands a Council. 17. Seditions against the Council. 18. The Council is held, and the Veneration of Images established. 19. Erroneous Opinion of the Council of Frankfort, regarding the Eighth General Council. 20. Persecution again renewed by the Iconoclasts.

CHAPTER IX.

Heresies of the Ninth Century, ... 201

ARTICLE I.—The Greek Schism commenced by Photius.

1. St. Ignatius, by means of Bardas, Uncle to the Emperor Michael, is expelled from the See of Constantinople. 2. He is replaced by Photius. 3. Photius

is consecrated. 4. Wrongs inflicted on St. Ignatius and on the Bishops who defended him. 5. The Pope sends Legates to investigate the Affair. 6. St. Ignatius appeals from the Judgment of the Legates to the Pope himself. 7. He is deposed in a False Council. 8. The Pope defends St. Ignatius. 9. The Pope deposes the Legates and Photius, and confirms St. Ignatius in his See. 10. Bardas is put to Death by the Emperor and he associates Basil in the Empire. 11. Photius condemns and deposes Pope Nicholas II., and afterwards promulgates his Error concerning the Holy Ghost. 12. The Emperor Michael is killed, and Basil is elected and banishes Photius.

ARTICLE II.—The Errors of the Greeks condemned in Three General Councils, ... 210

13, 14, 15. The Eighth General Council against Photius, under Pope Adrian and the Emperor Basil. 16. Photius gains over Basil, and in the mean time St. Ignatius dies. 17. Photius again gets Possession of the See. 18. The Council held by Photius rejected by the Pope; unhappy Death of Photius. 19. The Patriarch, Cerularius, revives and adds to the Errors of Photius. 20. Unhappy Death of Cerularius. 21, 22. Gregory X. convokes the Council of Lyons at the instance of the Emperor Michael; it is assembled. 23. Profession of Faith written by Michael, and approved of by the Council 24. The Greeks confess and swear to the Decisions of the Council. 25. They separate again. 26 Council of Florence under Eugenius IV.; the Errors are again discussed and rejected; Definition of the Procession of the Holy Ghost. 27. Of the Consecration in Leavened Bread. 28. Of the Pains of Purgatory. 29. Of the Glory of the Blessed. 30. Of the Primacy of the Pope. 31. Instructions given to the Armenians, Jacobites, and Ethiopians; the Greeks relapse into Schism.

CHAPTER X.

The Heresies which sprung up from the Eleventh to the Fifteenth Century, ... 223

ARTICLE I.—Heresies of the Eleventh Century.

1. Stephen and Lisosius burned for their Errors. 2. The new Nicholites and the Incestuosists. 3. Berengarius, and the Principles of his Heresy. 4. His Condemnation and Relapse. 5. His Conversion and Death.

ARTICLE II.—Heresies of the Twelfth Century, ... 226

6. The Petrobrussians. 7. Henry, and his Disciples. 8. Their Condemnation. 9. Peter Abelard, and his Errors concerning the Trinity. 10. His Condemnation. 11. His Conversion and Death. 12. His particular Errors. 13. Arnold of Brescia; his Errors and Condemnation. 14. Causes a Sedition, and is burned alive. 15. Gilbert de la Poree; his Errors and Conversion. 16. Folmar, Tanquelinus, and the Abbot Joachim; the Apostolicals and the Bogomiles. 17. Peter Waldo and his Followers under different Denominations —Waldenses, Poor Men of Lyons, &c. 18. Their particular Errors, and Condemnation.

ARTICLE III.—Heresies of the Thirteenth Century, . . . 234

19. The Albigenses and their Errors. 20. The Corruption of their Morals. 21. Conferences held with them, and their Obstinacy. 22. They create an Anti-Pope. 23. Glorious Labours of St. Dominick, and his stupendous Miracles. 24. Crusade under the Command of Count Montfort, in which he is victorious. 25. Glorious Death of the Count, and Destruction of the Albigenses. 26. Sentence of the Fourth Council of Lateran, in which the Dogma is defined in

CONTENTS.

PAGE.

Opposition to their Tenets. 27. Amalric and his Heresy; the Errors added by his Disciples; they are condemned. 28. William de St. Amour and his Errors. 29. The Flagellants and their Errors. 30. The Fratricelli and their Errors, condemned by John XXII.

ARTICLE IV.—Heresies of the Fourteenth Century, . . . 243

31. The Beghards and Beguines; their Errors condemned by Clement V. 32. Marsilius of Padua, and John Jandunus; their Writings condemned as heretical by John XXII. 33. John Wickliffe, and the Beginning of his Heresy. 34. Is assisted by John Ball; Death of the Archbishop of Canterbury. 35. The Council of Constance condemns forty-five Articles of Wickliffe. 36, 37. Miraculous Confirmation of the Real Presence of Jesus Christ in the Holy Eucharist. 38. Death of Wickliffe.

ARTICLE V.—Heresies of the Fifteenth Century—The Heresy of John Huss, and Jerome of Prague, ... 250

39. John Huss's Character, and the Commencement of his Heresy. 40. His Errors. 41. He is condemned in a Synod. 42. Council of Constance—he is obliged to appear at it. 43. He comes to Constance, and endeavours to escape. 44, 45. He presents himself before the Council, and continues obstinate. 46. He is condemned to death, and burned. 47. Jerome of Prague is also burned alive for his Obstinacy. 48. Wars of the Hussites—they are conquered and converted.

CHAPTER XI.

Heresies of the Sixteenth Century, ... 256

ARTICLE I.—Of the Heresies of Luther.

§ I.—The Beginning and Progress of the Lutheran Heresy.

1. Erasmus of Rotterdam, called by some the Precursor of Luther; his Literature. 2. His Doctrine was not sound, nor could it be called heretical. 3. Principles of Luther; his Familiarity with the Devil, who persuades him to abolish Private Masses. 4. He joins the Order of the Hermits of St. Augustin. 5 Doctrines and Vices of Luther. 6. Publication of Indulgences, and his Theses on that Subject. 7. He is called to Rome, and clears himself; the Pope sends Cardinal Cajetan as his Legate to Germany. 8. Meeting between the Legate and Luther. 9. Luther perseveres and appeals to the Pope. 10, 11. Conference of Ecchius with the Heretics. 12. Bull of Leo X., condemning forty-one Errors of Luther, who burns the Bull and the Decretals.

§ II.—The Diets and principal Congresses held concerning the Heresy of Luther, ... 264

13. Diet of Worms, where Luther appeared before Charles V., and remains obstinate. 14. Edict of the Emperor against Luther, who is concealed by the Elector in one of his Castles. 15. Diet of Spire, where the Emperor publishes a Decree, against which the Heretics protest. 16. Conference with the Zuinglians; Marriage of Luther with an Abbess. 17. Diet of Augsburg, and Melancthon's Profession of Faith; Melancthon's Treatise, in Favour of the Authority of the Pope, rejected by Luther. 18. Another Edict of the Emperor in Favour of Religion. 19. League of Smalkald broken up by the Emperor. 20. Dispensation given by the Lutherans to the Landgrave to have two Wives. 21. Council of Trent, to which Luther refuses to come; he dies, cursing the Council. 22. The Lutherans divided into fifty-six Sects. 23. The Second Diet of Augsburg, in which Charles V. published the injurious Formula of the Interim. 24, 25. The Heresy of Luther takes Possession of Sweden, Denmark, Norway, and other Kingdoms.

CONTENTS.

§ III.—Errors of Luther, ... 273

    26. Forty-one Errors of Luther condemned by Leo X. 27. Other Errors taken from his Books. 28. Luther's Remorse of Conscience. 29. His Abuse of Henry VIII.; his erroneous Translation of the New Testament; the Books he rejected. 30. His Method of celebrating Mass. 31. His Book against the Sacramentarians, who denied the Real Presence of Christ in the Eucharist.

§ IV.—The Disciples of Luther, ... 279

    32. Melancthon and his Character. 33. His Faith, and the Augsburg Confession composed by him. 34. Matthias Flaccus, Author of the Centuries. 35. John Agricola, Chief of the Antinomians; Atheists. 36. Andrew Osiander, Francis Stancaro, and Andrew Musculus 37. John Brenzius, Chief of the Ubiquists. 38. Gaspar Sneckenfield abhorred even by Luther for his Impiety. 39. Martin Chemnitz, the Prince of Protestant Theologians, and Opponent of the Council of Trent.

§ V.—The Anabaptists, ... 284

    40. The Anabaptists; they refuse Baptism to Children. 41. Their Leaders—Seditions and Defeat. 42. Are again defeated under their Chief, Munzer, who is converted at his Death. 43. They rebel again under John of Leyden, who causes himself to be crowned King, is condemned to a cruel Death, and dies penitent. 44. Errors of the Anabaptists. 45. They are split into various Sects.

ARTICLE II.—The Sacramentarians, ... 288

§ I.—Carlostad.

    48. Carlostad, Father of the Sacramentarians. 49. He is reduced to live by his Labour in the Field; he gets married, and composed a Mass on that Subject. 50. He dies suddenly.

§ II.—Zuinglius, ... 290

    51. Zuinglius, and the Beginning of his Heresy. 52. His Errors. 53. Congress held before the Senate of Zurich; the Decree of the Senate rejected by the other Cantons. 54. Zuinglius sells his Canonry, and gets married; Victory of the Catholics; and his Death.

§ III.—Ecolampadius; Bucer; Peter Martyr, . . . 293

    55. Ecolampadius. 56. Bucer. 57. Peter Martyr.

ARTICLE III.—The Heresies of Calvin, ... 296

§ I.—The Beginning and Progress of the Heresy of Calvin.

    58. Birth and Studies of Calvin. 59. He begins to broach his Heresy; they seek to imprison him, and he makes his Escape through a Window. 60. He commences to disseminate his Impieties in Angouleme. 61. He goes to Germany to see Bucer, and meets Erasmus. 62. He returns to France, makes some Followers, and introduces the "Supper;" he afterwards goes to Basle, and finishes his "Instructions." 63. He goes to Italy, but is obliged to fly; arrives in Geneva, and is made Master of Theology. 64. He is embarrassed there. 65. He flies from Geneva, and returns to Germany, where he marries a Widow. 66. He returns to Geneva, and is put at the Head of the Republic; the impious Works he publishes there; his Dispute with Bolsec. 67. He causes Michael Servetus to be burned alive. 68. Unhappy End of the Calvinistic Mission to Brazil. 69. Seditions and Disturbances in France on Calvin's Account; Conference of Poissy. 70. Melancholy Death of Calvin. 71. His personal Qualities and depraved Manners.

§ II.—Theodore Beza, the Huguenots, and other Calvinists, who disturbed France, Scotland, and England, ... 306

72. Theodore Beza; his Character and Vices. 73. His Learning, Employments, and Death. 74. Conference of St. Francis de Sales with Beza. 75. Continuation of the same Subject. 76, 77. Disorders of the Huguenots in France. 78. Horrors committed by them; they are proscribed in France. 79. Their Disorders in Flanders. 80. And in Scotland. 81. Mary Stuart is married to Francis II. 82. She returns to Scotland and marries Darnley, next Bothwell; is driven by Violence to make a fatal Renunciation of her Crown in favour of her Son. 83. She takes Refuge in England, and is imprisoned by Elizabeth, and afterwards condemned to Death by her. 84. Edifying Death of Mary Stuart. 85. James I., the Son of Mary, succeeds Elizabeth; he is succeeded by his Son, Charles I., who was beheaded. 86. He is succeeded by his Son, Charles II., who is succeeded by his Brother, James II., a Catholic, who died in France.

§ III.—The Errors of Calvin, ... 317

87. Calvin adopts the Errors of Luther. 88. Calvin's Errors regarding the Scriptures. 89. The Trinity. 90. Jesus Christ. 91. The Divine Law. 92. Justification. 93. Good Works and Free Will. 94. That God predestines Man to Sin and to Hell, and Faith alone in Jesus Christ is sufficient for Salvation. 95. The Sacraments, and especially Baptism. 96. Penance. 97. The Eucharist and the Mass. 98. He denies Purgatory and Indulgences; other Errors.

§ IV.—The different Sects of Calvinists, ... 323

99. The Sects into which Calvinism was divided. 100. The Puritans. 101. The Independents and Presbyterians. 102. The Difference between these Sects. 103. The Quakers and Tremblers. 104. The Anglo-Calvinists. 105. The Piscatorians. 106. The Arminians and Gomarists.

CHAPTER XII.

Heresies of the Sixteenth Century (continued), ... 327

ARTICLE I.—The Schism of England.

§ I.—The Reign of Henry VIII.

1. Religion of England previous to the Reformation. 2. Henry VIII. marries Catherine of Arragon, but becomes enamoured of Anna Boleyn. 3. The wicked Wolsey suggests the Invalidity of the Marriage; Incontinence of Anna Boleyn; Suspicion that she was the Daughter of Henry. 4. Catherine refuses to have her Cause tried by English Judges; Wolsey is made Prisoner and dies at Leicester. 5. Henry seizes on the Property of the Church, and marries Anna Boleyn. 6. He obliges the Clergy to swear Obedience to him, and Cranmer declares the Marriage of Catherine invalid. 7. The Pope declares Anna Boleyn's Marriage invalid, and excommunicates Henry, who declares himself Head of the Church. 8. He persecutes Pole, and puts More and Fisher to Death. 9. The Pope declares Henry unworthy of the Kingdom; the King puts Anna Boleyn to Death, and marries Jane Seymour. 10. The Parliament decides on six Articles of Faith; the Bones of St. Thomas of Canterbury are burned; Jane Seymour dies in giving Birth to Edward VI. 11. The Pope endeavours to bring Henry to a Sense of his Duty, but does not succeed. 12. He marries Anne of Cleves; Cromwell is put to Death. 13. Henry marries Catherine Howard, whom he afterwards put to Death, and then marries Catherine Parr. 14. His Remorse in his last Sickness. 15. He makes his Will and dies.

CONTENTS.

§ II.—Reign of Edward VI. 339

16. The Duke of Somerset, as Guardian of Edward VI, governs the Kingdom. 17. He declares himself a Heretic, and gives leave to the Heretics to preach; invites Bucer, Vermigli, and Ochino to England, and abolishes the Roman Catholic Religion. 18. He beheads his Brother, the Lord High-Admiral. 19. He is beheaded himself. 20. Death of Edward; the Earl of Warwick makes an attempt to get possession of the Kingdom, and is beheaded, but is converted, and dies an edifying Death.

§ III.—Mary's Reign, ... 343

21. Mary refuses the title of Head of the Church; repeals her Father's and Brother's Laws; Cranmer is condemned to be burned, and dies a Heretic: Mary sends off all Heretics from her Court. 22. Cardinal Pole reconciles England with the Church; her Marriage with Philip II., and Death.

§ IV.—The Reign of Elizabeth, ... 344

23. Elizabeth proclaimed Queen; the Pope is dissatisfied, and she declares herself a Protestant. 24. She gains over the Parliament through the Influence of three of the Nobility, and is proclaimed Head of the Church. 25. She establishes the Form of Church Government, and, though her Belief is Calvinistic, she retains Episcopacy, &c. 26. Appropriates Church Property; abolishes the Mass; the Oath of Allegiance; Persecution of the Catholics. 27. Death of Edmund Campion for the Faith. 28. The Pope's Bull against Elizabeth. 29. She dies out of Communion with the Church. 30. Her Successors on the Throne of England; Deplorable State of the English Church. 31. The English Reformation refutes itself.

ARTICLE II.—The Anti-Trinitarians and Socinians, . . . 350

§ I.—Michael Servetus.

32. Character of Servetus; his Studies, Travels, and False Doctrine. 32. He goes to Geneva; disputes with Calvin, who has him burned to Death.

§ II.—Valentine Gentilis, George Blandrata, and Bernard Ochino, 351

34. Valentine Gentilis; his impious Doctrine. 35. He is punished in Geneva, and retracts. 36. Relapses, and is beheaded. 37. George Blandrata perverts the Prince of Transylvania; disputes with the Reformers; is murdered. 38. Bernard Ochino; his Life while a Friar; his Perversion, and Flight to Geneva. 39. He goes to Strasbourg, and afterwards to England, with Bucer: his unfortunate Death in Poland.

§ III.—The Socinians, ... 356

40. Perverse Doctrine of Lelius Socinus. 41. Faustus Socinus; his Travels, Writings, and Death. 42. Errors of the Socinians.

CHAPTER XIII.

Heresies of the Sixteenth and Seventeenth Centuries, . . . 359

ARTICLE I.—Isaac Perieres, Mark Anthony de Dominis, William Postellus, and Benedict Spinosa.

1. Isaac Perieres, Chief of the Preadamites, abjures his Heresy. 2. Mark Anthony de Dominis; his Errors and Death. 3. William Postellus; his Errors, and Conversion. 4. Benedict Spinosa, Author of a new Sort of Atheism. 5. Plan of his impious System; his unhappy Death.

B

CONTENTS.

ARTICLE II.—The Errors of Michael Baius, ... 362

    6. Michael Baius disseminates his unsound Doctrine, and is opposed. 7. St. Pius V. condemns seventy-nine Propositions of Baius, and he abjures them. 8. Retractation written by Baius, and confirmed by Pope Urban VIII.

ARTICLE III.—The Errors of Cornelius Jansenius, . . . 365

    9. Cornelius, Bishop of Ghent, and Cornelius, Bishop of Ipres; his Studies and Degrees. 10. Notice of the condemned Work of Jansenius. 11. Urban VIII. condemns the Book of Jansenius in the Bull " In eminenti;" the Bishops of France present the Five Propositions to Innocent X. 12. Innocent condemns them in the Bull " Cum occasione ;" Notice of the Propositions. 13. Opposition of the Jansenists; but Alexander VIII. declares that the Five Propositions are extracted from the Book, and condemned in the sense of Jansenius; Two Propositions of Arnold condemned. 14. Form of Subscription commanded by the Pope to be made. 15. The Religious Silence. 16. *The Case of Conscience* condemned by Clement XI. in the Bull *Vineam Domini*. 17. The opinion, that the Pontificate of St. Paul was equal to that of St. Peter, condemned.

ARTICLE IV. 371

    18. Quesnel is dismissed from the Congregation of the Oratory. 19. He publishes several unsound Works in Brussels. 20. Is imprisoned, escapes to Amsterdam, and dies excommunicated. 21. The Book he wrote. 22. The Bull "Unigenitus," condemning the Book. 23. The Bull is accepted by the King, the Clergy, and the Sorbonne; the Followers of Quesnel appeal to a future Council. 24. Several Bishops, also, and Cardinal de Noailles, appeal to a future Council, likewise; but the Council of Embrun declares that the Appeal should not be entertained. 25. The Consultation of the Advocates rejected by the Assembly of the Bishops; Cardinal de Noailles retracts, and accepts the Bull; the Bull is declared Dogmatical by the Sorbonne and the Bishops. 26. Three Principles of the System of Quesnel.

ARTICLE V.—The Errors of Michael Molinos, ... 377

29. The unsound Book of Molinos called the "Spiritual Guide." 30. His impious Doctrine, and the Consequences deduced from it. 31. His affected Sanctity; he is found out and imprisoned, with two of his Disciples. 32. He is condemned himself, as well as his Works; he publicly abjures his Errors and dies penitent. 33. Condemnation of the Book entitled " The Maxims of the Saints."

SUPPLEMENTARY CHAPTER.

Heresies of the Eighteenth and Nineteenth Centuries, . . . 379

    1. Introductory Matter. 2. Rationalists. 3. Hernhutters, or Moravians. 4. Swedenborgians, or New Jerusalemites. 5. Methodism; Wesley. 6, 7. Doctrines and Practices of the Methodists. 8. Johanna Southcott. 9. Mormonism. 10. German Catholics.

CONTENTS. 19

REFUTATION OF HERESIES.

REFUTATION I.

The Heresy of Sabellius, who denied the Distinction of Persons in the Trinity, ... 391

§ I.—The real Distinction of the Three Divine Persons is proved, 391

§ II.—Objections answered, ... 396

REFUTATION II.

The Heresy of Arius, who denied the Divinity of the Word, . . 400

§ I.—The Divinity of the Word proved from the Scriptures, . 400

§ II.—The Divinity of the Word proved by the Authority of Holy Fathers and Councils, ... 411

§ III.—Objections answered, ... 415

REFUTATION III.

Of the Heresy of Macedonius, who denied the Divinity of the Holy Ghost, ... 420

§ I.—The Divinity of the Holy Ghost proved from Scriptures, from the Traditions of the Fathers, and from General Councils, 421

§ II.—Answer to Objections, ... 430

REFUTATION IV.

The Heresy of the Greeks, who assert that the Holy Ghost proceeds from the Father alone, and not from the Father and the Son, . 433

§ I.—It is proved that the Holy Ghost proceeds from the Father and the Son, ... 433

§ II.—Objections answered, ... 440

REFUTATION V.

Refutation of the Heresy of Pelagius, ... 443

§ I.—Of the Necessity of Grace, ... 443

§ II.—Of the Gratuity of Grace, ... 446

§ III.—The Necessity and the Gratuity of Grace is proved by Tradition; confirmed by the Decrees of Councils and Popes, 447

§ IV.—Objections answered, ... 449

REFUTATION VI.

Of the Semi-Pelagian Heresy, ... 451

§ I.—The Commencement of Faith and every good Desire is not from ourselves, but from God, ... 451

§ II.—Objections answered, ... 453

REFUTATION VII.

Refutation of the Heresy of Nestorius, who taught that in Christ there are two Persons, ... 457

§ I.—In Jesus Christ there is but the one Person of the Word alone, which terminates the two Natures, Divine and Human, which both subsist in the same Person of the Word, and, therefore, this one Person is, at the same time, true God and true Man, ... 458

Objections answered, ... 464

§ II.—Mary is the real and true Mother of God, . . . 466

The Objections of the Nestorians answered, . . . 469

REFUTATION VIII.

Refutation of the Heresy of Eutyches, who asserted that there was only one Nature in Christ, ... 470

§ I.—In Christ there are two Natures—the Divine and the Human Nature—distinct, unmixed, unconfused, and entire, subsisting inseparably in the one Hypostasis, or Person of the Word, ... 470

Objections answered, ... 477

REFUTATION IX.

Of the Monothelite Heresy, that there is but one Nature and one Operation only in Christ, ... 481

§ I.—It is proved that there are two distinct Wills in Christ, Divine and Human, according to the two Natures, and two Operations, according to the two Wills, ... 481

§ II.—Objections answered, ... 484

CONTENTS.

REFUTATION X.

The Heresy of Berengarius, and the pretended Reformers, concerning the Most Holy Sacrament of the Eucharist, ... 487

§ I.—Of the Real Presence of the Body and Blood of Jesus Christ in the Eucharist, ... 489

Objections against the Real Presence answered, ... 496

§ II.—Of Transubstantiation—that is, the Conversion of the Substance of the Bread and of the Wine into the Substance of the Body and Blood of Jesus Christ, ... 498

Objections against Transubstantiation answered, . . . 501

§ III.—Of the Manner in which Jesus Christ is in the Eucharist; the philosophical Objections of the Sacramentarians answered, 503

§ IV.—The Matter and Form of the Sacrament of the Eucharist, 509

REFUTATION XI.

Errors of Luther and Calvin, ... 514

Summary of the principal Points, viz.:—1. Free Will exists. 2. The Divine Law is not impossible. 3. Works are necessary. 4. Faith alone does not justify us. 5. Of the Uncertainty of Justification, Perseverance, and Eternal Salvation. 6. God is not the Author of Sin. 7. God predestines no one to Hell. 8. Infallibility of General Councils.

§ I.—Of Free Will, ... 514

§ II.—That it is not impossible to observe the Divine Law, . 516

§ III.—That Good Works are necessary for Salvation, and that Faith alone is not sufficient, ... 520

§ IV.—The Sinner is not justified by Faith alone, . . . 527

§ V.—Faith alone cannot render us secure of Justice, or Perseverance, or Eternal Life, ... 531

§ VI.—God cannot be the Author of Sin, ... 537

§ VII.—God never predestined any one to Eternal Damnation, without regard to his Sins, ... 543

§ VIII.—The Authority of General Councils, ... 553

REFUTATION XII.

The Errors of Michael Baius, ... 563

REFUTATION XIII.

The Errors of Cornelius Jansenius, ... 576

REFUTATION XIV.

The Heresy of Michael Molinos, ... 591

REFUTATION XV.

Berruyer's Errors, ... 597

§ I.—Berruyer says that Jesus Christ was made in time, by an operation *ad extra,* the natural Son of God, one subsisting in three Persons, who united the Humanity of Christ with a Divine Person, ... 599

§ II.—Berruyer says that Jesus Christ, during the three days he was in the Sepulchre, ceased to be a living Man, and, consequently, was no longer the Son of God. And when God again raised him from the dead, he once more generated him, and again made him the Son of God, ... 610

§ III.—Berruyer says that it was the Humanity alone of Christ that obeyed, prayed, and suffered, and that his Oblations, Prayers, and Meditations, were not Operations proceeding from the Word, as a physical and efficient Principle, but that, in this sense, they were actions merely of his Humanity, . . 613

§ IV.—The Miracles wrought by Jesus Christ were not performed by his own Powers, but obtained from his Father, by his Prayers, ... 623

§ V.—The Holy Ghost was not sent to the Apostles by Jesus Christ, but by the Father alone, at the Prayer of Christ, . 625

§ VI.—Other Errors of Berruyer on different Subjects, . . 626

Exhortation to Catholics, ... 634

AUTHOR'S PREFACE.

1. My object in writing this work is to prove that the Roman Catholic Church is the only true one among so many other Churches, and to show how carefully the Almighty guarded her, and brought her victoriously through all the persecutions of her enemies. Hence, as St. Iræneus says (*Lib.* 3, *cap.* 3, *n.* 2), all should depend on the Roman Church as on their fountain and head. This is the Church founded by Jesus Christ, and propagated by the Apostles; and although in the commencement persecuted and contradicted by all, as the Jews said to St. Paul in Rome: "For as concerning this sect (thus they called the Church), we know that it is gainsayed everywhere" (Acts, xxviii. 22); still she always remained firm, not like the other false Churches which in the beginning numbered many followers, but perished in the end, as we shall see in the course of this history, when we speak of the Arians, Nestorians, Eutychians, and Pelagians; and if any sect still reckons many followers, as the Mahometans, Lutherans, or Calvinists, it is easy to see that they are upheld, not by the love of truth, but either by popular ignorance, or relaxation of morals. St. Augustin says that heresies are only embraced by those who, had they persevered in the faith, would be lost by the irregularity of their lives. (St. Aug. de Va. Rel. c. 8.)

2. Our Church, on the contrary, notwithstanding that she teaches her children a law opposed to the corrupt inclinations of human nature, not only never failed in the midst of persecutions, but even gained strength from them; as Tertullian (Apol. cap. ult.) says,—the blood of martyrs is the seed of Christians, and the more we are mown down the more numerous we become; and in the 20th chapter of the same work he says,—the kingdom of Christ and his reign is believed, and he is worshipped by all nations. Pliny the Younger confirms this in his celebrated Letter to Trajan, in which he says that in Asia the temples of the gods were deserted, because the Christian religion had overrun not only the cities but even the villages.

3. This, certainly, never could have taken place without the power of the Almighty, who intended to establish, in the midst of idolatry, a new religion, to destroy all the superstitions of the false religion, and the ancient belief in a multitude of false gods adored by the Gentiles, by their ancestors, by the magistrates, and by the emperors themselves, who made use of all their power to protect it, and still the Christian faith was embraced by many nations who forsook a relaxed law for a hard and difficult one, forbidding them to pamper their sensual appetites. What but the power of God could accomplish this?

4. Great as the persecutions were which the Church suffered from idolatry, still greater were those she had to endure from the heretics which sprang from her own bosom, by means of wicked men, who, either through pride or ambition, or the desire of sensual license, endeavoured to rend the bowels of their parent. Heresy has been called a canker: " It spreadeth like a canker" (2 Tim. ii. 17); for as a canker infects the whole body, so heresy infects the whole soul, the mind, the heart, the intellect, and the will. It is also called a plague, for it not only infects the person contaminated with it, but those who associate with him, and the fact is, that the spread of this plague in the world has

injured the Church more than idolatry, and this good mother has suffered more from her own children than from her enemies. Still she has never perished in any of the tempests which the heretics raised against her; she appeared about to perish at one time through the heresy of Arius, when the faith of the Council of Nice, through the intrigues of the wicked Bishops, Valens and Ursacius, was condemned, and, as St. Jerome says, the world groaned at finding itself Arian (1); and the Eastern Church appeared in the same danger during the time of the heresies of Nestorius and Eutyches. But it is wonderful, and at the same time consoling, to read the end of all those heresies, and behold the bark of the Church, which appeared completely wrecked and sunk through the force of those persecutions, in a little while floating more gloriously and triumphantly than before.

5. St. Paul says: " There must be heresies, that they also who are reproved may be made manifest among you" (1 Cor. ii. 19). St. Augustin, explaining this text, says that as fire is necessary to purify silver, and separate it from the dross, so heresies are necessary to prove the good Christians among the bad, and to separate the true from the false doctrine. The pride of the heretics makes them presume that they know the true faith, and that the Catholic Church is in error, but here is the mistake: our reason is not sufficient to tell us the true faith, since the truths of Divine Faith are above reason; we should, therefore, hold by that faith which God has revealed to his Church, and which the Church teaches, which is, as the Apostle says, " the pillar and the ground of truth" (1 Tim. iii. 15). Hence, as St. Iræneus says, " It is necessary that all should depend on the Roman Church as their head and fountain; all Churches should agree with this Church on account of her priority of principality, for there the traditions delivered by the Apostles have always been preserved" (St. Iræn. lib. 3, c. 3);

---

(1) St. Hieron. Dial. adversus Lucifer.

and by the tradition derived from the Apostles, which the Church founded at Rome preserves, and the Faith preserved by the succession of the Bishops, we confound those who through blindness or an evil conscience draw false conclusions (*Ibid.*) " Do you wish to know," says St. Augustin, " which is the Church of Christ? Count those priests who, in a regular succession, have succeeded St. Peter, who is the Rock, against which the gates of hell will not prevail" (St. Aug. in Ps. contra part. Donat.): and the holy Doctor alleges as one of the reasons which detain him in the Catholic Church, the succession of Bishops to the present time in the See of St. Peter" (Epis. fund. *c.* 4, *n.* 5); for in truth the uninterrupted succession from the Apostles and disciples is characteristic of the Catholic Church, and of no other.

6. It was the will of the Almighty that the Church in which the true faith was preserved should be one, that all the faithful might profess the one faith, but the devil, St. Cyprian says (2), invented heresies to destroy faith, and divide unity. The enemy has caused mankind to establish many different churches, so that each, following the faith of his own particular one, in opposition to that of others, the true faith might be confused, and as many false faiths formed as there are different churches, or rather different individuals. This is especially the case in England, where we see as many religions as families, and even families themselves divided in faith, each individual following his own. St. Cyprian, then, justly says that God has disposed that the true faith should be preserved in the Roman Church alone, so that there being but one Church there should be but one faith and one doctrine for all the faithful. St. Optatus Milevitanus, writing to Parmenianus, says, also: " You cannot be ignorant that the Episcopal Chair of St. Peter was first placed in the city of Rome, in which one chair unity is observed by all" (St. Opt. *l.* 2, cont. Parmen.)

---

(2) St. Cyprian de Unitate Ecclesiæ.

7. The heretics, too, boast of the unity of their Churches, but St. Augustin says that it is unity against unity. "What unity," says the Saint, "can all those Churches have which are divided from the Catholic Church, which is the only true one; they are but as so many useless branches cut off from the Vine, the Catholic Church, which is always firmly rooted. This is the One Holy, True, and Catholic Church, opposing all heresies; it may be opposed, but cannot be conquered. All heresies come forth from it, like useless shoots cut off from the vine, but it still remains firmly rooted in charity, and the gates of hell shall not prevail against it" (St. Aug. lib. 1, de Symbol. ad Cath. *c.* 6). St. Jerome says that the very fact of the heretics forming a church apart from the Roman Church is a proof, of itself, that they are followers of error, and disciples of the devil, described by the Apostle as "giving heed to spirits of error and doctrines of devils" (1 Tim. iv. 1).

8. The Lutherans and Calvinists say, just as the Donatists did before them, that the Catholic Church preserved the true faith down to a certain period—some say to the third, some to the fourth, some to the fifth century—but that after that the true doctrine was corrupted, and the spouse of Christ became an adulteress. This supposition, however, refutes itself; for, granting that the Roman Catholic Church was the Church first founded by Christ, it could never fail, for our Saviour himself promised that the gates of hell never should prevail against it: "I say unto you that you are Peter, and on this rock I will build my Church, and the gates of hell shall not prevail against it" (Matt. xviii. 18). It being certain, then, that the Roman Catholic Church was the true one, as Gerard, one of the first ministers of Luther, admits (Gerard de Eccles. *cap.* 11, *sec.* 6) it to have been for the first five hundred years, and to have preserved the Apostolic doctrine during that period, it follows that it must always have remained so, for the spouse of Christ, as St. Cyprian says, could never become an adulteress.

9. The heretics, however, who, instead of learning from the Church the dogmas they should believe, wish to teach her false and perverse dogmas of their own, say that they have the Scriptures on their side, which are the fountain of truth, not considering, as a learned author (3) justly remarks, that it is not by reading, but by understanding, them, that the truth can be found. Heretics of every sort avail themselves of the Scriptures to prove their errors, but we should not interpret the Scripture according to our own private opinions, which frequently lead us astray, but according to the teaching of the Holy Church which is appointed the Mistress of true doctrine, and to whom God has manifested the true sense of the Divine books. This is the Church, as the Apostle tells us, which has been appointed the pillar and the ground of truth: "that thou mayest know how thou oughtest to behave thyself in the house of God, which is the Church of the living God, the pillar and the ground of truth." (1 Tim. iii. 15.) Hence St. Leo says, that the Catholic faith despises the errors of heretics barking against the Church, who, deceived by the vanity of worldly wisdom, have departed from the truth of the Gospel.—(St. Leo. Ser. 8 de Nat. Dim.)

10. I think the History of Heresies is a most useful study, for it shows the truth of our Faith more pure and resplendent, by showing how it has never changed; and if, at all times, this is useful, it must be particularly so at present, when the most holy maxims and the principal dogmas of religion are put in doubt: it shows, besides, the care God always took to sustain the Church in the midst of the tempests which were unceasingly raised against it, and the admirable manner in which all the enemies who attacked it were confounded. The History of Heresies is also useful to preserve in us the spirit of humility and subjection to the Church, and to make us grateful to God for giving us the

---

(3) Danes, Gen. Temp. Nat. in Epil.

grace of being born in Christian countries; and it shows how the most learned men have fallen into the most grievous errors, by not subjecting themselves to the Church's teaching.

11. I will now state my reasons for writing this Work; some may think this labour of mine superfluous, especially as so many learned authors have written expressly and extensively the history of various heresies, as Tertullian, St. Iræneus, St. Epiphanius, St. Augustin, St. Vincent of Lerins, Socrates, Sozymen, St Philastrius, Theodoret, Nicephorus, and many others, both in ancient and modern times. This, however, is the very reason which prompted me to write this Work; for as so many authors have written, and so extensively, and as it is impossible for many persons either to procure so many and such expensive works, or to find time to read them, if they had them, I, therefore, judged it better to collect in a small compass the commencement and the progress of all heresies, so that in a little time, and at little expense, any one may have a sufficient knowledge of the heresies and schisms which infected the Church. I have said in a small compass, but still, not with such brevity as some others have done, who barely give an outline of the facts, and leave the reader dissatisfied, and ignorant of many of the most important circumstances. I, therefore, have studied brevity; but I wish, at the same time, that my readers may be fully informed of every notable fact connected with the rise and progress of, at all events, the principal heresies that disturbed the Church.

12. Another reason I had for publishing this Work was, that as modern authors, who have paid most attention to historical facts, have spoken of heresies only as a component part of Ecclesiastical History, as Baronius, Fleury, Noel Alexander, Tillemont, Orsi, Spondanus, Raynaldus, Graveson, and others, and so have spoken of each heresy chronologically, either in its beginning, progress, or decay, and, therefore, the reader must turn over to different parts of the works to find out the rise, progress, and dis-

appearance of each heresy; I, on the contrary, give all at once the facts connected with each heresy in particular.

13. Besides, these writers have not given the Refutation of Heresies, and I give this in the second part of the Work; I do not mean the refutation of every heresy, but only of the principal ones, as these of Sabellius, Arius, Pelagius, Macedonius, Nestorius, Eutyches, the Monothelites, the Iconoclasts, the Greeks, and the like. I will merely speak of the authors of other heresies of less note, and their falsity will be apparent, either from their evident weakness, or from the proofs I bring forward against the more celebrated heresies I have mentioned.

14. We ought, then, dear reader, unceasingly to thank our Lord for giving us the grace of being born and brought up in the bosom of the Catholic Church. St. Francis de Sales exclaims: " O good God! many and great are the benefits thou hast heaped on me, and I thank thee for them; but how shall I be ever able to thank thee for enlightening me with thy holy Faith?" And writing to one of his friends, he says: " O God! the beauty of thy holy Faith appears to me so enchanting, that I am dying with love of it, and I imagine I ought to enshrine this precious gift in a heart all perfumed with devotion." St. Teresa never ceased to thank God for having made her a daughter of the Holy Church: her consolation at the hour of death was to cry out: " I die a child of the Holy Church—I die a child of the Holy Church." We, likewise, should never cease praising Jesus Christ for this grace bestowed on us—one of the greatest conferred on us—one distinguishing us from so many millions of mankind, who are born and die among infidels and heretics: " He has not done in like manner to every nation" (Psalm, cxlvii. 9). With our minds filled with gratitude for so great a favour, we shall now see the triumph the Church has obtained through so many ages, over so many heresies opposed to her. I wish to remark, however, before I begin, that I have written this Work amidst

the cares of my Bishoprick, so that I could not give a critical examination, many times, to the facts I state, and, in such case, I give the various opinions of different authors, without deciding myself on one side or the other. I have endeavoured, however, to collect all that could be found in the most correct and notable writers on the subject; but it is not impossible that some learned persons may be better acquainted with some facts than I am.

THE

HISTORY OF HERESIES,

AND

THEIR REFUTATION.

CHAPTER I.

HERESIES OF THE FIRST CENTURY.

1. Simon Magus. 2. Menander. 3. Cerinthus. 4. Ebion. 5. Saturninus and Basilides.
6. The Nicholites.

1. SIMON MAGUS (1), the first heretic who disturbed the Church, was born in a part of Samaria called Githon or Gitthis. He was called Magus, or the Magician, because he made use of spells to deceive the multitude; and hence he acquired among his countrymen the extraordinary name of "The Great Power of God" (Acts, viii. 10). "This man is the power of God which is called great." Seeing that those on whom the Apostles Peter and John laid hands received the Holy Ghost, he offered them money to give to him the power of communicating the Holy Ghost in like manner; and on that account the detestable crime of selling holy things is called Simony. He went to Rome, and there was a statue erected to him in that city, a fact which St. Justin, in his first Apology, flings in the face of the Romans: "In your royal city," he says, "he (Simon) was esteemed a god, and a statue was erected to him in the Island of the Tyber, between the two bridges, bearing this Latin inscription—SIMONI, DEO SANCTO." Samuel Basnage, Petavius, Valesius, and many others, deny this fact; but Tillemont, Grotius, Fleury, and Cardinal Orsi defend it, and adduce in favour of it the authority of Tertullian, St. Irenæus, St. Cyril of Jerusalem, St. Augustin, Eusebius, and Theodoret, who even says the statue was a bronze one. Simon broached many errors, which Noel Alexander enumerates and refutes (2). The principal ones

(1) Baron. Annal. 35, *d.* 23; N. Alex. Hist. Ecclesias. *t.* 5, *c.* 11, *n.* 1; Hermant. His. Con. 56, 1, *c.* 7; Van Ranst, His. Her. *n.* 1.   (2) Nat. Alex. *t.* 5, in fin. Dis. 24.

were that the world was created by angels; that when the soul leaves the body it enters into another body, which, if true, says St. Irenæus (3), it would recollect all that happened when it inhabited the former body, for memory, being a spiritual quality, it could not be separated from the soul. Another of his errors was one which has been brought to light by the heretics of our own days, that man had no free will, and, consequently, that good works are not necessary for salvation. Baronius and Fleury relate (4), that, by force of magic spells, he one day caused the devil to elevate him in the air; but St. Peter and St. Paul being present, and invoking the name of Jesus Christ, he fell down and broke both his legs. He was carried away by his friends; but his corporeal and mental sufferings preyed so much on him, that, in despair, he cast himself out of a high window; and thus perished the first heretic who ever disturbed the Church of Christ (5). Basnage, who endeavours to prove that St. Peter never was in Rome, and never filled the pontifical chair of that city, says that this is all a fabrication; but we have the testimony of St. Ambrose, St. Isidore of Pelusium, St. Augustin, St. Maximus, St. Philastrius, St. Cyril of Jerusalem, Severus Sulpicius, Theodoret, and many others, in our favour. We have, besides, a passage in Suetonius, which corroborates their testimony, for he says (lib. VI., cap. xii.), that, while Nero assisted at the public sports, a man endeavoured to fly, but, after elevating himself for a while, he fell down, and the Emperor's pavilion was sprinkled with his blood.

2. Menander was a Samaritan likewise, and a disciple of Simon Magus; he made his appearance in the year of our Lord 73. He announced himself a messenger from the "Unknown Power," for the salvation of mankind. No one, according to him, could be saved, unless he was baptized in his name, and his baptism, he said, was the true resurrection, so that his disciples would enjoy immortality even in this life (6). Cardinal Orsi adds, that Menander was the first who invented the doctrine of " Eons," and that he taught that Jesus Christ exercised human functions in appearance alone.

3. Cerinthus was the next after Menander, but he began to broach his doctrine in the same year (7). His errors can be reduced to four heads: he denied that God was the creator of the world; he asserted that the law of Moses was necessary for salvation; he also taught that after the resurrection Jesus Christ would establish a terrestrial kingdom in Jerusalem, where the just would spend a thousand years in the enjoyment of every sensual pleasure; and,

(3) St. Irenæus, de Heresi. *l.* 2, *c.* 58.   (4) Baron. Ann. 35, *n.* 14, ad 17; Fleury, His. Eccl. *t.* 1, *l.* 2, *n.* 23; St. Augus.; St. Joan. Chris.   (5) Baron. *n.* 17; Nat. Alex. *t.* 5, *c.* 11; Orsi, Istor. Eccl. *l.* 1, *n.* 20, and *l.* 2, *n.* 19; Berti. Brev. Histor. *t.* 1, *c.* 3.   (6) Fleury, loc. cit. *n.* 42; N. Alex. loc. cit. *art.* 2.   (7) N. Alex. *t.* 5, *c.* 11, *ar.* 5; Fleury, *t.* 1, *l.* 2, *n.* 42; Berti, loc. cit.; Orsi, *t.* 1, *l.* 2, *n.* 43.

finally, he denied the divinity of Jesus Christ. The account Bernini gives of his death is singular (8). The Apostle St. John, he says, met him going into a bath, when, turning to those along with him, he said, let us hasten out of this, lest we be buried alive, and they had scarcely gone outside when the whole building fell with a sudden crash, and the unfortunate Cerinthus was overwhelmed in the ruins. One of the impious doctrines of this heretic was, that *Jesus* was a mere man, born as all other men are, and that, when he was baptized in the river Jordan, *Christ* descended on him, that is, a virtue or power, in form of a dove, or a spirit sent by God to fill him with knowledge, and communicate it to mankind; but after Jesus had fulfilled his mission, by instructing mankind and working miracles, he was deserted by Christ, who returned to heaven, and left him to darkness and death. Alas! what impiety men fall into when they desert the light of faith, and follow their own weak imaginations.

4. Ebion prided himself in being a disciple of St. Peter, and could not even bear to hear St. Paul's name mentioned. He admitted the sacrament of baptism; but in the consecration of the Eucharist he used nothing but water in the chalice; he, however, consecrated the host in unleavened bread, and Eusebius says he performed this every Sunday. According to St. Jerome, the baptism of the Ebionites was admitted by the Catholics. He endeavoured to unite the Mosaic and Christian law, and admitted no part of the New Testament, unless the Gospel of St. Matthew, and even that mutilated, as he left out two chapters, and altered the others in many places. The ancient writers say that St. John wrote his Gospel to refute the errors of Ebion. The most impious of his blasphemies was, that Jesus Christ was the son of Joseph and Mary, born as the rest of men are; that he was but a mere man, but that, on account of his great virtue, the Almighty adopted him as his Son (9).

5. Saturninus and Basilides were disciples of Menander, whose history we have already seen; and they made some additions to the heresy of their master. Saturninus, a native of Antioch, taught, with Menander, as Fleury tells us (10), that there was one only Father, unknown to all, who created the angels, and that seven angels created the world and man. The God of the Jews, he said, was one of these rebellious angels, and it was to destroy him that Christ appeared in the form of man, though he never had a real body. He condemned matrimony and procreation as an invention of the devil. He attributed the Prophecies partly to the angels, partly to the devil, and partly to the God of the Jews. He also said, according to St. Augustin (Heres. iii.), that the Supreme Virtue—

---

(8) Bernin. Istor. del Eresia, *t.* 1, *c.* 1; St. Iren. *l.* 3, *c.* 4, de S. (9) N. Alex. loc. cit. *art.* 6; Fleury, loc. cit. *n.* 42. [N.B.—Fleury puts Ebion first, next Cerinthus, and lastly Menander.] (10) Fleury, *n.* 19.

that is, the Sovereign Father—having created the angels, seven of them rebelled against him, created man, and for this reason:— Seeing a celestial light, they wished to retain it, but it vanished from them; and they then created man to resemble it, saying, "Let us make man to the image and likeness." Man being thus created, was like a mere worm, incapable of doing anything, till the Sovereign Virtue, pitying his image, placed in him a spark of himself, and gave him life. This is the spark which, at the dissolution of the body, flies to heaven. Those of his sect alone, he said, had this spark; all the others were deprived of it, and, consequently, were reprobate.

6. Basilides, according to Fleury, was a native of Alexandria, and even exceeded Saturninus in fanaticism. He said that the Father, whom he called *Abrasax*, produced *Nous*, that is, Intelligence; who produced *Logos*, or the Word; the Word produced *Phronesis*, that is, Prudence; and Prudence, *Sophia* and *Dunamis*, that is, Wisdom and Power. These created the angels, who formed the first heaven and other angels; and these, in their turn, produced a second heaven, and so on, till there were three hundred and sixty-five heavens produced, according to the number of days in the year. The God of the Jews, he said, was the head of the second order of angels, and because he wished to rule all nations, the other princes rose up against him, and, on that account, God sent his first-born, *Nous*, to free mankind from the dominion of the angels who created the world. This *Nous*, who, according to him, was Jesus Christ, was an incorporeal virtue, who put on whatever form pleased him. Hence, when the Jews wished to crucify him, he took the form of Simon the Cyrenean, and gave his form to Simon, so that it was Simon, and not Jesus, was crucified. Jesus, at the same time, was laughing at the folly of the Jews, and afterwards ascended invisibly to heaven. On that account, he said, we should not venerate the crucifix, otherwise we would incur the danger of being subject to the angels who created the world. He broached many other errors; but these are sufficient to show his fanaticism and impiety. Both Saturninus and Basilides fled from martyrdom, and always cloaked their faith with this maxim—"Know others, but let no one know you." Cardinal Orsi says(11) they practised magic, and were addicted to every species of incontinence, but that they were careful in avoiding observation. They promulgated their doctrines before Menander, in the year 125; but, because they were disciples of his, we have mentioned them after him.

7. The Nicholites admitted promiscuous intercourse with married and single, and, also, the use of meats offered to idols. They also said that the Father of Jesus Christ was not the creator of the

(11) Orsi, *t.* 2, *l.* 3, *n.* 23.

world. Among the other foolish doctrines they held, was one, that darkness, uniting with the Holy Ghost, produced a matrix or womb, which brought forth four Eons; that from these four Eons sprung the evil Eon, who created the Gods, the angels, men, and seven demoniacal spirits. This heresy was of short duration; but some new Nicholites sprung up afterwards in the Milanese territory, who were condemned by Pope Nicholas II. The Nicholites called themselves disciples of Nicholas the Deacon, who, according to Noel Alexander, was esteemed a heresiarch by St. Eusebius, St. Hilarion, and St. Jerome. However, Clement of Alexandria, Eusebius, Theodoret, Baronius, St. Ignatius the Martyr, Orsi, St. Augustin, Fleury, and Berti, acquit him of this charge (12).

CHAPTER II.

HERESIES OF THE SECOND CENTURY.

1. Corpocrates. 2. Valentine. 3. Epiphanes. 4. Prodicus. 5. Tatian. 6. Severus. 7. Cerdonius. 8. Marcion. 9. Apelles. 10. Montanus. 11. Cataphrigians, Artotirites, Peputians, Ascodrogites, Pattalornichites. 12. Bardesanes. 13. Theodotus the Currier, Artemon, and Theodotus Argentarius. 14. Hermogenes.

1. CORPOCRATES was a native of Alexandria, or, as others say, of Samosata. His followers were called *Gnostics*—that is, learned or enlightened. He said that Jesus Christ was the son of Joseph, born as other men are, and distinguished from them by his virtue alone, and that the world was created by angels. Another blasphemous doctrine of his was, that, to unite ourselves with God, we should practise all the unclean works of concupiscence; our evil propensities should be followed in everything, for this, he said, was the enemy spoken of in the Gospel (1), to which we should yield, and, by this means, we show our contempt for the laws of the wicked angels, and acquire the summit of perfection; and the soul, he said, would pass from one body to another, till it had committed all sorts of unclean actions. Another of his doctrines was, that every one had two souls, for without the second, he said, the first would be subject to the rebellious angels. The followers of this hellish monster called themselves Christians, and, as a distinctive mark, they branded the lower part of the ear with a red iron. They paid the same veneration to the images of Pythagoras, Plato, and the other philosophers, as to that of Jesus Christ. Corpocrates lived in the year 160.

(12) Nat. Alex. *t.* 5, *diss.* 9; Baron. An. 68, *n.* 9; Orsi, *t.* 1, *n.* 64; Fleury, *t.* 1, *l.* 2, *n.* 21; Berti, loc. cit.   (1) N. Alex. *t.* 6, *c.* 3, *ar.* 2; Fleury, *l.* 3, *n.* 20; Berti, *t.* 1, *c.* 3; Bernin. *t.* 1. *c.* 2.

2. Valentine, who, it was supposed, was an Egyptian, separated himself from the Church, because he was disappointed in obtaining a bishopric. He came to Rome in 141, and abjured his errors, but soon again embraced them, and persevered in them till his death (2). He invented a fabulous genealogy of Eons or Gods; and another of his errors was, that Jesus Christ did not become incarnate in the womb of the Virgin Mary, but brought his body from heaven. He admitted in man a continual exercise of spirit, which, uniting with the flesh, rendered lawful every sensual pleasure; and he divided mankind into three classes—the carnal, the animal, and the spiritual. His followers, he said, were the spiritualists, and, on that account, were exempt from the necessity of good works, because, having arrived at the apex of perfection, and being certain of eternal felicity, it was useless for them to suffer, or observe the law. The carnal, he said, were excluded from eternal salvation and predestined to hell (3).

Three sects take their origin from Valentine. The first were called Sethites: These paid such honour to Seth, that they said Jesus Christ was born of him, and some went so far as to say that Jesus Christ and Seth were one and the same person. The second sect were called Cainites: These venerated as saints all those who the Scripture tells us were damned—as Cain, Core, the inhabitants of Sodom, and especially Judas Iscariot. The third were called Ophites: These said that *Wisdom* became a serpent, and on that account, they adored Jesus Christ as a serpent; they trained one of these reptiles to come out of a cave when called, and creep up on the table where the bread for sacrifice was placed; they kissed him while he crept round the bread, and, considering it then sanctified by the reptile, whom they blasphemously called Christ, they broke it to the people, who received it as the Eucharist (4).

Ptolemy and Saturninus were disciples of Valentine; but their master admitted thirty Eons, and they added eight more. He also had other disciples:—Heraclion, whose followers invoked over the dead certain names of principalities, and anointed them with oil and water; Marcus and Colarbasus taught that all truth was shut up in the Greek alphabet, and on that account, they called Christ Alpha and Omega (5); and Van Ranst adds to the list the Arconticites, who rejected the sacraments—Florinus, who said that God was the author of sin—and Blastus (6), who insisted that Easter should be celebrated after the Jewish fashion. The disciples of Valentine made a new Gospel, and added various books to the Canon of the Scriptures, as "The Parables of the Lord," "The

---

(2) Van Ranst, His. *p.* 20.   (3) Fleury, *t.* 1, *l.* 3, *n.* 26—27; Bernin. *t.* 1, *c.* 5; Graveson, *t.* 3, *p.* 49; N. Alex. *t.* 6, *c.* 3, *ar.* 6.   (4) Fleury, *t.* 1, *l.* 3, *n.* 30; Bernin. *t.* 1, *c.* 2; Van Ranst, *p.* 20.   (5) Fleury, *l.* 3, *n.* 30, *l.* 4, *n.* 9 & 10.   (6) Van Ranst, *p.* 22.

Prophetic Sayings and the Sermons of the Apostles." It is needless to add that all these were according to their own doctrines.

3. Epiphanes, the son of Corpocrates, besides defending the damnable opinions of his father, openly rejected the law of Moses, and especially the two last precepts of the Decalogue. He also rejected the Gospel, though he pretended to follow it (7).

4. Prodicus taught that it was lawful to deny the faith to avoid death; he rejected the worship of an invisible God, and adored the four elements and the sun and the moon; he condemned all prayers to God as superstitious, but he prayed to the elements and the planets to be propitious to mankind (8). This impious worship he always performed naked. Noel Alexander and Theodoret assign to this heretic the institution of the sect called Adamites; these always performed their religious exercises in their churches, or rather brothels, as St. Epiphanius calls them, naked, pretending by this to imitate the innocence of Adam, but, in reality, practising every abomination (9).

5. Tatian was born in Assyria, and was a disciple of St. Justin Martyr. He was the founder of the sect called Encratics, or Continent; he taught, with Valentine, that matter was uncreated and eternal; he attributed the Creation to God, but through the instrumentality of an inferior Eon, who said let there be light, not by way of command, but of supplication, and thus light was created. He denied, with Valentine, the resurrection of the dead, and human flesh he said was too unworthy to be united with the divinity in the person of Christ. He deprived man of free will, saying he was good and spiritual, or bad and carnal, by necessity, according as the seed of divine grace was infused or not into him; and he rejected the law of Moses, as not instituted by God, but by the Eon who created the world. Finally, he condemned matrimony, prohibited the use of flesh-meat and wine, and, because he used nothing but water in the consecration of the chalice, his disciples were called Hydroparastati, or Aquarii (10).

6. Severus was a disciple of Tatian; but differed from his master in some essential points, especially in admitting the law of Moses, the Prophets, and the Gospels. Julius Capianus, a disciple of Valentine, joined with Severus, and was the founder of the heresy of the Doceti, who said that Jesus had not a real, but an apparent, body. He wrote a book on continence, in which he quoted a passage of the spurious gospel used by the Egyptians, in which Jesus Christ is made to curse matrimony. In his commentaries on Genesis he says marriage was the forbidden fruit (11).

7. Cerdonius followed the doctrines of Simon, Menander, and

---

(7) Fleury, *l.* 3, *n.* 20; Bern. *t.* 1, *c.* 2.   (8) Bern. loc. cit.   (9) N. Alex. *t.* 6, *c.* 3, *ar.* 12; Gotti, Ver. Rel. *t.* 2, *c.* 27, *s.* 1; Bernin. loc. cit.   (10) Orsi, *t.* 2, *l.* 4, *n.* 11; Fleury, *t.* 1, *l.* 4, *n.* 8; Baron. An. 174, *n.* 3, 4; N. Alex. *t.* 6, *c.* 3, *ar.* 7. (11) Fleury, loc. cit. *n.* 8; Orsi, loc. cit. *n.* 12.

Saturninus; besides, he taught, with Manes, the existence of two first principles, or Gods, a good and a bad one, and admitted the resurrection of the soul, but not of the body. He rejected all the gospels, except St. Luke's, and mutilated that in several places (12).

8. Marcion was a native of the city of Sinope, in the province of Pontus, and the son of a Catholic bishop. In his early days he led a life of continence and retirement; but for an act of immorality he was cut off from the Church by his own father. He then went to Rome, and endeavoured to accomplish his restoration; but not being able to succeed, he, in a fit of rage, said—" I will cause an eternal division in your Church." He then united himself to Cerdonius, admitting two principles, and founding his doctrine on the sixth chapter of St. Luke, where it is said, a good tree cannot bring forth bad fruits. The good principle, he said, was the author of good, and the bad one of evil; and the good principle was the father of Jesus Christ, the giver of grace, and the bad one, the creator of matter and the founder of the law. He denied the incarnation of the Son of God, saying it was repugnant to a good God to unite himself with the filthiness of flesh, and that his soul should have for a companion a body infected and corrupt by nature. He also taught the existence of two Gods—one, the good God; the other, an evil one, the God of the Jews, and the creator of the world. Each of these Gods promised to send a Christ. Our Christ appeared in the reign of Tiberius, and was the good Christ; the Jewish Christ did not yet come. The Old Testament he rejected, because it was given by the bad principle, or God of the Jews. Among other errors, he said, that when Jesus descended into hell, he did not save Abel, or Henoc, or Noah, or any other of the just of the old law, because they were friends of the God of the Jews; but that he saved Cain, the Sodomites, and the Egyptians, because they were the enemies of this God (13).

9. Apelles, the most famous disciple of Marcion, was excommunicated by his master for committing a crime against chastity, and felt his disgrace so much that he fled to Alexandria. This heretic, among other errors, said that God created a number of angels and powers, and among the rest a power called the Lord, who created this world to resemble the world above, but not being able to bring it to perfection, he repented him of having created it (14). Van Ranst says that he rejected the Prophecies, and said the Son of God took a body of air which, at his ascension, dissolved into air again

10. Montanus, as Cardinal Orsi tells us (15), was born in Ardraba, an obscure village of Mysia. He first led such a mortified life that he was esteemed a saint; but, possessed by the demon of

---

(12) Fleury, *l.* 3, *n.* 30; Nat. Alex. *t.* 6, *c.* 3, *ar.* 4; Orsi, *t.* 2, *l.* 3, *n.* 44.
(13) Orsi, *t.* 2, *l.* 3, *n.* 45; N. Alex. *t.* 6, *c.* 3, *ar.* 5; Baron. Ann. 146, *n.* 9, &c.; Fleury, *t.* 1, *l.* 3, *n.* 34. (14) Fleury, loc. cit. *n.* 35. (15) Orsi, *t.* 2, *l.* 4, *n.* 17.

ambition, his head was turned. He began to speak in an extraordinary manner, make use of unknown words, and utter prophecies in contradiction to the traditions of the Church. Some thought him possessed by a spirit of error; others looked on him as a saint and prophet. He soon acquired a number of followers, and carried his madness to the utmost excess; among others who joined him were two loose women of the names of Prisca or Priscilla and Maximilla, and, seemingly possessed by the same spirit as himself, they uttered the most extraordinary rhodomontades. Montanus said that he and his prophetesses received the plenitude of the Holy Ghost, which was only partially communicated to others, and he quoted in his favour that text of St. Paul (1 Corinthians, xiii. 9), " By part we know, and by part we prophesy;" and they had the madness to esteem themselves greater than the apostles, since they had received the Holy Ghost promised by Jesus Christ in perfection. They also said that God wished, at first, to save the world, by means of Moses and the prophets; when he saw that these were not able to accomplish it, he himself became incarnate; but even this not sufficing, he descended in the Holy Ghost into Montanus and his prophetesses. He established nine fasting-days and three Lents in the year. Among other errors, he prohibited his disciples to fly from persecution, and refused to admit sinners to repentance, and prohibited second marriages (16). Eusebius tells us that he died miserably, having hanged himself (17).

11. The heresy of Montanus shot forth different branches, as the Cataphrigians, Artotirites, Peputians, Ascodrogites, and Pattalorinchites. The Cataphrigians were called from the nation to which Montanus belonged. The Eucharistic bread they used was made of flour and blood taken from the body of an infant by puncturing it all over; if the infant died he was considered a martyr, but if he survived he was regarded as high priest. This we learn from Noel Alexander (18). The Artotirites were so called, because, in the sacrifice of the Eucharist, they offered up bread and cheese. The Peputians took their name from an obscure village of Phrygia, where they held their solemn meetings; they ordained women priests and bishops, saying there was no difference between them and men. The Ascodrogites were no better than the ancient Bacchanalians; they used bottles which they filled with wine near the altars, saying that these were the new bottles Jesus Christ spoke of—" They shall put new wine into new bottles, and both are preserved." The Pattalorinchites were so called, because they wore a small stick in the mouth or nose, a sign of strict silence; they were so called, from *pattalos*, a stick, and *rinchos*, the nose (19).

(16) Euseb. Hist. Eccl. *l*. 5, *c*. 15. (17) Baron. An. 173, *n*. 20; N. Alex. *t*. 6, *sec*. 2. *c*. 3, *ar*. 8; Fleury, *t*. 1, *l*. 4, *n*. 5; Bernin. *t*. 1, *c*. 8; Orsi, *t*. 2, *l*. 4, *n*. 18. (18) Nat. Alex. cit. *ar*. 8, *n*. 11; St. Augus. & St. Cyril. [St. Epiphanius says it is the Peputians] (19) Van Ranst, His. Heres. *p*. 24 ; Vedia anche Nat. Alex. loc. cit.

12. Bardesanes, a native of Edessa, in Syria, lived in this age also. He was celebrated in the time of Marcus Aurelius for his learning and constancy in defending the faith. He told the Philosopher Apollonius, the favourite of the Emperor, who endeavoured to pervert him, that he was ready to seal his belief with his blood. He opposed the errors of Valentine; but, being educated in his school, he was infected with some of them, especially disbelieving the resurrection of the dead. He wrote many works in refutation of the heresies of his day, especially an excellent treatise on fate, which St. Jerome, in his catalogue of ecclesiastical writers, praises highly. We may truly say, with Noel Alexander, that the fall of so great a man is to be lamented (20).

13. Theodotus the Currier, so called on account of his trade, was a native of Byzantium, and he, along with Artemon, asserted, like Ebion and Cerinthus, that Christ was mere man. Besides this there was another Theodotus, called Argentarius, or the Banker, who taught that Melchisadech was Christ, or even greater than Christ, on account of that verse of the Psalms—" Thou art a priest for ever, according to the order of Melchisadech;" and his followers were afterwards called Melchisadechites (21).

14. Hermogenes said that matter was uncreated and eternal. Tertullian, Eusebius, and Lactantius refuted this error. He also taught that the devils would hereafter be united with matter, and that the body of Jesus Christ was in the sun (22).

CHAPTER III.

HERESIES OF THE THIRD CENTURY.

1. Praxeas.   2. Sabellius.   3. Paul of Samosata.   4. Manes.   5. Tertullian.   6. Origen.
7. Novatus and Novatian.   8. Nipos.   The Angelicals and the Apostolicals.

1. PRAXEAS, a native of Phrygia, was at first a Montanist, but afterwards becoming an enemy of Montanus, he caused him to be condemned by Pope Zepherinus, concealing his own heresy at the same time. Being soon discovered, he retracted his opinions, but soon afterwards openly proclaimed them. He denied the mystery of the Trinity, saying that in God there was but one person and one nature, whom he called the Father. This sole person, he said, descended into the womb of the Virgin, and being born of her by means of the incarnation, was called Jesus Christ. According to this impious doctrine, then, it was the Father who suffered death,

(20) Nat. Alex. t. 6, c. 3, ar. 9; Van Ranst, p. 24.   (21) N. Alex. loc. cit. ar. 10; Fleury, t. 1, l. 4, n. 33, 34.   (22) Fleury, loc. cit. n. 21; Alex. loc. cit. ar. 15.

and on that account his followers were called Patripassionists. The most remarkable among his disciples were Berillus, Noetus, and Sabellius. Berillus was Bishop of Bostris in Arabia; he said that Christ, before his incarnation, had no divinity, and in his incarnation had no divinity of his own, but only that of the Father. Noel Alexander says that Origen refuted him, and brought him back to the Catholic faith (1). Noetus, more obstinate in error, said that the Father, the Son, and the Holy Ghost were but one person and one God; he and his followers were cut off from the Church, and, as he died impenitent, he was refused Christian burial (2). The most celebrated promoter of this error was Sabellius.

2. Sabellius was born in the Ptolemais in Africa, and lived in the year 227. He shed a greater lustre, if we may say so, on the heresy of his master, and on that account this impious sect was called Sabellians. He denied the distinction of the three persons in the Trinity, and said they were but three names to distinguish the different operations of the Divinity. The Trinity, he said, was like the sun, in which we distinguish the light, the heat, and the form, though the sun be but one and the same. The light represents the Son, the heat the Holy Ghost, and the figure or substance of the sun itself the Father, who, in one person alone, contained the Son and the Holy Ghost (3). This error we will refute in the last part of the work.

3. Paul of Samosata was Bishop of Antioch. Before his appointment to the see he was poor, but afterwards, by extortion and sacrilege, by selling justice, and making false promises, he amassed a great deal of wealth. He was so vain and proud that he never appeared in public without a crowd of courtiers; he was always preceded by one hundred servants, and followed by a like number, and his own praises were the only subjects of his sermons; he not only abused those who did not flatter him, but frequently also offered them personal violence; and at length his vanity arrived at such a pitch that he had a choir of courtezans to sing hymns in his praise in the church; he was so dissolute in his morals that he had always a number of ladies of lax morals in his train. In fine, this impious prelate crowned all his crimes with heresy. The first of his blasphemies was, that Jesus Christ never existed until he was born of the Virgin, and hence he said he was a mere man; he also said that in Jesus there were two persons and two sons of God, one by nature and the other by adoption; he also denied the Trinity of the Divine persons, and although he admitted the names of the Father, and of the Son, and of the Holy Ghost, not, however, de-

---

(1) Nat. Alex. *t.* 7, *s.* 3, *c.* 3, *ar.* 1, ex Euseb.; Van Ranst, *p.* 65. (2) Nat. Alex. ibid. *c.* 3, *ar.* 7; Van Ranst, *p.* 48. (3) Nat. Alex. *t.* 7, *c.* 3, *ar.* 7; Orsi, *t.* 2, *l.* 5, *n.* 14; Hermant, *l.* 1, *c.* 60; Fleury, *l.* 7, *n.* 35.

nying, as Orsi thinks, personal existence to the Son and the Holy Ghost, yet he did not recognize either one or the other as persons of the Trinity, attributing to the Father alone the incarnation and passion (4). His disciples inserted those errors in their profession of faith, and in the formula of Baptism, but Noel Alexander says that it is uncertain whether Paul was the author of this heresy.

4. Manes was the founder of the Manicheans, and he adopted this name on account of taking to himself the title of the Paraclete, and to conceal the lowliness of his condition, since he was at first only a slave in Persia, but was liberated and adopted by an old lady of that country. She sent him to the public academy to be educated, but he made little progress in learning. Whatever he wanted in learning, he made up in impudence, and on that account he endeavoured to institute a new sect; and, to enlist the peasantry under the banner of his heresy, he studied magic with particular attention. To acquire a name for himself he undertook to cure the King of Persia's son, who was despaired of by the physicians. Unfortunately for him, however, the child died, notwithstanding all his endeavours to save him, and he was thrown into prison, and would have been put to death only he bribed the guards to let him escape. Misfortune, however, pursued him; after travelling through various countries, he fell again into the King's hands, who ordered him to be flayed alive with a sharp-pointed reed; his body was thrown to the beasts, and his skin hung up in the city gate, and thus the impious Manes closed his career. He left many followers after him, among whom was St. Augustin, in his youth, but, enlightened by the Almighty, he abandoned his errors, and became one of his most strenuous opponents (5).

The errors of Manes can be classed under the following heads: 1st. He admitted the plurality of Gods, alleging that there were two principles, one of good and the other of evil. Another of his errors was, that man had two souls—one bad, which the evil principle created together with the body; and another, good, created by the good principle, which was co-eternal, and of the same nature with God. All the good actions which man performs he attributes to the good soul, and all the evil ones he commits to the bad soul. He deprived man of free will, saying that he was always carried irresistibly forward by a force which his will could not resist. He denied the necessity of baptism, and entirely abolished that sacrament. Among many other errors, the Manicheans detested the flesh, as being created by the evil principle, and, therefore, denied that Jesus Christ ever took a body like ours, and they were addicted to every sort of impurity (6). They spread almost over the

(4) Orsi, t. 3, l. 8, n. 15; Gotti de Vera Rel. t. 2, c. 11, s. 2; N. Alex. t. 7, c. 3, ar. 8, sec. 2; Hermant, t. 1, c. 63; Fleury, t. 2, l. 8, n. 1. (5) Baron. Ann. 277, ex n. 1; Nat. Alex. t. 7, c. 3, ar. 9, sec. 1. (6) Nat. Alex. ibid. vide sec. 2; Hermant, t. 1, c. 65; Fleury, t. 2, l. 8, n. 10—12; Baron. Ann. 277, n. 1, & seq.; Graves in sec. 3.

entire world, and though condemned by many Popes, and persecuted by many Emperors, as Dioclesian, Gratian, and Theodosius, but especially by Justin and Justinian, who caused many of them to be burned alive in Armenia, still they were not annihilated till the year 1052, when, as Baronius relates, Henry II., finding some of them lurking in France, caused them to be hanged. The refutation of this heresy we have written in the book called the Truth of the Faith (7).

5. Tertullian was born, as Fleury (8) relates, in Carthage, and his father was a centurion in the Pretorian Bands. He was at first a Pagan, but was converted about the year 197, and was a priest for forty years, and died at a very advanced age. He wrote many works of the highest utility to the Church, on Baptism, Penance, Idolatry, on the Soul, on Proscriptions, and an Apology for the Christians, which has acquired great celebrity. Although in his book on Proscriptions he calls Montanus a heretic, still, according to the general opinion of authors, he fell into Montanism himself. Baronius says that he was cut off from the Church, and excommunicated by Pope Zepherinus (9). Tertullian was a man of the greatest austerity; he had the greatest veneration for continence; he practised extraordinary watchings, and on account of a dispute he had with the clergy of Rome, he attached himself to the Montanists, who, to the most rigid mortification, joined the belief that Montanus was the Holy Ghost. Noel Alexander proves, on the authority of St. Jerome, St. Hilary, St. Pacianus, St. Optatus, and St. Augustin, that he asserted the Church could not absolve adulterers, that those who married a second time were adulterers, and that it was not lawful to fly from persecution. He called the Catholics, Psichici, or Animals. Fleury says (10), that Tertullian taught that the soul was a body, of a palpable form, but transparent, because one of the Prophetesses heard so in a vision. Both Fleury and Noel Alexander say (11), that he forsook the Montanists before his death, but a sect, who called themselves Tertullianists after him, remained in Carthage for two hundred years, until the time of St. Augustin, when they once more returned to the bosom of the Church.

6. Origen was an Egyptian, and his early days were spent in Alexandria. His father was St. Leonidas the Martyr, who had him educated in every branch of sacred and profane literature (12). It is said his own father held him in the highest veneration, and that often while he slept he used to kiss his bosom, as the temple where the Holy Ghost dwelt (13). At the age of eighteen he was

(7) Verità della Fede, *part* 3. *c.* 2, *sec.* 2.   (8) Fleury, *t.* 1, *l.* 4, *n.* 47.
(9) Baron. Ann. 201, *n.* 3, & seq. ad 11; Fleury, *t.* 1, *l.* 25 & 26; Orsi, *t.* 3; *l.* 8, *n.* 28.   (10) Fleury, *t.* 1, *l.* 5, *n.* 25.   (11) Fleury, *t.* 1, *l.* 6, *n.* 3, cum St. Augus. & Nat. Alex. *t.* 6, *c.* 3, *ar.* 8, *n.* 9.   (12) Nat. Alex. *t.* 7, *ar.* 12.   (13) Fleury, *l.* 5, *n.* 2; Orsi, *l.* 5, *n.* 27.

made Catechist of the Church of Alexandria, and he discharged his duties so well that the very pagans flocked to hear him. Plutarch, who afterwards became an illustrious martyr of the faith of Christ, was one of his disciples. In the height of the persecution he never ceased to assist the confessors of Christ, despising both torments and death. He had the greatest horror of sensual pleasures, and it is related of him that for fear of offending against chastity, and to avoid temptation, he mutilated himself, interpreting the 12th verse of the 19th chapter of St. Matthew in a wrong sense (14). He refuted the Arabians, who denied the immortality of the soul, and converted Berrillus, as we have already seen, who denied the divinity of Jesus Christ. He also converted Ambrose from the errors of the Valentinians. He was so desirous of martyrdom, that his mother was obliged to take away his clothes, to prevent him from going to his father, who was in prison for the faith. All this, however, was to no purpose; he avoided her vigilance, flew to his father, and when he would not be allowed to speak to him, he exhorted him by letter to persevere in the faith. At the age of eighteen he was Prefect of the studies of Alexandria. When he was composing his Commentaries on the Scriptures, he dictated to seven or eight amanuenses at the same time. He edited different editions of the Scriptures, compiling the Tetrapla, the Hexapla, and the Octapla. The Tetrapla had four columns in each page; in the first was the version of the Seventy, or Septuagint, in the second that of Aquila, in the third that of Simmachus, and the fourth that of Theodotian. The Hexapla had six columns, and, besides the former, contained the Hebrew text and a Greek translation. Finally, the Octapla contained, besides the former, two other versions, compiled by some Hebrews. His name was so famous at that time that all the priests and doctors consulted him in any difficult matter. Presuming too much on his wisdom, he fell into different errors, by wishing to interpret many texts of Scripture in a mystical, rejecting the literal, sense. Those, he says, who adhere to the letter of the Scripture will never see the kingdom of God (15), hence we should seek the spirit of the word, which is hidden and mysterious. He is defended by some; but the majority condemn him, although he endeavoured to clear himself by saying that he wrote his sentiments merely as opinions, and subjected them to the judgment of his readers (16).

He was obliged to go into Achaia, a country at that time distracted by various heresies. In his journey he persuaded two bishops of Palestine whom he visited, that it would be of great service to the Church if he was ordained priest (17). Yielding to his suggestions they ordained him, and this so displeased Demetrius,

(14) Nat. Alex. *t.* 7, *ar.* 12.   (15) Origen, Stromata, *l.* 10.   (16) Orsi, *l.* 6. *n.* 61.   (17) Nat. Alex. ibid.; Orsi, *n.* 30.

Bishop of Alexandria, that in a council he deposed and excommunicated him. Several other bishops, however, received him in his misfortunes, and entertained him honourably. Orsi, on the authority of Eusebius, tells us (18), that in the persecution of Decius he was imprisoned a long time, loaded with irons, and a great iron ring on his neck; and that he was not only tortured in the legs in a horrible manner, but was likewise put on the rack. Dionisius, Eusebius says (19), wrote him a letter, or rather a small treatise, to animate and console him; and from that circumstance, Cardinal Orsi (20) proves the fallacy of Du Pin's conjecture, that the sentence passed against him by Demetrius was enforced under his successors Aracla and Dionisius. Origen did not long survive the torments he endured in that persecution. He died in Tyre, in the year 253, the sixty-ninth of his age (21).

Bernini tells us, on the authority of St. Epiphanius (22), (thinking, however, that this was foisted into St. Epiphanius's works by the enemies of Origen), that he denied the faith by offering incense to idols, to avoid the indignities and insults inflicted on him by an Ethiopian, and that he was then freed from prison, and his life spared. After that he went from Alexandria to Jerusalem, and at the request of the clergy and people went into the pulpit to preach. It happened, however, that opening the book of the Psalms, to explain them, the first words he read were those of the 49th Psalm: "God said to the sinner, why dost thou declare my justices and take my covenant into thy mouth?" Struck dumb with sorrow, he began to weep bitterly, and left the pulpit without saying a word. Not only St. Epiphanius, but Eusebius (23) before him, bear witness to Origen's fall. Although Bernini (24) says this story is quite fabulous, yet Petavius, Daniel Huet, Pagi, and especially Noel Alexander (25), say it is a fact. Roncaglia (26) is of opinion that Noel Alexander's arguments are groundless, and that Baronius's opinion carries more weight with it. We can decide nothing as to the salvation of Origen, though Baronius says that St. Simeon Salus saw him in hell; still, all is a mystery known to God alone. We know, however, on the authority of Baronius, that his doctrine was condemned by Pope Anastasius and Pope Gelasius, and afterwards by the fifth general council (27).

The substance of the errors of Origen, as well as I could collect from the works of Noel Alexander, Fleury, Hermant, Orsi, Van Ranst (who gives a great deal of information in a small space), and

---

(18) Orsi, *t.* 3, *l.* 7, *n.* 33. (19) Euseb. His. Eccl. *l.* 6. (20) Orsi, *t.* 3, *l.* 7, *n.* 33. (21) Orsi, loc. cit.; Hermant, *t.* 1, *c.* 68; Bar. Ann. 204, *n.* 8; V. Ranst, *p.* 42; Graves, *s.* 3. (22) Bernin. Istor. *t.* 1, *c.* 1, *p.* 125. (23) Euseb. *l.* 6; Hist. Eccl. *c.* 59. (24) Baron. Ann. 253, *n.* 117, & seq. cum Graves, loc. cit. (25) Petav. in Animadv. in St. Epiph. Heres. 64; Huetius, *l.* 1; Orig. *c.* 4; Pagius ad an. 251, *n.* 19; Nat. Alex. *t.* 7, *diss.* 15, *q.* 2, *art. unic.* (26) Ronc. not. in Natal. loc. cit. (27) Baron. Ann. 400, &c.

others, was all included in his *Periarchon*, or Treatise on Principles. This treatise, Fleury says, was translated by Rufinus, who endeavoured to correct it as much as possible. The intent of Origen in this work was to refute Valentine, Marcion, and Ebion, who taught that men are either essentially good or essentially wicked. He said that God alone was good and immutable, but that his creatures were capable of either good or evil, by making use of their free will for a good purpose, or perverting it for a wicked one. Another of his opinions was that the souls of men were of the same nature as the celestial spirits, that is, composed of spirit and matter; that they were all created before the beginning of the world, but that, as a punishment for some crimes committed, they were shut up in the sun, moon, and other planets, and even in human bodies, as it were in a prison, to punish them for a time; after which, being freed from their slavery by death, they went to heaven to receive the reward of their virtues, or to hell to suffer the punishment of their sins, but such rewards and punishments were not eternal. Hence, he said, the blessed in heaven could be banished from that abode of happiness for faults committed there, and that the punishment of the devils and the damned would not last for all eternity, because at the end of the world Jesus Christ would be again crucified, and they would participate in the general redemption. He also said that before the creation of this world there existed many others, and that after this had ceased to exist many more would be created, for, as God was never idle, so he never was without a world. He taught many other erroneous opinions; in fact his doctrine is entirely infected with the maxims of Plato, Pythagoras, and the Manicheans. Cassiodorus, speaking of Origen, says, I wonder how the same man could contradict himself so much; for since the days of the Apostles he had no equal in that part of his doctrine which was approved of, and no one ever erred more grossly in the part which was condemned. Cabassutius (28) says, that Pope Gelasius, following the example of Anastatius, gave this sentence relative to Origen in the Roman council:—" We declare that those works of Origen which the blessed Jerome does not reject can be read, but we condemn all others with their author."

After the death of Origen his followers disturbed the Church very much by maintaining and propagating his errors. Hermant (29) relates that Pope Anastatius had a great deal of difficulty in putting down the troubles occasioned by the Origenists in Rome, who got footing there under the auspices of Melania, by means of the priest Rufinus. The author of the notes on Fleury says, that Anastasius wrote to John of Jerusalem to inform him of how matters were

(28) Cabassut. Notit. Hist. Conc. Constan. II. an. 553, *n.* 14, in fin.   (22) Hermant, *t.* 1, *c.* 132.

going on, and that he, on that account, cut off Rufinus from the Church. In the reign of the Emperor Justinian, some Origenist monks who lived in a laura founded by St. Saba, under the abbot Nonnus, began to disseminate their errors among this brethren, and in a short time infected the principal laura, but were expelled by the abbot Gelasius. Favoured, however, by Theodore of Cesarea, they got possession of the great laura again, and expelled the greater part of the monks who disagreed with them. In the meantime, Nonnus died, and his successor George being deposed for immorality by his own party, the Catholic monks again got possession of the laura, and elected Conon, one of this party, abbot (30). Finally, in the twelfth canon of the second council of Constantinople, both Origen and all those who would persist in defending his doctrine were condemned (31).

7. Novatus and Novatian. Novatus was a priest of the Church of Carthage. St. Cyprian relates that he was a man of a turbulent disposition, seditious and avaricious, and that his faith was suspected by the bishops. He was accused of robbing the orphans and widows, and appropriating to his own use the money given him for the use of the Church. It is said he allowed his father to die of starvation, and afterwards refused to bury him; and that he caused the death of his wife by giving her a kick, and causing premature labour. He was also one of the principal agents in getting the deacon Felicissimus ordained priest without the leave or knowledge of St. Cyprian, his bishop, and was one of the principal leaders of the schism of Novatian, exciting as many as he could to oppose the lawful Pope, Cornelius (32).

We now come to speak of the character and errors of Novatian. Being possessed by an evil spirit he was baptized in bed during a dangerous fit of sickness, and when he recovered he neglected getting the ceremonies of baptism supplied, and never received confirmation, which, according to the discipline of the Church in those days, he ought to have received after baptism, and his followers, for that reason, afterwards rejected this sacrament. He was afterwards ordained priest, the bishop dispensing in the irregularity he incurred by being baptized in bed. Hence his ordination gave great umbrage both to the clergy and people. While the persecution was raging, the deacons begged of him to leave his place of concealment, and assist the faithful, who were dragged to the place of punishment; but he answered, that he did not henceforward intend to discharge the duties of a priest; that he had his mind made up for other objects. This was nothing less than the Popedom, which he had the ambition to pretend to, puffed up by the applause he received for his oratorical powers. At this time, Cornelius was elected Pope, and he, by intrigue, got himself consecrated privately by three

(30) Orsi, *t.* 18, *l.* 41, *n.* 1 & 5, ad 7.   (31) Orsi, al luogo, cit. *n.* 70.   (32) Baron. An. 254, *n.* 50; Nat. *t.* 7, *c.* 3, *ar.* 3, 4; Fleury, *t.* 1, *l.* 6, *n.* 51.

ignorant bishops whom he made intoxicated. Thus he was the first anti-Pope who ever raised a schism in the Church of Rome. But what will not ambition do? While he administered the Eucharist to his partizans, he exacted an oath from each of them, saying, "Swear to me, by the blood of Jesus Christ, that you will never leave my party and join Cornelius" (33).

The errors of Novatus and Novatian were the following:—they denied that the Church could use any indulgence with those who became idolaters through fear of persecution, or that she could grant pardon for any mortal sin committed after baptism, and they denied the sacrament of confirmation. Like the Montanists, they condemned second marriages, and refused communion on the point of death to those who contracted them (34).

8. These were not the only heretics who disturbed the Church during this century. Nipos, an Egyptian bishop, about the year 284, again raked up the errors of the Millenarians, taking the promise of the Apocalypse in a literal sense, that Jesus Christ would reign on earth for the space of a thousand years, and that the saints should enjoy all manner of sensual delights. The Angelicals offered the supreme adoration, which should be given to God alone, to the angels; adored them as the creators of the world, and pretended to lead angelic lives themselves. The Apostolicals said it was not lawful for any one to possess property of any sort, and that the riches of this life were an insurmountable obstacle to salvation. These heretics received no married persons into this sect (35).

CHAPTER IV.

HERESIES OF THE FOURTH CENTURY.

ARTICLE I.

SCHISM AND HERESY OF THE DONATISTS.

1, 2. Schism. 3. Heresy. 4, 5. Confutation of St. Augustin. Circumcellionists. 6. Conference commanded by Honorius. 7. Death of St. Marcellinus, and Council of Carthage.

1. IN order properly to understand the history of the Donatists, we must separate the schism from the heresy, for they were at first schismatics before they were heretics. Donatus the first was the author of the schism; a second Donatus was the father of the heresy, and he was called by his followers Donatus the Great. In the

(33) Nat. loc. cit.; Baron. n. 61, &c. Fleury, cit. n. 51; Hermant, t. 1, c. 48, 51. (34) Nat. Alex. ibid.; Van Ranst, p. 45, 46; (35) Nat. Alex. t. 7, c. 3, ar. 6, 9; Van Ranst, p. 47 & 64; Berti, t. 1, s. 3, c. 3.

beginning of the fourth century, Mensurius, Bishop of Carthage, was cited before the tyrant Maxentius on the charge of concealing in his house a deacon of the name of Felix, the author of a libel on the Emperor. Mensurius went to Rome to defend himself, and died on his way home. Cecilianus was elected by the general voice of the people to fill the vacant see, and was consecrated by Felix, Bishop of Aphthongum, and other prelates. His opponents immediately began to question the validity of his consecration, because it was performed by those bishops called *traitors* (traditores), who delivered up the Scriptures to the pagans. Another charge made against him was that he prohibited the faithful from supplying the confessors in the prisons with food. At the head of this conspiracy was a bishop of an African city, called "the Black Houses," whose name was Donatus; and it was very much strengthened by the intrigues of Lucilla, a Spanish lady then residing in Carthage. Cecilianus happened to come into collision with her while he was yet a deacon, because he reprimanded her for paying the veneration due to a holy martyr to a certain dead man, whose sanctity was never recognized by the Church. To revenge herself on him for this, she became the soul of the conspiracy, and by the influence of her wealth brought over to her party many of the bishops of Africa, who, uniting together in council, under the presidency of the secondary primate of Numidia, deposed Cecilianus in his absence, and elected a domestic of Lucilla's in his place, of the name of Majorinus, who was consecrated by Donatus (1).

2. Notwithstanding all this persecution, Cecilianus remained steadfast in the faith, which obliged the Donatists to have recourse to the Emperor Constantine. He referred the entire matter to St. Melchiades, the reigning Pope, who, in the year 315, or, according to others, in 316, assembled a council of nineteen bishops, and declared both the innocence of Cecilianus and the validity of his consecration. The Donatists were discontented with this decision, and again appealed to the Emperor; he used every means to pacify them, but seeing them determined to keep up the schism, he ordered Elianus, pro-consul of Africa, to investigate the matter, and find out whether the crime laid to the charge of Felix who consecrated Cecilianus (that of delivering up the Scriptures to the idolaters) was true. The conspirators, aware that this investigation was to take place, bribed a notary of the name of Ingentius to prove a falsehood; but, in his examination before the Proconsul, he acquitted both Felix and Cecilianus. The Emperor being informed of this was satisfied as to their innocence; but in order to appease the Donatists, and give them no cause of complaint, he caused another council to be convoked at Arles, to which

(1) Baron. Ann. 303, *n.* 29, & Ann. 306, *n.* 74 & 75; vide Fleury, Nat. Alex. Orsi, Van Ranst, & Hermant.

St. Silvester, who succeeded St. Melchiades in the year 314, sent his legate to preside in his name; and in that and the following year, Felix and Cecilianus were again acquitted by the council (2).

3. Nothing, however, could satisfy the Donatists; they even, according to Fleury (3), extended themselves as far as Rome. Heresy now was added to schism. The second Donatus, called by them Donatus the Great, put himself at their head; and although tinctured with the Arian heresy, as St. Augustin says (4), intruded himself into the See of Carthage, as successor to Majorinus. He was the first who began to disseminate the errors of the Donatists in Africa (5). Those consisted in the adoption of one false principle, which was the source of many others. This was, that the Church was composed of the just alone, and that all the wicked were excluded from it; founding this belief on that text of St. Paul, where he says that the Church of Christ is free from all stain: " Christ loved his Church, and delivered himself up for it, that he might present it to himself a glorious Church, not having spot or wrinkle" (Ephesians, v. 27). They also professed to find this doctrine in the twenty-seventh verse of the twenty-first chapter of the Apocalypse: " There shall not enter into it anything defiled." The adoption of this erroneous principle led them into many heretical consequences:—First, believing that the Church was composed of the good alone, they inferred that the Church of Rome was lost, because the Pope and bishops having admitted to their communion traitors, or those who delivered up the holy books into the hands of the Pagans, as they alleged Felix and Cecilianus to have done, and as the sour leaven corrupteth the entire mass, then the Church, being corrupted and stained by the admission of those, was lost,—it only remained pure in that part of Africa where the Donatists dwelt; and to such a pitch did their infatuation arrive, that they quoted Scripture for this also, interpreting that expression of the Canticles: " Shew me, O thou whom my soul loveth, where thou feedest, where thou liest in the mid-day" (the south), as relating to Africa, which lies in the southern part of the world. Another heretical inference of theirs was, that the sacrament of baptism was null and void if administered out of their Church, because a Church that was lost had not the power of administering the sacrament, and on that account they re-baptized all proselytes.

4. These two heretical opinions fall to the ground at once, by proving the falsity of the first proposition, that the Church consists of the good alone. St. Augustin proves clearly that these texts of St. Paul and St. John refer to the triumphant, and not to the militant Church, for our Redeemer, speaking of the militant

(2) Hermant, c. 78, &c.   (3) Fleury, t. 2, l. 10, n. 26.   (4) St. Augus. l. de Heres. c. 69.   (5) Orsi, t. 4, l. 11, n. 51 & 52.

Church, says, in many places, it contains both good and bad; in one place he likens it to a threshing floor, which contains both straw and grain: "He will thoroughly cleanse his floor, and gather his wheat into the barn, but the chaff he will burn with unquenchable fire" (Matt. iii. 12). In another place he compares it to a field sown with good seed, and cockle growing amongst it: "Let both grow," he says, "till the time of the harvest, and then I will say to the reapers, Gather up first the cockle and bind it into bundles to burn, but gather the wheat into my barn" (Matt. xiii. 3) (6).

5. The Donatists were not content with the crime of heresy, but committed a thousand others, if possible of a deeper dye. They destroyed the altars of the Catholics, broke the chalices, spilled the holy Chrism on the ground, and threw the holy Eucharist to the dogs. But St. Optatus Milevitanus (7) informs us that God did not suffer the indignity to his sacred body and blood to go unpunished, for the dogs getting mad turned on their own masters, and tore them, as if in revenge for the insult offered to the body of Jesus Christ. Not satisfied with tormenting the living, they outraged the dead, whom they dragged out of their graves, and exposed to the most unheard-of indignities. About this time, also, the Circumcellionists sprung from the Donatists. Their chiefs were Faber and Maxidus, and they were called Circumcellionists from running about from town to town and house to house. They were called by Donatus the chiefs of the saints; they boasted that they were the redressers of all wrong and injustice through the world, though nothing could be more unjust than their own proceedings. They gave liberty to slaves, and commanded debtors not to pay their debts, telling them they were freed from all obligation. Their cruelty equalled their fanaticism, for they went about in armed bands, and put to death those who did not become proselytes to their doctrine; but what was more astonishing than all was to see this fury turned against themselves, for many of them committed suicide by throwing themselves over precipices, some cast themselves into the fire, others drowned themselves or cut their throats, and endeavoured to induce others to follow their example, telling them that all who died so were martyrs; even women followed the example of their husbands in this madness, and St. Augustin tells us that even some, in a state of pregnancy, threw themselves down precipices. It is true that even the Donatist bishops endeavoured by every means to put a stop to such frightful fanaticism, and even called in the authority of the secular power to aid them, but they could not deny that they were their own disciples, and that they became the victims of such perverse doctrines from following their own example (8).

---

(6) Nat. Alex. *t.* 9, *diss.* 31.　　(7) St. Opt. *l.* 2, de Donatis.　　(8) Baron. An. 357, *n.* 15; V. Ranst; Fleury, *t.* 2, *l.* 11, *n.* 46; Hermant, *c.* 81.

6. The Emperors Constantine and Constans, sons of Constantine the Great and Valentinian, issued several edicts against the Donatists, but all was of little avail. In the reign of Honorius an edict was published, giving liberty to all sects to profess publicly their doctrines, but about the year 410 the Donatists, taking advantage of this, broke out into several acts of violence, which so exasperated Honorius that, at the suggestion of the Catholic bishops of Africa, he revoked the edict. He then published that law (L. 51, Codex Theodosianus), which punishes with confiscation of property the practice of any religion except the Catholic, and even with pain of death if the professors of any heretical doctrines should publicly assemble in their conventicles. In order, however, entirely to extinguish the heresy of Donatus, he sent the Imperial Tribune, Marcellinus, a man of the greatest learning and prudence, into Africa, with orders to assemble all the African bishops, both Catholics and Donatists, in Carthage, to proceed to a conference to see who was right and who was wrong, that peace should be established between them. The Donatists at first refused to come, but the edicts of Honorius were too strict to be avoided, and they consented, and the conference was held in the Baths of Gazilian. Two hundred and eighty-six Catholics and two hundred and seventy-nine Donatists assembled, but Marcellinus, to avoid confusion, would allow only thirty-six, eighteen on each side, to hold the conference, these eighteen to be chosen from among all the rest. The schismatics refused to obey the regulations of Marcellinus, and used every stratagem to avoid coming to the point; especially they endeavoured to cushion the question concerning the true Church, but, with all their art, they were, one day, drawn into it, and, seeing themselves caught, they could not help lamenting, saying, see how insensibly we have got into the bottom of the case. Then it was that St. Augustin, as we have already shown, proved clearer than the noon-day sun that the Church is not composed of the good alone, as the Donatists would have it, but of the good and the bad, as the threshing-floor contains both corn and chaff. Finally, after many disputations, Marcellinus gave his decision in favour of the Catholics (9).

7. Many were united to the Church, but many more persisted in their errors, and appealed to Honorius, who would not even admit them to an audience, but condemned to a heavy fine all those who would not join the Catholic Church, and threatened to banish all the Donatist bishops and priests who would persist in their opposition to his decree. Nothing could exceed their malice against the Catholics after that; they murdered the defender of the Church, Restitutus (10), and plotted with the Count Marinus the

---

(9) Orsi, *t.* 11, *l.* 25, *n.* 1, 24; Baron. Ann. 411, *n.* 24.   (10) Baron. An. 412, *n.* 1, &c.; Orsi, *n.* 28, 29.

destruction of Marcellinus. The means by which Marinus accomplished this were horrible. He caused St. Marcellinus to be imprisoned on a charge of high treason, alleging that he was one of the chief promoters of the rebellion of Heraclian, which he was most innocent of, and although he swore to his friend Cecilianus that he would liberate both St. Marcellinus and his brother Aprinus from prison, he ordered him the next day to be taken out to a lonesome place, and beheaded. Cardinal Orsi proves this on the authority of Orosius, St. Jerome, and St. Augustin. Thus Marcellinus died a martyr, but Marinus was punished for his injustice, being shortly after recalled by Honorius, and stripped of all his honours. In the Council of Carthage, in 348, or, as Hermant (11) has it, in 349, the Catholic bishops of Africa assembled in great numbers to thank the Almighty for putting an end to this sect, and the schismatical bishops then joined them. In this council it was prohibited to re-baptize those who were baptized in the faith of the Trinity, in opposition to the erroneous opinion of the Donatists, who declared the baptism administered out of their communion invalid. It was also forbidden to honour as martyrs those who killed themselves, and they were allowed the rites of burial through compassion alone. Cardinal Baronius says that this sect lasted till the time of Gregory the Great, who endeavoured to put an end to it altogether, and he also says that those heretics were the cause of the ruin of the Church of Africa (12).

Article II.

THE ARIAN HERESY.

SEC. I.—PROGRESS OF ARIUS, AND HIS CONDEMNATION BY THE COUNCIL OF NICE.

8. Origin of Arius. 9. His Errors and Supporters. 10. Synod of Bythinia. 11. Synod of Osius in Alexandria. 12. General Council of Nice. 13. Condemnation of Arius. 14—16. Profession of Faith. 17. Exile of Eusebius of Nicomedia, and insidious Letter of Eusebius of Cesarea. 18. Banishment of Arius. 19. Decree for the Meletians. 20. Decree for the Quartodecimans. 21. Canons. 22. End of the Council.

8. ARIUS was an African, born in that part of it called Lybia Cirenaica, and he went to Alexandria in the expectation of obtaining some ecclesiastical dignity. He was, as Baronius tells us, a man of great learning and science—of polished manners, but of a forbidding appearance—ambitious of glory, and fond of novelty (1). At first he was a follower of Meletius, Bishop of Lycopolis, in Upper Egypt. This bishop, in the beginning of the fourth century, though he taught nothing contrary to faith, still was deposed

---

(11) Hermant, c. 99.   (12) Baron. An. 591, &c.   (1) Baron. An. 319; Van Ranst, p. 70; Nat. Alex. t. 8, c. 3, ar. 3; Fleury, l. 10; Hermant, t. 1, c. 85; Orsi, l. 12, n. 2.

by St. Peter, Bishop of Alexandria, on account of many grievous crimes, one of which even was idolatry (2); and he then raised a great schism in Egypt against St. Peter, and went so far as to administer the ordination belonging by right to the Saint. Arius judged that he would have no great chance of advancing himself according to his wishes, by continuing a partizan of Meletius, so he made his submission to St. Peter, and was ordained deacon by him; but he, finding that he still continued to correspond with Meletius, turned him out of Alexandria. St. Peter was soon after put in prison for the faith, and about to be martyred. Arius endeavoured again to be received by him; and it was then, as Baronius (3) tells us, on the authority of the Acts of the martyrdom of St. Peter, that Christ appeared to the Saint with a torn garment, and said to him: "Arius has torn this; take heed lest you receive him into your communion." Alexander has strong doubts of the truth of this vision (4): but his arguments are not convincing, and it has been admitted into the Roman Breviary on the 26th of November, the feast of St. Peter. Arius, for all that, was promoted to the priesthood by Achilla, who succeeded St. Peter, martyred in 311, and got the charge of a parochial church called Baucal (5), in Alexandria. On the death of Achilla, Arius, who was now, as Fleury tells us, advanced in years, expected to succeed him; but St. Alexander was chosen, a man of great knowledge and most exemplary life. Arius began immediately to censure his conduct and condemn his doctrine, saying that he falsely taught that the Word, the Son of God, was equal to the Father, begotten by him from all eternity, and of the same nature and substance as the Father, which, he said, was the heresy of Sabellius. He then began to promulgate the following blasphemies:—1. That the Word was not from all eternity, but was brought forth out of nothing by the Father, and created, the same as one of ourselves; and, 2ndly, that Christ, according to his free will, was of a mutable nature, and that he might have followed vice, but that, as he embraced goodness, God, as a reward for his good works, made him a participator in the divine nature, and honoured him with the title of the Word, the Son, and of Wisdom (6). Noel Alexander says that these errors are taken from an impious work he wrote, called Thalia, and from an epistle of his to St. Alexander, referred to by St. Athanasius, and from the Synodical Epistle of the Council of Nice, quoted by Socrates, St. Epiphanius, and Theodoret. Noel Alexander also says, on the authority of St. Athanasius and Theodoret, that he taught that the Word in the Incarnation took a body without a soul, and that the soul was part of the divinity.

(2) Nat. Alex. ibid. *ar.* 2; St. Athan. cum. Socrat. & Theodoret; Orsi, *l.* 12, *n.* 41; Fleury, *l.* 11, *n.* 15.   (3) Baron. An. 310, *n.* 4 & 5.   (4) N. Alex. *t.* 8, *diss.* 9. (5) St.Epip. Her. 69, Theod. &c.   (6) Nat. Alex. *ar.* 3, *sec.* 2; Fleury, cit. *n.* 28; Baron. An. 315, *n.* 19 & 20; Hermant, *c.* 84.

9. Arius began at first privately to teach his errors; but he soon became so bold that he publicly preached them in his parish. St. Alexander at first tried to bring him back by admonition, but, finding that of no avail, he had recourse to more rigorous measures; and as some bishops were even then tainted with his heresy—especially Secundus of Ptolemais, and Theonas of Marmorica—he convoked a synod in Alexandria, in 320, at which nearly one hundred bishops from Lybia and Egypt assembled, besides a great number of priests. Arius was called before them, and publicly professed his errors; so the assembled Fathers excommunicated him and his adherents, and St. Alexander wrote from the synod an encyclical letter, giving an account of it to all the bishops of the Church (7). Notwithstanding this, Arius only became more obstinate, and made many proselytes, both men and women; and Theodoret says (8) he seduced several of his female followers. He then put himself under the protection of Eusebius of Nicomedia, a powerful and learned, but wicked man, who left his own bishopric of Beyrout, and intruded himself into the see of Nicomedia, through the influence of Constantia, the sister of Constantine. He wrote to St. Alexander, requesting him to receive Arius again into his communion; but the Holy Patriarch not only refused his request, but obliged Arius and all his followers to quit Alexandria (9).

10. Arius then went to Palestine, and succeeded in seducing several bishops of that and the neighbouring provinces, especially Eusebius of Cesarea, Aezius of Lidda or Hospolis, Paulinus of Tyre, Gregory of Beyrout, Athanasius of Anazarbus, and Theodotus of Laodicea. When St. Alexander heard of this, he complained very much of it, and wrote to several of the bishops of Palestine, who yielded to his advice, and forsook Arius. He then took refuge with his friend Eusebius of Nicomedia, and there he wrote his book called Thalia, interlarding it with low jests, to take the common people, and with all his blasphemies against the faith, to instil into the minds of every class the poison of his heresy (10). Eusebius called together a synod in Bythinia of bishops favourable to Arius, who wrote to several other bishops to interfere with St. Alexander to receive him again into his communion, but the saint was inflexible (11).

11. About this time Constantine gained the victory over Licinius, which gave him peaceable possession of the empire; but when he came to Nicomedia he was afflicted to hear of the dissensions between St. Alexander and Arius and the bishops of the East. Eusebius of Nicomedia, who had the first story for the Emperor, told him it was a matter of no great importance altogether, and did not touch on the integrity of the faith, and that all

---

(7) N. Alex. *ar.* 4, *s.* 1; Fleury, ibid.; Hermant, *c.* 86; Orsi. *l.* 1, *c.* 4. (8) Theodoret, Apol. 15. (9) Socrat. *l.* 1, *c.* 6; Orsi, *n.* 9; Fleury, loc. cit. (10) St. Athan. (11) Orsi, *l.* 12, *n.* 16; Fleury, *l.* 10, *n.* 37.

that was requisite was that both sides should be silent. So, to
believe that Jesus Christ was either God or a simple creature was
a matter of trifling importance; but this has always been the aim
of heretics, to make it appear that the dogmas they impugned were
of no great consequence. The Emperor being thus deceived, wrote
to St. Alexander (12), telling him it was unwise to disturb the
Church after this manner, and that the wisest way would be to
hold his tongue, and leave every one to follow his own opinions.
The disturbance in the East, however, only increased; so that, at
length, Osius, Bishop of Cordova in Spain, for thirty years, a man
of the greatest merit and learning, and who suffered a great deal
in the persecution of Maximilian, was sent to put an end to it.
Baronius and Van Ranst say he was sent by St. Sylvester; but the
general opinion, which Fleury and Noel Alexander, on the authority of Socrates, Eusebius, Sozymen, and Theodoret, adopt, is that
he was sent by the Emperor (13). When Osius arrived in Alexandria, and saw that the evil was greater than he imagined, he
summoned a synod of bishops in concert with St. Alexander, and
Arius and his followers were again excommunicated, and his errors
condemned (14).

12. After this new condemnation, Arius wrote to the Emperor
in his defence; but Constantine, now informed of his errors, answered him in a long letter, in which, after refuting his errors, he
proved him to be a malicious fool, and he also ordered that this letter
should be made public. The Arians were so annoyed at this that
they pelted the Emperor's statue, and disfigured the face of it; but
he showed his good sense, and proved himself a man of great moderation, on the occasion, for when his ministers urged him to
punish them, he, laughing, put his hand to his face, and said, "I
don't perceive they have hurt me," and took no more notice of the
matter (15). The fire of discord was not, however, extinguished,
but rather burned more violently every day. The Emperor then
judged it best to call together a general council, to put an end to
it; and appointed Nice, in Bythinia, not Nice, in Thrace, as the
place of meeting, and invited all bishops—both those of the Empire, and those beyond its borders—to assemble there, and provided
for all their expenses (16). The bishops of Asia, Africa, and
Europe were rejoiced at this, and came to the council; so that, in
the year 325, three hundred and eighteen bishops were assembled
in Nice, as Noel Alexander asserts, on the authority of St. Ambrose,
in contradiction to Eusebius, who reduces the number to two hundred and fifty (17). Oh, how glorious it was for the Church to
see so many pastors assembled in this council! Among them were

(12) Euseb. in Vit. Constant c. 63.   (13) Baron. An. 518, n. 88; Fleury, n. 42;
Van Ranst, p. 71.   (14) N Alex. ar. 4, sec. 1; Fleury, l. 10, n. 43; Orsi, l. 12, n.
21; Hermant, l. 1, c. 86.   (15) Orsi, l. 12, n. 24.   (16) Fleury, l. 11, n. 1; Orsi, l. 12,
n. 25.   (17) Baron. Ann. 325; Nat. Alex., Fleury, Ruf. Soc. St. Athanasius, & Soz.

many prelates bearing on their persons the marks of persecution suffered for the faith, especially St. Paphnutius, Bishop in the Thebaid, whose right eye was plucked out, and his left hand burned, in the persecution of Maximilian; St. Paul, Bishop of Neoceserea, who, by order of Licinius, lost the use of both his hands, the sinews being burned with a red iron; St. Potamon, Bishop of Thrace, whose right eye also was torn out for the faith; and many other ecclesiastics, who were tortured by the idolaters (18).

13. St. Sylvester seconded the pious intention of the Emperor, and assented to the council; and as his advanced age did not permit him to attend in person, he sent, as his legates, Vito and Vincentius, Roman priests, and Osius, Bishop of Cordova, to preside in his place, and regulate the sessions (19). Tillemont, in his history, at the year 325, doubts if Osius presided at this council; but not alone all the authors cited speak of him as president, but Maclaine, the English annotator of Mosheim, allows the fact. St. Athanasius calls Osius the chief and leader of the synod (20); and Gelasius Cizicenus, the historian of the fifth century, speaking of the Nicene Council, says Osius held the place of Sylvester, and, along with Vito and Vincentius, was present at that meeting. On the 19th of June, 325, the synod was opened in the great church of Nice, as Cardinal Orsi (21), following the general opinion, relates. The session, he says, held in the palace, in presence of Constantine, was not, as Fleury believes, the first, but the last one (22). The first examination that was made was of the errors of Arius, who, by Constantine's orders, was present in Nice; and being called on to give an account of his faith, he vomited forth, with the greatest audacity, those blasphemies he before preached, saying that the Son of God did not exist from all eternity, but was created from nothing, just like any other man, and was mutable, and capable of virtue or vice. The holy bishops hearing such blasphemies—for all were against him with the exception of twenty-two, friends of his, which number was afterwards reduced to five, and finally to two—stopped their ears with horror, and, full of holy zeal, exclaimed against him (23). Notwithstanding this, the council wished that his propositions should be separately examined; and it was then that St. Athanasius—brought from Alexandria by his bishop, St. Alexander—showed forth his prowess against the enemies of the faith, who marked him from that out, and persecuted him for the rest of his life. A letter of Eusebius of Nicomedia was read in the council, from which it appeared that he coincided in his opinions with Arius. The letter was publicly torn in his presence, and he was covered with confusion. The Eusebian party, notwithstanding, ceased not to defend the docrine of Arius; but they contradicted

---

(18) Theodoret, *l.* 1, *c.* 7; Fleury & Orsi. (19) Socrat. *l.* 1, *c.* 3; N. Alex. Orsi, Fleury. (20) St. Athan. Apol. de Fuga. (21) Orsi, *n.* 22, infra. (22) Fleury, *l.* 11, *n.* 10. (23) Ibid.

one another, and, by their very answers, showed the inconsistency of their opinions (24).

14. The Arians were asked by the Catholics: If they admitted that the Son of God was in everything like the Father—if he was his image—if he always existed—if he was unchangeable—if he was subsistent in the Father—if he was the power of God—if he was true God. At first the Arian party were undecided, whether they should admit all or only part of these terms; but the Eusebians, having whispered a while among themselves, agreed to admit them all. They could grant he was like the Father, they argued, and his image, since it is written in St. Paul (1 Cor. ii. 7), "that man is the image and glory of God;" they might say he was subsistent in the Father, since, in the Acts, xvii. 28, it is written, "in him we live, and move, and be;" that he always existed, since it is written of us (2 Cor. iv. 11), "For we who live are always delivered unto death for Jesus's sake," so that even we have always existed in the power and mind of God; that he was immutable, since it is written that nothing could separate us from the charity of God, "Nor life nor death shall be able to separate us from the love of God"—the power of God, for even soothsayers are called the power of God—the true God, for the Son of God, by his merits, he was made God, a name sometimes given unto men: "I said you are Gods" (John, x. 34) (25).

15. The Fathers of the Council, seeing how they thus distorted the Scriptures, and gave their own meaning to the texts, judged it necessary to avail themselves of a word which would remove all doubts, and could not be explained away by their adversaries, and this word was "consubstantial," which they considered as necessary to be introduced into the profession of faith, using the Greek word "omousion," the meaning of which is, that the Son is not only like, but is the very thing, the very substance, with the Father, as our Saviour himself says—"I and the Father are one" (John, x. 30). The Arians stoutly refused to admit this expression, for that one word did away with all subterfuges, and knocked away the last prop on which this heresy rested; they made, therefore, many objections, but all were overruled. We shall treat more fully of this in the third part of the work, The Theological Refutation of Errors.

16. The Emperor, Cardinal Orsi says, was anxious to be present at the last session of this synod, and wished it to be held in his palace, and came from Nicomedia to Nice for that purpose. When he entered the assembly, some discontented bishops handed him memorials, accusing their colleagues, and appealing to his judgment; but he ordered them to be burnt, making use of those remarkable expressions quoted by Noel Alexander (26), "God has made you priests, and has given you power even to judge ourselves,

(24) Socrat. *l.* 2, *c.* 8.   (25) Fleury, al. loc. cit. con. St. Athan.   (26) N. Alex. *ar.* 4, *sec.* 2; Rufin.; Theodoret, His. Eccles.

and we are properly judged by you, for you are given to us by God as Gods on this earth, and it is not meet that man should judge Gods." He refused to sit down on the low seat he had prepared for himself in the council until the bishops desired him; he then sat down, and all the bishops with his permission also took their seats (27). One of the fathers of the council—it is generally supposed Eustachius, Bishop of Antioch (28)—then arose and delivered an oration, in which he praised the Emperor's zeal, and gave God thanks for his victories. Constantine then spoke (29): It afforded him, he said, the greatest consolation to see so many fathers thus united in the same sentiments; he recommended peace to them, and gave every one liberty to speak his mind; he praised the defenders of the faith, and reproved the temerity of the Arians. The fathers then framed the decree in the following form, as Cabassutius gives it (30):—"We believe in one God, the Father Almighty, Creator of all things visible and invisible; and in One Lord, Jesus Christ, the Son of God, the only begotten Son of the Father; God of God, Light of Light, true God of true God, born, not made, consubstantial to the Father by whom all things were made in heaven and in earth; who for us died, for our salvation descended, became incarnate and was made man; he suffered and rose again the third day, and ascended into heaven, and again shall come to judge the quick and the dead; and in the Holy Ghost." This symbol, St Athanasius says (31), was composed by Osius, and was recited in the synod. The council then fulminated an anathema against any one who should say there was a time when the Son of God did not exist, or that he did not exist before he was born, or that he was made of those things that exist not; or should assert that he was of any other substance or essence, or created, or mutable, or convertible. All who speak thus of the Son of God, the Catholic and Apostolic Church anathematizes.

Baronius says (32), that the council then added to the hymn, "Glory be to the Father, &c.," the words, "As it was in the beginning, is now, and ever shall be, for ever, and ever. Amen."

17. The bishops of the opposite side were, as we have already seen, twenty-two at first, but they were reduced, as Sozymen (33) says, to seventeen; and even these, terrified by the threats of Constantine, and fearing to lose their sees, and be banished, all gave in with the exception of five (34); these were Eusebius of Nicomedia; Theognis of Nice; Maris of Chalcedon; Theonas of Marmorica; and Secundus of Ptolemais; and of these, three finally yielded, and the two first alone remained obstinate, and were deposed and

(27) Fleury *l.* 11, *n.* 10.   (28) Theod. *l.* 1, *c.* 7.   (29) Euseb. in vita Const. c. 12.   (30) Cabass. Not. Concil. *p.* 88, ex St. Athan. Socrat. Rufin. & Theod. (31) St. Athan. Hist. Arian. *n.* 42.   (32) Baron. Ann. 325, *n.* 173.   (33) Sozymen, *l.* 1, c. 28.   (34) Socrat. *l.* 1, c. 8.

banished (35). But while we condemn the temerity of those, we must acknowledge that they were more sincere than their colleagues, who subscribed the decrees, but were afterwards persecutors of the council and the Catholics. Eusebius of Cesarea especially merits reprobation on this score, for writing to his diocesans, as Socrates tells us (36), and publishing the formula of faith promulgated by the council, he says that he subscribed it merely for peace sake, and states, among other falsehoods, that the council approved the formula handed in by Eusebius of Nicomedia, when the fact was that it was not only rejected, but torn to pieces; that the word " consubstantial" was inserted to please the Emperor, when it was inserted by the fathers after the most mature deliberation, as a touchstone to distinguish the Catholics from the Arians. The fathers, he adds, in adopting this word intended merely to signify that the Son was of the Father, and not as a substantial part of him; and that the words, *born* and *not made*, merely meant that he was not made like other creatures, who were afterwards created by him, but of a more excellent nature. He concludes by saying that the council anathematized any one who would assert that the Son was made from nothing, and that he did not exist before he was born, in as far as such expressions are not found to be used in the Scriptures, and likewise because the Son, before he was generated, though he did not exist, was nevertheless existing *potentialiter*, as theologians say, in the Father, who was *potentialiter* from all eternity the creator of all things. Besides the proof afforded by this letter of his opinion, St. Jerome (37) says, that every one knows that Eusebius was an Arian. The fathers of the seventh synod, in the sixth Actio, declare " no one is ignorant that Eusebius Pamphilius, given over to a reprobate cause, holds the same opinions as those who follow the impiety of Arius." Valois remarks that this may have been said incidentally by the fathers, but Juenin (38) on the contrary proves that the synod came to this decision, after a strict examination of the arguments taken from his works.

18. Though Arius was abandoned by all except the two obstinate bishops, he still continued to defend his errors, so he was excommunicated by the council, and banished to Illiria, together with his partisans, by Constantine. All his writings, and especially the infamous Thalia, were likewise condemned by the Emperor and the council, and the Emperor published a circular or decree through the entire empire, ordering the writings of Arius to be everywhere burned, and denouncing the punishment of death against any one who would controvert this order (39).

19. The council having disposed of Arius, next suspended Me-

(35) Fleury, *l.* 11, *n.* 24; Orsi, *t.* 5, *l.* 12, *n.* 54.   (36) Orsi, ibid.   (37) St. Hieron. Epist. ad Ctesiphont.   (38) Juenin, Theol. *t.* 3, *ar.* 4, *sec.* 1.   (39) Fleury, *t.* 2, *l.* 11, *n.* 24; Orsi, *t.* 5, *l.* 12, *n.* 42.

letius, Bishop of Lycopolis, from all his episcopal functions, and especially from ordaining any one; but ordered, at the same time, that all his followers should be admitted to the communion of the Church on condition of renouncing his schism and doctrine (40).

20. The council likewise arranged the question of the celebration of Easter, which then made a great noise in Asia, by ordering that in future it should be celebrated not in the Jewish style, on the fourteenth day of the moon, but according to the Roman style, on the Sunday after the fourteenth day of the moon, which falls after the vernal equinox. This the council declared was not a matter of faith, but discipline (41); for whenever it speaks of articles of faith as opposed to the errors of Arius, the words, "This the Church believes," are used, but in making this order, the words are, " We have decreed," &c. This decree met with no opposition, but as we learn from the circular of Constantine, was embraced by all the Churches (42), and it is thought that the council then adopted the cycle of nineteen years invented by Meto, an Athenian astronomer, for fixing the lunations of each year, as every nineteenth year the new moon falls on the same day of the solar year as it did nineteen years before (43).

21. The council next decreed twenty canons of discipline; we shall mention some of the principal ones. 1st. The council excludes from the clergy, and deposes, all those who have voluntarily made themselves eunuchs, in opposition to the heresy of the Valerians, who were all eunuchs; but more especially to condemn those who justified and followed the example of Origen, through love of chastity (44). By the third canon, the clergy are prohibited from keeping in their houses any woman unless a mother, a sister, an aunt, or some person from whom no suspicion can arise. It was the wish of the council to establish the celibacy of bishops, priests, and deacons, and sub-deacons even, according to Sozymen, but they were turned from this by St. Paphnutius, who forcibly contended that it was quite enough to decree that those already in holy orders should not be allowed to marry, but that it would be laying too heavy an obligation on those who were married before they were admitted to ordination, to oblige them to separate themselves from their wives. Cardinal Orsi, however, says (45), that the authority of Socrates is not sufficient to establish this fact, since both St. Epiphanius, who lived in the time of the council, and St. Jerome (46), who was born a few years after, attest that no one was admitted to orders unless unmarried, or if married, who separated himself from his wife. It was ordained in the fourth canon that bishops should be ordained by all the co-provincial bishops, or at least by three with consent of the rest, and that the right of confirmation appertaining to the Metropolitan, should be strictly preserved. The

---

(40) N. Alex, *ar.* 4, *sec.* 2. (41) St. Athan. de Synod, *n.* 5; Nat. Alex. *ar.* 4, *sec.* 2. (42) Euseb. His. *l.* 3, *c.* 18, & Socrat. *l.* 1, *c.* 9. (43) Orsi, *t.* 5, *l.* 12, *n.* 42. (44) Ibid.; N. Alex. ibid. (45) Orsi, ibid.; Soc. *l.* 1. (46) Epiphan. Her. 59, & St. Hier. adv. Vigilan.

sixth canon says that the rights of the Patriarchal Sees shall be preserved, especially those of the See of Alexandria, over the Churches of Egypt, of Lybia, and of Pentopolis, after the example of the Bishop of Rome, who enjoys a similar authority over the Churches subject to his Patriarchate. Noel Alexander (47) has written a special dissertation to prove that the primacy of the Roman See is not weakened by this canon, and among other proofs adduces the sixth canon of the great council of Chalcedon: " The Roman Church always had the primacy;" and it is proved, he says, that after this canon was passed, the Bishop of Rome judged the persons of the other patriarchs, and took cognizance of the sentences passed by them, and no one ever complained that he usurped an authority which did not belong to him, or violated the sixth canon of the council of Nice.

22. Finally, the fathers wrote a circular letter addressed to all churches, giving them notice of the condemnation of Arius, and the regulation concerning the celebration of Easter. The Council was then dissolved, but before the bishops separated, Constantine had them all to dine with him, and had those who suffered for the faith placed near himself, and frequently kissed the scars of their wounds; he then made presents to each of them, and again recommending them to live in peace, he affectionately took leave of them (48). The sentence of exile against Eusebius and Theognis was then carried into execution; they were banished to Gaul, and Amphion succeeded Eusebius in the Bishopric of Nicomedia, and Chrestus, Theognis, in the See of Nice. It was not long, however, till the bishops of their party shewed that they accepted the decrees of the council through fear alone (49).

SEC. II.—OCCURRENCES UP TO THE DEATH OF CONSTANTINE.

23. St. Athanasius is made Bishop of Alexandria; Eusebius is recalled; St. Eustasius exiled, and Arius again taken into favour. 24. Council of Tyre. 25. St. Athanasius accused and exiled. 26. Arius banished from Alexandria. 27. His Perjury and horrible Death. 28. Constantine's Baptism and Death; Division of the Empire.

23. IN the following year, 326, St. Alexander, Patriarch of Alexandria, died, and St. Athanasius was elected his successor, with the unanimous consent of the bishops of Egypt and the people; when he heard of it he fled out of the way, but was discovered and obliged to yield to the wishes of the people and clergy. He was, therefore, placed on the episcopal throne of Alexandria (1), to the great joy of his fellow-citizens; but the Arians were highly discontented, and disseminated many calumnious reports regarding his elevation (2). About the same time Eusebius and Theognis pretended to be sorry for their errors, and having sent in writing a

(47) N. Alex. t. 8; Diss. 20. (48) Orsi, t. 5, l. 12. (49) Ibid. (1) Fleury, l. 11, n. 29. (2) Orsi, n. 80.

feigned retraction of their opinions to the principal bishops of the East, they were recalled by Constantine, and re-established in their sees. This conversion was only feigned, and they left no stone unturned to promote the interests of Arius. Among the rest, Eusebius succeeded, in a caballing council, at Antioch (3), in getting St. Eustatius, Arius's greatest opponent, deposed from that see, on a charge of adultery, got up against him by an infamous woman, the only witness in the case; but the calumny was soon after discovered, for the woman, falling sick, contradicted all she had previously charged him with (4). He, however, was banished and deposed, and Paulinus of Tyre, first, and, next, Eularius, were intruded into his see. Eularius dying soon after his intrusion, Eusebius of Cesarea, who previously had intruded himself into that church, was elected to succeed him; but he, having ulterior objects now in view, refused to go to Antioch, so Euphronius, a native of Cesarea, was first appointed, and after him Flacillus, both Arians; but many of the Catholics of Antioch would never hold communion with those intruded bishops (5). Eusebius of Nicomedia next intrigued successfully to establish Arius in the good graces of Constantine, and obtain permission for him to return to Alexandria. This he accomplished by means of an Arian priest, who was a great friend of Constantia, the Emperor's sister; and he induced her, when she was on the point of death, to request this favour from the Emperor. She did so, and Constantine said that, if Arius subscribed the decrees of the Council of Nice, he would pardon him. In fact, Arius was recalled, and came to Constantinople, and presented to the Emperor a profession of faith, in which he professed to believe, according to the Scriptures, that Jesus Christ was the Son of God, produced before all ages—that he was the Word by which all things were made (6). Constantine, believing that Arius had in reality now embraced the decisions of the Council, was satisfied with this profession; but he never adverted to the fact, that in this document the word "consubstantial" was omitted, and that the introduction of these words, "according to the Scriptures," was only a pretext of Arius to distort to his own meaning the clearest expression of the Scriptures, proving the divinity of the Son of God. He would not receive him, nevertheless, to his communion on his own authority, but sent him to Tyre, where a council was sitting, of which we shall treat presently, to undergo the scrutiny of the bishops; he wrote to the assembled prelates to examine Arius's profession of faith, and to see whether his retraction was sincere. The partizans of Eusebius were in great force in the Council of Tyre, so Arius, on his arrival, was immediately again received into communion (7).

(3) Orsi, *n.* 84; Nat. Alex. *a.* 4, *t.* 4; Fleury, ibid., *n.* 11. (4) Theodoret, *l.* 1, *t.* 22. (5) Orsi, *t.* 5, *l.* 12, *n.* 87, & 90. (6) Ibid. (7) Socrat. *l.* 1, *c.* 33; Sozom. Rufin. Nat. Alex. & Fleury.

24. We have now to speak of the cabal of Tyre, in which the Eusebians contrived to banish St. Athanasius from the see of Alexandria. Before, however, giving the history of this unjust expulsion, we should remark, that previously the Arians had plotted the destruction of the holy bishop, and charged him before the Emperor with many crimes (8). They accused him of having violated a virgin—of having killed Arsenius, the Bishop of Ipsele, in the Thebaid—of casting down an altar, and breaking a consecrated chalice; and they now renewed the same charges in the Council of Tyre (9). Constantine, at the request of his mother, St. Helen, had built the great Church of the Resurrection in Jerusalem, and had invited a great number of bishops to consecrate it with all solemnity; it was on this occasion that Eusebius of Nicomedia suggested to him that it would be well to collect all the bishops, before the consecration, into a council, to establish a general peace. The Emperor was most anxious for peace above all things; so he at once agreed, and selected Tyre as the most convenient place for the bishops to meet on their way to Jerusalem. Eusebius, who had planned the scheme, now got together all the bishops of his party, so that there were sixty bishops in all; but many of these were Catholics, and this number was increased soon after by the arrival of St. Athanasius, accompanied by Paphuntius, Potamon, and several other Egyptian bishops. St. Athanasius, seeing the storm he had to encounter, refused to come at first, but was constrained by Constantine, who threatened him with banishment in case of refusal (10). Eusebius next contrived that the Count Flavius should be present, to preserve order, as he said, and keep down any disturbance; but, in reality, to crush St. Athanasius and his friends. Flavius, accordingly, came, accompanied by a large body of troops, ready to seize on any one who opposed Eusebius's party (11).

25. The impious synod was now opened, and St. Athanasius, who, in right of his dignity, should preside, was obliged to stand as a criminal, to be tried for crimes he never was guilty of. When St. Potamon saw him in this position he was highly indignant with Eusebius of Cesarea, who was seated among the judges (12). "Tell me, Eusebius," said he, " how did it happen that, when we were both prisoners, in the days of persecution for the faith, my right eye was plucked out, but you left the prison safe and sound, without any mark of constancy; how could that have happened, unless you yielded to the will of the tyrant?" Eusebius, enraged at the charge, instead of making any defence, got up, and left the council, and the synod was dissolved for that day (13). St. Athanasius protested that he did not wish to submit himself to the

(8) Orsi, *l.* 12, *n.* 92.   (9) Ibid.   (10) Socrat. *l.* 1, *n.* 28.   (11) Orsi, *l.* 12, *n.* 96.   (12) Epiph. Her. 69.   (13) Orsi, *l.* 12, *n.* 97.

judgment of his enemies, but in vain. He was first accused by
two bishops of Meletius's party; and the principal charges they
brought against him were the violation of the virgin, the murder
of the bishop, and the desecration of the altar and chalice. This
last charge they could not bring any proof of, so they confined
themselves to the two former; and, to prove the crime of violation (14), they introduced into the synod a prostitute, who
declared that St. Athanasius had robbed her of her honour. The
Saint, however, knowing the plot beforehand, made one of his
priests, of the name of Timothy, stand forward; and he said to
the woman: "Do you mean to charge me with having violated
you?" "Yes," said the unfortunate wretch, thinking he was St.
Athanasius, "you have violated me—you have robbed me of my
virginity, which I dedicated to God." Thus this first calumny
was most triumphantly refuted, and the other charge was equally
proved to be unfounded. Among the other proofs they adduced
of the murder of Arsenius, they exhibited a hand which was cut
off from his dead body, they said, by St. Athanasius. But the fact
was thus (15):—When the Saint was first accused of the crime,
Arsenius lent himself to the Arian party, and concealed himself,
that his death might be proved. But he soon repented of such
wickedness, and, to clear St. Athanasius, he came to Tyre, and
confronted the Saint's accusers in the council; for while the
accusers were making the charge, and showing the dead hand as a
proof, Athanasius asked them, did they know Arsenius? They
answered, that they did. He then called forth the man they said
was dead, and told him to hold up his head, that all might recognize him. But even this would not stop their mouths, for they
then said, that he did not kill him, but cut off his hand only;
but Athanasius opened Arsenius's mantle, and showed that both
his hands were perfect. Beaten out of this last accusation, they
then said that it was all accomplished by magic, and that the Saint
was a magician. Finally, they said, that St. Athanasius (16)
forced persons to hold communion with him, by imprisoning some,
flogging and tormenting others, and that he even deposed and
flogged some bishops; and the winding up of the matter was, that
he was condemned and deposed. When St. Athanasius saw that
he was so unjustly deposed, he appealed to the Emperor in Constantinople, and acquainted him with all he suffered in the Council
of Tyre; and Constantine wrote to the bishops, who were yet
remaining in Jerusalem, reproving them for tumultuously smother-
ing the truth, and ordering them to come immediately to Constantinople, and account for their conduct (17). The Eusebians
obeyed the imperial order, and, saying nothing more about the

(14) Ibid., *n.* 93. (15) Orsi, *l.* 12, *n.* 24, ex St. Athan. Apol. contra Ar. *n.* 65.
(16) Nat. Alex. *t.* 8, *c.* 3; Hermant, *t.* 1, *c.* 92, & Fleury. (17) Orsi, cit.

murder of Arsenius, or the broken chalice, they invented a new charge against Athanasius—that he threatened to prevent the usual supply of grain from being sent from Alexandria to Constantinople. This was just the charge calculated to ruin him with the Emperor, who was so enraged, that he even threatened to put him to death; and, though the Saint refuted the accusation, he was condemned to banishment (18).

26. In the year 336 there was another council held in Constantinople, and the bishop of that city, St. Alexander, seeing that the Eusebians would have it all their own way, did everything in his power to prevent it, but could not succeed. The Eusebians then tried Marcellus of Ancira, the defender of St. Athanasius in the Council of Tyre, for some heresies alleged to have been written by him in a book, published in opposition to Asterius the Sophist, who composed a treatise filled with Arian errors. They, therefore, excommunicated and deposed Marcellus, as he was not one of their party, and elected, in his place, Basil, a partisan of Arius. This was only a secondary consideration, however. The principal reason the Arians had in assembling this council was to re-establish Arius in his place again, and confirm his doctrine. After Arius was received in Jerusalem to the communion of the bishops, he returned to Alexandria, hoping, in the absence of St. Athanasius, banished by Constantine, to be there received by the Catholics. In this he was disappointed—they would have nothing to do with him; but, as he had many partisans in the city, his residence there excited some commotion. When the Emperor was informed of this, he ordered him to come to Constantinople. It is said that the Eusebians induced the Emperor to give this order, hoping to have Arius received into the communion of the Church, in the imperial city; but in this they were most strenuously opposed by St. Alexander, and they, in consequence, threatened him that unless he received Arius into his communion on a certain day, they would have himself deposed. St. James, Bishop of Nisibis, then in Constantinople, said that prayers and penance alone could remedy these evils, and St. Alexander, taking his advice, gave up both preaching and disputing, and shut himself up alone in the Church of Peace, and remained there many nights, weeping and praying (19).

27. The Eusebians persuaded the Emperor that Arius held the doctrine of the Church, and it was, therefore, regulated that he should, the next Sunday, be received to the communion. The Saturday previous, however, Constantine, that he might be quite certain of the faith of Arius, ordered him to be called into his presence, asked him did he profess the faith of Nice, and insisted that he should give him a written profession of faith, and swear to it. Arius gave him the written profession, but a fraudulent one, and

(18) Orsi, cit.   (19) Fleury, Orsi, Socr. Sozymen, St. Epiphan. loc. cit.

swore that he neither then nor at any other time believed differently; some say that he had another profession of faith under his arm, and that it was to that one he intended to swear. However, the affair was arranged; it is certain that the Emperor, trusting to his oath, told St. Alexander that it was a matter of duty to assist a man who wished for nothing but his salvation. St. Alexander endeavoured to undeceive him, but finding he only irritated him more and more, held his tongue, and retired; he soon after met Eusebius of Nicomedia, who said to him, If you don't wish to receive Arius to-morrow, I will myself bring him along with me to the church. St. Alexander, grieved to the heart, went to the church accompanied by only two persons, and prostrating himself on the floor, with tears in his eyes, prayed to the Lord: O my God, either take me out of the world, or take Arius, that he may not ruin your Church. Thus St. Alexander prayed, and on the same day, Saturday, at three o'clock, the Eusebians were triumphantly conducting Arius through the city, and he went along, boasting of his re-establishment, but when he came to the great square the vengeance of God overtook him; he got a terrible spasm in the bowels, and was obliged to seek a place of retirement; a private place near the square was pointed out to him; he went in and left a servant at the door; he immediately burst open like Judas, his intestines, his spleen, and his liver all fell out, and thus his guilty soul took her flight to her Creator, deprived of the communion of the Church. When he delayed too long, his friends came to the door, and on opening it, they found him stretched on the floor in a pool of blood in that horrible state. This event took place in the year 336 (20).

28. In the following year, 337, Constantine died. He was then 64 years of age. He fell sick, and took baths in Constantinople at first, but receiving no benefit from them, he tried the baths of Helenopolis. He daily got worse, so went to Nicomedia, and finding himself near death, he was baptized in the Church of St. Lucian. Authors vary regarding the time and place of Constantine's baptism. Eusebius says that he was baptized in Nicomedia, a few hours before his death, but other writers assert that he was baptized in Rome by St. Sylvester, thirteen years before, in the year 324. Cardinal Baronius holds this opinion, and quotes many authorities in favour of it, and Schelestratus brings forward many Greek and Latin authorities to prove the same. The generality of authors, however, follow Eusebius, Socrates, Sozymen, Theodoret, and St. Jerome, Fleury, and Orsi, and especially Noel Alexander, who answers the arguments of Baronius, and cites for his own opinion St. Ambrose, St. Isidore, Papebrock, and the fathers of St. Maur. These last say that Constantine, being near his end, in Nicomedia, wished to receive from the bishops, in the church of St. Lucian, the imposi-

---

(20) Baron. Soc. Sozymen, Libellus, Marcel. & Fausti, *p.* 19; St. Epiphan. loc. cit.

tion of hands—a ceremony then in use previous to baptism, and practised with every catechumen. He was then carried to a castle, called Aquirion, a little distant from Nicomedia, and, having summoned the bishops, he received baptism with the greatest devotion. " Now," said he, " I feel myself truly happy." His officers then came to him, and, with tears in their eyes, expressed the wish they had for his restoration to health and long life; but he said, " I have now received the true life, and I have no other wish but to go and enjoy God." St. Jerome, in his Chronicle, says that he lapsed into Arian errors, but his festival is commemorated in the Greek Menalogy, according to Noel Alexander, on the 21st of May, and the same author wrote a dissertation to prove that he died a good Catholic, and all the ancients, he says, agree in that opinion with St. Athanasius, St. Hilary, St. Epiphanius, and St. Ambrose; and we have, likewise, the authority of the Council of Rimini, in the synodal epistle written to the Emperor Constantius, and quoted by Socrates, Theodoret, Sozymen, and St. Athanasius. Cardinal Orsi remarks that the baptism of Constantine, by Eusebius, ought not to render his faith suspected, and that this is no proof of a leaning to Arianism, as St. Jerome suspects, since we see how strenuously he defended the Council and doctrine of Nice, and especially since he recalled St. Athanasius from exile immediately after his baptism, notwithstanding the opposition of Eusebius of Nicomedia. Sozymen says that the Emperor left this order in his will, and that Constantine the Younger, when he sent back St. Athanasius to his see, declared that, in doing so, he was fulfilling the will of his father; and St. Athanasius attests that, at the same time, all the other Catholic bishops were reinstated in their sees (21).

29. Constantine died on the feast of Pentecost, the 23rd of May, 337, and divided the empire among his children and nephews. To Constantius the Elder he left all that was possessed by his father, Constans, and Gaul, Spain, and Britain besides; to Constantius the Second, Asia, Assyria, and Egypt; and to Constantius the Youngest, Africa, Italy, and Illyria; and to his nephews, Dalmatius and Hannibalianus, some provinces of less note. It was the will of the Almighty, however, that Constantine the Younger and Constans died, so the whole empire fell into the sway of Constantius, a great misfortune for the Church, for he was a violent persecutor, and Constantine and Constans were its friends (22).

(21) Socrates; Baron. An. 336; Auctores, cit.; Euseb. Vita Constant.; Schelestr. in Antiquit. &c. (22) Auctores, cit. ibid.

SEC. III.—THE EMPEROR CONSTANTIUS PERSECUTES THE CATHOLICS.

30. Eusebius of Nicomedia is translated to the See of Constantinople; Synods in Alexandria and Antioch. 31. Council of Sardis. 32. Council of Arles. 33. Council of Milan, and Exile of Liberius. 34. Exile of Osius. 35. Fall of Osius. 36. Fall of Liberius. 37. First Formula of Sirmium. 38. Second Formula of Sirmium. 39. Third Formula of Sirmium. 40. Liberius signs the Formula, &c. 41, 42. He signs the first Formula. 43. Return of Liberius to Rome, and Death of Felix. 44. Division among the Arians. 45-48. Council of Rimini. 49. Death of Constantius. 50. The Empire descends to Julian. The Schism of Lucifer.

30. ST. ALEXANDER, Patriarch of Constantinople, died about the year 340, at the age of ninety-eight, and Paul of Thessalonica was chosen his successor; but Constantius, who now publicly professed himself an Arian, being absent during the election, was highly indignant on his return to Constantinople, and, pretending that Paul was unworthy of the bishopric, joined with the Arian party, and had a council convoked, in which he procured the deposition of Paul and the appointment of Eusebius of Nicomedia, now, for the second time, translated to a new see, in opposition to the laws of the Church. About the same time another council was assembled in Alexandria, consisting of about a hundred bishops from Egypt, the Thebaid, Lybia, and Pentapolis, in favour of St. Athanasius, in which he was declared innocent of the calumnies laid to his charge by the Eusebians; but again, the following year, 341, a council was assembled in Antioch on the occasion of the dedication of the church of that city commenced by Constantine and finished by Constantius, consisting of ninety bishops; this was planned by Eusebius of Nicomedia and his partisans, and St. Athanasius was again deposed, and Gregory of Cappadocia, infected with the Arian heresy, was intruded into his place (1).

31. In the year 357, another council, consisting of many bishops, was assembled in Sardis, the metropolitan city of Dacia in Illyria, in which the Nicene Creed was confirmed, and St. Athanasius was again declared innocent, and restored to his see. There is no doubt but that this was a general council, as (in opposition to Peter of Marca) Baronius, Noel Alexander, Peter Annatus, Battaglini, and many others prove. St. Athanasius says that one hundred and seventy bishops were assembled, but among them were more than fifty orientals, and as these left Sardis to avoid the condemnation which they knew awaited them for their excesses, only about one hundred remained. It had, besides, all the requisites for a general council, for the convocation was general, as appears from the circular letters, and Archimides and Philosenus, priests, together with Osius, who was before president of the Council of Nice, presided as legates of Pope Julius. The Arians being aware that many well founded

(1) Fleury, N. Alex. & Bar. loc. con.

charges would be brought against them in the council, demanded that the bishops condemned in their synod should be expelled from the assembly of the prelates, otherwise they said they would go away themselves. This audacious proposal was universally rejected, so they fled to Philipopolis, and drew up a formula of faith, adapted to their errors, and this was afterwards promulgated as the formula of the Council of Sardis. Eight bishops of the Eusebian party were convicted of the crimes they were charged with, by the true Council of Sardis, and were deposed and condemned, for it is but just, said the fathers, that those should be separated from the Church who wish to separate the Son from the Father (2).

32. Constantius showed himself more favourable to the Catholic bishops after this council, and permitted them to return to their churches; he received St. Athanasius most graciously in Antioch, and gave an order in his favour, and allowed him to return to Alexandria, where he was received by the bishops of Egypt and by the people and clergy with the greatest demonstrations of joy. The Arians soon again, however, obtained the favour of Constantius, and St. Hilarion relates that Pope Liberius, who succeeded St. Julius in 342, wrote to him that the Eusebians wished to cheat him out of a condemnation of St. Athanasius, but that he, having received letters signed by eighty bishops, defending the saint, and, as he would not conscientiously act in opposition to the Council of Sardis, had declared him innocent. In the meantime, he sent to Constantius, who held his court at Arles, two legates, Vincentius of Capua and Marcellus, bishop in the Campagna, to implore of him to summon a synod in Aquileia to settle finally the cause of St. Athanasius, finally determine the articles of faith, and establish the peace of the Church. Constantius, we know not why, was highly offended at this request, and convoked a synod in Arles, and when the legates arrived there, they found that St. Athanasius had been already condemned by the synod, and that Constantius had published a decree of banishment against the bishops who refused to sign the condemnation. He then insisted that the legates should sign it likewise. Vincentius of Capua refused at first to do so, but he was beaten and threatened, so he yielded, and his colleague followed his example, and both promised to hold no more communication with St. Athanasius (3).

33. The Emperor now intended to crush the Catholic party for ever, and with this intention, assembled a council in Milan. Pope Liberius was anxious for the celebration of this council, as he thought it would unite the Church in the profession of the faith of Nice, but the Arians worked hard also to have it assembled, as they expected to obtain a general sentence of condemnation on St.

(2) Orsi, Fleury, St. Ath. Apol. loc. cit. (3) Orsi, cit. St. Hilar. Fragm. 5. Severus, Sulpici. His. *l.* 2 & seq.

Athanasius, and to establish their heresy; so, in the year 355, there were assembled over three hundred bishops in Milan. St. Eusebius of Vercelli was also summoned, but endeavoured to absent himself, knowing the plans of the Eusebians; he was, however, constrained to attend, and the Pope's legates themselves, Lucifer, Pancratius, and the Deacon Hilary, solicited him to come to Milan. On his arrival, the Arians endeavoured to induce him to sign the condemnation of St. Athanasius, having again renewed the fable of the broken chalice, &c. But St. Eusebius said, the first thing to be done was, that all should subscribe the formula of the Council of Nice, and then that other matters could be taken into consideration. St. Dionisius, Bishop of Milan, immediately prepared to subscribe to it, but Valens of Murcia snatched the pen and paper out of his hands, and said, that nothing ever would be concluded if that course was followed. When this came to the knowledge of the people, they murmured loudly, and complained that the bishops themselves were betraying the faith; so the Emperor, dreading a popular tumult, transferred the council to the church of his own palace, and told the assembled bishops that they should obey his edict in the affair, and sign a profession filled with all the errors of Arianism. He called especially on the Legate Lucifer, St. Eusebius, and St. Dionisius, and ordered them to subscribe the condemnation of St. Athanasius, and when they determinedly refused to do so, as being against the laws of the Church, he answered: "Whatever is my will is law, obey me or you shall be banished." The bishops then told him that he would have to answer to the Almighty if he used any violence towards them; but he became so indignant at being remonstrated with in this manner, that he actually drew his sword on them, and gave orders that they should be put to death, but when his passion cooled a little, he was satisfied with sending them into banishment, and they were sent off from the council, loaded with chains, under a guard of soldiers, to the place of their exile, where they had to endure a great deal of harsh treatment from the heretics. At the same time, Hilary, one of the legates, was stripped naked and cruelly flogged on the back, the Arians all the while crying out to him: "Why did you not oppose Liberius?" Constantius then appointed Ausentius in the place of St. Dionisius, and obliged Liberius to come to Milan. The Emperor, on Liberius's arrival, ordered him to condemn St. Athanasius, and, on his refusal to do so, gave him three days for consideration, and told him that if he refused he would also be sent into exile. Liberius persevered in his refusal, and was accordingly banished to Berea, in Thrace, of which Demophilus, a perfidious Arian, was bishop (4).

34. The great Osius was, next to Liberius, the great prop of the

---

(4) Sozymen, *l.* 4; Soc. *l.* 2; Fleury, Orsi, Ser. Sulp. *l.* 2.

Faith in the West, both on account of the holiness of his life, and his learning; he was at this time sixty years Bishop of Cordova, in Spain, and he showed his constancy in the persecution of Maximilian, by publicly confessing the faith. Constantius had him brought before him, and advised him to communicate with the Arians, and condemn St. Athanasius, but he resolutely refused to do either one or the other. Constantius allowed him to go away for that time; but soon after wrote to him, and threatened to punish him if he refused any longer to obey his will. Osius answered him with even greater firmness:—If you are resolved to persecute me, said he, I am prepared to shed my blood sooner than betray the truth; you may then save yourself the trouble of writing to me on the subject again. Tremble at the last judgment, and do not intermeddle with the affairs of the Church; God has given you the Empire, the government of the Church he has committed to us. Constantius sent for him once more, to induce him to yield, but, finding him inflexible, he banished him to Sirmium; he was then nearly in the hundredth year of his age.

35. We now have to treat of, first, the fall of Osius, and next of Liberius. The principal author of Osius's fall was Potamius, Bishop of Lisbon; he was at first a defender of the Faith, but Constantius gained him over by giving him possession of an estate of the Chancery; he, therefore, joined the Eusebians, and Osius, burning with zeal, denounced his impiety through all Spain. Potamius, thirsting for revenge, first got him banished to Sirmium, and then finding the Emperor there, he induced him to use such violent measures with him, that he broke down his resolution, and caused him to fall. The poor old man was weakened with torments; he was beaten so violently that his flesh was all torn, and he endured a long and violent torture; his strength failed him, he could suffer no more, and he unfortunately signed the second formula of Sirmium, condemning St. Athanasius, and holding communion with the Arians. Sozymen particularly mentions that Eudosius saw the letter of Osius, in which he disapproves of both the word *consubstantial*, and the words *like in substance*. He now was permitted to return again to Spain, but Gregory, Bishop of Alvira, refused to communicate with him on account of his prevarication. Two authors, followers of Lucifer, Faustus and Marcellinus, write that Osius died an unhappy death; but St. Athanasius, who, as Cardinal Orsi justly remarks, deserves more credit, says that at his death he declared he was subdued by violence, and thus fell into error, and that he anathematized the heresy of the Arians, and besought all who heard him to hold it in horror (5).

36. We now come to speak of the fall of Liberius. It is said

---

(5) Socrates, Sozymen, St. Hilary, Fragm. 2; St. Athanasius, His. Arian.; St. Augus. l. con.; Parmen. Nat. Alex. Fleury, loc. cit.

by some that Osius subscribed the second formula of Sirmium; now, to understand the fall of Liberius, it is necessary to have a knowledge of the three formulas of faith composed in Sirmium. Noel Alexander says that there was but one formula of Sirmium, and that the others were published elsewhere; but Baronius, and the generality of writers, hold that the whole three formulas were promulgated in the councils, or rather cabals, of Sirmium. There is no probability of the truth of what Socrates says, that the whole three formulas were promulgated in one and the same council. The Arians, when they got Liberius to sign one of the formulas, boasted, as Orsi says, that there was a union of faith between them, and that Liberius professed their faith. On the other hand, Orsi persuades himself that Liberius was innocent altogether, and supposes that he was liberated and allowed to return to Rome, on account of a promise made by Constantius to the Roman ladies, or to put an end to the disturbances which at that time distracted the city. The most generally received opinion, however, is that Liberius committed a great error, but that he did not fall into heresy. To make the matter clear we must investigate the Sirmium formula which he subscribed (6).

37. The first formula of Sirmium was adopted in the year 351, and in this, Photinus, Bishop of Sirmium, was again condemned, for he denied to Jesus Christ not only consubstantiality with the Father, but his Divinity, likewise; asserting, with Cerinthus, Ebion, and Paul of Samosata, that the Son of God had no existence before Mary. Photinus was previously condemned in the Council of Sardis; but he obtained from the Emperor the right of appeal to this Council of Sirmium, at which Constantius himself was present. Here his doctrine was condemned a second time, even by the Arians themselves, and the first formula, relating to the Arian heresy, was drawn up in Greek, and two anathemas were attached to it, as Noel Alexander tells us, on the authority of St. Athanasius and St. Hilary. The first was to this effect: " The Holy and Catholic Church does not recognize as belonging to her, those who say that the Son existed from any creation or substance, and not from God, or that there was a time when he did not exist." The second was that " if any one denied that Christ-God, the Son of God, was before all ages, and by whom all things were made, and that it was only from the time he was born of Mary that he was called Christ and the Son, and that it was only then his Deity commenced, let him be anathema." Noel Alexander thus Latinises the original Greek. " Eos qui dicunt: ex non ente, aut ex alio subsistente, et non ex Deo Filium extitisse, aut quod tempus, aut ætas fuit, quando ille non erat, alienos a se censet Sancta et Catholica Ecclesia. Si quis Christum Deum, Filium Dei ante secula,

---

(6) Socrates, Orsi, Sozymen; Nat. Alex. St. Athan. His. Arian.

administrumque ad universitatis opificium fuisse neget; sed ex quo tempore e Maria genitus est, Christum, et Filium appellatum fuisse, et principium suæ Deitatis tum accepisse dicat, anathema esto." Thus in this formula, it is laid down that the Son is God to all eternity, and that his Divinity is from eternity. St. Athanasius looked on this formula as impious. St. Hilary considered it Catholic; the truth is that, if it be considered absolutely in itself, it is Catholic, but, taken in the sense of the Arians, it is Arian (7).

38. The second formula was published also in Sirmium, but in the year 357, and it was written in Latin, and was subscribed by Potamius and Osius. This was totally Arian, for the words *consubstantial*, and *like in substance*, were rejected, as there was nothing about them in the Scriptures, and they were unintelligible to the human intellect. This was not the only blasphemous error introduced into this profession; for it was, besides, asserted, that the Father was, without any doubt, greater than the Son in honour, dignity, and Godship, and that the Son was subject to the Father, together with all things which the Father subjected to the Son. This formula St. Hilary calls blasphemous, and, in his Book of Synods, he thus describes it:—" Exemplum blasphemiæ apud Sirmium, par Osium et Potamium, conscriptæ (8)."

39. The third formula was likewise composed in Sirmium, but not for eight years after, that is in 359, and this was also in Latin, and St. Athanasius informs us, in his book on Synods, that it was this one which was presented to the Council of Rimini, by Valens and Ursacius. In this the word *substance* is rejected, but the Son is recognized as equal to the Father in all things:—" Vocabulum porro substantiæ, quia simplicius a Patribus positum est, et a populis ignoratur, et scandalum affert, eo quod in Scripturis non contineatur, placuit ut de medio tolleretur. Filium autem Patri per omnia similem dicimus, quemadmodum sacræ Litteræ dicunt, et docent." In the first formula, then, the word *consubstantial* is omitted, but the word *substantial* is retained. In the second, no mention is made of either word, nor even of the words *like unto;* and, in the third, the words *like unto* are retained and explained.

40. We now come to the case of Liberius. Constantius had promised the ladies of Rome that he would restore him again to his see; but had also promised the Eusebians that he would not liberate him till he communicated with them. He, therefore, laid his commands on Demophilus, Bishop of Berea, where Liberius was exiled, and on Fortunatus, Bishop of Aquileia, another apostate, to leave no means untried to make Liberius sign the formula of Sirmium, and the condemnation of St. Athanasius. Liberius was now three years in exile, broken down by solitude and flogging, and, above all, deeply afflicted at seeing the See of Rome occupied

(7) Auctores citati; Nat. Alex. l. cit.   (8) Nat. Alex.; Fleury, *l.* 13.

by an anti-Pope, the Deacon Felix, and thus he had the weakness to yield, and subscribed the formula, condemning at the same time St. Athanasius, and communicating with the Arian bishops.

41. It is a question among authors, which of the three formulas was subscribed by Liberius. Valesius says it was the third; but this has no foundation, for the third was not drawn up till 359, and St. Athanasius tells us that Liberius was then after returning to Rome. Blondel and Petavius say that it was the second he signed, and this is the general opinion followed by heretics, who strive thus to prove that the Catholic Church may fail. The Protestant Danæus numbers Liberius among the bishops who joined the Arians, and says that all historians are agreed that he signed this formula, and after that, he says, no one can deny that the Roman Church can err. But the general opinion held by Catholics, and which is, also, the most probable, and in which Baronius, N. Alexander, Graveson, Fleury, Juenin, Tournelly, Berninus, Orsi, Hermant, and Selvaggi, the learned annotator of Mosheim, join with Gotti, who gives it as the general opinion of Catholic authors, is, that it was the first formula he signed. There are very weighty reasons to prove that this opinion is founded on fact:—First—The formula subscribed by Liberius was the one drawn up at the time Photinus was condemned, and this was, indubitably, the first and not the second. Secondly—The formula he signed, and which was laid before him by Demophilus, was not drawn up by the Anomeans, or pure Arians, but by the Semi-Arians, to which sect Demophilus, Basil of Ancira, Valens, and Ursacius belonged. These did not admit that the Son was *consubstantial* with the Father, because they would not approve of the Nicene Creed, but said he was of the substance of the Father; and this was expressed in the first formula alone, but not in the second, in which both the words *substance* and *like unto* were omitted. These very bishops even who subscribed the first rejected the second in a synod purposely convoked in Ancira. Nor does it militate against this opinion, that the formula subscribed by Liberius was also subscribed by the Anomeans, for Constantine, who, as Socrates informs us, favoured the Semi-Arian party, obliged them to subscribe to it. Another proof is from Sozymen, who quotes a letter of Liberius, written to the Semi-Arians, in which he declares, that those who assert that the Son is not like to the Father in all things, and of the same substance, do not belong to the Church. From all this it is proved that Liberius signed the formula, from which the word *consubstantiality* was omitted, but which approved of the words *substantiality* and *like unto* (9).

(9) Tournelly, Theol. *t.* 2; Blondell. de Primatu, *p.* 48; Petav. in observ. St. Epiphan.; Danæus, Opus. de Her.; Baron. An. 357; Nat. Alex., Fleury, Graveson; Juenin, Theol. 40, 3 *ques.*; Bernin.; Hermant, *t.* 1; Orsi, *l.* 14; Gotti, de Ver. Rel.; Selvaggi, not. 52, ad Mosh.

42. Because St. Hilary calls the formula signed by Liberius a perfidy, the argument is not weakened, for Noel Alexander supposes that these words and the anathema hurled against Liberius, in St. Hilary's fragments, were foisted in by some other hand, for these fragments were written after the return of Liberius to Rome, when he most strenuously refused to approve of the formula of the Council of Rimini; others again, as Juenin, imagined that St. Hilary called the formula perfidious, taking it in the perverse sense as understood by the Arians, since speaking of it before (considered absolutely in itself), he called it a Catholic formula. Another argument is deduced from the Chronicle of St. Jerome, for he writes, that Liberius, conquered by a weary exile, subscribed to heretical pravity, and entered Rome almost like a conqueror. Noel Alexander says, that St. Jerome means by this, not that he signed a formula in itself heretical, but that he communicated with heretics, and although the communion with heretics was an error, it was not heresy itself. Another answer is, that St. Jerome might have written this under the belief that it was true, since, as Sozymen informs us, the heretics spread everywhere abroad, that Liberius, in subscribing the formula, not only denied the consubstantiality, but even the likeness of the Son to the Father; but, withal, we do not justify Liberius for condemning St. Athanasius and communicating with heretics. He afterwards refused to sign the formula of Rimini, and was, in consequence, obliged to conceal himself in the catacombs till the death of Constantius (10).

43. When Liberius returned to Rome, in the year 358, or the following year, according to Baronius, he was received, Orsi says, with the liveliest demonstrations of joy by the clergy and people; but Baronius says, that there was a large section of the people opposed to him on account of his fall, and that they adhered to Felix II., who, in the commencement, was a schismatic, and unlawfully ordained by three Arian bishops, to whose sect he belonged at the time. Nevertheless, when he learned the lapse of Liberius, he joined the Catholics, and excommunicated the Emperor; and he was thenceforth looked on as the lawful Pope, and Liberius as fallen from his office. However, as Baronius tells us, it appears from the Book of the Pontiffs, that he was taken and conveyed by the Imperial Ministers to Ceri, seventeen miles from Rome, and beheaded. The schismatic Marcellinus, quoted by Fleury, says, that Felix lived eight years after the return of Liberius; but Sozymen, on the contrary, tells us he died almost immediately after that event. Benedict XIV. says, that there is no doubt about the sanctity and martyrdom of Felix, but the learned are divided as to whether he died by the sword or by the sufferings he endured for Christ. Baronius says, that there was a doubt in the time of Gregory XIII.

(10) Nat. Alex. & cit.

as to whether the name of Felix II. should be expunged or not from the Martyrology, in which he was enumerated among the saints, and he was himself, he confesses, of the opinion that it should be done, on account of his illegal intrusion into the Popedom; but soon after he says, a marble sarcophagus was casually discovered buried in the earth, with some relics of saints on one side, and the body of St. Felix on the other, with this inscription, "The body of St. Felix, Pope and Martyr, who condemned Constantius;" and this discovery was made on the 19th of July, 1582, the day preceding the festival of St. Felix, and, on that account, his name was left undisturbed in the Martyrology. Baronius is opposed by N. Alexander, who denies that Felix II. ever was a true Pope; but Roncaglia, in his notes, and both the Pagi, contend for the contrary, and the Pagi prove, in opposition to Noel Alexander, that the Pope Felix commemorated in the Martyrology must necessarily be Felix II., not Felix I. (11).

44. We now come back once more to the Arians. When Osius and Liberius fell, they were already split up into a great many sects: some who followed the party of Acasius, Eudoxius, Eunomius, and Aesius, were called Anomeans—those were pure Arians, and they not alone rejected *consubstantiality*, but even the *likeness* of the Son to the Father; but the followers of Ursacius and Valens, though called Arians, did not follow the opinions of Arius in everything. Finally, those who followed the opinions of Basil of Ancyra, and Eustatius of Sebaste, were called Semi-Arians; these condemned the blasphemies of Arius, but did not admit the consubstantiality of the divine persons (12).

45. We have now to relate the events of the Council of Rimini, of sorrowful celebrity, in which, as St. Jerome says, the Nicene faith was condemned, and the whole world groaned, finding itself Arian. When the whole Church was in confusion about the articles of the faith, it was considered that the best way of arranging everything quietly, would be to hold two councils, one in Rimini in Italy, the other at Seleucia in the East. The Council of Rimini was held in 359, and was attended by more than four hundred bishops from Illyria, Italy, Africa, Spain, Gaul, and Britain, and among those there were eighty Arians, but the rest were Catholic. When they came to treat of matters of faith, Ursacius, Valens, and other heads of the Arian party produced a writing, and proposed that all should be satisfied with signing that, in which was laid down the last formula of Sirmium of the same year, in which, it is true, the word *substance* was rejected, but it was allowed that the Son was *like unto* the Father in all things. But the Catholic bishops unanimously

---

(11) Nat. Alex., Diss. 32; Sozymen, loc. cit.; Theolog. *l.* 2, *c.* 2; Baron. An. 359; Orsi, *t.* 6, *l.* 14; Baron. An. 357, & seq.; Sozymen, Bened. XIV., de Canon. S.S. *t.* 4.
(12) N. Alex. *t.* 9; Hermant. *t.* 1, *c.* 102.

answered that there was no necessity for any other formula, but that of the Council of Nice, and decreed that there should be no addition to or subtraction from that formula; that the word *substance* should be retained, and they again condemned the doctrine of Arius, and published ten anathemas against the errors of Arius, Sabellius, and Photinus. All the Catholics subscribed to this, but Ursacius. Valens and the Arians refused, so they themselves were judged heretics, and Ursacius, Valens, Caius, and Germinius were condemned and deposed by a formal act (13).

46. Ten bishops were now sent as legates from the council to the Emperor, bearers of the letters of the council, giving him notice that the fathers had decided that there should be nothing added to or taken from the Council of Nice, and that they regretted to find that Ursacius and Valens wished to establish another formula of faith, according to the document they presented to the council. The ten legates accordingly went, but the Arians sent ten likewise, along with Ursacius and Valens, and these arrived first and prejudiced the Emperor against the council, and presented him with the formula of Sirmium, which was rejected by the Council of Rimini. When the legates sent by the council arrived, they could not obtain an audience from the Emperor, and it was only after a long delay, that he sent an answer to the council, that he was about to proceed against the barbarians, and that he had given orders to the legates to wait for him in Adrianople, where he would see them on his return, and give them his final answer. The fathers of the council wrote again to Constantius, telling him that nothing would ever change them, and begging therefore that he would give an audience to the legates and let them depart. When the Emperor came to Adrianople, the legates followed him, and were taken to the small town of Nice, in the neighbourhood; and there they began to treat with the Arians against the express orders of the council, which particularly restricted them on this point. Partly by deception, and partly by threats, they were induced to sign a formula, worse even than the third formula of Sirmium; for not only was the word *substance* omitted, but the Son was said to be *like unto* the Father, but leaving out *in all things*, which was admitted in the Sirmium formula. They were, likewise, induced to revoke the deposition of Ursacius, and his companions, condemned by the council; and they signed the formula with their own hands (14).

47. The legates having put things in this state returned to Rimini, and Constantius then gave orders to his Prefect Taurus, not to permit the council to be dissolved, till the bishops had signed the *last* formula of Nice, and to send into banishment any bishops refusing their signature, if their number did not exceed fifteen. He likewise wrote a letter to the fathers of the council, prohibiting them from

(13) S. Hieron., Dialog., ad Lucifer. Fleury, *t.* 2. Orsi, cit. S. Athan. de Synod. Sozymen, *l.* 2. (14) Theod. *l.* 2, *c.* 19; Soz. *l.* 4; Soc. *l.* 2.

using the words *substantial* and *consubstantial*. Ursacius and Valens now returned to Rimini, and as their party was now in the ascendant, they seized on the church, and wrote to the Emperor that he was obeyed, and that the expressions he objected to were not allowed to be used any more. The Catholics, at first, made a show of constancy, and refused to communicate with the legates, who excused their error by alleging all they suffered at the Court of the Emperor; but by degrees they were tired out, their constancy failed, and they subscribed the same formula as the legates (15).

48. We cannot deny but that the bishops of Rimini committed a great error, but they are not so much to be blamed for bad faith, as for not being more guarded against the wiles of the Arians. This was the snare that was laid for them:—They were wavering as to whether they should sign the formula or not, and when they were all assembled in the church, and the errors attributed to Valens, who drew up the formula, were read out, he protested that he was not an Arian. " Let him be excommunicated," he exclaimed, " who asserts that Jesus Christ is not the Son of God, born of the Father before all ages. Let him be excommunicated who says that he is not *like unto* the Father, according to the Scriptures; or, he who says he is a creature like all other creatures —(how he conceals the poison, for he taught that Christ was a creature, but more perfect than all the others);—or that he is from nothing, and not from the Father; or that there was a time when he was not; or that anything was before him;—he who teaches any of those things let him be excommunicated." And all answered:—" Let him be excommunicated." These denunciations of anathema, so fraudulently put forward, threw the Catholics off their guard. They persuaded themselves that Valens was not an Arian, and were induced to sign the formula; and thus the Council of Rimini, which opened so gloriously, was ignominiously terminated, and the bishops got leave to return to their homes. They were not long, St. Jerome tells us, till they discovered their error; for the Arians, immediately on the dissolution of the council, began to boast of their victory. The word *substantial*, said they, is now abolished, and along with it the Nicene faith; and when it was said, that the Son was not a creature, the meaning was, that he was not like the other created beings, but of a higher order, and then it was that the world, St. Jerome says, groaning, found itself Arian. Noel Alexander proves, from St. Jerome, St. Ambrose, and others, and with very convincing arguments, too, that the bishops of Rimini, in subscribing that formula, did not violate the faith; for, taken in its obvious sense, it contained nothing heretical. While the Council of Rimini was in progress, there was another

(15) St. Hila. Fragmen. *p.* 453, Sulp. Ser. *l.* 2.

council held in Seleucia, at which many Arian bishops were present; but it was soon dismissed, for the bishops were so divided, that they could not agree to any formula (16).

49. After the Council of Rimini was dissolved, the Arians of Antioch, in the year 361, not satisfied with the formula adopted at the council, drew up another in which they said, that the Son was in everything unlike the Father, not alone in substance, but also in will, and that he was formed out of nothing, as Arius had already taught. Fleury counts sixteen formulas published by the Arians. Liberius, however, after his first error in subscribing the formula of Sirmium, as we have already related (No. 41), constantly refused, after his liberation in 360, to sign the formula of Rimini, and, as Baronius relates in his Acts of Pope Liberius, he was obliged to leave Rome and hide himself in the catacombs, where Damasus and the rest of his clergy went to see him, and he remained there until the death of Constantius in 361. St. Gregory of Nazianzen says that Constantius, just before his death, repented, but in vain, of three things:—Of the murder of his relatives; of having made Julian, Cæsar; and of causing such confusion in the Church. He died, however, in the arms of the Arians, whom he protected with such zeal, and Euzoius, whom he had made Bishop of Antioch, administered him baptism just before his death. His death put an end to the synods, and for a time restored peace to the Church; as St. Jerome says, "The beast dies and the calm returns" (17).

50. On the death of Constantius, the impious Julian the Apostate took the reins of empire, and, professing idolatry, commenced a most fierce persecution against the Church, not out of any liking for the Arians, but through hatred of Christianity itself. Before we speak of the other persecutions the Catholics had to endure from the Arians, we will relate the schism caused by the wretched Lucifer, Bishop of Cagliari, who, after all his labours and fortitude in defence of the Catholic Church, vexed because St. Eusebius would not approve of his having consecrated Paulinus Bishop of Antioch, separated himself from the communion, not only of St. Eusebius, but also of St. Athanasius and Pope Liberius; he was thus the founder of a new schism, and, in despite, retired to his see in Sardinia, where he died in 370, without giving any proof of returning once more to ecclesiastical unity. He was followed in his secession by some people in Sardinia and other kingdoms, and these added error to schism, by re-baptizing those who had been baptized by the Arians. It is worthy of remark, that Calmet, in his Sacred and Profane History (Book 65, No 110), tells us that the Church of Cagliari celebrated the feast of Lucifer

(16) S. Hieron. ad. Lucif. *n*. 17; Nat., Fleury, & Orsi, loc. con.; N. Alex. Dis. 33, *t*. 9.
(17) Baron. An. 359; St. Athan. de Synod.; Fleury, *l*. 14, *n*. 33; St. Greg. Naz. *Orat*. 21; Soc. *l*. 2, *c*. 47.

as a saint or holy personage, on the 20th of May. Benedict XIV., in his work de Sanctor. Canon. tome 1, lib. 1, cap. 40, says, that two archbishops of Sardinia having written for and against the sanctity of Lucifer, the Sacred Congregation of the Roman Inquisition, in the year 1641, imposed silence on both parties, under severe penalties, and decreed that the veneration of Lucifer should stand as it was. The Bollandists (die 20 Maii p. 207) strenuously defend this decree of the Sacred Congregation. Noel Alexander (sec. 4, cap. 3, art. 13). and D. Baillet (in vita Luciferi, 20 Maii) maintain, that the Lucifer whose feast is celebrated in the Church of Cagliari is not the personage we speak of, but another of the same name, who suffered martyrdom in the persecution of the Vandals.

SEC. IV.—PERSECUTION OF VALENS, OF GENNERIC, OF HUNNERIC, AND OTHER ARIAN KINGS.

51. Julian is made Emperor, and dies. 52. Jovian Emperor; his Death. 53. Valentinian and Valens Emperors. 54. Death of Liberius. 55, 56. Valens puts eighty Ecclesiastics to Death—his other Cruelties. 57. Lucius persecutes the Solitaries. 58. Dreadful Death of Valens. 59–61. Persecution of Genseric. 62–64. Persecution of Hunneric. 65. Persecution of Theodoric. 67, 68. Persecution of Leovigild.

51. On the death of Constantius, the impious Julian the Apostate succeeded to the Empire. At first he restored the Catholic bishops to their sees, but he soon began to persecute not only the bishops but the faithful in general, not because they were Catholics, but because they were Christians, for he declared himself an idolater and an enemy of Christ. He perished in the Persian war in the year 363. He was engaged in the heat of battle, when, beholding the Persians flying before his troops, he raised his arm to cheer on his own soldiers to the pursuit, when just at the moment, as Fleury relates, a Persian horseman let fly an arrow, which went through his arm, his ribs, and deep into the liver; he tried to pull it out, and even wounded his fingers in the attempt, but could not succeed, and fell over his horse. He was borne off the field and some remedies applied, and he felt himself so much better that he called for his horse and arms again to renew the fight, but his strength failed him, and he died on the same night, the 26th of June, being only thirty-one years and six months old, and having reigned but one year and eight months after the death of Constantius. Theodoret and Sozymen relate that when he felt himself wounded he filled his hand with blood, and threw it up towards heaven, exclaiming, "O Galilean, thou hast conquered!" Theodoret likewise relates, that St. Julian Saba the Solitary, while lamenting the threats uttered by Julian against the Church, suddenly turned to his disciples, with a serene and smiling coun-

tenance, and said to them, The wild boar which wasted the vineyard of the Lord is dead! and when the news of Julian's death afterwards reached them they found that he died at the very hour the holy sage announced the fact to them. Cardinal Orsi quotes the authority of the Chronicle of Alexander, which says that the horseman who executed the Divine vengeance on Julian was the martyr St. Mercurius, who, a hundred years previously, suffered in the persecution of Decius, and that this was revealed in a heavenly vision to St. Basil (1).

52. On the very day of Julian's death, the soldiers assembled and elected Jovian, the first among the Imperial guards, though he was not general of the army; he was much beloved for his fine appearance and for his great valour, of which he gave frequent proofs during the war. When Jovian was elected Emperor, he said, As I am a Christian I cannot command idolaters, for the army cannot conquer without the assistance of God. Then all the soldiers cried out, Fear not, Emperor, you command Christians. Jovian was delighted with this answer. He accepted the truce for thirty years offered by the Persians, and was most zealous in favouring the Catholics, opposing both the Arians and Semi-Arians. He restored peace to the Church, but it was of but short duration, for he died eight months after his elevation to the Empire, in the 33rd year of his age. The generality of authors, following St. Jerome, attribute his death to want of caution in sleeping in a room in which a large quantity of charcoal was burned, to dry the walls which were newly plastered, and thus died one of the greatest champions of the Church (2).

53. On the death of Jovian, Valentinian was elected by the army in 364. He was the son of Gratian, Prefect of the Pretorium, and he was banished by Julian, because, being a Christian, he had struck the minister of the idols, who sprinkled him with lustral water. He was solicited by the army to elect a colleague, as the Empire was attacked in various points by the barbarians, so he chose his brother Valens, declared him Emperor, and divided the Empire with him. Valentinian governed the West, when the Church enjoyed a profound peace, and Valens governed the East, where he kept up and even increased the dissensions already too rife there, and treated the Catholics with the greatest cruelty, as we shall shortly see.

54. Pope Liberius died in the year 366, and before his death had the consolation of receiving a deputation in Rome of several Oriental bishops, who were anxious to return to the unity of the Church. Liberius sat for fourteen years, and notwithstanding the error he fell into by signing the formula of Sirmium, he is called

(1) Fleury, *t.* 2, *l.* 14 & 15; Theod. *l.* 3; Philost. *c.* 2. (2) Orsi, cit. Theod. Fleury, loc. cit.; St. Hieron. Ep. 60.

a pontiff whose memory is in benediction by St. Basil, St. Epiphanius, and St. Ambrose. Orsi says that his name is found in some Greek Martyrologies, and that he was venerated by that Church as a saint, and Sandinus says that his name is still in the Martyrologies of Bede and of Wandelbert. St. Damasus, a man of great learning and sanctity, was elected Pope, at his death, but he was troubled for many years by the schism of Ursinus, commonly called Ursicinus, who sacrilegiously got himself elected Pope at the same time (3).

55. We now come to the reign of Valens, who was even a greater persecutor of the Church than Constantius. Eudosius, an Arian bishop, had a great influence over him, and, from his extraordinary anxiety to protect this bishop, he became a persecutor of the Catholics. Before he set out to undertake the war against the Goths, he was baptized by Eudosius, and, just as he was receiving the Sacrament, the bishop made him swear that he would persecute and banish from the country all the defenders of the Catholic faith; and Valens fulfilled this impious oath with dreadful exactness. The Arians, now strong in the Emperor's favour, began to maltreat the Catholics, and these, not being able to endure any longer the persecutions they were subjected to, deputed eighty ecclesiastics of great piety to go to Nicomedia, and implore Valens to put a stop to the violent measures of their enemies. Valens was outrageous at this proceeding, and commanded Modestes, Prefect of the Pretorium, to put them all privately to death. This impious order was barbarously obeyed by Modestes. He gave out that he was only sending them into banishment, lest the people should be incited to break out; and he had them all put on board a ship, and the sailors were ordered, when they were a good distance from the land, so that no one could observe them, to set fire to the vessel, and leave them to perish. The order, cruel as it was, was obeyed—the vessel was fired; but the Almighty deranged all their plans, for a strong wind immediately sprung up, and blew the vessel on shore while it was still burning, and it was then finally consumed (4).

56. Valens next sent many ecclesiastics of the Church of Edessa into exile. It is well known how he strove to banish St. Basil; but the hand of the Lord miraculously prevented it, for when he was about to sign the sentence, the pen was broken in his hand, and his arm was paralyzed. He, likewise, persecuted the Catholic followers of St. Meletius, and banished them from the churches; but these faithful Christians used to assemble at the foot of a mountain, and there, exposed to the winter's snow and rain, and the summer's sun, they praised God; but even then he dispersed them, and few cities in the empire but had to deplore the tyranny of Valens, and the loss of their pastors. St. Gregory of Nyssa gives a sad descrip-

(3) Sulpicius, *l.* 5; Fleury & Orsi, cit.; Sandinus, Vit. Pon. *t.* 1. (4) Fleury, ibid.; Theod. .4, *c.* 24; Soz. *l.* 6, *c.* 14; Soc. *l.* 4, *c.* 15.

tion of the desolation caused by the tyrant in many provinces. When he came to Antioch he put a great many to the torture, and ordered a great many to be drowned, and sent off a very great multitude into exile, into Palestine, Arabia, Lybia, and many other provinces (5).

57. The holy solitaries of Syria and Egypt, by their lives and miracles, were the great upholders of the faith of the people, and were, on that account, particularly odious to Valens. He, therefore, issued a decree, directed against those champions of the faith, obliging them to enrol themselves among his troops, intending to punish them severely in case of disobedience, and knowing well that they would not do as he ordained. Full scope was given by this to the Arians, to gratify their malignity, at the expense of these innocent men, and especially against the monks of St. Basil. Phontonius, who usurped the see of Nicomedia, exercised horrible cruelties against the Catholics; but even he was surpassed by Lucius, the pretended Bishop of Alexandria, who obtained possession of that see by cruelty, and retained it by the same means. When the law of Valens—that the monks should bear arms—was promulgated, Lucius left Alexandria, and, accompanied by the commander of the troops in Egypt, placed himself at the head of three thousand soldiers, and went to the deserts of Nitria, where he found the monks, not, indeed, prepared to fight, but to die for the love of Jesus Christ, and he put whole companies of them to death; but five thousand of them escaped his fury, and fled to a place of safety, and concealed themselves. Wearied out with killing and torturing these holy men, Lucius now seized on their chiefs, Isidore, Heraclides, Macarius of Alexandria, and Macarius of Egypt, and banished them to a marshy island in Egypt, where all the inhabitants were idolaters; but when they arrived at the shore, a child possessed by the devil was thrown at their feet, and the devil cried out—" O, servants of the true God, why do you come to drive us from this place, which we have possessed so long?" They prayed over the child, cast forth the devil, and restored the infant to his parents, and were received with the greatest joy by the people, who threw down the old temple of the idols they previously adored, and began to build a church in honour of the true God. When the news of this transaction was told in Alexandria, the people all cried out against their impious bishop, Lucius, who, they said, was warring, not against man, but against God, and he was so terrified with the popular excitement, that he gave the solitaries permission to return again to their deserts (6).

58. Valens was overtaken by the Divine vengeance in 378. The Goths extended their ravages to the very gates of Constantinople, and he was so lost to shame, that he thought of nothing all

(5) Auctor. cit.   (6) St Hieron. Chron.; St. Paulin. Ep. 29; Auctor. antea cit.

the while but enjoying himself in his capital. The people began to murmur loudly at this state of inaction, and he, at last, roused himself, and marched against the enemy. Theodoret relates, that, as he was leaving the city, a holy monk, called Isaac, who lived in the neighbourhood, thus addressed him:—" Where are you going to, Emperor, after having made war against God? Cease to war with the Almighty, and he will put an end to the war raging against you; but should you not do so, mark my words, you will go to battle, but the vengeance of God will pursue you—you will lose your army, and never return here again." " I will return," said Valens, in a rage, " and your life shall pay for your audacity;" and he immediately ordered that he should be sent to prison. The hermit's prophecy turned out too true. When Valens arrived in presence of the Goths, their king, Fritigern, sent him an embassy, asking for peace, and leave to establish himself and his people in Thrace. The Emperor rejected his offer; and, on the 9th of August, 378, both armies were drawn up in front of each other, and Fritigern again made proposals of peace. But while the Romans were deliberating on their answer, the division of Bacurius, Prince of the Iberians, was attacked, and the battle became general; and never, since the slaughter at Canne, did the Romans suffer such losses as on that day. When the night closed, Valens mixed himself up with some of his soldiers and fled, thinking thus to conceal himself; but he was wounded with an arrow, and fell from his horse, and was brought by his soldiers into the hut of a peasant by the way-side. He was scarcely there when a troop of Goths, looking for plunder, arrived, and, without knowing who was inside, endeavoured to break open the door; but when they could not succeed at once in doing so, they set fire to the hut, and went away, and the unhappy Valens was burned alive in the fifteenth year of his reign and the fiftieth of his age. This was, as Orosius writes, a just judgment of God: The Goths asked Valens for some bishops, to instruct them in the Christian religion, and he sent them Arians, to infect the poor people with their impious heresy; and so they were justly appointed afterwards, as ministers of the Divine justice, to punish him. On the death of Valens, Gratian became master of the whole empire, and this good prince gave liberty to the Catholics of the East, and peace to the Church (7).

59. We now have to treat of the persecution of the Catholics of Africa by Genseric, the Arian King of the Vandals. He commenced persecuting the Catholics in the year 437, with the intention of making Arianism the religion of all Africa, as St. Prosper writes. Immediately after conquering Carthage, he commenced a most cruel war against the Catholics, plundered the churches, and gave them as habitations to his vassals, after banishing the priests,

(7) Orsi, cit.; St. Pros. in Chron.

and taking away the sacred vessels; and, intending to have no religion but Arianism, he drove the bishops, not alone out of their churches, but out of the cities, and put many to death. He would not permit the Catholics, on the death of St. Deogratias, to elect another Bishop of Carthage, and he prohibited all ordinations in the province of Zeugitania, and in the Pro-consulate, where there were sixty-four bishoprics; the effect of this order was, that, at the end of thirty years, there were only three bishops in the province, and two of these were banished, and the third fled to Edessa. Cardinal Orsi, following the historian of the Vandalic persecution, says that the number of martyrs was very great. The history of four brothers, in particular, slaves of one of Genseric's officers, is very interesting:—These martyrs, finding it impossible to serve God according to their wishes in the house of their Vandal master, fled, and took refuge in a monastery near the city of Trabacca; but their master never ceased till he found them out, and brought them back to his house, where he loaded them with chains, put them in prison, and never ceased to torture them. When Genseric heard of it, instead of blaming the master for his cruelty, he only encouraged him to continue it, and the tyrant beat them with branches of the palm tree to that pitch, that their bones and entrails were laid bare; but, though this was done many days in succession, the following days they were always found miraculously healed. He next shut them up in a narrow prison, with their feet in stocks made of heavy timber; but the beams of the instrument were broken in pieces, like twigs, the next day. When this was told to Genseric, he banished them to the territories of a Pagan king, in the deserts of Africa. The inhabitants of their place of exile were all Pagans, but these holy brothers became apostles among them, and converted a great number; but, as they had no priest, some of them made their way to Rome, and the Pope yielded to their wishes, and sent a priest among them, who baptized a great number. When Genseric heard this, he ordered that each of the brothers should be tied to a car by the feet, and dragged through the woods till dead, and the barbarous sentence was executed. The very barbarians wept when they saw these innocent men thus torn to pieces, but they expired praying and praising God in the midst of their torments. They are commemorated in the Roman Martyrology, on the 14th of October (8).

60. Genseric was daily becoming more inimical to the Church, and he sent a person called Proculus into the province of Zeugitania, to force the bishops to deliver up the holy Books and all the sacred vessels, with the intention of more easily undermining their faith, when deprived, as it were, of their arms. The bishops refused to give them up, and so the Vandals took everything by force,

---

(8) Fleury, *t.* 4; Baron. An. 437 & 456; Orsi, cit.

and even stripped the cloths off the altars, and made shirts of them, but the Divine vengeance soon overtook Proculus, for he died raving mad, after eating away his own tongue. The Arians even frequently trampled the Holy Sacrament under their feet in the Catholic church. When the Catholics were deprived of their church they secretly opened another in a retired place, but the Arians soon heard of it, and collecting a body of armed men under the leadership of one of their priests, they attacked the faithful in their church; some rushed in at the door, sword in hand, others mounted to the roof with arrows, and killed a great many before the altar; a great many took to flight, but they were afterwards put to death in various ways by order of Genseric.

61. Genseric next issued a decree, that no one should be admitted into his palace or that of his son, unless he was an Arian, and then, as Victor Vitensis informs us, a person called Armogastes, who was in the court of Theodoric, one of the sons of Genseric, signalized himself for his constancy in the faith. Theodoric tried every means to make him apostatize, but in vain; he first made him promises of preferment; he next threatened him, and he then subjected him to the most cruel torments. He had his head and legs bound with cords twisted with the greatest possible force; he then was hung up in the air by one leg, with his head down, and when all this could not shake his constancy, he ordered him to be beheaded. He knew, however, that Armogastes would be venerated as a martyr by the Catholics, if this sentence were carried into execution, so he changed the sentence, and compelled him to dig the earth, and tend a herd of cows. While Armogastes was one day engaged in this humble employment under a tree, he begged a friend, a Christian of the name of Felix, to bury him after his death at the foot of that tree; he died in a few days after; and when his friend, in compliance with his request, set about digging his grave, he found in the spot a marble tomb, beautifully finished, and there he buried him. The name of St. Armogastes is marked in the Roman Martyrology on the 29th of March, and Archiminus and Saturus, who suffered likewise, are commemorated with him. Genseric used every artifice with Archiminus to cause him to apostatize, but when he could not shake his faith, he gave orders that he should be beheaded; but there was a private condition annexed; that was, that if he showed any symptoms of fear, the sentence should be executed; but if no terror could be remarked on him at the moment, that his life should be spared, lest he should be venerated as a martyr by the Catholics. He awaited death with the greatest intrepidity, and he was, consequently, spared. Saturus was in the service of Hunneric, the king's eldest son, and he was threatened with confiscation of his entire property, if he did not become an Arian; he yielded neither to the threats of the tyrant, nor to the tears of his wife, who came to see him one day with his

four children; and threw herself weeping at his feet, and embracing his knees, besought him to have pity on her and her poor children; but Saturus, unmoved, said: My dear wife, if you loved me you would not tempt me to send myself to hell; they may do with me as they please, but I will never forget the words of my Divine Master, that no one can be his disciple, unless he leaves all things to follow him. He thus remained firm, and he was despoiled of everything. Genseric died at length, in the year 477, the fiftieth of his reign over the Vandals, and forty-nine years after his landing in Africa. He made Hunneric heir to his kingdom, and settled the succession so that the oldest descendant of his, in the male line, should always be king.

62. Hunneric, in the beginning of his reign, reigned with clemency, but he soon showed the innate cruelty of his disposition, and he commenced with his own relatives. He put to death his brother Theodoric, and his young child, and he would likewise have put his other brother, Genton, out of the way, only he had the good fortune to be forewarned, and saved himself. He now began to persecute the Catholics; he commanded the holy bishop Eugenius, that he should not preach any more, and that he should allow no one, either man or woman, into the church. The saint answered that the church was open for all, and that he had no power to prohibit any one from entering. Hunneric then placed executioners at the door of the church, with clubs stuck over with spikes, and these tore off not only the hair but even the scalp of the persons who went in, and such violence was used that some lost their sight, and even some lost their lives. He sent away noblemen into the fields to reap the corn; one of these had a withered hand, so that he could not work, but he was still obliged to go, and by the prayers of his companions, the Almighty restored him the use of it. He published a decree that no one should be allowed to serve in the palace, or hold any public employment, if he were not an Arian; and those who refused obedience to this iniquitous order were despoiled of their properties, and banished into Italy and Sardinia; he likewise ordered that all the property of the Catholic bishops should go to the Crown after their death, and that no successor could be consecrated to any deceased bishop, until he paid five hundred golden crowns. He had all the nuns collected together, and caused them to be tormented with burning plates of iron, and to be hung up with great weights to their feet, to force them to accuse the bishops and priests of having had criminal intercourse with them; many of them died in these torments, and those who survived, having their skin burned up, were crooked all their lives after (9).

63. He banished to the desert, between bishops, priests, deacons,

(9) Orsi, *t.* 15 ; Fleury, *t.* 5, *l.* 30 ; N. Alex. *t.* 10.

and lay people, altogether four thousand nine hundred and seventy-six Catholics, and many among them were afflicted with gout, and many blind with age; Felix, of Abbitirus, a bishop, was for forty-four years paralyzed, and deprived of all power of moving, and even speechless. The Catholic bishops, not knowing how to bring him along with them, begged of the King to allow him to wear out the few days he had to live, in Carthage; but the barbarian answered: If he cannot go on horseback let him be tied with a rope, and dragged on by oxen; and they were obliged to carry him, thrown across a mule, like a log of wood. In the commencement of their journey they had some little liberty, but in a little while they were treated with the greatest cruelty; they were shut up together in a very narrow prison, no one allowed to visit them, crowded together one almost over the other, and no egress allowed for a moment, so that the state of the prison soon became horribly infectious; and, as Victor the historian relates, no torment could equal what they suffered—up to their knees in the most horrible filth, and there alone could they sit down, sleep, and eat the little quantity of barley given to them for food, without any preparation, as if they were horses. At length they were taken out of that prison, or rather sink, and conveyed to their destination; the aged, and those who were too weak to walk, were driven on with blows of stones, and prodded with lances, and when nature failed them, and they could not move on any longer, the Moors tied them by the feet, and dragged them on through stones and briars, as if they were carcases of beasts, and thus an immense number of them died, leaving the road covered with their blood.

64. In the year 483, according to Fleury and N. Alexander, Hunneric, wishing to destroy Catholicity altogether in Africa, commanded that there should be a conference held in Carthage between the Catholics and the Arians. The bishops, not alone of Africa, but of the Islands subject to the Vandals, assembled there, but as Cyril, the Arian Patriarch, dreaded that his sect would be ruined by the conference, it did not take place. The King was now highly incensed against the Catholics, and he privately sent an edict to all the provinces, while he had the bishops in Carthage, and on one and the same day all the churches of Africa were closed, and all the property belonging both to the churches and the Catholic bishops was given over to the Arians, following in that the decree laid down for the punishment of heretics in the laws of the Emperors. This barbarous decree was put into execution, and the bishops, despoiled of all they possessed, were driven out of Carthage, and all persons were ordered to give them neither food nor shelter, under pain of being burned themselves, and their houses along with them. Hunneric, at last, in the year 484, after committing so many acts of tyranny, and killing so many Catholics, closed his reign and his life by a most horrible death—he died rotten, and eaten up alive

by a swarm of worms; all his entrails fell out, and he tore his own flesh in a rage with his teeth, so that he was even buried in pieces. He was not altogether eight years on the throne when he died, and he had not even the satisfaction to leave the throne to his son Hilderic, for whom he had committed such slaughter in his family, because, according to the will of his father, Genseric, the crown descended to Guntamond, the son of his brother Genton; and he was succeeded, in 496, by Trasamond, who endeavoured to extirpate Catholicity totally in Africa, about the year 504. Among his other acts, he banished two hundred and twenty-four bishops, and among them was the glorious St. Fulgentius. On the death of Trasamond, in 523, he was succeeded by Hilderic, a prince, as Procopius writes, affable to his subjects, and of a mild disposition. This good King, Graveson tells us, was favourable to the Catholic religion, and he recalled St. Fulgentius and the other exiled bishops, and granted the free exercise of their religion to all the Catholics of his kingdom; but in the year 530, he was driven out of his kingdom by Glimere, an Arian, and then it was that the Emperor Justinian, to revenge his intimate friend, Hilderic, declared war against Glimere; and his general, Belisarius, having conquered Carthage and the principal cities, and subjected all Africa once more to the Roman Emperor, the Arians were banished, and the churches restored to the Catholics (10).

65. There were other persecutions by the Arians, after the death of Hunneric. Theodoric, King of Italy, and son of Theodomire, King of the Ostrogoths, was also an Arian, and persecuted the Catholics till his death, in the year 526. He ought, however, to be lauded for always keeping in his employment honest and learned ministers. One of them was the great Boetius, a man of profound learning, and a true Christian; but through the envy of his calumniators, he was cast into prison by his sovereign, and after being kept there a long time, was, at last, without being giving an opportunity of defending himself, put to death in horrible torments, his head being tied round with a cord, and that twisted till his eyes leaped out of their sockets. Thus died Boetius, the great prop of the faith in that age, in the year 524, and the fifty-fifth of his age. Theodoric likewise put to death Symmachus, a man of the highest character, in a most barbarous manner; and his crime was, that he was son-in-law to Boetius, and the tyrant dreaded that he would conspire against his kingdom. He also caused the death of the holy Pope John, in prison, by privations and starvation, and this holy man is venerated since in the Church as a martyr. Some inculpate this pontiff, for having induced the pious Emperor, Justin, to restore the churches to the Arians, but others deny his having done so. Cardinal Orsi says, that a great deal of obscurity

(10) Fleury, Orsi, Nal. *l.* con.; Graveson, His. Eccles. *t.* 3, Procopius, *l.* 1, de Bellow. Vand.

hangs over the transactions of this age; but, taking the anonymous commentator on Valesius as a guide, he does not think that the Pope obtained the restitution to the Arians of all their churches, but only of such as they were already in possession of, or such as were deserted, and not consecrated; and that he did this only that Theodoric might rest satisfied with this arrangement, and leave the Catholics in possession of their churches, and not turn them out, and give them up to the Arians, as it was feared he would. But Noel Alexander, Baronius, and Orsi himself—and with these Berti agrees—say, with more likelihood, that St. John refused to solicit the Emperor, at all, for the restitution of the churches to the Arians, and that this is proved from his second epistle to the Italian bishops, in which he tells them, that he consecrated, and caused to be restored to the Catholics in the East, all the churches in possession of the Arians; and it was on that account that he was put into prison by Theodoric, on his return to Italy, and died there on the 27th of May, 526, worn out with sufferings.

66. Theodoric, not satisfied with those acts of tyranny, as the above-mentioned anonymous writer informs us, published an edict on the 26th of August, giving to the Arians all the Catholic churches; but God, at length, had pity on the faithful, and he removed him by a sudden death. A dreadful flux brought him to death's door in three days; and on the very Sunday in which his decree was to be put into execution, he lost his power and his life. A cotemporaneous historian gives a curious account of the beginning of his sickness. He was going to supper, and the head of a big fish was placed before him; he immediately imagined that he saw the head of Symmachus, whom he had a little before put to death, and that it threatened him with eyes of fury. He was dreadfully alarmed; and, seized with sudden terror, he took to his bed, and told his physician, Elpidius, what he imagined; he then regretted sincerely his cruelty to Boetius and Symmachus, and between agitation of mind, and the racking of his bowels, he was soon dead. St. Gregory writes, that a certain hermit, in the island of Lipari, saw him in a vision after his death, barefooted, and stripped of all his ornaments, between St. John and Symmachus, and that they brought him to the neighbouring volcano, and cast him into the burning crater.

67. Leovigild, King of the Visigoths, in Spain, was likewise an Arian; he had two sons by his first wife, Hermengild and Reccarede, and he married a second time, Goswind, the widow of another King of the Visigoths. He married his son Hermengild to Ingonda, who was a Catholic, and refused to allow herself to be baptized by the Arians, as her mother-in-law Goswind, herself an Arian, wished. Not being able to induce her, by fair means, to consent, Goswind seized her one day by the hair, threw her on the ground, kicked her, and covered her over with blood, and then

stripped her violently, and threw her into a fountain of water, to re-baptize her by force; but nothing could induce her to change her faith, and she even converted her husband Hermengild. When Leovigild heard this, he commenced a persecution against the Catholics; many were exiled, and their properties confiscated; others were beaten, imprisoned, and stoned to death, or put out of the way by other cruelties. Seven bishops were also banished, and the churches were deprived of their possessions. Hermengild was cast into prison by his father, and, at the festival of Easter, an Arian bishop came to give him communion, but he refused to receive it from his hand, and sent him off as a heretic; his father then sent the executioners to put him to death, and one of them split open his head with a hatchet. This took place in the year 586, and this holy prince has been since venerated as a martyr.

68. The impious Leovigild did not long survive his son; he deeply regretted having put him to death; and, as St. Gregory tells us, was convinced of the truth of the Catholic religion, but had not the grace to embrace it, as he dreaded the vengeance of his people. Fleury, nevertheless, quotes many authorities to prove that Leovigild spent a week before his death deploring the crimes he committed, and that he died a Catholic in the year 587, the eighteenth of his reign. He left the kingdom to his son Reccarede, who became a Catholic, and received the sacrament of Confirmation in the Catholic church; and such was his zeal for the faith, that he induced the Arian bishops, and the whole nation of the Visigoths, to embrace it, and deposed from his employment, and cashiered from his army, all heretics. The beginning of his reign was thus the end of the Arian heresy in Spain, where it reigned from the conquest of that country by the barbarians, an hundred and eighty years before, in the beginning of the fifth century; and when the Emperor Justinian, by the victories of Belisarius, became master of Africa, about the year 535 (*chap.* 4, No. 64), the Catholic faith was also re-established. The Burgundians, in Gaul, forsook the Arian heresy under the reign of Sigismund, the son and successor of King Gontaband, who died in 516. Sigismund was converted to the faith in 515, by St. Avitus, Bishop of Vienne. The Lombards in Italy abandoned Arianism, and embraced the Catholic faith under their King, Rimbert, in 660, and have since remained faithful to the Church. Danæus thus concludes his essay on the heresy of the Arians: " This dreadful hydra, the fruitful parent of so many evils, was then extinguished, but after the lapse of about nine hundred years, in about the year 1530, was again revived in Poland and Transylvania, by modern Arians and Antitrinitarians, who, falling from bad to worse, have become far worse than the ancient Arians, and are confounded with Deists and Socinians" (11).

(11) Fleury, *t.* 5 ; Gregor. Jur. 9, *t.* 15 ; Danæus, Gen. Temp. *not. p.* 237.

Article III.

69-74. Heresy of Macedonius. 75-77. Of Apollinaris. 78. Of Elvidius. 79. Of Aetius. 80, 81. The Messalians. 82. The Priscillianists. 83. Jovinians. 84. Other Heretics. 85. Of Audeus, in particular.

69. As Arius uttered blasphemies against the Son, so Macedonius had the temerity to speak blasphemously of the Holy Ghost. He was, at first, an Arian, and was deputed to the Council or Cabal of Tyre, as legate of the Emperor Constantius. He was then intruded by the Arians into the See of Constantinople, as Socrates informs us, though Paul, the lawful bishop, was then alive, and he received ordination at the hands of the Arians. A horrible circumstance occurred at his induction into the Metropolitan See. He went to take possession in a splendid chariot, accompanied, not by his clergy, but with the imperial Prefect by his side, and surrounded by a powerful body of armed troops, to strike terror into the people. An immense multitude was assembled, out of curiosity to see the pageant, and the throng was so great, that the church, streets, and squares were all choked up, and the new bishop could not proceed. The soldiers set about clearing the way; they first struck the people with the shafts of their spears, and whether it was by orders of the bishop, or through their own ferocity, they soon began to wound and kill the people, and trampled on the slain and fallen; the consequence was, that three thousand one hundred and fifty dead bodies lay stretched in gore in the street; the bishop passed through, and as his entrance to the episcopal throne was marked by blood and slaughter, so his future government of the See was distinguished for vengeance and cruelty. In the first place, he began to persecute the friends of Paul, his competitor in the See; he caused some of them to be publicly flogged, confiscated the property of others, more he banished, and he marked his hatred of one in particular by causing him to be branded on the forehead, to stamp him through life with a mark of infamy. Several authors even say that, after he had banished Paul from the See, he caused him to be strangled at Cucusus, the place of his exile (1).

70. His rage was not alone directed against the friends of Paul, but against all who professed the faith of the Council of Nice; the wretch made use of atrocious torments to oblige them to receive communion from him. He used, as Socrates informs us, to have their mouths forced open with a wooden tongs, and the consecrated particle forced on them,—a punishment greater than death to the faithful. He used to take the children from their mothers, and have them most cruelly flogged in their mothers' presence; and the mothers themselves he used to torture by squeezing both their breasts under the lid of a heavy chest, and then caused them to be cut off with a sharp razor, or burned them with red coals, or with

(1) Bernin. *t.* 1; Coc. *l.* 1, *c.* 25; Danæus & Theod.

red-hot balls, and left them to die in prolonged tortures. As if it was not enough to torture and destroy the Catholics themselves in this manner, he vented his rage on their churches, which he destroyed to the very foundations, and the ruins he had scattered abroad.

71. One would think that these sacrilegious excesses were quite enough. But he was determined to do something more, and this was the last act he was permitted to perform as bishop. He had the audacity to disinter the body of Constantine, and transfer it from one tomb to another; but Constans could not stand this, so he ignominiously deposed him from the bishopric. While he was Bishop of Constantinople, he was only remarked for being a very bad man, and a Semi-Arian; but after his deposition, the diabolical ambition seized him, of becoming great in impiety, and the chief of a heresy; so, in the year 360, considering that preceding heresiarchs had directed their attacks against the Father and the Son, he determined to blaspheme the Third Person, the Holy Ghost. He, therefore, denied that the Holy Ghost was God, and taught that he was only a creature like the angels, but of a higher order.

72. Lambert Danæus says that Macedonius was deposed in the year 360, and was exiled to a place called Pilæ, where, in his old age, he paid the penalty of his crimes. But his heresy survived him: he had many followers, and the chief among them was Marantonius, Bishop of Nicomedia, and formerly his disciple, and, what was remarkable, he was distinguished for the regularity of his life, and was held in high esteem by the people. This heresy had many adherents in the monasteries of Monks, and among the people of Constantinople, but neither bishops nor churches till the reign of Arcadius, in the Arian domination. The Macedonians were principally scattered about Thrace, in Bithynia, along the Hellespont, and in all the cities of Cizica. They were, in general, people of moral lives, and observers of almost monastic regularity; they were usually called *Pneumatomachi,* from the Greek word signifying enemies of the Spirit (2).

73. The Macedonian heresy was condemned in several particular Councils. In the year 362, after the return of St. Athanasius, it was condemned in the Council of Alexandria; in 367, in a Council in Illyria; and in 373, in a Council held in Rome, by St. Damasus, for the condemnation of Apollinaris, whose heresy will be discussed presently. In the year 381, Macedonius was again condemned, in the Council of Constantinople (the first Constantinopolitan), and though only an hundred and fifty bishops were present, and these were all Orientals, this Council was recognized as a general one, by the authority of St. Damasus, and another Council of Bishops assembled in Rome immediately after, in 382. N. Alexander says:

(2) N. Alex. Bernin. *t.* 1, &c.

"This was a Council of the Oriental Church alone, and was only, *ex post facto*, Ecumenical, inasmuch as the Western Church, congregated in the Synod of Rome, under Pope Damasus, held the same doctrine, and condemned the same heresy, as the Oriental Church." And Graveson says: " This Council of Constantinople was afterwards reckoned a general one, for Pope Damasus, and the whole Church of the West, gave it this dignity and authority." An anonymous author says the same thing (Auctor Lib. Apparat. brev. ad Theol. & Jus Canon.) This Council is considered a General one, because it followed in everything what was previously defined in the Roman Council, to which the Eastern bishops were convoked, by letters of St. Damasus, presented to the bishops assembled in Constantinople, and what was decreed in that Council was confirmed in the other Synod, held in Rome, in 382. The Fathers of the Council wrote to St. Damasus, that he had, by his fraternal charity, invited them, by letters of the Emperor, to assist as members of the Council, to be held in Rome. The reader will find in the third volume the refutation of the heresy of Macedonius.

74. In this Council of Constantinople, besides the condemnation of the heresy of Macedonius, the heresies of Apollinaris and Eunomius were also condemned; and Maximus Cinicus, who seized on the See of Constantinople, was deposed, and St. Gregory of Nazianzen was confirmed in possession of it, but he, through love of peace, afterwards resigned it, and Neptarius was chosen in his place by the Council. Several canons, regarding the discipline of the Church, were passed, and the Nicene Creed was confirmed by the Council, and some few words were added to it concerning the mystery of the Incarnation, on account of the Apollinarists and other heretics, and a more ample explanation of the article regarding the Holy Ghost was added, on account of the heresies of the Macedonians, who denied his Divinity. The Nicene Creed says, of the incarnation of Jesus Christ, these words alone: " *Qui propter nos homines, et propter nostram salutem descendit, et incarnatus est, et homo factus. Passus est, et resurrexit tertia die; et ascendit in cœlos; et iterum venturus est judicare vivos, et mortuos; et in Spiritum Sanctum, &c.*" But the Symbol of Constantinople goes on thus: " *Descendit de cœlis, et incarnatus est de Spiritu Sancto ex Maria Virgine, et homo factus est. Crucifixus etiam pro nobis sub Pontio Pilato, passus, et sepultus est; tertia die resurrexit a mortuis secundum Scripturas, &c. Et in Spiritum Sanctum Dominum et vivificantem, ex Patre procedentem, et cum Patre et Filio adorandum et conglorificandum qui locutus est per Prophetas, &c.*" (3). Nicephorus (4) relates, that St. Gregory of Nyssa laid down the declaration of the Council in these words: " Et in Spiritum Sanctum

---

(3) Cabassutius, Not. Concil *p.* 136; Orsi, *t.* 8, *l.* 18, *n.* 71, & seq.; Fleury, *l.* 18, *n.* 1, & seq.; Nat. Alex. *t.* 1, diss. 37, *ar.* 2.   (4) Niceph. *l.* 12, *c.* 2.

Dominum et vivificantem, ex Patre procedentem, cum Patre et Filio coadorandum et conglorificandum, qui locutus est per Prophetas" (Act. Conc. Const.) When this was read in the Council, all the bishops cried out: "This is the faith of all; this is the orthodox faith; this we all believe" (5).

75. We have now to speak of Apollinaris, who was condemned in the same Council of Constantinople. He was Bishop of Laodicea, and St. Jerome's master in sacred literature; but he broached another heresy, concerning the person of Jesus Christ. His principal error, as Noel Alexander tells us, and on the authority of St. Epiphanius, St. Leo, St. Augustin, and Socrates (6), was, that he supposed the human nature of Jesus Christ only half human nature—he supposed that Christ had no soul, but that, in place of one, the Word made flesh answered as a soul to his body. He softened down this doctrine a little after, for then he admitted that Christ was not without a soul altogether, for he possessed that part of the sensitive soul, with which we see and feel in common with all other sensitive beings; but that he had not the reasoning part, or the mind, and the Word, he said, supplied that in the Person of Christ. This error is founded on the false philosophy of Plato, who wished to establish in man three substances, to wit—the body, the soul, and the mind.

76. The Apollinarists added three other errors; First, that the body of Christ, born of Mary, was consubstantial with the Divinity of the Word, and hence it followed that the Divinity of the Word was passible, and suffered, in reality, torments and death. Eranistes, an Apollinarist, contended that the Divine Nature suffered in the flesh, just as the soul suffers, conjoined with the body, in the sufferings of the body. But even in this illustration he was in error, because the body without the soul is not capable of suffering, and, when the body is hurt, it is the soul that suffers in reality, by the communication it has with the body; so that, according to their system, the Divine Nature would suffer, if the flesh, supposed to be consubstantial to the Divinity, was hurt. The second error was, that the Divine Word did not take flesh from the Virgin, but brought it down from heaven, and, on that account, they called the Catholics, who believed that the body of Christ was taken from Mary, *Homicolists*, and accused them of establishing, not a Trinity, but a Quaternity, of Persons, because, besides the three Divine Persons, they admitted a fourth substance, entirely distinct, Christ-God, and *Man*. Thirdly—The last error was, that the Divine substance of the Word was converted into flesh; but these three errors, N. Alexander says, were not taught by Apollinaris, but by his disciples (7). Apollinaris erred also in the doctrine of the Trinity,

(5) Bernini, *t.* 1, *p.* 316. (6) Nat. *t.* 8, *ar.* 3, ex St. Ephiph. Her. 77; St. Leo, Ser. de Nat. Dom.; St. Aug. de Her. *c.* 55; Socrat. *l.* 2, *c.* 36. (7) Nat. ibid.

by teaching that there were different degrees of dignity in the Trinity itself. He calls the Holy Ghost *great*, the Son *greater*, and the Father *greatest*. He, likewise, taught the errors of the Millenarians, and said that the Jewish rites ought to be resumed (8). Fleury and Orsi, likewise, give an account of his heresy (9).

77. The heresy of Apollinaris, especially that part of it referring to the Mystery of the Incarnation, was already condemned, in the year 362, by St. Athanasius, in the Council of Alexandria; it was also condemned, in 373, by St. Damasus in the Roman Council, and the same year Bernini tells us that Apollinaris died, the laughing-stock of the people, even of the children (10). An author, quoted by St. Gregory of Nyssa (11), relates, that Apollinaris, being in his dotage, gave the book containing his doctrines to a lady of Antioch, a disciple of his, to keep for him; this came to the knowledge of St. Ephraim the Syrian, who was then at Antioch, and he borrowed the book for a few days, from the lady: he took it home and pasted the leaves one to the other, so that nothing could open them, folded up the book, and sent it back again to the lady. Soon after this he had a Conference with Apollinaris, and they began to dispute about the doctrines of his book, in presence of a great many persons. Apollinaris, weakened in his intellect, on account of his great age, said that the answers to St. Ephraim's arguments would be all found in his book, and he sent to the lady for it; but when he tried to open the first page he found it pasted up, and the whole book just like a log of wood; he was so enraged that he dashed it violently to the ground and trampled on it, and ran out of the place as fast as ever he could, amid the laughter of the bystanders, who continued hooting after him as long as he was in sight. It is said that the poor old man took it so much to heart, that he fell sick and died. Finally, this heresy was condemned in the Second General Council (the first of Constantinople), as appears in the Synodical letters: "Nos præterea doctrinam Dominicæ Incarnationis integram & perfectam tenemus, neque dispensationem carnis Christi vel animæ, vel mentis expertem, vel imperfectam esse asserimus; sed agnoscimus Verbum Dei ante secula omnino perfectum hominem in novissimis diebus pro nostra salute factum esse" (12).

78. Among the followers of Apollinaris were the Antidicomarianites or adversaries of Mary. These said, following Elvidius, that she did not remain a virgin, but after the birth of Christ had other children by St. Joseph. St. Epiphanius (13), hearing that this error was prevalent in Arabia, refuted it in a long letter directed to all the faithful of that region. At the same time, and in the

---

(8) Nat. ibid.   (9) Fleury, *t.* 3, *l.* 17, *n.* 2-25; Orsi, *t.* 7, *l.* 16, *n.* 115.
(10) Bernin. *t.* 2, *s.* 4, *c.* 8.   (11) St. Greg. Niss. Serm. de St. Ephrem.   (12) N. Alex. *t.* 8, *c.* 3, *σ.* 1481.   (13) St. Epip. Her. 77, *n.* 26 & 78.

same country, another error altogether opposed to this was broached, that the Blessed Virgin was a sort of Deity. The followers of this sect were called Collyridians (14), because they worshipped the Virgin by offering her a certain sort of cakes called, in Greek, Collyrides. This superstition came from Thrace and Upper Sythica, and passed into Arabia. The women, especially, were almost all followers of this sect. On certain fast days every year they ornamented a car, and placed on it a square bench covered with a cloth; on this a loaf was placed, and, being offered to the Virgin, was then divided among the worshippers. St. Epiphanius, in combating this superstition, showed that women can never take any part in the priesthood, and that the worship they offered to the Virgin was idolatrous; for, although the most perfect of all creatures, she was still but a creature, and should not be honored like God with that oblation (15).

79. Aerius was ambitious of becoming Bishop of Antioch, and when Eustasius was elected to that See, he was devoured with envy. Eustasius did all in his power to gratify him; he ordained him priest, gave him the government of his hospital, and when, with all this, he could not prevent him from talking badly of him, he admonished him, tried to gain him over by more kindness, then threatened him, but all in vain. Aerius threw up the government of the hospital, and began to teach his errors to a number of followers, and when these were turned out not only of the churches, but even out of the towns and villages, they assembled in the woods and caverns, and even in the open fields, though sometimes covered with snow. This heresy sprung up in 370, but was never very extensive. Aerius was an Arian all out; but he added other errors of his own to the pre-existing heresy. These can be easily reduced to three heads: First—That there is no difference beween priests and bishops; Second—That prayers for the dead are useless; and, Third—That the observance of fasts and festivals, even of Easter, is only a Jewish rite, and useless (16).

80. The fourth century was also infested by the Messalians; these were wandering monks, who professed to abandon the world, though they were not properly monks at all. They were called Messalinians, or Messalians, from a Syriac word signifying prayer, and the Greeks called them Euchitians, for the same reason; they said that the whole essence of religion consisted in prayer (17). They were of two classes: the most ancient were Pagans, and had no connexion with Christians or Jews; they believed in a plurality of Gods, though they adored but one alone, whom they called the Almighty. It is supposed that these were the people called *Hypsisteri*, or *adorers*, of the Most High (18). Their oratories

(14) St. Epip. Her. 79.   (15) Fleury, *t.* 3, *l.* 17, *n.* 26; Orsi, *t.* 7, *l.* 7, *n.* 50.
(16) Nat. Alex. *t.* 8, *c.* 3, *art.* 15; Fleury, *t.* 3, *l.* 19, *n.* 36.   (17) St. Epip. Her. 88, *n.* 1.   (18) Supplem. *t.* 11, *n.* 80.

were large buildings, surrounded with porticos, but open to the sky; and they assembled there morning and evening, and, by the light of numerous lamps, sang hymns of praise to God, and they were called by the Greeks, Eusemites on that account (19). Those who called themselves Christians began to appear about the reign of Constans, but their origin is doubtful; they came from Mesopotamia, but they were established in Antioch, in 376, when St. Epiphanius wrote his Treatise on Heresies. St. Epiphanius says, that they took in too literal a sense the command of Jesus Christ, to leave everything and follow him, and they literally observed it; but they led an idle, vagabond life, begging and living in common, both men and women, so that, in the summer time, they used even to sleep together in the streets. They refused to do work of any kind, as they considered it wicked; they never fasted, and used to eat at an early hour in the morning—a practice totally opposed to the Oriental manner of fasting (20).

81. The following errors were taught and practised by them (21); they said that every man had, from his birth, a devil attached to him, who prompted him to all evil, and that the only remedy against him was prayer, which banished the devil, and destroyed the root of sin. They looked on the sacraments with indifference, and said the Eucharist did neither good nor harm, and that baptism takes away sin, just like a razor, which leaves the roots. They said the domestic devil is expelled by spitting and blowing the nose, and when they purified themselves in this manner, that they saw a sow and a number of little pigs come out of their mouths, and a fire that did not burn, enter into them (22). Their principal error consisted in taking the precept, to pray continually, in the literal sense; they did so to excess, and it was the parent of a thousand follies in this case; they slept the greater part of the day, and then began to say they had revelations, and prophesied things which never happened. They boasted that they saw the Trinity with the eyes of the flesh, and that they visibly received the Holy Ghost; they did very extraordinary things while praying; they would frequently jump forward with violence, and then say that they were dancing on the devil, and this folly became so glaring that they acquired the name of the *Enthusiasts* (23). They said that man's science and virtue could be made equal to that of God, so that those who once arrived at perfection, never could afterwards sin, even through ignorance. They never formed a separate community from the faithful, always denying their heresy, and condemning it as strongly as any one else, when they were convicted of it. Their founder was Adelphius, a native of Mesopotamia, and from him they were called Adelphians. The Messalians were con-

(19) St. Epiph. *n.* 3. (20) Theod. *t.* 4, *c.* 11. (21) Theod. Her. Fab. *l.* 4, *c.* 2; Nat. Alex. *t.* 8, *c.* 3, act 16; Fleury, *t.* 3, *l.* 19, *n.* 35. (22) St. Aug. Her. *l.* 5, *c.* 7. (23) St. Epip. Her. *n.* 3.

demned in a council, held in 387, by Flavian, Bishop of Antioch, and also in another council, held about the same time by St. Amphilochius, Bishop of Iconium, the Metropolis of Pamphilia (24). They were finally condemned in the first Council of Ephesus, especially in the seventh session, and they were proscribed by the Emperor Theodosius, in the year 428. It was a long time before this heresy was finally extinct in the East, and in 1018, during the reign of the Emperor Alexius Comnenus, another heresy sprung out of it, the followers of which were called Bonomilists, which signifies, in the Bulgarian language, the beloved of God. Their founder was Basil, a physician, or monk, who, after practising his errors for fifty-two years, and deluding a great number, was burned alive, with all his followers, by order of the Emperor. This unfortunate man promulgated many blasphemous opinions, principally taken from the Messalians and Manicheans; he said that we should use no prayer, except the "Our Father," and rejected every other prayer but that which, he said, was the true Eucharist; that we ought to pray to the devil even, that he might not injure us, and that we should never pray in churches, for our Lord says: "When you pray, enter into your chamber;" he denied the books of Moses, and the existence of the Trinity, and it was not, he said, the Son of God, who became incarnate, but the Archangel Michael. He published many other like opinions, so that there is little doubt but that he lost, not alone the faith, but his senses likewise (25).

82. About the year 380, the heresy of the Priscillianists first appeared in the East. The founder of this sect was an Egyptian of Memphis, of the name of Mark; he went to Spain, and his first disciples were, a lady of the name of Agapa, and Elpidius, a rhetorician, invited to join him by the lady. These two next wheedled Priscillian to join them, and from him the sect took its name. Priscillian was both noble and rich; he had a great facility of speech, but was unsettled, vain, and proud of his knowledge of profane literature. By his affable manners he gained a great number of followers, both noble and plebeian, and had a great number of women, especially, adherents, and soon the heresy spread like a plague over great part of Spain, and even some bishops, as Instantius and Salvianus, were infected by it. The foundation of this doctrine was Manicheism, but mixed up with the Gnostic, and other heresies. The soul, they said, was of the substance of God himself, and of its own will came on earth, passing through the seven heavens, to combat the evil principle, which was sown in the body of the flesh. They taught that we depended altogether on the stars, which decided our fate, and that our bodies depended on the signs of the zodiac, the *ram* presiding over the head, the *bull*

(24) Fleury, *t.* 3, *l.* 19, *n.* 25; Nat. Alex. *t.* 8, *c.* 3, *ar.* 16; Orsi, *t.* 8, *l.* 12, *n.* 78.
(25) Graveson, Hist. Eccl. *t.* 3, col. 2; Nat. Alex. *t.* 8, *c.* 4, *ar.* 5; Gotti. Ver. Rel. *t.* 2, *c.* 88, *s.* 2; Van Ranst, Hist. *sec.* xii. *p.* 195; Bernini, *t.* 2, *c.* 1.

over the neck, the *twins* over the back, and so on with the remainder of the Twelve Signs. They made merely a verbal profession of the doctrine of the Trinity, but they believed, with Sabellius, that the Father, and the Son, and the Holy Ghost, were one and the same thing, and that there was no real distinction of persons. They did not reject the Old Testament, like the Manicheans, but they explained everything in it allegorically, and they added many apocryphal books to the canonical ones. They abstained from meat, as an unclean thing, and separated married people, notwithstanding the repugnance manifested by those who were not followers of their sect, and this they did through hatred of procreation; for the flesh, they said, was not the work of God, but of the devil; but they used to assemble by night for prayer, and the lights being extinguished, indulged in revolting and promiscuous licentiousness; however, they denied all this when caught, and they taught their followers to practise the doctrine contained in the Latin distich: " Jura perjura, secretum prodere noli"—" Swear away, but never tell the secret." They used to fast on every Sunday, and even on Easter Sunday and Christmas-day, and on these days they used to hide themselves, and not appear at church; their reason for this conduct was their hatred of the flesh, as they believed that Christ was not really born or arose in the flesh, but only in appearance. They used to receive the Eucharist in the church, like other Christians, but they did not consume the species. They were condemned in the Council of Saragossa, by St. Damasus, and in several particular synods. Finally, Priscillian was condemned to death, at the instance of Ithacius, Bishop of Ossobona, in the year 383, by Evodius, appointed Prefect of the Pretorium by the tyrant Maximus (26).

83. St. Augustin (27) speaks of some heretics who lived about this time, and always went barefooted, and taught that all Christians were bound to do likewise (28).

84. Audæus, chief of the Audæans, was born in Mesopotamia, and was at first a man of exemplary life, and a strict observer of ecclesiastical discipline, but afterwards separated from the Church, and became founder of a sect. He celebrated Easter after the Jewish rite, and said that man was like to God corporeally; interpreting, in the plainest literal sense, that passage of Genesis, where the Lord says: " Let us make man in our own image and likeness;" and he and his followers were Antropomorphites. Noel Alexander says that the only error of the Audæans was in separating themselves from the Church, but as for the rest, they never deviated from the faith; but Petavius (29), and others, attribute to them the

(26) Nat. Alex. *t.* 8, *c.* 3, *ar.* 17; Fleury, *t.* 3, *l.* 17, *n.* 56, & *l.* 18, *n.* 30; Orsi, *t.* 8, *l.* 18, *n.* 44 & 100. (27) St. Augus. *l.* de Her. *c.* 68. (28) Nat. Alex. ibid. *ar.* 20. (29) App. Roncag. Nota, ad N. Alex. *t.* 8, *c.* 3, *ar.* 9; Diz. Portat. *t.* 1, Ver. Audæo; Berti, *t.* 1, *sec.* 4, *c.* 3.

errors of the Antropomorphites, since they attributed to God, literally, the corporeal members the Scripture mystically speaks of. He also taught some errors concerning the administration of the sacrament of penance, and died in the country of the Goths, in 370 (30).

CHAPTER V.

HERESIES OF THE FIFTH CENTURY.

ARTICLE I.

THE HERESIES OF ELVIDIUS, JOVINIANUS, AND VIGILANTIUS.

1. Heresy of Elvidius. 2. Errors of Jovinian. 3. Adverse Opinions of Basnage refuted. 4. Vigilantius and his Errors.

1. ELVIDIUS was a disciple of the Arian Ausentius, who was intruded into the See of Milan by the Emperor Constans, when he banished St. Dionisius. St. Jerome says he was a turbulent character, both as priest and layman; but, notwithstanding this high authority, it is doubtful whether he ever was a priest, because, as Noel Alexander says, he was a poor peasant, who scarcely knew his letters. He began to disseminate his heretical doctrines in the year 382. He said that the Blessed Virgin had other children by St. Joseph, besides our Lord, and he relied on the authority of Tertullian for this blasphemy; but St. Jerome proves that Tertullian never held such doctrine. St. Ambrose, St. Epiphanius, and especially St. Jerome refuted the errors of Elvidius. He drew three arguments from the Scriptures in support of his heresy: First.—That text of St. Matthew: "Before they came together she was found with child of the Holy Ghost" (Matt. i. 18). He, therefore, argued, as the text says "before they came together," it is a proof that they afterwards did so. Next he adduced the twenty-fifth verse of the same chapter: "And he knew her not until she brought forth her first-born son." Therefore, he argues he knew her after. St. Jerome, in his answer, says: "Should I grieve or smile at this folly?" He then asks, in derision: If any one should say that Elvidius was seized on by death before he did penance, is that a proof that he did penance after death? He then brings other texts of Scripture to refute him. Our Lord says to his apostles, "Behold I am with you all days even to the consummation of the world" (Matt. xxviii. 20); does that prove, says St. Jerome, that Jesus Christ will not be with his elect any more after the end of

(30) Nat. Alex. loc. cit.

the world? St. Paul says of Christ, "For he must reign until he hath put all his enemies under his feet" (Cor. xv. 25); so, when our Lord has conquered his enemies, he will reign no longer. In the book of Genesis it is said of the crow that left the ark, "That it did not return till the waters were dried up" (Gen. viii. 7); does it then follow that it returned to the ark when the waters were dried up? Away, then, with arguments of this sort, says St. Jerome (1); the Scripture here tells, not what was done, but what was not done—not what took place, but what did not. The second proof Elvidius adduces is taken from the text already mentioned (Matt. i. 25): "She brought forth her first-born son;" therefore, if he was her *first-born*, she must have had others after. St. Jerome answers this: The Lord commanded, that for every first-born a certain ransom should be paid a month after the birth (Numbers, xviii. 15, 16). Here, then, says St. Jerome, according to Elvidius, one might say: "How can I be obliged to pay a price for my first-born after a month; how can I tell whether I shall ever have a second? I must wait till a second is born to me, and then I can pay for the first-born." But the Scripture says itself, that the first-born is that which first "openeth the womb." The same is declared in Exodus, where it says: "The Lord slew every first-born in the land of Egypt" (Exod. xii. 29). Here there is no doubt, but that the text speaks of only-born as well as first-born. His third argument is from the text of St. Luke (viii. 19): "His mother and brethren came to him." Therefore, he had brothers; but St. Jerome proves, from a great many passages in the Scriptures, that first-cousins are also called brothers, and the brothers referred to in that text are St. James and St. John, the children of the other Mary, the sister of the Mother of God.

2. Jovinian shall now occupy our attention. He was a monk in Milan; and after spending the early years of his life in the austere practices of monastic life—fasting on bread and water, going barefooted, and labouring with his hands—he forsook his monastery, and went to Rome, where, as St. Ambrose (2) informs us, he began to disseminate his errors. After falling into this impiety he abandoned his mortified manner of living—went shod, and clothed in silk and linen garments—nourished and dressed his hair—frequented taverns, and indulged in play, banquets, delicate dishes, and exquisite wines—and still professed all along to be a monk, and led a life of celibacy, to avoid the responsibility of marriage. Preaching a doctrine pleasing to the senses, he soon had many followers of both sexes in Rome, who, having previously led chaste and mortified lives, now abandoned themselves to luxury, and got married. Jovinian was first condemned by Pope Siricus, in a Council, held in Rome, in the year 390, and soon after, in another Council, held

---

(1) St. Hieron. *l.* 1, Comment. in cap. ii, Matt.   (2) St. Ambrose, Ep. 41, *n.* 9.

by St. Ambrose, in Milan. In the end he was exiled by the Emperor Theodosius, and afterwards by Honorius, to Boas, a maritime town of Dalmatia, and died there in misery, in the year 412 (3). He taught many errors: First, that marriage and virginity were equally meritorious; secondly, that those once baptized can sin no more; thirdly, that those who fast and those who eat have equal merit, if they praise God; fourthly, that all have an equal reward in heaven; fifthly, that all sins are equal; sixthly, that the Blessed Virgin was not a virgin after giving birth to our Lord (4). This last error was followed by Hinckmar, Wickliffe, Bucer, Peter Martyr, Molineus, and Basnage (5), but has been ably refuted by St. Jerome, and condemned in a Synod by St. Ambrose. Petavius says, that all the Fathers unanimously profess the belief in the virginity of the Blessed Virgin, as fixed by a decree of the Catholic faith. St. Gregory says, that, as Jesus Christ entered into the house, where the apostles were assembled, with the doors shut, in the same manner, at his nativity, he left the inviolated cloister of Mary. The letter of Theodotus of Ancira was approved of by the General Council of Ephesus, in which, speaking of the Blessed Virgin, he says: the birth of Jesus Christ makes her a mother without injury to her virginity. The third canon of the Lateran Council, celebrated in the year 649, under Martin I., says: that he should be condemned, who does not confess that the Mother of God was always a virgin. A similar declaration was made in the Council of Trullus, in 692, and in the eleventh Council of Toledo, in 675 (6). He was also condemned by St. Gregory of Nyssa, St. Isidore Pelusiot, St. Proclus, St. John Chrysostom, St. John Damascenus, St. Augustin, St. Ambrose, St. Siricus Pope (who excommunicated him and his followers, in a synod held in Rome), St. Peter Chrysologus, St. Hilary, St. Prosper, St. Fulgentius, St. Eucherius, St. Paulinus, St. Anselm, St. Bernard, St. Peter Damian, and many others; and any one who wishes to see the opinions expressed by the Fathers, has only to look to Petavius's Theology (7). The text of Ezechiel: "This gate shall be shut, it shall not be opened," (Ezechiel, xliv. 2), is generally understood to refer to the perpetual virginity of the Mother of God, and St. Leo (8), Pope Hormisdas, Pelagius I., and the Council of Chalcedon, in the discourse addressed to the Emperor Marcion, all understood it thus.

3. Let us now hear what Basnage, and the heretics who hold the contrary opinion, have to say. Their first argument is founded on that text of Isaias: " Behold a virgin shall conceive, and shall bring forth a son" (Isaias, vii. 14), which St. Matthew, speaking of the Incarnation of the Divine Word, quotes (Matthew, i. 13). Basnage then argues on this text: The prophet says, that Mary con-

(3) Nat. Alex. *t.* 8, *c.* 3, *ar.* 19; Orsi, *t.* 9, *l.* 20, *n.* 27; Fleury, *t.* 3, *l.* 19.
(4) Nat. Alex. *t.* 8, *ar.* 19. (5) Basnage, ad an. 5, ante Dom. *n.* 25. (6) Col. Con. *t.* 1, col. *t.* 10, col. 1151. (7) Petav. Theol. Dog. 6, *l.* 14, *c.* 3. (8) St. Leo, Epist.

ceived as a virgin; but he does not say that she brought forth her son as a virgin. But what sort of argument is this? Because the text does not say that she was a virgin in the birth of her son, therefore, it is a proof that she did not bring him forth a virgin; whereas, the universal tradition of the Church, as we have seen, explains the text in its true sense, that she conceived a virgin, and brought forth our Lord a virgin. Basnage brings forth another argument, which he deems unanswerable. We read in St. Luke, he says: " After the days of her purification, according to the law of Moses, were accomplished, they carried him to Jerusalem, to present him to the Lord: as it is written in the law of the Lord, every male opening the womb shall be called holy to the Lord" (Luke, ii. 22). Now, says Basnage (and it is worthy of remark, with what temerity he threw overboard the doctrine of the Fathers, as opposed to Scripture, and the opinion of the learned), the opinion of the perpetual virginity of the Mother of God is generally held, and still it is opposed, both to Scripture and the opinions of the ancients. The narrative of St. Luke is quite plain: " When the days of her purification, &c." Mary was then subjected to the usual law of women after birth, not alone to avoid scandal, but as a matter of duty; and she was compelled, by the general discipline of the law, to offer a sacrifice for her purification. The days of her purification could not be accomplished if she had no necessity of purification. All his argument, then, is reduced to this, that Mary ought not to fulfil the days of her purification, if there was no necessity of purification; and, for all that, she was obliged (*coacta sit*) to fulfil the rite. This argument he took from Origen (9); but, as the Fathers of St. Maur say, truly, this was a blasphemy uttered by that Father (10); and justly, for all the Fathers have said with St. Basil (11), this virgin never was obliged to the law of purification; and this is clear, says the Saint, from the Scriptures; for in Leviticus, xii. 2, it is clearly proved that this law applies to ordinary mothers, but not to one who conceived by the Holy Ghost. " Scriptum est enim," says the holy Father, " mulier quæ conceperit semen, et peperit masculum, immunda erit septem diebus; hæc autem cum facta sit Emmanuelis Mater sine semine, pura, et intemerata est; imo postquam effecta est Mater, adhuc virgo permansit." Even Melancthon, Agricola, and the other Lutherans, as we read in Canisius (12), all say Mary had no necessity of purification. St. Cyril of Alexandria, the same author states, teaches that to assert the contrary is rank heresy. With all that, Basnage is not convinced, and he quotes a passage of St. Fulgentius, where he says: " Vulvam Matris Omnipotentia Filii nascentis aperuit.' But we have another passage, in St. Fulgentius himself, in which he declares that the Mother of

---

(9) Origen, Hom. 14. in Luc. (10) Patres. S. Maur. apud S. Hieron. *t.* 7, *p.* 285.
(11) St. Basil, in *cap.* 7; Isa. *n.* 201. (12) Canis. *l.* 4, *c.* 10, de Virg. Deip.

Christ was the only one who remained immaculate after giving birth to a son (13). But how are we then to understand "he opened the womb?"—this is to be understood, as St. Gregory of Nyssa explains it (14): "Solus ille haud ante patefactam virginalem aperuit vulvam;" that he preserved the virginity of his holy Mother. This is what St. Ambrose likewise says: "Hic (*Christus*) solus aperuit sibi vulvam" (15). And treating of the Mysteries against Jovinian, he says: "Why do you seek the order of nature in the body of Christ, when setting aside the order of nature, he was born of a virgin?" Basnage lauds St. Jerome as being of his opinion; but the passage he adduces is not to be found in St. Jerome's writings; besides, St. Jerome (16) says, in his Dialogues: "Christ alone opened the closed doors of the virginal womb, which, nevertheless, remained ever and always closed;" so that the very Fathers Basnage quotes in his favour, most expressly condemn the impious error he attempts to defend.

4. Vigilantius was a native of Comminges, near the foot of the Pyrenees, and of very low origin, having been a tavern-keeper for some time; somehow or other, he found leisure to study, and lead a pious life at the same time, so that he acquired the friendship of St. Paulinus, of Nola, who gave him a letter of recommendation to St. Jerome, and he undertook a journey to the Holy Land. This letter was so far useful to him, that St. Jerome, who knew him to be a man of relaxed morals, did not treat him as his hypocrisy deserved (17). He had the audacity to treat St. Jerome as a heretic, of the sect of Origen, because he saw him reading Origen's work; but the Saint, in the year 397, wrote to him (18), that he read these works, not to follow all their doctrine, but to take whatever was good out of them, and he exhorts him either to learn or be silent. Some years after, about the year 404, Riparius, a priest, wrote to St. Jerome, that Vigilantius began to dogmatize, speaking against the Relics of Martyrs and Vigils in churches. St. Jerome gave a summary answer, and promised to return again to the subject, and treat it more amply, when he would have read Vigilantius' work (19); and having soon after seen the production, be gave it a short but strong answer, because the monk Sisinius, who brought it to him, was in a hurry to return to Egypt (20). The following are the errors of Vigilantius, refuted by St. Jerome. First.—Like Jovinian, he condemned the practice of celibacy. Second.—He condemned the veneration of the relics of the martyrs; and called those who honoured them *Cinerists* and idolaters. Third.—He said it was a pagan superstition to light candles by day in their honor. Fourth.—He maintained that the faithful after death could no lon-

(13) St. Fulgent. *l.* 1, de vere Protest. *n.* 5. (14) St. Greg. Nys. Orat. de Occursu.
(15) St. Ambrose, *l.* 2, in Luc. *n.* 57. (16) St. Jerome, *l.* 2, Dial. contra Pelag. *n.* 4.
(17) St. Hier. Epis. 61. (18) St. Hier. Epis. 75. (19) Idem. Epis. ad Ripar. 55.
(20) St. Hier. *l.* con. Vigilan. c. 2.

ger pray for one another, and he founded this opinion on the apocryphal book of Esdras. Fifth.—He condemned public Vigils in the churches. Sixth.—He reprobated the custom of sending alms to Jerusalem. Seventh.—He totally condemned monastic life, and said that it was only making ourselves useless to our neighbours, if we embraced it. This sect was not condemned by any council, it had but few followers, and soon became extinct (21).

Article II.

ON THE HERESY OF PELAGIUS.

3. Origin of the Heresy of Pelagius. 6. His Errors and Subterfuges. 7. Celestius and his Condemnation. 8. Perversity of Pelagius. 9. Council of Diospolis. 10 & 11. He is condemned by St. Innocent, Pope. 12. Again condemned by Sozymus. 13. Julian, a follower of Pelagius. 14. Semi-Pelagians. 15. Predestination. 16 & 17. Godeschalcus.

5. PELAGIUS was born in Great Britain, and his parents were so poor, that in his youth he scarcely received any instruction in letters; he became a monk, but nothing more than a mere lay monk, and that was all the dignity he ever arrived at. He lived a long time in Rome, and was respected for his virtues by very many persons; he was loved by St. Paulinus (1); and esteemed by St. Augustin. He was looked on as a learned man, as he composed some useful books (2), to wit, three books on the Trinity, and a collection of passages of the Scripture on Christian Morality. He, unhappily, however, fell into heresy, while he sojourned at Rome, in regard to grace: and he took his doctrines from a Syrian priest, called Rufinus, (not Rufinus of Aquilea who disputed with St. Jerome). This error was already spread through the East (3); for Theodore, Bishop of Mopsuestia, had already taught the same errors as Pelagius; and deduced them from the same sources, the principles of Origen (4). This Rufinus, then coming to Rome, about the year 400, in the reign of Pope Anastasius, was the first introducer there of that heresy; but, as he was a cautious man, he did not publicly promulgate it himself, not to bring himself into trouble, but availed himself of Pelagius, who, about the year 405, began to dispute against the Grace of Jesus Christ. One day in particular, a bishop having quoted the words of St. Augustin, in his Confessions: "Lord, grant us what thou orderest, and order what thou wishest:" Pelagius could not contain himself, and inveighed against the author. He concealed his errors for a time, however, and only communicated them to his disciples to see how they would be received, and to approve or reject them afterwards,

(21) Fleury, *t*. 3, *l*. 22, *n*. 5; Orsi, t. 10, *l*. 25, *n*. 62; Nat. Alex. *t*. 10, c. 3, art. 1; Dict. Portatif. 4, ver. Vigilan. (1) St. Aug. de Gestis Pelagian. c. 52. (2) Gennad de Scriptur. c. 42. (3) Orsi, *t*. 11, *l*. 25, *n*. 42; Fleury, *t*. 4, *l*. 23, Nos. 1 & 2. (4) Orsi, ibid.

as suited his convenience (5). He afterwards became himself the disseminator of his heresy. We shall now review his errors.

6. The errors of Pelagius were the following: First.—That Adam and Eve were created mortal, and that their sin only hurt themselves, and not their posterity. Second.—Infants are now born in the same state that Adam was before his fall. Third.—Children dying without baptism, do not indeed go to heaven, but they possess eternal life. Such, St. Augustin testifies, were the errors of Pelagius (6). The principal error of Pelagius and his followers was, concerning Grace and Free-Will, for he asserted, that man, by the natural force of his free-will, could fulfil all the Divine precepts, conquer all temptations and passions, and arrive at perfection without the assistance of grace (7). When he first began to disseminate this pernicious error, which saps the whole system of our Faith, St. Augustin says, that the Catholics were horrified, and loudly exclaimed against him, so he and his disciples searched every way, for a loop-hole to escape from the consequences, and to mitigate the horror excited by so dreadful a blasphemy. The first subterfuge was this: Pelagius said that he did not deny the necessity of Grace, but that Grace was Free-Will itself, granted gratuitously by God, to men, without any merit on their part. These are his words, quoted by St. Augustin (8): "Free-Will is sufficient that I may be just, I say not without Grace;" but the Catholics said, that it was necessary to distinguish between Grace and Free-Will. To this Pelagius answered (and here is the second subterfuge), that by the name of Grace is understood the law or doctrine by which the Lord gave us the Grace to teach us how we are to live. "They say," St. Augustin writes (9), "God created man with Free-Will, and giving him precepts, teaches him how he should live, and in that assists him, inasmuch, as by teaching him, he removes ignorance." But the Catholics answered, that if Grace consisted in the Law alone given to man, the Passion of Jesus Christ would be useless. The Pelagians answered, that the Grace of Christ consisted in giving us the good example of his life, that we might imitate him; (and this was the third subterfuge,) and as Adam injured us by bad example, so our Saviour assisted us by his good example. Christ affords a help to us, not to sin, since he left us an example by living holily (10); but this example given by Christ, St. Augustin answers, was not distinct from his doctrine, for our Lord taught both by precept and example. The Pelagians seeing that their position regarding these three points was untenable, added a fourth subterfuge, that was, the fourth species of grace—the grace of the

(5) Fleury, ibid. n. 1, ex Mereat.   (6) St. Aug. de Gestis Pelagian. c. 34 & 35.
(7) Nat. Alex. t. 10, c. 3. art. 3; St. Fleury, l. e. n. 48; Tournelly, Comp. Theolog. t. 5, pt. 1, Disp. 1, a. 3.   (8) St. August. Serm. 26, al. 11, de Verb. Apost.   (9) Idem. l. de Spir. & littas. c. 2.   (10) Apud St. Augus. l. de Gratia Christi, c. 2.

remission of sins. They say, says St. Augustin (11), that the Grace of God is only valuable for the remission of sins, and not for avoiding future ones: and they say, therefore, the coming of Jesus Christ is not without its utility, since the grace of pardon is of value for the remission of past sins, and the example of Christ for avoiding future ones. The fifth subterfuge of the Pelagians was this: They admitted, as St. Augustin (12) tells us, the internal grace of illustration; but we should admit, with the holy doctor, that they admitted this illustration, solely *ex parte objecti*, that is, the internal grace to know the value of good and the deformity of bad works, but not *ex parte intellectus*, so that this grace would give a man strength to embrace the good and avoid the evil. We now come to the sixth and last shift: He finally admitted internal grace, not only on the part of the object, but on the part of human ability, strengthened by grace to do well; but he did not admit it as necessary according to our belief, but only as useful to accomplish more easily what is good, as St. Augustin explains it (13). Pelagius asserts, that Grace is given to us, that what is commanded to us by God should be more easily accomplished; but Faith teaches us that Grace is not only useful, but absolutely necessary to do good and avoid evil.

7. The Pelagian heresy was very widely extended in a little time. His chief disciple was Celestius, a man of noble family, and a eunuch from his birth. He practised as a lawyer for a time, and then went into a monastery; he then became a disciple of Pelagius, and began to deny Original Sin. Pelagius was reserved, but Celestius was free-spoken and ardent. They both left Rome a little before it was taken by the Goths, in 409. They went together, it is believed, first to Sicily, and afterwards to Africa, where Celestius thought to get himself ordained priest, in Carthage; but when the heresy he was teaching was discovered, he was condemned, and excommunicated by the Bishop Aurelius, and a Council summoned by him, in Carthage; he appealed from the Council to the Apostolic See, but, instead of going to Rome to prosecute his appeal, he went to Ephesus, where he was raised to the priesthood without sufficient caution; but when his heresy became manifest, he was banished from the city with all his followers (14). Notwithstanding all this, after the lapse of five years, he went to Rome to prosecute the appeal, but he was then condemned again, as we shall now see.

8. Pelagius, instead of repenting after the condemnation of Celestius, only became more obstinate in his errors, and began to teach them more openly. About this time the noble virgin, Demetriades, of the ancient Roman family of the Anicii, put into execution a

(11) St Augus. de Gratia Christi. *s.* lib. arb. *c.* 13. (12) Idem. lib. de Gratia, cap. 7 & 10.   (13) St. Augus. de Gratia Christi, *c.* 26.   (14) Orsi, *t.* 11, *l.* 25, *n.* 44; Fleury, *l.* 3, *n.* 3.

glorious resolution she had made. She had taken refuge in Africa when the Goths desolated Rome, and when her parents were about to marry her to a nobleman, she forsook the world, and, clothing herself in mean garments, as St. Jerome (15) tells us, consecrated her virginity to Christ. St. Jerome, St. Augustin, and even the Pope St. Innocent, congratulated this devout lady on the good choice she made. Pelagius also wrote a letter to her, in which, while he praises her, he endeavours to insinuate his poison. He used these words: *In hic merito cœteris præferenda es, quæ nisi ex te, et in te esse non possunt* (16). St. Augustin at once recognized the poison disseminated in this letter, and, explaining the words, *Nisi ex te et in te*, he says, as far as the second expression, *Nisi in te* (17), it is very well said; but all the poison is in the first part, he says, *Nisi ex te*, for the error of Pelagius is, that all that man does of good he does altogether *of himself*, without the assistance of grace. At the same time, when St. Jerome got notice of this letter of Pelagius, he also wrote to the lady (18), cautioning her against his doctrine, and from that out began to combat his heresy in several books, and especially in that of "The Dialogue of Atticus and Critobulus." St. Augustin likewise never ceased for ten years to combat the errors of Pelagius; and his books, "De Natura et Gratia," "De Gratia Christi," "De Peccato Originali," &c., prove how successfully he refuted them.

9. When Pelagius saw that he was not cordially received in Africa, he went to Palestine, where John, Bishop of Jerusalem, received him; and in a Council held with his clergy, instead of condemning him, as he ought, he only imposed silence on both parties (19). In the year 415, a council of fourteen bishops was held in Diospolis, a city of Palestine; and here Pelagius, as Cardinal Baronius (20) tells us, induced the bishops to agree to the following propositions, all Catholic, indeed, and opposed to the errors promulgated by him and Celestius: First.—Adam would not have died had he not sinned. Second.—The sin of Adam is transfused into the whole human race. Third.—Infants are not such as Adam was previous to his fault. Fourth.—As in Adam all die, according to the Apostle, so in Christ all will be vivified. Fifth.—Unbaptized infants cannot obtain eternal life. Sixth.—God gives us assistance to do good, according to St. Paul (1 Tim. vi. 17). Seventh.—It is God that gives us grace to do every good work, and this grace is not given to us according to our merits. Eighth.—Grace comes to us, given gratuitously by God, according to his mercy. Ninth.—The children of God are those who daily say, "forgive us our sins," which we could not say if we were entirely without sin. Tenth.—Free-will exists, but it must be assisted by Divine help. Eleventh.

(15) St. Hier. Ep. 8, ad Demetr. (16) Apud St. Augus. Ep. 143. (17) St. Aug. ibid. (18) St. Hier. Ep. 8, ad Demetr. (19) Orsi, *t.* 25, *n.* 111; Fleury, *l* 23, *n.* 18, & seq. (20) Baron. Ann. *a.* 415, *n.* 23.

—The victory over temptations does not come from our own will, but from the grace of God. Twelfth.—The pardon of sins is not given according to the merits of those who ask it, but according to the Divine Mercy. Pelagius confessed all these truths, and the council of bishops, deceived by his hypocrisy, admitted him to the communion of the Church (21); but in this they acted imprudently, for, although his errors were condemned, he was personally justified, which gave him a far greater facility of disseminating his errors afterwards, and, on this account, St. Jerome, speaking of this Synod, calls it a miserable one (22), and St. Innocent the Pope refused to admit him to his communion, although he was informed of the retraction of his errors in that Synod, for he truly suspected that his confession was only feigned. The subsequent conduct of Pelagius proved the penetration of the holy Pontiff, for, as soon as he was freed from the obedience of those bishops, he returned to his vomit, and rejected the truths he had then professed, and especially on the point of grace, as St. Augustin remarks (23), he said, that Divine grace was necessary to do what was right more easily, but the good depended directly on our own free will, and this grace he called the *grace of possibility*. St. Augustin (24), writing against this false novelty, indites this great sentence: " God, by co-operating in us, perfects that which he began by operating: for we are worth nothing for any pious work without him operating, that we may wish it, or co-operating when we do wish it." Pelagius, hoping that the proceedings of the Council of Diospolis would be buried in darkness, wrote four books afterwards against the " Dialogue" of St. Jerome, and entitled his work " De Libero Arbitrio" (25).

10. The affairs of Pelagius did not take such a favourable turn in Africa as they did in Palestine, for in the following year, 416, the Bishop Aurelius summoned another Council in Carthage, in which both he and Celestius were again condemned; and it was decided to send a Synodal letter to the Pope St. Innocent, that he might confirm the decree of the Council by Pontifical authority (26); and, about the same time, another Council of sixty-one Numidian Bishops was held in Milevis, and a letter was likewise written to the Pope, calling on him to condemn the heresy (27). Pope Innocent answered both Synodal letters in 417; confirmed the Christian doctrine held by the councils concerning grace (28); and condemned Pelagius and Celestius, with all their adherents, and declared them separated from the communion of the Church. He answered, at the same time, and in the same strain, the letters of five other bishops, who had written to him on the same subject;

(21) Fleury, *l.* 23, *n.* 20. (22) St. Hier. Ep. 79. (23) St. Aug. de Her. *c.* 88. (24) St. Aug. de Grat. & lib. arb. *c.* 17. (25) Orsi, *l.* 25, *n.* 117, ex St. Aug. *l.* de Gest. Pel. *c.* 33. (26) Nat. Alex. *t.* 10, *c.* 3, *ar.* 4, *s.* 4; Fleury, ibid. *n.* 20; Orsi, *t.* 11, *l.* 25, *n.* 121. (27) Nat. Alex. ibid. *s.* 5; Fleury, loc. cit.; Orsi, *n.* 122. (28) St. Innoc. Ep. 181, *n.* 8 & 9, & Ep. 182, *n.* 6.

and, among other remarks, says, that he found nothing in Pelagius's book which pleased him, and scarcely anything which did not displease him, and which was not deserving of universal reprobation (29). It was then that St. Augustin, as he himself mentions (30), when Pope Innocent's answer arrived, said: "Two Councils have referred this matter to the Apostolic See. Rescripts have been sent in answer; the cause is decided."

11. We should remark that St. Prosper (31) writes, that St. Innocent the Pope was the first to condemn the heresy of Pelagius:

> Pestem subeuntem prima recidit
> Sedes Roma Petri, quæ pastoralis honoris
> Facta caput mundi, quidquid non possidet armis,
> Religione tenet.

But how can St. Prosper say that St. Innocent was the first to condemn this heresy, when it was already condemned in 412 by the first Council of Carthage, and by the second in 416, and by the Council of Milevis? Graveson (32) answers, that these Councils considered it their duty to refer the condemnation of Celestius and Pelagius to the Apostolic See, and, on that account, St. Prosper writes, that the first condemnation proceeded from the Pope. Garner (33) says that the Pelagian heresy was condemned by twenty-four Councils, and, finally, by the General Council of Ephesus, in 431 (34), for up to that time the Pelagians had not ceased to disturb the Church.

12. When Pelagius and Celestius heard of the sentence pronounced against them by St. Innocent, they wrote him a letter filled with lies and equivocations, appealing to his supreme tribunal from the sentence passed on them by the bishops of Africa; and, as St. Innocent had died, and St. Zozymus was elected in his place, Celestius went to Rome himself to endeavour to gain his favour. St. Zozymus was, at first, doubtful how he ought to act in the matter; but the African bishops suggested to him that he ought not to interfere with a sentence passed by his predecessor, and when the holy Pontiff was better informed of the deceits of Pelagius and Celestius, and especially of the flight of the latter from Rome, when he heard that the Pope was about to examine the cause more narrowly, he was convinced of their bad faith, and condemned their doctrine (35).

13. The author of the *Portable Dictionary* (36) writes, that Pelagius, after his condemnation by Pope Zozymus, and the proclamation subsequent, issued against him by the Emperor Honorius from Rome, went to his beloved Palestine, where he was before so well received; but as his impiety and hypocrisy were now well

(29) Fleury, *t.* 4, *l.* 23, *n.* 34; Orsi, *t.* 11, *l.* 25, *n.* 129.   (30) St. Aug. Serm. 131, *n.* 10.   (31) St. Prosp. In Carm. de Ingratis.   (32) Graveson, *t.* 3, *col.* 2. (33) Garner. ap. Danes Temp. not. *p.* 240.   (34) Act. 5 & 7, *can.* 1 & 4, ap. Danes, ibid. *p* 241; & vide Fleury, *l.* 25, *n.* 58.   (35) Hermant, *t.* 1, *c.* 124; Orsi, *l.* 26, *n.* 16 & 17.   (36) Diz. Port. verb. Pelagio.

known, he was driven out of that province. We do not know afterwards what became of him, but it is probable that he returned to Britain to disseminate his doctrines, and that it was this which induced the bishops of Gaul to send St. Germain de Auxerre there to refute him. The Pelagian heresy was finally extinguished in a short time, and no one was bold enough openly to declare himself its protector, with the exception of Julian, son and successor to Memorius, in the See of Capua. He was a man of talent, but of no steadiness, and the great liveliness of his understanding served to ruin him, by inducing him to declare himself an avowed professor of the heresy of Pelagius. His name is celebrated on account of his famous disputes with St. Augustin, who at first was his friend, but afterwards, in defence of religion, was obliged to declare himself his adversary, and pursued him as a heretic. He was afterwards banished out of Italy, and went to the East, and after wandering in poverty for a long time through various regions, he at last was obliged to support himself by teaching school. It is said he died in Sicily in the reign of the Emperor Valentinian (37). The refutation of the Pelagian heresy will be found in the last volume of this work.

14. Several years had rolled by since St. Augustin had successfully combated the Pelagian heresy, when, in the very bosom of the Church, a sort of conspiracy was formed against the Saint, including many persons remarkable for their learning and piety; this happened about the year 428, and they were called Semi-Pelagians. The chief of this party was John Cassianus, who was born, as Genadius informs us, in the Lesser Scythia, and spent part of his time in the monastery of Bethlehem. From that he came first to Rome, and then to Marseilles, where he founded two monasteries, one of men and one of women, and took the government of them according to the rules he had practised, or seen observed, in the monasteries of Palestine and Egypt; these rules he wrote in the first four books of twelve he published under the title of Monastic Instructions. What is more to the purpose we treat of, he endeavoured to bring into notice and establish his erroneous sentiments on the necessity of Grace, in his thirteenth Collation or Conference; and to give more weight to his errors, he puts them into the mouth of Cheremon, one of the solitaries of Panefisum, a place in Egypt, who, he said, was well instructed in all the disputes about Grace, but which, as Orsi says (38), were never spoken of at all when Cassianus was in Egypt; nor could any one, in any human probability, ever imagine that such a dispute would be raised in the Church. Nevertheless, he, as it were, constituted that holy monk as a sort of judge between Pelagius and St. Augustin, and puts into his mouth a condemnation, more or less of both, as if St. Augustin had erred in attributing too much to Grace,

(37) Hermant, *t.* 1, *c.* 124.   (38) Orsi, *t.* 12, *l.* 17, *n.* 59.

by attributing to it even the first movements of the will to do what is right, and that Pelagius erred in attributing too much to Free-Will, by denying the necessity of Grace to carry out good works. Cassianus thought, in the meanwhile, that he had found out a means of reconciling both parties, Catholics and heretics; but it was only combating one error by another, and his erroneous doctrine was followed by many persons of the greatest piety in Gaul, and especially in Marseilles, who willingly imbibed the poison, because mixed with many Catholic truths in his works. The Semi-Pelagians then admitted the necessity of Grace, but they were guilty of a most pernicious error, in saying, that the beginning of salvation often comes to us from ourselves without it. They added other errors to this, by saying that perseverance and election to glory could be acquired by our own natural strength and merits. They said, likewise, that some children die before baptism, and others after, on account of the foreknowledge God possesses of the good or evil they would do if they lived (39).

15. Cassianus died in 433, and was considered a saint (40); but the Semi-Pelagians were condemned in the year 432, at the request of St. Prosper, and St. Hilary, by Pope Celestine I., in a letter written by him to the bishops of Italy. They were also condemned in 529, by Pope Felix IV., in the Synod of Orange, and, immediately after, in the Synod of Valence; and both these councils, as Noel Alexander testifies (41), were confirmed by Pope Boniface II. At the end of the work will be found the refutation of this heresy.

16. In the year 417, according to Prosper of Tyre, or in the year 415, according to Sigisbert, arose the heresy of the Predestinarians (42); these said that good works were of no use to those, for salvation, whom God foreknows will be lost; and that if the wicked are predestined to glory, their sins are of no harm to them. Sigisbert's words are (43): " Asserebant nec pie viventibus prodesse bonorum operum laborem, si a Deo ad damnationem præsciti essent: nec impiis obesse, etiamsi improbe viverent." Noel Alexander says that a certain priest of the name of Lucidus (44), having fallen into the errors of the Predestinarians, and his opinions becoming notorious, he was obliged to retract them by Faustus de Ries, on the authority of a council held at Arles, in 475; he obeyed, and signed a retraction of the following errors: First.—The labour of human obedience is not to be joined to Divine Grace. Second.— He should be condemned who says, that after the fall of the first man, the freedom of the will is entirely extinct. Third.—Or who says that Christ did not die for all men. Fourth.—Or who says that the foreknowledge of God violently drives men to death, or that those who perish, perish by the will of God. Fifth.—Or who

(39) Nat. Alex. *t.* 10, *c.* 3, *a.* 7 & 8; Orsi, loc. cit. *n.* 60 & 61; Fleury, *t.* 4, *l.* 21, *n.* 56 & seq. (40) Nat. *l.* cit. *ar.* 7, *s.* 4. (41) Nat. Al. *l.* cit. *ar.* 10, in fin. (42) Nat. Al. *t.* 10, *c.* 3, *ar.* 5. (43) Sigisbert in Cron. an. 415. (44) Nat. loco cit.

says that whoever sins, dies in Adam, after lawfully receiving baptism. Sixth.—Or who says that some are deputed to death eternal, and others predestined to life. This heresy, or these errors, were condemned in the Council of Lyons, in the year 475. It is a question among the learned, whether the Predestinarians ever existed as a heretical body. Cardinal Orsi and Berti (45), with Contenson, Cabassutius and Jansenius deny it; but Tournelly (46), with Baronius, Spondanus, and Sirmond, held the contrary opinion, and Graveson quotes Cardinal Norris (47) in their favour, and Noel Alexander thinks his opinion probable (48).

17. In the ninth century, Godeschalcus, a German Benedictine monk, lived, who is generally considered a real Predestinarian. He was a man of a turbulent and troublesome disposition. He went to Rome through a motive of piety, without leave of his superiors, and usurping the office of a preacher without lawful mission, disseminated his maxims in several places, on which account he was condemned in a Synod, held on his account, in Mayence, in 848, by the Archbishop Rabanus, and sent to Hincmar, Archbishop of Rheims, his superior. Hincmar, in another, held in Quercy, again condemned him, deprived him of the sacerdotal dignity, and after obliging him to throw his writings into the fire with his own hand, shut him up in close confinement in the monastery of Haut Villiers, in the diocese of Rheims. Two Councils were held in Quercy on this affair; one in 849, in which Godeschalcus was condemned, and the other in the year 853, in which four canons were established against his doctrine, and which we shall hereafter quote. Finally, Hincmar being at Haut Villiers, the monks of the monastery told him that Godeschalcus was near his end, and anxious for his eternal welfare, he sent him a formula of Faith to sign, that he might receive Absolution and the Viaticum, but he rejected it with disdain. Hincmar could then do no more, but after his departure, he wrote to the monks, telling them that in case of the conversion of Godeschalcus, they should treat him as he had given them verbal directions to do; but if he persevered in his errors, that they should not give him the sacraments, or ecclesiastical burial. He died unchanged, and without sacraments, and he was deprived of Christian burial (49).

18. His errors, Van Ranst informs us, were these following: First.—As God has predestined some to eternal life, so he predestines others to everlasting death, and forces man to perish. Second.—God does not wish the salvation of all men, but only of those who are saved. Third.—Christ died for the salvation of the elect alone, and not for the redemption of all men. These three propositions of

---

(45) Orsi, *t.* 15, *l.* 35, *n.* 83; Berti, Hist. *t.* 1, *s.* 5, *c.* 4. (46) Tour. *t.* 4, *p.* 1, D. 3, concl. 3. (47) Graves. Hist. *t.* 3, coll. 2, *p.* 19. (48) Nat. Alex. *t.* 10, *c.* 3, *a.* 2, *p.* 144, and Dis. Prop. *p.* 461. (49) Fleury, *t.* 7, *l.* 41, *n.* 41 & 49, & *l.* 50, *n.* 48; Van Ranst, *s.* 9, *p.* 153.

Godeschalcus are also contained in a letter written by Hincmar to Nicholas I. "He says," writes Hincmar, "that the old Predestinarians said, that as God predestined some to eternal life, so he predestined others to everlasting death" (50); and Rabanus, in his Synodical letter to Hincmar, says: "He (Godeschalcus) taught that there are some in this world, who, on account of the predestination of God, who forces them to go to death, cannot correct themselves from sin; as if God, from the beginning, made them incorrigible and deserving of punishment to go to destruction. Second.—He says that God does not wish all men to be saved, but only those who are saved. Third.—He says that our Lord Jesus Christ was not crucified and died for the salvation of all, but only for these who are saved" (51). The four canons established in the Council of Quercy against Godeschalcus, as Cardinal Gotti (52) writes, were these following: First.—There is only one predestination by God, that is to eternal life. Second.—The free will of man is healed by means of Grace. Third.—God wishes all men to be saved. Fourth.—Jesus Christ has suffered for all.

19. As to the judgment we should pass on the faith of Godeschalcus, some modern writers, as Christian Lupus, Berti, Contenson, and Roncaglia (53), defend it, by thus explaining his three propositions: As to the first, the predestination to death; they say that it can be understood of the predestination to punishment, which God makes after the prevision of sin. As to the second, that God does not wish the salvation of all; it can be understood of his not wishing it efficaciously. And, as to the third, that Jesus Christ had not died for the salvation of all; it can, likewise, be understood that he did not die efficaciously. But on the other hand, as Tournelly writes, all Catholic doctors previous to Jansenius (with the exception of some few, as Prudentius, Bishop of Troyes, in France; Pandal, Bishop of Lyons; and Loup, Abbot of Ferrieres), condemned them as heretical, and, with very good reason; many modern authors, of the greatest weight, as Sirmond, Cardinal de Norris, Mabillon, Tournelly, and Noel Alexander, are of the same opinion (54). As far as our judgment on the matter goes, we say, that if Godeschalcus intended to express himself, as his defenders have afterwards explained his words, he was not a heretic; but, at all events, he was culpable in not explaining himself more clearly; but, as Van Ranst very well remarks, his propositions, as they are laid before us, and taking them in their plain, obvious sense, are marked with heresy. As he did not explain himself

---

(50) Tournelly, Theol. Comp. *t.* 5, *p.* 1, Disp. 4, *ar.* 3. (51) Tourn. loc. cit. (52) Gotti. *t.* 2, Vict. adv. Her. *c.* 84, *s.* 2. (53) Lupus Not. ad conc. 1 Rom.; Berti, Theol. *l.* 6, c. 14, *prop.* 3, & Hist. *s.* 9, *c.* 4; Contens. Theol. *l.* 8; De Prædest. *app.* 1, *s.* 3; Roncaglia, Animad. ap. N. Alex. *t.* 13, *diss.* 5. (54) Sirmond. Tract. de Præd. Har. Card. de Noris, *l.* 2; Hist. Pelag. c. 15; Mabillon, ad sec. iv. Bened. Tournelly, Theol. *t.* 5, loc. cit. *p.* 142; Gotti, loc. supra cit. c. 84, *s.* 2; Nat. Alex. loc. cit. *t.* 13, *diss.* 5.

according as his friends do who defend him, and he showed so much obstinacy in refusing to accommodate himself to his superiors, and as he died so unhappily, as we have already related, we may reasonably doubt of his good faith, and have fears for his eternal salvation.

Article III.

THE NESTORIAN HERESY.

20. Errors of Nestorius, and his Elevation to the Episcopacy. 21. He approves of the Errors preached by his Priest, Anastasius; his Cruelty. 22. He is contradicted, and other Acts of Cruelty. 23. St. Cyril's Letter to him, and his Answer. 24. The Catholics separate from him. 25. Letters to St. Celestine, and his Answer. 26. He is admonished; Anathemas of St. Cyril. 27. The Sentence of the Pope is intimated to him. 28. He is cited to the Council. 29. He is condemned. 30. The Sentence of the Council is intimated to him. 31. Cabal of John of Antioch. 32. Confirmation of the Council by the Legates, in the Name of the Pope. 33. The Pelagians are condemned. 34. Disagreeable Affair with the Emperor Theodosius. 35. Theodosius approves of the Condemnation of Nestorius, and sends him into Banishment, where he dies. 36. Laws against the Nestorians. 37. Efforts of the Nestorians. 38. The same Subject continued. 39. It is condemned as heretical to assert that Jesus Christ is the adopted Son of God. 40–43. Answer to Basnage, who has unjustly undertaken the Defence of Nestorius.

20. THE heresy of Pelagius was scarcely condemned by the African Councils, when the Church had to assemble again to oppose the heresy of Nestorius, who had the temerity to impugn the maternity of the Mother of God, calling her the Mother, not of God, but of Christ, who, he blasphemously taught, was a mere man, as, with a similar impiety, Ebion, Paul of Samosata, and Photinus, had done before, by asserting that the Word was not hypostatically united with Christ, but only extrinsically, so that God dwelled in Christ as in his temple. Nestorius was born in Germanicia, a small city of Syria, and, as Suidas, quoted by Baronius, informs us, was a nephew of Paul of Samosata, and was brought up in the monastery of St. Euprepius, in the suburbs of Antioch (1). He was ordained priest by Theodotus (2), and appointed his catechist, to explain the faith to the catechumens, and defend it against heretics; and, in fact, he was most zealous in combating the heretics who then disturbed the Eastern Church—the Arians, the Apollinarists, and the Origenists—and professed himself a great admirer and imitator of St. John Chrysostom. He was so distinguished for his eloquence, though it was only of a vain and popularity-hunting sort, and his apparent piety, for he was worn, pale, and always poorly clad, that he was placed in the See of Constantinople, in place of Sisinnius, in the year 427, according to N. Alexander, or

(1) Nat. Alex. *t.* 10, *c.* 3, *a.* 12, *s.* 1; Baron. Ann. 428, *n.* 1, & seq.; Orsi, *t.* 12, *l.* 28, ex *n.* 1, & Fleury, *t.* 4, *l.* 24, *n.* 54. (2) Evagr. Hist. *l.* 1, *c.* 5.

428, according to Hermant and Cardinal Orsi. His elevation, however, was not only legitimate, but highly creditable to him, for after the death of the Patriarch Sisinnius, the Church of Constantinople was split into factions about who should succeed him, which induced the Emperor Theodosius the Younger to put an end to it all, by selecting a bishop himself; and, that no one should complain of his choice, he summoned Nestorius from Antioch, and had him consecrated Bishop, and his choice was highly pleasing to the people (3). It is said, also, that at the first sermon he preached (4), he turned round to the Emperor, and thus addressed him: " Give me, my Lord, the earth purged from heretics, and I will give you heaven; exterminate the heretics with me, and I will exterminate the Persians with you."

21. Theodosius hoped that his new Patriarch would in all things follow in the steps of his predecessor, Chrysostom; but he was deceived in his hopes. His virtue was altogether Pharisaical, for, under an exterior of mortification, he concealed a great fund of pride. In the beginning of his reign, it is true, he was a most ardent persecutor of the Arians, the Novatians, and the Quartodecimans; but, as St. Vincent of Lerins tells us, his chief aim in this was only to prepare the way for teaching his own errors (5). " He declared war against all heresies, to make way for his own." He brought a priest from Antioch with him, of the name of Anastasius, and he, at the instigation of the Bishop, preached one day the blasphemous doctrine that no one should call Mary the Mother of God, because she was only a creature, and it was impossible that a human creature could be the Mother of God. The people ran to Nestorius, to call on him to punish the temerity of the preacher; but he not only approved of what was said, but unblushingly went into the pulpit himself, and publicly defended the doctrine preached by Anastasius. In that sermon, called afterwards by St. Cyril (6) the Compendium of all Blasphemy, he called those Catholics blind and ignorant, who were scandalized by Anastasius preaching, that the Holy Virgin should not be called the Mother of God. The people were most anxiously waiting to hear what the Bishop would say in the pulpit, when, to their astonishment, he cried out: " How can God, then, have a mother? The Gentiles ought to be excused, who bring forward on the stage the mothers of their Gods; and the Apostle is a liar, when, speaking of the Divinity of Christ, he says that he is without father, without mother, without generation: no, Mary has not brought forth a God. What is born of the flesh is nothing but flesh; what is born of the spirit is spiritual. The creature does not bring forth the Creator, but only a man, the instrument of the Divinity."

(3) Orsi, *t.* 12, *l.* 28, *n.* 1. Nat. Alex. *t.* 10, *c.* 3, *art.* 12. (4) Fleury, *t.* 4, *l.* 21, *n.* 54; Nat. loc. cit. (5) Apud. (6) Orsi, loc. cit. *n.* 8; Serm. 1, ap. More.

22. It has always been the plan with heretics to sustain this error by accusing the Catholics of heresy. Arius called the Catholics Sabellians, because they professed that the Son was God, like unto the Father. Pelagius called them Manicheans, because they insisted on the necessity of Grace. Eutyches called them Nestorians, because they believed that there were two distinct natures in Christ—the Divine and the human nature; and so, in like manner, Nestorius called them Arians and Apollinarists, because they confessed in Christ one Person, true God and true man. When Nestorius thus continued to preach, not alone once, but frequently, and when the whole burden of his sermons was nothing but a blasphemous attack on the doctrine of the Church, the people of Constantinople became so excited, that, beholding their shepherd turned into a wolf, they threatened to tear him in pieces, and throw him into the sea. He was not, however, without partisans, and although these were but very few, they had, for all that, the support of the Court and the Magistracy, and the contests even in the church became so violent, that there was frequently danger of blood being spilled there (7). Withal, there was one person who, while Nestorius was publicly preaching in the church(8), and denying the two generations of the Word, the Eternal and the Temporal, boldly stood forward, and said to his face: "It is so, nevertheless; it is the same Word, who, before all ages, was born of the Father, and was afterwards born anew of a virgin, according to the flesh." Nestorius was irritated at the interruption, and called the speaker a miserable, ribald wretch; but as he could not take vengeance as he wished on him,—for, though but then a layman (he was afterwards made Bishop of Dorileum, and was a most strenuous opponent of Eutyches, as we shall see in the next chapter), he was an advocate of great learning, and one of the agents for the affairs of his Sovereign,—he discharged all the venom of his rage on some good Archimandrites of monks, who came to inquire of him whether what was said of his teaching was true—that he preached that Mary brought forth only a man—that nothing could be born of the flesh but flesh alone —and suggested to him that such doctrine was opposed to Faith. Nestorius, without giving them any reply, had them confined in the ecclesiastical prison, and his myrmidons, after stripping them of their habits, and kicking and beating them, tied them to a post, and lacerated their backs with the greatest cruelty, and then, stretching them on the ground, beat them on the belly.

23. The sermons of Nestorius were scattered through all the provinces of the East and West, and through the monasteries of Egypt, likewise, where they excited great disputes. St. Cyril, Bishop of Alexandria, hearing of this, and fearing lest the heresy

---

(7) Orsi, *l.* 28, *n.* 9.   (8) Orsi, *n.* 10; Fleury, *t.* 4, *l.* 25, *n.* 6.

should take root, wrote a letter to all the monks of Egypt (9), in which he instructs them not to intermeddle in such questions at all, and, at the same time, gives them excellent instructions in the true Faith. This letter was taken to Constantinople, and St. Cyril was thanked by several of the magistrates; but Nestorius was highly indignant, and got a person named Photius to answer it, and sought every means to be revenged on St. Cyril. When this came to the knowledge of the Saint, he wrote to Nestorius (10): "This disturbance," he says, "did not commence on account of my letter, but on account of writings scattered abroad (whether they are yours or not is another thing), and which have been the cause of so many disorders, that I was obliged to provide a remedy. You have, therefore, no reason to complain of me. You, rather, who have occasioned this disturbance, amend your discourses, and put an end to this universal scandal, and call the Holy Virgin the Mother of God. Be assured, in the meantime, that I am prepared to suffer everything, even imprisonment and death, for the Faith of Jesus Christ." Nestorius answered, but his reply was only a threatening tirade (11): "Experience," said he, "will shew what fruit this will produce; for my part, I am full of patience and charity, though you have not practised either towards me, not to speak more harshly to you." This letter proved to St. Cyril that nothing more was to be expected from Nestorius, and what followed proved the truth of his conjecture.

24. There was a bishop of the name of Dorotheus in Constantinople, who was such a sycophant to Nestorius, that while the Patriarch was one day in full assembly, seated on his throne, he rose up and cried out: "If any one says that Mary is the Mother of God, let him be excommunicated." When the people heard this blasphemy so openly proclaimed, they set up a loud shout and left the church (12), determined to hold no more communion with the proclaimers of such an impious heresy (13); for, in fact, to excommunicate all those who said that Mary was the Mother of God, would be to excommunicate the whole Church—all the bishops, and all the departed saints, who professed the Catholic doctrine. There is not the least doubt but that Nestorius approved of the excommunication announced by Dorotheus, for he not only held his peace on the occasion, but admitted him to the participation of the Sacred Mysteries. Some of his priests, on the contrary, after having publicly given him notice in the assembly, and seeing that he still persisted in not calling the Holy Virgin the Mother of God, and Jesus Christ, by his nature, true God (14), now openly

(9) St. Cyril, Ep. ad Mon. *n.* 3, apud.; Fleury, *t.* 4, *l.* 25, *n.* 3; Orsi, *l.* 28, *n.* 14. (10) Epis. ad Nestor. *c.* 6, ap.; Fleury, ibid. (11) Fleury, ibid. (12) St. Cyril, Ep. ad Nest. *c.* 10, ap.; Fleury, *l.* 25. (13) St. Cyril, ad Acac. *c.* 22. (14) Libell. Basil. *c.* 30, *n.* 2.

forsook his communion; but he prohibited not only those, but all who previously had preached against his opinion, from preaching; so that the people, deprived of their usual instructions, said: "We have an Emperor, but we have not a Bishop." A monk, burning with zeal, stepped forward while Nestorius was going into the church, and thought to prevent him, calling him a heretic, but the poor man was immediately knocked down, and given into the hands of the Prefect, who first caused him publicly to be flogged, and then sent him into exile (15).

25. St. Cyril wrote again to Nestorius, but seeing his obstinacy, and that the heresy was spreading in Constantinople, through favour of the Court, he wrote several letters, or, rather, treatises, to the Emperor Theodosius, and to the Princesses, his sisters, concerning the true Faith (16). He wrote likewise to Pope Celestine, giving him an account of all that took place, and explaining to him the necessity there was that he should oppose the errors of Nestorius (17). Nestorius himself, at the same time, had the boldness to write a letter to St. Celestine, likewise, in which he exaggerates his great labours against the heretics, and requires also to know why some bishops of the Pelagian party were deprived of their Sees; he thus wrote, because he had kindly received those bishops in Constantinople, and the Pelagians were not included in an edict he procured from Theodosius against the heretics; for, as Cardinal Orsi remarks, he adhered to the Pelagian opinion, that Grace is given to us by God, according to our own merits. He also wrote that some called the Blessed Virgin the Mother of God, when she should only be called the Mother of Christ, and on that account he sent him some of his books; this letter is quoted by Baronius (18). St. Celestine having read both letters, summoned a Council in Rome, in the month of August, 430, for the examination of the writings of Nestorius, and not only were his blasphemies condemned, but he was even deposed from his bishopric, if, ten days after the publication of his sentence, he did not retract his errors, and the Pope charged St. Cyril with the execution of the sentence (19).

26. St. Cyril, in discharge of the commission to which he was appointed by the Pope, convoked a Council, in Alexandria, of all the bishops in Egypt, and then in the name of the Council wrote a Synodical letter to Nestorius, as the third and last admonition; telling him that if, in the term of ten days after the receipt of that letter, he did not retract what he had preached, those Fathers would have no more communication with him, that they would no longer consider him as a bishop, and that they would hold communion with all clergymen and laymen deposed or excommunicated by him (20).

(15) Nat. Alex. *t.* 10, *c.* 3, *a.* 12, *s.* 2; Fleury, *l.* 25, *n.* 3; Orsi, *t.* 12, *l.* 28, *n.* 37, & seq. (16) Con. Ephes. *p.* 1, *c.* 3, *n.* 6. (17) Conc. Ephes. *p.* 1, *c.* 14. (18) Baron. An. 430, *n.* 7. (19) Fleury, *t.* 4, *l.* 25, *n.* 10, & seq; Nat. Alex. cit. *ar.* 12 & 3. (20) Conc. Ephes. *p.* 1, *c.* 26.

The Synodical letter also contained the profession of Faith and the anathemas decreed against the Nestorian errors (21). These, in substance, are an anathema against those who deny that the Holy Virgin is Mother of the Incarnate Word, or deny that Jesus Christ is the only Son of God, true God and true Man, not alone according to his dignity, but through the hypostatic union of the Person of the Word with his most Holy Humanity. These anathemas are fully and distinctly expressed in the letter.

27. St. Cyril appointed four Egyptian bishops to certify to Nestorius the authenticity of this letter, and two others—one to the people of Constantinople, and another to the abbots of the monasteries, to give them notice likewise of the letter having been expedited. These prelates arrived in Constantinople on the 7th of the following month of December, 430 (22), and intimated to Nestorius the sentence of deposition passed by the Pope, if he did not retract in ten days; but the Emperor Theodosius, previous to their arrival, had given orders for the convocation of a General Council, at the solicitation—both of the Catholics, induced to ask for it by the monks, so cruelly treated by Nestorius, and of Nestorius himself, who hoped to carry his point by means of the bishops of his party, and through the favour of the Court. St. Cyril, therefore, wrote anew to St. Celestine, asking him (23), whether, in case of the retractation of Nestorius, the Council should receive him, as bishop, into communion, and pardon his past faults, or put into execution the sentence of deposition already published against him. St. Celestine answered, that, notwithstanding the prescribed time had passed, he was satisfied that the sentence of deposition should be kept in abeyance, to give time to Nestorius to change his conduct. Nestorius thus remained in possession of his See till the decision of the Council. This condescension of St. Celestine was praised in the Council afterwards, by the Legates, and was contrasted with the irreligious obstinacy of Nestorius (24).

28. As St. Celestine could not personally attend the Council, he sent Arcadius and Projectus, Bishops, and Philip, a priest, to preside in his place, with St. Cyril appointed President in chief. He gave them positive orders that they should not allow his sentence against Nestorius to be debated in the Council (25), but to endeavour to have it put into execution. He wrote to the Council to the same effect, and notified the directions he had given to his Legates, and that he had no doubt but that the Fathers would adhere to the decision he had given, and not canvass what he already had decided, and, as we shall see, everything turned out most happily, according to his wishes. When the celebration of Easter was concluded, the bishops all hastened to Ephesus, where the Council

(21) Apud Bernini, *t.* 1, *sec.* 5, *c.* 4, *p.* 452, & Orsi, *t.* 12, *l.* 28, *n.* 48. (22) Orsi, *t.* 13, *l.* 29, *n.* 1, *ar.* 2. (23) Celest. Ep. 161. (24) Orsi, loc. cit. *n.* 1, in fin. (25) Celest. Epis. 17, apud ; Orsi, ibid. *n.* 2.

was convoked for the 7th of June. Nestorius, accompanied by a great train, was one of the first to arrive, and soon after, St. Cyril, accompanied by fifty Egyptian bishops, arrived, and in a little time two hundred bishops, most of them Metropolitans and men of great learning, were assembled. There was no doubt about St. Cyril presiding as Vicar of Pope Celestine, in the Council of Ephesus; for, in several acts of the Synod itself, he is entitled President, even after the arrival of the Apostolic Legates, as is manifest from the fourth act of the Council, in which the Legates are mentioned by name after St. Cyril, and before all the other bishops. It appears, even from the opening act of the Council, before the arrival of the Legates, that he presided in place of Celestine, as delegate of his Holiness the Archbishop of Rome. Graveson (26), therefore, justly says: " That they are far from the truth, who deny that Cyril presided at the Council of Ephesus, as Vicar of Pope Celestine." St. Cyril, therefore, as President (27), gave notice that the first Session of the Synod would be held on the 22nd of June, in St. Mary's Church, the principal one of Ephesus, and, on the day before, four bishops were appointed to wait on Nestorius, and cite him to appear next day at the Council. He answered, that if his presence was necessary, he would have no objection to present himself; but then, in the course of the same day, he forwarded a protest, signed by sixty-eight bishops, against the opening of the Council, until the arrival of other bishops who were expected (28). St. Cyril and his colleagues paid no attention to the remonstrance, but assembled the next day.

29. On the appointed day the Council was opened; the Count Candidianus, sent by Theodosius, endeavoured to put it off, but the Fathers having ascertained that he was sent by the Emperor solely with authority to keep order and put down disturbance, determined at once to open the Session, and the Count, accordingly, made no further opposition. Before they began, however, they judged it better to cite Nestorius a second and third time, according to the Canons, and sent other bishops to him in the name of the Council, but they were insulted and maltreated by the soldiers he had with him as a body-guard. The Fathers, therefore, on the day appointed, the 22nd of June, held the first Session, in which, first of all, the second letter of St. Cyril to Nestorius was read, and the answer of Nestorius to St. Cyril, and they called out immediately, with one accord (29): " Whoever does not anathematize Nestorius, let him be anathema. Whoever communicates with Nestorius let him be anathema. The true faith anathematizes him. We anathematize all the letters and dogmas of Nestorius." St. Celestine's letter was next read, in which he fulminates a sentence

(26) Graveson, *t.* 3, *sec.* 5, *col.* 4.   (27) Orsi, *l.* 29, *n.* 12.   (28) Orsi, loc. cit. *n.* 12.   (29) In actis Con. Ephes. ap. Bernin. *sec.* 4, *c.* 4, *p.* 458.

of deposition against Nestorius, unless he retracts in ten days (30). Finally, the sentence of the Council was pronounced against him: It begins, by quoting the examination, by the Fathers, of his impious doctrines, extracted from his own writings and sermons, and then proceeds: " Obliged by the Sacred Canons, and the Epistle of our Holy Father and Colleague, Celestine, Bishop of the Roman Church, we have been necessarily driven, not without tears, to pronounce this melancholy sentence against him. Therefore, our Lord Jesus Christ, whom he has insulted by his blasphemies, deprives him, through this Holy Council, of the Episcopal dignity, and declares him excluded from every Assembly and College of Priests (31)." This sentence was subscribed by one hundred and eighty-eight bishops. The Session lasted from the morning till dark night (32), though the days were long at that season, the 22nd June, and the sun did not set in the latitude of Ephesus, till seven o'clock in the evening. The people of the city were waiting from morning till night, expecting the decision of the Council, and when they heard that Nestorius was condemned and deposed, and his doctrine prohibited, and that the Holy Virgin was declared to be the Mother of God in reality, they all, with one voice, began to bless the Council and praise God, who cast down the enemy of the Faith, and of his Holy Mother. When the bishops left the church, they were accompanied to their lodgings by the people with lighted torches. Women went before them, bearing vases of burning perfume, and a general illumination of the whole city manifested the universal joy (33).

30. The following day, the foregoing sentence was intimated to Nestorius, and a letter sent to him as follows: " The Holy Synod, assembled in the Metropolis of Ephesus, to Nestorius, the new Judas. Know that you, on account of your many discourses, and your obstinate contumacy against the Sacred Canons, have been deprived, on the 22nd of this month, of all Ecclesiastical dignity, according to the Ecclesiastical Decrees sanctioned by the Holy Synod" (34). The sentence was published the same day through the streets of Ephesus, by sound of trumpet, and was posted up in the public places; but Candidianus ordered it to be taken down, and published an edict, declaring the Session of the Council celebrated null and void. He also wrote to the Emperor, that the decision of the Council was obtained by sedition and violence; and the perfidious Nestorius wrote another letter to Theodosius to the same effect, complaining of the injustice done to him in the Council, and requiring that another General Council should be convened, and all the bishops inimical to him excluded (35).

(30) Orsi, *t.* 13, *l.* 29, *n.* 18. (31) Orsi, *n.* 21; Fleury, *t.* 4, *l.* 25, *n.* 42. (32) Epis. Cyr. *t.* 3, Conc. (33) Fleury & Orsi, loc. cit. (34) Apud Bernin. *sec.* 5, *c.* 4; Nat. Alex. *t.* 10, *c.* 3, *ar.* 12, *s.* 6. (35) Orsi, *l.* 29, *n.* 23, & seq.

31. Several bishops of the Nestorian party, who had signed the protest, were even shocked at his impiety, and convinced of the justice of the sentence passed against him, joined the Council (36). But when everything appeared to be about to settle down peaceably, John, Bishop of Antioch, raised another storm (37), in conjunction with other schismatical bishops, to the number of forty; and, either to please Chrisaphius, Prime Minister of the Emperor, and a great friend of Nestorius, or because it went to his heart to see his friend and fellow-citizen (Nestorius was a citizen of Antioch) condemned, he had the hardihood to summon a Cabal in the very city of Ephesus, and then to depose St. Cyril, and St. Mennon, Bishop of Ephesus, and to excommunicate all the other bishops of the Synod, because, as they said, they trampled on and despised the orders of the Emperor. St. Cyril and the other bishops took no notice of such rash attempts, but, on the contrary, the Council put forth its authority, and deputed three bishops to cite John, as chief of the Cabal, to account for his insolence, and after being twice more cited, and not appearing, the Council, in the fifth Session, declared John and his colleagues suspended from ecclesiastical communion, till such time as they would repent of their fault, and that, if they obstinately persevered, they would be proceeded against, according to the Canons, to the last extremity (38). Finally, in the year 433, John, and the other bishops of his party, subscribed the condemnation of Nestorius, and St. Cyril received him to his communion, and thus peace was re-established between the Metropolitans of Alexandria and Antioch (39).

32. We will, however, return to the Council, and see what was decided on in the subsequent Sessions, and, which we have postponed, the end of the Cabal of John of Antioch. Shortly after the first Session, the three Legates of St. Celestine arrived at Ephesus —Philip, Arcadius, and Projectus—and they came not alone in the Pope's name, but also of all the bishops of the West. The second Session was then held in the palace of St. Mennon, Bishop of the See, and the Legates took the first place (40). First of all, they wished that the letter of St. Celestine, sent by them to the Council, should be read. And when the Fathers heard it, they all agreed to the sentiments expressed in it by the Pope. Philip then thanked the Council, and said: " You, by these acclamations, have united yourselves as holy members with your head, and have manifested that you well know that the Blessed Apostle, Peter, is the head of all the faithful, and chief of the Apostles." Projectus then moved that the Council would put into execution what was mentioned in the letter of the Pope. Fermus, Bishop of Cesarea, in Cappadocia, answered, that the holy Synod, guided by the antecedent letters of the Pope, to St. Cyril, and to the Churches of Constantinople and

(36) Orsi, n. 25.   (37) Cabassu. not. Con. sec. 5, n. 17, & Orsi, n. 33.   (38) Orsi, l. cit. n. 49.   (39) Orsi, t. 13, l. 30, n. 28.   (40) Orsi, n. 42.

Antioch, had already put it into execution, and pronounced a canonical judgment against the contumacious Nestorius. The next day, therefore, all the acts of the Council, and the sentence of the deposition of Nestorius, were read, and then the Priest Philip thus spoke: "No one doubts that St. Peter is the chief of the Apostles, the column of the Faith, and the foundation of the Catholic Church, and that he received the keys of the kingdom from Jesus Christ, and He lives even to-day, and exercises, in his successor, this judgment. Therefore, his Holiness Pope Celestine, who holds the place of St. Peter, having sent us to this Council to supply his place, we, in his name, confirm the Decree pronounced by the Synod against the impious Nestorius; and we declare him deposed from the priesthood and the communion of the Catholic Church; and, as he has contemned correction, let his part be with him, of whom it is written, 'another shall receive his Bishopric.'" The Bishops Arcadius and Projectus then did the same, and the Council expressing a wish that all the acts of the two Sessions should be joined with those of the first preceding one, that the assent of all the Fathers might be shown to all the acts of the Council, it was done so, and the Legates subscribed the whole (41).

33. This being done, the Fathers of the Council wrote a Synodical epistle to the Emperor, giving him an account of the sentence fulminated against Nestorius and his adherents, as the Pope, St. Celestine, had already decided, and charged his Legates with the execution of it in their name. They then subjoined the confirmation of the sentence by the Papal Legates, both in their own name and the name of the Council of the Western Bishops, held in Rome (42). The Council, besides, wrote another letter to St. Celestine, giving him an account of all that had been done, both against Nestorius, and against John, Patriarch of Antioch. They also notified to him the condemnation of the Pelagians and Celestians, and explained to him how the Pelagians disturbed the East, looking for a General Council to examine their cause; but that, as the Fathers had read in the Synod the Commentaries of the Acts of the deposition of these bishops, they considered that the Pontifical Decrees passed against them should retain all their force. Cardinal Orsi (43) writes, that there is a great deal of confusion regarding the Synod of Ephesus, but there is no doubt but that the Pelagians were condemned in this Council as heretics, by the assembled bishops of the world. The symbol composed by Theodore of Mopsuestia was also condemned in this Council, and every other formula, except that of the Council of Nice, was prohibited (44). Here, however, Cardinal Orsi justly remarks (45), that that does not prohibit the Church, when she condemns any heresy not formally condemned by the Council of Nice, from making additions neces-

(41) Orsi, *l.* 29, *n.* 42, & seq.   (42) Orsi, loc. cit.   (43) Orsi, *l.* 29, *n.* 52.
(44) Baron. Ann. 431, *n.* 98 & 99.   (45) Orsi, *n.* 58.

sary for clearing up the truth, as the Council of Constantinople had done already, and other Councils did since that of Ephesus. The heresy of the Messalians (*Art.* 3, *chap.* 4, *n.* 80) was also condemned in this Council, and a book, entitled *The Ascetic*, was anathematized at the same time (46).

34. When all was concluded, the Fathers wrote to Theodosius, requesting leave to return to their Churches; but the letter containing this request, as well as all the former ones they wrote to Constantinople, was intercepted by Count Candinianus, who placed guards on the roads for that purpose (47); while, at the same time, the letters of John of Antioch, and the schismatical bishops of his party, stuffed with lies and calumnies regarding the proceedings of the Council, had already arrived some time at Constantinople; and thus it happened, that the Emperor, poisoned, on the one side, by the false accounts furnished him, and vexed, on the other, with the Fathers of the Council, for, as he believed, not having written to him, and informed him of what they had done in the affair of Nestorius, wrote to them that all the acts of the Synod, as done against his orders, were to be considered invalid, and that everything should be examined anew; and therefore, Palladius, the bearer of the Emperor's letter to Ephesus, commanded, on his arrival, that none of the Fathers should be permitted to leave the city (48). The Fathers were confounded when they discovered how they were calumniated, and prevented from giving the Emperor a faithful account of all that had been done in the case of Nestorius, and the Patriarch of Antioch; they, therefore, devised a plan to send a trusty messenger (49), disguised as a beggar, with copies of all the letters they had already written, but which were intercepted, enclosed in a hollow cane, such as poor pilgrims usually carried. They wrote, likewise, to several other persons in Constantinople, so that when the good people of that city discovered the intrigues of the enemies of the Council, they went in a crowd along with the Monk St. Dalmatius, who, for forty-eight years previously, had never left his monastery (50), and all the Archimandrites, singing hymns and psalms, to address the Emperor in favour of the Catholics. Theodosius gave them audience in the Church of St. Mocius, and St. Dalmatius, ascending the pulpit, said: " O Cæsar, put an end, at length, to the miserable imposture of heresy; let the just cause of the Catholics prevail for ever." He then proceeded to explain the rectitude of the acts of the Council, and the insolence of the schismatics. Theodosius, moved by the reasons adduced, revoked his orders (51), and, concerning the dispute between St. Cyril and the Patriarch of Antioch, he said he wished to try the cause

(46) Baron. *n.* 101; Orsi, *n.* 61. (47) Baron. Ann. 451, *n.* 104. (48) Baron. *n.* 105 & 107. (49) Baron. Ann. 451, *n.* 108; Cabass. *sec.* v. 17; Fleury, *t.* 4, *l.* 26, *n.* 6. (50) Orsi, *t.* 13, *l.* 30, *n.* 28. (51) Baron. Ann. 431, *n.* 113.

I

himself, and commanded, therefore, that each of them should send some of his bishops to Constantinople.

35. The Legates had now left the Council for Constantinople, but, when matters were just settling down, another storm arose, for the Count Ireneus, a great patron of the schismatics, came to Ephesus, and informed the Emperor that Nestorius was no more a heretic than Cyril and Mennon, and that the only way to pacify the Church of the East was to depose the whole three of them together. At the same time, Acacius, Bishop of Berea, an honest and righteous man, but who, deceived by Paul, Bishop of Emisenum, joined the party of John of Antioch, wrote to the Emperor, likewise, against St. Cyril and St. Mennon; so Theodosius thought it better to send (52) his almoner, the Count John, to Ephesus, to pacify both parties. When the Count came to Ephesus, he ordered that Nestorius, Cyril, and Mennon should be put into prison: but the Catholic bishops immediately wrote to the Emperor, praying him to liberate the Catholic bishops, and protesting that nothing would induce them ever to communicate with the schismatics. In the meanwhile, the concerns of the Empire all went wrong; the Roman army was cut to pieces by the Goths, in Africa, and the few survivors were reduced to slavery. The clergy of Constantinople clamoured in favour of the Catholics, and they were assisted in their zealous exertions by St. Pulcheria, who opened the eyes of her brother to the impositions of the Nestorians (53). The Emperor, at length, assured of the wickedness of the schismatics, and the virtue of the Catholics, ordered St. Cyril and St. Mennon to be liberated, and gave leave to the bishops to return home to their Sees; he confirmed the deposition of Nestorius, and ordered him to shut himself up once more in his old monastery of St. Euprepius, and there learn to repent; but as he, instead of exhibiting any symptoms of sorrow for his past conduct, only continued to infect the monks of the monastery with his heretical opinions, he was banished to the Oasis between Egypt and Lybia (54), and soon after, as Fleury informs us, was transferred to Panapolis, and from Panapolis to Elephantina, and, from thence, back again to another place near Panapolis, where, at last, he died in misery, worn out by years and infirmities. Some say that, through desperation, he dashed his brains out; others, that the ground opened under him and swallowed him; and others, again, that he died of a cancer, which rotted his tongue, and that it was consumed by worms engendered by the disease—a fit punishment for that tongue which had uttered so many blasphemies against Jesus Christ and his Holy Mother (55).

36. Nestorius was succeeded in the See of Constantinople by Maximinian, a monk untainted in the Faith, and Theodosius

(52) Baron. n. 126 & 127.   (53) Baron. n. 159.   (54) Fleury, t. 4, l. 26, n. 34.
(55) Baron. Ann. 520, n. 67; Cabass. sec. 5, n. 18; Orsi, t. 18, l. 30, n. 74; Nat. t. 10, c. 3, ar. 12, n. 18, s. 10; Hermant, t. 1, c. 148.

deprived Count Ireneus of his dignity (56). The Emperor next, in the year 435, made a most rigorous law against the Nestorians. He ordered that they should be called Simonians, and prohibited them from having any conventicle, either within or without the city; that if any one gave them a place of meeting, all his property should be confiscated, and he prohibited all the books of Nestorius treating of Religion. Danæus (57) says, that the heresy of Nestorius did not end with his life; it was spread over various regions of the East, and, even in our own days, there are whole congregations of Nestorians on the Malabar coast, in India.

37. When the Nestorians saw their chief rejected by all the world, and his works condemned by the Council of Ephesus and the Emperor, they set about disseminating the writings of the Bishops Theodore and Diodorus, who died in communion with the Church, and left a great character after them in the East (58). The Nestorians endeavoured to turn the writings of those prelates to their own advantage, and pretended to prove that Nestorius had taught nothing new, but only followed the teaching of the ancients, and they translated those works into various languages (59); but many zealous Catholic bishops, as Theodosia of Ancyra, Acacius of Meretina, and Rabbola of Edessa, bestirred themselves against the writings of Theodore of Mopsuestia. When St. Cyril heard of the matter, he also wrote against those books, and purposely composed a declaration of the Symbol of Nice, in which, with great particularity and diffuseness, he explains the doctrine of the Incarnation (60).

38. We should also remark, that Theodoret being soon after re-established in his See, by the Council of Chalcedon, after subscribing the condemnation of Nestorius and of his errors; and Ibas being likewise reinstated, after retracting the errors imputed to him, and anathemátizing Nestorius, the Nestorians made a handle of that, to insinuate that their doctrines were approved of by the Council of Chalcedon, and thus they seduced a great many persons, and formed a numerous party. God sent them, however, a powerful opponent, in the person of Theodore, Bishop of Cesarea, who prevailed on the Emperor Justinian to cause the writings of Theodore against St. Cyril, and the letter of Ibas, on the same subject, to be condemned. Justinian, in fact, condemned the works of these bishops, and of Theodore of Mopsuestia, and requested Pope Vigilius to condemn them also, which he did, after mature examination in his *Constitution*, and approved of all that was decided in the fifth General Council, the second of Constantinople, held in the year 533 (61), as we shall see in the next chapter. The condemnation of these

(56) Baron. *n*. 177 & 181.   (57) Dan. temp. not. *p*. 241.   (58) Liberat. Brev. c. 10.   (59) Coll. Sup. c. 199.   (60) Fleury, *t*. 4, *l*. 26, *n*. 36.   (61) Berti, *t*. 1, *sec*. vi. c. 2.

works, afterwards called *The Three Chapters*, put an effectual stop to the progress of Nestorianism (62); but still there were, ever since, many, both in the East and West, who endeavoured to uphold this impious heresy.

39. The most remarkable among the supporters of Nestorianism were two Spanish bishops—Felix, Bishop of Urgel, and Elipandus, Archbishop of Toledo; these maintained that Jesus Christ, according to his human nature, was not the natural, but only the adopted, Son of God, or, as they said, the nuncupative, or Son in name alone. This heresy had its origin about the year 780. Elipandus preached this heresy in the Asturias and Gallicia, and Felix in Septimania, a part of Narbonic Gaul, called at a later period, Languedoc. Elipandus brought over to his side Ascarieus, Archbishop of Braga, and some persons from Cordova (63). This error had many opponents, the principal were Paulinus, Patriarch of Aquilea; Beatus, a priest and monk in the mountains of Asturias; Etherius, his disciple, and afterwards Bishop of Osma; but its chief impugner was Alcuinus, who wrote seven books against Felix, and four against Elipandus. Felix was first condemned in Narbonne, in the year 788, next in Ratisbon, in 792, and in 794, in a Synod held at Frankfort, by the bishops of France, who, as Noel Alexander tells us, condemned him with this reservation (64): " Reservato per omnia juris privilegio Summi Pontificis Domini et Patris nostri Adriani Primæ Sædis Beatissimi Papæ." This error was finally twice condemned in 799, in Rome, under Adrian and Leo III. (65). Felix abjured his errors in the Council of Ratisbon, in 792; but it appears he was not sincere, as he taught the same doctrine afterwards. In the year 799, he was charged with relapsing by Alcuinus, in a Synod held at Aix-la-Chapelle; he confessed his error, and gave every sign of having truly returned to the Church, but some writings of his, discovered after his death, leave us in doubt of the sincerity of his conversion, and of his eternal happiness. This was not the case with Elipandus, for, though he resisted the truth a long time, he at length bowed to the decision of the Roman Church, and died in her communion, as many authors, quoted by Noel Alexander, testify (66).

40. Who would believe that, after seeing Nestorius condemned by a General Council, celebrated by such a multitude of bishops, conducted with such solemnity and accuracy, and afterwards accepted by the whole Catholic Church, persons would be found to defend him, as innocent, and charge his condemnation as invalid and unjust. Those who do this are surely heretics, whose chief study has always been to reject the authority of Councils and the

---

(62) Hermant. *t.* 1, *c.* 202. (63) Fleury, *t.* 6, *l.* 44, *n.* 50. (64) N. Alex. *t.* 12, *s* 8, *c.* 2, *a.* 3, *f.* 2. (65) Graves, *t.* 3; Colloq. 3, *p.* 55. (66) Nat. Alex. loc. cit. *c.* 2, *a.* 3. *f.* 1.

Pope, and thus sustain their own errors. The history of Nestorianism would be incomplete without a knowledge of the modern defenders of the heresy, and the arguments made use of by them. Calvin was the first to raise the standard, and he was followed by his disciples, Albertin, Giles Gaillard, John Croye, and David de Roden. This band was joined by another Calvinistic writer, in 1645, who printed a work, but did not put his name to it, in which he endeavours to show that Nestorius should not be ranked with the heretics, but with the doctors of the Church, and venerated as a martyr, and that the Fathers of the Council of Ephesus ought to be considered Eutychians, as well as St. Cyril, St Gregory Thaumaturgus, St. Dionisius of Alexandria, St. John Chrysostom, and St. Hilary, who give it such praise. This book was refuted by the learned Petavius, in the year 1646, in the sixth book of his work on Theological Dogmas. Finally, Samuel Basnage, in his Annals (67), has joined with Calvin and the other authors above-named, and has taken up the defence of Nestorius; he has even the hardihood to declare, that the Council of Ephesus had filled the world with tears.

41. We shall let Basnage speak for himself. He says, first, the Council of Ephesus was not a General one, but only a particular Synod, as the bishops refused to wait either for the Pope's Legates, or for the other bishops of the East. As far as the Legates are concerned, we see (No. 28.) that St. Cyril assisted at the Council from the beginning, and that he had been already nominated by the Pope as President; that a few days after, the other Legates arrived, and that they confirmed the Council. It is true all the bishops of the East did not attend it, for eighty-nine bishops seceded, and formed a cabal apart, in the very city of Ephesus, in which they deposed St. Cyril; but a few days after, the eighty-nine were reduced to thirty-seven, among whom were the Pelagian bishops, and several others already deposed; and the rest, when their eyes were opened to the truth, united themselves to the Fathers of the Council, so that Theodoret, who at first adhered to the party of John of Antioch, wrote to Andrew of Samosata: " Pars maxima Israelis consentit inimicis, pauci vero valde sunt salvi, ac sustinent pro pietate certamen:" but John himself, afterwards, together with Theodoret and the rest who repented, subscribed to the Council, which then was recognized as Ecumenical by the whole Church. With what face, then, can Basnage say that it was a particular, and not a General Council?

42. Basnage says next (68), that it is a false supposition of Noel Alexander, that Nestorius taught that there were two persons in Christ, or denied that Mary was the true Mother of God, and he was condemned, he says, only because he was not well understood;

(67) Basnage, ad an. 141, n. 13.   (68) Basnage, l. cit. ad an. 430.

but how does he prove this as to the maternity of the Blessed Virgin? By saying that Nestorius, in a certain letter he wrote to John of Antioch, admits, that as far as the words of the Gospel go, he has no objection that the Virgin should be piously called the Mother of God, but these words he afterwards interpreted in his own way. But why should we lose time in trying to interpret these obscure and equivocal expressions of his, when he expressly declares more than once, that Mary was not the Mother of God, otherwise the Gentiles ought to be excused for adoring the mothers of their gods. " Has God," he says, " a Mother?—therefore Paganism is excusable. Mary brought not forth God, but she brought forth a man, the instrument of the Divinity." These are his own words, quoted by Basnage himself, and he also relates that the monks of the Archimandrite Basil, in their petition to the Emperor Theodosius, stated that Nestorius (69) said, that Mary only brought forth a man, and that nothing but flesh could be born of the flesh, and, therefore, they required, that in a General Council, the foundation of the Faith should be left intact, that is, that the Word with the flesh, taken from Mary, suffered and died for the Redemption of mankind. We have, besides, a letter written by Nestorius to the Pope St. Celestine (70), in which he complains that the clergy, " aperte blasphemant, Deum Verbum tamquam originis initium de Christotocho Virgine sumsisse. Sed hanc Virginem Christotochon ausi sunt cum modo quodam Theotocon dicere, cum Ss. illi Patres per Nicæam nihil amplius de S. Virgine dixissent, nisi quia Jesus Christus incarnatus est ex Spiritu Sancto de Maria Virgine;" and he adds, " Verbum Theotocon ferri potest propter inseparabile Templum Dei Verbi ex ipsa, non quia ipsa Mater sit Verbi Dei, nemo enim antiquiorem se parit:" thus, he denies in the plainest terms, that the Blessed Virgin is Theotocon, the Mother of the Word of God, but only allows her to be Christotocon, the Mother of Christ; but St. Celestine answers him (71): " We have received your letters containing open blasphemy," and he adds that this truth, that the only Son of God was born of Mary, is the promise to us of life and salvation.

43. Let us now see what Nestorius says of Jesus Christ. No nature, he says, can subsist without its proper subsistence, and this is the origin of his error, for he therefore gives two persons to Christ, Divine and human, as he had two natures, and he therefore said that the Divine Word was united to Christ after he was formed a perfect man with appropriate human subsistence and personality. He says: " Si Christus perfectus Deus, idemque perfectus homo intelligitur, ubi naturæ est perfectio, si hominis natura non subsistit" (72)? He also said that the union of the two natures was

(69) Habetur in Sess. 4; Con. Col. 1103. (70) Sess. 4; Con. Col. 1021. (71) Tom. 4; Con. Col. 1023. (72) Tom. 5; Con. Col 1004

according to grace, or by the dignity or honor of Filiation given to the Person of Christ, and he, therefore, in general, did not call the union of the two natures a union at all, but propinquity, or inhabitation; he thus admits two united, or more properly speaking, conjoined natures, but not a true unity of person, and by two natures understands two personalities, and therefore could not bear to hear it said in speaking of Jesus Christ, that God was born, or suffered, or died. In his letter to St. Cyril, quoted by Basnage, he says: "My brother, to ascribe birth, or suffering, or death, to the Divine Word by reason of this appropriation, is to follow the Pagans or the insane Apollinares." These expressions prove that he did not believe that the two natures were united in one Person. When his priest Anastasius, preaching to the people, said: "Let no one call Mary the Mother of God, it is not possible that God should be born of man," and the people, horrified with the blasphemy, called on Nestorius to remove the scandal given by Anastasius, he went up into the pulpit, and said: "I never would call him God, who has been formed only two or three months," and he never called Jesus Christ God, but only the temple or habitation of God, as he wrote to St. Cyril. It is proper, he said, and conformable to ecclesiastical tradition, to confess that the body of Christ is the temple of Divinity, and that it is joined by so sublime a connexion to his Divine self, that we may say his Divine nature appropriates to itself something which otherwise would belong to the body alone. Here, then, are the very words of Nestorius himself, and nothing can be more clear than that he means to say that Christ is only the temple of God, but united to God in such a manner by Grace, that it might be said that the Divine nature appropriated the qualities proper to humanity. Now, Basnage does not deny that these are the letters and expressions of Nestorius, and how then can he say that he spoke in a pious and Catholic sense, and that the Council of Ephesus, by his condemnation, filled the world with tears, when Sixtus III., St. Leo the Great, and the fifth General Council, together with so many other doctors and learned writers, received the Council of Ephesus as most certainly Ecumenical, and all have called and considered Nestorius a heretic. Basnage, however, prefers following Calvin and his adherents, instead of the Council of Ephesus, the fifth Council, the Pope, and all the Catholic doctors. Selvaggi, the annotator of Mosheim, is well worthy of being read on this question (73); he has six very excellent reflections, and makes several useful remarks about Luther and the other modern heretics, who seek to discredit St. Cyril and the Council of Ephesus. It is the interest of all heretics to weaken the authority of Councils, that there may be no power to condemn them, and expose their errors to the world. But I remark that the devil has

---

(73) Selvag. in Mosheim, *Part II.* n. 82, *p.* 729.

made it a particular study to ruin, by his partisans, the credit of the Council of Ephesus, to remove from our sight the immense love which our God has shown us, by becoming man and dying for our love. Men do not love God, because they do not reflect that he has died for love of them, and the devil endeavours not only to remove this thought from our minds, but to prevent us from thinking it even possible.

Article IV.

THE HERESY OF EUTYCHES.

SEC. I.—THE SYNOD OF ST. FLAVIAN.—THE COUNCIL OR CABAL OF EPHESUS, CALLED THE "LATROCINIUM," OR COUNCIL OF ROBBERS.

44. Beginning of Eutyches; he is accused by Eusebius of Dorileum. 45. St. Flavian receives the Charge. 46. Synod of St. Flavian. 47. Confession of Eutyches in the Synod. 48. Sentence of the Synod against Eutyches. 49. Complaints of Eutyches. 50. Eutyches writes to St. Peter Chrysologus, and to St. Leo. 51. Character of Dioscorus. 52 & 53. Cabal at Ephesus. 54. St. Flavian is deposed, and Eusebius of Dorileum. 55. The Errors of Theodore of Mopsuestia. 56. Death of St. Flavian. 57. Character of Theodoret. 58 & 59. Writings of Theodoret against St. Cyril. Defence of Theodoret. 60. Dioscorus excommunicates St. Leo. 61. Theodosius approved the Council or Cabal, and dies. 62. Reign of St. Pulcheria and Marcian.

44. THE heresy of Eutyches sprung up (1) in the year 448, eighteen years after the Council of Ephesus. Eutyches was a monk and priest; he was also the abbot of a monastery near Constantinople, containing three hundred monks; he was a violent opponent of his Archbishop, Nestorius, and accused him at the Council of Ephesus, where he went in person to testify to his prevarications, so that he was considered by the friends of St. Cyril as one of the staunchest defenders of the Faith (2). St. Leo having received a letter from him, informing him that Nestorianism was again raising its head (3), answered him, approving of his zeal, and encouraging him to defend the Church; imagining that he was writing at the time against the real Nestorians, while he, in that letter, meant all the while the Catholics, whom he looked upon as infected with Nestorian principles (4). Eusebius, Bishop of Dorileum, in Phrygia, was also one of the most zealous opponents of Nestorius, for, while yet only a layman, in the year 429, he had the courage to stand up and reprove him publicly for his errors (5). (No. 22. supra.) The conformity of their opinions, therefore, made him a friend of Eutyches, but in the course of their intimacy he, at length, perceived that he (Eutyches) went too far and fell into heretical propositions (6). He endeavoured then for a long time, by reasoning

(1) Nat. Alex. *t.* 10, *c.* 3, *ar.* 13, *s.* 1; Baron. An. 448, ex. *n.* 19; Hermant, *t.* 1, c. 155; Fleury, *t.* 4, *l.* 27, *n.* 23. (2) Liberat. Brev. c. 11. (3) St. Leo, Ep 19, *l.* 6. (4) Fleury, *t.* 4, *l.* 27, *n.* 23. (5) Sulp. *l.* 25, *n.* 2, ap. Fleury, cit. *n.* 23. (6) Orsi, ibid. *n.* 16, Fleury, cit. *n.* 23; Nat. Alex. *t.* 10, *ar.* 13, *s.* 2.

with him, to bring him round; but, when he saw it was all in vain, he gave up his friendship and became his accuser. Even before that the Orientals (7) had already denounced the errors of Eutyches to the Emperor Theodosius; but he so adroitly turned aside the charge, that, instead of being arraigned, he became the accuser. The bishops of the East exclaimed, that Eutyches was infected with the errors of Apollinares, but as it was an old trick to charge with the profession of this false doctrine the adversaries of Nestorius, and especially all who defended the anathemas of St. Cyril; and as those same bishops had before defended Nestorius, and even still upheld the doctrine of Theodore of Mopsuestia, no one took any notice of their accusation of Eutyches on the present occasion. The unfortunate man had then nothing to fear from the charges of those bishops, but when Eusebius of Dorileum took up the matter it wore a more serious aspect. Eusebius then, having frequently admonished him privately, and seeing that this had no effect on him, considered himself now bound by the Gospel to denounce him to the Church, and, accordingly, laid the matter before St. Flavian, Archbishop of Constantinople (8).

45. St. Flavian foresaw, that a judicial process and condemnation of Eutyches would occasion a great deal of tumult, for he was venerated by the people, and respected by the Court, as a man who, having dedicated himself to God from his infancy, had now grown grey in monastic solitude, and never went outside of his cloister for a day, only when he joined with St. Dalmatius, to defend the Council of Ephesus; the Archbishop, therefore, advised Eusebius to act with the greatest caution. Eutyches was also protected by the Eunuch Chrisaphius, whose godfather he was, and joined with Dioscorus, Bishop of Alexandria, in opposing the Oriental bishops, who were the first to accuse him of heresy; it would appear, then, that in intermeddling at all with the matter, that St. Flavian and Eusebius were joining the enemy, and opposing both the Court and Dioscorus, and thus occasioning a great disturbance in the Church; but neither this, nor any other consideration, could restrain the zeal of Eusebius, so St. Flavian was obliged to receive the charge, and let justice take its course.

46. While this was going on, St. Flavian held a Synod for the adjustment of some disputes between Florens of Sardis, the Metropolitan of Lydia, and two bishops of the same province. When this case was concluded (9), the Bishop of Dorileum arose, and presented a document to the Council, requiring that it should be read and inserted in the Acts. The document was read, and in it Eusebius charged Eutyches with blaspheming Jesus Christ, with speaking with disrespect of the Holy Fathers, and with accusing

(7) Orsi, t. 14. l. 32, n. 9. (8) Orsi, ibid n 16; Fleury, l. c. (9) Orsi, loc. cit. n. 17; Fleury, l. 27. n. 24.

himself, whose whole study it was to make war with heresy, with being a heretic; he demanded, therefore, that Eutyches should be cited to appear before the Council, to give an account of his expressions, and he promised that he would be prepared to convict him of heresy, and thus, those whom he had perverted could see the evil of their ways and repent. When the paper was read through, St. Flavian besought Eusebius to see Eutyches once more in private, and try to bring him to a better sense. Eusebius answered, that he had done so over and over already, and could bring many witnesses to prove it, but all in vain, and he, therefore, again begged of the Council, at any cost, to summon Eutyches, that he might not lead others astray, as he had already perverted a great number. Still, however, St. Flavian wished that Eusebius should try once more the effect of a private remonstrance, but he refused, as he had so often made the attempt already and could not succeed. The Synod, at length, received the charge against Eutyches, and deputed a priest and deacon to wait on him, and summon him to appear at the ensuing Session of the Council to clear himself. The second Session was then held, and in that, the two principal letters of St. Cyril, on the Incarnation of the Word, were read, that is, his second letter to Nestorius, approved by the Council of Ephesus, and the other to the Council of John of Antioch, after the conclusion of the peace. When these letters were read, St. Flavian said, that his Faith was, that Jesus Christ is perfect God and perfect man, composed of body and soul, consubstantial to his Father, according to his Divinity, and consubstantial to his Mother, according to his humanity, and that from the union of the two natures—Divine and human, in one sole *hypostasis* or person, there results but one Jesus Christ, after the Incarnation of the Word; and all the other bishops made the same profession. Other Sessions were held, and other citations were sent to Eutyches, calling on him to appear and justify himself, but he refused, and alleged as an excuse, that he never left his convent, and, besides, that he was then sick (10).

47. Towards the close of the seventh Session, Eutyches presented himself before the Council, for he could no longer refuse the repeated citations he received, but the Fathers were surprised to see him enter, accompanied by a great troop of soldiers (11), of monks, and of officers of the Prefect of the Pretorium, who would not allow him to enter the Council, till the Fathers promised to send him back safe again. He came into the Council hall, and he was followed by the " Great Silenciary" (an officer so called among the Romans, whose duty it was to preserve the peace of the Imperial Palace), who presented, and read an order from the Emperor, commanding that the Patrician

(10) Orsi, *n.* 18.   (11) Fleury, *l.* 27, *n.* 28 ; Orsi, *t.* 14, *l.* 32. *n.* 23, Baron. Ann. 448, *n.* 48 ; Hermant, *t* 1, *c* 155.

Florentius should attend the Council for the conservation of the Faith. Florentius came, and then Eusebius of Dorileum the accuser, and Eutyches the accused, were placed both standing in the midst of the Council. The letter of St. Cyril to the Orientals, in which the distinction of the two natures is expressed, was then read. Eusebius then said: Eutyches does not agree to this, but teaches the contrary. When the reading of the Acts was concluded, St. Flavian said to Eutyches: You have heard what your accuser has said; declare, then, if you confess the union of the two natures in Christ? Eutyches answered that he did. But, replied Eusebius, do you confess the two natures, after the Incarnation; and do you believe that Jesus Christ is consubstantial to us, according to the flesh or not? Eutyches, turning to St. Flavian, answered: I came not here to dispute, but to declare what my opinion is; I have written it in this paper, let it be read. St. Flavian said, Read it yourself. I cannot read it, said Eutyches. He then made this confession: "I adore the Father with the Son, and the Son with the Father, and the Holy Ghost with the Father and the Son. I confess his coming in the flesh, taken from the flesh of the Holy Virgin, and that he has been made perfect man for our salvation." Flavian again asked him: Do you now confess, here present, that Jesus Christ has two natures? "Hitherto, I have not said so," said he, "now I confess it." Florentius asked him: If he professed that there are two natures in Christ, and that Jesus Christ is consubstantial to us? Eutyches answered: "I have read in Cyril and Athanasius, that Christ was of two natures, and I, therefore, confess that our Lord was, before his Incarnation, of two natures, but after these were united, they do not say any longer that he had two natures, but only one; let St. Athanasius be read, and you will see that he does not say two natures." Eutyches did not advert, that both his propositions were open heresy, as St. Leo well remarks in his letter: The second proposition, that is, that Christ, after the union of the two natures, was of only one nature. The human nature, as Eutyches said, being absorbed in and confounded with the Divine nature, would prove, that the Divinity itself in Christ had suffered and died, and, that the sufferings and death of Christ were only a mere fable. The first proposition was no less heretical than the second, that Christ, previous to his Incarnation, had two natures—for this could only be sustained by upholding the heresy of Origen, that the souls of men were all created before the beginning of the world, and then, from time to time, sent to inhabit the bodies of men.

48. When Eutyches spoke thus, Basil of Seleucia said to him: "If you do not say that there were two natures after the union, you admit a mixture or confusion." Florentius replied: "He who does not admit two natures in Christ, does not believe as he ought." Then the Council exclaimed: "Faith ought not to be forced. He

will not submit; what do you exhort him for?" St. Flavian then, with consent of the bishops, pronounced the sentence in these terms: "Eutyches, Priest, and Archimandrite, is fully convicted, both by his past acts, and his present confessions, to hold the errors of Valentine and Apollinares, and more so, as he has had no regard to our admonitions: therefore, weeping and sighing for his total loss, we declare, on the part of Jesus Christ, whom he blasphemes, that he is deprived of every priestly grade, of our communion, and of the government of his monastery; and we make known this, that all those who hold any conversation or communication with him shall be excommunicated" (12). Here are the words of the decree, as quoted by Noel Alexander (13): "Per omnia Eutiches, quondam Presbyter et Archimandrita, Valentini et Apollinaris perversitatibus compertus est ægrotare, et eorum blasphemias incommutabiliter sequi; qui nec nostram reveritus persuasionem, atque doctrinam, rectis noluit consentire dogmatibus. Unde illacrymati, et gementes perfectam ejus perditionem, decrevimus per Dominum N. Jesum Christum, quem blasphematus est, extraneum eum esse ab omni officio sacerdotali, et a nostra communione, et primatu monasterii; scientibus hoc omnibus, qui cum eo exinde colloquentur, aut eum convenerint, quoniam rei erunt et ipsi pœne excommunicationis." This sentence was subscribed by thirty-two bishops, and twenty-three abbots, of whom eighteen were priests, one a deacon, and four laymen. When the Council was terminated, Eutyches said to the Patrician Florentius, in a low voice, that he appealed to the Council of the Most Holy Bishop of Rome, and of the Bishops of Alexandria, of Jerusalem, and of Thessalonica, and Florentius immediately communicated it to St. Flavian, as he was leaving the hall to go to his own apartment. This expression, thus privately dropped (14), gave a handle to Eutyches afterwards to boast that he had appealed to the Pope, to whom he wrote, as we shall soon see.

49. This pretended appeal did not prevent St. Flavian from publishing the sentence of excommunication, but Eutyches made use of it, to publish a great many false charges against the Synod, which he accused of trampling on all the rules of justice in his regard. The sentence of the Council was published, by order of St. Flavian, in all the monasteries, and subscribed by their Archimandrites; but the monks of the monastery Eutyches governed, instead of separating themselves from his communion, preferred to remain without sacraments, and some of them even died without the viaticum, sooner than forsake their impious master. Eutyches complained very much of St. Flavian, for calling on the heads of the other monasteries to subscribe his sentence, as a novelty never

(12) Fleury. *t.* 4, *l.* 27, *n.* 28; Orsi. *t* 14. *l.* 52, *n.* 28. (13) Nat. Alex. *t.* 10, *c.* 3, *art.* 13. *sec.* 4. (14) St. Leo, Epis. 20, *al.* 8.

before used in the Church, not even against heretics; but, on the other hand, it was a new thing to find an Abbot chief of a heretical sect, and disseminating his pestilent errors in the monasteries. He also complained that St. Flavian had removed his protests, posted up in Constantinople, against the Council, and which were a tissue of abuse and calumny, as if he had any right to stir up the people against a Council now closed, or to defend his pretended innocence by calumnious libels (15).

50. He next wrote to St. Peter Chrysologus, Bishop of Ravenna, complaining of the judgment of St. Flavian, with the intention of gaining the favour of this holy bishop, who had great influence with the Emperor Valentinian and his mother Placida, who in general resided at Ravenna. St. Peter answered him, that, as he had not received any letter from Flavian, nor heard what that bishop had to say in the matter, he could give no opinion on the controversy, and he exhorts him to read and obey whatever the Pontiff, St. Leo, would write to him: "Above all things we advise you, honourable brother, obediently to attend to whatever is written by his Holiness the Pope, since St. Peter, who lives and presides in his See, affords to those who seek it the truth of Faith." This letter is found in Bernini and Peter Annatus (16). Both Eutyches and St. Flavian wrote afterwards to St. Leo; Eutyches, to complain of the grievances he asserted were inflicted on him by the Council of Constantinople, and St. Flavian, to explain the just cause he had to depose and excommunicate Eutyches. St. Leo having received the letter of Eutyches before that of St. Flavian, wrote to him (17), wondering that he had not already written to him what he thought of the matter, for he could not make out from the letter of Eutyches the reason of his excommunication. He, therefore, ordered him to inform him immediately of the whole transaction, and especially of the erroneous doctrine for which he was condemned, that, as the Emperor wished, an end might be put to this discord and peace restored, especially as Eutyches professed his willingness to be corrected, if it was proved he had erred. St. Flavian answered the Pope, giving him a full account of everything, and, among the rest, that Eutyches, in place of repenting, was only endeavouring to disturb the Church of Constantinople, by wicked libels and petitions to the Emperor, for a revision of the Acts of the Synod at which he was condemned, and making charges to the effect that the Acts were falsified. In fact, on the 8th of April, 449, another assembly was held in Constantinople, by order of the Emperor, and St. Flavian (18) was obliged to present his profession of Faith, in which he declares, that he recognizes in Jesus Christ two natures after the Incarnation, in one Person, and that he did

(15) Orsi, cit. n. 33. (16) Bernin. t. 1, sec. 5, c. 6, p. 510; Petr. Anat. Ap. par ad Theol. l. 4, de Script. Eccl. art. 30. (17) St. Leo, Epis. 20, ap. Orsi, ibid. n. 24, 25; Fleury, n. 31, 32. (18) Liberat. Brevia. c. 11.

not also refuse to say *one nature* of the Divine Word, if the words *incarnate* and *humanized* were also used, and he excommunicated Nestorius and all who divided Jesus Christ into two persons (19). No other matter of importance was decided in that meeting.

51. In the meantime, Dioscorus, Patriarch of Alexandria, at the instigation of Eutyches, and urged on by Chrysaphius, his protector, wrote to the Emperor, that it was necessary to convoke a General Council, and he obtained an order for it through the influence of Chrysaphius. Before we proceed, however, it will be necessary to give an insight into the character of Dioscorus, as we shall have to speak frequently of his wickedness hereafter. He concealed his vices under an exterior of virtue, to obtain the bishopric of Alexandria (20), in which, for his own misfortune, he was successful; he was avaricious, immoral, and furiously violent. When placed on the Episcopal throne of Alexandria, he threw aside all restraint; treated most cruelly those ecclesiastics who were honoured by St. Cyril; some he reduced to beggary, and even burned their houses, and tortured them in prison; others he sent into banishment. He kept improper women in his palace, and publicly bathed with them, to the insufferable scandal of the people. He so persecuted the nephews of St. Cyril, deprived them of all their property, that he drove them as wanderers through the world, while he made a show with their property, distributing it among the bakers and tavern-keepers of the city, that they might sell better bread and wine (21). He was charged with many homicides, and with causing a famine in Egypt by his insatiable avarice. It is even told of him, that a lady having left her property to the hospitals and the monasteries, he ordered it to be distributed among the actors and prostitutes of Alexandria. Hermant asserts (22) that he followed the errors of the Origenists and the Arians: such was the protector of Eutyches. Now to the subject.

52. Theodosius convoked the Council, in Ephesus, for the 1st of August, 449 (it was not held, however, till the 8th), and sent his diploma to Dioscorus, appointing him President, with power to assemble whatever bishops he pleased to try the case of Eutyches. Never, perhaps, before was the world disgraced by such acts of injustice as were committed by Dioscorus in that Synod, which has been justly called, by ecclesiastical writers, the *Latrocinium Ephesinium*, or meeting of robbers at Ephesus; for he, abandoning himself to his innate ferocity, used horrible violence towards the Catholic bishops, and even towards the two Legates, Hilary, Deacon of the Roman Church, and Julius, Bishop of Pozzuoli, sent by St. Leo to represent him at the Council. When these saw the Holy See excluded from the presidency of the Council, in their persons, for

---

(19) Fleury, *t.* 4, *l.* 97, *n.* 31; Nat. Alex. *c.* 3, *art.* 13, *sec.* 6, 7. (20) Hermant, *t.* 1, *c.* 156. (21) Baron. Ann. 444, *n.* 33, ex. Lib. (22) Hermant, loc cit.

Dioscorus, who usurped the first place, they judged it better to take the last place, and to appear no longer as Legates of the Pope, when they saw his authority slighted. Lucretius, the Pope's Legate in the Council of Chalcedon, charged Dioscorus with this after, and called him to answer for his audacity, in holding a Synod in Ephesus, without the authority of the Apostolic See, which never, he said, has been lawful, nor has ever been done; and he could not have made this charge, if Hilary and Julius had been received in the Council as Legates of the Pope (23). Nevertheless, they several times requested that the letter of Pope Leo should be read (24); but Dioscorus would never allow it, calling for other documents to be read, according to his own pleasure; neither would he allow any examination of Articles of Faith, fulminating anathemas against any one who would allude to it. It was quite enough, he said, to hold by what was decided in the Councils of Nice and Ephesus, and, since they had decided that, no novelty should now be introduced to interfere with their decisions (25).

53. Dioscorus now called on Eutyches to read his profession of Faith, and the impious heresiarch anathematized Apollinares and Nestorius, or any one that would assert that the flesh of Jesus Christ came down from heaven. When he came to this passage, Basil of Seleucia interrupted him, and asked him to explain the manner in which he believed the Word had taken human flesh? but he gave him no answer, nor did the heads of the Synod, as they ought to have done, oblige him to explain himself, for this was the principal point of the whole question; for, if the Divine nature destroyed the human nature in the Incarnation, or the human nature was confounded with the Divine nature, as the Eutychians asserted, how could it be said that the Word of God took human flesh? However, without waiting for the answer to the question of Basil, the notary was ordered to proceed with the reading of the document of Eutyches, in which he complained of the sentence passed on him, and concluded by requiring that his persecutors should be punished (26). When this statement of Eutyches was read, St. Flavian said that it was but just that his accuser, Eusebius of Dorileum, should be heard likewise, but not only this was refused, but St. Flavian himself was told that he was not allowed to speak, as the Emperor had given positive orders that none of those who had passed judgment on Eutyches before should be allowed to say a word without leave of the Synod (27).

54. The Acts of the Synod, held by St. Flavian, were then read, and also the two letters of St. Cyril to Nestorius and John of Antioch, in which St. Cyril approved of the expression of the two natures. Eustatius of Beyroot, a partisan of Eutyches, then re-

(23) Liberat. Brevia. c. 12. (24) Orsi, n. 41. (25) Orsi, n. 52. (26) Orsi, n. 53. (27) Orsi, n. 14, l. 32, n. 54.

marked to the Council that St. Cyril, in two other letters written to Acacius of Melitis and Valerian of Iconium, did not use the words, two natures, but the one nature of the Divine Word Incarnate, and thus this Eutychian bishop wished to make it appear that St. Cyril held the same faith as Eutyches; but this was all a calumny against St. Cyril, for the saint, in a thousand passages of his writings, had expressly spoken of the two natures of Christ, and besides the expression, the one nature of the Incarnate Word only meant the *union* in Christ of two distinct natures, the Divine and human. And this was most clearly expressed soon after, in the Council of Chalcedon, in which it was laid down that these words, used first by St. Cyril, and afterwards by St. Flavian, were only used in that sense, and an anathema was pronounced against any one using the expression, " the one nature," with the intention of denying that the flesh of Christ was consubstantial with ours. The votes given in the Council held by St. Flavian were next read, and when the vote of Basil of Seleucia, that two natures should be required in Christ, was read out, all the Egyptians and the monks, followers of Barsuma, cried out: " Let him be cut in two who speaks of two natures in Christ; he is a Nestorian heretic." It was then read out that Eusebius of Dorileum had pressed Eutyches to confess two natures in Christ, and when the same party heard this, they cried out with all their force; " To the pile with Eusebius, let him be burned alive; as he has divided Jesus Christ, let him be cut in two halves himself" (28). Dioscorus being now assured of the suffrages of the bishops, for some adhered to him through liking, and more through terror, called on every one to give his sentence; and thus the faith of Eutyches was approved of, and he was re-established in his dignity, and the monks, his adherents, who were excommunicated by St. Flavian, were again received into communion (29).

55. The great object which Dioscorus had in view, however, was the deposition of St. Flavian and of Eusebius of Dorileum, and he therefore ordered the decree of the Synod antecedent to that of Ephesus to be read, prohibiting, under pain of anathema and deposition, any other Symbol but that of Nice to be used. The intention of the Council, in passing this law, was to reject the malignant Symbol of Theodore of Mopsuestia, in which, as Rabbula, Bishop of Edessa (30), relates, the Nestorian blasphemy was introduced, and it was professed: First.—That the Holy Virgin was not the real Mother of God. Second.—That man was not united to the Word according to the substance, but through good will. Third.—That Jesus Christ ought to be adored but only as the image of God. Fourth.—That the flesh of Jesus Christ availeth nothing. Theodore,

(28) Orsi, *n.* 55. (29) Orsi, *n.* 56; Baron. Ann. 448, *n.* 91, ad 93.
(30) Fleury, *t.* 4, *l.* 26, *n.* 36, in fine.

besides, denied original sin, and on that account, when Julian and his fellow-Pelagians were banished out of Italy by the Pope St. Celestine, they went to Theodore, who, as Marius Mercator informs us, received them kindly. Cassianus (31) also tells us that the Pelagians taught the same errors as Nestorius and Theodore, that is, that Christ was but a mere man, and they meant to prove by that proposition that it was possible for a man to be without original sin, as he was so; and hence they deduced as an inference, that other men might be without sin, likewise, if they wished to be so. But to the point; the intention of the Council then was to reject the Symbol of the impious Theodore, as it was afterwards declared in the fifth Ecumenical Council, in which, as we shall see in the following chapter, the *Three Chapters* were condemned, as was also Theodore and his writings; but it was not the intention of the Council of Ephesus, nor did it ever prohibit the use of other words, besides those used in the Council of Nice, when these expressions are only used to express more clearly the sense of any Catholic dogma, impugned by some new heresy not taken into consideration by the Council of Nice. Still, Dioscorus, intent on the condemnation of St. Flavian and Eusebius, ordered that the Decree of the Council of Ephesus should be read, and then immediately called on the notaries, and without any form of trial, or giving St. Flavian any time to defend himself, ordered one of the notaries to read the sentence of deposition against these two bishops, on the false charge that they had introduced novelties in Faith, and had not adhered to the words of the Symbol of Nice (32). St. Flavian instantly put into the hands of the Legates of the Pope an appeal against the sentence (33). Several bishops, horrified at such a glaring act of injustice, endeavoured to soothe Dioscorus; some of them even throwing themselves at his feet, and embracing his knees, besought him to revoke the sentence, but all to no avail, for he told them he would sooner cut out his own tongue than revoke it; and when they still, in the most pressing manner, continued to implore him to change his mind, he stood up on the steps of the throne and cried out: " Are you then determined to create a sedition; where then are the Counts?" The Counts at once came into the church with a strong body of soldiers, and were joined by the partisans of Dioscorus and the monks of Barsumas, so that the church became a scene of tumult and confusion. The bishops all fled, some to one part of the edifice, some to another, but the doors were all bolted, and guarded, so that no one could escape. Dioscorus then, to give a finishing stroke to this villany, presented a blank paper to the bishops, that they might subscribe the sentence, and those who showed any disposition to refuse, were threatened

(31 Cassian. *l.* 1, de Incar. contra Nestor. *c.* 2 & 3.   (32) Fleury, *l.* 27, *n.* 41.
(33) Orsi, *l.* 33, *n.* 58 ; Baron. Ann. 499, *n.* 92.

with deposition, banishment, and even with death, as partisans of the Nestorian heresy. On all sides shouts arose: " Cut them in pieces if they say there are two natures." The soldiers obliged them to sign their names, and if they refused, beat them with clubs, threatened them with drawn swords, and even wounded some of them, so that the church was sprinkled with their blood. The bishops, thus constrained, finally all signed the sentence of deposition, but said, when the Synod was dissolved, that it was not they, but the soldiers, who deposed St. Flavian; but this excuse went but a little way to justify them, for no Christian, let alone a bishop, should, through fear, condemn an innocent man, or betray the truth (34).

56. The wretch Dioscorus was so enraged at the appeal of St. Flavian, that, not satisfied with having deposed and banished this holy bishop, he laid violent hands on him, and became his executioner, or, at all events, the cause of his death, for he was so blinded with passion, that he struck him on the face, kicked him in the stomach, and throwing him on the ground, trampled on his belly. Timothy Eleurus, and Peter Mongus, who afterwards disgraced the episcopal throne of Alexandria, and the impious Barsumas, who cried out in the Synod: " Kill him, kill him," were also parties to his death, and it is on that account, that when Barsumas presented himself afterwards in the Council of Chalcedon, they cried out: " Turn out the murderer Barsumas; cast the murderer to the beasts." St. Flavian did not die on the spot, but being dragged to prison, and given in the hands of the guards the next day to be conveyed to the place of his banishment, after three days' weary travelling, he arrived at Epipa, a city of Lydia, and then gave up his holy soul into the hands of his Maker. This is the account Cardinal Orsi gives of his death (35), and Fleury and Hermant agree with him in the particulars; and it is on this account the Fathers of the Council of Chalcedon did not scruple to give him the title of Martyr (36). Eusebius of Dorileum escaped, because he was not allowed admission into this impious meeting; he was deposed and condemned to exile, but escaped to Rome, where St. Leo received him into his communion, and retained him with himself, till his departure for the Council of Chalcedon. In the meanwhile, Dioscorus continued to publish anathemas and suspensions against those bishops who he any ways suspected were opposed to the doctrines of Eutyches; he condemned Theodoret, Bishop of Cyrus, as a heretic, in his absence, and proscribed his works, on account of his having written against the anathemas of St. Cyril (37). It is necessary, in order to explain the injustice of condemning Theodoret as a heretic, to give some account of this learned and remarkable man.

(34) Orsi, *n.* 59 & 60. (35) Orsi, *t.* 14, *l.* 32, *n.* 62; Fleury, *t.* 4, *l.* 27, *n.* 41; Hermant, *t.* 1, *c.* 157. (36) Orsi, *t.* 14, *l.* 33, *n.* 62; vide Fleury, *t.* 4, *l.* 67, *n.* 41, *t.* 1; Ber. *p* 552. (37) Orsi, *n.* 68.

57. Cardinal Orsi (38) very justly remarks, that if Theodoret never was so unfortunate as to oppose for some time St. Cyril, the great defender of the Faith, against Nestorius, his name, at the present day, would be venerated like the venerable names of St. Basil, St. Chrystostom, and St. Gregory, whose equal, perhaps, he was both in virtue and learning. He was born in Antioch (39), about the end of the fourth century. After the death of his parents, who were both rich and noble, he sold all his property, and gave it to the poor, reserving nothing for himself. He retired to the solitude of a monastery, and spent the greater part of the day in prayer, and the remainder in the study of literature, both sacred and profane. His master, unfortunately, was Theodore of Mopsuestia, of whose errors we have already spoken (*n.* 48), but he did not infect his disciple with them. He was forced from his solitude, and against his will made Bishop of Cyrus, a small, but very populous See, with eight hundred churches. The desire of assisting the many poor souls in his diocese infected with heresy, overcame his attachment to his solitude, and his repugnance to accept of any dignity, so he gave up his whole soul to the discharge of his pastoral duties, nourishing the piety of his people, and combating the heresies which infected part of his diocese; and he succeeded in rescuing eight villages from the darkness of the heresy of Marcion.

58. On reading the anathematisms of St. Cyril (40), he wrote against them, and in no measured terms, and appeared rather to favour Nestorius than St. Cyril, who laboured to convince him of his mistake. Although he appeared to recognize only one Christ alone, and called the Holy Virgin the Mother of God, still, his arguments would lead us to believe, that he divided Christ into two persons, and gave Mary the title of Mother of God, in the sense of Nestorius, that is, mother of him who was the temple of God. St. Cyril, withal, justified him, and said, that though his mode of expressing himself was rash, that they agreed in Faith, and he therefore writes (41), that he did not wish to fall out with Theodoret, as long as he confessed that God was not separated from human nature, and that Christ was not separated from the Divinity, but was both God and man. On the other hand, Theodoret (42), being in Antioch when the letters of Pope St. Celestine and St. Cyril were received, joined with John, Patriarch of Antioch, and wrote to Nestorius, that he should not disturb the Church, by denying to Mary the title of the Mother of God, because, said he, that cannot be denied without corrupting the truth of the Incarnation of the Word. It cannot be doubted, but that Theodoret was somewhat reprehensible in his writings against the anathematisms of

(38) Orsi, *t.* 12, *l.* 28, *n.* 49. (39) Nat. Alex. *t.* 10, *c.* 4, *n.* 28 ; Orsi, loc. cit. *n.* 50.
(40) Orsi, *l.* 28, *n.* 62. (41) St. Cyril, Apol. cap. (42) Orsi, *t.* 13, *l.* 30, *n.* 66 & seq.

St. Cyril, and the Cabal of Ephesus, and in his defence of Theodore and Nestorius, and those productions were condemned in the second Council of Constantinople; but we should not forget, that he erred, not in holding the doctrines of Nestorius, but in believing that St. Cyril was an upholder of the doctrines of Apollinares; so that when he read (43) St. Cyril's letter to Acacius of Berea, in which the saint clears himself from the imputation of being a favourer of the doctrines of Apollinares, and professes, that he firmly believes that the body of Christ was animated by a reasoning soul, and expresses his detestation of the confusion of the two natures, and declares that he holds the nature of the Word to be impassable, but that Christ suffered according to the flesh; he at once, thinking that St. Cyril had now forsaken the doctrine of Apollinares (44), and no longer believed in the confusion of the two natures, felt quite happy, and said, that St. Cyril now followed the pure doctrine of the Fathers, and wrote him a loving letter, because, as he said, he now recognized in the Incarnation of the Word, one Son alone, and one Christ alone, with the distinction of the two natures; St. Cyril cordially answered him, and this was the commencement of a friendly correspondence between them (45).

59. Theodoret next wrote his work Eranistes (the Beggar), against the Eutychians (46), and, on that account, through the calumnies of Eutyches, he was first confined by the Emperor to his Diocese of Cyrus, and was afterwards deposed by Dioscorus, in the Cabal of Ephesus, but he appealed from this sentence to St. Leo, and subsequently retired to his old monastery, near Apamea (47). He was afterwards recalled from exile, by Marcian (48), and St. Leo declared him innocent, and reinstated him in the See of Cyrus (49). Finally, in the Council of Chalcedon, after publicly anathematizing Nestorius, and all who did not call the Virgin Mary the Mother of God, and divided Jesus Christ into two Sons, he was received by all the Fathers, and declared worthy of being restored to his See (50). It is supposed that he lived to the year 458, and that, towards the end of his life, he composed the treatise on Heretical Fables (51).

60. We now come back to the impious Synod of Ephesus. The majority of the bishops having now subscribed the condemnation of St. Flavian, the few, who refused to lend themselves to this iniquity, were sent into banishment by Dioscorus. These few confessors alone, and Hilary, the Pope's Legate, were the only members who had the courage to protest, and declared that a cabal like that would never be approved of by the Pope, or be received, as it undermined the Apostles' Creed, and that they never would,

(43) Orsi, *t.* 13, *l.* 30, *n.* 12.   (44) Orsi, *n.* 13.   (45) Orsi, *t.* 13, *l.* 30, *n.* 67.
(46) Orsi, *t.* 14, *l.* 32, *n.* 10 & 11.   (47) Orsi, *t.* 14, *l.* 32, *n.* 68 & seq. ad 85.
(48) Orsi, *t.* 14, *l.* 33, *n.* 3.   (49) Orsi, ibid. *n.* 20.   (50) Orsi, ibid. *n.* 70.
(51) Orsi, ibid *n.* 20.

through terror, give up the Faith they professed (52). Dioscorus, in the meanwhile, having now closed the meeting, returned in joy and triumph to Alexandria, and to such a pitch did his arrogance then arrive, that he solemnly published a sentence of excommunication against St. Leo, and partly by cajolery, and partly by terror, obliged about ten bishops, who returned with him to Egypt, to subscribe to it, though they did it weeping, and lamenting the horrible impiety they were called on to perform (53). Orsi (54) says, on the authority of the statement made to the Council of Chalcedon by Theodore, a deacon of Alexandria, that Dioscorus was guilty of this act of madness in Nice, beyond the bounds of Egypt (55).

61. When St. Leo heard of these atrocious proceedings, he wrote to Theodosius, explaining to him the deplorable state to which religion was reduced by Dioscorus, but all in vain, for the Emperor, gained over by his courtiers, in favour of Eutyches, and regardless of the prayer of the Pope, and the sage advices of the Princess Pulcheria, instead of punishing the efforts the Eutychians were making, re-established Eutyches himself in all his honours, condemned the memory of St. Flavian, and approved of all that was done in Ephesus (56). He, therefore, wrote to St. Leo, that as the Council of Ephesus had examined everything according to the rules of justice and of the Faith, and as those unworthy of the dignity of the priesthood were deprived of it, so those who were worthy were re-established in the grade they before held (57). Such was the answer of Theodosius; but God, who always watches over his flock, though he sometimes appears to sleep, soon after removed this prince out of the world, in the year 450, the 59th of his age; previous to his death, however, as Orsi remarks (58), he listened to the remonstrances of his holy sister, and gave several proofs of his sorrow for having favoured Eutyches. As he died without issue he left the Empire to his sister, St. Pulcheria, whose piety and wisdom soon healed the disorders caused by the weakness of her brother, in allowing himself to be governed by his courtiers. Though no one could be found more worthy to govern the Empire alone than she was, still her subjects were anxious that she should marry, and give them a new Emperor. She was, however, now advanced in years, and besides, had made a vow of perpetual virginity; anxious, therefore, to please her subjects, and at the same time remain faithful to her promises to God, she gave her hand to the Senator Marcian, of whose probity and regard for herself, personally, she was perfectly convinced, and who, she well knew, was better qualified than any other to govern the Empire; and his subsequent conduct proved, that her opinion of his good-

(52) Orsi, *t.* 14, *l.* 13, *n.* 61. (53) Hermant, *t.* 1, *c.* 157; Fleury, *t.* 4, *l.* 27, *n.* 41.
(54) Orsi, *t.* 14, *l.* 32, *n.* 97. (55) Libel. Theo. æt. Con. Chal. *v.* Fleury, *l.* cit.
(56) Hermant, *t.* 1, *c.* 157. (57) Orsi, *l.* 32, *n.* 90. (58) Orsi, loc. cit. *n.* 101.

ness was not unfounded. In the beginning of his career, this great man was only a private soldier, but his wisdom and prudence elevated him to the senatorial rank (59).

SEC. II.—THE COUNCIL OF CHALCEDON.

62. A Council is assembled in Chalcedon, under the Emperor Marcian and the Pope St. Leo. 63. The cause of Dioscorus is tried in the first Session. 64. He is condemned. 65. Articles of Faith defined, in opposition to the Eutychian Heresy, according to the Letter of St. Leo. 66. Privileges granted by the Council to the Patriarch of Constantinople. 67. Refused by St. Leo. 68. Eutyches and Dioscorus die in their obstinacy. 69. Theodosius, Head of the Eutychians in Jerusalem. 70. His Cruelty. 71. Death of St. Pulcheria and of Marcian. 72. Timothy Eleurus intruded into the See of Alexandria. 73. Martyrdom of St. Proterius, the true Bishop. 74. Leo succeeds Marcian in the Empire. 75. Eleurus is expelled from the See of Alexandria, and Timothy Salofacialus is elected. 76. Zeno is made Emperor; he puts Basiliscus to Death. Eleurus commits Suicide. 77. St. Simon Stilites. 78. His happy Death. 79. Peter the Stammerer intruded into the See of Alexandria.

62. MARCIAN was proclaimed Emperor on the 24th of August, in the year 450, and on assuming the imperial power, recognizing in his elevation the work of God, he at once began to advance His glory, and try every means to banish heresy from his dominions. With that intention he wrote two letters to Pope Leo, praying him to convoke a Council, and preside at it in person, or, at all events, to send his Legates, and strive to give peace to the Church. St. Pulcheria wrote to St. Leo likewise, and informed him of the translation of the body of St. Flavian to Constantinople, and also that Anatolius, the Patriarch of that city, had already subscribed the letter he (the Pope) had sent to St. Flavian, against the heresy of Eutyches; that all who had been banished were now recalled; and she prayed him to do what was in his power to have the Council celebrated (1). The Pope was highly delighted that what he sought for so anxiously, during the reign of Theodosius, was now in his power, but he requested that the Council should be put off for a time, for the Huns, under Attila, overran Italy, and the bishops could not, with safety, proceed to the place of meeting. The barbarians were soon after defeated by the Franks, and St. Leo now set about convening the Council, and at once sent as his Legates to Constantinople, Pascasinus, Bishop of Lillibeum, in Sicily; Julian, of Cos; Lucentius, of Ascoli; and Basil, and Boniface, priests of the Roman Church (2). The Emperor, at first, was desirous that the Council should be held in Nice, but for just reasons he was satisfied afterwards that it should be transferred to Chalcedon. This Council was celebrated, in the year 451, in the great Church of St. Euphemia, Virgin and Martyr; and St. Leo (3) says, it was attended by six hundred bishops; but Liberatus and Marcellinus (4) tell us the

---

(59) Hermant, t. 1, c. 158. (1) Fleury, t. 4, l. 27, n. 48, in fin. (2) Orsi, t. 14, l. 35, n. 28 & 29. (3) St. Leo, Epis. 52. (4) Lib. Brev. c. 13, & Mar. in Chron.

number was six hundred and thirty; and Nicephorus (5) raises it to six hundred and thirty-six.

63. The first matter the Council deliberated on in the first Session, held on the 8th of October, 451, was the examination of the conduct of the impious Dioscorus. He went to the Synod with the hope that his party would be still all-powerful through the bishops who subscribed the acts of the Cabal of Ephesus, but Pascasinus, standing up, said that Dioscorus should not take his seat in the Council, but should present himself as a criminal, to be judged: and seeing him then seated among the bishops, he called on the judges and the Senate to have him expelled, otherwise he and his colleagues would leave the Council. The imperial ministers demanded from the Legate his reasons for calling for the expulsion of Dioscorus, and then Lucentius, another of the Legates, answered that he had dared to summon a Synod, without the authority of the Apostolic See, which never was lawful, nor ever before done (6). Dioscorus then took his seat in the middle of the church, and Eusebius, of Dorileum, likewise, as his accuser, on account of the sentence pronounced against himself and against St. Flavian, and he demanded that the Acts of the Council of Ephesus should be read. The letter of the Emperor for the convocation of the Council was first read, and Theodoret, on account of his writings against St. Cyril, was at first prevented from taking his place among the Fathers; but as St. Leo and the Emperor Marcian had re-established him in his See, he was introduced as one of the members. His enemies, however, immediately began tumultuously to oppose his admission, so the imperial officers ordered him to sit also in the middle as an accuser, but without prejudice to his rights, and he was afterwards re-established in his See by the Council itself, after anathematizing the errors of Nestorius, and subscribing the definition of Faith, and the Epistle of the Pope, St. Leo (7). The Acts of the *Latrocinium* of Ephesus were next read, and the Profession of Faith of St. Flavian, and the imperial judges asked the Council if it was Catholic. The Legates answered in the affirmative, as it coincided with the letter of St. Leo. Many of the bishops then, who sat with Dioscorus's party, went over to the other side, but he, though left alone almost, as only a few Egyptian bishops held on to him, still persevered in maintaining the Eutychian errors, and asserting that after the union of the Divinity with the humanity of Christ we should not say those were two natures, but only one in the Incarnate Word. When the reading of the Acts was finished, the imperial minister declared that the innocence of St. Flavian and Eusebius of Dorileum was fully established, and that those bishops who had caused them to be deposed should undergo the same sentence themselves; and thus the first Synod was concluded (8).

(5) Vide Nat. Alex. *t.* 10, *c.* 4, *a.* 13, *s.* 17.   (6) Acta, Con. Chal.   (7) Orsi, *l.* 23, *n* 45, 47 & 70.   (8) Orsi, ibid. *n.* 49.

64. The second Synod was held on the 10th of October, to decide on the Faith that should be held; the two creeds of Nice and Constantinople, the letter of St. Leo, and the two letters of St. Cyril were read, and the bishops then exclaimed: "We all believe the same. Peter has spoken by the mouth of Leo; anathema to him who does not believe likewise." A petition, presented by Eusebius, against the injustice practised by Dioscorus was then read, but he had left the church. Three bishops were sent to summon him before the Council, but on various false pretences he refused to appear, though cited three times. The Legates then, in the name of the Pope, declared him excommunicated and deposed from his bishopric, and all the bishops, both verbally and in writing, confirmed the sentence, which was sanctioned, likewise, by Marcian and St. Pulcheria (9). Some monks of the Eutychian party now presented themselves before the Synod; the principal among them were Carosus, Dorotheus, and Maximus. When these and their party entered the church (and among them was Barsumas, at whose appearance the bishops all cried out: "Out with the murderer of St. Flavian"), they impudently demanded that Dioscorus and the other bishops who came with him from Egypt, should be admitted as members of the assembly, and in case this demand was rejected, they would separate themselves, they said, from the communion of the Council. They received for answer, that in that case they would be deposed, and that if they persevered in disturbing the Church, they would be punished, as creators of sedition, by the secular power; but, as they pertinaciously persevered, the Council gave them thirty days for consideration, at the expiration of which they would be punished as they deserved (10).

65. After this the bishops subscribed the Dogmatical Epistle of St. Leo, and set about definitively arranging the articles of Faith in opposition to the heresy of Eutyches; a formula composed by Anatolius, Patriarch of Constantinople, and some other bishops, was read, but was not received by the Pope's Legates (11), for it said that Christ was *in* two natures, but it did not say that he was *of* two natures. The bishops, who pertinaciously declared that nothing should be added to the ancient symbols, were thus reasoned with by the judges; Dioscorus, said they, is satisfied that it should be declared that Christ is *in* two natures, but will not allow that he is *of* two natures; on the other hand, St. Leo says that there are in Christ two natures united, without confusion or divisibility, whom, then, will you follow, Leo or Dioscorus? Then all cried out: "We believe as Leo believes; he has properly expounded the Faith; whosoever contradicts it is a Eutychian." The judges then added: "So you agree to the definition, according to the judgment of our

(9) Nat. Alex. *t.* 10, *c.* 3, *ar.* 13, *s.* 17; Orsi, ibid. *n.* 50 & 55. (10) Orsi, *t.* 14, *l.* 33, *n.* 59, 60.   (11) Or-i, *t.* 14, *l.* 33, *n.* 62.

Holy Father, that there are in Christ two natures, united without confusion or division." Thus the clamours were finally stopped, and a formula adopted (12), in which it was declared, that the Fathers took for the rule of their definition the symbols of the two Councils of Nice and Constantinople, which were also the rule for that adopted in the Council of Ephesus, in which Pope Celestine and St. Cyril presided; in continuation it was said, that although the forementioned symbols were sufficient for the full knowledge of the Faith, nevertheless, as the inventors of new heresies had adopted new expressions, and corrupting the doctrine of the Mystery of the Incarnation, some of them denied to the Virgin the title of the Mother of God, and others taught that the nature of the Divinity and of the humanity were one and the same, and that the Divine nature was passible in Christ, therefore the holy Council confirmed both the Faith of the three hundred and eighteen Fathers of Nice, and of the one hundred and fifty Fathers of Constantinople; and, as the Council of Constantinople has added some words to the Creed of Nice, not because it was deficient in anything essential, but more clearly to explain the doctrine regarding the Holy Ghost, in opposition to those who denied the Divinity of the third Person of the Trinity, thus, with a similar intention, the Council of Chalcedon, in opposition to those who wish to corrupt the doctrine of the Incarnation, and say, that one nature alone was born of the Virgin, or deny two natures to Christ, besides the two forenamed symbols admits the synodical letter of the Blessed Cyril, and lastly, the letter of St. Flavian, against the errors of Eutyches, which corresponds with the letter of St. Leo, in which these are condemned, who divide the "Only-begotten" into two Sons; and those who attribute the Passion to his Divine nature; and those who, of the Divinity and the humanity, make one nature alone; and those who say the flesh of Christ is celestial, or of any other substance than flesh; and those who blasphemously teach, that before the union there were two natures in Christ, but only one after the union. The Council, therefore, teaches that there is only one Lord Jesus Christ in two natures, without division, without change, and without confusion; that the difference of the two natures was never removed on account of the union, but that each remains properly the same, both one and the other concurring in one person alone, and in one substance, so that Jesus Christ is not divided into two persons, but is always the same, only Son, and only-begotten Word, God. The Council finally prohibited the teaching or holding of any other Faith, or any other symbol to be composed for the use of the Catechumens, renewing after this manner the order of the Council of Ephesus, notwithstanding the abuse Dioscorus made of it. When the definitive decree was read, it was uniformly received

(12) Fleury, *t.* 4, *l.* 28, *n.* 21; & Orsi, loc. cit. *n.* 61.

by all the Fathers, and first the Legates, and next all the Metropolitans, put their signatures to it (13).

66. When all these matters had been defined, the Council made other regulations, and especially in the sixteenth and last Session, by the twenty-eighth Canon, the privilege of ordaining the Metropolitans of Pontus, of Asia, and of Thrace, who were before subject to the Patriarch of Antioch, was confirmed to Anatolius, Patriarch of Constantinople. This privilege was already granted to the Bishop of Constantinople by a Council of one hundred and fifty bishops, held in that city, in the time of Theodosius the Great, on the plea that as Constantinople had become the seat of empire, and the second Rome in the East, it was only proper that it should be decorated with the primacy of honour, second only to Rome itself, especially as it was already in possession of the honour for sixty or seventy years past. The Legate Pascasinus, Bishop of Lilibeum, opposed this Canon. It was, he said, contrary to the ancient Canons of the Church, and especially to the sixth Canon of the Council of Nice, in which it was recognized that the Church of Alexandria, Antioch, and Jerusalem, took precedence of Constantinople, not to speak of the Church of Rome, which always enjoyed the primacy; but notwithstanding the opposition, the Fathers remained firm to the arrangement they decreed (14).

67. The bishops then wrote to St. Leo, giving him a statement of all that was done in the Council, and asking for his confirmation of their proceedings. In their Synodical epistle they recognize the Pope as the faithful interpreter of St. Peter, and acknowledge that he presided at the Synod as head over the members. They first praise his epistle, and next inform him of the sentence fulminated against Dioscorus, on account of his obstinacy, and the re-union of the repentant bishops, and all these things, they said, were effected with the assistance of the Pontifical Vicars. They made some other regulations, they said, on the presumption that his Holiness would confirm them, and especially they confirmed the primacy of honour to the Archbishop of Constantinople, for the reasons already stated (15). Besides this Synodical letter, the Emperor Marcian, St. Pulcheria, and Anatolius, wrote without the least delay to St. Leo, begging him, notwithstanding the opposition of the Legate, to confirm the twenty-eighth Canon of the Council in favour of the See of Constantinople (16); but, although he was extremely desirous of obliging Marcian and St. Pulcheria, still he never would agree to the violation of the Canons of the Council of Nice, and he answered them that the prerogatives of the See of Antioch should be preserved (17).

68. Before we go any further we shall relate the fate of Eutyches

(13) Orsi, *t.* 14, *l.* 33, *n.* 66. (14) Orsi, *t.* 14, *l.* 33, *n.* 78 & 79. (15) Orsi, *l.* cit. *n.* 84. (16) Orsi, *l.* cit. *n.* 82 & 83. (17) Fleury, *t.* 14, *l.* 28, *n.* 33; Orsi, *n.* 86.

and Dioscorus. Eutyches was banished by order of the Emperor, in 450, but being confined in the vicinity of the city of Constantinople, St. Leo (Ep. 75, edit. Rom.) wrote to St. Pulcheria (18), and afterwards to Marcian (Epis. 107), that he heard from Julian of Cos, that even in his exile he continued to infect the people with his pestilent doctrines, and continued to disseminate his errors; he therefore besought the Emperor to banish him to some deserted neighbourhood. The Emperor complied with this request of the Pope; Eutyches was banished to a distant place, and there died as he lived in sinful obstinacy (19). Dioscorus was banished to Gangres, in Paphlagonia, and soon after died without repentance, on the 4th of September, 454, leaving some impious writings, composed by him, in favour of the Eutychian heresy, which were afterwards condemned to be burnt by the Emperor Marcian (20).

69. The followers of Eutyches and Dioscorus continued for many ages to disturb the Church, and there were several among these leaders of perdition who excited others, and caused a great deal of harm. The Council of Chalcedon was scarcely over, when some monks from Palestine, who refused submission to the decree of the Council, excited several other monks of that country to join them, proclaiming that the Council had taken the part of Nestorius, obliging the faithful to adore two persons in Christ, as they had decided on two natures. The chief of these was a monk of the name of Theodosius (21), who was expelled by his bishop from his monastery on account of his vices, but still retained the monastic habit. He succeeded in gaining over to his side a great many monks in Palestine, through favour of Eudoxia, the widow of the Emperor Theodosius, who after his death retired to that country, to spend the remainder of her days (22). I have said he gained over a great many monks, but not all of them, for, as Evagrius (23) relates, there were very many among those solitaries who led a most holy life, and we cannot, therefore, believe that all followed the impious Theodosius. When Juvenal returned from the Council to his See of Jerusalem he strove in vain to bring these blinded men to reason, but instead of succeeding they not only did not repent, but had the audacity to attempt to force him to anathematize the Council and St. Leo, and, on his refusal, collected a mob of the most depraved characters and took possession of Jerusalem; they burned several houses, killed a number of persons, opened the prisons, and closed the gates of the city to prevent the escape of Juvenal, and then proceeded to elect the wretch Theodosius Bishop of the See (24).

70. When Theodosius was thus so iniquitously placed in the episcopal throne of Jerusalem he endeavoured to have Juvenal assassi-

(18) Orsi, t. 14, l. 33, n. 4; Fleury, ibid. l. 28, n. 55. (19) Berni, t. 1, c. 6, p. 584.
(20) Orsi, t. 14, l. 33, n. 55, in fin. 133. (21) Evag. l. 2, c. 5. (22) Ap. Orsi, t. 14, l. 35, n. 91. (23) Evag. l. 1, c. 31. (24) Orsi, l. cit. n. 90.

nated, and employed a wretch for that purpose; but this assassin, as he could not come at Juvenal, who escaped to Constantinople, joined some other wretches along with him, and killed St. Saverianus, Bishop of Schytopolis (commemorated in the Roman Martyrology, on the 21st of February), and some of his adherents. He next set about establishing himself in his usurped See, by persecuting all who opposed his tyranny; some he caused to be cruelly tormented, he burned the houses of others, and, in particular, he put to death a deacon of the name of Athanasius, and not satisfied with his murder had his body dragged through the city and cast to the dogs. Athanasius is commemorated in the Martyrology, on the 5th of July (25). He next set out on a visitation through the Dioceses of the Patriarchate, accompanied by the monks of his party, and many others of dissipated characters, who spread desolation and destruction wherever they went. He drove several bishops from their churches, and he even had some of them killed, and put his own partisans in their Sees; one of these, Theodotus, he ordained Bishop of Joppa, and another, Peter of Iberia, Bishop of Majuma; and it was from one of these afterwards that the impious Eleurus, the usurper of the See of Alexandria, received consecration (26). When Marcian was informed of the tyranny and insolence of Theodosius and his monks he appeased the sedition by proclaiming a pardon to all who would return to the obedience of the Church, and when he saw himself abandoned by his followers he privately fled. After various wanderings he came to the convent of Sinai and begged the monks to receive him, but they refused, so he fled on to Arabia, and concealed himself in the solitudes of that region. His usurpation lasted only a year and eight months, from the beginning of the year 452, till August, 453, when Juvenal returned to Jerusalem, and again took possession of his See (27).

71. About this time, that is in the year 453, St. Pulcheria died; though the learned have agreed as to the year, they have not as to the day of her death; but the Greeks in their Menelogues, and the Latins in their Martyrologies, celebrate her festival on the 10th of September. St. Leo, in one of his Epistles (Ep. 90), says in her praise, that she was possessed of the royal power, and the sacerdotal learning and spirit, with which she offered to God a perpetual sacrifice of praise: and to the zeal of this holy Empress he ascribed the stability of the Faith against the heresies of Nestorius and Eutyches. She preserved her virginity in marriage, and by her example induced her sisters also to consecrate themselves to God. She built many hospitals, founded several monasteries, and erected a great number of churches, especially in honour of the Divine Mother, and the Church soon venerated her as a saint (28). Four years after, in

(25) Orsi, *t.* 14, *l.* 33, *n.* 94.   (26) Orsi, *n.* 111.   (27) Orsi, cit. loc. 33, *n.* 131.
(28) Orsi, *t.* 15, *l.* 34, *n.* 12 & 13.

the year 467, the Emperor Marcian died. St. Leo calls him a prince of blessed memory, and the Greeks celebrate his festival on the 17th of February. We have already seen how great was his piety, and with what fervour he opposed every enemy of the Faith (29).

72. We shall now speak of the principal followers of Eutyches. The second hero of iniquity was Timothy Eleurus, a priest, but who before his ordination wore the monastic habit, though merely as a mask of piety. He was of a most ambitious character, so that scarcely had he heard of the deposition of Dioscorus, when he considered he had pretensions to the Diocese of Alexandria, but when St. Proterius was elected in place of Dioscorus, he was filled with rage, and began to declaim against the Council of Chalcedon. He succeeded in getting over to his side four or five bishops and some monks, infected like himself with the errors of Apollinares, and thus had the boldness to separate himself from the communion of Proterius. When Marcian was informed of this schism he endeavoured to extinguish it, but could not succeed, so St. Proterius assembled a Synod of all Egypt, and condemned Eleurus, Peter Mongos his companion, and those few bishops and monks who adhered to him. With all that St. Proterius was obliged to be constantly on his guard against him, although he was sent into banishment by the Emperor, and only with difficulty saved his life during the reign of the Emperor Marcian (30). At the Emperor's death he renewed his pretensions, set at nought the decree of banishment he laboured under, returned to Egypt, and endeavoured to drive St. Proterius from the Church of Alexandria. He concealed himself in a monastery of Alexandria, and to induce the monks to join his party he used to go about their cells in the night time, telling them in a feigned voice that he was an angel sent from heaven to admonish them to separate themselves from Proterius, and elect Timothy Eleurus for their bishop. Having by these schemes gained over many monks to his side, he sent them into Alexandria to excite the people against St. Proterius and the Council of Chalcedon. When all was prepared, and the people sufficiently excited, he came forth into the city, accompanied by his schismatical bishops, Peter Mongos, his monks, and several other monks, accomplices of his schism, and caused himself to be proclaimed bishop in the church. He immediately got himself consecrated by two bishops of his party, and at once began to ordain deacons, priests, and bishops for the Egyptian churches, and gave orders that all those ordained by St. Proterius should be expelled, unless they attached themselves to his party (31).

73. Count Dionisius, the military commander of the province,

(29) Orsi, *t.* 15, *l.* 34, *n.* 12 & 13,   (30) Orsi, *t.* 14, *l.* 33, *n.* 105.   (31) Orsi, *t.* 15, *l.* 34, *n.* 15; Fleury, *t.* 4, *l.* 29, *n.* 2.

on hearing this came to Alexandria, and finding that Timothy had left the city, took measures to prevent his return. His partisans were outrageous at hearing this, and sought St. Proterius to take away his life; this was on Good Friday, the 29th of March, in the year 457. When Proterius saw the outbreak he took refuge in the baptistery of the church, but the schismatics, regardless both of the sanctity of the day and the age of this sainted pastor, broke into the baptistery, and finding St. Proterius there in prayer, gave him several wounds and killed him with a blow of a sword. They were not even satisfied with his death; they tied a rope to his body and exposed it in the street before all the people, proclaiming that that was the body of Proterius. They next dragged the body through the whole city, and tore it in pieces, then tore out the entrails and devoured them, and the remainder of the body they burned and cast the ashes to the wind. Eleurus, who in all probability was the mover of this tragic occurrence, now more proud than ever, gave a public festival in rejoicing for the death of St. Proterius, and prohibited the sacrifice of the Mass to be offered up for him; and even to manifest more strongly the hatred he had for the holy bishop, he caused all the episcopal chairs in which he had sat to be broken and burned, and all the altars on which he had celebrated to be washed with sea-water; he persecuted all his family and relations, and even seized on his paternal property; he took his name out of the dyptichs of the church, and substituted his own name and that of Dioscorus, but with all that he could not prevent the entire Church from venerating Proterius as a saint and martyr (32). The Greek Church has enrolled him among the Martyrs on the 28th of February. Eleurus now began to exercise all the episcopal functions; he distributed the property of the Church just as his fancy led him among his partisans, and he even had the temerity to anathematize the sacred Council of Chalcedon, together with all those who received it, and especially the Pope St. Leo, Anatolius, and the other Catholic bishops, declaring that this Council had favoured Nestorius. He also persecuted the monasteries of monks and nuns who adhered to the Council. In the commencement of his career he had but few bishops partisans, but he quickly ordained others, and sent them abroad to drive the Catholic bishops out of their churches (33), but he made an unhappy end of it, as we shall see hereafter (n. 76), committing suicide.

74. Marcian was succeeded in the Empire by Leo, in the year 459, who followed his predecessor's example in vigorous opposition to the heretics, especially the Eutychians: he therefore promulgated an edict through all the East, confirming all the laws passed by his predecessors, and especially the law of Marcian in de-

(32) Orsi, n. 16, &c.; Baron. An. 457, n. 28.   (33) Orsi, t. 15, l. 33, n. 17, & Fleury, t. 4, l 29, n 2.

fence of the Council of Chalcedon. As he found that the followers of Eutyches were the most troublesome to the Church, he considered, acting on the advice of some of his councillors, that it would be well to convoke a new Synod to put a final stop to all controversy. He therefore wrote to the Pope that he considered it would be advantageous to the Church and satisfactory to the recusants, if the Decrees of the Council of Chalcedon were re-examined (34). St. Leo, however, enlightened him on the point, and besought him in the name of the whole Church not to allow the authority of the Council to be called in doubt, or that to be re-examined which had already been decided with such exactitude; there never would be wanting persons, he said, to cavil at the decisions of any Synod, for it is always the practice of heretics to re-examine dogmas of Faith already established, with the intention of obscuring the truth. The Emperor, convinced of the truth of the Pontiff's reasons, thought no more of a new Council. In the following year, 453, he wrote again to the Pope that a great many Eutychians were desirous of being instructed in the truth of the Faith, and were disposed to retract their errors as soon as they would be convinced of their falsehood, and they therefore prayed that at least a conference might be held between them and the Catholics, to which the Pope's own Legates might come. St. Leo in answer promised to send his Legates for the good of religion, but he besought the Emperor totally to set his face against the conference, for he again explained to him that the only intention the heretics had was to throw doubt on what was already definitively settled (35).

75. Leo, in fact, sent Legates to urge on the Emperor to banish Eleurus from Alexandria, where he impiously persevered in persecuting the Church, and he succeeded at last, for the Emperor published an edict against Eleurus, and gave orders to Stila, commander of the troops in Egypt, to drive him out of the city and banish him to Gangres in Paphlagonia, where Dioscorus had been banished before, and ended his days. Eleurus remained there for some time, but as he continued to excite disturbances by holding schismatical meetings, the Emperor confined him in the Crimea, where he was kept till the year 476, when Basiliscus usurped the Empire. Before he was sent to exile he obtained permission, through some of his friends, to come to Constantinople, and feigning himself a Catholic, obtained pardon, and was restored to the See of Alexandria. When St. Leo was informed of this he wrote to the Emperor (36) that although the profession of Faith made by Eleurus might be sincere, yet the horrible crimes he committed would render him eternally unworthy of the bishopric (37). The Emperor then gave orders that no matter what took place, he should

(34) Orsi, *t.* 15, *l.* 34, *n.* 18 & 19.   (35) Orsi, loc. cit. *n.* 48.   (36) St. Leo, Epis. 137, al. 99.   (37) Fleury, *t.* 4, *l.* 29, *n.* 13; Orsi, *n.* 61 & 62.

be banished out of Alexandria, and another bishop elected in his place. This order was executed, and by common consent of the clergy and people, Timothy Salofacialus was chosen, a man of sound faith and virtuous life, and totally different from his predecessor.

76. The Emperor Leo died in 474, and was succeeded by his nephew Leo the Younger. He was crowned, but dying soon after, was succeeded by his father Zeno; but during Zeno's reign Basiliscus, a relation of Leo Augustus, and a Roman general, seized on the Empire in the year 476. He was a follower of the Arian heresy, and he therefore recalled Eleurus from exile, in which he had now spent eighteen years, and sent him back to Alexandria, to take possession of that See (38). Zeno, however, regained his throne, by means of the generals who before betrayed him, and banished Basiliscus, who held the Empire a year and a half, into Cappadocia, and there shut him up in a tower with his wife, Zenonida, and his child, and starved him to death, and sent orders, at the same time, that Eleurus should be again banished; but it was told him that the unfortunate man was now decrepit with years, so he allowed him to die in his native place, Alexandria. He gave orders, however, that he should be deprived of the government of the Church, and that Salofacialus should be reinstated (39), but before these commands were received in Egypt, Eleurus had ceased to live, for he cut short his days by poison, under the dread of being again banished from Alexandria. His followers said that he had foretold the day of his death (40), but there is nothing wonderful in that, when he died by his own hand (41).

77. In this same year, 459, died that great saint, Simon Stilites, the wonder of the world. The Innovators deride the life of this great saint, especially the Protestant Mosheim and his annotator, Archibald M'Lain (42). They say that St. Simon Stilites, to get nearer to heaven, even in the flesh, built his column; and they assert, that the whole story of his life is nothing but a romance invented by certain ecclesiastical writers. But, in the erudite works of the learned priest Julius Selvaggi, whom I before lauded, it is proved (*Note* 75), that the life of St. Simon is not nonsense, but a prodigy of holiness. There can be no doubt of the authenticity of his history, as Cardinal Orsi (43) proves by many authorities, both ancient and modern, as Evagrius (44), Theodoret (45), the ancient writers of the lives of St. Theodosius, St. Ausentius, and of Eutinius, Fleury (46), the erudite Canon Mazzocchi (47), and several others; so that it would be mere rashness to doubt it. As St.

(38) Fleury, *t.* 4, *l.* 29, *n.* 45. (39) Orsi, *t.* 15, *l.* 35, *n.* 66 & 68. (40) Liberat. Breviar. *c.* 16. (41) Fleury, *l.* 29, *n.* 49 ; cum Gennad. de Scrip. Ecclesias. *n.* 80. (42) Mosheim, Hist. Ecclesias. *cen.* v. *p.* 2, *c.* 5, *n.* 12; M'Lain, ibid. (43) Orsi, *t.* 12, *l.* 27, *n.* 14. (44) Evagrius, *l.* 1, *c.* 33. (45) Theod. Philoch. *c.* 26. (46) Fleury, *t.* 4, *l.* 29, *n.* 7. (47) Mazzocchi, *t.* 3, in Com. in Cal.; Neop. *p.* 585.

Simon was a great defender of the Church against the errors of the Eutychians, it will not be irrelevant to give here a short account of his life. He was born in the village of Sisan, on the frontiers of Syria, or, as Theodoret says, of Aria. Up to the age of thirteen, he kept his father's sheep, but after that he gave himself entirely up to God, and lived in several monasteries; but even the austere lives of the monks did not satisfy him, so he accustomed himself to live alone on the top of a column he had built. Moved by a particular divine instinct, he several times changed from one pillar to another, but the last one was forty cubits high, and on that he lived for thirty years till his death, exposed to the sun of summer and the snows of winter. This pillar was so narrow at the top, that he had scarcely room on it. He only ate once a-week, and spent several Lents in the year without any food at all. His only employment was prayer. Besides other exercises of piety, he made a thousand inclinations every day, so performed that he touched his feet with his head, and this caused a great ulcer on his belly, and three of the vertebræ of his spine were displaced, and he had painful ulcers in his thighs, which bled a great deal. The holy monks of Egypt, dreading lest a life of such penance might be dictated only by some extravagant notions, and wishing to test his obedience, and see by that whether it was pleasing to God, sent him a command to come down from his pillar. When the saint heard the word obedience, he immediately prepared himself to descend, but the messenger then said, as he had been instructed: Stop where you are, Simon, for we now know that it is the will of God that you should live on this pillar (48). I pass over many wonderful things in his holy and penitential life, but the most wonderful thing of all was to see the thousands of conversions this unlettered saint wrought from this pillar,—not alone of sinners and heretics, but even of the pagans themselves. People from the most remote regions came to the foot of his column, for his fame had extended through the world. Some he brought out of the darkness of infidelity to the light of faith,—others he led from the ruin of their sins to a holy life; many he saved from the pestilence of heresy—especially of that of Eutyches, which then infested the Church to a great extent. He wrote a most powerful letter to the Emperor Theodosius (49), praying him to labour with all his might for the defence of the Council of Chalcedon.

78. The death of St. Simon was just as stupendous as his life (50). He died in the year 449, and the time of his death was revealed to him forty years previously. Just before his death, a dreadful earthquake took place at Antioch; so the people all crowded round the pillar of the servant of God to beg his prayers in that awful

(48) Orsi, t. 12, l. 17, n. 14, infra ex Theod. exc. l. 2. (49) Evagrius, l. 2, c. 20. (50) Orsi, t. 15, l. 34 & 57.

calamity, and it would appear as if God had purposely collected so many persons together, that they might be witnesses of his holy death, and honour his remains. His last sickness lasted five days; and, on the day of his death, the 2nd of September, he recommended to God all his disciples then present. He then made three genuflections, and raised his eyes in ecstasy three times to heaven. The immense multitude, who surrounded him and came to witness his happy transit, all cried out with a loud voice for his benediction. The saint then looked round to the four parts of the world, raised up his hands, recommended them to God, and blessed them. He again raised his eyes to heaven, struck his breast three times, laid his head on the shoulder of one of his disciples, and calmly expired. His sacred body was brought to Antioch, which was four miles distant. The coffin was borne by bishops and priests, and innumerable torches blazed and censors burned around. Martirius, Bishop of Antioch, and several other bishops, were in the procession. The General Ardaburius, at the head of 6,000 soldiers, twenty-one counts, and many tribunes, and the magistracy of the city, also attended. When the sacred remains were brought into the city, they were buried in the great church commenced by Constantine and finished by Constans, and his was the first body laid there. A magnificent church, described by Evagrius, was afterwards built near his pillar (51). St. Simon had a perfect imitator in St. Daniel, who also lived on a pillar, and was a powerful defender of the Church against the partisans of Eutyches (52). These are miracles which the Catholic faith alone produces, and which are never seen among heretics. Plants of this sort cannot grow in a soil cursed by God;—they can only take root in that Church where the true faith is professed.

79. We will now revert to the impious heroes of the Eutychian heresy. When Timothy Eleurus died, the heretical bishops of the province, by their own authority, chose in his place Peter Mongos, or Moggos, that is, the "Stammerer" (53). He was before archdeacon, and he was consecrated at night by one schismatical bishop alone. The Emperor Zeno, when informed of this, determined not to let it pass unpunished; he therefore wrote to Antemius, Governor of Egypt, to punish the bishop who ordained Mongos, and to drive Mongos himself out of Alexandria, and to restore Timothy Salofacialus to his See. This was in 477, and the Emperor's orders were immediately executed (54). Salofacialus having died in the year 482, John Thalaia was elected in his place; but as he was not on terms with Acacius, Bishop of Constantinople, that prelate worked on the Emperor to banish him, and place Mongos once more in the See of Alexandria. He succeeded in his plans,

(51) Orsi, cit., n. 57.   (52) Orsi, t. 15, l. 35, n. 62.   (53) Orsi, t. 15, l. 35, n. 66, 68.   (54) Fleury, l. 29, n. 49, ex Gennad. de Scrip. Eccles. n. 80.

by representing to the Emperor that Mongos was a favourite with the people of Alexandria, and that, by placing him in that See, it would not be difficult to unite in one Faith all the people of that Patriarchate. The Emperor was taken with the suggestion, and wrote to the Pope Simplicius to re-establish Mongos in the Alexandrian See; but the Pope told him he never would put his hand to such an arrangement. The Emperor was very angry at this refusal, and wrote to Pergamius, Duke of Egypt, and to Apollonius, the Governor, to drive John out of the See of Alexandria, which he held at the time, and to replace him by Peter Mongos (55).

SEC. III.—THE HENOTICON OF THE EMPEROR ZENO.

80. The Emperor Zeno publishes his Henoticon. 81. Mongos anathematizes Pope St. Leo and the Council of Chalcedon. 82. Peter the Fuller intrusted with the See of Antioch. 83. Adventures and Death of the Fuller. 84. Acacius, Patriarch of Constantinople, dies excommunicated.

80. ACACIUS, with the assistance of the protectors of Mongos, induced the Emperor to publish his famous Henoticon, or Decree of Union, which Peter was to sign as agreed on in resuming possession of the See of Alexandria. This decree was afterwards sent to all the bishops and people, not only of Alexandria, but of all Egypt, Lybia, and Pentapolis (1). This is the substance of the edict: "The abbots, and many other venerable personages, having asked for the re-union of the Christians, to put an end to the sad effects of division, by which many have remained deprived of baptism and the holy communion, and numberless other disorders have taken place. On this account we make known to you that we receive no other creed, but that of the three hundred and eighteen Fathers of Nice, confirmed by the one hundred and fifty Fathers of Constantinople, and followed by the Fathers of Ephesus, who condemned Nestorius and Eutyches. We likewise receive the Twelve Articles of Cyril, and we confess that our Lord Jesus Christ is God, the only Son of God, who has become incarnate in truth, is consubstantial to the Father, according to his Divinity, and consubstantial to us according to his humanity; he descended and is incarnate from the Holy Ghost of the Virgin Mary—(Noel Alexander thus transcribes it: 'ex Spiritu Sancto de Maria Virgine;' but it would be better to have said, as in the first Council of Constantinople, ' de Spiritu Sancto ex Maria Virgine,'—*chap.* iv. *n.* 74), Mother of God, and is one Son alone, and not two Sons. We say that it is the same Son of God who wrought miracles, and voluntarily suffered in the flesh; and we receive not those who divide or confound the two natures, or who only admit a simple appearance of Incarnation. We excommunicate whoever believes, or at any other time has believed differently, either in Chalcedon,

---

(55) Fleury, ad cit. *n.* 49.　　(1) Evagr. *l.* 3, *c.* 14.

or in any other Council, and especially Nestorius, Eutyches, and their followers. Unite yourself to the Church, our Spiritual Mother, for she holds the same sentiments." This is the copy Fleury (2) gives, and the one adduced by N. Alexander corresponds with it, in every respect (3). Cardinal Baronius rejects the Henoticon, as heretical (4); but N. Alexander justly remarks, that it does not deserve to be stamped as heretical, for it does not establish the Eutychian heresy, but, on the contrary, impugns and condemns it; but he wisely adds, that it injured the cause of the Faith, and favoured the Eutychian heresy, inasmuch as it said nothing about St. Leo's Epistle or the definition of the Council of Chalcedon on the words *of two* and *in two* natures, which is the touchstone against the perfidy of the Eutychian heresy (5).

81. Let us now return to Peter Mongos, who was placed on the throne of Alexandria, received the Henoticon, and caused it to be received not only by his own party, but by the friends of St. Proterius likewise, with whom he did not refuse to communicate, not to give cause to suspect his bad faith; and on the celebration of a festival in Alexandria, he spoke to the people in the church in favour of it, and caused it to be publicly read. While he was acting thus, however, he excommunicated the Council of Chalcedon and the Epistle of St. Leo, he removed from the Dyptichs the names of St. Proterius and of Timothy Salofacialus, and substituted those of Dioscorus and Eleurus (6). Finally, this faithful companion and imitator of Eleurus, after persecuting the Catholics in various ways, ended his days in the year 490 (7).

82. We have now to speak of another perfidious Eutychian priest, who, in the same century, about the year 469, caused a great deal of harm to the Church of Antioch. This was Peter the Fuller. At first he was a monk in the monastery of Acemeti, in Bythinia, opposite Constantinople, and was by trade a fuller, from which he took his name. He then went to Constantinople, and, under the appearance of piety, gained the favour of the great, and, in particular, of Zeno, the son-in-law of the Emperor Leo, who began to look on him with a favourable eye. Zeno brought him with himself to Antioch, and he set his eye on that See, and induced Zeno to protect him. He commenced by calumniating Martyrius, Bishop of Antioch, and accused him of being a Nestorian. Having thus, by means of a great number of friends of his, Appollinarists, got up a disturbance in the city, he persuaded Zeno that the only way to re-establish peace was to drive Martyrius out of the city, and then he stepped into his place. The first way he showed himself was, by adding to the Trisagion of the Mass, Holy, Holy, Holy, the words " who was crucified for us," to show that he believed that the

(2) Fleury, *t.* 4, *l.* 29, *n.* 53.   (3) Nat. Alex. *t.* 10, *c.* 3, *a.* 15, *s.* 4.   (4) Baron. Ann. 428.   (5) Nat. Alex. loc. cit.   (6) Fleury, *t.* 4, *l.* 29, *n.* 54.   (7) Nat. Alex. *t.* 10, *c.* 3, *ar.* 14, *s.* 5; Fleury, *t.* 5, *l.* 30, *n.* 21.

Divinity was crucified in the person of Christ (8). Martyrius went to Constantinople, and appealed to the Emperor, and Peter did the same, and brought with him a bill of calumnious charges against the bishop; but Leo condemned the usurpation of the fuller, and sent Martyrius back with honour to his See. On his arival in Antioch, Martyrius found a large party opposed to him, and though he tried, he could not bring them to terms; he therefore resolved to withdraw, and said publicly in the church: "I reserve to myself the dignity of the priesthood, but I renounce a disobedient people and a rebellious clergy. When the Fuller thus saw the See again vacated, he took possession of it once more, and was recognized as Patriarch of Antioch. When this was told to St. Gennadius, he (9) informed the Emperor, and he at once gave orders that Peter should be sent in exile to the Oasis; but he had knowledge of the sentence beforehand, and saved himself by flight (10).

83. On the death of the Emperor Leo, in the year 474, Zeno was declared his successor; but as Basiliscus had seized on the sovereign power in 476, as we have already seen (he was brother to the Empress Verina), the Fuller was reinstated by him in the See of Antioch. In the following year, 477, Zeno recovered his dominions, and had him deposed in a Council of the East, and John, Bishop of Apamea, was elected in his place (11). John only held the See three months; he was driven out also, and Stephen, a pious man, was chosen in his place; but he had governed only a year when the heretics rose up against him, stabbed him to death in his own church with sharp-pointed reeds, and afterwards dragged his body through the steets, and threw it into the river (12). Another bishop of the name of Stephen was now ordained, and Peter the Fuller was sent in banishment to Pitiontum, on the frontiers of the empire, in Pontus; but he deceived his guards, and fled to another place (13), and in the year 484 was a third time re-established in the See of Antioch, with the consent of Acacius, who had himself so often condemned him (14). At length, after committing a great many acts of injustice against several churches, and stained with cruelty, he died in 488, having retained his See since his last usurpation little more than three years. Thus, in the end of the fifth century, the Divine justice overtook the chiefs and principal supporters of the Eutychian heresy, for the Fuller died in 488, Acacius in 489, Mongos in 490, and Zeno in 491.

84. Speaking of Acacius, it would be well if those who are ambitious for a bishopric would reflect on the miserable end of this unhappy prelate. He succeeded a saint, St. Gennadius, on the throne of Constantinople in 472; but he did an immensity of injury

(8) Fleury, *t.* 4, *l.* 29, *n.* 30; Orsi, *t.* 15, *l.* 35, *n.* 18; Nat. Alex. *t.* 10, *c.* 3, *art.* 17. (9) Liberat. Breviar His. Eutych. (10) Orsi, loc. cit. (11) Orsi, ibid. *n.* 64 & 69. (12) Orsi, vide ibid.; Fleury, loc. cit. *n.* 49, in fin. ex Evagr. *l.* 3, *c.* 10. (13) Fleury, ibid. *n.* 50. (14) Fleury, *t.* 5, *l.* 30, *n.* 17; Nat. Alex. loc. cit.

to the Church, for, although not infected with the heresy of the Eutychians, he was their great protector, and, by his bad practices, kept alive a great schism, which was not extinguished till thirty years or more after his death (15). He was accused to the Pontiff, St. Felix, of many negligences of duty, and especially of communicating with the impious Mongos, who had anathematized the Council of Chalcedon and the Epistle of St. Leo. The Pope admonished him to repent; but, taking no notice of his remonstrances, he deposed and excommunicated him, and in that state he lived for the remainder of his life, and died so (16). At his death, in fine, we are horrified at reading of the ruin of religion all over the East, for the churches were either in possession of heretics, or of those who communicated with heretics, or, at least, of those who, by communicating with heretics, were separated from the communion of Rome; and almost all this evil originated in the protection given by Acacius to the enemies of the Church. While I write this I tremble. A bishop myself, and considering how many, on account of being exalted to that dignity, have prevaricated and lost their souls—many, I say, who, if they had remained in a private condition, would be more easily saved. I abstract altogether from the question, whether he who looks for a mitre is in a state of mortal sin, but I cannot understand how any one, anxious to secure his salvation, can wish to be a bishop, and thus voluntarily expose himself to the many dangers of losing their souls, to which bishops are subject.

CHAPTER VI.

HERESIES OF THE SIXTH CENTURY.

ARTICLE I.

OF THE ACEPHALI, AND THE DIFFERENT SECTS THEY SPLIT INTO.

1. Regulation made by the new Emperor, Anastasius, to the great Detriment of the Church. 2. Anastasius persecutes the Catholics; his awful Death. 3. The Acephali, and their Chief, Severus. 4. The Sect of the Jacobites. 5. The Agnoites. 6. The Tritheists. 7. The Corruptibilists. 8. The Incorruptibilists. 9. Justinian falls into this Error. 10. Good and bad Actions of the Emperor. 11, 12. The Acemetic Monks; their Obstinacy.

1. WHEN Zeno died, the Catholics hoped for peace: but, in 491, Anastasius was elected Emperor, and he commenced a long and fierce persecution against the Church (1). In his private life he appeared a pious man; but when he was raised to the Empire, and

(15) Orsi, 15, *l.* 35, *n.* 27.   (16) Orsi, *t.* 16, *l.* 36, *n.* 27, 28.   (1) Orsi, *t.* 16, *l.* 36, *n.* 57.

saw all the Churches of the world split into different factions, so that the Western bishops would not communicate with the Eastern, nor even the Easterns among themselves, and wishing to see no novelty introduced, as he said, he gave orders (2) that all the Churches should remain in the same state he found them, and banished from their Sees any bishops who introduced novelties. Nothing could be better than this, if all the Churches were united in the profession of the true Faith; but as there were several at that time which did not adhere to the Council of Chalcedon, to make a law, that no Church should change its ancient usage, was the best possible means of perpetuating discord, and this was precisely the effect it produced.

2. Although Anastasius had shown some signs of piety, still Euphemius, Patriarch of Constantinople, who had narrowly watched his sentiments in regard of the Faith, considered him a heretic, and opposed his exaltation with all his might (3); he never even would consent to it, till he had from him a sworn promise, and signed, besides, with his own hand, binding him to defend the Council of Chalcedon. All this Anastasius did; but he not only broke his promise afterwards, but endeavoured (4) to destroy all proof of it, by requiring the restoration of the paper he had signed and sworn to, which was kept in the treasury of the Church; for the retention of such a document, he said, was an insult to the Empire, as if the word of a Prince was not worthy of faith by itself. He favoured the heretics, and persecuted the Catholics, especially the Patriarch Euphemius, whom he succeeded in deposing (5). He favoured, above all others, the Eutychians, who principally infested the Church at that time. He could not, however, be called an Eutychian himself; he was rather one of the sect of *Existants* or *Tolerators*, who permitted every religion except the Catholic (6). He died at last, in the year 518, on the 9th of July, and in the ninetieth, or, at all events, the eighty-eighth year of his age, having constantly persecuted the Church during the twenty-seven years he reigned. According to the account of Cyril, Bishop of Scythopolis, in the life of St. Saba, quoted by Orsi and Fleury (7), he had an unhappy end. St. Saba, he says, came to Aila, where St. Elias, Patriarch of Jerusalem, was banished. They used to take their meals together, at the hour of noon every day; but on the 9th of June, the Patriarch did not make his appearance till midnight, and, when he entered, he said, Do you eat, for I will not nor cannot eat any more. He then told St. Saba, that, at that very hour, the Emperor was dead, and that he should follow him before ten days, to meet him at the bar of Divine justice, and, in fact, on the 20th of July, he slept in the Lord, in the eighty-eighth year of his age, having taken

(2) Orsi, *n.* 68.   (3) Evagr *l.* 3, *c.* 32; Orsi, *t.* 16, *l.* 35, *n.* 37, con. Theodoret.
(4) Orsi, loc. cit. *n.* 70.   (5) Orsi, *n.* 112.   (6) Orsi, *t.* 19, *l.* 37, *n.* 21.   (7) Orsi, *t.* 17, *l.* 38, *n.* 34; Fleury, *t.* 5, *l.* 31, *n.* 33.

no food for eight days previously. St. Elias, and St. Flavian, Patriarch of Constantinople, who also died in exile, banished by Anastasius for defending the Council of Chalcedon, are commemorated in the Roman Martyrology, on the 4th of July (8). The circumstances of the Emperor's death were remarkable: On the night of the 9th and 10th of July a dreadful thunder-storm raged over his palace. Terrified with the frequent flashes of lightning, but much more on account of his sins, he imagined that God was now about to chastise him for his iniquities, and he fled wandering from chamber to chamber; he, at last, retired into a private cabinet, and was there found dead, whether from the effects of terror, or struck by lightning, authors are undecided. This was the end of this bad man, after twenty-seven years' persecution of the Church of God. On the day of Anastasius's death, Justin was invested with the Imperial dignity; he was a prince (9) always obsequious to the Apostolic See, and zealous in combating heresies, and establishing unity and peace in the Church. He reigned nine years, and was succeeded by Justinian, of whom we shall speak by-and-by, and he was succeeded, in 565, by his nephew, Justin II., who began his reign well, but soon fell into dreadful excesses, though he never lost the Faith, and died, at last, with sentiments of Christian piety (10).

3. The heresies which disturbed the Church in this century were almost all offshoots from the stock of Eutychianism. Those from whom the Catholics suffered most were the Acephali, who were also Eutychians. They were called Monophysites, as they believed only one nature in Christ (11); but as they separated themselves from Mongos, the pretended Bishop of Alexandria, and refused to adhere, either to the Catholic party, or to their bishop, Mongos, they were called Acephali, or Headless. They were not without a chief, withal—one Severus, from the city of Sozopolis, in Pisidia. He was a Pagan in the beginning of his days, and it is thought he never sincerely renounced his errors; he went to Beyroot to study law, and was convicted there of idolatry and magical practices, so, to escape the punishment his infamies deserved, he pretended to embrace Christianity. He was baptized in Tripoli, in Phenicia (12), but he was not eight days a Christian, when he forsook the Catholic communion, and threw himself into the arms of the party who had separated from Mongos, and he rejected from that out both the Council of Chalcedon and the Henoticon of Zeno. He was a man of corrupt morals, but to gain credit with the monks he professed the monastic life in the monastery of the abbot Nefarius, in Egypt; but he was there discovered to be a heretic and expelled, and he then went to Constantinople, where he some time after found himself at the head of two hundred monks, and of many other

(8) Orsi, *t.* 19, *l.* 42, *n.* 89.   (9) Orsi, *t.* 19, *l.* 39, *n.* 37, in fin.   (10) Orsi, *t.* 19, *l.* 43, *n.* 67.   (11) Orsi, loc cit. *n.* 68.   (12) Orsi, *t.* 16, *l.* 37, *n.* 62, cum Evagr. *l.* 3, *n.* 33.

heretics (13), and with them committed many excesses, without regard to either the laws or the judges. Anastasius, who then reigned, desirous of upsetting the Council of Chalcedon, winked at his crimes, and thus, under favour of that impious sovereign, he succeeded in driving out of Constantinople the bishop of the See, Macedonius, and substituting Timothy, treasurer of the city, in his place, who had the hardihood to cause the Trisagion, composed by Peter the Fuller, to favour the Eutychian doctrines, to be publicly sung in the Church (14). Timothy, likewise, through favour of the Emperor, got Severus elected Bishop of Antioch, and Flavian banished (15); and he, on the very day he took possession of his See, anathematized the Council of Chalcedon and the Epistle of St. Leo.

4. The Acephali were split into several sects. The Jacobites are among the most remarkable; these took their name from a Syrian monk of the name of James, a disciple of Severus. He preached the Eutychian heresy in Armenia and Mesopotamia; and from that time the Syrian Catholics, who received the Council of Chalcedon, were called Melchites, or Royalists, from the Syrian word *Melk*, a King, because they followed the religion of the Emperors, that is of the Emperors who received the Council of Chalcedon. The Jacobites professed the error of Eutyches, that Christ suffered in the flesh, and they added other errors to this, especially in Armenia, for there they denied that the Word had taken flesh from the Virgin, but taught that the Word itself was changed into flesh and merely passed through the Virgin; they do not mix water with the wine in the celebration of Mass; celebrate Easter the same time as the Jews; do not venerate the cross until it is baptized the same as a human being; when they make the sign of the cross they do it with one finger alone, to signify that they believe in one nature; they observe singular fasts, and during the Lent they cannot eat eggs or cheese unless on Holy Saturday.

5. The Agnoites or *Ignorants* were founded by Themistius, a deacon of Alexandria. This Eutychian taught that Christ, being of one nature alone, composed out of, or confounded rather, between the Divinity and humanity, was, even according to the Divinity, ignorant of many things, as he in particular himself alludes to his ignorance of the day of judgment: " But of that day or hour no man knoweth, neither the angels in heaven, nor the Son, but the Father" (Mark, xiii. 32); and this ignorance, he said, was just as natural to him as the other inconveniences, hunger, thirst, and pain, which he suffered in this life (16). St. Gregory (17), however, explains the text by saying that Christ did not know it as far as his humanity was concerned, but that he knew it by the union of

(13) Orsi, *n*. 63. (14) Orsi, *n*. 71. (15) Orsi, *n*. 72 (16) Fleury, *t*. 5, *l*. 33, *n*. 2; Nat. Alex. *t*. 11, *c*. 3, *a*. 3; Gotti, loc. cit. (17) St. Greg. *l*. 10, Ep. 89, *a*. 42.

the humanity with the Divinity. God made man, he says, know the day and the hour by the power of his Divinity.

6. The chief of the Tritheists was John, a grammarian of Alexandria; he was known by the name of Philoponos the labourer. He objected to the Catholics, that if they recognized two natures in Christ they should admit two persons; but he was answered that nature was one thing and person another: for, if nature and personality were one and the same thing, we should admit three natures in the Trinity as there are three persons. This reasoning was so convincing to Philoponos that he at once admitted its force, but it led him into a much greater error, for he recognized three distinct natures in the Trinity, and, therefore, admitted three distinct Gods, and hence his followers were called *Tritheists* (18). He wrote likewise against the resurrection of the flesh (19). With these exceptions he believed in Christianity, and defended it against Proclus of Licia, a Platonic philosopher who attacked it at the time.

7. From this hot-bed of error two other sects sprung up, the Corruptibilists and the Incorruptibilists. Theodosius, a monk, founded the Corruptibilists, who believed that Christ had a corruptible body. These erred, not because they said that the Word had in Christ taken a corruptible body by its nature, and subject to hunger and thirst and sufferings, but because they asserted that Christ by necessity was subject to these sufferings, in the same manner as all of us were subject to them, so that he should undergo them whether he willed or not (20). The Catholic doctrine is that the Word had in the body of Christ put on the common sufferings of mankind, hunger, weariness, pain, and death, not through necessity, as they are of necessity with us, the punishment of original sin, but of his own free will on account of his unbounded charity which induced him to come " in the likeness of sinful flesh" (Romans, viii. 3), to condemn and punish sin in the flesh. And in the same manner, says St. Thomas (21), our Saviour wished to assume the passions of the mind, sorrow, fear, weariness, not in the same way as they are in us, opposed to reason, for all the motions of the sensitive appetites in Christ were ordered according to reason, and were on that account called in him *propassions;* for passion in itself, says the angelic doctor, is so called when it rules over reason, but it is propassion when it remains in and does not extend beyond the sensitive appetite.

8. St. Julian of Halicarnassus was the head of the Phantasiasts or Incorruptibilists. These taught that the body of Christ was by its nature incorruptible and free from all passions, so that he suffered neither hunger nor thirst, nor weariness nor pain, but that

(18) Fleury & Nat. Alex. *l.* cit. Berti, Brev. His. *t.* 1, *s.* 6, *c.* 3.   (19) Niceph. *l.* 18, *c.* 47, 48.   (20) Gotti, *l.* cit. *c.* 76, *s.* 6, *n.* 7.   (21) St. Thomas, *p.* 2. *q.* 15, *a.* 4.

is directly opposed to the words of the Gospel: "When he had fasted........he was hungry" (Matt. iv. 2); "Fatigued from his journey, he sat down" (John, iv. 6). The Eutychians were favourable to this doctrine, for it corresponded with their own, that there was only one, an impassable, nature in Christ (22). Julian wrote in favour of the Incorruptibilists and Themistius of the Corruptibilists, and they both stirred up such a commotion among the people of Alexandria, that they burned each other's houses, and murdered each other on account of their difference of opinion (23).

9. We should here remark that the Emperor Justinian fell into the error of the Incorruptibilists. Who could have imagined that this prince, who showed himself so zealous against heretics, and, above all, against the Eutychians, should have died, as many suppose he did, a heretic himself, and infected with the pestilential dogmas of Eutyches. Fleury and Orsi (24) both attribute his fall to his overweening desire of meddling by his edicts in matters of Faith which God has committed to the heads of his Church. He had the misfortune to have as a most intimate confidant, Theodore, Bishop of Cesarea, a concealed enemy of the Council of Chalcedon, and a friend of the Acephali, and at his instigation he promulgated an edict in the year 564, in which he declared that the body of Christ was incorruptible, so that after it was formed in the Virgin's womb, it was no longer capable of any change or natural passion, no matter how innocent, as hunger and thirst, so that although he ate before his death, he only did so in the same manner as after his Resurrection, without having any necessity of food. If the body of Christ, therefore, was not capable of any natural passion, he suffered nothing in the flesh, neither in life nor death, and his passion was merely an appearance without any reality. Isaias, therefore, uttered a falsehood when he said, "Surely he hath borne our infirmities, and carried our sorrows" (Isaias, liii. 4). So did St. Peter, where he says, "Who his own self bore our sins in his body upon the tree" (1 Peter, ii. 24). Even Christ himself stated what was false when he said, "My soul is sorrowful unto death" (Matt. xxvi. 38); and then exclaiming on the cross, "My God, my God, why hast thou forsaken me?" (Matt. xxvii. 46). All this would be false if Christ was insensible to internal and external sufferings. O ingratitude of mankind. Christ died of pain on a cross for the love of man, and men say that he suffered nothing in reality, only in appearance. Justinian required that this doctrine should be approved of by all the bishops, and he was particularly anxious to induce six learned African bishops to give it their approbation, but they resisted, and were accordingly separated, and shut up in six different churches in Constantinople (25). St.

(22) Gotti, *l.* cit. ex Liberat. in Brev. c. 20.   (23) Gotti, ibid.   (24) Fleury, *t.* 5, *l.* 34, *n.* 8, cum Evagr. *l.* 4, *n.* 30 ; Orsi, *t.* 19, *l.* 42, *n.* 78.   (25) Fleury, *l.* cit.

Eutychius, Patriarch of Constantinople, opposed it likewise, and laboured in vain to undeceive the Emperor. He was driven from his See and another put in his place, and all the patriarchs and many other bishops refused to sign their approbation (26). When the Oriental bishops were required to subscribe, they said they would follow the example of Anastasius, Patriarch of Antioch, and Justinian, therefore, used every effort to induce him to agree to it, but he sent the Emperor an answer in which he learnedly proved that the body of Christ, as to the natural and innocent passions, was corruptible, and when informed that it was the Emperor's intention to banish him, he prepared a sermon to take leave of his people, but he never published it, as Justinian died at midnight, the 13th of November, 566, the eighty-fourth year of his age, after a reign of thirty-nine years and eight months (27).

10. Cardinal Baronius (28) says that the Emperor's death was sudden and unexpected, but it was most serviceable to the Empire, which was daily falling from bad to worse, God revenging the injuries inflicted on the bishops of his Church, and preventing, by his death, that fire from spreading, which he enkindled. Evagrius and Nicephorus (29) remark, that he died just at the time he had decreed the exile of St. Anastasius and other Catholic priests, although the order had not been yet promulgated. This Evagrius, a contemporaneous author, as Orsi (30) remarks, gave it as his deliberate opinion that Justinian, having filled the world and the Church with tumult and confusion, only received from God, in the end, that condign punishment his crimes deserved. Baronius adds (31), that although the name of Justinian was not removed from the Ecclesiastical Registers, like that of other heretics, and though the sixth Council and several Pontiffs had entitled him Pious and Catholic, we should not be surprised if his falling off from the Faith was not published in any public decree. However, his other crimes, the banishment of so many bishops, his cruelties to so many innocent persons, his acts of injustice in depriving so many of their properties, prove that he was, at all events, unjust and sacrilegious, if not a heretic.

11. Besides these sects of the Acephali, another sect of the Acemetic* monks sprung up in this century. This was another sprout of Nestorianism, and it was thus discovered. During the reign of Pope Hormisdas, the Scythian monks took on themselves

---

(26) Evagr. *l.* 4, *n.* 83. (27) Fleury, *l. c. n.* 11. (28) Baron. Ann. 565, *n.* 1. (29) Evagr. *l.* 4, *c.* 40; Niceph. *l.* 16, *c.* 31. (30) Orsi, *t.* 19, *l.* 42, *n.* 84. (31) Baron. loc cit. *n.* 3.

---

* Acemetic, or *sleepless* monks, were a celebrated order in the East. They were called the sleepless, because night and day they kept up Divine psalmody without intermission; the community was divided into three sections, and each spent eight hours out of the twenty-four singing the praises of God.—TRANS.

to sustain, as a necessary article of Faith, that one of the Trinity was made flesh, and they sent a deputation to Rome to get a decree from the Pope to that effect; he, however (32), refused to accede to their wishes, dreading that some leaven of Eutychianism might be concealed in the proposition, and that they wished besides to throw discredit on the Council of Chalcedon and the Epistle of St. Leo, as deficient in the definition of the expressions necessary to condemn the Nestorian and Eutychian heresy. On the other hand, that proposition was embraced by all the Oriental Churches as a touchstone against the Nestorian heresy, and was impugned by the Acemetic monks alone, who, it is true, in the time of Zeno and Anastasius, had fought strenuously against the heresy of Eutyches, but becoming too warm against the Eutychians, began to agree with the Nestorians, not alone denying that one of the Trinity was made flesh, but also that the Son of God suffered in his flesh, and that the Blessed Virgin was really and truly the Mother of God (33).

12. The Emperor Justinian undertook the defence of the proposition upheld by the monks of Scythia, and wrote to Pope John II. for his approbation, and gave his letter in charge to two bishops—Ignatius, Archbishop of Ephesus, and Demetrius of Philippi. When the Acemetic monks got a knowledge of this proceeding, they sent two of their body to Rome—Cyrus and Eulogius—to defend their cause (34); so Pope John had the matter most particularly examined. We know, for certain, that Anatolius, deacon of the Roman Church, wrote to Ferrandus, a deacon in Africa, a man of most profound learning and of great sanctity, who, having previously expressed a doubt as to whether this proposition was admissible or not, now, after a rigorous examination, answered that there should be no hesitation in admitting it. Among other proofs, he adduces the words of St. Paul: "Take heed to yourselves and to the whole flock wherein the Holy Ghost hath placed you bishops, to rule the Church of God, which he hath purchased with his own blood" (Acts, xx. 28). Now when the Apostle says that God hath shed his blood, every one must understand that he shed the blood of the flesh he had taken from the Virgin, and that it is not God the Father, nor God the Holy Ghost, but God the Son, who has done so, as the Scripture declares in several places: "For God so loved the world as to give his only begotten Son" (John, iii. 16): "He hath spared not even his own Son, but delivered him up for us all" (Rom. viii. 32): if, therefore, we can say that God has shed his blood for us, we can also say that one of the Persons of the Trinity shed his blood and suffered in the flesh. After a rigorous examination, therefore, Pope John answered the Emperor, and authentically gave his approbation to the proposition, that one of

(32) Orsi, *t.* 17, *l.* 39, *n.* 123. (33) Orsi, loc. cit. (34) Fleury, *t.* 5, *l.* 32, *n.* 35; Orsi, ibid. *n.* 24.

the Trinity suffered in the flesh. He then strove to get the Acemetic monks who had come to Rome, to accept his definition, but they obstinately refused, and he was obliged to separate them from the communion of the Church (35). We should remark that the letter of Pope John did not contradict the letter of Pope Hormisdas, for this Pope did not condemn the proposition, but only withheld his approbation for just causes, lest, as Roncaglia says, a hasty definition at the time might divide some from the unity of the Church (36).

ARTICLE II.

THE THREE CHAPTERS.

13. Condemnation of the Three Chapters of Theodore, Ibas, and Theodoret. 14, 15. Defended by Vigilius. 16. Answer to the Objection of a Heretic, who asserts that one Council contradicts another.

13. It was during this sixth century that the controversy about the *Three Chapters* was carried on. These were: First.—The books of Theodore of Mopsuestia, in which it was clear he taught the heresy of Nestorius (*supra, cap.* v. n. 48); Second.—The letter of Ibas to Maris of Persia, in which he condemned alike St. Cyril and Nestorius, and praised Theodore of Mopsuestia: and, Thirdly. —The writings of Theodoret, Bishop of Cyrus, against the twelve anathematisms of St. Cyril. This controversy grievously disturbed the Church, but it was put at rest by the condemnation of these Three Chapters, in the year 553, in the fifth General Council, the second of Constantinople. The Emperor Justinian hurried on the condemnation of Theodore and his writings, the letter of Ibas to Maris the Persian, and the writings of Theodoret against St. Cyril, and finally, the sentence received the approbation of Pope Vigilius, in his famous *Constitutum*. Danæus (1) says that Vigilius was opposed to the celebration of this Council, but as he had not the power to prevent it, and foresaw that a ruinous schism would spring from his objection, he gave his assent, and, confirmed by the assent of the Holy See, it now ranks among the Ecumenical Councils.

14. Pope Vigilius was blamed for his conduct in regard to this Council, and for so frequently changing his judgment regarding the condemnation of the Three Chapters, but Cardinal Norris (2), after relating all his changes, defends him—as does Peter of Marca— and says that his inconstancy was not weakness but prudence. "Vigilius," he says, "was a most tenacious upholder of Pontifical authority, even setting at defiance the Sovereign himself, as appears from his actions. He is reproached with inconstancy of mind, and too great a facility in changing his opinions, for in the case of the

(35) Fleury, *t.* 5, *l.* 32, *n.* 39; Gotti, *t.* 2, loc. cit. *c.* 77, *l. t.* 8; Orsi, loc. cit. *n.* 128.
(36) Roncaglia, Not. apud.; Nat. Alex. *t.* 11, *c.* 3, *ar.* 2.   (1) Danes.; Nat. Temp. *p.* 255.   (2) De Norris; Diss. Histor. de Syn. v. c. d.

Three Chapters he was often inconsistent, and more than once was opposed to his previous opinions. In the beginning, while he was yet in Sicily, he defended the Three Chapters; but, if we are to believe Victor, he had already promised to Theodora Augusta that he would condemn them. When he came to Constantinople he suspended Menna for condemning the Three Chapters; but he was soon after reconciled to him, and juridically condemned them himself. Three years after he revoked his judgment, published a new Constitution, and denied that they could be condemned; but he held this opinion for only a few months, for he forwarded an epistle to Eutyches, declaring the Constitution of no effect, and coming to the Synod, he proscribed the Three Chapters." That most learned man, Peter of Marca (*lib.* iii., De Concordia Sacerdotii & Imperii, *cap.* 13), testifies that this inconstancy of Vigilius has been considered prudence by the learned; he calls it dispensation, for at one time he acted up to the rigour of law and canons, and then again dispensed with them for the sake of Faith and public tranquillity.

15. Peter of Marca, therefore, says that the Popes at all times, in questions relating to discipline, have acted according to the rules of prudence; sometimes, when necessary, using all the rigour of the canon, at other times the dispensing power—called by the Greeks, *Economy*, by the Latins, *Dispensation*—to preserve the union of the faithful and the peace of the Church. Cardinal Orsi (3) remarks, besides, that it was the last Constitution or Judgment alone that was proposed to the Church by Vigilius as a peremptory decree, and, as theologians say, pronounced *ex Cathedra.* He was unwilling, at first, to condemn the Three Chapters, because he feared to give a handle to the Nestorians to throw discredit on the Council of Chalcedon, which, it was said, approved of the Three Chapters; but when, on one hand, he perceived that the Eutychians more vigorously attacked the Council of Chalcedon, which they said (though it was not the case) had approved of these Chapters; and, on the other, the Nestorians, laying hold of that, boasted that this Council was favourable to the doctrine of Nestorius; then, indeed, he was convinced that it was necessary to condemn them absolutely, and he accordingly gave a decree to that effect, in unison with the Fathers of the Council of Constantinople, which is, therefore, as Tournelly says (4), considered one of the Ecumenical Councils, as it was approved of by Vigilius, and also by some of his successors, as Pelagius II., Leo II., &c., and Photius, according to Orsi, mentions the same thing in his writings.

16. How does it happen though, says Maclain, the annotator of Mosheim (5), that in the Council of Chalcedon the writings of Ibas and Theodoret were not condemned, and they themselves were

---

(3) Orsi, *t.* 7, *l.* 39, *n.* 84.   (4) Tournelly, Theol. Comp. *t.* 3 ; append. *a.* 2, de Con. Constan. 2, *p.* 998.   (5) Mosheim, Hist. Eccles. Centur. 6, par. 2, *c.* 3, *p.* 839.

praised for the purity of their Faith, and, for all that, the Council of Constantinople condemns their writings? the decision of the Council of Constantinople then is, he says, opposed to that of Chalcedon, and is a proof that both the Councils and the Doctors differ among themselves. Thus, he endeavours to prove the fallibility of General Councils of the Catholic Church, as these two Councils were opposed to each other. But as Selvaggi, in his sixteenth note, very fairly remarks, this is altogether false, for the Three Chapters were not approved of by the Council of Chalcedon; in fact, as Tournelly also remarks, they were neither approved nor rejected; they were altogether passed over in that Council, lest, by condemning them, more disturbance would be raised in the Church, already distracted by the Nestorians. Peter of Marca explains the omission of the condemnation, on the authority of St. Cyril (6). Cyril, he says, prudently teaches that rigorous rules must sometimes be tempered by dispensation, as people at sea frequently throw some of their merchandise overboard to preserve the rest; and in his Epistle to Proclus of Constantinople, he tells him that the Council of Ephesus acted in this manner, for the Synod, indeed, condemned the heretical impiety, but in this condemnation prudently abstained from mentioning the name of Theodorus, lest many, led away by their respect for his person, would forsake the Church itself.

17. Juenin (7) tells us that the books of Origen were condemned in this Council, and the following errors of his especially were noted: First.—That the souls of men are created before they are united to their bodies, and that they are joined to the body as a place of punishment. Second.—That the heavens, the sun, the moon, the stars, and the waters above the heavens, are animated and reasoning powers. Third.—That in the general resurrection, our bodies will arise all in a round form, and that the pains of the damned and of the devils will have an end some time or other. Fourth.—That in some future ages Jesus Christ will be again crucified for the devils, and that the wicked spirits who are in heaven will inflict this suffering on him. Juenin also remarks that the condemnation of these erroneous doctrines does not appear clearly, from the original Acts of the second Council of Constantinople, as in the edition of L'Abbe, but that Cardinal Norris clearly shows that they were condemned there, though Garner maintains that it was not in this Council they were condemned at all, but in the Constantinopolitan Council, celebrated under Menna.

(6) Mos. loc. cit. (7) Juenin, Theol. t. 1, ar. 5, s. 2, ver. Quinto.

CHAPTER VII.

THE HERESIES OF THE SEVENTH CENTURY.

ARTICLE I.

OF MAHOMETANISM.

1. Birth of Mahomet, and Beginning of his False Religion. 2. The Alcoran filled with Blasphemy and Nonsense.

1. THE impious sect of Mahometanism sprung up in this century. I have already written the history of Mahomet in my work on the "Truth of the Faith" (1), but I consider it necessary to give a short sketch of it here. Mahomet, the founder of this destroying sect, which has spread over the greater—perhaps, the greatest part of the Christian world, was born in Arabia, in 568, according to Fleury (2), and his family was amongst the most illustrious of that peninsula. His uncle put him to trade on the death of his father, and when twenty-eight years of age, he became, at first the factor, and, soon after, the husband of a rich and noble widow, called Cadijah (3). He was brought up an idolater; but, as he grew old, he determined, not alone to change his own religion, but that of his countrymen, who, for the greater part, were idolaters also, and to teach them, as he said, the ancient religion of Adam, of Abraham, of Noah, and of the Prophets, among whom he reckoned Jesus Christ. He pretended to have long conversations with the Archangel Gabriel, in the cave of Hera, three miles from Mecca, where he frequently retired. In the year 608, being then forty years of age (4), he began to give out that he was a Prophet, inspired by God, and he persuaded his relatives and domestics of this first, and then began publicly to preach in Mecca, and attack idolatry. At first, the people did not very willingly listen to him, and asked him to prove his mission by a miracle; but he told them that God sent him to preach the truth, and not to work miracles. The impostor, however, boasts of having wrought one, though ridiculous in the extreme: a piece, he says, fell off from the moon once into his sleeve, and he fixed it on again; and it is said that this is the reason for the Mahometans adopting the half moon as the device of their Empire. He gave out, in the commencement of his career, that God commanded him not to force any one to embrace his religion, but the people of Mecca having risen up against him, and driven him from their city, he then declared that God commanded him to pursue the

(1) Ver. del Fede, *part* 3, *c.* 4, nota a.   (2) Fleury, *t.* 7, *l.* 38, *n.* 1.   (3) Nat. Alex. *t.* 12, c. 12, *a.* 2.   (4) Fleury, loco cit.

infidels with arms, and thus propagate the Faith; and from that till his death he was always at war. Now Lord of Mecca, he made it the Metropolis of the Faithful, and before his death he saw almost all the tribes of the Arabian peninsula subject to his spiritual and temporal sway.

2. He composed the Koran (*Al Koran*—the book), assisted, as some think, by Sergius, a monk. It is a collection of precepts, taken from the Mosaic and Christian Law, together with many of his own, and interspersed with fables and ridiculous revelations. He recognizes the Divine mission of Moses and Jesus Christ, and admits many parts of the Scriptures; but his law, he says, is the perfection of the Jewish and Christian law, and he is the reformer of these codes, though, in truth, it is totally different from both one and the other. He professes that there is but one God; but in his Alcoran he relates many trivialities unworthy of the Supreme Being, and the whole work is, in fact, filled with contradictions, as I have shown in my book on the "Truth of the Faith." Jews or Christians, he says, may be saved by the observance of their respective laws, and it is indifferent if they exchange one for the other; but hell will be for ever the portion of the infidels; those who believe in one God alone will be sent there for a period not exceeding, at most, a thousand years, and then all will be received into the House of Peace, or Paradise. The Mahometan Paradise, however, is only fit for beasts; for filthy sensual pleasure is all the believer has to expect there. I pass over all the other extravagances of the Koran, having already, in the "Truth of the Faith," treated the subject more fully.

3. The Mahometans shave the head, and leave only a lock of hair on the crown, by which they hope Mahomet will take them up to heaven, even out of hell itself. They are permitted to have four wives by their law, and they ought, at least, to have one; they may divorce each wife twice. It is prohibited to dispute on the Alcoran and the Scriptures; and the devil appears to have dictated this precept himself, for, by keeping those poor people in ignorance, he keeps them in darkness. Mahomet died in 631, in the sixty-third year of his age, and nine years after he was recognized as sovereign of Arabia. He saw almost the whole peninsula subject to his sway, and for four hundred leagues to the North and South of Medina no other sovereign was known. He was succeeded by Aboubeker, one of his earliest disciples, and a great conqueror likewise. A long line of caliphs united in their own persons the spiritual and royal power of the Arabian Empire. They destroyed the Empire of Persia; and Egypt, and Syria, and the rich provinces and kingdoms of the East yielded to their arms (5).

(5) Fleury, *t.* 6, *l.* 38, *n.* 4, 5.

Article II.

HERESY OF THE MONOTHELITES.

4. Commencement of the Monothelites; their Chiefs, Sergius and Cyrus. 5. Opposed by Sophronius. 6. Letter of Sergius to Pope Honorius, and his Answer. 7. Defence of Honorius. · 8, Honorius erred, but did not fall into any Error against Faith. 9. The Ecthesis of Heraclius, afterwards condemned by Pope John IV. 10. The Type of the Emperor Constans. 11. Condemnation of Paul and Pyrrhus. 12. Dispute of St. Maximus with Pyrrhus. 13. Cruelty of Constans; his violent Death. 14. Condemnation of the Monothelites in the Sixth Council. 15. Honorius condemned in that Council, not for Heresy, but for his Negligence in repressing Heresy.

4. IN the year 622, according to Noel Alexander (1), or 630, according to Fleury (2), the Monothelite heresy sprang up; and this was its origin:—some bishops who had received the Council of Chalcedon, recognizing two natures in Christ, still asserted that as both natures were but one person, we should only recognize in him one operation (3). N. Alexander (loco cit.) says, that the founder of this error was Sergius, Patriarch of Constantinople; he communicated his opinions to Theodore, Bishop of Pharan, in Arabia, and he answered him that his sentiments were the same. It happened also about this time that the Emperor Heraclius was in Gerapolis in Upper Syria, when he was visited by Athanasius, Patriarch of the Jacobites, a crafty and wicked man; he gained the Emperor's confidence, who promised to make him Patriarch of Antioch, if he would receive the Council of Chalcedon. Athanasius pretended to receive it, and confessed the two natures; he then asked the Emperor, if, having received the two natures, it was necessary to recognize in the person of Christ two wills and two operations, or one alone. This question posed him, and he wrote to Sergius, Patriarch of Constantinople, and asked also the opinion of Cyrus, Bishop of Phasis, and both persuaded him that he should confess in Christ one will alone, and only one operation, as he was only one person. The Eutychian Athanasius was quite satisfied with this false doctrine, because if we recognize in Christ only one operation, we should, according to the Eutychian system, only recognize one nature also. Thus, Sergius, Theodore, Bishop of Pharan, Athanasius, and Cyrus, joined together, and as, on the death of George, Patriarch of Alexandria, Cyrus was raised to that dignity, and Athanasius was immediately appointed Patriarch of Antioch, three of the Eastern Patriarchs embraced the heretical doctrine, that there was but one will in Jesus Christ; and on that account, this sect was called the Monothelites, from the two Greek terms composing the word, and signifying one will (4). Sophronius,

---

(1) Baron. Ann. 163, n. 4; Nat. Alex. t. 12, c. 2, a. 1, sec. 2.   (2) Fleury, t. 6, l. 37, n. 41.   (3) Fleury, al luogo cit.   (4) Fleury, loc. cit.; Van Ranst. sec. 6, p. 125; Herm. Hist. t. 1, c. 235.

Patriarch of Jerusalem, remained faithful to the Church, and never could be induced to embrace the heresy.

5. Cyrus, being now Patriarch of Alexandria, formed a union there of all the Theodosians, a very numerous Eutychian sect. This act of union was concluded in 633, and contains nine articles; but the seventh is the one that contains all the poison of heresy. This asserts that Christ is the Son himself, who produces the divine and human operations by means of one *theandric* operation alone; that is, we may say, a human-divine operation, both divine and human at the same time—so that the distinction exists not in reality, but is only drawn by our understandings (5). Cyrus gave these articles to be examined by the monk Sophronius; but when he read them, he threw himself at the bishop's feet, and, with tears, implored of him not to promulgate them, as they were contrary to Faith, and conformable to the doctrine of Apollinares. Cyrus, however, would not listen to him, but published the act of union, and Sophronius, seeing he could make no impression in Alexandria, betook himself to Constantinople, to lay the affair before Sergius; but he being one of the firmest supporters of the error, refused to see him, and, under pretext of re-uniting all the heretics of Egypt, approved the doctrine of Cyrus (6).

6. Sophronius returned again to the East, and was elected this same year, 633, Patriarch of Jerusalem, much to the displeasure of Sergius, who endeavoured to blacken him in the estimation of Pope Honorius, to whom he wrote a long letter filled with deceit and lies. He pretends to have been ignorant altogether of the question of two wills, until Cyrus of Phasis wrote to him, and laid great stress on a pretended work of Menas, formerly Bishop of Constantinople, written to support Monothelism. Some of the Fathers, he says, teach one operation in Christ, but not one of them ever speaks of two, and he then falsely reports that St. Sophronius, when he was made Patriarch of Jerusalem, entered into an agreement with him not to say anything about the controversy at all. The Pope, ignorant of the artifices of Sergius, answered him, and commended him for putting a stop to this novel doctrine (the two operations in Christ, maintained by Sophronius), as only calculated to scandalize the simple, and he then adds: "We confess one will alone in Jesus Christ, for the Divinity did not assume our sin, but our nature, as it was created before it was corrupted by sin. We do not see that either the Sacred Scriptures or the Councils teach one or two operations. That Jesus Christ is one alone, operating by the Divinity and humanity, the Scriptures prove in many places; but it is of no consequence to know whether by the operation of the Divinity or of the humanity we should admit one or two operations. We should leave this dispute to the grammarians. We ought to reject these

(5) Epist. Cyri, *p.* 952, ap. Fleury, loc. cit. *n.* 42.   (6) Fleury, cit. *n.* 42.

new expressions, lest the simple, hearing of two operations, might consider us Nestorians, or perhaps might count us Eutychians, if we recognize one operation alone in Christ" (7).

7. Not alone the heretical, but even some Catholic writers, have judged, from these expressions of Pope Honorius, that he fell into the Monothelite heresy; but they are certainly deceived; because when he says that there is only one will in Christ, he intends to speak of Christ as man alone, and in that sense, as a Catholic, he properly denies that there are two wills in Christ opposed to each other, as in us the flesh is opposed to the spirit; and if we consider the very words of his letter, we will see that such is his meaning. " We confess one will alone in Jesus Christ, for the Divinity did not assume our sin, but our nature, as it was created before it was corrupted by sin." This is what Pope John IV. writes to the Emperor Constantine II., in his apology for Honorius: " Some," said he, " admitted two contrary wills in Jesus Christ, and Honorius answers that by saying that Christ—perfect God and perfect man—having come to heal human nature, was conceived and born without sin, and therefore, never had two opposite wills, nor in him the will of the flesh ever combated the will of the spirit, as it does in us, on account of the sin contracted from Adam." He therefore concludes that those who imagine that Honorius taught that there was in Christ but one will alone of the Divinity and of the humanity, are at fault (8). St. Maximus, in his dialogue with Pyrrhus (9), and St. Anastasius Bibliothecarius (10), make a similar defence for Honorius. Graveson, in confirmation of this (11), very properly remarks, that as St Cyril, in his dispute with Nestorius, said, in a Catholic sense, that the nature of the Incarnate Word was one, and the Eutychians seized on the expression as favourable to them, in the same manner, Honorius saying that Christ had one will (that is, that he had not, like us, two opposite wills—one defective, the will of the flesh, and one correct, the will of the Spirit), the Monothelites availed themselves of it to defend their errors.

8. We do not, by any means, deny that Honorius was in error, when he imposed silence on those who discussed the question of one or two wills in Christ, because when the matter in dispute is erroneous, it is only favouring error to impose silence. Wherever there is error it ought to be exposed and combated, and it was here that Honorius was wrong; but it is a fact beyond contradiction, that Honorius never fell into the Monothelite heresy, notwithstanding what heretical writers assert, and especially William Cave (12), who says it is labour in vain to try and defend him from his charge. The learned Noel Alexander clearly proves that it cannot be laid

(7) Fleury, t. 6, l. 37, n. 43, 44. (8) Fleury, loc. cit. l. 28, n. 25. (9) Nat. Alex. t 12, dis. p. 3. (10) Anasta. Præf. ad Joan. Diacon. (11) Graveson, Hist. Ecclesi, t. 3, p. 48, c. 3. (12) Cave, Hist. St. Leo, Monoth.

to his charge (13), and in answer to the great argument adduced by our adversaries, that in the Thirteenth Act of the Sixth Council it was declared that he was anathematized—" Anathematizari prævidimus, et Honorium eo quod invenimus per scripta, quæ ab eo facto sunt ad Sergium, quia in omnibus ejus mentem secutus est, et impia dogmata confirmavit"—replies that the Synod condemned Honorius, not because he formally embraced the heresy, but on account of the favour he showed the heretics, as Leo II. (*Optimo Concilii Interprete*, as N. Alex. calls him) writes to Constantine Pogonatus in his Epistle, requesting the confirmation of the Synod. In this letter Leo enumerates the heretics condemned, the fathers of the heresy, Theodore of Pharan, Cyrus of Alexandria, Sergius, Pyrrhus, Paul and Peter, successors in the See of Constantinople; he also anathematizes Honorius, not for embracing the error, but for permitting it to go on unmolested: " Qui hanc Apostolicam Ecclesiam non Apostolicæ Traditionis doctrina lustravit, sed profana proditione immaculatam maculari permisit." He also writes to the Spanish bishops, and tells them that Theodore, Cyrus, and the others are condemned, together with Honorius, who did not, as befitted his Apostolical authority, extinguish the flame of heretical doctrine in the beginning, but cherished it by negligence. From these and several other sources, then, Noel Alexander proves that Honorius was not condemned by the Sixth Council as a heretic, but as a favourer of heretics, and for his negligence in putting them down, and that he was very properly condemned, for the favourers of heresy and the authors of it are both equally culpable. He adds that the common opinion of the Sorbonne was, that although Honorius, in his letters, may have written some erroneous opinions, still he only wrote them as a private doctor, and in no wise stained the purity of the faith of the Apostolic See; and his letters to Sergius, which we quoted in the last paragraph, prove how different his opinions were from those of the Monothelites.

9. On the death of Honorius, in 638, the Monothelite heresy was very much extended by the publication of the Ecthesis of the Emperor Heraclius. This was an edict drawn up by Sergius himself, and published in the name of Heraclius. It was called Ecthesis, the Greek word for *exposition*, as it contained an exposition of the Faith regarding the question of one or two operations in Jesus Christ. It commences by an exposition of the Faith regarding the Trinity, speaks of the Incarnation, and distinguishes two natures in the single person of Christ, and it then proceeds: " We attribute all the operations of Christ, Divine and human, to the Incarnate Word, and we do not permit it to be said or taught that there are one or two operations, but rather, according to the doctrines of the Ecumenical Councils, we declare that there is one Jesus Christ

---

(13) Nat. Alex. *t.* 11, Hist. Ecclesias. Diss. II. Prop. 3.

alone, who operates things both Divine and human, and that both one and the other operations proceed from the same Incarnate Word, without division or confusion; for although the expression of one or two natures has been made use of by some of the Fathers, still others look on it as strange, and dread lest some may avail themselves of it to destroy the doctrine of the two natures in Christ. On the other hand, the expression of two operations scandalises many, as it was never made use of by any of the principal Doctors of the Church, and because it appears to be the same thing to admit two contrary wills in Christ, as to admit two Persons. And if the impious Nestorius, although he admitted two Sons, did not dare to say that there were two wills—nay, more, he declared that in the two Persons supposed by him, there was only one will—how then can Catholics, who recognize one Jesus Christ alone, admit in him two wills, and even one will contrary to the other? We, therefore, following in all things the Holy Fathers, confess in Christ one will alone, and we believe that his flesh, animated with a rational soul, never of itself made any movement contrary to the Spirit of the Word which was united in one Person." Such was the famous Ecthesis of Heraclius, confirmed afterwards by its author, Sergius, in a Cabal or Council held by him in Constantinople; we perceive that in the commencement it prohibits the expression of one or two operations, to deceive the people, but afterwards the dogma of one will, the formal heresy of the Monothelites, is maintained (14). This Ecthesis was sent to Pope Severinus, but, either because it did not come to hand, or that he died before it reached Rome, we hear nothing of its condemnation then, but it was subsequently condemned by Pope John IV. (15).

10. Notwithstanding the condemnation of the Ecthesis, the Monothelite heresy still continued to flourish, through the malice of Pyrrhus and Paul, the successors of Sergius in the See of Constantinople. Paul pretended, for a long time, to be a Catholic, but at length he threw off the mask, and induced the Emperor Constans to publish, in 648, an edict called the " Type," or formula, imposing silence on both parties. In this formula there is a summary review of the reasons on both sides, and it then proceeds: " Wherefore, for the future, we forbid all our Catholic subjects to dispute about one or two wills or operations, without prejudice, however, to what was decided by the approved Fathers, relative to the Incarnation of the Word. We wish, therefore, that they should hold by the Holy Scriptures, the five General Councils, and the simple expressions of the Fathers, which doctrine is the rule of the Church, without either adding to, or diminishing, anything, nor explaining anything by the private opinions of others, but let

(14) Nat. Alex. *t.* 12, *c.* 2, *s*, 2, *n.* 4; Fleury, *t.* 6, *l.* 38. *n.* 21.   (15) Fleury, loc. cit. *n.* 22.

everything be in the same state as it was before this controversy sprung up at all, and as if it had never taken place. Those who will dare to contravene this decree, if they are bishops or clergymen, they shall be deposed; if monks, excommunicated and banished from their monasteries; if in public employments, cashiered; if private individuals, their property shall be confiscated; and all others shall suffer corporal punishment, and be transported." Such is the " Type" of Constans (16).

11. We should here remark, that on the death of Sergius, he was succeeded by Pyrrhus, and he resigned the See, of his own free-will, afterwards, on account of disputes he had with his people, and Paul, the Econome of the Cathedral Church, was elected in his place (17), and he followed the heretical doctrines of both his predecessors. Pope Theodore laboured hard, both by writing to him and through his Legates, to bring him back to the Catholic Faith, but finding it all in vain, at length, by a formal sentence, deposed him (18). It is supposed that this took place in the same Council in which Theodore condemned Pyrrhus, for after he had made his retractation in Rome at the Pope's own feet, as he had promised St. Maximus he would do, when he disputed with him in Africa (as we shall see hereafter), he went to Ravenna, and again relapsed into Monothelitism. It is probable he was induced by the Exarch, who was a heretic himself, to take this step, hoping to regain his See of Constantinople, and in fact he again got possession of it in the year 655. When Pope Theodore heard of his relapse, he convoked a partial Synod of bishops and the Roman clergy, and pronounced an anathema and sentence of deposition against him, and not only that, but he had the chalice with the consecrated blood of the Redeemer brought to him, dipped the pen in it, and thus signed the awful sentence with the precious Blood of Christ (19).

12. We have spoken of the dispute of Pyrrhus with St. Maximus the Abbot, in Africa. The controversy was about the one or two wills and operations, and it is worthy of remark how forcibly the learned St. Maximus refuted him. If Christ is one, said Pyrrhus, he should only will as one person, and, consequently, he has but one will. Tell me, Pyrrhus, said St. Maximus, Christ is certainly only one, but he is, at the same time, both God and man. If, then, he is true God and true man, he must will as God and as man in two different manners, though but one person all the time, for as he is of two natures, he must certainly will and operate according to the two natures, for neither of these natures is devoid of will, nor devoid of operation. Now, if Jesus Christ willed and operated according to the two natures, he had, as they were, two,

(16) Nat. Alex. loc. cit. n. 6; Fleury, loc. cit. n. 45. (17) Fleury, t. 6, l. 38, n. 24, in fine. (18) Anast. in Theod. Con. Lat. s. 2, p. 116. (19) Fleury, loc. cit.

we must admit that he had two natural wills and two essential
operations, and as the two natures did not divide him, so the two
wills and operations essentially attached to the two natures did not
actually divide him, and being united in Christ did not prevent
him from being one alone. But, Pyrrhus replied, it is not possible,
for as there are several wills there should be several persons. Then
you assert, said St. Maximus, that as there are many wills there
must be many persons to wish; but if you go by this rule, you must
also admit, reciprocally, that as many persons as there are, so many
wills must there be; but if you admit this, you must grant that
there is but one Person, as Sabellius teaches, for in God and in the
three Divine Persons there is but one will alone, or, you must
grant that as there are in God three persons, so there are three
wills, and consequently three natures, as Arius taught, if according
to the doctrine of the Fathers the number of wills must correspond
to the number of persons. It is, therefore (concludes St. Maximus), not true that wherever there are many wills, there are many
persons, but the real truth is that when several natures are united
in the same person, as in Jesus Christ, there are several wills and
operations, though only one person. Pyrrhus raised more difficulties, but St. Maximus answered them all so clearly that he was
at last convinced, and promised him that he would go to Rome,
and retract his errors at the feet of the Pope, which he soon after
did, and presented to his Holiness the instrument of his retractation (20); but again, as we have seen, relapsed.

13. But to return to the Type of Constans; that, together with
all the Monothelite doctrine, was condemned in Rome in a Synod
held by Pope Martin; and in consequence, the holy Pontiff was
bitterly persecuted by Constans, and ended his days in the Crimea, in 654, where he was banished (21). Constans himself, after
practising so many cruelties against the Pope and the faithful,
especially in Syracuse, was called away by God, in the year 668,
the twenty-seventh year of his reign, and met an unhappy end.
He went into the bath along with an attendant, who killed him
with a blow on the head, inflicted with the vessel used for pouring
out water, and instantly took to flight; his attendants, astonished
at his long delay in the bath, at last went in to see what was the
matter, and found him dead (22). Cardinal Gotti (23) says, he
also put St. Maximus to death; and among his other acts of cruelty
related by Noel Alexander (24), on the authority of Theophanes,
Cedrenus, Paul the deacon, &c., is the murder of his brother Theodosius. He first got him ordained a deacon through envy, by the
Patriarch Paul, but he never after enjoyed peace of mind, for
he frequently dreamed he saw his brother clad in the diaconal

---

(20) Fleury, t. 6, l. 38, n. 36 & 40 (21) Danæus, Temp. Natio. p. 158. (22) Fleury, t 6, l. 39, n. 42. (23) Gotti, Vic. adver. Her. c. 68, f. 4, n. 41. (24) Nat. Alex. t. 12, c. 5, ar. 3.

robes, and holding a chalice filled with blood in his hand, and crying out to him, "Drink, brother, drink."

14. The scene was changed. Constantine Pogonatus, son to Constans, mounted the Imperial throne; he was a lover of faith and justice, and lost no time in procuring the assembly of the Sixth General Council in Constantinople, in 680 (25), which was presided over by the Legates of Pope Agatho. Noel Alexander informs us that authors are not agreed as to the number of bishops who attended; Theophanes and Cedrenus reckoned two hundred and nineteen, while Photius only counts one hundred and seventy. This Council was happily brought to a conclusion in eighteen Sessions, and on the 18th of October, the definition of the Faith, in opposition to the heresy of the Monothelites, was thus worded: "We proclaim........ that there are in Christ two natural operations, invisibly, inconvertibly, inseparably, and unconfusedly, according to the doctrine of the Fathers." This definition was subscribed by all the Fathers (26). Thus was concluded the Sixth General Council; the zeal of the prelates was seconded by the approbation and authority of the Emperor, whose faith was lauded by the assembled Fathers, and he was decorated with the title of the Pious Restorer of Religion. The Pope, St. Leo II., the successor of Agatho, who died during the celebration of the Council, confirmed its decisions and decrees, and as Graveson (27) says, confirmed by his Apostolic authority this Sixth Council, and ordained that it should be numbered among the other General Councils.

15. We should here remark, that Cardinal Baronius (28), to wipe off the stain of heresy from Pope Honorius, says, that the Acts of this Council have not been handed down to us fairly, but were corrupted through the artifice of Theodore, the Bishop of Constantinople. But Graveson properly remarks, that this conjecture is not borne out by the learned men of our age, because (as he says) Christian Lupus, Noel Alexander, Anthony Pagi, Combesis and Garner, clearly prove the authenticity of the Acts. Graveson (29), besides, remarks that several follow Cardinal Bellarmine's opinion, and endeavour to clear Honorius, by saying, that the Fathers of the Council were in error in the examination and judgment of Honorius; but, he adds, it is very hard to believe that all the Fathers, not alone of this Council, but also of the Seventh and Eighth General Councils, who also condemned Honorius, were in error, when condemning his doctrine. I think it better, then, to keep on the highway, and conclude, that Honorius can, by every right, be cleared from the Monothelite heresy, but still was

(25) Nat. Alexander, *t.* 12, *c.* 2, *a.* 1, *s.* 4; Herm. *c.* 240; Fleury, *t.* 6, *l.* 4, *n.* 11; Berti, *t.* 1, *sec.* 7, *c. a.*   (26) Tourncly. Theol. Com. *t.* 3, in appen. *p.* 304.
(27) Graveson, Hist. Ecclesias. *t.* 3, *p.* 60; Collog. 4.   (28) Baron. ap. Grav
(29) Grav. loc. cit. *p.* 27.

justly condemned by the Council, as a favourer of heretics, and for his negligence in repressing error. Danæus (30) says the same thing; there is no open heresy in the private letter of Honorius to Sergius, but he is worthy of condemnation for his pusillanimity in using ambiguous words to please and keep on terms with heretics, when it was his duty to oppose them strenuously in the beginning. Hermant says (31), that Honorius was condemned, because he allowed himself to be imposed on by the artifices of Sergius, and did not maintain the interests of the Church with the constancy he should have done. It is dreadful to see the blindness and obstinacy of so many prelates of the Church poisoned by this heresy. Among the rest, Noel Alexander tells us, was Macarias, Patriarch of Antioch, who was present at the Council (32), who, when the Emperor and the Fathers asked him if he confessed two natural wills, and two natural operations in Christ, answered that he would sooner allow himself to be torn limb from limb, and thrown into the sea; he was very properly deposed, and excommunicated by the Synod. The same author informs us (33,) that the heresy continued to flourish among the Chaldeans, even since the Council (but they abandoned it in the Pontificate of Paul V.), and among the Maronites and Armenians, likewise; among these last another sect, called Paulicians, from one Paul of Samosata, took root in 653. They admitted the two principles of the Manicheans, denied that Mary was the Mother of God, and taught several other extravagances enumerated by Noel Alexander (34). Before I conclude this chapter, I wish to make one reflection; we see how it displeases the powers of hell, that mankind should be grateful to our Redeemer, and return him love for love; for the devil is constantly labouring to sow amongst Christians, by means of wicked men, so many heresies, all tending to destroy the belief of the Incarnation of the Son of God, and, in consequence, to diminish our love for Jesus Christ, who, by the assumption of the flesh of man, has constituted himself our Saviour. Such were the heresies of Sabellius, of Photinus, of Arius, of Nestorius, of Eutyches, and of the Monothelites; some of these have made of Christ an imaginary personage, some deprived him of the Divinity, others again of his humanity, but the Church has always been victorious against them.

(30) Danæus Temp. Not. *p.* 259. (31) Hermant, *t.* 5, *c.* 242. (32) Nat. Alexander, *t.* 12, *ar.* 1, *s.* 4. (33) Nat. Alexander, *t.* 12, *c.* 2, *ar.* 12, *s.* 2, in fine. (34) Nat. Alexander, loc. cit. *a.* 3.

CHAPTER VIII.

HERESIES OF THE EIGHTH CENTURY.

THE HERESY OF THE ICONOCLASTS.

1. Beginning of the Iconoclasts. 2, 3. St. Germanus opposes the Emperor Leo. 4. He resigns the See of Constantinople. 5. Anastasius is put in his place; Resistance of the Women. 6. Cruelty of Leo. 7. Leo endeavours to put the Pope to Death; Opposition of the Romans. 8. Letter of the Pope. 9. A Council is held in Rome in Support of the Sacred Images, but Leo continues his Persecution. 10. His Hand is miraculously restored to St. John of Damascus. 11. Leo dies, and is succeeded by Constantine Copronymus, a greater Persecutor; Death of the impious Patriarch Anastasius. 12. Council held by Constantine. 13. Martyrs in Honour of the Images. 14. Other tyrannical Acts of Constantine, and his horrible Death. 15. Leo IV. succeeds to the Empire, and is succeeded by his Son, Constantine. 16. The Empress Irene, in her Son's Name, demands a Council. 17. Seditions against the Council. 18. The Council is held, and the Veneration of Images established. 19. Erroneous Opinion of the Council of Frankfort, regarding the Eighth General Council. 20. Persecution again renewed by the Iconoclasts.

1. THE first and fifth Acts of the Eighth General Council attest that the Gentiles, the Jews, the Marcionites, and the Manicheans, had previously declared war against sacred images, and it again broke out in the year 723, in the reign of Leo Isaurus. About this period, a captain of the Jews, called Sarantapechis (or four cubits), induced the Caliph Jezzid to commence a destructive war against the sacred images in the Christian churches, promising him a long and happy reign as his reward. He, accordingly, published an edict, commanding the removal of all images; but the Christians refused to obey him, and six months afterwards God removed him out of the way. Constantius, Bishop of Nacolia, in Phrygia, introduced this Jewish doctrine among Christians. He was expelled from his See, in punishment of his perfidy, by his own diocesans, and ingratiated himself into the Emperor's favour, and induced him to declare war against images (1).

2. Leo had already reigned ten years, when, in the year 727, he declared publicly to the people, that it was not right to venerate images. The people, however, all cried out against him; and he then said, he did not mean (2) to say that images should be done away with altogether, but that they should be placed high up, out of the reach, that they should not be soiled by the people kissing them. It was manifest his intention was to do away with them altogether; but he met the most determined resistance from St. Germanus, Patriarch of Constantinople, who proclaimed his willingness to lay down his life for the sacred images, which were always venerated in the Church. The holy pontiff wrote many

---

(1) Nat. Alex. *t.* 12, *sec.* 8, *c.* 2, *a.* 1; Hermaut, *t.* 1, *p.* 283; Fleury, *t.* 6, *l.* 42, *n.* 1; Baron. Ann. 723, *n.* 17, & vide Ann. 726, *n.* 3.   (2) Nat. Alex. loc. cit.; Fleury, loc. cit.

letters to those bishops who held on to the Emperor's opinion, to turn them from their evil ways, and he also wrote to Pope Gregory II., who answered him in a long letter, approving of his zeal, and stating what was the doctrine of the Catholic Church in the veneration of the sacred images which he was contending for (3).

3. The Emperor continued his rage against images, and the displeasure of the people of Continental Greece and the islands of the Cyclades at length broke out into open rebellion. Zeal for religion was the motive assigned for this outbreak, and one Cosimus was elected as their Emperor, and they marched to Constantinople to have him crowned. They fought a battle near Constantinople, under the leadership of Cosimus, Agallianus, and Stephanus, but were totally defeated; so Agallianus threw himself into the sea, and Stephanus and Cosimus were taken and beheaded. Leo was emboldened by this victory to persecute the Catholics with greater violence. He sent for the Patriarch, St. Germanus, and strove to bring him over to his way of thinking; but (4) the saint told him openly, that whoever would strive to abolish the veneration of images was a precursor of Antichrist, and that such doctrine had a tendency to upset the mystery of the Incarnation; and he reminded him of his coronation oath, not to make any change in the traditions of the Church. All this had no effect on the Emperor; he continued to press the Patriarch, and strove to entrap him into some unguarded expression, which he might consider seditious, and thus have a reason for deposing him. He was urged on to adopt this course by Anastasius, a disciple of the Patriarch, but who joined the Emperor's party, and was promised the See of Constantinople, on the deposition of St. Germanus. The saint, knowing the evil designs of Anastasius, gave him many friendly admonitions. One day, in particular, he was going in to see the Emperor, and Anastasius followed him so closely that he trod on his robe: "Do not be in a hurry," said the saint; "you will be soon enough in the hyppodrome" (the public circus), alluding to his disgrace fifteen years afterwards, when the Emperor Constantine, who placed him in the See of Constantinople, had his eyes plucked out, and conducted round the hyppodrome, riding on an ass, with his face to the tail; but, for all that, kept him in the See, because he was an enemy to the sacred images. The Emperor, in the meanwhile, continued a bitter enemy of the Patriarch St. Germanus, and persecuted, not alone the Catholics who venerated the sacred images, but those also who honoured the relics of the saints, and invoked their intercession, not knowing, or, perhaps, not wishing to learn, the difference between the supreme worship, which we

---

(3) Fleury, *t.* 6, *l.* 42, *n.* 3.   (4) Fleury, loc. cit. *n.* 4, ex Theophil.

Catholics pay to God, and that veneration which we pay to relics and holy images (5).

4. The Emperor convoked a Council in the early part of the year 730 (6), in which he made a decree against sacred images, and wanted the Patriarch to subscribe it, but he firmly refused, and preferred resigning his dignity; he threw off his pallium, and said: " It is impossible, my Lord, that I can sanction any novelty against the Faith; I can do nothing without a General Council;" and he left the meeting. The Emperor was enraged, and sent some armed officials to eject him from the archiepiscopal palace, which they did with blows and outrages, not even respecting his venerable age of eighty years. He went to the house of his family, and lived there as a monk, and left the See of Constantinople, which he had governed for fourteen years, in a state of the greatest desolation. He then died a holy death, and the Church venerates his memory on the 12th of May (7).

5. A few days after the banishment of St. Germanus, Anastasius was appointed Patriarch of Constantinople, and, by force of arms, was put in possession of the See. The impious usurper at once gave up all power over the churches to the Emperor, and he having now no one to contradict him, began vigorously to enforce his decree against the holy images. In the vestibule of the imperial palace at Constantinople, there was an image of our Redeemer crucified, held in extraordinary veneration by the people, as it was believed to have been erected by Constantine, in memory of the cross that appeared to him in the heavens. Leo intended to begin with this most sacred image, and he ordered Jovinus, one of his guards, to throw it down; a number of women, who were present, endeavoured to dissuade him from the sacrilegious attempt, but he despised their supplications, mounted on a ladder, and gave three blows with an axe on the face of it. When the women saw this, they dragged back the ladder, threw him on the ground, killed him, and tore him in pieces. Withal, the holy image was cast to the earth and burned, and the Emperor put in its place a plain cross, with an inscription telling that the image was removed, for the Iconoclasts venerated the cross, and only did away with images representing the human figure. The women, after killing Jovinus, ran off to the bishop's palace, hurled stones against it, and poured out all sorts of abuse on Anastasius: " Wretch that you are," said they, " you have usurped the priesthood only to destroy everything sacred." Anastasius, outrageous at the insult, went at once to the Emperor, and had the women all put to death; ten more suffered along with them, and the Greek Church honours them as martyrs on the 9th of August (8).

6. The Emperor Leo, a man of no learning himself, was a bitter

(5) Fleury, t. 6, l. 42, n. 4. (6) Theoph. Ann. 10, p. 340, ap. Fleury, loc. cit. Baron. Ann. 754, n. 42. (7) Fleury, loc. cit. (8) Fleury, t. 6, l. 42, n. 5.

persecutor of learned men, and abolished the schools of sacred literature, which flourished from the time of Constantine. There was a library founded by the ancient Emperors near the imperial palace of Constantine, containing over three thousand volumes. The librarian, Lecumenicus, was a man of great merit, and he superintended the labours of twelve professors, who taught gratuitously both the sacred and the profane sciences. This learned corporation had so high a character, that even the Emperor himself could not make any unusual ordinance without consulting them. Leo used every means in his power, both threats and promises, to induce these professors to give their sanction to his proceedings; but when he found it was all in vain, he surrounded the library with faggots and dry wood, and burned both the professors and the literary treasures together. Partly by threat, and partly by seduction, he got all the inhabitants of Constantinople to bring together into the middle of the city all the images of the Redeemer, the Blessed Virgin, and the saints, and burn them, and the paintings in the churches were all destroyed and covered over with whitewash. Many refused obedience, and he beheaded some, and mutilated others, so that many clergy, monks, and even lay people suffered martyrdom (9).

7. When the news of this persecution reached Italy, the images of the Emperor were thrown down and trampled (10), and when he sent his impious decree against holy images to Rome, and threatened Pope Gregory II. to depose him, if he resisted its execution, the Pontiff rejected the impious command, and prepared to resist him as an enemy to the Church, and wrote to the faithful in all parts, to put them on their guard against this new error. The people of the Pentapolis, and the army quartered in the Venetian territory, refused obedience to the Imperial decree, and proclaimed that they would fight in defence of the Pope Paul the Exarch of Ravenna, the Emperor, who sent him his orders, and all who would obey them, were anathematized, and Chiefs were elected. All Italy, at last, in a general agreement, resolved to elect another Emperor, and conduct him to Constantinople; but the Pope having still some hopes of the conversion of Leo, used all his influence to prevent this plan being put into execution. While things were in this state, Exilaratus, Duke of Naples, and his son Adrian, Lord of Campania, persuaded the people of that province to obey the Emperor, and kill the Pope, but both father and son were taken by the Romans, and killed by them, and as it was reported that Peter, the Duke of Rome, had written to the Emperor against the Pope, he was driven out of the city by the people. The people of Ravenna were divided into two factions, one party for the Pope, another for the Emperor; they broke out at last into open warfare, and the

---

(9) Baron. An. 754, n. 37; Fleury, loc. cit. n. 5, con Anas. in Greg. II. & Theophil. 15, p. 543, &c. (10) Fleury, loc. cit. n. 6.

Patrician Paul, Exarch of Ravenna, was killed. While all this was going on, the Lombards conquered several strong places of Emilia and Auxumum, in the Pentapolis, and finally took Ravenna itself. Gregory II., therefore, wrote to Ursus, Duke of Venice, or rather of the Province of Ravenna, called Venice, to unite with the Exarch, then in Venice, and recover the city for the Emperor. But the Emperor was only more outrageous, and sent the Patrician Eutychius, a eunuch, to Naples, who sent one of his creatures to Rome, to procure the Pope's death, and the death of the chief people of the city likewise; when this was discovered, the people wanted to kill the Patrician, but the Pope saved his life. The whole people then, rich and poor, swore that they would die before they would allow the Pope, the defender of the Faith, to be injured. The ungrateful Patrician sent messengers to the Lombard Dukes, and offered them the most tempting bribes if they would desert the Pope, but they, already acquainted with his perfidy, joined with the Romans, and took the same oath as they did to defend the Pope (11).

8. Anastasius, the newly-elected Patriarch of Constantinople, sent his Synodical letter to Pope Gregory II., but the Pope knowing him to be a supporter of the Iconoclasts, refused to recognize him as a brother, and gave him notice that if he did not return to the Catholic Faith, he would be degraded from the priesthood (12). Gregory did not long survive this; he died in the February of 731, and was succeeded by Gregory III., who, in the beginning of his reign, wrote to the Emperor an answer to a letter sent to his predecessor, rather than to him. In this able production he thus speaks: "You confess a holy Faith in your letters, in all its purity, and declare accursed all who dare to contradict the decisions of the Fathers. What, therefore, induces you to turn back, after having walked in the right road for ten years? During all that time, you never spoke of the holy images, and now, you say that they are the same as the idols, and that those who venerate them are idolaters. You are endeavouring to destroy them, and do not you dread the judgment of God; scandalising, not alone the faithful, but the very infidels? Why have you not, as Emperor and chief of the Christian people, sought the advice of learned men? they would have taught you why God prohibited the adoration of idols made by men. The Fathers, our masters, and the six Councils, have handed down as a tradition, the veneration of holy images, and you refuse to receive their testimony. We implore of you to lay aside this presumption." He then speaks of the doctrine of the Church regarding the veneration of images, and thus concludes: "You think to terrify me by saying: I will send to Rome, and will break the statue of St. Peter, and I will drag away Pope Gregory in chains,

(11) Fleury, *t.* 6. *l.* 42, *n.* 6.   (12) Theoph. *ar.* 13, *p.* 343, apud; Fleur. loc. cit. *n.* 7.

as Constans did Martin. Know, then, that the Popes are the arbiters of peace between the East and the West, and as to your threats, we fear them not" (13).

9. He wrote a second letter to Leo soon after, but neither the first nor second reached him, for a priest of the name of George, to whom they were entrusted, was afraid to present them, so the Pope put him under penance for his negligence, and sent him again with the same letters, but the Emperor had the letters detained in Sicily, and banished the priest for a year, and would not allow him to come to Constantinople (14). The Pope was highly indignant that his letters were despised, and his Legate, George, detained, so he felt himself called on to summon a Council in Rome, in 732 (15), which was attended by ninety-three bishops, and by the consuls, the nobility, the clergy, and people of Rome, and in this assembly it was ordained that all those who showed disrespect to holy images should be excluded from the communion of the Church, and this decree was solemnly subscribed by all who attended. The Pope again wrote to the Emperor, but his letters were detained a second time, and the messengers kept in prison for a year, at the termination of which, the letters were forcibly taken from him, and he was threatened and maltreated, and sent back to Rome. All Italy joined in a petition to the Emperor to re-establish the veneration of the holy images, but even this petition was taken from the messengers by the patrician Sergius, governor of Sicily, and they, after a detention of eight months, were sent back, after having received cruel treatment. The Pope, however, again wrote to the Emperor, and to the Patriarch Anastasius, but all in vain, and Leo, enraged with the Pope and his rebellious subjects in Italy, sent a great fleet against them, but it was shipwrecked in the Adriatic. This increased his fury, so he raised to a third higher the capitation tax in Calabria and Sicily, and obliged a strict registry to be kept of all the male children that were born, and confiscated in all the countries where his power reached in the East, the estates belonging to the patrimony of St. Peter. He continued to persecute all who still venerated the holy images; he no longer, indeed, put them to death, lest they should be honoured as martyrs, but he imprisoned them, and tortured them first, and then banished them (16).

10. About this time the cruel persecution of St. John of Damascus took place. This saint defended, in Syria, the honour due to the sacred images, so Leo endeavoured to ruin him by an infamous calumny; he had him accused as a traitor to the Saracen Caliph Hiokam, and the false charge proved by a forged letter; the caliph called his council together, and the saint was con-

---

(13) Fleury, t. 6, l. 42, n. 7 & 8.   (14) Fleury, loc. cit. n. 9.   (15) Anast. in Greg. III., n. 8 & 9 apud; Fleury, l. 42, n. 16.   (16) Fleury, t. 6, l. 42, n. 16 & 17.

demned, and sentenced to have his hand cut off as a traitor. His innocence was, however, miraculously proved; animated with a lively faith, he went before an image of the Blessed Virgin, whose honour he constantly defended, placed his amputated hand in connexion with the stump of his arm, prayed to the Holy Mother that his hand might be again united to his body, that he might be able to write again in her defence; his prayer was heard, and he was miraculously healed (17). Noel Alexander says (18), that the wonderful things related of St. John of Damascus are proved from th book of the Life of St. John of Jerusalem.

11. The Almighty, in the end, took vengeance on the crimes of the Emperor, and evils from all sides fell thick upon him; pestilence and famine ravaged both the city and country, and the fairest provinces of Asia were laid waste by the Saracens. He became a prey to the most direful and tormenting maladies himself, and died miserably in 741, leaving the Empire to his son Constantine Copronimus. He surpassed his father in wickedness, his morals were most debased, and he had no principle of religion; not alone satisfied with destroying the images and relics of the saints, he prohibited all from invoking their intercession. His subjects could no longer bear with his vices, so they rose up against him, and proclaimed his relative, Artavesdes, Pretor of Armenia, Emperor. This prince, brought up in the Catholic Faith, re-established the veneration of sacred images; and Religion began to hope once more for happy days, but Constantine recovered the Empire, took Constantinople, and Artavesdes fell into his hands with his two sons, Nicephorus and Nicetus, and he deprived all three of sight. The justice of God now overtook the false Patriarch, Anastasius; he ordered him to be led through the city, as we have already remarked, mounted on an ass, with his face to the tail, and to be severely flogged; but as he could find no one wicked enough to carry out his designs, he continued him in the Patriarchate; he enjoyed the dignity but a short time after this disgrace; he was attacked by a horrible cholic, in which the functions of nature were disgustingly reversed, and he left the world without any signs of repentance (19).

12. Constantine, raging more furiously against sacred images every day, wished to have the sanction of ecclesiastical authority for his impiety; he accordingly convoked a General Council, as Danæus tells us, in 754, in Constantinople, and three hundred and thirty-eight bishops assembled, but the Legates of the Apostolic See, or the bishops of the other Patriarchates, were not present. Theodore, Bishop of Ephesus, and Palla, or Pastilla, Bishop of Perga, at first presided, but the Emperor afterwards appointed

(17) Hermant, *t*. 1, *c*. 187; Gotti, *t*. 2. c. 80, *s*. 1, *n* 15, 16, 17.   (18) Natal. *t*. 12, *c*. 2, *a*. 1, *s*. 1.   (19) Hermant, *t*. 1, *c*. 289; Baron. 763, *n*. 19.

Constantine, a monk, President, a man whose only law was the Emperor's will, and who, having been a bishop, was degraded and banished from his see, on acconnt of his scandalous vices. In the Cabal which they had the hardihood to call the Seventh General Council, all honour shown to the images and saints was condemned as idolatry, and all who approved of recurring to the intercession of the Blessed Virgin were anathematized. We find no decision against relics, or against the Cross, which they held in great veneration, for they obliged every one to swear on the Cross to receive the decree of their Council, and to do away with the veneration of images. Thus, we always remark, as a particular characteristic of heresy, the spirit of contradiction.

13. When this Council was brought to a close, the Emperor redoubled his persecutions against the Catholics. Several bishops and several solitaries, who forsook their cells to defend the Faith, received the crown of martyrdom. Among these, three holy Abbots are particularly remembered;—the first was St. Andrew Calabita; he had the courage to charge the Emperor to his face with impiety; he called him another Valens, a second Julian, and he was ordered to be flogged to death: he suffered in 761, and the Church honours his memory on the 17th of October (20). The second was the Abbot Paul; he was taken by Lardotirus, Governor of the Island of Theophanus. This wretch placed on the ground an image of Jesus Christ on one side, and the rack on the other. "Now, Paul," said he, "choose whichever you like; trample on that image, or you shall be put on the rack." "O Jesus Christ, my Lord," said the Saint, "may God never permit me to trample on your holy image," and throwing himself on the ground, he most devoutly kissed it. The Governor was furious, and commanded that he should be stripped;—he was stretched on the rack; the executioners squeezed him from head to heels, and bored all his limbs with iron nails; he was then suspended by his feet, his head down, and roasted alive, in that posture, with a great fire (21). The third was St. Stephen, Abbot of Mount Auxentium; he was first of all exiled to the Island of Proconesus, near the Hellespont, for two years; afterwards brought to Constantinople, and put into prison, with chains on his hands, and his feet in the stocks. There he had the consolation to meet three hundred and forty-two monks from different countries —some had their noses cut off; some their eyes pulled out, or their hands or ears cut off; some were covered all over with scars, from the floggings they had received; and many were afterwards put to death, and all this because they would not subscribe the decree against holy images. After being detained forty days in prison, a number of the imperial satellites came there one day, furiously calling on the guards to bring out Stephen of Auxentium. The

(20) Fleury, *t.* 6, *l.* 43, *n.* 32.   (21) Fleury, loc. cit. *n.* 46.

saint came boldly forward, and said: "I am he whom you seek;" they immediately threw him on the ground, tied a rope to the irons on his legs, and dragged him through the streets, kicking and trampling him on the head and body, and striking him with clubs and stones all the way. When they dragged him as far as the Oratory of St. Theodore the Martyr, just outside the first gate of the Pretorium, he raised up his head and recommended himself to the intercession of the Martyr. "See," said Philomatus, one of his tormentors, "the scoundrel wishes to die a martyr," and he at once struck him on the head with a heavy club, and killed him. The murderer immediately fell to the ground, the devil entered into him, and took possession of him, and he died a death of torment. They still withal continued dragging along the body of St. Stephen; the ground was covered with his blood, and his limbs were torn from his body. If any one refused to insult the sacred remains, he was looked on as an enemy to the Emperor. They came at last to a convent of nuns, and the saint's sister was one of the community; they thought to make her come out and throw a stone at the remains of her brother, with her own hand; but she concealed herself in a tomb, and they were foiled in their savage intent. Finally, they threw the body of the saint into a pit, at the Church of the Martyr St. Pelagia, where the Emperor commanded that the bodies of malefactors and Pagans should be buried. This saint was martyred in the year 767 (22).

14. The churches themselves did not escape the fury of Constantine; numberless sacrileges were committed in them by his soldiers. When the decree of the Council was promulgated in the provinces, the heretics at once commenced the destruction of all pictorial and sculptural ornaments; the images were burned or broken, the painted walls whitewashed, the frames of the paintings were burned (23); in a word, more barbarity was exercised in the name of a Christian Emperor than under any of his Pagan predecessors. Michael, the Governor of Anatolia (24), collected together, by order of the Emperor, in the year 770, all the religious men of the province of Thrace in a plain near Ephesus, and then addressed them: "Whosoever wishes to obey the Emperor, let him dress himself in white, and take a wife immediately; but those who refuse it shall lose their eyes, and be banished to Cyprus." The order was immediately put into execution. Many underwent the punishment (though some apostatized), and were numbered among the Martyrs. The next year the governor sold out all the monasteries, both male and female, with all the sacred vessels, stock, and entire property, and sent the proceeds to the Emperor; he burned all their books and pictures, burned also whatever reliquaries he could lay hands

---

(22) Fleury, *t.* 6, *l.* 43, *n.* 36.   (23) Fleury, *n.* 8.   (24) Nat. Alex. *t.* 12, *c.* 2, art. 1, *s.* 2; Fleury, *t.* 6, *l.* 44, *n.* 7.

on, and punished those who had them in their possession as guilty of idolatry. Some he put to death by the sword, more expired under the lash; he deprived an immense multitude of sight; he ordered the beards of others to be anointed with oil and melted wax, and then set on fire; and more he banished, after subjecting them to various tortures. Such was the furious persecution by Constantine of the venerators of holy images; but with all his cruelty, he could not destroy religion, and in the end God destroyed him, by an extraordinary sickness, in the year 775. According to Danæus, his death was like that of Antiochus, and his repentance of the same sort as that of his prototype (25). Fleury says (26), that Constantine having cast his eye on a crown of gems presented to the Patriarchal Church by the Emperor Heraclius, seized it; but he had scarcely put it on his head, when he was covered with carbuncles, and tortured besides with a violent fever, and that he died in the most excruciating agony. Van Ranst adds (27), that he died consumed by an internal fire, and crying out that he was burning alive as a penalty for the irreverence he showed to the images of the Mother of God.

15. Constantine Copronimus was succeeded by his son, Leo IV.; he pretended to be a Catholic in the commencement of his reign, with the intention of cementing his authority, and more especially he expressed his wishes that the Mother of God should be treated with the greatest respect; he permitted the Religious scattered in the late persecution to inhabit their monasteries once more, and assisted them to do so, and he appointed Catholic bishops to the Sees; but when he felt himself firmly established on the throne he threw off the mask and renewed the persecution with all his father's fury: he even banished the Empress Irene, his wife, because he suspected that in private she venerated the holy images, and nothing would induce him to see her again. His reign, however, was short; he was attacked by a strange disorder like his father's, and died, having only reigned about five years. He had associated his son Constantine in the Empire with him, but as he was only ten years old at his father's death, his mother, the Empress Irene, took the reins of government, and under her pious care the Christian religion flourished once more. Paul, then Patriarch of Constantinople, was attacked with a severe sickness and took the sudden resolution of retiring into a monastery, and declared to the Empress that against his conscience he condemned the veneration of images to please the Emperor Copronimus. Withal, he was a virtuous man, and the Empress endeavoured to force him to resume the government of his Church, but he was firm in his refusal, and said he would spend the remainder of his days weeping for his sins (28).

(25) Hermant, t. 1, c 299, 300.   (26) Fleury, l. 41, n. 16.   (27) Van Ranst, s c. 8. p 147   (28) Hermant, t. 1, c. 304, 305.

16. Tarasius, as yet a layman, and who had been Secretary of State, was, with the good will of all, appointed to succeed Paul; but as the See was separated from the communion of the other patriarchates, he accepted it solely on condition that as soon as possible a General Council should be convoked, to re-unite all the Churches in one faith. This condition was agreed to by all, and he was consecrated Patriarch, and immediately sent his professsion of faith to Pope Adrian, and at the same time the Empress also wrote to the Holy Father, both in her own and her son's name, imploring him to consent to the convocation of a General Council, and to assist at it himself in person to re-establish the ancient tradition in regard to the veneration of holy images, and if he could not attend himself, at least to send his Legates. The Pope answered this letter of the Empress, and besought her to use all her influence to get the Greeks to pay the same veneration to holy images as did the Romans, following the tradition of the Fathers; and should it be found impossible, he says, to re-establish this point without a General Council, the first thing of all to be done should be, to declare the nullity of the false Council, held in the reign of the Emperor Leo. He besides required that the Emperor should send a declaration sworn in his own name, and in the names of the Empress his mother, of the Patriarch, and of the whole Senate, that the Council should enjoy full and perfect liberty (29).

17. The Pope then sent two Legates to Constantinople—Peter, Archpriest of the Roman Church, and Peter, Abbot of the Monastery of St. Saba, and they arrived at their destination while the Emperor and Empress were in Thrace. The Iconoclast bishops, who were more numerous and supported by a great number of the laity, took courage from this, and insisted that it was necessary to maintain the condemnation of images, and not allow a new Council. The Emperor and Empress returned to Constantinople, and the 1st of August of the year 786 was appointed for opening the Council in the Church of the Apostles. The evening before, however, the soldiers went to the baptistery of the church, crying out that they would have no Council. The Patriarch notified this to the Empress; but, notwithstanding the disturbance, it was determined not to postpone the Council, and it was opened the following day. When the bishops were assembled, and while the Synodical letters were being read, the soldiers, urged on by the schismatical bishops, came round the church, and, thundering at the doors, told the assembled prelates that they would never allow what was decreed under the Emperor Constantine to be revoked, and they then burst into the church with drawn swords, and threatened the Patriarch and bishops with death. The Emperor sent his own body-guards to restrain them, but they could not succeed, and the schismatical bishops sung the

(29) Fleury, *t.* 6, *l.* 44, *n.* 25.

song of victory. The Patriarch and the Catholic bishops went into the Sanctuary, in the meantime, and celebrated the Holy Mysteries, without showing any signs of fear; but the Empress sent him word to retire for that time, and avoid the extremity the schismatics might be led to. Every one then went to his own lodging, and the disturbance was quelled. The Empress then, in the ensuing month, brought in a reinforcement of new troops from Thrace, and sent out of the city all those, together with their families, who had served under her father-in-law, Constantine, and were tainted with his errors (30).

18. Being thus secured against the violence of the soldiery and the intrigues of the chiefs of the sedition, on the May following, in the year 787, the bishops were again called on to hold the Council in Nice, in Bythynia; and, on the 24th of September (31), the same year, the first Session was held in the Church of St. Sophia, in that city. Three hundred and fifty bishops, the Legates of the Apostolic See, and of the three Patriarchal Sees, and a great number of monks and Archimandrites, attended. The Legates of Pope Adrian presided in this Council, as we gather from the Acts, in which they are named before the Patriarch Tarasius, and before the Legates of the other Patriarchal Sees. Graveson remarks that the statement of Photius, that Tarasius presided in the Seventh Council, is as false as what he asserts in another place, that the Patriarchs of Constantinople presided at all the former General Councils. Seven Sessions were held in this Council. In the first Session the petition of a great many bishops was read, condemning the heresy of the Iconoclasts, and asking pardon at the same time for having subscribed the false Council of Copronimus. The Council having examined their case admitted them to mercy, and re-established them in their dignity; but deferred the admission of those bishops who had lived for a long period in heresy. In the Second Session the letter of Pope Adrian to the Emperor, and to Tarasius, was read, and several other bishops were re-established in their Sees. In the Fourth Session, several proofs of the veneration of holy images were read from the Scriptures and from the Holy Fathers. In the Fifth, it was proved that the Iconoclasts had drawn their erroneous doctrines from the Gentiles, the Jews, the Manicheans, and the Saracens. In the Sixth, chapter by chapter of everything that was defined in the late Cabal of Constantinople was refuted (32); and, in the Seventh Session, the veneration of sacred images was defined. Cardinal Gotti (33) gives the Decree in full; this is the substance of it: "Following the tradition of the Catholic Church, we define that, in the same manner as the image of the precious cross, so should be likewise venerated, and placed in churches, on

(30) Fleury, *t.* 6, *l.* 44, 28. (31) Fleury, *n.* 39; Nat. Alex. *t.* 11, *c.* 3, *d.* 3; Graves, *t.* 3, *col.* 4. (32) Fleury, *t.* 6, *l.* 44, *n.* 29. (33) Gotti, Ver. Rel. *t.* 2, *c.* 80, *s.* 4.

walls in houses, and streets, the images of our Lord Jesus Christ, of the Holy Mother of God, of the Angels, and of all the Saints. For those who frequently have before their eyes, and contemplate those sacred images, are more deeply impressed with the memory of those they represent, and give them an honorary adoration, but do not, indeed, offer them that real adoration which Faith teaches should be given to God alone; for the honour paid to the image is referred to the principal, and he who venerates an image venerates the person it represents." It then anathematizes all those who profess or teach otherwise, and who reject the images, crosses, pictures, or relics, which the Church honours. This Decree was subscribed by all the bishops.

19. When the Acts of this Council were brought to France, the bishops of that nation (34), assembled in a Synod, in Frankfort, absolutely rejected them; and so did Charlemagne, in the "Four Books," either composed by him, or more properly published in his name, in the year 790, and called the Four Caroline Books. But as Selvaggi, in his notes on Mosheim, remarks (35), all this was caused by an error of fact, as the Frankfort Fathers believed that the Fathers of Nice decided that images should be absolutely worshipped, and this he proves from the Second Canon of the Council of Frankfort itself. " A question has been submitted to us," it says, " concerning the new Synod the Greeks have holden in Constantinople, relative to the worship of images, in which it is reported to have been decided, that those should be anathematized who would not worship them. This doctrine we totally reject:" " Allata est in medium quæstio de nova Græcorum Synodo, quam de adorandis Imaginibus Constantinopoli fecerunt, in qua scriptum habebatur, ut qui Imaginibus Sanctorum, ita ut Deificæ Trinitatis servitium, aut adorationem non impenderent, anathema judicarentur. Qui supra sanctissimi Patres nostri omnimodis adorationem renuentes contempserunt atque consentientes condemnaverunt." This mistake occurred, as Danæus says, on account of the unfaithful version of the Acts of the Council of Nice received in France, and translated from the Greek; whereas the Council of Nice itself, as we have already seen, makes the distinction between honorary reverence and absolute adoration very clearly.

20. Besides, Graveson informs us, that the French bishops did not consider this Council of Nice as a General one at all, but merely a Greek national Synod, since it was almost altogether composed of Eastern bishops, and they did not see the customary letter of confirmation from the Pope to the Emperor and to the whole Church; but, as Danæus says, as soon as the matter was cleared up, there was no longer any disagreement. Still, he says, in the ninth century, several Emperors, adherents of the Iconoclasts, renewed

(34) Graves. Hist. Eccl. t. 3, col. 1.   (36) Selvag. nota, 65, ad t. 10, Mosh. p. 1063.

the persecution of the Catholics, and especially Nicephorus, Leo the Armenian, Michael the Stammerer, and, above all, Theophilus, who surpassed all the rest in cruelty. He died, however, in 842, and the Empress Theodora, his wife, a pious and Catholic lady, administered the empire for her son, Michael, and restored peace to the Church, so that the Iconoclasts never after disturbed the peace of the Eastern Church. This erroneous doctrine began to spring up in the West in the twelfth century—the Petrobrussians first, and then the Henricians and Albigenses followed it. Two hundred years after, the same error was preached by the followers of Wickliffe; by the Hussites, in Bohemia; by Carlostad, in Wittemburg, though against Luther's will; and by the disciples of Zuinglius and Calvin, the faithful imitators of Leo and Copronimus; and those, as Danæus says, who boast of following the above-named masters, should add to their patrons both the Jews and the Saracens. I have explained the doctrine of the veneration of holy images in my dogmatic work on the Council of Trent (*sess.* 25, *sec.* 4, *n.* 35), in which this matter is discussed, and the veneration due to the holy images of the Trinity, of the Cross, of Jesus Christ, of his Divine Mother, and the Saints, is proved from tradition, and from the authority of Fathers, and ancient history; and the objections made by heretics are there answered likewise.

CHAPTER IX.

HERESIES OF THE NINTH CENTURY.

ARTICLE I.

THE GREEK SCHISM COMMENCED BY PHOTIUS.

1. St. Ignatius, by means of Bardas, Uncle to the Emperor Michael, is expelled from the See of Constantinople. 2. He is replaced by Photius. 3. Photius is consecrated. 4. Wrongs inflicted on St. Ignatius and on the Bishops who defended him. 5. The Pope sends Legates to investigate the Affair. 6. St. Ignatius appeals from the Judgment of the Legates to the Pope himself. 7. He is deposed in a False Council. 8. The Pope defends St. Ignatius. 9. The Pope deposes the Legates and Photius, and confirms St. Ignatius in his See. 10. Bardas is put to Death by the Emperor, and he associates Basil in the Empire. 11. Photius condemns and deposes Pope Nicholas II., and afterwards promulgates his Error concerning the Holy Ghost. 12. The Emperor Michael is killed, and Basil is elected and banishes Photius.

GODESCHALCUS, of whom we have already spoken (*chap.* 5, *art.* 2, *n.* 17), was charged with Predestinarianism in this century; but, as we have already heard his history, we now pass on to the great Greek schism.

1. In the reign of the Emperor Michael, the Church of Constantinople was governed by the Patriarch, St. Ignatius. This great prelate was son to the Emperor Michael Curopalates; and when his

father was dethroned, he was banished to a monastery, and there brought up in all the penitential austerities of monastic life. His virtues were so great, that, on the death of Methodius, Bishop of Constantinople, he was placed in the vacant See, and his appointment gave universal satisfaction; but his fortitude in defence of the Faith and of the rights of his Church, raised up for him many powerful enemies, and among them, three wretches who were unceasing in their persecution of him—Bardas, uncle to the Emperor, Photius, and Gregory Asbestas, Bishop of Syracuse. Bardas, wishing to be sole master in the Empire of his nephew, Michael, had either procured the death or banishment of all who stood in his way at court. He even shut up in a monastery his own sister, the Empress Theodora, because he could not bend her in all things to his wishes, and then began a persecution against St. Ignatius, because he refused to give her the veil (1). What irritated him, above all, against the saint was, he had repudiated his wife, and lived publicly with his step-daughter, a widow. St. Ignatius admonished him of the scandal he was giving; but he took so little note of this that he presented himself one day in the church to partake of the holy mysteries, and the saint then excommunicated him. Bardas threatened to run him through with his sword, and from that out never ceased misrepresenting him to the Emperor, and at last, on the 23rd of November, in the year 858, got him banished out of the patriarchal palace, and exiled to the island of Terebintum (2), and sent after him several bishops, patricians, and some of the most esteemed judges, to induce him to renounce the bishopric. Their journey was all in vain; and Bardas then promised to each of the bishops the See of Constantinople if they deposed St. Ignatius, and these unfortunate prelates lent themselves to the nefarious scheme, though every one of them had previously taken an oath that he would not vote for the Patriarch's deposition, unless he was convicted of a canonical fault; but they were all deceived in the end, for Bardas, after promising that the Emperor would give the bishopric to each of them, persuaded them that it would be most grateful to the Emperor if each one, when called, would at first, through humility, as it were, refuse it; and they took his advice. The Emperor sent for each of them, and proffered the bishopric; every one declined at first, and was not asked a second time, so that their villany was of no use to them (3).

2. The Patriarch chosen by the Court was the impious Photius, a eunuch of illustrious birth, but of the most inordinate ambition. He was a man of great talent, cultivated by the most arduous study, in which he frequently spent the whole night long, and as he was wealthy he could procure whatever books he wanted; he thus became one of the most learned men of his own or of any former age.

(1) Hermant, *t.* 1, *c.* 341.   (2) Van Ranst, *p.* 162.   (3) Fleury, *t.* 7, *l.* 50, *n.* 2.

He was a perfect master of grammar, poetry, rhetoric, philosophy, medicine, and all the profane sciences; he had not paid much attention to ecclesiastical learning, but became a most profound theologian when he was made Patriarch. He was only a mere layman, and held some of the highest offices in the Court; he was Protospathaire and Protosecretes, or Captain of the Guards, and Chief Secretary. We cannot say much for his religious character, for he was already a schismatic, as he joined Gregory, Bishop of Syracuse, a man convicted of several crimes, and whose character was so bad, that when St. Ignatius was elected Bishop of Constantinople, he would not permit him to attend at his consecration, and Gregory was so mortified at the insult that he dashed to the ground the wax candle he held in his hand as an attendant at the consecration, and publicly abused Ignatius, telling him that he entered into the Church, not as a shepherd but as a wolf. He got others to join with him, and formed a schism against the Patriarch, so that the saint was in the end obliged, in the year 854, to pass sentence of deposition against him in a Council (4). Noel Alexander remarks that St. Ignatius deposed Gregory from the See of Syracuse, because the churches of that province were subject to the Patriarch of Constantinople, as Sicily then formed part of the Empire of the East, but, in order to confirm the sentence, he appealed to Benedict III., who, having again examined the affair, confirmed what was decided, as Nicholas I. attests in his sixth epistle to Photius, and his tenth epistle to the clergy of Constantinople (5).

3. Such was Gregory, with whom Photius was leagued, and as this last was elected Bishop of Constantinople, not according to the canons, but solely by the authority of Bardas, he was at first rejected by all the bishops, and another was elected by common consent. They adhered to their resolutions for many days, but Bardas by degrees gained them over. Five still held out, but at length went with the stream, and joined the rest, but only on condition that Photius would swear to it, and sign a paper, promising to renounce the schism of Gregory, and to receive Ignatius into his communion, honouring him as a father, and to do nothing contrary to his opinion. Photius promised everything, and was accordingly consecrated, but by the very same Gregory, and took possession of the See (6).

4. Six months had not yet passed over, since his consecration, and he had broken all his oaths and promises; he persecuted St. Ignatius, and all the ecclesiastics who adhered to him; he even got some of them flogged, and by promises and threats induced several to sign documents, intended for the ruin of his sainted predecessors. Not being able to accomplish his design, he laid a plot, with the

(4) Fleury, loc. cit. n. 3.　　(5) Nat. Alex. t. 13, Dis. 4, s. 2.　　(6) Nat. Alex. loc. cit. s. 2; Fleury, t. 7, l. 50, n. 3, Baron. An. 858, n. 25.

assistance of Bardas, that the Emperor should send persons to take informations, to prove that St. Ignatius was privately conspiring against the state. Magistrates and soldiers were immediately sent to the island of Terebintum, where St. Ignatius dwelt, and endeavoured by every means, even resorting to torture, to prove the charge, but as nothing came out to inculpate him, they conveyed him to another island, called Jerium, and put him in a place where goats were kept, and, in a little time after, brought him to Prometum, near Constantinople, where he underwent cruel sufferings, for they shut him up in a confined prison, and his feet were fastened to the stocks by two iron bars, and the captain of his guard struck him so brutally with his clenched fist, that he knocked two of his teeth out. He was treated in this brutal manner, to induce him to sign a renunciation of his See, to make it appear, that of his own free will he gave up the patriarchate. When the bishops of the province of Constantinople were informed of this barbarous proceeding, they held a meeting in the Church of Peace, in that city, declared Photius deposed, and anathematized him and all his adherents; but he, supported by Bardas, called together a Council in the Church of the Apostles, in which he deposed and anathematized St. Ignatius, and, as several bishops complained loudly of this injustice, he deposed them likewise, and put them in prison along with Ignatius. Finally, in the month of August of the year 859, St. Ignatius was banished to Mytilene, in the island of Lesbos, and all his adherents were banished from Constantinople, many of them severely beaten, and one, who complained against this act of injustice, had his tongue cut out (7).

5. Photius could not but see that he was very much censured for all this, so he sent some of his partisans to Rome, to Pope Nicholas, to request that he would send his Legates to the East, under the pretext of extinguishing the remains of the Iconoclastic heresy, but in reality, to sanction the expulsion of St. Ignatius by their presence, and the Emperor wrote to the Pope on the same subject, at the same time (8). When the Imperial Ambassador and the Legates of Photius arrived in Rome, the Pope deputed two Legates, Rodaldus, Bishop of Porto, and Zacchary, Bishop of Anagni, to arrange the affairs of the Iconoclasts, by holding a Council, and deciding any supplementary matters necessary to carry out the provisions of the Seventh Council, and regarding the affair of Photius himself, as he received neither a letter nor messenger from St. Ignatius (for his enemies deprived him of all intercourse with the Holy See), he directed his Legates to take juridical informations on the spot, and forward them to him. On the arrival of the Legates in Constantinople (9), they were kept three months by the

(7) Bar. An. 859, n. 54; Fleury, loc. cit. n. 3 & 4; Nat. Alex. loc. cit. (8) Fleury, loc. cit. n. 4, cum Anas. in Nic. 4. (9) Nat. Alex. t. 13; Diss. 4, s. 3, ex Epis. 6, Nichol.

Emperor and Photius, and even not permitted to speak with any one, except those appointed to visit them, lest they might be informed of the true state of things regarding the deposition of St. Ignatius. They were made to understand that if they did not bend, in all things, to the Emperor's will (10), they would be banished to a place where nothing but a miserable death awaited them. At first they resisted, but finally, after spending there eight months, yielded, and soon after, Photius called together a Council in Constantinople, which was attended by them and three hundred and eighteen bishops, but, as Noel Alexander remarks (11), they were merely the nominal Legates of the Pope, for that meeting did not even preserve the forms of a General Council, as it was the Emperor himself who presided, and everything was done according as he wished, at the instigation of Photius.

6. When the Council was assembled, a message was sent to St. Ignatius, to appear and defend his cause; he at once put on his Pontifical ornaments, and went on foot, accompanied by bishops and priests, and a great number of the monks and the laity, but on his way he was met by the patrician, John, who, on the part of the Emperor, prohibited him, under pain of death, from appearing in the Pontifical robes, but merely in the habit of a simple monk. He obeyed, and presented himself in this garb in the Church of the Apostles; he was there separated from the friends who accompanied him, and brought alone into the Emperor's presence, who loaded him with abuse. Ignatius asked leave to speak, and then asked the Pope's Legates what brought them to Constantinople. They answered, that they came to try his case. The Saint asked them if they brought letters for him from the Pope, and was told they had not, as he was no longer considered as Patriarch, having been deposed by a Council of his province, and that, therefore, they were there to judge him. "Then banish the adulterer Photius, first of all," said St. Ignatius, "and if you cannot do that, you are no longer judges." The Emperor, said they, wishes us to be judges; but the Saint peremptorily refused to recognize them as such, and appealed to the Pope, on the authority of the fourth Canon of the Council of Sardis, which decrees, that, "If a bishop be deposed, and he declares that he has a defence to make, no one must be elected in his place till the Pontiff of the Roman Church decides his case."

7. Notwithstanding this, seventy-two false and bribed witnesses were examined, and deposed that the Saint had been guilty of tyranny in the government of his church, and that he was intruded into the See by the secular power, and that, therefore, he should, according to the Apostolical Canon, be deposed: "If any bishop obtain his See by secular powers, let him be deposed." On this

---

(10) Nichol. Ep. 9.   (11) Nat. Alex. loc. cit. s. 4.

testimony, the bishops of the Council, if it could be called such (with the exception of Theodulus of Ancira, who hated the injustice), and the Legates, deposed St. Ignatius, all crying out, *unworthy, unworthy* (12). He was then handed over to the executioners, to be tormented till he would sign his own deposition; they first nearly starved him for a fortnight, and afterwards hung him up by the feet over a deep pit, which was the tomb of Copronimus, and dashed him from side to side till the marble lining of the tomb was stained with his blood. When he was thus reduced to the last extremity, and scarcely breathing, one Theodore, a bravo employed by Photius, took hold of his hand and forcibly made him sign a cross on a sheet of paper, which he brought to Photius, who then wrote on it himself: "I, Ignatius, unworthy Bishop of Constantinople, confess that I have not been lawfully appointed, but have usurped the throne of the Church, which I have tyrannically governed." But even after this act of villainy, Photius did not consider himself safe, so he laid a plot with Bardas, and sent soldiers to take St. Ignatius, who, after his liberation from prison, lived at home with his mother, but he escaped in the disguise of a poor man, carrying two baskets slung on a pole over his shoulder. Six light horsemen were sent after him, with directions to kill him wherever he was found, but God delivered him out of their hands. For forty days, Constantinople was shaken by earthquakes, and so Bardas and the Emperor gave him leave to retire to his monastery, and live in peace (13), though he was again banished.

8. In the meantime the Legates returned to Rome loaded with presents by Photius, and merely told the Pope verbally that Ignatius was deposed by the Council, and Photius confirmed. Two days after, Leo, Secretary to the Emperor, arrived in Rome, and presented a letter to the Pope from the Emperor, containing a long defence of the acts of the Council, and of Photius. Nicholas began then to suspect that his Legates had betrayed him, and so he immediately summoned together all the bishops then present in Rome, and publicly declared in presence of the secretary Leo himself, that he never had sent his Legates either to depose Ignatius or confirm Photius, and that he never had, nor ever would consent to either one or the other (14). He wrote both to the Emperor and to Photius to the same effect (Epis. 9) and wrote likewise another letter to all the faithful of the East (Epis. 4), in which, by his apostolic authority, he particularly commands the other patriarchs of the East to hold the like sentiments regarding Ignatius and Photius, and to give all possible publicity to this letter of his. Photius, in the meantime, without taking any notice of this letter of his Holiness, planned that a certain monk, of the

---

(12) Baron. Ann. 861, n. 1; Nat. Alex. cit. s. 4, & Bernin. s. 9, c. 9, ex Niceta in Vit. St. Ig. Nat. (13) Nat. Alex. loc. cit. s. 4; Fleury, t. 7, c. 53, n. 12, 13, 14, 18, 19, & Nat. Alex. t. 14; diss. 14, s. 6. (14) Nichol. Epis. 13.

name of Eustrates, should present himself in Constantinople, pretending that he had been sent to the Pope by Ignatius as the bearer of a letter, complaining of all he had suffered; but he said the Pope did not even deign to receive him, but on the contrary, sent a letter by him to Photius, assuring him of his friendship. Photius immediately brought these two letters to the Emperor and to Bardas; but when the whole matter was sifted, it was discovered that it was all a scheme got up by Photius, and Bardas felt so indignant at the imposition, that he commanded that the monk Eustrates should receive a severe flogging (15).

9. The Pope convoked a Council of several provinces, which was held in the beginning of the year 863, first in St. Peter's, and then in the Lateran Church, to try the Legates for betraying the Roman Church. One alone of them, the Bishop Zacchary, made his appearance (Rodoaldus being in France), and he being convicted, on his own confession, of having signed the deposition of Ignatius, contrary to the orders of the Pope, was excommunicated and deposed by the Council, and the following year the same was decreed in regard to Rodoaldus, in another Council held in the Lateran, and he was threatened with anathema, if he ever communicated with Photius, or *opposed St. Ignatius. Besides, in this first Lateran Council, Photius was deprived of all sacerdotal offices and honours, on account of his many crimes, and especially for having got himself ordained, he being a layman, by Gregory, the schismatical Bishop of Syracuse, and for having usurped the See of Ignatius, and daring to depose and anathematize him in a Council; besides, for having bribed the Legates of the Holy See to contravene the orders of the Pope, for having banished the bishops who refused to communicate with him, and, finally, for having persecuted, and continuing to persecute, the Church. It was then decreed, that if Photius should continue to hold possession of the See of Constantinople, or prevent Ignatius from governing it, or should exercise any sacerdotal function, that he should be anathematized, and deprived of all hope of communion, unless at the hour of death alone. Gregory, Bishop of Syracuse, was condemned in the same manner, for having dared to exercise ecclesiastical functions after his deposition, and for consecrating Photius Bishop. It was finally decreed that Ignatius never was deposed, from his See, and that for the future every cleric should be deposed, and every layman anathematized, who would show him any opposition (16).

10. When the Emperor Michael heard of the decrees of the Roman Council, he wrote a most abusive letter to Pope Nicholas, threatening him with his displeasure if he did not revoke his judgment (17). The Pope answered him (Epis. 70), that the Pagan

---

(15) Fleury, loc. cit. n, 15, 18, 19, & Nat. Alex. t. 13, diss. 14, s. 6. (16) Baron. Ann 663. n. 3; Fleury, t, 7, l. 50, n. 19, 26. (17) Nichol. Epis. 8.

Emperors were princes and pontiffs, but that after the coming of Jesus Christ the two powers were divided, as temporal things were different from spiritual things, and Noel Alexander particularly calls attention to these expressions in the Pope's letter: "It is plain that as there is no higher authority than the Apostolic See, that no one can revoke its judgments; nor is it lawful for any one to pass judgment on its judgments, since, according to the canons, appeals come to it from all parts of the world; but from it no one is permitted to appeal." He then says, that the case of Ignatius and Photius can only be decided by appearing in person, or by deputy, in Rome, when both can state their causes of complaint, and defend themselves (18). Some time after the Emperor took the field to conquer Crete, and was accompanied by his uncle, Bardas, who was so strongly suspected of being a traitor, that he resolved to put him to death. He was in the Emperor's tent when he saw the soldiers come to take him, and he threw himself at his nephew's feet, imploring mercy, but his prayer was in vain; he was dragged out and cut to pieces, and a piece of his flesh was carried round the camp in mockery, fixed on a spear, and thus, in the year 886, the unfortunate Bardas closed his mortal career. The Emperor immediately returned to Constantinople, and appointed Basil, the Macedonian, who was one of the chief instigators of the death of Bardas, prime minister, and as he was aware of his incapacity in governing by himself, he soon after associated him in the Empire, and had him solemnly crowned (19).

11. Although Photius lost his protector, he did not lose heart; he continued to retain the Emperor's friendship, and ingratiated himself with Basil. He was abandoned by many of his adherents after he incurred the censure of the Pope, and he then bitterly persecuted them whenever he could; some he deprived of their dignities, some he imprisoned, and he banished the hermits from Mount Olympus, and burned their cells (20). On the 13th of October, 866, the Pope sent three Legates to Constantinople to appease the Emperor and put an end to the discord caused by Photius; but they were arrested in Bulgaria by an imperial officer, who treated them very disrespectfully, and told them that the Emperor would have nothing to say to them, so when they perceived the treatment they were likely to receive if they proceeded to Constantinople, they returned to Rome (21). It came to the knowledge of Photius at the same time that the Pope had sent other Legates to the Bulgarians to protest against the new mode of unction introduced by him (Photius) among them, in the administration of the sacrament of Confirmation, and he felt so indignant at this interference, that he summoned a Council which he called an Ecumenical one, in

(18) Fleury, loc. cit. n. 41; Nat. Alex. cit. s. 6.   (19) Fleury, n. 42.
20) Fleury, loc. cit. n. 11.   (21) Nat. Alex. t. 13, diss. 4, s. 7; Fleury, n. 52, 53.

which he got the two Emperors, Basil and Michael, to preside, and had it attended by the Legates of the other patriarchal Sees, and by many bishops of the patriarchate of Constantinople, to revenge himself on the Pope. Persons came forward there and made several charges against Pope Nicholas. Photius received the accusations, and tried the cause, and finally condemned the Pope for many supposed crimes, and deposed and excommunicated him and all who would hold communion with him. Twenty-one bishops were mad enough to approve of and subscribe this sacrilegious sentence, and Photius afterwards forged nearly a thousand other signatures to the same document (22). He had now lost all respect for the Pope, and his insolence arrived at such a pitch, that he sent a circular letter of his composition to the Patriarch of Alexandria, condemnatory of several practices and doctrines of the Roman Church, as the fast on Saturdays, the celibacy of the clergy, but, above all, the doctrine of the procession of the Holy Ghost not from the Father alone, but from the Father and Son (23). Baronius (24) even says, that he taught that every man had two souls. He obtained the Emperor's permission to summon a second Council in Constantinople, and having done so, he again excommunicated and deposed the Pope (25).

12. In the year 867, the Emperor Michael was killed, while drunk, by his own guards, at the instigation of Basil, whose life he sought on account of some disagreements they had. When Basil thus obtained the undivided sovereignty of the Empire, he banished Photius from the See of Constantinople, and exiled him to a distant monastery (26), and the next day he sent the imperial galley to the island where the Patriarch, St. Ignatius, was confined, to convey him back to Constantinople, and received him with the highest honours on his arrival, and solemnly put him in possession of his See once more (27). He sent orders then to Photius to restore all the documents with the Emperor's signature he had in his possession; but he sent back word, that as he left the palace by the Emperor's command in a hurry, he left all his papers behind him; but while he was making this excuse to the prefect sent to him by Basil, his officers perceived the servants of Photius busy in hiding several bags filled with documents, with leaden seals appended to them; these were immediately seized on and brought to the Emperor, and among other papers, two books beautifully written were found, one containing the Acts of the imaginary Council condemning Ignatius, and the other the Synodical letter against Pope Nicholas, filled with calumnies and abuse (28). Basil then wrote to Pope Nicholas, giving him an account of the expulsion of Photius and

(22) Baron Ann. 663, *n.* 13; Nat. Alex. cit. *s.* 7. (23) Fleury, *t.* 7, *l.* 52, *n.* 55, 56. (24) Baron. Ann. 869, *n.* 49. (25) Nat. Alex. loc. cit. & Grav. *t.* 3, *s.* 9, *coll.* 4. (26) Baron. Ann. 367, *n.* 92; Nicetas in Vita St. Ignatii, *p.* 1226. (27) Fleury, *t.* 7, *l.* 51, *n.* 1, 2. (28) Nat. Alex. loc. cit. *s.* 9, & Fleury, loc. sit.

the re-establishment of Ignatius; but this letter was delivered into the hands of Adrian II., in 868, the successor of Nicholas, who died in 867. Adrian answered the Emperor, and said that he would put into execution, in regard to Photius and Ignatius, whatever was decided by his predecessor (29), and the same year he condemned the Council of Photius in a Council held at Rome, and the book we mentioned was burned there, being first thrown on the ground with this anathema: " Cursed at Constantinople, be again cursed at Rome" (30).

Article II.

THE ERRORS OF THE GREEKS CONDEMNED IN THREE GENERAL COUNCILS.

13, 14, 15. The Eighth General Council against Photius, under Pope Adrian and the Emperor Basil. 16. Photius gains over Basil, and in the mean time St. Ignatius dies. 17. Photius again gets Possession of the See. 18. The Council held by Photius rejected by the Pope; unhappy Death of Photius. 19. The Patriarch, Cerularius, revives and adds to the Errors of Photius. 20. Unhappy Death of Cerularius. 21, 22. Gregory X. convokes the Council of Lyons at the instance of the Emperor Michael; it is assembled. 23. Profession of Faith written by Michael, and approved of by the Council. 24. The Greeks confess and swear to the Decisions of the Council. 25. They separate again. 26. Council of Florence under Eugenius IV.; the Errors are again discussed and rejected; Definition of the Procession of the Holy Ghost. 27. Of the Consecration in Leavened Bread. 28. Of the Pains of Purgatory. 29. Of the Glory of the Blessed. 30. Of the Primacy of the Pope. 31. Instructions given to the Armenians, Jacobites, and Ethiopians; the Greeks relapse into Schism.

13. POPE ADRIAN (1) made arrangements to celebrate a General Council in Constantinople, which was accomplished in the year 869, in the reign of the Emperor Basil; he sent three Legates to preside in his name: Donatus, Bishop of Ostia, Stephen of Nepi, and Marinus, one of the seven deacons of the Roman Church, who was afterwards Pope. The Legates proceeded to Constantinople, and were most honourably received by the Emperor; he sent all the officers of the palace to meet them at the gate of the city, and they were received there by the clergy in their robes likewise. They were then presented to the Emperor in his palace, and he received them with all honour and reverence, kissed the Pope's letters when presented to him, and told them that he, as well as all the bishops of the East, were for two years waiting for the decision of the Roman Church, their mother, and he therefore most earnestly besought them to make every endeavour to re-establish union and peace. The day for the opening of the Council was then appointed.

(29) Fleury, loc. cit. n. 18. (30) Baron. Ann. 868, n. 38; Nat. Alex. loc. cit. s. 9, & Fleury, cit. n. 19. (1) Nat. Alex. s. 11, & Graveson, t. 3, coll. 3, p. 153.

14. The Legates presided in this Council in the name of the Pope; although in the eighth and tenth Act Basil and his two sons, Constantine and Leo, are called Presidents, still, as Noel Alexander (2) remarks, the Emperor is called the President, not because of any authority he held in the Synod, but because he was honoured as the protector of the Church, but not as the judge of ecclesiastical affairs. The first Session was held on the 5th of October, in the year 869, and eight others were held, the last in the February of 870. The bishops and priests who had joined the schism presented themselves in the fifth Session, and were mercifully received again. Photius also came forward, but when he was asked by the Legates whether he received the exposition of Pope Nicholas, and of his successor Pope Adrian, he refused to answer (3). He was pressed for a reply, but he only said: "God understands what I mean, though I do not speak." "But," said the Legates, "your silence will not preserve you from condemnation." "Jesus Christ," said he, "was silent, likewise, and was condemned." They told him that if he wished to be reconciled to the Church, he should confess his crimes, and all the wrongs he had inflicted on Ignatius, and promise to recognize him as his pastor for the future, still he continued silent; then the patrician Baanes addressed him, and said: "My Lord Photius, your mind is now confused, so the Council gives you time to think on your salvation; go, you shall be again recalled." He made his appearance again in the seventh Session, with the crozier in his hand, but it was taken from him, for the Council said he was a wolf, and not a shepherd; he was again asked if he was willing to retract his errors, but he answered, that he did not recognize the Legates as his judges. Several other questions were put to him, but he answered them in a haughty manner, so he was anathematized in these words: "Anathema to Photius the invader, the schismatical tyrant, the new Judas, the inventor of perverse dogmas." In these and such like terms was he condemned, and, together with him, Gregory of Syracuse, and all their followers, who persevered in their obstinacy (4).

15. Twenty-seven Canons were promulgated in this the Eighth General Council. Among the rest it was decreed, that all the orders conferred by Photius were invalid, and that the churches and altars he consecrated should be consecrated again. All bishops and clerks who continued to hold by his party were deposed, and all who held with him that man had two souls were anathematized. It was prohibited, under pain of deposition, to consecrate bishops, at the command of the Sovereign (5). All the works of Photius were burned in the midst of the Assembly; the definitions of the other seven General Councils were received, and the Council was

(2) Nat. Alex. *t.* 13; Diss. 4, *s.* 12. (3) Baron. Ann. 869, *n.* 28. (4) Baron. Ann. 869, *n.* 37, & Fleury, *t.* 7, *l.* 51, *n.* 29, & seq. (5) N Alex. *sec.* 22, & Fleury, *l.* 51. *n.* 55.

closed. It was afterwards confirmed by Pope Adrian, at the request of the Fathers (6), who besought him to confirm the decrees of this General Synod as his own, that the words of truth and the decrees of justice should be received through the whole world confirmed by his authority. It is worthy of remembrance what Nicetas tells us of this Council (7), that the Fathers signed the decree with a pen dipped in the sacred blood of Jesus Christ. The Emperor Basil did not look sufficiently to the safety of the Legates on their return to Rome; and the consequence was, that they were seized by the Sclavonians, and robbed of all they had, the original Acts of the Council among the rest, with the autograph signatures of the Fathers. They were freed from captivity by the joint exertions of the Pope and the Emperor, and, on the 22nd of December, 870, arrived in Rome. The Pope received through another channel the authentic copy of the Synodical Acts, and confirmed the Council (8). The cause of the Emperor's displeasure with the Legates was, because they refused to accede to the wishes of the ambassadors of the King of Bulgaria, in Constantinople, who wished to be subjected, not to the Roman Church, but to the See of Constantinople, and the Legates of the other oriental patriarchates seconded this request (9).

16. Photius, in the meantime, never ceased to asperse the Council. He wrote several letters to that effect to his friends, and one, especially to a monk of the name of Theodosius (10), in which he says; " Why do you wonder that those who have been themselves condemned presume to judge the innocent? Have you not examples? Caiphas and Pilate were judges; my God Jesus was the accused." He then alludes to the examples of St. Stephen, St. James, St. Paul, and so many martyrs, who had to appear before judges worthy of being put to death a thousand times. " God," said the impious Photius, " disposes of everything for our advantage." Noel Alexander and Fleury tell us, that, during the whole ten years of his exile, he never ceased plotting and scheming to injure the holy Patriarch, St. Ignatius, and to get back to the See himself, and he left no means untried to accomplish his purpose. He laid one plan, in particular, to ingratiate himself into the Emperor's favour: he wrote a genealogy and prophecy on a piece of old parchment, and in the antique Alexandrian character. This was called " Beclas," the name of Basil's father. In this he pretended that Basil, though his father was but a man of low birth, was descended from Tiridates, King of Armenia, and that his reign would be longer and happier than that of any of his predecessors. He got this bound up in an old cover, and privately conveyed into the Imperial library. He then got one of his friends, as great a

(6) N. Alex. loc. cit. (7) Nicep. ap. Fleury, loc. cit 46. (8) Hermant, t. 1, c. 374. (9) Fleury, t. 7, l. 31, n. 44, 49. (10) Fleury, loc. cit. n. 41. (11) Nat. Alex. t. 7, diss. 4, sec. 25; Fleury, t. 8, l. 53, n. 1, ex Nicet.

schemer as himself, to suggest to the Emperor, that there was not a man in the Empire who could interpret that but Photius. The Emperor took the bait, and recalled him, and he soon ingratiated himself into his good graces, and endeavoured to obtain permission from St. Ignatius, through the sovereign's influence, to exercise episcopal functions; but the saint never would permit him, for, as he was excommunicated by a Council, he said he could not be rehabilited, unless by another Council; but, notwithstanding, he administered orders, and exercised other episcopal duties (12). The holy Patriarch, Ignatius, died in the year 878, the eightieth year of his age, and there are strong suspicions, according to Noel Alexander, and Van Ranst, that Photius was the author of his death. Fleury says (13), that Stilianus, the Metropolitan of Neocesarea, wrote to Pope Stephen, and openly charged Photius with employing some wretches to take away the holy Patriarch's life. Both the Greek and Latin Churches honour the memory of St. Ignatius on the 23rd of October.

17. Three days had not elapsed since the death of St. Ignatius, and Photius managed to mount the Patriarchal throne once more, and at once began to banish, flog, and incarcerate the servants of his holy predecessor. He restored some of the deposed bishops; and those who rejected his communion, and adhered to the Council, he delivered into the hands of his relative, Leo Catacalus, who gained over many of the weak by torments, and punished the constancy of many more with death (14). He was most desirous of having the sanction of Pontifical authority for his re-establishment, and tried numberless schemes to accomplish it. Among the rest, he sent a letter to the Pope then reigning, John VIII., telling him that he was forced to resume the See, and he surreptitiously obtained the signatures of the other Oriental Patriarchs to this, by pretending that it was a contract for purchase to be secretly made. He sent another letter, forged in the name of St. Ignatius (then dead), and several other bishops, begging of the Pope to receive Photius, and he sent along with those, letters from the Emperor, which he obtained in his favour (15). When the Pope received those letters, in Rome, in the year 879—desirous of not displeasing the Emperor, especially—he answered, that, for the good of the Church, and for peace sake, he was willing to dispense with the Decrees of the Eighth Council, and of his predecessors, and receive Photius into his communion, but only on condition of giving public proofs of penance, in a Council, to be held in presence of his Legates, then in Constantinople, and he, accordingly, sent Peter, a Cardinal, as his Legate, to preside at a Council in his name. Cardinal Baro-

(12) Nat. Alex. *sec.* 25; Baron. Ann. 878, *n.* 53; Fleury, *t.* 8, *l.* 53, *n.* 1, & seq.; Van Ranst, *p.* 154.   (13) Fleury, cit. *l.* 53, *n.* 52.   (14) Nat. Alex. loc. cit. *sec.* 25. (15) Fleury, loc. cit. *n.* 3, 4; N. Alex. eod. *sec.* 25.

nius, Noel Alexander, Fleury (16), and several others, severely censure this condescension of the Pope; but Peter de la Marca excuses him (17), for, solicited as he was by the Emperor, and having the authority of his predecessors, Leo, Gelasius, and Felix, and of the Council of Africa, all which teach that the rigour of the law must be dispensed with in time of necessity, he naturally considered that the good of the Church required he should yield the point, and thus, with the consent of the other Patriarchs, he consented that Photius should retain possession of the See.

18. Photius put the finishing stroke to his plans on the arrival of the Legate in Constantinople; he deceived him, by asking for the Pope's letter that he might translate it into Greek, and when he got it into his hands, he curtailed it, and interpolated it to suit his own purpose, as Cardinal Baronius shows, and on the strength of this deception, a Council was held, called the Eighth General Council by the schismatic Greeks, though it was nothing more than a Cabal, for though it was attended by four hundred and eighty bishops, they were all adherents of Photius, and he presided himself and carried everything just as he liked, in opposition to the sentiments of the Legate and the Pope. This Council was closed after five Acts, and the impious Photius was re-established, in the Pope's name, in the See of Constantinople. When Pope John learned what passed in Constantinople, as Noel Alexander (18) relates, he had sent anew his Legate, Maximus, to Constantinople, to annul by Apostolical authority all that had been done in that wicked Council; and the Legate proceeded with courage, and confirmed, in the Pope's name, the condemnation of Photius, decided by the General Council; this so displeased the Emperor, that he cast the Legate into prison, and kept him there for thirty days, but, withal, the Pope confirmed the decrees passed against Photius by his predecessors, Nicholas I. and Adrian II., and again solemnly excommunicated him. Cardinal Gotti (19) adds, that this sentence of John VIII. was, after the death of Basil, which took place in 886, put into execution by his son and successor, Leo VI., the philosopher. Fleury tells us (20) that the Emperor sent two of his principal officers to the Church of Sancta Sophia, and they went into the gallery, and publicly read all the crimes of Photius, and then banished him from the Metropolitan See, and sent him to an Armenian monastery, where he died, but we do not know how or when. Cedrenus (21), in his annals, however, says, that the Emperor ordered his eyes to be put out, as suspected of rebellion; and Noel Alexander says he died obstinately in his schism, and separated from the communion of the Church.

(16) Baron. Ann. 879, t. 10; N. Alex. t. 13, diss. 4, sec. 26; Fleury, t. 8, l. 53, n. 7. (17) De Marc. de Concordia, Sac. & Imp. l. 3, c. 14. (18) Nat. Alex. loc. cit sec. 28. (19) Gotti, Ver. Relig. t. 2, c. 85, sec. 1. (20) Fleury, t. 53, n. 51. (21) Apud Gotti, loc. cit.

19. Noel Alexander (22) says that the schism was extinguished on the death of Photius, but that it broke out again; but Danæus (23) says, that, on the contrary, his death left it as it was, and that it broke out with more violence in the time of Nicholas Chrisobergus, Patriarch, in 981, of Sisinnius, his successor, in 995, and, more than all, in the reign of Sergius, also Patriarch, who sent, in his own name, to the bishops of the East, the encyclical letter written by Photius against the Pope. It gained new strength in the eleventh century, under the Patriarch Michael Cerularius. This prelate was of noble birth, but proud and intriguing; and he was imprisoned in a monastery, by the Emperor Michael Pophlaganius, and was not released till the reign of the Emperor Constantine Monomachus, in the year 1043; he uncanonically seized on the See of Constantinople, but naturally fearing the censures of the Pope for this act of violence, he laboured to bring to maturity the seeds of division, previously sown between the two Churches. He commenced the attack, by writing a letter to John, Bishop of Trani, in Apulia, charging the Roman See with holding erroneous doctrines regarding the procession of the Holy Ghost from the Father and the Son; that the soul, after leaving purgatory, went directly to enjoy beatitude before the General Resurrection; that the Pope usurped the authority of Universal Pastor, without having any authority to do so, and more, that the Latins, by consecrating the Eucharist in unleavened bread, followed the Jewish practice of celebrating the Pasch in unleavened bread. In making a charge of this sort against the Roman Church, he was most surely astray, for our Lord celebrated the Pasch on the first day of the feast of the unleavened bread; and then, according to the precept of God himself, in Exodus, it was unlawful to have even in the house leavened bread: " Seven days there shall not be found any leaven in your houses" (Exod. xii.); and, besides, there was a most ancient tradition handed down direct from St. Peter himself, as Christian Lupus (24) says, that Christ offered up the Sacrifice in unleavened bread, and such was indubitably the universal practice, during the first centuries in the West, unless, for a short time, when the discipline was changed, lest the Christians should be scandalised, as if they were Judaising. It is true, the Greeks have always made use of leavened bread; and by doing so, never offended against Faith, for one Church has never reprobated the custom of another; but Cerularius was altogether astray in accusing the Latin Church of heresy, for using unleavened bread.

20. Pope Leo, to extinguish the fire of schism which was every day spreading more widely, sent as his Legates to the East, Umbert, Bishop of Silva Candida, the Cardinal Archdeacon of Rome, and

(22) Nat. Alex. s. 29. (23) Danæus tem. net. p. 271. (24) Chris. Lupus. p. 3, Conc. Diss. de Act. St. Leo VII.

Peter, Archbishop of Amalphi; they brought letters from the Pope to the Emperor Constantine, threatening to excommunicate Cerularius, unless he desisted from censuring the Roman Church, on account of the custom of celebrating with unleavened bread. The question then was discussed in Constantinople itself, and the Latin practice was justified; but Cerularius refused all along to meet the Legates, and continued to give them every opposition in his power. The Legates, despairing of any change in him, after celebrating Mass one day in St. Sophia, publicly laid the letter of excommunication on the altar. This only exasperated him more, and he removed the Pope's name from the Diptychs, and following the Legates' example, he excommunicated them, and sent letters through all Asia and Italy, filled with calumnies and abuse of the Roman Church. He lived and died obstinately in schism; he was banished to Proconesus by the Emperor, Isaac Comnemus, who deposed him from the patriarchate, and he there ended his days (25).

21. The schism was not extinguished at his death, but spread more widely; and though several Greek Churches in the eleventh and following centuries continued in communion with the Roman Church, still the breach was every day becoming wider, till Constantinople was conquered by the Latins. Union was again restored under the Frankish monarchy, from the reign of Baldwin, the first Latin Emperor of Constantinople, in 1204, till 1261; but when Constantinople was re-taken by Michael Paleologus, the Greeks renewed the schism, which, to all appearance, they had eternally forsaken, and for the four subsequent centuries the Churches were disunited, till the chastisement of God bore heavily on the sinful Empire. Michael Paleologus (26) sent a Franciscan doctor to Gregory X., the bearer of letters requesting a union between the Greek and Roman Churches once more, and he wrote to St. Louis, King of France, also, to induce him to co-operate to the same end. The Pope was most desirous to accede to his wishes, and he sent four friars of the Order of St. Francis (or according to others, two of the Franciscan and two of the Dominican Order), as his Legates, to conclude a peace. This happened in 1272, and he convoked a General Council at the same time to meet in two years after in Lyons, to concert with the Christian Sovereigns for the conquest of the Holy Land; to reform some matters of discipline; but principally to re-unite the Greek and Latin Churches; and to facilitate this object, so dear to his heart, he sent a formula of Faith to the Emperor by the four religious delegates, which the Greek bishops were called on to sanction. He prayed the Emperor to come to the Council himself, or, at all events, to send his Legates, and he also invited the Patriarch of Constantinople and the other Greek bishops to the Council.

(25) Bernin. *t.* 3, *sec.* xi. *c.* 6; Van Ranst, *sec.* 10, *p* 171; Bask. *t.* 2, *sec.* 11, *c.* 3. (26) Nat. Alex. *t.* 17. *diss.* 7, de Con. Lug. 11, *a.* 1; Graveson, *t.* 4, *coll.* 4, *p.* 116.

22. At the appointed time the Council assembled in Lyons, and besides the Latin prelates, two of the Greek Patriarchs—Pantaleon, of Constantinople, and Opizio, of Antioch, and several other Greek bishops, attended. Five hundred bishops altogether, seventy abbots, and about one thousand inferior prelates, were assembled. St. Bonaventure was also present, and took the first place after the Pope, and to him was committed, by his Holiness, the whole arrangement of the Council. The Pope had summoned St. Thomas of Aquin, likewise, but he died on his way thither, in the convent of Fossa Nova. The ambassadors of the Kings of France, England, and Sicily were also in attendance. Several authors, among others Trithemius and Platina, assert that the Emperor Michael was present, but Noel Alexander proves (27) indubitably, that he was not, but only his ambassadors, and it is on that account that his letter was read in the Council, and approved of, because the ambassadors, in his name, took an oath assenting to the union, and besides, Pope Gregory, immediately on the conclusion of the Council, wrote to him an account of all that had taken place there, which he assuredly would not have done had he been present in person.

25. In the fourth Session, the letter of the Emperor Michael Paleologus was read, professing the Faith taught by the Roman Church, as laid down in the formula sent to him by the Pope. In this, he professes that the Holy Ghost proceeds from the Father and the Son, the existence of Purgatory, the validity of consecration with unleavened bread, and finally the Primacy of the Pope. Noel Alexander (28), and Raynaldus (29), quote his words: " That the Holy Roman Church has full and plenary primacy and principality over the whole Catholic Church, and that it received the plenitude of power in the Apostle St. Peter, whose successor the Roman Pontiff is, through Christ himself; and, as it is bound, above all others, to defend the truth of the Faith, so its judgment should be definitive, in all controversies regarding faith. That all persons having any ecclesiastical business can appeal to it, and that it can examine and judge all ecclesiastical cases, and all other churches owe it reverential obedience. The plenitude of power consists in this, that it admits the other Church to a part of its solicitudes, and it honours others, but above all the Patriarchal Churches, with divers privileges, never, however, giving up its prerogatives, both in General Councils and elsewhere, but always keeping the purity of the Faith, as faithfully explained;" and then he adds: " We, of our own free will, confess and receive the Primacy of the Holy Roman Church." He then begs of the Pope to allow the Symbol or Creed to be sung in the Greek Church, as it was before the schism, and to permit the Greeks to observe the

(27) Nat. Alex. cit. *a*. 2, *n*. 1.　　(28) Nat. Alex. cit. *n*. 2.　　(29) Raynal. Ann. 1274, *n*. 14.

same rites as before, when not opposed to Faith, to the Divine Commandments, to the Old or New Testament, to the Doctrines laid down by General Councils or Holy Fathers, and received by the Councils, celebrated under the spiritual power of the Roman Church. The letters of the several Greek bishops were then read, submitting themselves to the power of the Roman Church, and professing in all things the same episcopal obedience to the Apostolic See as their fathers did before the schism.

24. When these letters were read, George Acripolita, the *great Logothete*, or High Chancellor, the Emperor's Ambassador, renounced the schism in his name, professed the Faith of the Roman Church, and recognized the Primacy of the Roman Pontiff; he also took an oath, promising that the Emperor never would depart from his faith and obedience. The Legates of the Greek bishops did the same, and now the Council having approved and accepted the profession of Faith, the Synodical Constitution was promulgated: " We confess," said the Fathers, " with a faithful and devout profession, that the Holy Ghost proceeds eternally from the Father and the Son, not as from two principles, but, as from one principle, not from two spirations, but one spiration. The Holy Roman Church, the Mother and Mistress of all Churches, has always professed, and firmly holds and teaches this Doctrine, and this is also the true and unchangeable opinion of the orthodox Fathers and Doctors, both of the Latin and Greek Churches. But as some, on account of not knowing this undoubted truth, have fallen into various errors, we, wishing to prevent any from going the same false way, in future, with the approbation of the Sacred Council, condemn and hand over to reprobation all who presume to deny, that the Holy Ghost eternally proceeds from the Father and the Son, or who dare to assert that the Holy Ghost proceeds from the Father and the Son as from two principles and not from one." The Council closed at last, and Gregory sent back the Greeks to their own country, loaded with presents, and wrote to the Emperor Michael, and to his son, Andronicus, congratulating them on the completion of the Synod. The Emperor was so highly pleased that all was so happily concluded, and as Joseph, the Patriarch of Constantinople, who was always opposed to the union, would not now give his consent to it, he obliged him to renounce his dignity, and retire to a monastery, and had John Veccus elected in his place, and he imprisoned, banished, and even put to death, some ecclesiastics and nobles, who refused to receive the decrees of the Council (30).

25. Two Synods were held in Constantinople in the year 1276, under Pope John XXI., in which the Patriarch Veccus, and the other Greek bishops, professed the Faith, according to the rule

---

(30) Nat. Alex. loc. cit. *a.* 2, *n.* 6, ex Nicephor. *l.* 5, & aliis.

laid down by the Roman Church; and the Emperor Michael and his son Andronicus wrote to the Pope, that all that the Roman Church believes and teaches was confirmed by these Synods. The Emperor wrote another letter in 1278 to Nicholas III., the successor of John, informing him that he used every means in his power to consolidate the union, but that so many outbreaks occurred, and so many plots were laid against him, that he feared he would be deposed if he tried any further, and he begged of his Holiness not to be angry if he appeared to yield a little in so delicate an affair. The end of the matter was, that the Greeks, with few exceptions, every day more and more separated themselves from the union they had sworn to, and at last Martin IV., the successor of Nicholas III., excommunicated the Emperor, Michael Paleologus, in 1281, as a supporter of the Greek schism and heresy, and forbade all princes, lords, and universities, and the authorities of all cities and towns, under pain of personal excommunication and local interdict, from having any connexion with him, as long as he was under ban of excommunication. Noel Alexander, on the authority of two authors, says that the Pope excommunicated the Emperor at the instigation of Charles, King of Sicily, who hoped that when Michael was by this measure deprived of assistance, he could easily banish him from the throne, and place his son-in-law on it; but Roncaglia, in his notes on Alexander, shows that Martin having renewed the excommunication the following year (as Raynaldus relates, *Ann.* 1281, *N.* 8), proves that the only reason he could have for doing it was, that the Emperor broke faith, and gave up the union he had sworn to maintain (31).

26. This schism continued for about a hundred and twenty years longer, from the Council of Lyons, till the year 1439, when the Greeks were reduced almost to the last extremity, for the Almighty permitted the Turks to punish them, and, after conquering the greater part of their Empire, now threatened their total destruction. In their distress, they now made overtures for a re-union with the Roman Church once more, and Pope Eugenius IV., who was extremely desirous of acceding to their wishes, convoked a Council principally for this object, in Ferrara; and when the plague broke out in that city, afterwards in Florence, and invited the Emperor, the Patriarchs, and the other Greek bishops, to attend. The Emperor John Paleologus accepted the invitation, and the Patriarch of Constantinople, the two chief Metropolitans, Basil Bessarion, Archbishop of Nice, and Mark, Archbishop of Ephesus, several other Greek bishops, seven hundred other distinguished personages, and a hundred and sixty Latin bishops, assembled in Florence. The points of disagreement, which were the same as those decided on in the Council of Lyons (32), were again examined. The word, *Filioque*,

(31) Nat. Alex. *t.* 17, *diss.* 7, *a.* 2, per totum.   (32) Spondan. ad Ann. 1438, *n.* 28.

"and from the Son," which was added to the Creed by the Latin Church, to explain that the Holy Ghost proceeds both from the Father and the Son, as from one principle, was again debated. Mark, the Greek Archbishop of Ephesus, was the most strenuous opposer of this addition; it was unlawful, he said, to add anything to the ancient Symbols of the Church, but our Theologians replied, that the promise made by Jesus Christ to assist his Church was not confined to any period, but lasts till the end of time: "Behold, I am with you all days, even to the consummation of the world" (Matt. xxviii. 20). The word *Consubstantial* was not, said they, in the Creed at first; and for all that the Council of Nice thought it necessary to add it, to put an end to the subterfuges of the Arians, and explain that the Word was of the same substance as, and in all things equal to, the Father. The Councils of Ephesus and Chalcedon, also, made an addition to the Nicene Creed, to explain the two natures of Christ, Divine and human, against Nestorius, who taught that he was a mere man; and against Eutyches, who asserted that the human was absorbed by the Divine nature. Hence they argued that the words, "and from the Son," were added to the Symbol; not to prove that the ancient Symbols were imperfect, but to declare more clearly the truth of the Faith, and that the declaration of the truth ought not to be called an addition, but rather an explanation. The Council, therefore, defined: "That this truth should be believed by all Christians; that the Holy Ghost is eternally from the Father and the Son, and that his essence and being is both from the Father and the Son, and that he proceeds eternally from both, as from one principle, and by one spiration; and that this is what the Holy Fathers mean by saying that he proceeds from the Father by the Son; and when the Greeks speak of the Son as the cause, and the Latins the principle, together with the Father, of the subsistence of the Holy Ghost, they both mean the same thing." Here are the words: "Diffinimus, ut hæc fidei veritas ab omnibus Christianis credatur, quod Spiritus Sanctus ex Patre, et Filio æternaliter est; et essentiam suam, suumque esse subsistens habet ex Patre simul et Filio; et ex utroque æternaliter tanquam ab uno principio, et unica spiratione procedit, declarantes, quod id quod SS. Patres dicunt ex Patre per Filium precedentem Spiritum Sanctum; ad hanc intelligentiam tendit, ut per hoc significetur, Filium quoque esse secundum Græcos quidem causam, secundum Latinos vero principium subsistentiæ Spiritus Sancti, sicut et Patrem. Et quoniam omnia quæ Patris sunt, Pater ipse unigenito Filio suo gignendo dedit, præter esse Patrem, hoc ipsum quod Spiritus Sanctus procedit ex Filio, ipse Filius a Patre æternaliter habet, a quo etiam æternaliter genitus est. Diffinimus insuper, explicationem verborum illorum *Filioque*, veritatis declarandæ gratiæ, et imminente tunc necessitate, ac rationabiliter Symbolo fuisse appositam."

27. The question of the validity of the consecration of the Eucha-

rist in unleavened bread was then discussed, but the parties soon agreed on this, as there was no doubt that wheaten bread was the essential matter of the Sacrament, and it was but a matter of discipline, whether it was leavened or unleavened; and it was then defined that each priest should follow the custom of his own Church, whether of the East or the West.

28. Purgatory, and the state of beatitude the just enjoy, previous to the General Resurrection, was then discussed. Both parties soon agreed on these points, for as to Purgatory, the Greeks never denied its existence, but they taught that the stains of sin are there purged away by the penalty of sorrow, and not of fire; and they, accordingly, at once agreed to the definition of the Council, which decided that the souls are purged from the stain of sin, in the next life, by punishment, and that they are relieved by the suffrages of the faithful, and especially by the sacrifice of the Mass, but does not specify either the penalty of sorrow or of fire; and the Council of Trent, in the Twenty-fifth Session, in the Decree on Purgatory, decided the same, though many of the Holy Fathers, as St. Ambrose, St. Augustin, St. Gregory, Bede, and the Angelic Doctor, St. Thomas, particularly mention the penalty of fire, as I have remarked in my Dogmatic Work on the Council of Trent, in opposition to the Innovators (33); and they found their opinion on the text of St. Paul (1 Cor. iii. 12). The following is the decree of the Council: " Item (*definimus*) si vere pœnitentes in Dei charitate decesserint, antequam dignis pœnitentiæ fructibus de commissis satisfecerint, et omissis, eorum animas pœnis purgatoriis post mortem purgari, et ut a pœnis hujusmodi releventur, prodesse eis Fidelium vivorum suffragia, missarum scil. sacrificia, orationes, et eleemosynas, et alia pietatis officia, secundum Ecclæsia instituta."

29. The Greeks also accepted the definition of the Council, that the just enjoy the beatific vision previous to the General Resurrection. This is the Decree: " Illas (*Animas*) etiam, quæ post contractam peccati maculam, vel in suis corporibus, vel eisdem exutæ corporibus (prout superius dictum est), sunt purgatæ, in Cœlum mox recipi, et intueri clare ipsum Deum trinum, et unum sicuti est, pro meritorum tamen diversitate, alium alio perfectius; illorum autem animas, qui in actuali mortali peccato, vel solo originali decedunt mox in infernum descendere, pœnis tamen disparibus puniendas." Theologians commonly teach that the blessed will not have the fulness of beatitude till after the General Judgment, when their souls will be united with their bodies. This St. Bernard (34), speaking of the two stoles of the blessed, says: " The first stole is the happiness itself, and the rest of the soul; but the second is immortality and the glory of the body."

(33) In cit. Sogg. 25, *n.* 7, & 27. (34) S. Bernard, *t.* 1, q. 1033; Serm. 3, om. SS. *n.* 1.

30. The greatest dispute was concerning the primacy of the Pope, and Mark of Ephesus not only obstinately opposed this doctrine to the end of the Council, but after its conclusion, as we shall see, succeeded in again perverting the Greeks. The Greeks, indeed, admitted that the Pope was the head of the Church, but would not allow that he could receive appeals from sentences passed by the four Patriarchal Sees of the East, or convoke a General Council without their assent. They were so firm on this point especially, that there would be no hope of agreement had not Basil Bassarion, the Archbishop of Nice, suggested a mode of reconciling both parties, by putting in the clause: " Saving the rights and privileges of the Greeks;" and to this the Greeks at last consented, for they then maintained their privilege, and at the same time confessed their subjection to the Roman Church; for the very word privilege implies a concession from a superior power, and thus the power of the Pope over all Christian Churches is confirmed. " We define," says the Council, " that the Holy Apostolic See, and the Roman Pontiff, has the primacy over the whole world, and that the Pope is the successor of St. Peter, the Prince of the Apostles, and our Father and Doctor; and that full power has been given him by our Lord Jesus Christ, in St. Peter, to feed, rule, and govern the Universal Church, as is contained in the Acts of the Universal Councils and the Sacred Canons. We also renew the order laid down by the Sacred Canons, in regard to the other venerable patriarchs, that the Patriarch of Constantinople should have the second place after the Holy Roman Pontiff, the Patriarch of Alexandria the third, of Antioch the fourth, and of Jerusalem the fifth, saving all their rights and privileges."

31. When all this was concluded, and before the Council was dismissed, the Armenians arrived in Florence, on the invitation of the Pope, as their provinces were infected with errors. The Armenian Patriarch sent four delegates, who were most kindly received by the Pope, and as they were extremely ignorant, his Holiness judged it proper to cause a compendium of the whole Christian doctrine to be drawn up, which they should swear to profess, and take with them as a rule for their countrymen. This Instruction or Decree was accepted and sworn to by the Armenians, and is quoted at length by Cardinal Justinian and Berninus (35). The Jacobites also, on the invitation of the Pope, were represented in the Council by the Abbot of St. Anthony, sent by the Armenian Patriarch. The ambassadors of the sovereign of Ethiopia, the *Prester John* of that age, presented themselves at the Council likewise, and promised obedience to the Roman Church, and a book of instructions was given them by the Pope, when he transferred the Council from Florence to Rome (36). This peace, however, was but of

(35) Card. Justin. in Concil. Floren. par. 3, *p.* 263, & ap. Bernin. *t.* 4, *s.* 5, 6, *p.* 134.
(36) Rainal. Ann. 1442, *n.* 1 & 2.

short duration, for the Greeks, on their return home, again fell back into their former errors, principally at the instigation of the wicked Mark of Ephesus. The chastisement of God soon overtook that fickle people; in 1453, Mahomet II. took Constantinople by assault, and gave it up to sack and slaughter; the infuriated soldiery slew all who came in their way, cast down the altars, profaned the monasteries, and despoiled the wretched inhabitants of all their property. Thus fell the Empire of the East, after eleven centuries of a glorious existence. The Greeks continue, to the present day, obstinately attached to their errors; they are the slaves of the Turks in their ancient capital. That noble Church, that gave to the world Athanasius, Gregory, Basil, and so many other learned and holy doctors, now lies trampled under foot, vice usurping the place of virtue, and ignorance seated in the chair of learning. The Greek Church, in a word, the mother of many saints and doctors of the Church, has, on account of its separation from the Roman See, fallen into a state of deplorable barbarity and wretched slavery (37).

CHAPTER X.

THE HERESIES WHICH SPRUNG UP FROM THE ELEVENTH TO THE FIFTEENTH CENTURY.

WE pass over the tenth century, because in that age no new heresy sprung up in the Church; but Danæus (1) says, that there was both great ignorance aud great disunion in the West, so that even the Apostolic See was not exempt from intrusions and expulsions. Graveson (2) states the same, and says, that it was a great mark of Divine protection, that, amid so many evils, a schism did not arise in the Church.

ARTICLE I.

HERESIES OF THE ELEVENTH CENTURY.

1. Stephen and Lisosius burned for their Errors. 2. The new Nicholites and the Incestuosists. 3. Berengarius, and the Principles of his Heresy. 4. His Condemnation and Relapse. 5. His Conversion and Death.

1. THE first heresy of this century was an offshoot of Manicheism, or, rather, a collection of errors, which may be called Atheism itself. It was first discovered in Orleans, in France, where it was introduced by an Italian lady, and was embraced by many persons, but especially by two ecclesiastics, of the name of Stephen

---

(37) Hermant. t. 2, c. 201; Berti, Br. H. t. 2, s. 16, c. 5. (1) Danes, gen. tem. not. p. 275. (2) Graveson, Hist. Ecclesias. t. 3, sec. 10, coll. 2.

and Lisosius, who were considered both holy and learned men. They taught, that all that the Scriptures say about the Trinity and the creation of the world is mere nonsense, as the heavens and the earth are from all eternity, and never had a beginning. They denied the Incarnation and the Passion of Christ, and, consequently, the value of baptism. They condemned matrimony, and denied that good works were rewarded, or evil ones punished, in the next life. They used to burn an infant eight days old, and preserved his ashes for the viaticum of the sick. A Norman gentleman, called Arefastus, informed Robert, King of France, of the practices and doctrines of those wretches, and he, at once, went to Orleans himself, accompanied by the queen, and a number of bishops. These prelates finding Stephen and Lisosius obstinate in their errors, held a Synod, and deposed and degraded them, and they were then, by the king's orders, brought outside the city, shut up in a cabin with several of their followers, and burned alive (1).

2. The new Nicholites also made their appearance in this century. These were some clergymen in holy orders, who preached that it was lawful for them to marry. The sect, called Incestuosists, also then disturbed the Church. These taught that it was lawful to contract marriage within the four prohibited degrees of consanguinity (2).

3. The remarkable heresy of Berengarius also sprung up in this century, and it is one of the prodigies of Divine mercy, to see that this heretic, after so many relapses, in the end died a true penitent and in communion with the Church. Berenges, or Berengarius, was born in the early part of this century, in Tours; he first studied in the school of St. Martin, and then went to prosecute his studies at Chartres, under Fulbert, the bishop of that city. A certain author (3), speaking of his haughtiness, says, that while only a scholar he cared but very little for his master's opinions, and despised altogether anything coming from his fellow-students; he was not, however, deeply grounded in the abstruse questions of philosophy, but took great pride in quibbles, and strange interpretations of plain words. His master, Fulbert, well aware of his petulant genius, and his desire of novelty, frequently advised him to follow in everything the doctrine of the Fathers, and to reject all new doctrines. He returned to Tours, and was received among the chapter of the church of St. Martin, and was appointed a dignitary, the master of the school, as it was called. He next became treasurer of the church, and then went to Angers, and was appointed archdeacon by the Bishop Eusebius Bruno, one of his own scholars. It was in Angers, according to Noel Alexander and Graveson (4),

---

(1) Fleury, *t.* 8, *l.* 58, *n.* 53 & 55; Graves. *t.* 3, *sec.* 11, *coll.* 5; Gotti, Ver. Relig. *t* 2, *c.* 86, *sec.* 1; Berti, *sec.* 11, *c.* 3; Van Ranst, *sec.* 11, *p.* 173, & seq. (2) Van Ranst, *sec.* 11, *p.* 167; Berti, Brev. Hist. *sec.* 11, *c.* 3. (3) Quidmond. *l.* 1, de Corp. Xti. ver. in Euch. (4) Nat. Alex. *t.* 14, *sec.* 11, *c.* 4, *art.* 2; Graves., *t.* 3, *sec.* 11, *col.* 3.

that he first began, about the year 1047, to disseminate his errors; and Baronius says, that the Bishop Eusebius connived at it, though Noel Alexander acquits him (5). At first, he attacked the sacrament of matrimony, the baptism of infants, and other dogmas of the Faith; but he soon gave up all other questions, and confined himself to one alone—the denial of the Real Presence of the Body and Blood of Christ in the Eucharist. He attacked Paschasius Radbert, who, in 831, wrote a learned treatise on the Eucharist, aud held up to admiration John Scotus Erigena, who flourished in the ninth century, and is believed to have been the first who attacked the Real Presence of Christ in the Holy Eucharist. Cardinal Gotti, however, remarks, that Berenger is looked on as the founder of this heresy, as the Church was obliged to summon several Councils to condemn it, as we shall see hereafter (6).

4. Berengarius was first condemned in the year 1050, in a Roman Council, held under Pope St. Leo IX., but he took so little notice of this, that he called it the Council of Vanity. He was condemned, likewise, in the Council of Vercelli, held the same year, and that Council also condemned the book of John Scotus. He was again condemned in a Council held in Paris, under the reign of King Henry I.; and Victor II., the successor of St. Leo, condemned him in a Synod, held in Florence, in the year 1055. In the same year he abjured his errors—convinced by Lanfranc that he was wrong—in a Council held at Tours, and swore never again to separate himself from the Faith of the Catholic Church; but his subsequent conduct proved that he was not sincere in this recantation. In the year 1059, therefore, Pope Nicholas II. convoked a Council in Rome of 113 bishops, and then Berengarius again made his profession of Faith, according to the form prescribed to him, and swore again never to deviate from it, and threw his own works and those of John Scotus into a great fire, which was lighted in the midst of the Council. Still he was unchanged; on his return to France he again relapsed, and even wrote a book in defence of his heresy, and in defiance of the Church of Rome. Alexander II., the successor of Nicholas, paternally admonished him by letter; but he not only obstinately held out, but even sent him a disrespectful answer. Maurilius, Archbishop of Rouen, therefore, considered himself obliged to adopt extreme measures, and in a Council, held in 1063, excommunicated him and all his followers, and the Decrees of this Council were confirmed by another, held in Poictiers, in 1075. Finally, St. Gregory VII., to put an end to the scandal altogether, convoked a Council, in Rome, of one hundred and fifty bishops, in 1079, in which the Catholic doctrine was confirmed, and Berengarius, confessing himself convinced, took an oath to the following

(5) Nat. Alex. *t.* 14, *diss.* 1, *art.* 4.   (6) Gotti, Ver. Rel. *t.* 2, *c.* 87, *sec.* 1 & 2; Fleury, *t.* 8, *l.* 59, *n.* 65; Graves. loc. cit.

effect: "I confess that the bread and wine placed on the altar are substantially converted into the true flesh and blood of Jesus Christ, by the mystery of sacred prayer and the words of our Redeemer, not alone by the sign and virtue of a Sacrament, but by the truth of substance, &c." (7)

5. Notwithstanding all this, when Berengarius returned to France, he again retracted his confession by another writing (8); but in the year following, 1080, he obtained from the Divine Mercy the grace of a true conversion, and in a Council, held at Bordeaux, retracted this last work of his, and confirmed the profession of Faith he made at Rome; and he survived this last retraction for nearly eight years, and in the year 1088, at the age of nearly ninety years, he died a true penitent, in communion with the Church, after spending these eight years in retirement in the island of St. Cosmas, near Tours, doing penance for his sins (9). William of Malmesbury (10) says, that when just about to die, Berengarius exclaimed, remembering all the perversions his heresy had caused: "To-day Jesus Christ shall appear to me—either to show me mercy on account of my repentance, or, perhaps, to punish me, I fear, for having led others astray." St. Antoninus, De Bellay, Mabillon, Anthony Pagi, Noel Alexander, Graveson, and several other authors, assert that his repentance was sincere, and that he never relapsed during the last years of his life—a remarkable exception to so many other heresiarchs, who died in their sins.

Article II.

HERESIES OF THE TWELFTH CENTURY.

6. The Petrobrussians. 7. Henry, and his Disciples. 8. Their Condemnation. 9. Peter Abelard, and his Errors concerning the Trinity. 10. His Condemnation. 11. His Conversion and Death. 12. His particular Errors. 13. Arnold of Brescia; his Errors and Condemnation. 14. Causes a Sedition, and is burned alive. 15. Gilbert de la Poree; his Errors and Conversion. 16. Folmar, Tanquelinus, and the Abbot Joachim; the Apostolicals and the Bogomiles. 17. Peter Waldo and his Followers under different Denominations—Waldenses, Poor Men of Lyons, &c. 18. Their particular Errors, and Condemnation.

6. The Petrobrussians made their appearance at this time; they were followers of a monk, Peter of Bruis, who, tired of the restraint of the cloister, apostatized, and fled to the province of Arles, and, about the year 1118, began to preach his errors in that neighbourhood. These may be reduced to five heads, as Peter, Abbot of Cluny (1), tells us: First.—He rejected the baptism of infants till they came to the use of reason. Second.—He rejected altars and churches, and said they should be destroyed. Third.—He prohi-

(7) Fleury, t. 9, l. 62, n. 60; N. Alex. loc. cit. art. 17; Gotti, loc. cit. s. 3. (8) Mabillon, præf. 2, sec. 6, n. 31. (9) Fleury, t. 9, l. 63, n. 40. (10) Villel. Malmesb. de Rebus Angl. l. 3. (1) Bibli. Cum. p. 1120.

bited the veneration of the Cross. Fourth.—He rejected the sacrifice of the Mass, and the sacrament of the Eucharist. Fifth.—He rejected prayers and suffrages for the dead. It is very likely, Graveson says (2), that these errors were condemned in the Third Canon of the Council of Toulouse, in the year 1119, at which Pope Celestine II. presided, and that they were again condemned in the Second Council of Lateran, under Innocent II. It is the opinion of some, that Peter of Bruis was a follower of the Manichean doctrine; but Noel Alexander and Cardinal Gotti (3) are of the contrary opinion, because he baptized with water, made use of flesh-meat, and venerated both the Old and New Testaments, all which the Manicheans rejected. He had a horrible death. He collected together a great number of crosses on Good Friday, in the town of St. Giles, in the diocese of Nismes, and making a great fire with them, he caused a great quantity of meat to be roasted at it, and distributed it to his followers, but the Archbishop of Arles got him into his power some time after, and sentenced him to be burned alive (4).

7. After the death of this unfortunate man, another monk, named Henry, some say an Italian, others a Provenceal (5), took his place, and about the year 1142 increased the numbers of the sect, and added new errors to those of his master. He was highly esteemed for his learning and piety, and on that account disseminated his errors most extensively in several places, especially in the diocese of Mans; but before he proceeded to that city himself, he sent two of his disciples, bearing, like himself, a cane with an iron cross on the top, and they obtained leave for him to preach in that city, from the Bishop Ildebert. When he began to preach, his eloquence soon drew crowds after him, and he so excited the fury of the populace against the priests that they looked on them as excommunicated, and would have burned down their dwellings, robbed them of their property, and even stoned them to death, if the principal people of the city had not opposed these violent proceedings. The Bishop Ildebert himself was not allowed to pass free by Henry's followers, so he banished him from his diocese, and received two of his disciples, whose eyes were opened to his errors, and abandoned him (6). After his banishment from Mans, he first went to Poictiers, and next to Toulouse, where he principally added to his followers. St. Bernard describes (Epis. 241) the ruinous consequences that ensued from his preaching in that city; the priests, the churches, the festivals, the sacraments, and all holy things, were treated with supreme contempt; people died without confession, and without the Viaticum; and baptism was refused to children. He even adds,

---

(2) Graves. Hist. *t.* 3, *sec.* 12, *coll.* 2. (3) Nat. Alex. *t.* 14, *sec.* 12, *c.* 4, *art.* 4; Gotti, Ver. Rel. *t.* 2, *c.* 89, *s.* 1. (4) Gotti, loc. cit. *n.* 10, *l.* 69, *n.* 24; N. Alex. loc. cit.; Graves. loc. cit. (5) Gotti, *c.* 79, *sec.* 2. (6) Nat. Alex. cit. *art.* 7; Fleury, cit. *n.* 24.

that Henry himself shamelessly spent what he got at his sermons at the gaming-table, and that so great was his depravity, that he frequently, after preaching in the day, spent the night in houses of ill fame. When the Pope, Eugene III., learned that the number of the heretics was daily increasing in Toulouse, he sent thither, as Legate, the Cardinal Bishop of Ostia, Alberic, and he took along with him, Godfrey, Bishop of Chartres, and St. Bernard, who, by his sermons, conferences, and miracles, converted many from their evil ways, and accordingly, in his epistle to the people of Toulouse, in 1147 (Ep. 242), he says: "We thank God that our sojourn among you was not an idle one, and although we tarried but a short time with you, still our presence was not unprofitable."

8. The Legate, Alberic, published a sentence of excommunication against all holding any communication with the Henricians, or with their protectors. St. Bernard promised Henry himself that he would receive him as a monk into Clairvaux, in case it was his wish to retire and do penance (7); but the unfortunate man always shunned him. The saint still continued to follow his traces, and wherever he went and preached, went after him and preached likewise, and generally re-converted those who had fallen by him. He was taken at last, and put in chains into the hands of the bishop, and he, as Noel Alexander tells us, delivered him up to the Legate Apostolic, and it is supposed that he was by him condemned to perpetual imprisonment, that he might not have any longer an opportunity of preaching his heresy (8).

9. Peter Abelard was born in 1079, in the village of Palais, three leagues from Nantes. At first he taught philosophy and theology with great credit, but the disastrous consequences of an intrigue with Heloise, the niece of Fulbert, a canon of Paris, drove him from the world, and he retired, to bury his shame and regret in the Abbey of St. Denis, and took the monastic habit at the age of forty years (9). He soon got tired of the life of the cloister, and went to the territories of the Count of Champagne, and opened a school which soon became celebrated, and it was there he published his book, filled with several errors concerning the Trinity. His work was condemned by Conon, Bishop of Palestrina, the Pope's Legate, in a Council held in Soissons in 1121, and Abelard was summoned there, and obliged to cast the book into the fire with his own hands, and was then given into the keeping of the Abbot of St. Medard of Soissons, who received orders to keep him in close custody in a monastery (10).

10. Notwithstanding all this, Abelard continued for eighteen years teaching theology and writing works tainted with various errors. St. Bernard, when this came to his knowledge, endeavoured

(7) Fleury, n. 25.   (8) Nat. Alex. loc. cit.   (9) Fleury, t. 10, l. 67, n. 22.
(10) Fleury, loc. cit. n. 21; Nat. Alex. t. 15, diss. 7, a. 7.

to get him to change his sentiments, without giving him any pain; but though Abelard promised amendment, there was no change, and knowing that there was soon to be a Council at Sens, he called on the archbishop, and complained that St. Bernard was privately speaking against his works, and begged the archbishop to summon the saint to the Council, promising publicly to defend his writings. St. Bernard at first refused; but finally conquered his repugnance, and although not prepared for the dispute, attended on the appointed day, the 2nd of June, 1140. He produced Abelard's book in the assembly, and quoted the errors he marked in it; but Abelard, instead of answering, judging that the Council would be opposed to him, appealed to the Pope previous to the delivery of the sentence, and left the meeting. Though the bishops did not consider his appeal canonical, still, out of respect for the Pope, they did not condemn Abelard in person; but St. Bernard having proved that many propositions in the book were false and heretical, they condemned these, and then forwarded an account of the whole proceedings to Innocent II., requesting him to confirm their condemnatory sentence by his authority, and to punish all who would presume to contravene it (11). St. Bernard wrote to the same effect to Innocent, and the Pope not only condemned the writings of Abelard, but his person likewise, imposing perpetual silence on him as a heretic, and excommunicating all who would attempt to defend him (12).

11. Abelard was on his way to Rome to prosecute his appeal, but happening to pass by Clugni, he had a meeting with Peter the Venerable, the Abbot of that monastery, and with the Abbot of Citeaux, who came on purpose to reconcile him with St. Bernard. The Abbot of Clugni joined his entreaties to those of his brother of Citeaux, and persuaded him to go and see St. Bernard, and retract the errors this holy doctor charged him with. Abelard yielded at last; he went to Citeaux, became reconciled to St. Bernard and returned to Clugni, and being there informed that the condemnation of the Council was confirmed by the Pope, he resolved to abandon his appeal, and to remain in that abbey for the remainder of his life. The abbot offered to receive him with all his heart, if the Pope had no objection. Abelard wrote to the Pope, and obtained his consent, and then became an inmate of the Abbey of Clugni. He lived there for two years, wearing the habit of the convent, and leading a life of edification, and even gave lessons to the monks; but he was obliged, on account of a heavy fit of sickness, to go for change of air to the Priory of St. Marcellus, in Burgundy, and he died there on the 21st of April, in the year 1142, the 63rd of his age, and went to enjoy, we hope, eternal happiness (13).

(11) Fleury, t. 10, l. 68, n. 61, 62; Nat. Alex. c. 1.   (12) Fleury, loc. cit. n. 67; Nat. Alex. art. 8 in fine.   (13) Nat. Alex. loc. cit. art. 12, & Fleury, loc. cit.

12. The following errors were attributed to Peter Abelard: First.—He said that the names of the Father, Son, and Holy Ghost, are improperly attributed to God, and that they only describe the plenitude of the Supreme Good. Second.—That the Father has a plenary power, the Son a certain power, but that the Holy Ghost has not any power. Third.—That the Son is of the substance of the Father, but that the Holy Ghost is not of the substance of the Father and the Son. Fourth.—That we can do good without the assistance of grace. Fifth.—That Jesus Christ, as God and man, is not a third Person of the Trinity. Sixth.—That mankind derives from Adam the penalty alone, but not the fault of original sin. Seventh.—That no sin is committed with desire or with delectation, or with ignorance (14). Graveson (15) says that Abelard asserted in his Apology that these errors were falsely attributed to him by the ignorance or malice of others, and Berenger, Bishop of Poictiers, one of his disciples, also wrote an Apology in defence of his master. But then the authority of St. Bernard, the Decrees of the Council, and the condemnation of Innocent II., should have more weight with us than these Apologies. Graveson and Alexander justly remark, that although Abelard may undoubtedly have been the author of these heretical propositions, still, that he cannot be called a heretic, as he repented and abjured them. Cardinal Gotti (16), speaking of him, says: "There is no doubt but that he rendered himself suspected in explaining the Articles of the Faith, so that at one time he seems an Arian, then a Sabellian, next a Macedonian, now a Pelagian, and frequently a founder of a new heresy altogether; but he finally wiped away all stains by his retractation."

13. Arnold, of the city of Brescia, in Italy, lived also in this century. He went to study in Paris under Abelard, and was infected with his master's errors. He then returned to Brescia, and to gain an opinion of sanctity, took the monastic habit, and, about the year 1138 (17), began to preach and dogmatise against the truth of the Faith. He was more flippant than profound, and always attached to new opinions. His sentiments regarding Baptism and the Eucharist were not Catholic, but his principal declamations were against monks, priests, bishops, and the Pope. Those monks, he said, would be damned who possessed estated property—the priests who held property also—and the bishops who were in possession of lordships or feudalties would share the same fate; the clergy, he said, should live on the tithes and oblations of the people alone. The effect of his sermons of this nature was to cause the clergy of Brescia and the neighbouring cities to be despised and contemned by the people, and he was, therefore, charged by his

(14) Fleury, n. 61, Alex. art. 5, ex Ep. St. Bernar. (15) Graveson, t. 3, sec. 12, coll. 3. (16) Gotti, Ver. Rel. t. 2, c. 90, s. 3, cum Baron. Ann. 1140, n. 11, & seq. (17) Nat. Alex. t. 14, s. 12, c. 3, art. 8.

bishop and others, before the Second Council of Lateran, held in 1139, by Pope Innocent II.; and the Council condemned and imposed perpetual silence on him (18). When Arnold heard of this sentence, he fled to Zurich, in the diocese of Constance, and did a great deal of harm there, as the austerity of his life gave authority to his words, and he was, besides that, supported by the nobles of the country. When St. Bernard heard this, he wrote to the Bishop of Zurich (Epis. 195), exhorting him to be on his guard against so dangerous a character, and to put him in prison, as the Pope had commanded, because if he rested satisfied with only banishing him out of his own diocese, he would be allowing the plague to infect some other place. He also wrote to Guido, the Pope's Legate, with whom it was said Arnold had taken refuge (Epis. 146), putting him on his guard in like manner.

14. In the first year of the Pontificate of Eugenius III., 1145, Arnold went to Rome, and blew up the coals of a sedition already enkindled. He went about saying that the dignity of the Senate and the Order of Knights should be re-established, and that the Pope had no right to the government of Rome, as his power was spiritual alone. The Romans, excited by these discourses, rose up against the authority of the Prefect of Rome, tore down some of the houses of the nobility and cardinals, and maltreated, and even wounded, some of them (19). While Arnold was stirring up this sedition, he was taken prisoner by Gerard, Cardinal of St. Nicholas, but was rescued by the Viscounts of the Campagna, and fell into the hands of Frederic Barbarossa, then King of the Romans, and when he went to Rome he was met by three cardinals, sent to him by Adrian IV., and they, in the Pope's name, demanded that Arnold should be delivered up to them. Frederic gave him up at once, and he was brought back to Rome, and according to the sentence passed on him by his judges, was burned to death in public, and his ashes cast into the Tiber. Such was the end of this disturber of Rome and of the world, as Van Ranst calls him, in 1155 (20).

15. Gilbert de la Poree, a native of Poictiers, was at first a canon of that city, and afterwards its bishop, in 1141. From the very first day he began to study philosophy, he was so taken with logical subtleties, that when he afterwards applied himself to scholastic theology, which was then just beginning to be developed, he wished to judge everything by the rules of philosophy, and to use them as a standard for the articles of the Faith; and hence the origin of his errors. He said that the Divine Essence was not God, and that the *proprietates* of the Persons are not the Persons themselves; that the Divine Nature did not become incarnate, but only

(18) Fleury, *t.* 10, *l.* 68, *n.* 55; Gotti, loc. cit. *s.* 1; Nat. Alex. loc. cit. (19) Nat. Alex. loc. cit.; Fleury, *t.* 10, *l.* 69, *n.* 10; Gotti, loc. cit. (20) Van Ranst, Hist. *p.* 148; Fleury, *t.* 10, *l.* 70, *n.* 1; Nat. Alex. & Gotti, loc. cit.

the person of the Son, and that baptism is received alone by those predestined to glory. He was charged with these errors in the year 1145, and Pope Eugenius III., to whom the complaint was made, ordered his accusers to have the whole affair investigated in a Council in Paris. The Synod was accordingly held, and St. Bernard attended, and strenuously combated his errors; but nothing was decided till the following year, in which a Council was held in Rheims, at which the Pope himself attended, and condemned Gilbert's doctrine. He at once bowed to the decision of the Pontiff, abjured his errors, was reconciled to his accusers, who were two of his own archdeacons, and returned with honour to his diocese (21).

16. Other heretics disturbed the peace of the Church in this century. One of these was Folmar, Principal of the Church of Trieffenstein, in Franconia; he said that in the Eucharist the blood alone of Jesus Christ was received under the appearance of wine, and the flesh alone, not the bones or the members, under the appearance of bread, and that it was not the Son of Man that was received, but the flesh alone of the Son of Man. He, however, soon retracted, and abjured his errors in a letter he wrote to the bishops of Bavaria and Austria (22). Tanquelinus taught that the reception of the Holy Eucharist was of no avail for salvation, and that the ministry of priests and bishops was of no value, and was not instituted by Christ. He infected the city of Antwerp, but it was afterwards purged from this heresy by St. Norbert, founder of the Premonstratensians and Archbishop of Magdeburg (23). Joachim, an abbot in Calabria, lived also in this century; he fell into some errors regarding the Trinity, in a treatise he wrote against Peter Lombard; he denied that the three Divine Persons are one and the same as the Divine Nature, and he also said that in the mystery of the Trinity, essence generates essence, insinuating by that, that each Divine Person has a particular essence. This was a renewal of the Tritheism of John Philiponus, infected with the Eutychian heresy, who taught that there are three natures in the Trinity, confounding the three Persons with the three natures. This treatise was condemned in the Fourth Council of Lateran, celebrated by Innocent III., in 1215. Joachim, however, had previously died in 1201, and submitted all his writings to the judgment of the Church, so Honorius III., the successor of Innocent, would not have him considered as a heretic (24). The Apostolicals also infested the Church about this time; among other errors, they condemned marriage, and even bound themselves by a vow of chastity, though the licentiousness of their lives showed

(21) Nat. Alex. *t.* 14, *s.* 12, *c.* 4, *a.* 9; Graveson, His. Eccl. *t.* 3, *sec.* 12, *coll.* 3; Fleury, *t.* 10, *l.* 69, *n.* 23. (22) Nat Alex. *t.* 14, *s.* 12, *c.* 4, *ar.* 12. (23) Nat. loc. cit. *ar.* 6. (24) Graves *t* 3, *s.* 12, Coll. 3; Fleury, *t.* 11, *l.* 77, *n.* 46; Berti, *s.* 12, 3; Van Ranst, *p.* 214.

what little regard they had for that angelic virtue (25). We have already spoken of the Bogomiles (*Chap.* iv. *N.* 81), treating of the heresy of the Messalians. We have now to investigate the history of the Waldenses

17. Peter Waldo, the founder of the sect of the Waldenses, began to preach his heresy in the year 1160, on the occasion of the sudden death of a great personage in Lyons, who dropped dead in the presence of a great many people. He was so terrified at the occurrence, that he immediately distributed a large sum of money to the poor, and a great many people joined him out of devotion, and became his followers. He was a man of some learning, and began to explain the New Testament to his followers, and taught several errors. The clergy immediately took up arms against him, but he set them at defiance, telling his followers that they (the clergy) were both ignorant and corrupt, and that they were envious of his exemplary life and learning. Such is the origin of the Waldenses, according to Fleury, Alexander, and Gotti (26); but Graveson gives another account (27); he says, that Peter Waldo, having either heard or read the 19th chapter of the Gospel of St. Matthew, in which our Lord tells us that we should sell our goods, and give the price to the poor, persuaded himself that he was called on to renew the Apostolic life, and accordingly sold his property, gave all to the poor, and led a life of poverty himself. A person of the name of John, terrified at the sudden death already spoken of, sold his patrimony, likewise, and joined him; many others followed their example, and in a little time the sect became so numerous, that in the diocese of Poictiers alone they had forty-one schools. From these seats of iniquity sprung several sects, enumerated by Rainer (28), who for seventeen years was a Waldensian, but his eyes at length being opened to their impiety, he forsook them, joined the Catholic Church, and became a distinguished member of the Order of St. Dominick. The different sects that sprouted out from the parent stock took various names; they were called Waldenses, from Peter Waldo; Lyonists, or poor men of Lyons, from the city whence they originated; Picards, Lombards, Bohemians, Bulgarians, from the provinces they overran; Arnaldists, Josepeists, and Lollards, from Doctors of the sect; Cathari, from the purity of heart they boasted of; Bons Hommes, or good men, from their apparent sanctity and regularity of life; Sabbatists, or Insabatists, either from the peculiar shoe or sandal, with a cross cut on the top, which they wore, or because they rejected the celebration of the Sabbath and other festivals (29).

18. The Waldenses fell into very many errors, which Rainer, quoted by Noel Alexander, enumerates (30). We will only men-

(25) N. Alex. loc. cit. *ar.* 11. *c.* 4, *ar.* 13; Gotti, *t.* 2, *c.* 93, *s.* 1. Opusc. de Hæret. lc. cit. *ar.* 13, *s.* 2, & seq.
(26) Fleury, *t.* 11, *l.* 73, *n.* 55; Nat. Alex. *t.* 14,
(27) Graves. *t.* 3, *s.* 12, Coll. 3. (28) Rainer,
(29) Graves. loc. cit. & Nat. Alex. loc. cit. (30) Nat. Alex.

tion the principal ones here. The Roman Church, they said, failed in the time of Pope St. Sylvester, when it entered into the possession of temporal property, and that they alone were the true Church, as they followed the Apostles and the Gospel in holding no possessions. The Pope, they said, was the head of all errors, the bishops, Scribes, and the religious, Pharisees. Tithes ought not to be paid, as they were not paid in the primitive Church. They only believed in two sacraments, Baptism and the Eucharist, and baptism, they said, was of no use to infants. A priest falling into mortal sin, according to them, lost the power of absolving and consecrating, and, on the contrary, a good layman has the power of giving absolution. They rejected indulgences, and the dispensations of the Church, the fasts commanded to be observed, and all the ceremonies of the Roman Church. They abhorred holy images and the sign of the Cross even; denied the distinction between mortal and venial sin, and said it was unlawful to take an oath, even in judgment. These heretics were first condemned by Alexander III., in 1163; in the Synod of Tours, in 1175 or 1176; in the Synod of Lombes, in 1178; in one held in Toulouse by Peter, Cardinal and Legate of the Pope; in the Third General Council of Lateran, in 1179; in the Fourth General Council of Lateran, in 1215; and finally, in the Constitution of Gregory IX., "Cap. Excommunicamus, 15 de Herat." in which all the heretics of all the above-named sects are anathematized (31).

Article III.

HERESIES OF THE THIRTEENTH CENTURY.

19. The Albigenses and their Errors. 20. The Corruption of their Morals. 21. Conferences held with them, and their Obstinacy. 22. They create an Anti-Pope. 23. Glorious Labours of St. Dominick, and his stupendous Miracles. 24. Crusade under the Command of Count Montfort, in which he is victorious. 25. Glorious Death of the Count, and Destruction of the Albigenses. 26. Sentence of the Fourth Council of Lateran, in which the Dogma is defined in Opposition to their Tenets. 27. Amalric and his Heresy; the Errors added by his Disciples; they are condemned. 28. William de St. Amour and his Errors. 29. The Flagellants and their Errors. 30. The Fratricelli and their Errors, condemned by John XXII.

19. THE heretics called the Albigenses, sprung from the Waldenses, made their appearance in this century, and were so called, because they first spread themselves in the territory of the city of Albi, or that part of Narbonic Gaul called Albigensum, and subsequently in the province of Toulouse (1). Graveson (2) says that the impurities of all other heresies were joined in this one sect. This sect was in existence previous to the reign of Innocent III., but it was so strong in the year 1198, that Cesarius (3), a contem-

(31) Nat. Alex. loc. cit. s. 7.   (1) Nat. Alex. t. 16, c. 3, ar. 1.   (2) Graves. t. 3, s. 12, Coll. 3.   (3) Cæsar Heisterb. Dial. Mirac. Diss. 5, c. 2.

poraneous author, says, that almost all the pure grain of the Faith of the people was turned into tares. Spondanus gives the following list of their errors (4): First.—They received the New Testament alone, rejecting the Old, with the exception of the passages quoted by our Lord, and his Apostles; they, likewise renounced all Catholic Doctors, and when asked for an account of their Faith, they said they were not bound to answer. Second.—They taught that there were two Gods, a good and a bad one; the good one, the author of the New Testament, and the Creator of all invisible things; the bad one, the author of the Old Testament, the Creator of man, and of all visible things. Third.—They said that baptism was useless to infants. Fourth.—That an unworthy priest had not power to consecrate the Eucharist. Fifth.—That matrimony was nothing more than concubinage, and that no one could be saved in that state, and still their morals were most corrupt. Sixth.—That no one should obey either bishops or priests, unless they have acquired the qualities required by the Apostles; and that they have no power in the Sacraments or in Divine things, and that no one, therefore, should pay tithes to them. Seventh.—That churches should not be dedicated to God or the Saints, and that the faithful are not bound to pray or to give alms, either to the poor or to churches, and that it was quite sufficient to confess to any one at all, and that penance was of no use. Noel Alexander (5), besides these errors, enumerates several others, as that the Fathers of the Old Testament were all damned; that St. John the Baptist was a demon; that the Roman Church is the harlot of the Apocalypse; that the resurrection of the body is all a lie; that the Sacraments are all false, and that the Eucharist, Confirmation, Orders, and the Mass are nothing more than superstitions; that the souls of men are no other than the rebellious spirits who fell from heaven; that there was no purgatory, and they blasphemously applied to the Virgin Mother of God a term we dread to make use of.

20. They led most horribly immoral lives. Lucas Tudensis (6) horrifies us by recounting what he heard from some of them who forsook the sect, and joined the Catholic Church. Murder, cheating, theft, and usury were quite common among them, but their impurities were above all of the most horrible description; the nearest relatives had no regard to the decencies of life, or the very laws of nature itself. The old people, he says, are blasphemous and cruel; the young ripe for every wickedness; the children, from the universal depravity, belonging to no father in particular, are depraved from their childhood; and the infants imbibe the most pernicious errors with their mothers' milk; the women, without shame or modesty, go about among their neighbours, making others as bad as them-

---

(4) Spondan. Epit. Baron. ad Ann. 1181. (5) Nat. Alex. loc. cit. s. 2.
(6) Lucas Tuden. l. 3, adv. Albig.

selves. Among the other proofs of their impiety, Cesarius (7) tells us, that when they were besieged by the Catholics in Bessiers, they indecently defiled a book of the Gospels, and threw it from the walls into the ranks of the besiegers, amidst a shower of arrows, crying out: " Behold your law, wretches."

21. The Albigenses laboured to gain proselytes not alone by persuasion, but by force of arms likewise; and the Catholics, therefore, found it necessary to have recourse not alone to preaching, but were obliged to summon the power of the Prince to their aid. Peter of Castlenau and Rodulph, Cistercian monks, together with their Abbot, Arnold, appointed Apostolic Legates by Innocent III., were the first to oppose them. The holy Bishop of Osma joined them, and without attendance or money, like the Apostles, they proceeded on foot to preach to the heretics, and their first conference was held in Montreal, in the diocese of Carcasonne. They disputed for fifteen days in presence of judges chosen for the purpose, and the heretics were convinced, but the judges being favourable to the heretical party, suppressed the sentence, and would not even give up the Acts of the disputation. The preachers remained in the city to instruct the people, and supported themselves by begging from door to door. The Abbot of Citeaux and twelve of his monks, together with the Bishop of Osma, spread themselves through the country, preaching and disputing with the heretics. The Bishop of Osma and some other prelates held another conference with the Albigenses in Pamiers, and the heretics were so confounded that the judge of the Conference, a nobleman of the city, abjured his errors, and more followed his example every day (8). The Cistercian, Peter of Castlenau, the Pope's Legate, having found it necessary to excommunicate Raymond, Count of Toulouse, the chief favourer of the heretics, was summoned before him to clear himself from charges laid against him; he went accordingly, but nothing was decided on in the interview; the Count even uttered threats against him when he was about to take his departure, and sent two of his servants to accompany him. One of them, while the Legate was passing the Rhone, ran him through with a lance. Peter at once felt that the wound was mortal. "God pardon me," said he, " as I pardon you," and died shortly after. Pope Innocent, when informed of his death, declared him a martyr, and excommunicated his murderers and all their accomplices, and gave orders to the bishops of the provinces of Arles and Narbonne and the neighbouring territories again to excommunicate the Count of Toulouse (9).

22. A few years after the Albigenses elected a person of the name of Bartolomew, an anti-Pope. He resided on the borders of Dal-

---

(7) Cæsar. *l.* 5, de Demon. (8) Gotti, Ver. Rel. *t.* 2, *c.* 94, *s.* 3. (9) Fleury, *t.* 11, *l.* 76, *n.* 86; Gotti, loc. cit.; Nat. Alex. loc. cit.

matia and Bulgaria, and was the chief adviser of the heretics. He appointed another person of the same name as his vicar, and he took up his residence in the territory of Toulouse, and sent round to all the neighbouring cities his principal's letters, headed, "Bartholomew, servant of the servants of the holy Faith, to N. N. health." This vicar pretended to consecrate bishops and regulate the Church (10), but the Almighty soon put a stop to all by the death of the anti-Pope (11).

23. It is now time to speak of the glorious labours of St. Dominick, who may justly be called the exterminator of the Albigenses He was engaged nine years, according to Graveson, or seven, according to Van Ranst, in battling with them, and finally he instituted the Order of Preachers, to bring back the strayed sheep to the fold of the Catholic Church. He attended the Bishop of Osma at the conference he held with the heretics, and was a most strenuous opponent of their errors, both by preaching and writing, and God confirmed his exertions by miracles. Peter de Valle Sernai, a Cistercian monk (12), relates the following miracle, and says he had it from the man himself in whose possession the paper was. After the conference of Montreal, St. Dominick wrote down the texts he cited on a sheet of paper, and gave it to one of the heretics to peruse them at his leisure. The next evening several Albigenses were seated round a fire considering it, when one of them proposed to throw the paper into the fire, and if it burn, said he, that is a proof that our faith is the true one, but should that not be the case, we must believe the Catholic faith. All agreed, the paper was cast into the flames, and, after lying there some time, it leaped out unscorched. All were surprised; but one of the most incredulous among them suggested that the experiment should be tried again; it was done so, and the result was the same. Try it a third, said the heretic; a third time it was tried, and with the same effect. But for all that they agreed to keep the whole affair a secret, and remained as obstinate as before. There was a soldier present, however, somewhat inclined to the Catholic faith, and he told it to a great many persons (13). God wrought another more public miracle through his servant in Fois, near Carcasonne; he challenged the heretics, in one of his sermons, to a formal disputation, and each party agreed to bring, in writing, to the Conference, their profession of Faith, and the principal arguments in support of it. The saint laid down his document, the heretics did the same; they then proposed that each paper should be thrown into the fire, to leave the judgment to God. St. Dominick, inspired by the Almighty, immediately cast his paper into the flames; the heretics also threw in theirs, which was immediately burned to ashes, while the saint's

(10) Parisius, Hist. Anglic. an. 1223. (11) Fleury, *t.* 11, *l.* 78, *n.* 60; Gotti, loc. cit.; Nat. Alex. loc. cit. *s.* 2. (12) Pat. Vallis. Ser. His. Albig. *c.* 7. (13) Nat. Alex. *t.* 16, *c.* 3; Gotti, Ver. Rel. *t.* 2, *c.* 94, cap. 3.

remained intact on top of the burning coals. Three times it was cast into the fire, and always came forth untouched by the flames (14).

24. Neither miracles nor missions had any effect on the Albigenses, however, who every day became more powerful, under the protection of several princes, and especially of Raymond, Count of Toulouse. Pope Innocent III., therefore, considered it necessary at last to call on the Catholic princes to free the Church from these enemies, and therefore wrote to Philip, King of France, and to the other princes of that kingdom, and likewise to the bishops and faithful, calling on them to take up arms for the extermination of these heretics, and granting them the same indulgences as were granted to those who put on the cross for the liberation of the Holy Land. This Bull was published in 1210, and immediately a great number of soldiers, not only from France but elsewhere, enrolled themselves in this crusade under the command of Count Simon of Montfort. The Albigenses numbered a hundred thousand, the Crusaders only twelve hundred, and Count Montfort was advised not to risk an engagement; but he said: "We are numerous enough, for we fight for God and God for us." He divided his small army into three bodies, and made a feint, as if about to march on Toulouse, but turned on the vanguard of the enemy, and attacked them with such fury, that at first they wavered, and finally took to flight. Montfort, encouraged by this success, gave orders to his three small divisions to unite, and, without loss of time, attacked the main body of the enemy, among whom was the King of Arragon. The Count broke through the ranks, and singled out the King; he charged him with his lance, but Montfort, parrying the blow with one hand, seized the King with the other, and unhorsed him, and his esquire immediately dispatched the fallen monarch. The enemy was panic-struck with the King's death, and fled in every direction, and the Crusaders cut them down almost without opposition. It is said that between the Albigenses and the Arragonese twenty thousand fell that day, with only a loss of six or seven persons to the Catholics (15). The letters written by the French bishops to all the churches of Christendom, on the occasion of this glorious and stupendous victory, are still extant (16).

25. Count Montfort, after so many glorious actions in defence of the Faith, died gloriously, like Judas Maccabeus, at the second siege of Toulouse. He was told that the enemy were concealed in the trenches; but he armed, and went to the church to hear Mass, and recommended himself and his cause to God. While he was hearing Mass, he was informed that the people of Toulouse were attacking the troops who had charge of the besieging engines; but he refused to move until, as he said, he had heard Mass, and seen

(14) Gotti, loc. cit. (15) Nat. Alex. loc. cit. s. 4; Gotti, loc. cit. s. 4; Bernin. t. 3; ec. 13, c. 1; Graveson, t. 4, sec. 33; Coll. 3. (16) Rainald. Ann. 1213, n. 60.

his God on the altar. Another messenger came in haste to tell him his troops were giving way, but he dismissed him, saying: "I want to see my Redeemer." After adoring the Sacred Host, he raised up his hands to heaven, and exclaimed: "Now thou dost dismiss thy servant, O Lord, according to thy word, in peace, because mine eyes have seen thy salvation. Now," said he, "let us proceed, and die, if necessary, for him who died for us." His soldiers rallied at once when he appeared among them; but he approached too near to the engines, and a stone from one of them struck him in the head, and he had barely time to recommend himself to God and the Blessed Virgin, when his spirit fled. This was on the 25th of June, 1218 (17). After the death of this great champion of the Lord, and martyr of Christ, as Peter de Valle Sernai (18) calls him, Louis VIII., King of France, prosecuted the war, and in the year 1236 took Avignon from the enemy, after a siege of three months, and several other strong places besides. St. Louis IX., by the advice of Pope Gregory IX., prosecuted the war, and having taken the city of Toulouse, the young Count Raymond—for his wicked father met with a sudden death—signed a treaty of peace, on the conditions prescribed to him by the King and the Pope's Legate, the principal one of which was, that he would use all his power to extirpate the Albigensian heresy in his territory. The heretics, thus deprived of all assistance, dwindled away by degrees, and totally disappeared, as Graveson tells us (19), though Noel Alexander and Cardinal Gotti say that they were not totally put down (20).

26. These heretics having been previously condemned in particular Synods, at Montilly, Avignon, Montpelier, Paris, and Narbonne, were finally condemned in the Fourth General Council of Lateran, celebrated and presided over by Pope Innocent III., in 1215. In the first Chapter of this Council it was decreed, in opposition to these heretics, "that there was one universal principle, the Creator of all, visible and invisible, corporeal and spiritual things, who by his Almighty power, in the beginning of time, created from nothing both spiritual and corporeal, angelic and earthly beings, and man likewise, as consisting of body and spirit. The devil, and all other evil spirits, were created by God good, according to their nature, but became bad of themselves, and man sinned at the suggestion of the devil. The Holy Trinity, undivided, as to its common essence—divided, as to its personal *proprietates*—gave saving doctrine to mankind, by Moses and the Holy Prophets, and other servants, according to the properly-ordained disposition of time; and, at length, Jesus Christ, the only-begotten Son of God, by the whole Trinity in common, incarnate of Mary, ever Virgin, conceived by the co-operation of the Holy Ghost, and made true man,

---

(17) Fleury, *t.* 11, *l.* 78, *n.* 18; Nat. and Gotti, loc. cit.   (18) Pet. Vallises. His. Albig. *c.* 86.   (19) Grav. loc. cit.   (20) Nat. Alex. loc. cit. *sec.* 4, & Gotti, loc. cit.

composed of a rational soul and a real body, one person in two natures, more clearly pointed out to us the way of life; who, according to his Divinity, being impassible and immortal, was made passible and mortal, according to his humanity, and suffered and died on the wood of the Cross for the salvation of mankind, descended into hell, arose from the dead, and ascended into heaven; but he descended in the spirit, arose in the flesh, and in both ascended into heaven, and shall come in the end of the world to judge both the living and the dead, and shall render to each—both the reprobate and the elect—according to their works. For all shall arise in the same bodies they now have, to receive, according to their deserts, either rewards or punishment—the wicked, eternal punishment with the devil—the good, eternal glory with Christ. There is one universal Church of all the faithful, out of which there is no salvation, in which Jesus Christ is, at the same time, priest and sacrifice, and his body and blood is truly contained under the appearance of bread and wine, the bread being, by the Divine power, transubstantiated into the body, and the wine into the blood, that we might receive from him what he received from us to perfect the mystery of Unity; and no one but a priest rightly ordained according to the keys of the Church, which Jesus Christ himself granted to the apostles, and to their successors, can consecrate this holy Sacrament. The Sacrament of Baptism, consecrated to the invocation of the undivided Trinity, Father, Son, and Holy Ghost, properly administered in water, both to infants and adults, by any person, according to the form of the Church, is available to salvation. And should any one, after receiving baptism, fall into sin, he can be always healed by true repentance. Not virgins alone, and those who observe continence, but married persons, likewise, pleasing God by true faith and good works, shall deservedly obtain eternal happiness (21).

27. In this century also lived Amalric, or Amaury, a priest, a native of Bene, near Chartres. He studied in Paris, and was a great logician, and taught this science with great applause. He then applied himself to the study of Sacred Scripture and theology, and as he was fond of newfangled opinions, he had the rashness to teach that every Christian ought to believe himself a *natural* member of Christ, and that no one could be saved unless he so believed. The University of Paris condemned this opinion in 1204, but Amalric refused to submit to the sentence, and appealed to Innocent III., and went to Rome to prosecute his appeal in person; the Pope, however, confirmed the sentence, and obliged him to make a public abjuration in the presence of the University. He obeyed the Pope's orders in 1207, but his heart belied what his lips uttered, and so great was his chagrin that he soon after died.

(21) Nat. Alex. *t.* 16, *c.* 3, *s.* 5; Gotti, *t.* 2, *c.* 94.

His disciples added new errors to those taught by their master. The power of the Fathers, they said, lasted only during the period of the Mosaic Law; the New Law lasted from that till their own times—that is, twelve hundred years; and then the Law of the Holy Ghost began, when all sacraments, and all other assistances to salvation ceased, and every one could be saved by the grace of the Holy Ghost alone, without any act of his own. The virtue of charity, they said, caused that that which before was sinful, if done through charity was sinful no longer, and thus, under the pretext of charity, they committed the most impure actions. They asserted that the body of Christ was only in the Consecrated Host as in any other bread, and that God spoke as much through Ovid as through St. Augustin, and they denied the Resurrection, heaven, and hell, for those who thought about God as they did had heaven in themselves, and those who fell into mortal sin had hell in their own bosoms (22). Raul of Nemours, and another priest, laboured assiduously to discover these heretics in several dioceses, not only many of the laity, but also some priests, being infected with it, and, when they discovered them, had them conveyed to Paris, and put in the bishop's prison. A Council of Bishops and Doctors was held in 1209, in which some of those unfortunate people retracted; but others obstinately refused, and were degraded, and handed over to the royal power, and were, by orders of the King, burned outside the gates of Paris; and the bones of Amalric were exhumed at the same time, and burned, and thrown on the dunghill. It was also ordered, that Aristotle's Metaphysics, which was the fountain of this heresy, should be burned likewise, and all persons were prohibited, under pain of excommunication, from reading or keeping the work in their possession. In this Council were, likewise, condemned the books of David of Nantz, who asserted that God was the *Materia Prima*. St. Thomas wrote against him in 1215 (23). The heresy of Amalric was condemned in express terms, in the Fourth General Council of Lateran, cap. ii. (24).

28. William de St. Amour, a doctor of Sorbonne, and canon of Beauvais, lived in this century also. He wrote a work, entitled, " De Periculis adversus Mendicantes Ordines," in opposition to the friars, who made a vow of poverty, in which he asserted that it was not a work of perfection to follow Christ in poverty and mendicancy, and that, in order to be perfect, it was necessary, after giving up all we had, either to live by manual labour, or to enter into a monastery, which would afford all the necessaries of life; that the Mendicant Friars, by begging, acted contrary to the Holy Scriptures, and that it was not lawful for them to teach the laity, to preach, to be enrolled as Masters in Colleges, or to hear the

(22) Fleury, *t.* 11, *l.* 67, *n.* 59; Nat. Alex. *c.* 16, *l.* 3, *a.* 2; Graveson, *t.* 4, *sec.* 13, *coll.* 3.   (23) St. Thomas, 1, *p.* 9, 3, *ar.* 8.   (24) Fleury, Nat. Alex. Graveson, loc. cit.

confessions of the laity. This work was condemned by Pope Alexander IV., in the year 1252, and publicly burned, and the following year the author was banished from all the dominions of France, and a few years after, died a miserable exile (25).

29. In the year 1274, the sect of the Flagellants sprung up, and first made its appearance in Perugia, and thence spread on, even to Rome itself. A torrent of vice had overspread the Italian Peninsula about that time, and a violent spirit of reaction commenced. All were seized on by a new sort of devotion, and old and young, rich and poor, nobles, and plebeians—not alone men, but even ladies—terrified with the dread of Divine judgments, went about the streets, in procession, nearly naked, or, at least, with bared shoulders, beating themselves with scourges, and imploring mercy. Even the darkness of the night, and the rigors of winter, could not subdue their enthusiasm. Numerous bodies of penitents —sometimes even as many as twelve thousand—marched in procession, preceded by priests, and crosses, and banners; and the towns, and villages, and plains, resounded with their cries for mercy. A great change for the better in the morals of the people was the first fruit of this wonderful movement—enemies were reconciled, thieves restored their ill-gotten wealth, and all were reconciled to God, by confession. They used to scourge themselves twice a day, it is said, for thirty-three days, in honour of the thirty-three years of our Lord's life, and sung, at the same time, some canticles in honour of his Sacred Passion. From Italy this practice spread into Germany, Poland, and other kingdoms; but, as neither the Pope nor the bishops approved of this public form of penance, it speedily degenerated into superstition. They said that no one could be saved unless by adopting this practice for a month; they used to hear the confessions of each other, and give absolution, though only lay people; and they had the madness to pretend that even the damned were served by their penance. Pope Clement VI. formally condemned this heresy, and wrote to the bishops of Germany, Poland, Switzerland, England, and France, on the subject, which proves how widely it was spread; he also wrote to all secular princes, calling on them to scatter these hypocrites, to disperse their conventicles, and, above all, to imprison their leaders (26).

30. Another sect—the offspring of an ill-judged piety also— sprung up in this century, that of the Fratricelli. This sect originated with Peter of Macerata and Peter of Fossombrone, two apostate Franciscan friars, who, playing on the simplicity of Pope Celestine V., got permission from him to lead an eremetical life, and observe the rule of St. Francis to the very letter. Boni-

---

(25) Fleury, *t.* 12, *l.* 84, *n.* 30; Nat. Alex. *t.* 16, *c.* 3, *ar.* 7; Berti, Brev. Histor. *sec.* 13, *c.* 3. (26) Nat. Alex. *t.* 16, *sec.* 13, *art.* 5; Fleury, *t.* 13, *l.* 84, *n.* 62.

face VIII., Celestine's successor, soon saw that this institute was a source of error, which was spreading every day more widely, and he, accordingly, in express terms, condemned it; but, notwithstanding this sentence, the Fratricelli every day increased in numbers, and openly preached their tenets. John XXII., therefore, found it necessary to publish a Bull against them in 1318, and, as Noel Alexander relates, condemned the following errors adopted by them :—First.—They taught that there were two churches, one carnal, abounding in delights, and stained with crime, governed by the Roman Pontiff and his prelates; the other spiritual, adorned with virtue, clothed in poverty, to which they alone, and those who held with them, belonged, and of which they, on account of their spiritual lives, were justly the head. Second.—That the venerable churches, priests, and other ministers, were so deprived both of the power of order and jurisdiction, that they could neither administer the sacraments, nor instruct the people, as all who did not join their apostacy were deprived of all spiritual power, for (as they imagined), as with them alone holiness of life was found, so with them alone authority resided. Third.—That in them alone was the Gospel of Christ fulfilled, which hitherto was either thrown aside or totally lost among men (27).

Article IV.
HERESIES OF THE FOURTEENTH CENTURY.

31. The Beghards and Beguines; their Errors condemned by Clement V. 32. Marsilius of Padua, and John Jandunus; their Writings condemned as heretical by John XXII. 33. John Wickliffe, and the Beginning of his Heresy. 34. Is assisted by John Ball; Death of the Archbishop of Canterbury. 35. The Council of Constance condemns forty-five Articles of Wickliffe. 36, 37. Miraculous Confirmation of the Real Presence of Jesus Christ in the Holy Eucharist. 38. Death of Wickliffe.

31. THE Beghards and Beguines sprung up in Germany in this century. Van Ranst (1) draws a distinction between the good Beghards, who, in Flanders, especially, professed the third rule of the Order of St. Francis, and the heretics; and also between the Beguines, ladies, who led a religious life, though not bound by vows, and the heretical Beguines, whose conduct was not remarkable for purity. The religious Beguines deduce their origin either from St. Begghe, Duchess of Brabant, and daughter of Pepin, Mayor of the Palace to the King of Austrasia, or from Lambert le Begue, a pious priest, who lived in 1170. The origin of the name adopted by the heretics is uncertain; but the followers of the Fratricelli were called by that name in Germany and the Low Countries, as were also the followers of Gerard Segarelli and Dulcinus, who both were burned alive for their errors. The doctrines professed by the Beghards was as absurd as it was impious. Man, said they, might arrive at such

(27) Nat. Alex. loc. cit.   (1) Van Ranst, Hist. Heres. p. 221.

a degree of perfection, even in this life, as to become totally impeccable, and even incapable of advancing any more in grace, and when he arrives at this state, he should no longer fast or pray, for sensuality is then so entirely subjected to reason and the spirit, that anything the body desires may be freely granted to it. Those who have arrived at that pitch of perfection are no longer subject to human obedience, or bound by the precepts of the Church. Man can, even in the present life, being thus perfect, obtain final beatitude, as well as he shall obtain it hereafter in the realms of the blessed, for every intellectual nature is in itself blessed, and the soul does not require the light of glory to see God. It is only imperfect men who practise acts of virtue, for the perfect soul throws off virtue altogether. " Mulieris osculum (cum ad hoc natura non inclinet) est mortale peccatum, actus autem carnalis (cum ad hoc natura inclinet) peccatum non est maxime cum tentatur exercens." When the body of Christ is elevated, a perfect man should not show any reverence, for it would be an imperfection to descend from the summit of his contemplation, to think on the Eucharist or on the humanity of Christ. It is remarkable that many of their opinions were adopted by the Quietists in a subsequent century. Clement V. condemned these heretics in a General Council, held in Vienne, in Dauphiny, in 1311.

32. Marsilius Menandrinus, of Padua, and John Jandunus, of Perugia, also lived in this century. Marsilius published a book, called " Defensorum Pacis," and Jandunus contributed some additions to it. The errors scattered through the work were condemned by Pope John XXII., as heretical, and refuted by several theologians, especially by Noel Alexander, who gives the following account of them (2). When Christ paid tribute to Cæsar, he did it as matter of obligation and not of piety, and when he ascended into heaven he appointed no visible head in the Church, left no Vicar, nor had St. Peter more authority than the rest of the Apostles. It is the Emperor's right to appoint, remove, and punish prelates, and when the Papal See is vacant he has the right of governing the Church. All priests, not even excepting bishops and the Pope, have, by the institution of Christ, equal authority and jurisdiction, unless the Emperor wishes that one should have more power than another. The whole united Church has not the power to punish any man, and no bishop or meeting of bishops can inflict a sentence of excommunication or interdict, unless by authority of the Prince. Bishops, collectively or individually, can no more excommunicate the Pope than he can them. The dispensation for marriages, prohibited by human law alone, and not by Divine law, belongs, of right, to the Prince. To the Prince, by right, it belongs to give a definitive judgment, in regard to persons about to be

(2) Nat. Alex. *t.* 16, *c.* 3, *ar.* 13, *p.* 193.

ordained, and bishops should not ordain any one without his authority. We will now speak of Wickliffe, the leader of all the so-called Reformers.

33. John Wickliffe began to preach his heresy in 1374, some say because he was disappointed in the bishopric of Winchester.* He was learned in scholastic theology, which he taught at Oxford, and was a favourite preacher, always followed by the people. He led an austere life, was meanly clothed, and even went barefooted. Edward III. died, and was succeeded by his grandson, Richard, the son of Edward, the Black Prince, who was then only eleven years of age; and his uncle, the Duke of Lancaster, was a man of very lax sentiments in regard to religion, and extended his protection to Wickliffe, who openly preached his heresy (3). Gregory IX., who then governed the Church, complained to the Archbishop of Canterbury and the Bishop of London, that they were not active enough in putting a stop to this plague, and he wrote on the same subject to the King and the University of Oxford (4). A Synod of Bishops and Doctors was accordingly summoned, and Wickliffe was cited to appear and account for himself; he obeyed the summons, and excused himself by explaining away, as well as he could, the obnoxious sense of his doctrine, and putting another meaning on it. He was then only admonished to be more prudent for the future—was absolved, and commanded to be silent from thenceforward (5).

34. Wickliffe was assisted by a wicked priest of the name of John Ball, who escaped from the prison where his bishop had confined him for his crimes, and joined the Reformers, who gladly received him. The subject of his discourses to the people was, that all ranks should be levelled, and the nobility and magistracy done away with, and he was joined by over an hundred thousand levellers. They laid their demands before the sovereign, but could not obtain what they desired; they considered that the Archbishop of Canterbury, Simon Sudbury, a good man in the main, but too weak a disposition to cope with the troubles of the times, influenced the sovereign's mind against them; they resolved on his death, therefore, and stormed the tower, where he had taken refuge, and found him praying, and recommending his soul to God. He addressed them mildly, and tried to calm their rage, but his executioner, John Sterling, stepped forward, and told him to prepare for death. The good bishop then confessed that

(3) Nat. Alex. *s.* 6, *n.* 1; Gotti, loc. cit. *n.* 2.   (4) Gotti, ib. *n.* 3 ; Nat. Alex. 6, *n.* 1 ; Grav. loc. cit.   (5) Nat. Alex. *s.* 6, *n.* 1 ; Gotti, ibid. *n.* 5, & Grav. loc. cit.

---

* I believe the holy author was misled in this fact; it is generally supposed that the primary cause of his rancour against the monastic orders and the Court of Rome were his expulsion from the wardenship of Canterbury Hall, into which he had illegally intruded himself.—*See* LINGARD, vol. iv. c. 2.

he deserved that punishment for not being more vigorous in the discharge of his duties, perhaps, and stretched forth his neck to receive the fatal stroke; but whether it was that the sword was blunt, or the executioner awkward, his head was not cut off till he received eight blows (6). Berninus, quoting Walsingham (7), says, that the executioner was immediately possessed by the devil, and that he ran through the streets with the sword hanging round his neck, boasting that he had killed the archbishop, and entered the city of London to receive his reward; this was, however, different from what he expected, for he was condemned to death, and Ball was hanged and quartered, at the same time, together with his accomplices.

35. William of Courtenay being appointed archbishop, in place of Sudbury, held a Synod in London, and condemned twenty-four propositions of Wickliffe—ten of them, especially—as heretical. These were afterwards condemned by the University of Paris, and by John XXIII., in a Council held at Rome, and, finally, in the eighth Session of the Council of Constance, in 1415, in which forty-five articles of Wickliffe were condemned—the greater part as heretical, the rest as erroneous, rash, &c.—and among these the twenty-four condemned previously were included. The following are the errors condemned by the Council, as Noel Alexander quotes them (8): The material substance of bread and wine remains in the Sacrament of the Altar, and the *accidence* of the bread is not without the substance in the Eucharist. Christ is not identically and really there in his proper presence. If a bishop or priest be in mortal sin he cannot consecrate, nor ordain, nor baptize. There is nothing in Scripture to prove that Christ instituted the Mass. God ought to obey the devil. If one be truly contrite, all external confession is superfluous and useless. If the Pope is foreknown and wicked, and, consequently, a member of the devil, he has no power over the faithful. After Urban VI. no other Pope should be elected, but, like the Greeks, we should live under our own laws. It is opposed to the Holy Scriptures that ecclesiastics should have possessions. No prelate should excommunicate any one, unless he knows him to be already excommunicated by God, and he who excommunicates otherwise is, by the act, a heretic, or excommunicated himself. A prelate excommunicating a clergyman who appeals to the King, or to the Supreme Council of the realm, is, by the fact, a traitor to the King and the realm. Those who cease to preach, or to listen to the Word of God, on account of the excommunication of man, are excommunicated, and in the judgment of God are traitors to Christ. Every deacon and priest has the power of preaching the Word of God, without any authority from the Holy See or a Catholic Bishop. No one is a civil lord—no

(6) Gotti, loc. cit. *n.* 5; Van Ranst, dicto, *n.* 241; Bernin. *t.* 3, *c.* 9.   (7) Bernin. loc. cit. *c.* 9, con. Richard, Ann. 1381, ex Walsingh.   (8) Nat. Alex. *t.* 16, *sec.* 14, *c.* 3, *art.* 22, *s.* 6; Gotti, ibid.; Van Ranst.

one a prelate—no one a bishop, while he is in mortal sin. Temporal lords can, whenever they please, take temporal goods from the Church. *Possessionatis habitualiter delinquentibus id est ex habitu non solum actu delinquentibus.* The people can, whenever they please, punish their delinquent lords. Tithes are merely eleemosynary offerings, and the parishioners have the right, whenever they please, of keeping them from their prelates on account of their sins. Special prayers applied by prelates or religious to any one individual, are of no more value to him than general ones *cæteris paribus.* Any one giving charity to friars is excommunicated by the fact. Any one entering a religious order, either mendicant or endowed, becomes weaker, and less able to observe the commandments of God. The Saints who founded religious orders sinned by doing so. Religious living in orders do not belong to the Christian religion. Friars are obliged to live by the labour of their hands, and not by receiving the oblations of the faithful. Those who oblige themselves to pray for others, who provide them with the things of this life, are guilty of simony. The prayer of the *foreknown* availeth nothing. All things happen through absolute necessity. The confirmation of youth, the ordination of priests, and the consecration of places, are reserved to the Pope and bishops, on account of the temporal gain and honour they bring. Universities and the studies, colleges, degrees and masterships in them, are only vain things introduced from paganism, and are of no more utility to the Church than the devil himself. The excommunication of the Pope, or of any other prelate, is not to be feared, because it is the censure of the devil. Those who found convents sin, and those who enter them are servants of the devil. It is against the law of Christ to endow a clergyman. Pope Sylvester and the Emperor Constantine erred by endowing the Church. All members of the mendicant orders are heretics, and those who give them alms are excommunicated. Those who become members of any religious order are by the fact incapable of observing the Divine commandments, and, consequently, can never enter the kingdom of heaven till they apostatize from their institute. The Pope, and all his clergy having possessions, are heretics, by holding these possessions; and temporal lords, and the rest of the laity who consent to their holding them, are heretics also. The Roman Church is the synagogue of Satan, and the Pope is not the proximate and immediate Vicar of Christ. The Decretal Epistles (canon law) are apocryphal, and seduce from the faith of Christ, and the clergymen are fools who study them. The Emperor and secular lords have been seduced by the devil to endow the Church with temporalities. It is the devil who introduced the election of the Pope by the cardinals. It is not necessary for salvation to believe that the Roman Church is supreme among all other Churches. It is folly to believe in the indulgences of the Pope and bishops.

The oaths which are taken to corroborate contracts and civil affairs are unlawful. Augustin, Benedict, and Bernard are damned, unless they repented of having possessions, and of instituting and entering into religious orders; and so from the Pope to the lowest religious they are all heretics. All religious orders altogether are invented by the devil.

36. Enumerating these errors, I cannot help remarking that Wickliffe, the Patriarch of all the modern heretics, attacks especially the Real Presence of Jesus Christ in the Eucharist, as we see in his first three propositions, and in this he was followed by all the modern heresiarchs; but God at the same time confirmed the faith of his people by extraordinary miracles; and I will just mention three of them (among a great number), on the authority of authors of the first character. Nicholas Serrarius (9) relates, that when the Wickliffites first began to attack this dogma of the Faith in 1408, the following miracle took place: a priest, called Henry Otho, was one day saying Mass in Durn, in the diocese of Wurtzburg, and through his want of caution upset the chalice, and the Sacred Blood was spilled all over the corporal. It appeared at once of the real colour of blood, and in the middle of the corporal was an image of the Crucifix, surrounded with several other images of the head of the Redeemer crowned with thorns. The priest was terrified, and although some other persons had already noticed the accident, he took up the corporal and laid it under the altar-stone, that it might decay in some time and nothing more would be known about it. God, however, did not wish that such a miracle should be concealed. The priest was at the point of death, and remorse of conscience troubled him even more than the agony he was suffering; he could bear it no longer, but confessed all, told where the corporal was concealed, and then died immediately. All was found to be as he stated, and God wrought other miracles to confirm its truth. The magistrates investigated the whole affair with the greatest caution and deliberation, and sent an authentic account of it to the Pope, and he published a brief, dated the 31st of March, 1445, inviting all the devout faithful to ornament and enlarge the church honoured by so stupendous a miracle.

37. Thomas Treter (10) relates the next miracle. Some Jews bribed an unfortunate Christian servant woman to procure a consecrated Host for them, and when they got it they brought it into a cavern, and cut it in little bits on a table with their knives, in contempt of the Christian Faith. The fragments immediately began to bleed, but instead of being converted by the miracle, they buried them in a field near the city of Posen, and went home. A Christian child soon after, who was taking care of some oxen, came into the field, and saw the consecrated particles elevated in the air, and

(9) Serar. Moguntinar. Rerum, *l.* 5.   (10) Treter. de Mirac. Eucharis.

shining as if made of fire, and the oxen all on their knees, as if in adoration. He ran off at once, and told his father, and when he found the fact to be as the child stated, he gave notice to the magistrates and the people. Crowds immediately followed him to the place, and all saw the particles of the Sacred Host shining in the air, and the oxen kneeling in adoration. The bishop and clergy came at once in procession, and collecting the holy particles into the pixis, they brought them to the church. A little chapel was built on the spot soon after, which Wenceslaus, King of Poland, converted into a sumptuous church, where Stephen Damaleniski, Archbishop of Gnesen, attests that he saw the sacred fragments stained with blood.

Tilman Bredembach (11) relates that there lived in England, in 1384, a nobleman of the name of Oswald Mulfer; he went to his village church one Easter, to receive his Paschal Communion, and insisted on being communicated with a large Host. The priest, fearful of his power, if he denied him, placed the large Host on his tongue, but in the very act the ground opened under his feet, as if to swallow him, and he had already sunk down to his knees, when he seized the altar, but that yielded like wax to his hand. He now, seeing the vengeance of God overtaking him, repented of his pride, and prayed for mercy, and as he could not swallow the Host —for God would not permit him—the priest removed it, and replaced it in the Tabernacle; but it was all of the colour of blood. Tilman went on purpose to visit the place where this miracle happened: he saw, he says, the Host tinged with blood, the altar with the marks of Oswald's hands, and the ground into which he was sinking still hollow, and covered with iron bars. Oswald himself, he says, now perfectly cured of his pride, fell sick soon after, and died with sentiments of true penance.

38. We now come back to Wickliffe, and see his unhappy end. On the feast of St. Thomas of Canterbury, in 1385, he prepared to preach a sermon, not in honour of, but reprobating the saint; but God would no longer permit him to ravage his Church, for a few days after, on St. Sylvester's day, he was struck down by a dreadful palsy, which convulsed him all over, and his mouth, with which he had preached so many blasphemies, was most frightfully distorted, so that he could not speak even a word, and as Walsingham (12) informs us, he died in despair. King Richard prohibited all his works, and ordered them to be burned. He wrote a great deal, but his principal work was the Trialogue between Alithia, Pseudes, and Phronesis—Folly, Falsehood, and Wisdom. Several authors wrote in refutation of this work, but its own contradictions are a sufficient refutation, for the general characteristic of heretical writers is to contradict themselves (13). The University

---

(11) Bredembach in Collat. *l.* 1, *c.* 35.   (12) Walsingham, ap. Bernin. *t.* 3, *c.* 9; Van Ranst, *p.* 241; Varillas, *t.* 1, *l.* 1, & Gotti, loc. cit.   (13) Graveson, *t.* 4, *sec.* 15, *coll.* 31; Bernin. *t.* 3, *l.* 9, *p.* 609, *c.* 8.

of Oxford condemned two hundred and sixty propositions extracted from Wickliffe's works; but the Council of Constance included all his errors in the one hundred and forty-five articles of his it condemned.

Article V.

HERESIES OF THE FIFTEENTH CENTURY.

THE HERESY OF JOHN HUSS, AND JEROME OF PRAGUE.

39. John Huss's Character, and the Commencement of his Heresy. 40. His Errors. 41. He is condemned in a Synod. 42. Council of Constance—he is obliged to appear at it. 43. He comes to Constance, and endeavours to escape. 44, 45. He presents himself before the Council, and continues obstinate. 46. He is condemned to death, and burned. 47. Jerome of Prague is also burned alive for his Obstinacy. 48. Wars of the Hussites—they are conquered and converted.

39. In the reign of Wenceslaus, King of Bohemia, and son of the Emperor Charles IV., about the beginning of the fifteenth century, the pestilence of the heresy of Wickliffe first made its appearance in Bohemia. The University of Prague was then in a most flourishing condition; but the professors who had the management of it kept up a very lax system of discipline. They were of four nations, each of which enjoyed equal privileges in that seat of learning—Bohemians, Saxons, Bavarians, and Poles; but mutual jealousies blinded them to the danger the Catholic faith was exposed to, for want of due vigilance. Such was the state of things when John Huss, one of the Bohemian professors, obtained a privilege from the King, that in all deliberations of the University the vote of the Bohemian nation alone should count as much as the three others together. The German professors were so much offended at this ordinance, that they left Prague in a body, and settled in Leipsic, where they contributed to establish that famous University, and thus the government of the whole University of Prague, we may say, fell into the hands of John Huss (1). This remarkable man was born in a village of Bohemia, called Huss, and from which he took his name, and his parents were so poor, that at first the only means of learning he had was by accompanying a gentleman's son to school as attendant; but being a man of powerful mind, he by degrees worked himself on, until he became the chief professor of the University of Prague, which he infected, unfortunately, with heresy. Having, as we have seen, ousted the German professors, and become almost supreme in his college, it unfortunately happened that one of Wickliffe's disciples, Peter Payne, who had to fly from England, arrived in Prague, and brought along with him the works of his master. These works fell

(1) Coclæus, Hist. Hussit. Æneas Silv. Hist. Bohem. c. 35; Bernin. t. 4, sec. 15, c. 2, p. 9; Graves. t. 4, coll. 8, p. 75; Gotti, Ver. &c. c. 105.

into the hands of Huss, and though filled with blasphemy, pleased him by the bold novelty of their doctrines, and he imagined that they were well calculated to make an impression on the ardent minds of the youth of the University. He could not at once begin to teach them, for he was one of the doctors who, a little while before, had subscribed the condemnation of Wickliffe's errors (2), so he contented himself, for the present, with merely making them subjects of discussion with his pupils; but little by little he became more bold, and not alone among the students of the University, but even among the people in the churches, he disseminated the pestilence. At length, he threw off the mask altogether, and preaching one day in the Church of SS. Matthias and Matthew, in Prague, he publicly lauded the works of Wickliffe, and said, if he were dying, all he would desire is to be assured of the same glory that Wickliffe was then enjoying in heaven.

40. He next translated some of Wickliffe's works into Bohemian, especially the Trialogue, the worst of them all. He was joined at once by several priests of relaxed morals, and also by several doctors, discontented with the unjust distribution of church patronage, which was too often conferred on persons whose only qualification was nobility of birth, while humble virtue and learning was neglected. Among the doctors who joined him was Jerome of Prague, who, in the year 1408, had, like Huss, condemned the errors of Wickliffe, but now turned round, and even accused the Council of Constance of injustice for condemning them. Sbinko, Archbishop of Prague, summoned a Synod, which was attended by the most famous doctors, and condemned the propositions broached by Huss, and he was so enraged at this, that he endeavoured to stir up the people to oppose it; the archbishop, accordingly, excommunicated him, and sent a copy of the condemnation of his doctrine to Pope Alexander V., but Huss appealed to the Pope, who was badly informed, he said, of the matter, and in the meantime, the archbishop died, and thus Bohemia became a prey to heresy. Huss was now joined by Jacobellus of Misnia, and Peter of Dresden, who went about preaching to the people against the error the Church was guilty of, as they said, in refusing the people communion under both kinds, and proclaimed that all who received under one kind were damned. John Huss and his followers took up this new doctrine, and so deeply was the error implanted in the minds of the Bohemian Hussites, that even all the power of the imperial arms could scarcely eradicate it.

41. Noel Alexander enumerates the errors of Huss under thirty heads (3). We will only take a succinct view of the most important ones. The Church, he said, was composed of the predestined

---

(2) Nat. Alex. *sec.* 14, *c.* 3, *a.* 22, *sec.* 6; Æneas Silv. Hist Bohem. *c.* 35.   (3) Nat. Alex. *sec.* 15, *c.* 2, *a.* 1, *sec.* 2.

alone (*Art.* 1, 3, 5, 6); and the two natures, the Divinity and the humanity, are one Christ (*Art.* 4). Peter neither was nor is the head of the Catholic Church (*Art.* 7, 10, 11); and civil and ecclesiastical lords, as prelates and bishops, are no longer so while in mortal sin (*Art.* 30); and he says the same of the Pope (*Art.* 20, 22, 24, 26). The Papal dignity is derived from the power of the Emperor (*Art.* 9); and ecclesiastical obedience is an invention of the priests (*Art.* 15). Everything the wicked man does is wicked, and everything the virtuous man does is virtuous (*Art.* 16). Good priests ought to preach, though they be excommunicated (*Art.* 17, 18); and in *Art.* 19, he reprobates ecclesiastical censures. It was an act of iniquity to condemn the forty-five articles of Wickliffe (*Art.* 25). There is no necessity of a head to rule the Church, for the apostles and other priests governed it very well before the office of Pope was introduced (*Art.* 27, 28, 29). These are, in substance, the errors of John Huss. Van Ranst (*p.* 275) remarks, that it appears from his own works, that he always held the belief of the Real Presence, and when, in the fifteenth Session of the Council, he was accused of teaching that, after the consecration, the substance of bread remained in the Eucharist, he denied that he ever either taught or believed so. He also admitted sacramental confession, with its three parts, as we do—Extreme Unction, and all the other sacraments—prayers for the dead—the invocation and intercession of saints. How unjustly, then, says the same author, do the Lutherans and Calvinists condemn in the Church of Rome these dogmas held by Huss himself, whom they venerate as a witness of the truth, and through whom they boast that they have derived the original succession of their churches!

42. We now come to speak of the sad end the obstinacy of Huss brought him to. The Pope condemned Wickliffe and his errors, in a Synod held in Rome, in 1413. When this came to the knowledge of Huss, he published several invectives against the Fathers composing the Synod, so the Pope found himself obliged to suspend him from all ecclesiastical functions, the more especially as he had been cited to Rome, but refused to come. In the year 1414, a General Council was held in the city of Constance, at which twenty-nine Cardinals, four Patriarchs, and two hundred and seven prelates assisted, and the Emperor Sigismund attended there in person also (4). John Huss was summoned by the Emperor to present himself before the Council and defend his doctrine, but he refused to leave Prague until he was furnished by him with a safe conduct. The Emperor gave him the protection he demanded, and he, accordingly, came to Constance, puffed up with the idea, that he would, by his reasoning, convince the Fathers of the Council that he was right. He was quite satisfied, also, that in case even the Council

(4) Labbe, *t.* 12, conc.

should condemn him, he was quite safe, on account of the Imperial safe conduct; but it is extraordinary that he never adverted to the clause inserted in it, granting him security as far as he was charged with crimes, but not in regard to errors against the Church (5); for it was stated that he would be exempt from all penalty in regard to his faith, if he would obey the decisions of the Council, after being heard in his defence, but not if he still obstinately remained attached to his errors. But, as we shall see, he refused to obey these conditions. The Lutherans, therefore, are unjust in charging us with upholding that maxim, that faith is not to be kept with heretics, and alleging that as their excuse for not coming to the Council of Trent. Our Church, on the contrary, teaches that faith must be observed with even infidels or Jews, and the Council of Basil faithfully observed the guarantee given to the Hussites, though they remained obstinately attached to their errors.

43. When Huss arrived in Constance, before he presented himself to the Council he fixed his safe conduct to the door of the Church; and while he remained at his lodging, never ceased to praise Wickliffe, and disseminate his doctrines; and, although he was excommunicated by his bishop in Prague, he used to say Mass in a chapel; but when the archbishop heard of this, he prohibited him from celebrating, and his subjects from hearing his Mass (6). This frightened him, and when he saw the charges that would be made against him, and received an order from the Council not to quit the city, he trembled for his safety, and attempted to escape; he, accordingly, disguised himself as a peasant, and concealed himself in a cart load of hay, but was discovered by a spy, who was privately placed to watch him, and notice being given to the magistrates of the city, he was taken. This took place on the third Sunday of Lent. He was asked, why he disguised himself in this way, and hid himself in the hay? He said it was because he was cold. He was put on a horse, and taken to prison, and he then appealed to the safe conduct given him by the Emperor; but his attention was directed to the clause giving him security only as far as he was charged with certain crimes, but not for any erroneous doctrines concerning the Faith, and he was told, that it was decided that he should prove his cause not to be heretical, and if not able to do that, either retract, or suffer death (7). He was now truly terrified; but seeing several Bohemians around him, who accompanied him to the Council, he threw himself from the horse among them, and thus thought to escape, but was immediately seized again, and confined in the Dominican Convent, but attempting to escape from that, he was transferred to a more secure prison (8).

(5) Varillas His. &c., *t.* 1, *l.* 11, *p.* 25; Gotti, Ver. Rel. 105, *s.* 3, *n.* 1. (6) Coclæus, His. Huss. *t.* 2; Varillas, loc. cit.; Gotti, cit. (7) Gotti, loc. cit. sec. 3, *n.* 3. (8) Gotti, ibid.; Van Ranst, *p.* 279; Varillas, loc. cit.; Bernin. *t.* 4; Rainaldus, Ann. 1415, *n.* 32.

45. He was summoned from his prison to appear before the Council, and defend himself, and as the Council had already condemned the forty-five articles of Wickliffe, he trembled for his own fate. Witnesses were formally examined to prove the errors he had both preached and written, and a form of abjuration was drawn up by the Council for him to sign, for it was decided by the Fathers, that he should not alone retract verbally, but also subscribe the abjuration of his heresy in the Bohemian language. This he refused to do; but he presented a paper himself, in which he declared that he could not conscientiously retract what he was asked to do, but the Council refused to receive it. The Cardinal of Cambray endeavoured to induce him to sign a general retractation, as everything charged against him had been proved; and he promised him, in that case, the Council would treat him most indulgently. Huss then made an humble answer: he came, he said, to be taught by the Council, and that he was willing to obey its decrees. A pen was handed to him, accordingly, to sign his retractation, in Bohemian, as was commanded in the beginning; but he said that the fear of signing a lie prevented him. The Emperor himself even tried to bend his obstinacy; but all in vain. The Council, accordingly, appointed the 6th of July to give the final decision; but before they came to extremities, the Fathers deputed four bishops and four Bohemian gentlemen to strive and bring him round, but they never could get a direct retractation from him. The appointed day at last arrived. He was brought to the Church, in presence of the Council, and asked, if he would anathematize the errors of Wickliffe; he made a long speech, the upshot of which was that his conscience would not allow him to do so.

46. Sentence was now pronounced on him; he was declared obstinately guilty of heresy, and the Council degraded him from the priesthood, and handed him over to the secular power. He made no remark while the sentence was read, intending, after the reading was finished, to say what he intended, but he only commenced to speak, when he was ordered to be silent. He was now clothed in the sacerdotal vestments, which were immediately after stripped off him, and a paper cap was put on his head, inscribed: "Behold the Heresiarch!" Louis, Duke of Bavaria, then took him, and handed him over to the ministers of justice, who cut off his hair in the very place where the pile was prepared to burn him. He was now tied to the stake, but before fire was put to the pile, the Duke of Bavaria again besought him to retract, but he answered, that the Scriptures tell us we should obey God, and not man. The Duke then turned his back on him, and the executioner applied the torch; when the pile began to light, the hypocrite was heard to exclaim: "Jesus Christ, Son of the living God, have mercy on me;" words inspired by the vainglorious desire of being considered to have died a martyr's death, but we should not

forget that the devil has martyrs, and infuses into them a false constancy, and as St. Augustin says: "It is not the punishment, but the cause, that makes a martyr;" that is, the confession of the true Faith. The flames burned so fiercely, that it is thought he was immediately suffocated, for he gave no other signs of life. His ashes were cast into the lake, and thus the scene closed on John Huss (9).

47. We have now to speak of Jerome of Prague, who having joined Huss in his errors, was his companion in a disgraceful death and perdition. He was a layman, and joined Huss in all his endeavours to disseminate his errors, led astray himself, first by Wickliffe's works, and next by the preaching of his master. He came to Constance to try and be of some assistance to Huss, but was taken and obliged to appear before the Council, together with his patron, but he was not finally tried for a year after the death of Huss. A lengthened process was instituted against him, and it was proved, as Raynaldus tells us (10), that he preached the same errors as Wickliffe and Huss, that he was guilty of several excesses, and had caused several seditious movements in divers kingdoms and cities. When first brought before the Council in 1414, he confessed that he was wrong, and said that he was satisfied to abjure his heresy, even according to the formula required by the Council. He, therefore, got permission to speak with whom he pleased, and he then was so imprudent as to tell his friends that his retractation was extorted from him, not by conscience, but because he was afraid of being condemned to be burned alive, but that now he should defend his doctrines to the death. When he was discovered, he was obliged to appear again before the Council, in 1415, and when the Patriarch of Constantinople called on him to clear himself from the new charges laid against him, he spoke out plainly, and said that his former abjuration was extorted by the dread of being burned alive; that he now held as true all the articles of Wickliffe, and that he was anxious to expiate at the stake the fault of his former retractation. The Fathers of the Council still charitably gave him time to repent, but, at last, in the twenty-fifth Session, after the Bishop of Lodi endeavoured by every means in his power to induce him to retract, he was declared an obstinate heretic, and handed over to the civil magistrate, who had him led to the pile. Even then, several persons endeavoured to get him to retract, but he said that his conscience would not allow him; he took off his clothes without any assistance, was tied to the stake, and the pile was fired. His agony was much longer than that of John Huss, but, like him, he died without any signs of repentance (11).

48. The unhappy end of John Huss and Jerome of Prague did not put a stop to the progress of their doctrines; on the contrary,

(9) Varill. loc. cit. *p.* 48 ; Gotti, loc. cit. *s.* 3, *n.* 8 ; Van Ranst, 279. (13) Rainal' Ann. 1415, *n.* 13 & seq. (11) Varil. *p.* 51, *l.* 1; Gotti, *c.* 105 ; Bern. *t.* 4, *c.* 4.

as Varillas writes (12), the Hussites, irritated at the punishment of their leader, united together in Bohemia, ruined the churches, seized on the properties of the monasteries, and attempted the life of their king, Wenceslaus; and though they desisted at the time, they were sorry they did not accomplish it after, and they would have done so even then had Wenceslaus not died in the meantime. They then elected Zisca as Commander-in-Chief, and declared war against the Emperor Sigismund, who succeeded his brother Wenceslaus on the throne of Bohemia, and, having gained four victories, they forced him to quit his kingdom. Although Zisca lost both his eyes in battle, he still commanded his countrymen, but was attacked by the plague and died, having previously ordered that his skin should be tanned and converted into the covering of a drum, that even after his death he might terrify his enemies. After Zisca's death the sect was divided into Orphans, Orebites, and Thaborites, who, though disagreeing among themselves, all united against the Catholics. When those heretics got a Catholic priest into their power, they used to burn him alive, or cut him in two halves. When the Council of Basil was assembled, they sent delegates there to make peace with the Church, having previously obtained a safe conduct, but all to no purpose, as on their return into Bohemia the war raged with greater fury, and, having collected a powerful army, they laid siege to the capital, but were encountered by Mainard, a noble Bohemian, and totally routed. Sigismund then again got possession of his kingdom, and made peace with the Hussites, who abjured their heresy, promised obedience to the Pope, and were absolved by him from all censures, on the 5th of July, 1436 (13).

CHAPTER XI.

THE HERESIES OF THE SIXTEENTH CENTURY.

ARTICLE I.

OF THE HERESIES OF LUTHER.

SEC. I.—THE BEGINNING AND PROGRESS OF THE LUTHERAN HERESY.

1. Erasmus of Rotterdam, called by some the Precursor of Luther; his Literature. 2. His Doctrine was not sound, nor could it be called heretical. 3. Principles of Luther; his Familiarity with the Devil, who persuades him to abolish Private Masses. 4. He joins the Order of the Hermits of St. Augustin. 5. Doctrines and Vices of Luther. 6. Publication of Indulgences, and his Theses on that Subject. 7. He is called to Rome, and clears himself; the Pope sends Cardinal Cajetan as his Legate to Germany. 8. Meeting between the Legate and Luther. 9. Luther perseveres and appeals to the Pope. 10, 11. Conference of Ecchius with the Heretics. 12. Bull of Leo X., condemning forty-one Errors of Luther, who burns the Bull and the Decretals.

1. WE have now arrived at the sixteenth century, in which, as in a sink, all the former heresies meet. The great heresiarch of

(12) Varil. Dis. *t.* 1, *t.* 2; Gotti, *c.* 105; Van Ranst, *p.* 281.   (13) Van Ranst, *p.* 382; Bernini, loc. cit.

this age was Luther; but many writers assert that Erasmus was his predecessor, and there was a common saying in Germany that Erasmus (1) laid the egg, and Luther hatched it (2). Erasmus was born in Holland; his birth was illegitimate, and he was baptized by the name of Gerard, which he afterwards changed to the Greek name Erasmus—in Latin, Desiderius (3). At an early age he was received among the Regular Canons of St. Augustin, and made his religious profession; but, weary of a religious life, and regretting having made his vows, he left the cloister and lived in the world, having, it is supposed, obtained a Papal dispensation. He would certainly have conferred a benefit on the age he lived in, had he confined himself to literature alone; but he was not satisfied without writing on theological matters, interpreting the Scriptures, and finding fault with the Fathers; hence, as Noel Alexander says of him, the more works he wrote the more errors he published. He travelled to many Universities, and was always honourably received, on account of his learning; but a great many doubted of his faith, on account of the obscure way he wrote concerning the dogmas of religion; hence, some of the Innovators, friends of Erasmus, often availed themselves of his authority, though he frequently endeavoured to clear himself from the imputation of favouring them, especially in a letter he wrote to Cardinal Campeggio (4).

2. A great contest at that time was going on in Germany, between the Rhetoricians and Theologians. The Rhetoricians upbraided the Theologians with their ignorance, and the barbarism of the terms they used. The Theologians, on the other hand, abused the Rhetoricians for the impropriety and profaneness of the language they used in the explanation of the Divine Mysteries. Erasmus, who took the lead among the Rhetoricians, began by deriding, first, the style, and, next, the arguments of the Theologians; he called their theology Judaism, and said that the proper understanding of ecclesiastical science depended altogether on erudition and the knowledge of languages. Many writers openly charge Erasmus with heresy: he explained everything just as it pleased himself, says Victorinus (5), and vitiated everything he explained. Albert Pico, Prince of Carpi, a man of great learning (6), and a strenuous opponent of the errors of Erasmus, assures us that he called the Invocation of the Blessed Virgin and the saints idolatry; condemned monasteries and ridiculed the Religious, calling them actors and cheats, and condemned their vows and rules; was opposed to the celibacy of the clergy, and turned into mockery Papal indulgences, relics of saints, feasts and fasts, and auricular confession; asserts that by Faith alone man is justified (7), and even

---

(1) Rainald. Ann. 1516, *n.* 91; Bernin. *t.* 4. *sec.* 26, *c.* 2, *p.* 255. (2) Gotti, Ver. Rel. *c.* 108, *sec.* 2, *n.* 6. (3) Nat. Alex. *t.* 19, *sec.* 15, *c.* 5, *art.* 1, *n.* 12.
(4) Nat. Alex. loc. cit. (5) Victor. in Scholiis ad Epist. Hier. Ep. 30.
(6) Rainald. & Bernin. loc. cit. (7) Alberto Pico, *l.* 20.

throws a doubt on the authority of the Scripture and Councils (8). In the preface to one of his works he says (9), it is rash to call the Holy Ghost God. " Audemus Spiritum Sanctum appellare Deum, quod veteres ausi non sunt." Noel Alexander informs us (10), that in 1527 the Faculty of Paris condemned several propositions taken from his works, and that at the Council of Trent the Cardinals appointed by Paul III. to report on the abuses which needed reformation, called on him to prohibit in the schools the reading of the Colloquies of Erasmus, in which are many things that lead the ignorant to impiety. He was, however, esteemed by several Popes, who invited him to Rome, to write against Luther, and it was even reported that Paul III. intended him for the Cardinalship. We may conclude with Bernini, that he died with the character of an unsound Catholic, but not a heretic, as he submitted his writings to the judgment of the Church, and Varillas (11) says he always remained firm in the Faith, notwithstanding all the endeavours of Luther and Zuinglius to draw him to their side. He died in Basle in 1536, at the age of 70 (12).

3. While Germany was thus agitated with this dispute, the famous brief of Leo X. arrived there in 1613; and here we must introduce Luther. Martin Luther (13) was born in Eisleben, in Saxony, in 1483. His parents were poor, and when he afterwards acquired such a sad notoriety, some were not satisfied without tracing his birth to the agency of the devil (14), a report to which his own extraordinary assertions gave some colour at the time, since he said in one of his sermons to the people, that he had eaten a peck of salt (15) with the devil, and in his work " De Missa Privata," or low Mass, he says he disputed with the devil on this subject, and was convinced by him that private Masses should be abolished (16). " Luther," said the devil, " it is now fifteen years that you are saying private Masses;—what would the consequence be, if on the altar you were adoring bread and wine? would you not be guilty of idolatry?" " I am a priest," said Luther, "ordained by my bishop, and I have done everything through obedience." " But," added the devil, " Turks and Gentiles also sacrifice through obedience, and what say you if your ordination be false?" Such are the powerful reasons which convinced Luther. Frederick Staphil (17) relates a curious anecdote concerning this matter. Luther at one time, he says, endeavoured to exorcise a girl in Wittemberg, possessed by an evil spirit, but was so terrified that he tried to escape, both by the door and window, which to his great consternation were both made fast;—finally one of his companions broke open the door with a hatchet, and they escaped (18).

(8) Alberto, *l.* 11, 12. (9) Erasm. advers. Hil. *t.* 12; Bernin. loc. cit. (10) Nat. Alex. cit. *art.* 10, *n.* 12. (11) Varill. *t.* 1, *l.* 7, *p.* 322. (12) Nat. Alex. loc. cit. (13) Gotti, Ver. Rel. *t.* 2, *c.* 108, *sec.* 2; Baron. Ann. 1517, *n.* 56; Varillas Istor. &c. *t.* 1, *l.* 3, *p.* 129; Hermant, Histor. Concili, *t.* 2, *c.* 227. (14) Gotti, cit. *sec.* 2, *n.* 3. (15) Nat. Alex. loc. cit.; Gotti, loc. cit. *sec.* 2, *n.* 2. (16) Gotti, *sec.* 5, *n.* 2. (17) Staphil. Resp. contra Jac. Smidelin, *p.* 404. (18) Varillas loc. cit. *l.* 14, *p.* 31.

4. If Luther was not the child of Satan, however, few laboured so strenuously in his service. His name originally was *Luder;* but as the vulgar meaning of that word was not the most elegant, he changed it to Luther. Applying himself at an early age to literature, he went to Erfurt, in Thuringia, and at the age of twenty years graduated as a Master of Philosophy. While pursuing his legal and philosophical studies in that University, he happened to take a walk in the country with a fellow-student, who was struck dead by lightning at his side. Under the influence of terror, and not moved by devotion, he made a vow to enter into religion, and became an Augustinian Friar, in the Convent of Erfurt (19). "It was not," he says, "by my own free will I became a monk, but terrified by a sudden death, I made a vow to that effect." This took place in 1504, in the 22nd year of his age, and was a matter of great surprise to his father and friends, who previously never perceived in him any tendency to piety (20).

5. After his profession and ordination he was commanded by his superiors, as an exercise of humility, to beg through the streets, as was the custom of the Order at that period. He refused, and in the year 1508 left the Convent and Academy of Erfurt, in which he was employed, greatly to the satisfaction of his colleagues in that University, who could not bear his violent temper, and went to Wittemberg, where Duke Frederick, Elector of Saxony, had a little before founded a University, in which he obtained the chair of Philosophy. He was soon after sent to Rome, to settle some dispute raised in his Order, and having satisfactorily arranged everything, he returned to Wittemberg, and received from Andrew Carlostad, Dean of the University, the dignity of Doctor of Theology. The entire expense of taking his degree was borne by the Elector, who conceived a very great liking for him (21). He was certainly a man of fine genius, a subtle reasoner, deeply read in the Schoolmen and Holy Fathers, but, even then, as Cochleus tells us, filled with vices—proud, ambitious, petulant, seditious, evil-tongued—and even his moral character was tainted (22); he was a man of great eloquence, both in speaking and writing, but so rude and rugged, that in all his works we scarcely find a polished period; he was so vain of himself, that he despised the most learned writers of the Church, and he especially attacked the doctrines of St. Thomas, so much esteemed by the Council of Trent.

6. Leo X., wishing, as Hermant tells us (23), to raise a fund for the recovery of the Holy Land, or, according to the more generally received opinion (24), to finish the building of St. Peter's Church, commenced by Julius II., committed to Cardinal Albert, Arch-

---

(19) Luther Præfat. ad lib. de Vot. Mon. (20) Nat. Alex. ibid. *sec.* 1, *n.* 1; Gotti, loc. cit. *sec.* 2. (21) Hermant, Histor. Conc. *t.* 1, *c.* 228; Nat. Alex. *t.* 19, *art.* 11, *sec.* 1, *n.* 1; Van Ranst, Hær. *p.* 298; Gotti, Ver. Rel. *c.* 108, *sec.* 2, *n.* 6. (22) Nat. Alex. *sec.* 1, *n.* 3; Hermant, loc. cit.; Van Ranst, loc. cit. (23) Hermant, loc. cit. *c.* 227. (24) Nat. Alex., Gotti, Van Ranst, Bernino, &c.

bishop and Elector of Mayence, the promulgation of a brief, granting many indulgences to those who contributed alms for this purpose. The archbishop committed the publication of these indulgences to a Dominican Doctor, John Tetzel, who had already discharged a similar commission in aid of the Teutonic Knights, when they were attacked by the Duke of Muscovy, and who was reputed an eloquent preacher. This was highly displeasing to John Staupitz, Vicar-General of the Augustinians, and a great favourite of the Duke of Saxony; he, therefore, with the Duke's permission, charged Luther with the duty of preaching against the abuse of these indulgences. He immediately began to attack these abuses, and truth compels us to admit that abuses had crept into the mode of collecting these alms, which scandalized the people. He, however, not only preached against the abuses which existed, but against the validity of indulgences altogether, and immediately wrote a long letter to the Archbishop of Mayence, in which he gave an exaggerated account of the errors preached in their distribution, such as, that whoever took an indulgence was certain of salvation, and was absolved from all punishment and penalties of sin, and to this letter he tacked ninety-five propositions, in which he asserted that the doctrine of indulgences altogether was a very doubtful matter. He did not rest satisfied with sending them to the archbishop; he posted them on the doors of the Church of All Saints in Wittemberg, sent printed copies of them through all Germany, and had them publicly sustained by his scholars in the University. He was answered by Father Tetzel in Frankfort, who proved the doctrine of the Church, and as he was armed with inquisitorial powers, condemned these propositions as heretical. When this came to Luther's ears, he retorted in the most insolent manner, and from these few sparks, that fire was kindled which not only ran through Germany, but through Denmark, Norway, Sweden, and the most remote countries of the North (25).

7. In the year 1518, Luther sent his conclusions to the Pope in a pamphlet, entitled "Resolutiones Disputationum de Indulgentiarum virtute;" and in the preface he thus addresses him: "Holy Father, prostrate at your Holiness' feet I offer myself with all I possess; vivify or destroy, call, revoke, reject as you will, I recognize your voice as the voice of Christ, presiding and speaking in you; if I deserve death, I refuse not to die" (26). With such protestations of submission did he endeavour to deceive the Pope, but as Cardinal Gotti (27) remarks, in this very letter he protests that he adopts no other sentiments than those of the Scriptures, and intends merely to oppose the schoolmen. Leo X. having now received both Luther's and Tetzel's writings, clearly saw the poison

(25) Hermant, c. 228; Van Ranst, p. 299; Gotti, c. 108, sec. 3, n. 3.   (26) Ap. Van Ranst, Hist. p. 300.   (27) Gotti, sec. 2, n. 8.

which flowed from the pen of the former, and accordingly summoned him to Rome to defend himself. Luther excused himself on the plea of delicate health, and the want of means to undertake so long a journey, and added, that he had strong suspicions of the Roman judges; he also induced the Duke of Saxony, and the University of Wittemberg, to write to his Holiness to the same effect, and to request him to appoint judges in Germany to try the cause (28). The Pope dreaded to entrust the case to the decision of the Germans, as Luther already had a powerful party in his own country; he therefore sent as his Legate a *latere*, Thomas Vio, called Cardinal Cajetan, commissioning him to call on the secular power to have Luther arrested, and to absolve him from all censures in case he retracted his errors, but should he obstinately persist in maintaining them, to excommunicate him (29).

8. On the Legate's arrival in Augsburg, he summoned Luther before him, and imposed three commandments on him: First.—That he should retract the propositions asserted by him. Secondly.—That he should cease from publishing them; and finally, that he should reject all doctrines censured by the Church. Luther answered that he never broached any doctrine in opposition to the Church; but Cajetan reminded him that he denied the treasure of the merits of Jesus Christ and his saints, in virtue of which the Pope dispensed indulgences, as Clement VI. declared in the Constitution *Unigenitus;* that he also asserted that to obtain the fruit of the sacraments it was only required to have the faith of obtaining them. Luther made some reply, but the cardinal, smiling, said he did not come to argue with him, but to receive his submission, as he had been appointed (30). Luther was alarmed at finding himself in Augsburg, then totally Catholic, without a safe conduct (although Noel Alexander (31) says he obtained one from Maximilian; Hermant, Van Ranst, and Gotti deny it (32), and Varillas wonders at his boldness in presenting himself without it), and asked time for reflection, which was granted him, and on the following day he presented himself before the Legate, together with a notary public, and four senators of Augsburg, and presented a writing signed with his own hand, saying that he followed and revered the Roman Church in all her acts and sayings, past, present, and to come, and that if ever he said anything against her, he now revoked and unsaid it. The cardinal, well aware that he had written several things which were not in accordance with the Catholic Faith, wished to have a still more ample retractation, but still he flattered himself that the one obtained was so much gained. Luther, however, soon slipped through his fingers, for he then persisted that he had neither

(28) Gotti, ibid. *n.* 9, & Van Ranst, loc. cit. (29) Nat. Alex. *t.* 19, *ar.* 11, *sec.* 4; Gotti, loc. cit. *sec.* 2, *n.* 20; Hermant, *t.* 2, *c.* 229. (30) Hermant, *c.* 230. (31) Nat. Alex. loc. cit. *sec.* 4. (32) Hermant, cit. *c.* 230; Van Ranst, *p.* 302; Gotti, *sec.* 3, *n.* 10.

said nor written anything repugnant to the Scriptures, Fathers, Councils, Decretals, or reason; that his propositions were true, and that he was prepared to defend them, but, nevertheless, that he would submit them to the judgment of the three Imperial Academies of Basle, Fribourg, and Louvain, or of Paris (33).

9. The Cardinal still insisted on the three primary conditions. Luther asked time to answer in writing, and the next day presented a document, in which he advanced many opinions, not only against the value of indulgences, but also against the merits of the saints, and good works, propping up his opinions by false reasoning. Cardinal Cajetan heard him out, and then told him not again to appear before him, unless he came prepared to retract his heresy. Luther then left Augsburg, and wrote to the Cardinal, saying, that his opinions were founded on truth, and supported by reason and Scripture, but, notwithstanding, it was his wish still to subject himself to the Church, and to keep silence regarding indulgences, if his adversaries were commanded to keep silent, likewise (34). The Cardinal gave him no answer, so Luther, fearing sentence would be passed against him, appealed from the Cardinal to the Pope, and had the appeal posted on the Church doors (35). Van Ranst censures Cajetan for not imprisoning Luther, when he had him in Augsburg without a safe conduct, knowing him to be a man of such deceitful cunning, and so extinguishing, in its commencement, that great fire, which consumed so great a part of Europe, by introducing to the people a religion so much the more pernicious, as it was so favourable to sensual license. Luther himself, afterwards, deriding the whole transaction, says (36): "I there heard that new Latin language, that teaching the truth was disturbing the Church, and that denying Christ was exalting the Church." It is then he appealed, first to the Pope, and afterwards from the Pope to the Council (37).

10. The Legate, seeing the obstinacy of Luther, wrote to the Elector Frederick, telling him that this friar was a heretic, unworthy of his protection, and that he should send him to Rome, or at all events banish him from his States. The Elector immediately transmitted the letter to Luther, who, on his escape from the power of the Legate, began to make the most rabid attacks on the Pope, calling him tyrant and Antichrist: "He (the Pope) has refused peace," said he, "then let it be war, and we shall see whether Luther or the Pope shall be first hurt." Notwithstanding his boasting, the Legate's letter to the Elector terrified him, and he indited a most humble letter, declaring himself guiltless of any crime against Faith, and praying for a continuance of his protection (38). Hermant says

(33) Nat. Alex. *ar.* 11, *sec.* 4, *n* 1; Gotti, *c.* 108, *sec.* 3, *n.* 10. (34) Nat. Alex. loc. cit.; Van Ranst, *p.* 302. (35) Van Ranst, *p.* 302. (36) Luther, *t.* 1; Oper. *p.* 208. (37) Gotti, *sec.* 3, *n.* 11. (38) Gotti, *c.* 108, *sec.* 3, *n.* 12; Van Ranst, *p.* 302; Nat. Alex. *sec.* 4, *n.* 1; Hermant, *c.* 229.

the Elector protected Luther, not only on account of his affection for his newly founded University of Wittemberg, on which he shed so much lustre, but also through hatred to the Elector Albert, of Mayence, Luther's most determined enemy (39). This protector of Luther, however, met with a dreadful death, as if to mark the judgment of God. While hunting, he was attacked with apoplexy, accompanied with dreadful convulsions; Luther and Melancthon immediately posted off to assist, or rather to ruin him, in his last agony, but they could not obtain from him a single word; he had lost the use of all his senses, the most dreadful convulsions racked every one of his limbs, his cries were like the roar of a lion, and he died without sacraments, or without any signs of repentance.

11. On the 9th of November, 1518, Leo X. published a Bull, on the validity of indulgences, in which he declared that the Supreme Pontiff alone had the right of granting them without limitation, from the treasures of the merits of Jesus Christ; that this was an article of Faith, and that whoever refused to believe it should be excluded from the communion of the Church. Ecchius, a man of great learning, and Pro-Chancellor of Ingoldstad, began to write about this time, and subsequently, in 1519, he had a conference with Luther, through the instrumentality of Duke George, uncle of the Elector Frederick, a good Catholic. This conference took place in Duke George's city of Leipsic, and in his own palace. After debating on many questions there, they agreed to leave the whole matter to the decision of the Universities of Erfurt and Paris. The University of Paris, after an examination of the writings on each side, received the doctrine of Ecchius, and condemned that of Luther. One hundred and four of his propositions were censured, which excited his ire to a great pitch against that University. The following year there was another conference between Luther, accompanied by Carlostad and Ecchius, in which, in six discussions, the doctrines of free-will, of grace, and of good works, were argued by Carlostad. Luther followed, and disputed on Purgatory, the power of absolving sins, reserving cases, the primacy of the Pope, and indulgences. In this conference, his doctrines were not so heretical as soon after the dispute, for then the force of truth obliged him to admit the Papal primacy, though he said it was of human, not divine right; he also acknowledged a Purgatory, and did not altogether reject indulgences, solely condemning the abuse of them. The same year his doctrines were condemned by the Universities of Cologne and Louvain (40).

12. In the year 1519, the Emperor Maximilian I. died, and there was an interregnum of six months, during which Luther gained many adherents in Wittemberg, not only among the youth

(39) Hermant, c. 229; Nat. Alex. sec. 4. n. 1 ; Van Ranst, p. 302.   (40) Van Ranst, p. 303 ; Varillas, l. 3, p. 48.

of the University, who afterwards scattered themselves through all Saxony, but some of the Professors, and even some of the clergy, secular and regular, became his disciples. Leo X. seeing his party every day gaining strength, and no hope of his retractation, then published in Rome his famous Bull, "Exurge Domine," in which he condemned forty-one of his principal errors as heretical (see Third Part of this history), and sent his Commissaries to publish it in Germany, ordering, at the same time, his books to be publicly burned in Rome. His Holiness, however, even then exhorts Luther and his followers to return to the fold, and promises to receive with clemency whoever returns before the expiration of two months, at the expiration of which, he orders his Commissaries to excommunicate the perverse, and hand them over to the secular power. The two months being passed, he published another Bull, declaring Luther a heretic, and also that all who followed or favoured him incurred all the penalties and censures fulminated against heretics (41). Luther, as soon as he heard of the publication of the first Bull of 1520, and the burning of his books in Rome, burned in the public square of Wittemberg the Bull, and the Book of the Decretals of the Canon Law, saying: "As you have opposed the saints of the Lord, so may eternal fire destroy you;" and then, in a voice of fury, exclaimed: " Let us fight with all our strength against that son of perdition, the Pope, the Cardinals, and all the Roman sink of corruption; let us wash our hands in their blood (42)." From that day to the day of his death, he never ceased writing against the Pope and the Catholic Church, and from the year 1521 to 1546, when he died, he brought to light again, in his works, almost every heresy of former ages. Cochleus, speaking of Luther's writings, says (43): " He thus defiled everything holy; he preaches Christ, and tramples on his servants; magnifies faith, and denies good works, and opens a license to sin; elevates mercy, depresses justice, and throws upon God the cause of all evil; finally, destroys all law, takes the power out of the hands of the magistrate, stirs up the laity against the clergy, the impious against the Pope, the people against princes."

SEC. II.—THE DIETS AND PRINCIPAL CONGRESSES HELD CONCERNING THE HERESY OF LUTHER.

13. Diet of Worms, where Luther appeared before Charles V., and remains obstinate. 14. Edict of the Emperor against Luther, who is concealed by the Elector in one of his Castles. 15. Diet of Spire, where the Emperor publishes a Decree, against which the Heretics protest. 16. Conference with the Zuinglians; Marriage of Luther with an Abbess. 17. Diet of Augsburg, and Melancthon's Profession of Faith; Melancthon's Treatise, in Favour of the Authority of the Pope, rejected by Luther. 18. Another Edict of the Emperor in Favour of Religion. 19. League of Smalkald

---

(41) Hermant, *t.* 1, *c.* 230. (42) Gotti, *c.* 108, *n.* 13. (43) Cochleus de Act. & Script. Luth. Ann. 1523.

broken up by the Emperor. 20. Dispensation given by the Lutherans to the Landgrave to have two Wives. 21. Council of Trent, to which Luther refuses to come; he dies, cursing the Council. 22. The Lutherans divided into fifty-six Sects. 23. The Second Diet of Augsburg, in which Charles V. published the injurious Formula of the Interim. 24, 25. The Heresy of Luther takes Possession of Sweden, Denmark, Norway, and other Kingdoms.

13. THE first Conference was in the Imperial Diet, assembled in Worms. Luther still continued augmenting his party, and pouring forth calumnies and vituperations against the Holy See. At the request of the Pope, Charles V. then wrote to the Elector of Saxony, to deliver up Luther, or, at all events, to banish him from his territories. The Elector, on receipt of the letter, said that as the Diet was now so near, it would be better to refer the whole matter to its decision. Luther was most anxious to appear in this illustrious assembly, hoping, by his harangue, to obtain a favourable reception for his doctrine, especially as at the request of his patron, the Elector, he obtained not only permission to attend, but also a safe conduct from the Emperor himself. The Diet assembled in 1521, and Luther arrived in Worms, on the 17th of April. Ecchius asked him, in the name of the Emperor, if he acknowledged himself the author of the books published in his name, and if it was his intention to defend them. He admitted the books were his; but as to defending them, he said, as that was an affair of importance to the Word of God, and the salvation of souls, he required time to give an answer. The Emperor gave him a day for consideration, and he next day said, that among his books some contained arguments on religion, and these he could not conscientiously retract; others were written in his own defence, and he confessed that he was guilty of excess in his attacks on his adversaries, the slaves of the Pope, but that they first provoked him to it. Ecchius required a more lucid answer. He then turned to the Emperor, and said he could not absolutely retract anything he had taught in his lectures, his sermons, or his writings, until convinced by Scripture and reason, and that both Pope and Councils were fallible judges in this matter (1).

14. The Emperor, perceiving his obstinacy, after some conversation with him, dismissed him. He might then have arrested him, as he was in his power, but he disdained violating the safe conduct he himself had given him. Notwithstanding, he published, on the 26th of May, an edict, with consent of the Princes of the Empire, and of its Orders and States, in which he declared Luther a notorious and obstinate heretic, and prohibited any one to receive or protect him, under the severest penalties. He moreover ordained, that, after the term of the safe conduct expired, which was twenty days, he should be proceeded against wherever found (2); and he

(1) Nat. Alex. sec. 14, n. 4; Varill. t. 1, l. 4, dalla, p. 175; Van Ranst, p. 304.
(2) Nat. Alex. loc. cit.; Van Ranst, p. 205.

would not have escaped, were it not for the Elector Frederick, who bribed the soldiers who escorted him, and had him conveyed to a place of security. A report was then spread abroad, that Luther was imprisoned before the expiration of the safe conduct, but the Elector had him conveyed to the Castle of Watzberg, near Alstad, in Thuringia, a place which Luther afterwards called his Patmos. He remained there nearly ten months, well concealed and guarded, and there he finished the plan of his heresy, and wrote many of his works. In the works written here, Luther principally attacked the scholastic Theologians, especially St. Thomas, whose works, he said, were filled up with heresies. We should not wonder he called the works of St. Thomas heretical, who centuries before had confuted his own pestilential errors (3).

15. In the year 1529, another Diet was held in the city of Spire, by the Emperor's orders, in which it was decided, that in these places in which the edict of Worms was accepted, it should be observed; but that wherever the ancient religion was changed, and its restoration could not be effected without public disturbances, matters should remain as they were until the celebration of a General Council. It was, besides, decided that Mass should freely be celebrated in the places infected with Lutheranism, and that the Gospel should be explained, according to the interpretation of the Fathers approved by the Church. The Elector Frederick of Saxony, George of Branderburg, Ernest and Francis, Dukes of Luneburg, Wolfgang of Anhalt, and fourteen confederate cities (thirteen, according to Protestant historians), *protested* against this Decree, as contrary to the truth of the Gospel, and appealed to a future Council, or to some judge not suspected, and from this protest arose the famous designation of Protestant (4).

16. The same year another Conference, composed of Lutherans and Zuinglians, or Sacramentarians, was held in Marpurg, under the patronage of the Landgrave of Hesse, to endeavour to establish a union between their respective sects. Luther, Melancthon, Jonas, Osiander, Brenzius, and Agricola appeared on one side, and Zuinglius, Ecolampadius, Bucer, and Hedio, on the other. They agreed on all points, with the exception of the Eucharist, as the Zuinglians totally denied the Real Presence of Christ. Several other Conferences were held to remove, if possible, the discussion of doctrine objected to then by the Catholics, but all ended without coming to any agreement. In this the Providence of God is apparent; the Roman Church could thus oppose to the innovators that unity of doctrine she always possessed, and the heretics were always confounded on this point (5). About this period Luther married an abbess of a convent. His fellow-heresiarch Zuinglius, also a priest,

(3) Hermant, c. 230, 231; Van Ranst, loc. cit. (4) Nat. Alex. t. 9, sec. 4, n. 9, ex Sleidano, l. 6; Van Ranst, p. 306; Hermant, t. 2, c. 244. (5) Van Ranst, p. 306; Nat. Alex. loc. cit. n. 10.

had already violated his vows, by a sacrilegious marriage, and Luther would have done the same long before, only he was restrained by the Elector of Saxony, who, though a heretic, shuddered at the marriage of a religious, and protested he would oppose it by every means in his power. On the other hand, Luther was now quite taken with Catherine Bora, a lady of noble family, but poor, and who, forced by poverty, embraced a religious life, without any vocation for that state, in a convent at Misnia, and finally became abbess. Reading one of Luther's works, she came across his treatise on the nullity of religious vows, and requested him to visit her. He called on her frequently, and finally induced her to leave her convent, and come to Wittemberg with him, where, devoid of all shame, he married her with great solemnity, the Elector Frederick, who constantly opposed it, being now dead; and such was the force of his example and discourses, that he soon after induced the Grand Master of the Teutonic Order (6) to celebrate his sacrilegious nuptials, likewise. Those marriages provoked that witticism of Erasmus, who said that the heresies of his day all ended, like a comedy, in marriage.

17. In the July of 1530, the famous Diet of Augsburgh was held. The Emperor and all the princes being assembled at the Diet, and the feast of Corpus Christi falling at the same time, an order was given to the princes to attend the procession. The Protestants refused, on the plea that this was one of the Roman superstitions; the Elector of Saxony, nevertheless, whose duty it was to carry the sword of state before the Emperor (7), consulted his theologians, who gave it as their opinion, that in this case he might consider it a mere human ceremony, and that, like Naam, the Syrian, who bowed down before the idol, when the king leaned on his arm in the temple, he might attend. In this Diet the Catholic party was represented by John Ecchius, Conrad Wimpin, and John Cochleus, and the Lutheran by Melancthon, Brenzius, and Schnapsius. The Lutheran princes presented to the Emperor the Profession of Faith, drawn up by Philip Melancthon, who endeavoured as much as possible to soften down the opinions opposed to Catholicity. This is the famous Confession of Augsburg, afterwards the creed of the majority of Lutherans. In those Articles they admitted: First.—That we are not justified by faith alone, but by faith and grace. Second.—That in good works not only grace alone concurs, but our co-operation likewise. Third.—That the Church contains not only the elect, but also the reprobate. Fourth.—That free-will exists in man, though without Divine grace he cannot be justified. Fifth.—That the saints pray to God for us, and that it is a pious practice to venerate their memories on certain days, abstracting, however, from either approving

(6) Varillas, *t.* 1, *p.* 306; Hermant, *t.* 2, *c.* 243.   (7) Nat. Alex. loc. cit, *sec.* 4, *n.* 11; Van Ranst, *p.* 307.

or condemning their invocation. In ten other chapters of less importance they agree with Catholics. They agreed, likewise, in saying that Jesus Christ is present in the Eucharist, in each species, and did not condemn the laity who communicated in one kind only. They allowed the jurisdiction of bishops, and that obedience was due to them by pastors, preachers, and priests, in spiritual matters, and that censures published by them, according to the rule of Scripture, are of avail. The Emperor, hoping it would render easier the establishment of peace, joined to the commissions two jurists for each side, along with Ecchius and Melancthon; but this Conference never was closed, because, as Sleidan tells us, Melancthon was not permitted by Luther to sign the treaty, although he was most anxious for the establishment of peace, as he declares in his letter to the Legate Campeggio: "We have no dogma," he says, "different from the Roman Church; we are ready to yield her obedience, if, in her clemency, she will relax or wink at some little matters. We still profess obedience to the Roman Pontiff, if he does not cast us off" (8). Varillas (9) mentions a curious fact relative to this. When Francis I., King of France, invited Melancthon to Paris, to teach in the University (in which he did not succeed), he received from him a pamphlet, in which he laid it down as a principle, that it was necessary to preserve the pre-eminence and authority of the Roman Pontiff, to preserve the unity of doctrine. Nothing could exceed Luther's rage when he heard of this, and he told Melancthon that he had a mind to break with him altogether, and that he was now about to ruin the religion it cost him twenty years' labour to establish, by destroying the authority of the Pope.

18. The Zuinglians presented their Confession of Faith at the same Diet, in the name of the four cities of Strasburg, Constance, Meningen, and Lindau, which differed from the Lutheran only in the doctrine of the Eucharist. At the breaking up of the Diet, the Emperor promulgated an edict, in which the Lutheran Princes and cities were allowed, until the 15th of April following, to wait for a General Council, and again become united with the Catholic Church, and the rest of the Empire. It was forbidden them to allow any innovations in religious matters, or any works contrary to religion to be published in their respective territories, and ordained that all should unite in opposition to the Anabaptists and Zuinglians. The Lutherans refused to accept these articles, and all hopes of peace being at an end, asked leave to depart. Before they left, however, the Emperor published an edict, subscribed by the remaining Princes and Orders of the Empire, that all should persevere in the ancient religion, condemning the sects of the Anabaptists, Zuinglians, and Lutherans, and commanding all to hold themselves in

(8) Nat. Alex. loc. cit. *n.* 11 ; Hermant, *c.* 244.   (9) Varillas, *t.* 1, *l.* 10, *p.* 445, *coll.* 1.

readiness to attend at the Council, which he promised he would induce the Pope to summon in six months (10).

19. The Protestants refused obedience to this Decree, and met in Smalcald, a city of Franconia, and there, in 1531, formed the famous League of Smalcald, to defend with force of arms the doctrines they professed; but they refused the admission of the Zuinglians into this League, on account of their errors regarding the Holy Sacrament. This was the cause of the famous battle of Mulberg, on the Elbe, in 1547, in which Charles V. was victorious, and John, Elector of Saxony, and Philip, the Landgrave, the two chiefs of the heretical party in Germany, were made prisoners (11). The whole power of Protestantism would have been broken by this defeat, had not Maurice of Saxony, the nephew of the imprisoned Elector, taken up arms against Charles (12). The Landgrave obtained his liberty, but was obliged to beg pardon of the Emperor prostrate at his feet, and surrender his States into his hands (13).

20. This Philip is the same who obtained, in 1539, from Luther and other faithful Ministers of the Gospel, as they called themselves, that remarkable dispensation to marry two wives at the same time. Varillas says (14), that the Landgrave, though previous to his marriage he always led a moral life, could not, after the loss of his faith, content himself with one wife, and persuaded himself that Luther and the theologians of his sect would grant him a dispensation to marry another. He well knew whom he had to deal with; he assembled them in Wittemberg, and though they well knew the difficult position in which they were placed, and the scandal they would give by yielding to his wishes, still his influence had greater weight with them than the laws of Christ or the dictates of their consciences. Varillas (*P.* 531) gives the rescript in full by which they dispense with him. They say they could not introduce into the New Testament the provisions of the Old Law, which permitted a plurality of wives, as Christ says they shall be *two* in one flesh, but they likewise say that there are certain cases in which the New Law can be dispensed with; that the case of the Prince was one of these; but that, in order to avoid scandal, it would be necessary that the second marriage should be celebrated privately, in the presence of few witnesses; and this document is subscribed by Luther, Melancthon, Bucer, and five other Lutheran Doctors. The marriage was soon after privately celebrated in presence of Luther, Melancthon, and six other persons. The Landgrave died, according to De Thou, in 1567.

21. The Council of Trent was opened on the 13th of December, 1545, under Paul III., was continued under Julius III., and being

(10) Nat. Alex. *sec.* 4, *n.* 10, in fin. ex Cochlæo in Act. Lutheri & Sleidano, *l.* 7; Van Ranst, *p.* 307.   (11) Nat. Alex. *sec.* 4, *n.* 13; Hermant, *t.* 2, *c.* 245.   (12) Van Ranst, *p.* 307; Nat. Alex. *t.* 19, *c.* 10, *sec.* 4, *n.* 1.   (13) Nat. Alex. loc. cit.   (14) Varillas, *t.* 1, *l.* 7, *p.* 530, c. 2.

many times suspended for various causes, was formally concluded under Pius IV., in December, 1563. Luther frequently called on the Pope to summon a General Council, but now that it was assembled, he would not attend it, knowing full well his doctrines would be there condemned. First, he appealed from the Legate to the Pope, then from the Pope not sufficiently informed to the Pope better informed, then from the Pope to a Council, and now from the Council to himself. Such has been the invariable practice of heresiarchs; to refute the decisions of the Pope they appeal to a Council, condemned by a Council, they reject the decisions of both. Thus Luther refused to attend the Council, and after his death his example was followed by the other Protestants, who refused even to avail themselves of the safe conduct given to them for that effect. While the Fathers were making preparations for the Fourth Session, news of Luther's death was brought to Trent; he went to Eisleben towards the end of January, at the invitation of some of his friends, to arrange some differences, when he was then told he was invited to the Council. He exclaimed in a rage: " I will go, and may I lose my head if I do not defend my opinions against all the world; that which comes forth from my mouth is not my anger but the anger of God" (15). A longer journey, however, was before him; he died in the sixty-third year of his age, on the 17th of February, 1546. After eating a hearty supper and enjoying himself, jesting as usual, he was a few hours after attacked with dreadful pains, and thus he died. Raging against the Council a little before his death, he said to Justus Jonas, one of his followers: " Pray for our Lord God and his Gospel, that it may turn out well, for the Council of Trent and the abominable Pope are grievously opposed to him." Saying this he died, and went to receive the reward of all his blasphemies against the Faith, and of the thousands of souls he led to perdition. His body was placed in a tin coffin, and borne on a triumphal car to Wittemberg, followed by his concubine, Catherine, and his three sons, John, Martin, and Paul, in a coach, and a great multitude both on foot and horseback. Philip Melancthon preached his funeral oration in Latin, and Pomeranius in German. Pomeranius also composed that inscription for his tomb, worthy alike of the master and the disciple: " Pestis eram vivus, moriens ero mors tua Papa"— " I was the plague of the Pope while living, dying I will be his death" (16).

22. The Lutherans were invited to the Council by various briefs of the Popes, but always refused to attend (17). They were afterwards summoned by the Emperor Ferdinand, on the re-opening of the Council; but they required conditions which could not be granted (18). They at first split into two sects, Rigorous and Re-

(15) Cochleus in Actis Lutheri.   (16) Gotti, c. 105, s. 5, n. 7; Van Ranst, p. 308; Bernin. t. 4, sec. 16, c. 5, p. 454; Varillas, t. 2, l. 14, p. 34.   (17) Varillas, t. 2, l. 24, p. 366.   (18) Varillas, l. 25, p. 393.

laxed Lutherans (19), and these two, as Lindan afterwards informs us, were divided into fifty-six sects (20).

23. In another Diet, celebrated in Augsburg, in 1547, the Emperor Charles V. restored the Catholic religion in that city; but in the following year, as Noel Alexander (21) tells us, he tarnished his glory by publishing the famous *Interim*, thus usurping the authority to decide on questions of Faith and ecclesiastical discipline. We should, says Noel Alexander, hold this Interim in the same detestation as the Enoticon of Zeno, the Ecthesis of Heraclius, and the Tiphos of Constans. In the year 1552, he again tarnished his honour, for after routing Maurice of Saxony, he made peace with him, and granted freedom of worship in his states to the professors of the Confession of Augsburg. In the year 1556 he gave up the government of the Empire to his brother Ferdinand, King of the Romans, and retired to the Jeromite Monastery of St. Justus, in Estremadura, in Spain, giving himself up to God alone, and preparing for death, which overtook him on the 21st of September, 1558, in the fifty-eighth year of his age (22).

24. Luther's heresy, through the instrumentality of his disciples, soon spread from Germany into the neighbouring kingdoms, and first of all it infected Sweden. This kingdom, at first idolatrous, received the Catholic Faith in 1155, which was finally established in 1416, and continued the Faith of the nation till the reign of Gustavus Erickson. Lutheranism was introduced into this country in 1523 by Olaus Petri, who imbibed it in the University of Wittemberg; along with many others, he gained over King Gustavus, who gave leave to the preachers to propound, and to all leave to follow, their doctrines, and also permitted the religious to marry. It was his wish that the old ceremonies should be kept up, to deceive the people; but he caused all the ancient books to be burned, and introduced new ones, written by heretics; thus in four years Lutheranism was established in Sweden. Gustavus, at his death, left the crown to his son, Eric XIV.; but his reign was but short, for his younger brother, John, declared war against him, and dethroned him in 1569. Before John came to the crown, he was a good Catholic, and desired to re-unite Sweden to the Church, especially as the Pope sent him an excellent missioner to strengthen him in the Faith. He commenced the good work by publishing a liturgy opposed to the Lutheran, and intending gradually to abolish the heresy. He then wrote to the Pope, saying, he hoped to gain Sweden altogether to the Faith, if his Holiness would grant four conditions: First.—That the nobility should not be disturbed in the possession of the ecclesiastical property they held. Second.—That the married bishops and priests should have liberty to retain

(19) Varill. *t.* 2, *l.* 17, *p.* 122, & *l.* 24, *p.* 364. (20) Lindan, Epist., Roræm in Luther. (21) Nat. Alex. *t.* 19, *c.* 10, *art.* 5, *p.* 321. (22) Nat. Alex. loc. cit. *c.* 10, *art.* 5.

their wives. Third.—That communion should be given in both kinds. Fourth.—That the Church service should be celebrated in the vulgar tongue. The Pope consulted the cardinals, but refused his request, as he could not well grant him what he refused to so many other princes. When this answer arrived, the King was already wavering in his determination to support the true Faith, fearful of causing a revolt with which he was threatened; this unfavourable answer decided him, and he gave up all hopes, and followed the religion of his States. His Queen, a zealous Catholic, a sister of Sigismund Augustus, King of Poland, was so much affected by the change in her husband's dispositions, that she survived but a short time. In twelve months after the King followed her, and left the throne to his son Sigismund, then King of Poland. Charles of Sudermania, who governed the kingdom in the Sovereign's absence, usurped the crown, and his crime was sanctioned by the States, who declared Sigismund's right to the crown null and void, on account of his religion. Charles, therefore, being settled on the throne, established Lutheranism in Sweden. He was succeeded by his son, Gustavus Adolphus, one of the greatest enemies Catholicity had either in Sweden or Germany; but his daughter Christina renounced the throne, sooner than give up the faith she embraced, and lived and died in the Catholic Church. She left the kingdom to Charles Gustavus, her cousin, who reigned for six years, and transmitted it to his son, Charles V., and to the present day no other religion but Lutheranism is publicly professed in Sweden (23).

25. Denmark and Norway underwent a similar misfortune with Sweden. Idolatry was predominant in Denmark till the year 826, when the Catholic religion was established by Regnor I., and continued to be the only religion of the kingdom, till in 1523 Lutheranism was introduced by Christian II. The judgment of God, however, soon fell on him, as he was dethroned by his subjects, and banished with all his family. His uncle, Frederick, was chosen to succeed him. He gave liberty to the Protestants to preach their doctrine, and to his subjects to follow it. Not, however, content with this, he soon began a cruel persecution against the bishops, and against every Catholic who defended his religion, and many sealed their religion with their blood. This impious monarch met an awfully sudden death while he was banqueting on Good Friday, and was succeeded by Christian III., who completed the final separation of Denmark from the Catholic Church. Thus, in a short time, Lutheranism became dominant in these kingdoms, and continues to hold its sway there. There are many Calvinistic congregations in Denmark, as Christian permitted the Scotch Presbyterians to found churches there. There

(23) Historia Relig. Jovet, *t.* 2, *p.* 324.

are also some Catholics, but they *were* obliged to assemble privately for the Holy Sacrifice, and even now, though the spirit of the age is opposed to persecution, they labour under many restraints and disabilities. Norway, till lately, and Iceland at the present day, belongs to Denmark, and Lutheranism is likewise the religion of these countries, though the people, especially in the country parts, preserve many Catholic traditions, but they were till lately destitute of priests aud sacrifice.* In Lapland, some Pagans remain as yet, who adore the spirits of the woods, and fire, and water; they have no Catholic missioner to instruct them. There are, indeed, but few Catholics altogether in the Northern kingdoms. Formerly, the Dominicans, Franciscans, Carthusians, Cistercians, and Brigittines, had convents there, but now all have disappeared (24).

SEC. III.—ERRORS OF LUTHER.

26. Forty-one Errors of Luther condemned by Leo X. 27. Other Errors taken from his Books. 28. Luther's Remorse of Conscience. 29. His Abuse of Henry VIII.; his erroneous Translation of the New Testament; the Books he rejected. 30. His Method of celebrating Mass. 31. His Book against the Sacramentarians, who denied the Real Presence of Christ in the Eucharist.

96. FIRST in order, come the forty-one propositions of Luther, condemned by Leo X. in his Bull, *Exurge Domine*, published in 1520, which is found in the Bullarium of Leo X. (Constit. 40), in Cochleus's account of Luther's proceedings, and also in Bernini's (1) works. They are as follows: First.—It is a usual, but a heretical opinion, that the Sacraments of the New Law give justifying grace to those who place no hindrance in the way. Second.—To deny that sin remains in a child after baptism is, through the mouth of Paul, to trample both on Christ and Paul. Third.—The tendency to sin (*Fomes peccati*), although there is no actual sin, delays the soul, after leaving the body, from entering into heaven. Fourth.—The imperfect charity of one about to die necessarily induces a great fear, which of itself is enough to make the pains of purgatory, and excludes from the kingdom. Fifth.—That the parts of penance are three—contrition, confession, and satisfaction; is founded neither in Scripture, nor in the ancient Holy Christian Doctors. Sixth.—Contrition, which is obtained by examination, recollection, and detestation of sins, by which a person recollects his years in the bitterness of his soul, pondering on the grievousness, the multitude, and the foulness of

(24) Joves, cit. *p.* 343.   (1) Bernin. *t.* 4, *sec.* 16, *c.* 2, *p.* 285.

---

* N.B.—A Vicar Apostolic has been appointed to Sweden and Norway. In 1856, a Prefect Apostolic, Abbé Djonvoski, has been appointed for Iceland, Lapland, Greenland, and the Arctic Regions of America.

his sins, the loss of eternal beatitude, and the incurring eternal damnation; this contrition only makes a man a hypocrite, and a greater sinner. Seventh.—That proverb is most true, and better than all the doctrine about conditions given as yet: the highest penance is not to act so again, and the best penance is a new life. Eighth.—Presume not by any means to confess venial sins, and not even every wicked sin; for it is impossible that you should know all your mortal sins, and hence, in the primitive Church only these manifestly mortal were confessed. Ninth.—When we wish clearly to confess everything, we act as if we wished to leave nothing to the mercy of God to pardon. Tenth.—Sins are not remitted to any one, unless (the priest remitting them) he believes they are remitted—yea, the sin remains unless he believes it remitted; for the remission of sin and the donation of grace is not enough, but we must also believe it is remitted. Eleventh.—You should on no account trust you are absolved on account of your contrition, but because of the words of Christ: "Whatsoever thou shalt loose." Hence, I say, trust, if you obtain the priest's absolution, and believe strongly you are absolved, and you will be truly absolved, no matter about contrition. Twelfth.—If by impossibility you should confess without contrition, or the priest should absolve you only in joke, and you, nevertheless, believe you are absolved, you are most certainly absolved. Thirteenth.—In the Sacraments of Penance and the Remission of Sins, the Pope or bishop does no more than the lowest priest—nay, if a priest cannot be had, any Christian, even woman or child, has the same power. Fourteenth.—No one ought to answer a priest that he is contrite, nor ought a priest to ask such a question. Fifteenth.—They are in great error who approach the Sacrament of the Eucharist with trust, because they have confessed, are not conscious to themselves of any mortal sins, have said the prayers and preparations for Communion—all these eat and drink unto themselves judgment; but if they believe and trust, they will then obtain grace: this faith alone makes them pure and worthy. Sixteenth.—It seems advisable that the Church, in a General Council, should declare that the laity should communicate under both kinds, and the Bohemians who do so are not heretics but schismatics. Seventeenth.—The treasures of the Church, from which the Pope grants indulgences, are not the merits of Christ or his saints. Eighteenth.—Indulgences are pious frauds of the faithful, and remission of good works, and are of the number of those things that are lawful, but not expedient. Nineteenth.—Indulgences are of no value to those who truly obtain them for the remission of the punishment due to the Divine justice for their actual sins. Twentieth.—They are seduced who believe indulgences are salutary and useful for the fruit of the spirit. Twenty-first.—Indulgences are necessary only for public crimes, and should be granted only to the hardened and impatient. Twenty-second.—

For six classes of persons indulgences are neither useful nor necessary—to wit, the dead, those on the point of death, the sick, those who are lawfully impeded, those who have not committed crimes, those who have committed crimes, but not public ones, and those who mend their lives. Twenty-third.—Excommunications are merely external penalties, and do not deprive a man of the common spiritual prayers of the Church. Twenty-fourth.—Christians should be taught rather to love excommunication than to fear it. Twenty-fifth.—The Roman Pontiff, the successor of Peter, is not the Vicar of Christ instituted by Christ himself in St. Peter, Vicar over all the Churches of the world. Twenty-sixth.—The word of Christ to St. Peter, "Whatsoever thou shalt loose upon earth," &c., extended but to what St. Peter himself alone had bound. Twenty-seventh. —It is not certainly in the power of the Pope or the Church by any means to lay down articles of faith nor laws of morals, nor good works. Twenty-eighth.—If the Pope with a great part of the Church should think so and so, although not in error, it is, nevertheless, neither sin nor heresy to think the contrary, especially in a matter not necessary to salvation, until by a General Council one thing is rejected and the other approved. Twenty-ninth.—We have a way open to us for weakening the authority of Councils, and freely contradicting their acts, and judging their decrees, by freely confessing whatever appears true, no matter whether approved or condemned by any Council. Thirtieth.—Some of the articles of John Huss, condemned in the Council of Constance, are most Christian, most true, and most evangelical, such as not even the universal Church could condemn. Thirty-first.—The just man sins in every good work. Thirty-second.—A good work, be it never so well performed, is a venial sin. Thirty-third.—It is against the will of the spirit to burn heretics. Thirty-fourth.—To fight against the Turks is to oppose the will of God, who punishes our iniquities through them. Thirty-fifth.—No man can be certain that he is not in a constant state of mortal sin on account of the most hidden vice of pride. Thirty-sixth.—Free will after sin is a matter of name alone, and while one does what is in him he sins mortally. Thirty-seventh.—Purgatory cannot be proved from the Holy Scriptures contained in the Canon of Scripture. Thirty-eighth.—The souls in purgatory are not sure of their salvation—at least all of them; nor is it proved by reason or Scripture that they are beyond the state of merit or of increasing charity. Thirty-ninth.—The souls in purgatory continually sin, as long as they seek relief and dread their punishment. Fortieth.—Souls freed from purgatory by the suffrages of the living, enjoy a less share of beatitude than if they satisfied the Divine justice themselves. Forty-first.—Ecclesiastical prelates and secular princes would do no wrong if they abolished the medicant orders.

27. Besides the errors here enumerated and condemned by the

Bull, there are many others mentioned and enumerated by Noel Alexander, and Cardinal Gotti (2), extracted from various works of Luther, as from the treatise " De Indulgentiis," " De Reformatione," " Respon. ad lib. Catharini," " De Captivitate Babilonica," "Contra Latomum," " De Missa privata," "Contra Episc. Ordinem," " Contra Henricum VIII. Regem," " Novi Testamenti Translatio," " De Formula Missæ et Communionis," " Ad Waldenses, &c.," " Contra Carlostadium," " De Servo arbitro," " Contra Anabaptistas," and other works, printed in Wittemberg, in several volumes. Here are some of his most remarkable errors: First.—A priest, though he does it in mockery or in jest, still both validly baptizes and absolves. Second.—It is a foul error for any one to imagine he can make satisfaction for his sins, which God gratuitously pardons. Three.—Baptism does not take away all sin. Fourth.—Led astray by wicked doctors, we think we are free from sin, by baptism and contrition; also that good works are available for increasing merit, and satisfying for sin. Fifth.—Those who have made it a precept, obliging under mortal sin to communicate at Easter, have sinned grievously themselves. Sixth.—It is not God, but the Pope, who commands auricular confession to a priest. Whoever wishes to receive the Holy Sacrament, should receive it entire (that is under both kinds), or abstain from it altogether. Seventh.—The right of interpreting Scriptures is equal in the laity as in the learned. Eighth.—The Roman Church in the time of St. Gregory was not above other churches. Ninth.—God commands impossibilities to man. Tenth.—God requires supreme perfection from every Christian. Eleventh.—There are no such things as Evangelical Counsels; they are all precepts. Twelfth.—We should give greater faith to a layman, having the authority of Scripture, than to a Pope, a Council, or even to the Church. Thirteenth.—Peter was not the Prince of the Apostles. Fourteenth.—The Pope is the Vicar of Christ by human right alone. Fifteenth.—A sin is venial, not by its own nature, but by the mercy of God. Sixteenth.—I believe a Council and the Church never err in matters of Faith, but as to the rest, it is not necessary they should be infallible. Seventeenth.—The primacy of the Roman Pontiff is not of Divine right. Eighteenth.—There are not Seven Sacraments, and for the present there should only be established Baptism, Penance, and the Bread. Nineteenth.—We can believe, without heresy, that real bread is present on the altar. Twentieth.—The Gospel does not permit the Mass to be a sacrifice. Twenty-first.—The Mass is nothing else but the words of Christ: " Take and eat, &c.," the promise of Christ. Twenty-second.—It is a dangerous error to call Penance, and believe it to be, the plank after shipwreck. Twenty-third.—It is impious to assert that the sacraments are efficacious signs of

(2) Nat. Alex. *t.* 19, *art.* 11, *sec.* 2; Gotti, *c.* 108, *sec.* 4; Tournelly, Comp. Thol. *t.* 5, *p.* 1, *diss.* 5, *art.* 2.

grace, unless we should say that when there is undoubted faith, they confer grace. Twenty-fourth.—All vows, both of religious orders and of good works, should be abolished. Twenty-fifth.—It is sufficient for a brother to confess to a brother, for to all Christians that were, has been addressed: " Whatsoever ye shall bind on earth." Twenty-sixth.—Bishops have not the right of reserving cases. Twenty-seventh.—A change of life is true satisfaction. Twenty-eighth.—There is no reason why Confirmation should be reckoned among the sacraments. Twenty-ninth.—Matrimony is not a sacrament. Thirtieth.—Impediments of spiritual affinity, of crime, and of order, are but human comments. Thirty-first.—The Sacrament of Orders was invented by the Pope's Church. Thirty-second.—The Council of Constance erred, and many things were rashly determined on, such as, that the Divine essence neither generates nor is generated, that the soul is the substantial form of the human body. Thirty-third.—All Christians are priests, and have the same power in the words and sacraments. Thirty-fourth.—Extreme Unction is not a sacrament; there are only two sacraments, Baptism and the Bread. Thirty-fifth.—The Sacrament of Penance is nothing also, but a way and return to Baptism. Thirty-sixth.—Antecedent grace is that movement which is made in us without us, not without our active and vital concurrence (as a stone which is merely passive to physical acts), but without our free and indifferent action. It was thus Luther explained efficacious grace, and on this he founded his system, that the will of a man, both for good and evil, is operated upon by necessity; saying, that by grace a necessity is induced into the will, not by coaction, for the will acts spontaneously, but by necessity; and in another place, he says, that by sin the will has lost its liberty, not that liberty which theologians call *a coactione*, but *a necessitate*, it has lost its indifference.

28. In his book on the Sacrifice of the Mass, we may perceive how remorse torments him. " How often," he says, " has my heart beat, reprehending me—Are you always wise? Do all others err? Have so many centuries passed in ignorance? How will it be if you are in error, and you lead so many along with you to damnation? But at length Christ (the devil he should have said) confirmed me."

29. In the year 1522, Henry VIII. wrote a book in defence of the Seven Sacraments. Luther, answering him, calls him a fool, says he will trample on the crowned blasphemer, and that his own doctrines are from heaven. In the same year he published his German translation of the New Testament, in which learned Catholics discover a thousand errors; he rejects altogether the Epistle of St. Paul to the Hebrews, the Epistles of St. James and St. Jude, and the Apocalypse; he made many changes after the first edition, no less than thirty-three in the Gospel of St. Matthew alone. In the words of St. Paul, *chap.* iii. *v.* 3, " For we account a man to be justified by

Faith without the works of the law," he adds the word *alone*, " by Faith alone." In the Diet of Augsburg, some one said to him, that the Catholics spoke very loudly of this interpretation, when he made that arrogant answer: " If your Papist prattles any more about this word *alone*, tell him that Doctor Martin Luther wishes it to be so; sic volo, sic jubeo, sit pro ratione voluntas—I wish so, I order so, let my will be sufficient reason for it."

30. In the year 1523 he composed his book, " De Formula Missæ et Communionis;" he abolished the Introits of the Sundays, all the festivals of saints, with the exception of the Purification and Annunciation of the Blessed Virgin; he retained the Kyrie, the Gloria, and *one* Collect, the Epistle, the Gospel, and the Nicene Creed, but all in the vulgar tongue; he then passed on to the Preface, omitting all the rest; he then says: " Who, the day before he suffered," &c, as in the Catholic Sacrifice of the Mass, but the words of the Consecration are chaunted as loud as the Pater Noster, that they may be heard by the people. After the Consecration, the Sanctus is sung, and the Benedictus qui venit said; the bread and the chalice is elevated immediately after the Pater Noster is said, without any other prayer, then the Pax Domini, &c. The Communion follows, and while that is going on, the Agnus Dei is sung; he approves of the Orationes Domine Jesu, &c., and Corpus D. N. J. C. custodiat, &c. He allows the Communion to be sung, but in place of the last Collect, chaunts the prayer, Quod ore sumpsimus, &c., and instead of the Ita Missa est, says Benedicamus Domine. He gives the chalice to all, permits the use of vestments, but without any blessing, and prohibits private Masses. To prepare for Communion, he says confession may be permitted as useful, but it is not necessary. He allows Matins to be said, with three lessons, the Hours, Vespers, and Complin.

31. In the year 1525, Carlostad attacked the doctrine of the Real Presence of Christ in the Holy Sacrament, saying that the word *this* did not refer to the bread, but to the body of Christ crucified. Luther opposed him in his book, " Contra Prophetas seu Fanaticos;" in this he first speaks of images, and says that in the law of Moses it was images of the Deity alone which were prohibited; he before admitted the images of the saints and the cross. Speaking of the Sacrament he says, by the word *hoc, this*, the bread is pointed out, and that Christ is truly and carnally in the supper. The bread and the body are united in the bread, and (speaking of the Incarnation) as man is God, so the bread is called his body and the body bread. Thus Luther falsely constitutes a second hypostatic union between the bread and the body of Christ. Hospinian quotes a sermon Luther preached against the Sacramentarians, where, speaking of the peace they wished to have established, if the Lutherans would grant them the liberty to deny the Real Presence, he says: " Cursed be such concord which tears asunder and despises the Church." He

then derides their false interpretation of the words, "This is my body." He commences with Zuinglius, who says the word *is* is the same as *signifies*. " We have the Scripture," says Luther, " which says, This *is* my body; but is there any place in the Scriptures where it is written, This *signifies* my body." He then ridicules the interpretation of the others. " Carlostad," he says, " distorts the word *this;* Ecolampadius tortures the word *body;* others transpose the word *this;* and say, my body which shall be delivered for you is *this;* others say, *that* which is given for you, *this* is my body; others maintain the text, this is my body, for my commemoration; and others again say, this is not an article of Faith." Returning, then, on Ecolampadius, who said it was blasphemous to assert that God was kneaded, baked, and made of bread, he retorts: " It would also, I suppose, be blasphemous to say God was made man, that it was most insulting to the Divine Majesty to be crucified by wicked men, and concludes by saying: " The Sacramentarians prepare the way for denial of all the articles of Faith, and they already begin to believe nothing." Speaking of Transubstantiation, he says: " It makes but little difference for any one to believe the bread to remain or not to remain in the Eucharist, if he believe in Transubstantiation." In an agreement made with Bucer, at Wittemberg, in 1526, he granted that the body and blood of Christ remained in the Sacrament only while it was received.

SEC. IV.—THE DISCIPLES OF LUTHER.

32. Melancthon and his Character. 33. His Faith, and the Augsburg Confession composed by him. 34. Matthias Flaccus, Author of the Centuries 35. John Agricola, Chief of the Antinomians; Atheists. 36. Andrew Osiander, Francis Stancaro, and Andrew Musculus. 37. John Brenzius, Chief of the Ubiquists. 38. Gaspar Sneckenfield abhorred even by Luther for his Impiety. 39. Martin Chemnitz, the Prince of Protestant Theologians, and Opponent of the Council of Trent.

32. PHILIP MELANCTHON, Luther's chief and best beloved disciple, was a German, born in Britten, in the Palatinate, of a very poor family, in the year 1497. He was a man of profound learning, and, at the age of twenty-four, was appointed one of the professors of Wittemberg by the Duke of Saxony. There he became imbued with Lutheran opinions, but as he was a man of the greatest mildness of manner, and so opposed to strife that he never spoke a harsh word against any one, he was anxious to bring about a union between all the religions of Germany; and on that account in many points smoothened down the harsh doctrines of Luther, and frequently, in writing to his friends, as Bossuet, in his History of the Variations, tells us, he complained that Luther was going too far. He was a man of great genius, but undecided in his opinions, and so fond of indifference that his disciples formed themselves into a sect called Indifferentists, or Adiaphorists. The famous Confession

of Augsburg was drawn up by him at the Diet, and his followers were on that account sometimes called Confessionists (1).

33. He divided his Confession into twenty-one articles, and stated his opinions with such moderation, that Luther afterwards complained that Philip, in endeavouring to smoothen down his doctrine, destroyed it (2). He admitted the liberty of human will, rejected the opinion of Luther, that God is the author of sin, and approved of the Mass. All these points were opposed to Luther's system. He was at length so tired with the way matters went on among the Reformers, that he intended to leave them altogether, and retire into Poland, there to wait the decision of the Council, whatever it should be (3). His opinions were very unsteady regarding matters of Faith; thus, he says, man can be justified by Faith alone; and his rival, Osiander, says he changed his mind fourteen times on this one subject. He was selected to arrange a treaty of peace with the Sacramentarians, but notwithstanding all his endeavours he never could succeed (4). Gotti, quoting Cochleus (5), says, that with all his anxiety to smoothen down any harsh points in the system, he only threw oil and not water on the flames. He died in Wittemberg in 1556, according to Van Ranst, or in 1560, according to Gotti, at the age of sixty-one. Many authors relate that, being at the point of death, his mother said to him: "My son, I was a Catholic; you have caused me to forsake that Faith; you are now about to appear before God, and tell me truly, I charge you, which is the better Faith, the Catholic or the Lutheran?" He answered: "The Lutheran is an easier religion, but the Catholic is more secure for salvation" (6). Berti relates (7) that he himself composed his own epitaph, as follows:—

"Iste brevis tumulus miseri tenet ossa Philippi,
Qui qualis fuerit nescio, talis erat."

These are not the words of Faith, and would imply that he much doubted of his eternal salvation.

34. Matthias Flaccus Illiricus, born in Albona in Istria, had the misfortune to study in Wittemberg, under Luther, and became afterwards the Chief of the Rigid Lutherans. He was the principal of the compilers of the Centuries of Magdeburg, an Ecclesiastical History, published in 1560, and to refute which Cardinal Baronius published his celebrated Annals Flaccus died in Frankfort, in 1575, at the age of fifty-five. He disagreed in many things with Luther. Striger (8) sustained an erroneous opinion, bordering on Pelagianism, that original sin was but a slight accident, which did not substantially corrupt the whole human race;

(1) Nat. Alex. t. 19, a. 11; s. 3, n. 4; Gotti, Ver. Rel. s. 109, sec. 3; Van Ranst, p. 308; Hermant, c. 241. (2) Hermant, loc. cit. (3) Varillas Hist. 20, 2, l. 24, p. 363. (4) Varillas, s. 1, l. 8, p. 364. (5) Gotti, loc. cit. n. 2. (6) Floremund. l. 2, c. 9; Van Ranst, & Gotti, loc. cit.; & Nat. Alex. loc. cit. n. 10. (7) Berti, H.st. sec. 16, c. 3. (8) Ap. Spondam. ad an. 1560, n. 32.

and Flaccus, on the contrary, renewing the blasphemous errors of the Manicheans, said that original sin was the substance itself of man, which deprived him of free will, and of every good movement, and drove him necessarily on to evil, from which faith in Jesus Christ alone could save him. On that account, he denied the necessity of good works for salvation, and his followers were called Substantialists (9).

35. John Agricola was a townsman of Luther, and was for a time his disciple, but became afterwards the founder of a sect, called Antinomians, or Law Opposers, for he rejected all authority of law, and taught that you may become a sensualist, a thief, a robber, but if you believe you will be saved (10). Varillas says that Luther brought the errors of Agricola before the University of Wittemberg, as subversive of all the value of good works, and, on their condemnation, he retracted them; but after Luther's death he went to Berlin, and again commenced teaching his blasphemies, where he died, without any sign of repentance, at the age of seventy-four (11). Florimundus calls the Antinomians Atheists, who believe in neither God nor the devil.

36. Andrew Osiander was the son of a smith in the Mark of Brandenburg. He taught that Christ was the justifier of mankind, not according to the human, but according to the Divine nature (12); and opposed to him was Francis Stancaro, of Mantua, who taught that Christ saved man by the human nature, not by the Divine nature (13). Thus Osiander taught the errors of Eutyches, and Stancaro those of Nestorius (14). In answer to the first, we have to remark that, although it is God that justifies, still he wishes to avail himself of the humanity of Christ (which was alone capable of suffering and making atonement), as of an instrument for the salvation of mankind. The Passion of Christ, says St. Thomas (15), is the cause of our justification, not, indeed, as a principal agent, but as an instrument, inasmuch as the humanity is the instrument of his Divinity, and hence the Council of Trent has declared (*Sess.* 6, *Cap.* 7) the efficient cause of this justification is God—the meritorious cause is Jesus Christ, who, on the wood of the Cross, merited for us justification (16), and satisfied for us to God the Father. In answer to Stancaro, who teaches that Christ saved mankind, as man alone, but not as God, we have but to consider what is already said, because if Christ, according to the flesh, deserved for man the grace of salvation, nevertheless, it was the Divinity, and not

(9) Gotti, c. 109, *sec.* 7, *n.* 1, 2; Van Ranst, *p.* 310; Varillas, *t.* 1, *l.* 17, *p.* 122, & *t.* 2, *l.* 24, *p.* 363; Nat. Alex. *t.* 19, *a.* 11, *sec.* 3, *n.* 10. (10) Nat. Alex. *t.* 19, *a.* 11, *sec.* 3, *n.* 7; Gotti, c. 109, *sec.* 5, *n.* 7; Van Ranst, *p.* 310. (11) Varillas, *t.* 1, *l.* 11, *p.* 512. (12) Remund. in Synopsi, *l.* 2, *c.* 16. (13) Gotti, loc. cit. *sec.* 6, *n.* 1 ad 6; N. Alex. loc. cit. *n.* 8; Van Ranst, cit. *p.* 310. (14) Gotti, *sec.* 7, *n.* 8; Van Ranst, loc. cit.; Nat. Alex. loc. cit. *n.* 11. (15) St. Thomas, *p.* 3, *q.* 64, *ar.* 1. (16) Gotti, *sec.* 7, *n.* 8; Van Ranst, *p.* 310.

the humanity, which granted this grace to man. Andrew Musculus, of Lorraine, opposed both Osiander and Stancaro, but with just as great a heresy, for he taught that the Divine nature of Christ, as well as the human nature, died on the Cross. This was nothing else but the blasphemy of Eutyches, that the Divinity suffered for the salvation of mankind (17). Remund (18) tells us, that at that period new churches were every day forming in every corner of Germany, and changing as quickly as the moon, and that two hundred sects existed at one time among the Reformers. No wonder that Duke George of Saxony said that the people of Wittemberg could not tell to-day what their faith would be to-morrow.

37. John Brenzius, a Suabian, and Canon of Wittemberg, was already a priest, when he became the disciple of Luther, and imitated his master in taking a wife. He taught that the concupiscence which remains in the soul after Baptism is a sin, contrary to the Council of Trent, which declares that the Catholic Church never understood that concupiscence should be called a sin, but that it is from sin, and inclines to sin. He also said that the body of Christ, by the personal union with the Word, is everywhere, and, consequently, that Jesus Christ is in the Host before consecration; and, explaining the words, "This is my body," he says that denotes that the body of Christ is already present. Hence the sect who acknowledged him as their chief was called Ubiquists (19), and even Luther was one of his adherents (20).

38. Gaspar Schwenkfeldt, a noble Silesian, and a man of learning, while Luther was attacking the Church, took up arms also against her, and attacked the Lutherans as well. We should not mind the Scriptures, he says, as they are not the word of God, only a dead letter, and, therefore, should only obey the private inspirations of the Holy Ghost; he condemns sermons and spiritual lectures, for, in the Gospel of St. Matthew, we are told that we have but one Master, and he is in heaven. He taught, at the same time, the errors of the Manicheans, of Sabellius, of Photius, and also of Zuinglius, denying the Real Presence of Christ in the Eucharist. Osius says the devil's gospel commenced with Luther, but was brought to perfection by this monster of hell, who had more followers in many parts of Germany and Switzerland than the arch-heretic himself (21). Gotti informs us, that he sent a messenger to Luther, with his writings, begging of him to correct them; but he, seeing them filled with abominable heresies, returned him the following answer: " May your spirit, and all those who participate with Sacramentarians and Eutychians, fall into perdi-

---

(17) Gotti, loc. cit. sec. 6.   (18) Remund. in Synopsi, *l.* 2, *c.* 14, *n.* 2.   (19) Nat. Alex. *t.* 1, *sec.* 3, *n.* 8, 9; Gotti, *sec.* 6, *n.* 8 ad 10; Van Ranst, *p.* 293.   (20) Bossuet, Istor. *l.* 2, *n.* 41.   (21) Gotti, *c.* 109, *sec.* 5, *n.* 6; Van Ranst, *p.* 311.

tion." After Luther's death, this sect increased somewhat; but in a Synod, held at Naumburg, in 1554, by Bucer, Melancthon, and some others, all the author's works were condemned (22).

39. Martin Chemnitz was a poor woolcomber's son, in the Mark of Brandenburg. He was born in 1522, and followed his father's business until the age of fourteen, when he commenced his studies in Wittemberg. His Theological Professor was Melancthon, who was so well satisfied with the progress he made, that he called him the Prince of Protestant Theologians. He taught Theology in Brunswick, for thirty years, and died in 1586, the sixty-fourth year of his age. Chemnitz laboured strenuously along with Bucer, to bring about an agreement between the Lutherans and Sacramentarians, but without effect. He published many works, but his principal one is the " Examen Con. Tridentini," in which he endeavours to upset the decisions of the Council. He does not admit, as Canonical, any books of Scripture only those approved of by all the Churches, not those approved of by Councils alone; he praises the Greek and Hebrew text, and rejects the Vulgate wherever it disagrees with them; he rejects tradition, but believes in free will, and thinks that, with the assistance of grace, it can accomplish something good. He says that man is justified by Faith alone, through medium of which the merits of Christ are applied to him, and that good works are necessary to salvation, but still have no merit. Baptism and the Eucharist, he says, are properly the only sacraments—the rest are but pious rites; and in the Eucharist he rejects both the Transubstantiation of the Catholics, and the Impanation of the Lutherans, but does not decide whether the body of Christ is really present in the bread and wine; he merely says it is not a carnal presence, that Christ is there alone in the actual use of the Communion and that it must always be taken under both kinds. He admits that the Mass may be called a sacrifice, but not a true sacrifice, only under the general denomination of a good work. It is not necessary, he says, speaking of the sacrament of Penance, to confess all our sins, but he allows the absolution of the Minister, though not as coming from the Minister himself, but from Christ, through his promise. Purgatory, according to him, cannot be proved from Scripture. We should honour the saints, their images, and relics, but not have recourse to their intercession, and we should observe the Sundays, but no other festival (23).

(22) Gotti, loc. cit.   (23) Apud, Gotti, c. 109, sec. 7, n. 1 ad 7.

SEC. V.—THE ANABAPTISTS.

40. The Anabaptists; they refuse Baptism to Children. 41. Their Leaders—Seditions and Defeat. 42. Are again defeated under their Chief, Munzer, who is converted at his Death. 43. They rebel again under John of Leyden, who causes himself to be crowned King, is condemned to a cruel Death, and dies penitent. 44. Errors of the Anabaptists. 45. They are split into various Sects.

40. THE Anabaptists were likewise the spawn of Lutheranism. The chief doctrine of those heretics was, that children should not be baptized in infancy, as, not having come to the use of reason, they were incapable of real belief and salvation, according to the words of the Gospel: " He that believeth, and is baptized, shall be saved; he that believeth not shall be condemned" (Mark, xvi. 16); hence they were called Anabaptists, as they taught that those who were baptized in infancy should be re-baptized. Now this error sprung from Luther himself, who asserted it was better to leave infants without baptism than to baptize them when they had no Faith of their own (1). These unfortunate persons, however, should remember, that in the text of the Gospel quoted it is adults that are meant, who are capable of actual Faith, for infants, who are incapable of it, receive the grace of the Sacrament through the Faith of the Church in which they are baptized, and as, without any actual fault of theirs, they contract original sin, it is but just that they should receive the grace of Jesus Christ without actual Faith, for, as St. Augustin writes (2), as they are sick with the weight of another's sin, they are healed by another's confession, and are saved. Our Lord says in St. Matthew, xix. 14: " Suffer little children to come to me, for of such is the kingdom of heaven." As, therefore, little children can acquire the kingdom of heaven, so can they receive baptism, without which no one can enter into heaven. The Church has received it as a tradition from the Apostles, so says Origen (3), to give baptism to infants, and St. Irenæus, Tertullian, St. Gregory of Nazianzen, St. Ambrose, St. Cyprian, and St. Augustin, all bear witness to the same practice. Hence, the Council of Trent, anathematizing those who asserted that persons baptized before they came to the use of reason should be re-baptized, uses the following words: " If any one should say that children having received baptism should not be numbered among the faithful, because they have not actual Faith, and therefore when they come to the years of discretion, that they should be re-baptized, or that it is better to omit baptism than to baptize in the Faith of the Church alone those who have not actual Faith, let him be anathema."

---

(1) Gotti, Ver. Rel. t. 2, c. 110, sec. 1, n. 1.   (2) August. Serm. 176, alias 10, de Verb. Apost.   (3) Orig. t. 2, p. 35, St. Iren. p. 147, n. 4 ; Tertul. p. 231 ; St. Greg. Naz. t. 1, p. 658 ; St. Amb. t. 1, p. 849; St. Cypr. Epist. ad Fidum, n. 59 ; St. Aug. Serm. 10, de Verb. Apost. alias 177.

This Canon condemns most clearly both the Anabaptist and Lutheran heresies.

41. The chief of the Anabaptists was Nicholas Stork, or Storchius, sometimes also called Pelargus. He was at first a disciple of Luther, but soon the head of a new heresy, which he preached in 1522, saying it was revealed to him from heaven. Being banished from Wittemberg, he went to Thuringia, where, together with his first error, he preached many others, such as that all men enjoy universal freedom from restraint, that all property is common, and should be equally divided, and that all bishops, magistrates, and princes who opposed his true Church should be put to death (4). Here he was joined by Thomas Munzer, a priest, a follower of Luther, also, who pretended to lead a most mortified life, and boasted of having frequent ecstacies and extraordinary communications from the Deity. He abused the Pope for teaching too severe a doctrine, and Luther for promulgating too lax a one. He everywhere censured Luther's morals and conduct, accused him of debauchery and lasciviousness, and said it was impossible to believe God would make use of so wicked a man to reform his Church. Through Luther's influence, he and all his followers were banished from Saxony (5). He then went to Thuringia, and preached the same errors as Storchius, especially in Munster, teaching the country people that they should not obey either prelates or princes. In a short time he rallied round him the great body of the Anabaptists, and led forth three hundred thousand ignorant peasants (6), causing them to forsake their spades for the sword, and promising them the assistance of God in their battles. These poor deluded creatures at first did a great deal of harm, but when regular troops were brought against them, they were soon, notwithstanding their immense numbers, completely routed, not being trained to the use of arms. Those who escaped the slaughter marched towards Lorrain, with the intention of devastating that province; but the Count Claude of Guise, brother to the Duke of Lorrain, slaughtered twenty thousand of them in three victories which he gained (7). Sleidan (8) says that these poor peasants, when they were attacked by the troops, appeared quite demented, and neither defended themselves nor fled, but began to sing a popular hymn, imploring the assistance of the Holy Ghost, whose protection, according to Munzer's promises, they expected.

44. In the meantime, while Munzer, with his Anabaptist followers, were ravaging Thuringia, they were encountered by an army commanded by Duke George of Saxony, who promised them peace if they laid down their arms; but Munzer, thinking himself lost if the conditions were accepted, encouraged them to refuse all

---

(4) Nat. Alex. *t.* 18, *art.* 11, *sec.* 12; Gotti, loc. cit. *n.* 2. *p.* 266. (6) Varillas, *p.* 270; Hermant, Hist. *t.* 2, *c.* 239. Varill. *p.* 267. (8) Ap. Gotti, ibid. *n.* 7, ex Sleidan, *l.* 5.

(5) Varillas, *t.* 1, *l.* 6, (7) Hermant, loc. cit. ;

accommodation, and to kill the officer who bore a flag of truce to them. This treachery infuriated the soldiers, who immediately attacked them; they made a stout resistance at first, encouraged by Munzer, who told them he would catch the balls of the enemy in his sleeve, and such was the effect this promise had on them, that many of them stood firm before the cannon of the enemy. This did not, however, last long; the greater part fled, and the rest were taken prisoners. Munzer fled with the rest, and, without being recognized, hid himself in Franchausen, pretending to be sick; he was there discovered, taken and condemned, along with Pfeiffer, an apostate Premonstratensian Canon, to have his head cut off in Mulhausen. This war lasted five months, and it is said cost the lives of a hundred and thirty-five thousand peasants (9). Pfeiffer died an obstinate heretic. Munzer's death is related in different ways—some say he died with the greatest boldness, and challenged the Judges and Princes, telling them to read the Bible, the word of God; and these were his last words. But the more general opinion is, and Noel Alexander says it can be relied on as fact, that previous to his death he retracted his errors, confessed to a priest, received the Viaticum, and after offering up some devout prayers, bared his neck to the executioner's sword (10).

45. Munzer's death, and the slaughter of so many of the peasantry, did not put an end to this sect. In the year 1534, nearly nine years after his death, a number of people in Westphalia rebelled against their Princes, and seized the city of Munster, when they elected, as their chief, John of Leyden, the son of a Dutch tailor. His first act was to banish the bishop and all the Catholics of the city, and then pretending to have a revelation from heaven, he caused his followers to crown him King, saying he was elected to that dignity by God himself, and he called himself Rex Justitiæ hujus Mundi; he preached polygamy, and put it in practice by marrying sixteen wives, at the same time; he rejected the Eucharist, but, sitting at a table, distributed bits of bread to his followers, saying: " Take, and eat, and ye shall announce the death of the Lord ;" and at the same time the Queen, that is, one of his wives, dispensed the chalice, saying: " Drink, and you shall announce the death of the Lord." He next selected twenty disciples, and sent them as Apostles of God, to preach his doctrine, but all these unfortunates were taken and condemned to death, along with himself, in the year 1535 (11). The mercy of the Lord be praised for ever, since he extended it to John of Leyden; he shewed himself a sincere penitent, and bore, with the most admirable patience, the cruel death and torments inflicted on him; he was three times tortured

(9) Nat. Alex. *t.* 29, *cit. sec.* 12, Gotti, *cit. cap.* 110, *sec.* 1, *n.* 7. (10) Nat. Alex. loc. cit.; Gotti, *n.* 8; Varill. *p.* 288; Van Ranst, *sec.* 16, *p.* 313; Hermant, *c.* 239. (11) N. Alex. cit. *a.* 12, *n.* 2; Varill. *p.* 427; V. Ranst, p. 315; Her. *t.* 241.

with pincers by two executioners for two hours, and he bore it all without a murmur, saying he deserved it for his sins, and imploring the Divine Mercy; his companions died in their obstinacy (12), and Hermant says, that his sect has spread its roots into many Christian kingdoms (13).

46. The errors of the Anabaptists were: First.—That children should not be baptized, but only adults capable of reason. Second.—That no Christian could be a civil magistrate. Third.—It is in no case lawful for Christians to swear. Fourth.—War is unlawful to Christians.

47. The Anabaptists soon split into several sects—some say fourteen, some, even seventy. Some were called Munzerites, after Thomas Munzer; some who preferred voluntary poverty, Huttites, from John Hut; others, Augustins, from Augustin Boehem, who taught that heaven would not be opened till after the day of judgment; others, Buholdians, from John (Buhold) of Leyden, whose history we have just given—these preached polygamy, and wished to destroy all the wicked; some Melchiorists, from Melchior Hoffman, who taught that Christ had but one nature, that he was not born of Mary, and various other errors; some were called Mennonites, from Mennon—these held heretical opinions regarding the Trinity; some Davidians, the followers of one George, who called himself the Third David, the true Messiah, the beloved Son of God, born of the Spirit, not of the flesh, the pardoner of sins; he died in 1556, and promised to rise again in three years. This vain prophecy had some truth in it, for three years afterwards, the Senate of Basle caused him to be disinterred, and his remains burned along with his writings. The Clancularists, when asked if they were Anabaptists, denied it; they had no churches, but preached in private houses and gardens. The Demonists, following the errors of Origen, said the devils would be saved in the end of the world. The Adamites appeared naked in public, having, as they asserted, recovered the pristine innocence of Adam. The Servetians, followers of Michael Servetus, joined to the errors of the Anabaptists blasphemies against the Trinity and Jesus Christ. The Condormientes slept together without distinction of sex, and called this indecency the new Christian Charity. The Ejulants, or Weepers, said there was no devotion so pleasing to God as weeping and wailing. Noel Alexander and Van Ranst enumerate many other classes of these fanatics (14).

(12) Varill. *p.* 436. (13) Her. loc. cit.; V. Ranst, *p.* 314. (14) Nat. Alex. *t.* 19, *art.* 11, *n.* 4; Van Ranst, *p.* 315, & seq.

ARTICLE II.

THE SACRAMENTARIANS.

SEC. I.—CARLOSTAD.

48. Carlostad, Father of the Sacramentarians. 49. He is reduced to live by his Labour in the Field; he gets married, and composed a Mass on that Subject. 53. He dies suddenly.

48. THE father of the Sacramentarians was, as Van Ranst informs us, Andrew Carlostad; he was born in the village from which he took his name, in Franconia, and was Archdeacon of the church of Wittemberg. He was, it is said, the most learned man in Saxony, and was, on that account, a great favourite with the Elector Frederick; he it was who admitted Luther to the Doctorship, and afterwards became his follower in heresy. His pride, however, would not allow him to remain a disciple of Luther, and thus he became chief of the Sacramentarians, teaching, in opposition to Luther, that Christ was not really present in the Eucharist, and, therefore, that the word *this* (this is my body) did not refer to the bread, but to Christ himself, who was about to sacrifice his body for us, as if he were to say: "This is my body which I am about to deliver up for you." Another error he taught in opposition to Luther, was the doctrine of the Iconoclasts, that all crucifixes and images of the saints should be destroyed, and he carried his infidelity to such a pitch in Wittemberg that he abolished the Mass, trampled on the consecrated Host, and broke the altars and images (1). When this came to Luther's ears, who was then concealed in his Patmos of Watzberg, he could restrain himself no longer, and even against the will of the Elector, went to Wittemberg, and caused the altars and images to be restored; and not being able to convince Carlostad of his errors, he deprived him of his benefices and dignities by authority of the Elector, who had him seized, and banished from his territories along with the woman he married. Carlostad went to Orlemond in Thuringia, and there wrote that wicked treatise, De Cœna Domini (2), which contains in full his heretical opinions. It happened one day, as Berti tells us (3), that Luther came to this town, and Carlostad, in revenge for the treatment he received from him, caused him to be pelted with stones, and to fly from the place. It may be as well here to give Bossuet's account of the war between Luther and Carlostad: In the year 1524, Luther preached in Jena, in presence of Carlostad, who went to visit him after the sermon, and blamed him for the

(1) Nat. Alex. *t.* 19, *s.* 3; Gotti, Ver. Rel. c. 109, *s.* 1; Van Ranst, *s.* 16, *p.* 217; Hermant, *t.* 1, *c.* 231; Varillas, *t.* 1, *l.* 3, *p.* 148.   (2) Hermant, *c.* 234; Gotti, *s.* 1, *n.* 2; Varillas, *t.* 1, *l.* 3, *p.* 211.   (3) Berti, Brev. Hist. *s.* 3.

opinion he held regarding the Real Presence. Luther, in a tone of mockery, told him he would give him a gold florin if he would write against him, and took out a florin and handed it to Carlostad, who pocketed it, and they then drank together to cement the bargain; thus the war commenced. Carlostad's parting benediction to Luther was: " May I see you broken on the wheel!" " And may you break your neck before you quit the town!" rejoined Luther. Behold, says Bossuet, the acts of the new apostles of the Gospel (4).

48. Notwithstanding all that had passed, Carlostad's friends interfered, and finally induced Luther to permit him to return to Wittemberg, but he agreed to this only on condition that he would not oppose his doctrine for the future. Carlostad, however, ashamed to appear in Wittemberg in the poor state he was reduced to, chose rather to live in another town, where he was reduced to such poverty, that he was obliged to become a porter, and afterwards to turn to field labour along with his wife for subsistence (8). We may here remark, that Carlostad was the first of all the priests of the new Gospel who married. In the year 1525, he married a young lady of good family, and he composed a sacrilegious service of Mass, on the occasion of his abominable nuptials. Octavius Lavert and Raynaldus have preserved some parts of it* (6).

50. The just chastisement of God, however, always pursues the impious, and thus we see him and his wife, who, being a lady, was ashamed to beg, obliged to earn a scanty subsistence, which they could not always obtain, by working as common field labourers (7). Some time afterwards he went to Switzerland, hoping to get a kind reception from the heretics of that country, whose doctrine regarding the Sacrament of the Altar coincided with his own. But Zuinglius or Zuingle, wishing to have no competitor, gave him a very cool reception; he then went to Basle, where he was appointed preacher, and where a sudden death overtook him in the midst of his sins (8). Varillas says, that he was seized with apoplexy, coming down from the pulpit, after declaiming against the Real Presence, and dropped dead (9). It was also told at the time, that whilst he was preaching a man of fearful mien appeared to him, and

(4) Bos. Stor. del Variaz. *l.* 2, *n.* 12. (5) Gotti, *c.* 109, *n.* 3, ex Cochleo, ad an. 15, 25; V. Ranst, *p.* 217; Var. 242. (6) Octavius Lavert. *p.* 117. (7) Rinal. *an.* 1523, *n.* 74. (8) Varillas, *l.* 8, *p.* 359. (9) Lancis. *t.* 4, Ist. *s.* 16, *c.* 3; Var. loc. cit.

---

* Deus qui post tam longam et impiam Sacerdotum tuorum cæcitatem Beatum Andream Carlostadium ea gratia donare dignatus es, ut primus, nulla habita Papistici Juris ratione, uxorem ducere ausus fuerit, da quæsumus ut omnes Sacerdotes recepta sana mente, ejus vestigia sequentes ejectis concubinis aut eisdem ductis ad legitimum consortium thori convertantur.
Oremus—Nos ergo concubinis nostris gravati, te Deus poscimus, ut illius, qui Patres nostros sectatus antiquos tibi placet, nos imitationem gaudeamus in æternum.

that immediately one of his children ran to him telling him that he had seen the same vision, and that it said to him: "Tell your father that in three days I will deprive him of life, breaking his head." All that is known for certain is that he died suddenly, and died, as he had lived, without any signs of repentance.

SEC. II.—ZUINGLIUS.

51. Zuinglius, and the Beginning of his Heresy. 52. His Errors. 53. Congress held before the Senate of Zurich; the Decree of the Senate rejected by the other Cantons. 54. Zuinglius sells his Canonry, and gets married; Victory of the Catholics; and his Death.

51. ULRIC ZUINGLIUS was born of an obscure family in a poor village of Switzerland, called Mildenhausen, some say in Moggi; he was at first parish priest of two rural parishes, and was afterwards promoted to a parish in Zurich (1). In his early days he was a soldier, but hoping to better his condition, he changed the sword for the gown, and being a man of talent, became a most eloquent preacher. Hearing, in 1519, that indulgences were to be published in Switzerland, as had been done in Germany, he hoped that would be a favourable occasion for him to acquire notoriety, and advance himself in the estimation of the Court of Rome. But in this he was disappointed; a Franciscan, Father Sampson, was sent by the Pope to publish the Swiss indulgences, and with power to prohibit any one else from doing so, unless with his permission. Zuinglius, seeing his hopes frustrated, imitated the example of Luther in Saxony, and began to preach, first, against indulgences—then against the power of the Pope—and from that passed on to other errors against the Faith (2).

52. The following were his principal tenets: First.—The Mass is not a sacrifice, but only a commemoration of the sacrifice once offered on the Cross. Second.—We have no necessity of any intercessor but Christ. Third.—Christ is our justificator; and here he deduced, that our works are no good as ours, but only as the works of Christ. Fourth.—Marriage is fitted for all. Fifth.—Those who make a vow of chastity are held by presumption. Sixth.—The power which the Pope and bishops arrogate to themselves has no foundation in Holy Writ. Seventh.—The confession made to a priest is not for remission of sin, but should be made solely to obtain advice. Eighth.—The Holy Scripture recognizes no Purgatory. Ninth.—The Scripture knows no other priests but those who announce the Word of God. He preached other errors regarding free will. Luther attributed everything to grace for salvation; Zuinglius, on the contrary, following the Pelagians, to free will and the force of nature. He broached many other errors regarding

(1) Nat. Alex. t. 19, sec. 16, art. 11, c. 3, n. 2; Gotti, Ver. Rel. c. 100, s. 2, n. 1; Varillas, t. 1, l. 4, p. 155. (2) Apud. Nat. Alex. s. 3, n. 2; Gotti, loc. cit. n. 1.

the sacraments, original sin, and other points, but his chief blasphemies were against the Holy Eucharist, which turned even Luther against him, who at first called him the strong champion of Christendom, but ended by calling him a heretic. He first said that the Eucharist was a remembrance of the passion of Christ, but, as Varillas remarks, then came the difficulty, that the Apostle says the Eucharist is to be eaten, but not the remembrance, and he five times changed his mode of explaining the communion; he rejected the Transubstantiation of the Catholics, the Impanation of the Lutherans, and the explanation given by Carlostad (*N.* 48). He then began to teach, that in the words, "This is my body," the word *is* has the same meaning as *signifies*, that is, this bread signifies the body of Christ; but still the difficulty was not solved, for he could nowhere find that the word *est* was used for *significat* (3), when one morning, at break of day, a spirit, whether a black or white one he does not remember, spoke to him, and said: "Ignorant man, read the twelfth chapter of Exodus, where it is said, For it is the phase, that is the passage, of the Lord." Behold, said he, here the word *is* stands for the word signifies; and thus he began to teach, that as the Pasch of the Jews was but a mere figure of the passing of the Lord, so the Eucharist was the figure of Christ sacrificed on the Cross. To authenticate this discovery of his, he got the translation of the New Testament printed, and where the text says, "This is my body," he inserted, this "signifies my body"(4). Nothing, however, can be more foolish than this argument, for in Exodus the explanation is annexed: This is the *Phase*, that is the *passage*, of the Lord; but surely the text of the Gospel does not give any explanation, that the words "this *is* my body," refer not to the body, but to the figure of Jesus Christ (5). This error we refute at length in the Confutation X., No. 11.

53. Zuinglius printed sixty-seven propositions, by way of doubt, and placarded them in all the towns of the diocese of Constance. The Dominicans preached against them as heretical, and offered to convince Zuinglius of his errors in a public disputation. Zuinglius accepted the challenge, but the Dominicans understood that it was to take place in the presence of the judges appointed by the Bishop of Constance, while he, on the other hand, insisted it should be held in presence of the Senate of Zurich, composed of two hundred laymen, the majority of whom knew not how to read or write; in this move he was successful, for the Senate thought themselves competent judges in religious matters, and would not yield their pretended right to any one; in effect, the Congress took place in their presence, and the bishop not being able to prevent it, sent his Vicar-General to try and bring matters to some rational arrangement.

---

(2) Zuinglius, *l.* de Subsid. Euch. (4) Hermant, *t.* 1, *c.* 237. (5) Gotti, loc. cit. *n.* 4; Varill. *l.* 7, *p.* 304; Nat. Alex. loc. cit.

This took place, according to Varillas, in 1524, and the Senate commanded all the ecclesiastics of Zurich to attend. Zuinglius first read his Theses, and explained them without meeting with any interruption; he then asked if any one had any reply to make; the Vicar-General answered, that a great deal of what he set forth was an absurdity. Zuinglius replied in his defence. The Vicar-General answered that he was sent by his bishop neither to dispute nor give decisions, that it was a Council alone should decide, and then was silent; the other ecclesiastics were asked if they had anything to say; they followed the Vicar-General's example, and were silent also; the Senate, therefore, gave the palm of victory to Zuinglius, and made a Decree, that thenceforward the pure Gospel (according to Zuinglius) should be preached in all Zurich, that no more notice should be taken of traditions, and that the Mass and the adoration of the Eucharist should be abolished (6). This decree was opposed by the other Cantons, and in the year 1526 another public disputation was held in Swiss Baden (7), between Zuinglius and Ecolampadius, on the one side, and Ecchius and some others, on the Catholic side, in which the arguments of Ecchius were so convincing, that by a formal Decree, the Swiss recognized the Real Presence of Christ in the Eucharist, the invocation of saints, and veneration of sacred images, and purgatory, and condemned the doctrine of Luther and Zuinglius.

54. In the year 1528, Zuinglius sold his prebend, and married, shamelessly asserting that he had not sufficient confidence in himself to resist the vice of incontinence (8), and in the same year the Canton of Berne united with Zurich in embracing his doctrine. Basle, Schaffhausen, St. Gall, and three others, soon followed this example; Lucerne, Switz, Zug, Uri, and Underwalden, remained Catholic, and were soon after obliged to go to war with the heretical cantons, for the following reason (9). The Catholic party deposed two officers who embraced the Zuinglian doctrines; they were received by the Zuinglians, who provided them with places, and through revenge, prevented the merchants who supplied the Catholic cantons with corn, as they do not produce enough for their own consumption, from passing through their territories. The Catholics complained of this, as an infraction of the Confederation League, but were told they were only treated as they deserved, for insulting the new religion. Eight thousand Catholics took the field in October, 1532; fifteen hundred of the Zurich troops were entrenched outside the city; the Catholics assaulted them in that position and put them to flight. Twenty thousand of the Zurich troops then marched out to attack the Catholics, and Zuinglius, against the advice of his friends, insisted on marching

(6) Varill. *t.* 1, *l.* 5, *p.* 214. (7) Gotti, *c.* 109, *s.* 2, *n.* 11. (8) Varill. *l.* 7, *p.* 304; Hermant. *c.* 237; Nat. Alex. *c.* 19, *art.* 12, *s.* 3, *n.* 2. (9) Varill. *l.* 8, *p.* 354; Gotti, loc. cit. *n.* 13.

at their head. The Catholics, with their small number, would have no chance against this army in the open field, so they posted themselves in a narrow pass; they were here assaulted by the Zuinglians, and victory was for some time doubtful, till Zuinglius, while valiantly leading on his troops, was struck to the earth; his followers, thinking he was killed, immediately took to flight, and were pursued by the Catholics with great slaughter, who are said to have killed five thousand Zuinglians, with only the loss of fifteen on their own side (10). Zuinglius was found by two Catholics, who did not know him, among a heap of the slain, prostrate on his face, but still breathing; they asked him if he wished for a confessor, but got no answer; another now came up, who immediately killed him, and told their commanders; by their orders he was quartered and burned, and some of his followers collected his ashes, and kept it as a relic (11). He was killed on the 11th of October, 1532, in the forty-fourth year of his age, according to Hermant, but Natalis, Gotti, and Van Ranst, say he was forty years old. The war was not yet ended; five other battles were fought, and the Catholics were always victorious; peace was at length concluded, on condition that each canton should freely profess its own religion, and thus, with few interruptions, it has continued to the present day (12). Before I dismiss this subject, I will mention a few words of a sermon, or letter, of his, to Francis I. of France, in which he speaks of the glory that Kings are to expect in heaven: "There," he says, " you will see the Redeemer and the redeemed; there you will behold Abel, Noe, Abraham, Isaac; there you will see Hercules, Theseus, Numa, the Catos, the Scipios, &c." This was the language of this new Church Reformer after his apostacy; he places, along with Christ and the holy patriarchs, in heaven, the idolaters, and the Pagan gods. Bossuet, in his History of the Variations (13), gives a large extract from this letter.

SEC. III.—ECOLAMPADIUS; BUCER; PETER MARTYR.

55. Ecolampadius. 56. Bucer. 57. Peter Martyr.

55. JOHN ECOLAMPADIUS, a faithful follower of Zuinglius, was a Greek linguist, and held the situation of tutor to the Prince Palatine's children; his friends injudiciously importuned him to become a monk, so he entered into the Order of St. Brigit, and made his profession (1); but we may judge of his intentions, when we are told that he said: " If I make six hundred vows, I will not observe one of them, unless I like it." " Why," says Florimund (2), " should we wonder at his leaving the cloister, when such were his sentiments on entering it? In a few years he laid aside the cowl, and

(10) Varill. *t.* 1, *l.* 4, *p.* 355.   (11) Nat. Alex. loc. cit.; Gotti, *n.* 13, & Van Ranst, *p.* 318.   (12) Varill. loc. cit. *p.* 358, & seq.   (13) Bossuet, Hist. de Variat. *l.* 2, *n.* 19.   (1) Nat. Alex. *t.* 19, *s.* 3, *n.* 3.   (2) Florimund in Synopsi. *l.* 2, *c.* 8, *n.* 9.

married, as he said, by the inspiration of the Holy Ghost, and became a follower of Zuinglius, who appointed him Superintendent of Basle (3). He followed Zuinglius's doctrine regarding the Real Presence, but not his explanation of *est* by *significat* (see *N.* 48), as he explained the text, " this is my body," by " this is the figure of my body" (4). How strange that not one of the new apostles of the Gospel could agree with the other! He died in the year 1532, at the age of forty-nine, only a month after Zuinglius's death, to him a source of the most poignant grief. Luther said he was found dead in his bed, strangled by the devil, a generally received opinion at that time, according to Noel Alexander; others say he died of an ulcer in the *os sacrum;* the general opinion, however, is, that he was found dead in his bed. Many writers, Varillas says (5), tell us that he several times attempted to take away his own life, and that he poisoned himself. Cardinal Gotti quotes others (6), who assert, that a short time previous to his death, he was heard to exclaim: " Alas, I shall soon be in hell;" and also that, just before his death, he said: " I, uncertain and fluctuating in the Faith, have to give an account before the Tribunal of God, and see whether my doctrine is true or false" (7). Foolish man, he had the Church, the pillar and the ground of truth, which condemned his doctrine, and he wished to have it tried at that Tribunal, where, if he found it false (as it was), there would be no remedy to ward off eternal perdition.

56. Martin Bucer was the son of a poor Jew in Strasbourg, who left him, at his death, on the world without any one to look to him, and only seven years of age. He was taken in by the Dominicans to serve Mass and assist the servants of the Convent; but finding him endowed with great talents, they gave him the habit of the Order, and put him to study (8). He soon became a great proficient in sacred and profane literature, and received Holy Orders, Cardinal Gotti says (9), without being baptized. He was so taken with Luther's doctrine on celibacy, that he apostatized, and not only married once, but three times successively, saying, that as a divorce was allowed to the Jews on account of the hardness of their hearts, it was also permitted to Christians of an extraordinary temperament (10). To the errors of Luther he added others: First.—That Baptism is necessary as a positive precept, but that it is not necessary for salvation. Second.—That there is no Church which does not err in morals and faith. Third.—That before we are justified by God we sin in every good work we do, but that after our justification the good we perform we do through necessity. Fourth.—That some are so formed by God for the marriage state, that they cannot be forbidden to marry. Fifth.—That usury is not contrary

(3) Gotti, loc. cit *n.* 15. (4) Gotti, *n.* 16, & Nat. Alex. loc. cit. (5) Varill. *l. 8,* p. 356. (6) Gotti, *n.* 17. (7) Gotti, *c.* 109, *s.* 2, in fine. (8) Gotti, *t.* 2, *c.* 109, *s.* 4; Varil. *t.* 1, *l.* 8, *p.* 363. (9) Gotti, loc. cit. *n.* 1. (10) Varil. loc. cit.

to the Divine command. Sixth.—He admitted the Presence of
Christ in the Holy Sacrament, but said it was not real, but took
place solely by faith. On this account he passed over to the sect of
the Sacramentarians, and quarrelled with Luther, and it was in defence of that sect he wrote his dialogue, "Arbogastus" (11). He
was selected by the Landgrave as the most likely person to unite
the Zuinglians and Lutherans; but though he held many conferences, he never could succeed, for Luther never would give up the
Real Presence of Christ in the Sacrament. He left Strasbourg,
where he lived and taught a long time, and in 1549, in the reign of
Edward VI., went to England to join Peter Vermigli, commonly
called Peter Martyr, who, two years previously, was appointed
Professor of Theology in Oxford. He had not been three years in
England when he died, at the age of sixty-one, in Cambridge, in
1551; and Cardinal Gotti says (12), he was tormented with remorse
of conscience in his last moments. His bones were exhumed and
burned, by order of Queen Mary, in 1556.

57. The other celebrated disciple of Zuinglius who, especially in
England, endeavoured to disseminate his errors, was Peter Vermigli,
a Florentine, commonly called Peter Martyr. He was born in
Florence, in 1500, of a noble, but reduced family. His mother,
who was acquainted with the Latin language, taught him till he
was eighteen years of age, when, according to some authors, he took
the Carthusian habit, but the general opinion is, that he became a
Canon Regular (13) of St. Augustin, in the Monastery of Fiesole.
In his novitiate he gave indications of great talent, and was, after
his profession, sent to Padua, where he was taught Greek, Hebrew,
and Philosophy. He thence went to Bologna to study theology,
and returned with a great stock of learning (14). He next turned
his attention to the pulpit, and preached several Lents in the principal cities of Italy. While preaching in the Cathedral of Naples,
he had the misfortune to become acquainted with a Spanish lawyer
of the name of Valdes, who, by reading Luther's and Calvin's
works, became infected with their heresies, and fearing to be discovered in Spain, where the stake awaited him, went to Germany,
but the climate not agreeing with him, he came to Naples, and contracted a friendship with Peter Martyr, and then made him a Sacramentarian. As soon as he tasted the poison himself he began to
communicate it to others who used to meet him in a church. This
had not gone on long when he was charged with his errors before
the Nuncio, and immediately called to Rome. His brethren in
religion, with whom he always lived on the best terms, and who
certainly believed him innocent, took up his defence most warmly,
and he was most fully acquitted and dismissed. From Rome he

(11) Gotti, loc. cit. *n.* 2, 3; Varil. *t.* 1, *l.* 8, *p.* 364. (12) Varil. *l.* 11, *p.* 297.
(13) Gotti, loc. cit. *n.* 5. (14) Varillas, *t.* 2, *l.* 17, *p.* 106; Dizion. Port. alla parola
Vermigli.

went to Lucca, where he thought he could establish a Zuinglian congregation, with less risk to himself than in Naples, and he succeeded so far, that among others he made four proselytes among the Professors of the University. They were in a little while discovered and obliged to fly to the Protestant Cantons of Switzerland, where they soon became ministers. Peter being discovered also, and not knowing where to fly, turned his steps likewise to Switzerland, hoping that his disciples there would procure a Professorship for him. He went first to Zurich, and afterwards to Basle; but as he wished to make himself the master of all, he met but a cool reception in either place. He then went to Bucer, in Strasbourg, who received every heretic, and procured him immediately a Professorship of Theology. He remained there till called to England, where he went with a nun he married, and was received with great honour in London, and was appointed to a Chair in Oxford, with double the salary that was promised to him. He returned to Strasbourg, in 1553, and finally went to teach his blasphemies in Zurich, where he died in 1562, loaded with fruits of perdition, for besides the many years he taught his errors in all these places, he composed and left after him also a number of works to sustain them (15).

ARTICLE III.

THE HERESIES OF CALVIN.

SEC. II.—THE BEGINNING AND PROGRESS OF THE HERESY OF CALVIN.

58. Birth and Studies of Calvin. 59. He begins to broach his Heresy; they seek to imprison him, and he makes his Escape through a Window. 60. He commences to disseminate his Impieties in Angouleme. 61. He goes to Germany to see Bucer, and meets Erasmus. 62. He returns to France, makes some Followers, and introduces the "Supper;" he afterwards goes to Basle, and finishes his "Instructions." 63. He goes to Italy, but is obliged to fly; arrives in Geneva, and is made Master of Theology. 64. He is embarrassed there. 65. He flies from Geneva, and returns to Germany, where he marries a Widow. 66. He returns to Geneva, and is put at the Head of the Republic; the impious Works he publishes there; his Dispute with Bolsec. 67. He causes Michael Servetus to be burned alive. 68. Unhappy End of the Calvinistic Mission to Brazil. 69. Seditions and Disturbances in France on Calvin's Account; Conference of Poissy. 70. Melancholy Death of Calvin. 71. His personal Qualities and depraved Manners.

58. JOHN CALVIN was born on the 10th of July, 1509, in Noyon, in the ancient province of Picardy, some say he was born in Bourg de Pont; but the almost universal opinion is, that he was born in the city itself, and Varillas (1) says that the house in which he first saw the light was afterwards razed to the ground by the people, and that a person who subsequently rebuilt it was hanged at the door. He was the third son of Gerard Caudin (he afterwards changed his

(15) Varillas, *l.* 17, *p.* 106; Berti, Hist. *sec.* 16. *c.* 3; Van Ranst, *sec.* 16, *p.* 391; Dizion. Portat. loc. cit. (1) Varillas, Istor. della Rel. *t.* 1, *l.* 12, *p.* 450.

name to Calvin), the son of a Flemish saddler, and Fiscal Procurator to the Bishop of Noyon, and receiver to the chapter. He obtained a chaplaincy for his son when he was twelve years old, and afterwards a country curacy in the village of Martville, which he some time after exchanged for the living of Pont l'Elveque (2). Endowed with those benefices, he at an early age applied himself with the greatest diligence to study, and was soon distinguished for talents, which God gave him for his service, but which he perverted to his own ruin, and to the ruin of many nations infected with his heresy. When he had gone through his preliminary studies, his father sent him to Bourges to study law under Andrew Alciati; but wishing to learn Greek, he commenced the study of that language under Melchior Walmer, a concealed Lutheran, and a native of Germany, who, perceiving the acute genius of his scholar, by degrees instilled the poison of heresy into his mind, and induced him to give up the study of law, and apply himself to theology (3); but Beza confesses that he never studied theology deeply, and that he could not be called a theologian.

59. In the meantime Calvin's father died, and he returned home, and without scruple sold his benefices, and went to Paris, where, at the age of twenty-three, he first began to disseminate his heresy (4). He then published a little treatise on "Constancy," in which he advised all to suffer for the truth as he called his errors. This little work was highly lauded by his friends, but it is only worthy of contempt, as it contains nothing but scraps of learning badly digested, injurious invectives against the Catholic Church, great praises of those heretics condemned by the Church, whom he calls martyrs of the truth, and numberless errors besides. The publication of this work, and the many indications Calvin had given of using his talents against the Church, aroused the attention of the Criminal Lieutenant, John Morin, who gave orders to arrest him in the College of Cardinal de Moyne, where he then lodged. Calvin, however, suspected what was intended, and while the officers of justice were knocking at the door, he let himself down from the window (5) by the bedclothes, and took refuge in the house of a vine-dresser, as Varillas informs us (6,) with whom he changed clothes, and left his house with a spade on his shoulder. In this disguise he was met by a canon of Noyon, who recognized him, and inquired the meaning of this masquerade. Calvin told him everything, and when his friend advised him to return, and retract his errors, and not cast himself away, he, it is said, answered: "If I had to begin again, I would

---

(2) Varillas, al. loc. cit ; Nat. Alex. *t.* 19, *a.* 13, *sec.* 1, *n.* 1 ; Gotti, Ver. Rel. *t.* 2, c. 111, *sec.* 1, *n.* 1 ; Hermant, Hist. de Conc. *t.* 2, *c.* 271; Van Ranst, Hist. Hær. *p.* 119; Berti, Hist. *sec.* 16, *c.* 3, *p.* 161 ; Lancist, Hist. *t.* 4, *sec.* 16, *c.* 5. (3) Nat. loc. cit. *n.* 1; Gotti, ibid. *n.* 3; Hermant, cit. *c.* 271 ; Varil. al. loc. cit. *p.* 451. (4) Gotti, cit. *c.* 111, *n.* 5 ; Van Ranst, *p.* 320; Varill. *t.* 1. *l.* 10, *p.* 452. (5) Van Ranst, *p.* 330; Gotti, loc. cit. *n.* 5 ; N. Alex loc. cit. *s.* 1, *n.* 1. (6) Varillas, 10, *p.* 345.

not forsake the Faith of my fathers; but now I am pledged to my doctrines, and I will defend them till death;" and an awful and terrible death awaited him, as we shall see hereafter. Varillas adds, that while he resided afterwards in Geneva, a nephew of his asked him if salvation could be obtained in the Catholic Church, and that Calvin could not find it in his heart to deny it, but told him he might be saved in that Church.

60. He escaped into Angouleme, and for three years taught Greek, as well as he could from the little he learned from Walmar, and his friends procured him lodgings in the house of the parish priest of Claix, Louis de Tillet, a very studious person, and possessor of a library of 4,000 volumes, mostly manuscripts. It was here he composed almost the entire of the four books of his pestilent Institutes, the greater part of which he took from the works of Melancthon, Ecolampadius, and other sectaries, but he adopted a more lucid arrangement, and a more elegant style of Latinity (7). As he finished each chapter he used to read it for Tillet, who at first refused his assent to such wicked doctrine; but by degrees his Faith was undermined, and he became a disciple of Calvin, who offered to accompany him to Germany, where a Conference with the reforming doctors, he assured him, would confirm him in the course he was adopting. They, accordingly, left for Germany, but had not gone further than Geneva when Tillet's brother, a good Catholic, and Chief Registrar of the Parliament of Paris, joined them, and prevailed on his brother to retrace his steps and renounce his Calvinistic errors. In this he happily succeeded; the priest returned, and was afterwards the first in his district to raise his voice publicly against Calvinism (8).

61. Calvin continued his route to Germany, and arrived at Strasbourg, where Bucer was labouring to unite the Lutherans and Zuinglians in doctrine, but never could succeed, as neither would consent to give up their peculiar tenets on the Real Presence of Christ in the Eucharist. Calvin, seeing the difficulties he was in, suggested to him a middle way to reconcile both parties—that is, to propose as a doctrine that in the reception of the Eucharist it is not the flesh, but the substance or power of Jesus Christ that is received; this, he imagined, would reconcile both parties. Bucer, however, either because he thought Luther never would give up his own particular views, or, perhaps, jealous that the idea did not originate with himself, refused to adopt it. Calvin next visited Erasmus with a letter of recommendation from Bucer, in which he told Erasmus to pay particular attention to what would drop from him; he did so, and after some conversation with him, told his

(7) Nat. Alex. *t.* 19, *a.* 13, *s.* 1; Gotti, *c.* 3, *s.* 1, *n.* 3; Van Ranst, *p.* 330; Varil. *l.* 30, *p.* 454. (8) Varil. cit *p.* 454; Gotti, loc. cit. *n.* 6.

friends that he saw in that young man one who would be a great plague to the Church (9).

62. Calvin, finding it difficult to make many proselytes to his Sacramentarian doctrines in Germany, returned to France in 1535, and went to Poictiers, where at first, in the privacy of a garden, he began to expound his tenets to a few, but his followers increasing, he transferred his chair to a hall of the University, called Ministerium, and here the Calvinistic teachers took the name of ministers, as the Lutherans called themselves preachers. Calvin sent out from this several ministers to the neighbouring towns and villages, and, by this means, made a great many proselytes (10). It was there he first published the forty articles of his heresy, and it was there also he introduced the Supper, or Manducation, as he called it, which was privately celebrated in the following manner: First, some part of the Testament relative to the Last Supper was read, then the minister made a few observations on it, but in general the burden of these discourses was the abuse of the Pope and of the Mass, Calvin always saying that in the New Testament no mention is made of any other sacrifice than that of the Cross. Bread and wine were then set on the table, and the minister, instead of the words of consecration, said: " My brethren, let us eat of the bread and drink of the wine of the Lord, in memory of his passion and death." The congregation were seated round a table, and the minister, breaking off a small portion of bread, gave it to each, and they ate it in silence; the wine was dispensed in like manner. The Supper was finished by a prayer, thanking God for enlightening them, and freeing them from Papistical errors; the Our Father and the Creed was said, and they swore not to betray anything that was there done. It was, however, impossible to conceal the existence of this new Church of Poictiers, and as the Royal Ordinances were very rigorous against innovators, and Calvin felt that he could not be safe in Pictou, he went to Nerac in Aquitaine, the residence of Margaret, Queen of Navarre, a patroness of the new doctrine. Even here he was not in safety, as Royal edicts were every day published against heretics, so he went to Basle, where he employed himself in preparing his four books of the Institutes for the press. He was twenty-six years of age when he published this work, with the motto, " I came not to send peace, but a sword;" showing, like a true prophet, the great evils this work would bring on France, and every other country where its pestilential doctrines would be embraced (11).

63. While Calvin was at Basle he felt a great desire to propagate his doctrine in Italy, where Luther could make no way; and understanding that Renee, daughter of Louis XII. of France, and wife of Hercules of Este, Duke of Ferrara, was a woman fond of

(9) Van Ranst, *s.* 16. *p.* 323 ; Nat. Alex. loc. cit. *n.* 1 ; Varill *p.* 459. (10) Varill. *l.* 10, *p.* 457 ; Hermant, *t.* 2, *c.* 271 ; Nat. Alex. *s.* 1, *n.* 1 ; Gotti, *c.* 111, *s.* 2, *n.* 1. (11) Nat Alex. *t.* 19, *c.* 13, *n.* 2 ; Van Ranst, *p.* 321, Gotti, *c.* 111, *s.* 2, *n.* 4.

novelties, and a proficient not only in philosophy and mathematics, but also fond of dabbling in theology, he went to visit her, and, after some time, succeeded in making her one of his followers, so that he held privately in her chamber several conferences with her and others of the party. When this came to the Duke's ears, he was very angry, and bitterly reproved the Duchess, obliging her to give up the practice of the new religion, and all the favour Calvin could obtain was leave to quit his States. He then at once fled from Ferrara to France, for fear of the Inquisition, which was very active just then, on account of the disturbed state of religious opinions in Europe (12). In the year 1536 he went to Geneva, which the year before rebelled against the Duke of Turin, and cast off, along with its allegiance, the Catholic religion, at the instigation of William Farrell; and the Genevese, to commemorate their infamy, placed a public inscription on a bronze tablet, as follows: " Quum anno Domini MDXXXV. profligata Romani Antichristi tyrannide, abrogatisque ejus superstitionibus, sacrosancta Christi Religio hic in suam puritatem, Ecclesia in meliorem ordinem singulari beneficio reposita, et simul pulsis fugatisque hostibus, Urbs ipsa in suam libertatem non sine insigni miraculo restituta fuerit; S. P. Q. G. Monumentum hoc perpetuæ memoriæ causa fieri, atque hoc loco erigi curavit, quo suam erga Deum gratitudinem testatem faceret." Farrell, perceiving that Calvin would be of great assistance to him in maintaining the new doctrines he had introduced into Geneva, used every means in his power to induce him to stay, and got the magistrates to appoint him Preacher and Professor of Theology (13). One of his first acts after his appointment was to burn the images of the saints which adorned the Cathedral, and to break the altars. The table of the high altar was formed of a slab of very precious marble, which a wretch called Perrin caused to be fitted up in the place of public execution, to serve as a table for cutting off the heads of the criminals; but by the just judgment of God, and at Calvin's instigation, though the cause is not known, it so happened that in a short time he was beheaded on the same stone himself (14).

64. Calvin fixed his residence in Geneva, but he and Farrell were accused, in 1537, of holding erroneous opinions concerning the Trinity and the Divinity of Jesus Christ (15). Their accuser was Peter de Charles, a Doctor of Sorbonne, who had been a Sacramentarian, and Minister of Geneva; he charged Calvin, who said the word Trinity was a barbarism, with denying the Unity of God in three Persons; besides, he had stated in his Catechism, that the Saviour on the cross was abandoned by his Father, and driven into

(12) Varill *t.* 1, *l.* 10, *p.* 465; Van Ranst, *p.* 321.   (13) Apud Berti, Brev. Hist. *t.* 2, *s.* 16, *c.* 2, *p.* 162.   (14) Nat. Alex. loc. cit. *n.* 2; Van Ranst, *p.* 221; Gotti, *c.* 111, *s.* 1, *n.* 6.   (15) Gotti, ibid.

despair, and that he was condemned to suffer the pains of hell, but his detention, unlike that of the reprobate, which endures for eternity, only lasted for a short time; from this Charles argued that Calvin denied the Divinity of Christ. Calvin cleared himself and Farrell from these charges, and his accuser was banished from Geneva, a most fortunate circumstance for him, as it opened his eyes to Divine grace. He went to Rome, and obtained absolution for his errors, and died in the Catholic Church. This affair concluded, Calvin had a serious dispute with his confrere Farrell, who, following the custom of Berne, used unleavened bread for the Supper, while Calvin insisted on using leavened bread, saying it was an abuse introduced by the scholastic Papists, to use the other. The magistrates, however, were in favour of the use of unleavened bread. Calvin, anxious to differ as much as possible from Zuinglius (16), preached to the people, and got them to declare in his favour, so much so that Easter being now nigh they said they would not communicate unless with leavened bread (17). The magistrates, jealous of their authority, appointed a minister called Maré to administer the Sacrament, with unleavened bread, in St. Peter's Church; but Calvin frightened him so much that he hid himself, and the magistrates then commanded that there should be no communion that day, and banished both Calvin and Farrell from the city (18).

65. Calvin went to Berne to plead his cause, but met with another adventure there. A Flemish Catholic, of the name of Zachary, was at that time before the Council of Berne; he held a disputation about matters of Faith with Calvin; in the midst of it he took out a letter, and asked him if he knew the writing. Calvin acknowledged it was written with his own hand; the letter was then read, and found to contain a great deal of abuse of Zuinglins (19). The meeting immediately broke up, and he, seeing Berne was no longer a place for him, went to Strasbourg, where he was again received by his friend Bucer, and appointed Professor of Theology, and minister of a new church, in which he collected together all the French and Flemings who embraced his doctrine; here also, in the year 1538, he married one Ideletta, the widow of an Anabaptist, with whom he lived fourteen years, but had no children, though Varillas says he had one, but it only lived two days (20).

66. Calvin sighed to return to Geneva, and in 1541 was recalled. He was received with every demonstration of joy and respect, and was appointed Chief of the Republic. He then established the discipline of his sect, and the Senate decreed that

(16) Varill. *l.* 12, *p.* 512, & Nat. Alex. *a.* 13 ; *s.* 1, *n.* 1.   (17) Nat. cit. *n.* in fin. ; Gotti, *s.* 2, *n.* 7.   (18) Nat. Alex. loc. cit. *n.* 3 ; Varill. *p.* 513 ; Van Ranst, *p.* 121 ; Gotti, c. 111, *s.* 2, *n.* 8.   (19) Varill. *l.* 11, *p.* 514.   (20) Gotti, *s.* 2, *n.* 9 ; Varill. loc. cit. Nat. Alex. ibid.

thenceforward the ministers or citizens could never change the statutes promulgated by him. He then also published his great French Catechism, which his followers afterwards translated into various languages, German, English, Flemish, Erse, Spanish, and even Hebrew. He then also published his pestilent books, entitled *Defensio Sacræ Doctrinæ, De Disciplina, De Necessitate Reformandæ Ecclesiæ*, one against the *Interim* of Charles V., and another against the Council of Trent, called *Antidotum adversus Conc. Tridentinum* (21). In the year 1542, the Faculty of Sorbonne, by way of checking the errors then published almost daily, put forth twenty-five Chapters on the Dogmas of Faith we are bound to believe; and Calvin seeing all his impious novelties condemned by these chapters, attacked the venerable University in the grossest manner, so as to call the Professors a herd of swine (22). In the year 1543, he procured a union between his sect and the Zuinglians, and being thus safe in Geneva, which he was cautious not to leave, he encouraged his followers in France to lay down their lives for the Faith, as he called his doctrines; and these deluded creatures, while Francis I. and Henry II. were lighting fires to burn heretics, deceived by Calvin and his ministers, set at nought all punishments, even death itself—nay, some of them cast themselves into the flames, and Calvin called their ashes the ashes of Martyrs (23). In the year 1551, he had a great dispute in Geneva with Jerome Bolsec, who, though an apostate Carmelite, nevertheless could not tolerate the opinions of Luther and Calvin concerning free will, who denied it altogether, and said, that as God predestined some to grace and paradise, so he predestined others to sin and hell. He could not agree with Calvin in this, and he accordingly induced the magistrates to banish Bolsec from Geneva and its territories as a Pelagian, and with a threat of having him flogged, if he made his appearance there again. Happily for Bolsec, this sentence was put in execution: he then began to reflect on the evil step he had taken, again returned to the Catholic Church, and wrote a great deal against Calvin's doctrine, who answered him in his impious work *De Æterna Dei Prædestinatione* (24).

67. About the year 1553, Calvin caused Michael Servetus to be burned, and thus he, who, in the dedication of his work to Francis I., called the magistrates who burned heretics Diocletians, became, in the case of Servetus, a Diocletian himself. These are the facts of the case (25): Calvin procured from the Fair of Frankfort the dialogues of Servetus, in which he denied the Trinity, and published several other errors we shall see hereafter. When he read this, he immediately marked his prey, as he had an old grudge

(21) Nat. Alex. *t.* 19, *ar.* 13, *sec.* 1; *n.* 4, & seq.; Gotti, *c.* 111, *sec.* 2, *n.* 10. (22) Gotti, *n.* 11.   (23) Gotti, *n.* 11-14.   (24) Nat. Alex. cit. *sec.* 1, *n.* 8. Gotti, loc. cit. *n.* 14.   (25) Varillas, *t.* 2, *l.* 20.

against him, since once he proved him in a disputation to have made a false quotation. Servetus was passing through Geneva, on his way to Italy, and as it was Sunday, Calvin was to preach that evening after dinner. Servetus was curious to hear him, and expected to escape observation. He was betrayed, however, to Calvin, who was just going into the pulpit, and he immediately ran to the house of one of the Consuls to get an order for his arrest, on a charge of heresy. By the laws of Geneva it was ordered, that no one should be imprisoned, unless his accuser would consent to go to prison also. Calvin, accordingly, got a servant of his to make the charge, and go to prison, and in the servant's name, forty charges were brought against Servetus. Undergoing an examination, he asserted that the Divine Word was not a person subsisting, and hence it followed, that Jesus Christ was but a mere man. Calvin was then summoned, and seeing that Servetus was condemned by that avowal of his opinions, he proposed that his condemnation should be sanctioned, not by the Church of Geneva alone, but by the Churches of Zurich, Basle, and Berne, likewise. They all agreed in condemning him to be burned to death by a slow fire, and the sentence was carried into execution on the 17th of October, 1553 (26). Varillas quotes a writer who asserts, that when Servetus was led to punishment he cried out: "O God, save my soul; Jesus, Son of the Eternal God, have pity on me." It is worthy of remark, that he did not say, Eternal Son of God, and hence it appears that he died obstinately in his errors, by a most horrible death, for being fastened to the stake by an iron chain, when the pile was lighted, a violent wind blew the flames on one side, so that the unhappy wretch was burning for two or three hours before death put an end to his torment, and he was heard to cry out: "Wo is me, I can neither live nor die." Thus he perished at the age of thirty-six (27). In the following year Calvin, to defend himself from the charge of being called a Diocletian, published a treatise to prove that by Scripture and Tradition, and the custom of the first ages, it was lawful to put obstinate heretics to death. This was answered by Martin Bellius; but Theodore Beza wrote a long rejoinder in defence of Calvin, and thus we see how inconsistently heretics act in blaming the Catholic Church at that time, for making use of the secular arm to punish heresy, when in theory and practice they did the same themselves.

68. In the year 1555, the Calvinists had the vanity to send a mission to America, to endeavour to introduce their poisonous doctrines among these simple people. For this purpose, Nicholas Durant, a zealous French Calvinist, equipped three vessels, with consent of the King, in which he and many other Calvinists, some

---

(26) Varillas, *t.* 2, *l.* 20, *p.* 219; Gotti, *c.* 111, *sec.* 3, *n.* 1; Nat. Alex. loc. cit. *sec.* 1, *n* 9. (27) Varillas, *l.* 20, *p.* 221.

of them noblemen, embarked for Brazil, under the pretext of a commercial speculation; but their primary object was to introduce Calvinism. When Calvin heard of this, he sent two ministers to accompany them—one of the name of Peter Richer, an apostate Carmelite; the other a young aspirant of the name of William Carter. In the month of November this impious mission arrived in Brazil, but turned out a total failure, as the two ministers could not agree on the doctrine of the Eucharist, for Richer said that the Word made flesh should not be adored, according to the words of St. John, " the Spirit quickeneth, the flesh availeth nothing," and hence he deduced, that the Eucharist was of no use to those who received it. This dispute put an end to the mission, and Durant himself, in the year 1558, publicly abjured Calvinism, and returned to the Church, which he afterwards defended by his writings (28).

69. In the year 1557, a number of Calvinists were discovered in Paris clandestinely celebrating the Supper by night in a private house, contrary to the Royal Ordinances. One hundred and twenty were taken and imprisoned, and a rumour was abroad, that many enormities were committed in these nocturnal meetings. They were all 'punished, and even some of them were burned alive (29). In the year 1560, the Calvinistic heresy having now become strong in France, the conspiracy of Amboise was discovered. This was principally directed against the princes of the House of Guise, and Francis II., King of France, and Louis, Prince of Conde, and brother of the King of Navarre, was at the head of it. Calvin mentioned this conspiracy in a letter to his friends Bullenger and Blauret, in which he admits that he was acquainted with it, but says he endeavoured to prevent it. It is easy to see, however, his disappointment at its failure. It is said by some authors that this was the time when the French Calvinists first adopted the name of Huguenots (30). The Conference of Poissy was also held at this time. Calvin expected that his party would have the victory; in this he was disappointed; but the heretics, thus beaten, remained as obstinate as ever, and began to put on such a bold face that they preached publicly in the streets of Paris. A scandalous transaction took place on this account: A minister, named Malois, was preaching near the church of St. Medard; when the bell rang for vespers, the heretics sent to have it stopped, as it prevented them from hearing the preacher. The people in the church continued to ring on, when the Calvinists, leaving the sermon, rushed furiously into the church, broke the images, cast down the altars, trampled on the Most Holy Sacrament, wounded several ecclesiastics, and

(28) Nat. Alex. *t.* 19, *ar.* 13, *sec.* 1, *n.* 10; Varillas, *l.* 21, *p.* 256; Gotti, *c.* 111, *sec.* 3, *n.* 5.   (29) Gotti, loc. cit. *n.* 6.   (30) Varillas, *l.* 23, *n.* 331; Gotti, loc. cit. *n.* 8.

then dragged thirty-six of them, tied with ropes, and covered with blood, through the streets of the city to prison. Beza wrote a flaming account of this victory of the Faith, as he called it, to Calvin.

70. At length the day of Divine vengeance for the wretched Calvin drew nigh; he died in Geneva, in 1564, on the 26th day of May, in the 54th year of his age. Beza says he died calmly; but William Bolsec, the writer of his life, and others, quoted by Noel Alexander and Gotti (31), assert that he died calling on the devil, and cursing his life, his studies, his writings, and, at the same time, exhaling a horrible stench from his ulcers, and thus he appeared before Christ, the Judge, to answer for all the souls lost, or to be lost, through his means.

71. Varillas, in his account of Calvin's character and personal qualities, says (32) he was endowed by God with a prodigious memory, so that he never forgot what he once read, and that his intellect was so acute, especially in logical and theological subtleties, that he at once discovered the point on which everything hinged in the doubts proposed to him. He was indefatigable in studying, in preaching, in writing, and in teaching, and it is wonderful how any man could write so many works during the time he lived, and, besides, he preached almost every day, gave a theological lecture every week, on every Friday, held a long conference with his followers on doubts of faith, and almost all his remaining time was taken up in clearing up and answering the knotty questions of his friends. He was very temperate both in eating and drinking, not so much through any love of the virtue of abstinence, as from a weakness of stomach, so that he was sometimes two days without eating. He suffered also from hypochondria, and frequent headachs, and hence his delicate health made him melancholy. He was very emaciated, and his colour was so bad, that he appeared as if bronzed all over. He was fond of solitude, and spoke but little. He was graceless in his delivery, and frequently, in his sermons, used to break out in invectives against the Catholic Church and people. He was prompt in giving advice or answers, but proud and rash, and so rude and intractable, that he easily fell out with all who were obliged to have any communication with him (33). He was very vain of himself, and on that account affected extreme gravity. He was the slave of almost every vice, but especially hatred, anger, and vindictiveness, and on that account Bucer, though his friend, in a letter of admonition to him, says he is a mad dog, and as a writer inclined to speak badly of every one. He was addicted to immorality, at all events in his youth, and Spondanus says (34), he was charged even with

(31) Nat. Alex. sec. 1, n. 16; Gotti, ibid. n. 9. (32) Varillas, t. 1, l. 10, p. 459.
(33) Spondan. ad an. 1564; Nat. Alex. ar. 13, sec. n. 16; Gotti, loc. cit. sec. 3, n. 10;
Varillas, l. 12, t. 1, l. 10, p. 450. (34) Spondan. ad an. 1534.

U

an unnameable offence, and Bolsec even says in his life of him, that he was condemned to death for it in Noyon, but that, through the intercession of the bishop, the punishment was changed to branding with a red-hot iron. Varillas says (35), that in the registry of Noyon a leaf is marked with this condemnation, but without mentioning the offence: but Noel Alexander says (36) positively, that both the certificate of the condemnation and the offence was preserved in Noyon, and that it was shown to, and read by, Berteler, Secretary to the Republic of Geneva, sent on purpose to verify the fact. Cardinal Gotti says (37), that when he taught Greek in Angouleme the same charge was brought against him by his scholars, and that he was condemned there likewise. Such are the virtues attributed to the pretended Reformers of the Church (38).

SEC. II.—THEODORE BEZA, THE HUGUENOTS, AND OTHER CALVINISTS WHO DISTURBED FRANCE, SCOTLAND, AND ENGLAND.

72. Theodore Beza; his Character and Vices. 73. His Learning, Employments, and Death. 74. Conference of St. Francis de Sales with Beza. 75. Continuation of the same Subject. 76, 77. Disorders of the Huguenots in France. 78. Horrors committed by them; they are proscribed in France. 79. Their Disorders in Flanders. 80. And in Scotland. 81. Mary Stuart is married to Francis II. 82. She returns to Scotland and marries Darnley, next Bothwell; is driven by Violence to make a fatal Renunciation of her Crown in favour of her Son. 83. She takes Refuge in England, and is imprisoned by Elizabeth, and afterwards condemned to Death by her. 84. Edifying Death of Mary Stuart. 85. James I., the Son of Mary, succeeds Elizabeth; he is succeeded by his Son, Charles I., who was beheaded. 86. He is succeeded by his Son, Charles II., who is succeeded by his Brother, James II., a Catholic, who died in France.

72. At Calvin's death, he left the direction of the unfortunate city of Geneva to Theodore Beza, a worthy successor of his, both in life and doctrines. He was born on the 24th of June, 1519, in Vezelais, in Burgundy, of a noble family, and was educated by his uncle, who sent him to Paris to study humanity, and afterwards to Orleans to learn Greek under Melchior Wolmar, Calvin's master, first in Greek and next in heresy. His appearance was agreeable, his manners polished, and he was a great favourite with all his acquaintance. He led, when young, an immoral life, and wrote several amatory poems; he had an intrigue with a tailor's wife in Paris, of the name of Claudia, and he has been charged with even more abominable crimes. His uncle resigned a priorate, which he held, in his favour, and likewise made him his heir; but he spent not only that and his paternal property, but even stole the chalices and ornaments of a church belonging to the natives of Burgundy, in Orleans, of which he was procurator. For this he was imprisoned,

(35) Varillas, loc cit. (36) Nat. Alex. cit. n. 16. in fin. (37) Gotti, sec 1, n 6. (38) Remundus, l. 1, c. 9, n. 3.

but soon liberated, and soon after he published in Paris a shocking epigram regarding a person named Audabert, which induced the Court of Paris to order his imprisonment. This terrified him, for if convicted of the crime he was charged with, the penalty was burning alive. He was reduced to the greatest poverty, for he not only ran through his property, but also sold his priorate for twelve hundred crowns, and even in this transaction he was guilty of dishonesty, for he prevailed on the agents of his benefice to pay him the revenue of it before it came due. Covered with infamy, he changed his name to Theobald May, and fled to Geneva, taking Claudia with him, whom he then married, though her husband was still living. He presented himself to Calvin, who, finding he studied under Wolmar, received him, and procured him a professorship of Greek, and from that he was promoted to a professorship of Theology in Lausanne. The ministers of that city, though apostates, yet having a knowledge of the crimes already committed by Beza, and seeing the debauched life he led, refused to admit him to the ministry, but he was sustained by Calvin, whom he venerated almost to adoration, so that he was called *Calvinolator*, the adorer of Calvin (1).

73. In his teaching he surpassed even Calvin in impiety, for the one admitted, though obscurely, the body of Christ in the Eucharist, but the other said, in the Conference of Poissy, that the body of Christ was as far from the Eucharist as heaven is from the earth; and although he was obliged to retract, nevertheless, in a letter of his, he again repeats the same sentiment (2); and one of his companions, as Spondanus tells us, said, what wonder is it that Beza does not believe that, when he scarcely believes in the existence of God (3)? On the occasion of the outbreak of the Calvinists against the priests of the Church of St. Medard (*N*. 69), he boasted not only of the insult to the Church and the priests, but especially of the horrible profanation of the Holy Eucharist. He wrote a letter of congratulation to the Queen of England, praising her for assisting to plant the Faith in France by blood and slaughter; and when he went to the Congress of Worms, where Calvin sent him to try and gain friends for his sect, and Melancthon asked him, " Why the French caused so many disasters in France?" He said, " They only did what the Apostles had done before them." " Why, then," said Melancthon, do you not suffer stripes as the Apostles did?" Beza made him no answer, but turned his back on him. Although nearly seventy years old when his wife Claudia died, he married a very young widow, of whom we shall have occasion to speak hereafter. Florimund (4) says that a nobleman of Guienne returning from Rome in the year 1600, called on Beza, and found him a venerable

(1) Gotti, *c.* 114, *sec.* 4, *n.* 1, 6; Varillas, *t.* 2, *l.* 18, 137. (2) Berti, Brev. Hist. *t.* 2, *sec.* 16, *c.* 1. (3) Spondan. ad An. 1561, *n.* 19. (4) Florimund, Remund. *l.* 8, *c.* 17, *n.* 6.

old man, with a long white beard, and in his hand a beautifully bound little volume. When the gentleman asked him what it contained, he showed him that it was a book of sonnets, and said: "Sic tempus fallo"—" I thus cheat time." "Oh," said the gentleman to a friend of his, "is it thus this holy man, with one foot already in Charon's bark, passes his time?" Beza continued for forty-one years after Calvin's death to govern the Church of Geneva, or rather to poison it by his bad example and doctrine; he was, however, called to account for all before God, in the year 1605, the eighty-fifth of his age (5) Let not the reader wonder that I have said so much about the vices of Luther, Calvin, and Beza. I have done so on purpose, that every one may understand that God did not send such men to reform his Church, but rather the devil to destroy it. In this, however, no heresiarch ever can or ever has succeeded, for our Lord has promised to protect it to the end of the world, "and the gates of hell shall not prevail against it."

74. I will here relate a conference St. Francis de Sales had with Beza, about the year 1597, as we find it in the saint's life (6). Clement VIII. desired St. Francis to see Beza and try could he convert him. The saint made his way into Geneva, at the risk of his life, and called on Beza, whom he found alone. He commenced by begging Beza not to believe all he heard of him from his enemies. Beza answered that he always considered St. Francis a man of learning and merit, but that he regretted seeing him devote his energies to prop up anything so weak as the Catholic religion. St. Francis then asked him if it was his opinion that a man could be saved in the Catholic Church? Beza demanded a little time before he would give his answer; he went into his study, remained walking about for a quarter of an hour, and then coming out said: "Yes; I believe that a man may be saved in the Catholic Church." "Why, then," said St. Francis, "have you established your Reformation with so much bloodshed and destruction, since, without any danger, a man may be saved, and never leave the Catholic Church?" "You have put obstacles in the way of salvation," said Beza, "in the Catholic Church, by inculcating the necessity of good works; but we, by teaching salvation by faith alone, have smoothened the way to heaven." "But you," said St. Francis, "by denying the necessity of good works, destroy all human and divine laws, which threaten punishment to the wicked, and promise rewards to the good; and Christ says, in the Gospel, that not only those who do evil, but, likewise, those who omit to do the good commanded to be done, shall suffer eternal punishment. It is necessary, also," said he, "in order to know the true Faith, that there should be some judge from whom there is no appeal, and to whose judgment all

---

(5) Gotti, loc. cit. n. 7, 10.   (6) Vita di St. Francesco di Sales, da Pietro Gallo, l. 2, c. 21, 22.

should submit; for otherwise disputes never would have an end, and the truth never could be found." Beza then began talking about the Council of Trent, and said that the only rule of Faith was the Scriptures, and that the Council did not follow them. St. Francis answered that the Scriptures had different meanings, and that it was necessary that their true sense should be decided by the Church. "But," said Beza, "the Scriptures are clear, and the Holy Ghost gives to every one the internal understanding of their true sense." "How, then, does it happen," said St. Francis, "if the Scripture be clear, and the Holy Ghost inspires the true sense of it to every one, that Luther and Calvin, both, in the opinion of the Reformers, inspired by God, held the most opposite opinions in the most important questions of religion. Luther says that the real body of Christ is in the Eucharist; Calvin, on the other hand, that it is only the virtue of Christ. How, then, can we know, when so great a difference exists, to which of the two, Luther or Calvin, the Holy Ghost has revealed the truth? Besides, Luther denies the Canonicity of the Epistle of St. James, and of some other books of the Holy Scriptures; Calvin admits it. Whom are we to believe?" They had now been disputing for three hours, and when Beza saw himself thus hemmed up in a corner, he lost his temper, and only answered the saint's arguments by abuse. St. Francis then, with his accustomed meekness, said he did not come to give him any annoyance, and took his leave.

75. Some time after, again at the request of the Pope, St. Francis paid him a second visit, and, among many things then discussed, they argued specially concerning Free Will, for Calvin blasphemously asserted, that whatever man does, he does through necessity —that if he is predestined he does what is good—if he is not, he does what is evil. The saint proved the doctrine of Free Will so clearly, both from the Old and the New Testament, that Beza was convinced of its truth, and, cordially taking St. Francis by the hand, said that he daily prayed to God, that if he was not in the right way, he might lead him to it. This shows the doubts he entertained of his new Faith; for those who are certain that they profess the true Faith, never pray to God to enlighten them to adopt another, but to confirm and preserve them in the Faith they profess. Finally, St. Francis, thinking him now better disposed after this acknowledgment, spoke to him plainly, and told him, that now his years should lead him to reflect whether he was not letting the time of mercy pass by, and preparing himself for the day of justice— that, as he was now near the close of life, he should defer his conversion no longer, but return immediately to the Church he had forsaken—that if he feared the persecution he would suffer from the Calvinists, he should remember he ought to suffer everything for his eternal salvation; but as Luther himself remarked, it is hard to expect that the head of any sect will forsake the doctrines he has

taught others, and become a convert. Beza said that he did not despair of salvation in his own Church. The saint then, seeing that his heart was made of stone, left him, under a promise of returning soon again to visit him; but this was not in his power, for the Genevese put guards to watch their minister, and determined to put St. Francis to death if he ever came again. Some say that Beza was anxious to see him again, and that he retracted his errors, and that on that account his friends gave out that the violence of his sickness deranged his mind; but we know nothing of this for certain, and it is most probable that he died as he lived. The writer of St. Francis's life says, also, that Des Hayes, Governor of Montargis, being in Geneva, and conversing familiarly one day with Beza, asked him why he remained in his new sect? He pointed out to him a young woman in his house, and said, this is what retains me; and it is supposed that this was his second wife, whom he married when he was seventy years old.

76. We have now to speak of the French Calvinists, or Huguenots, as they are generally called, as is supposed, from the Castle of Hugon, near Toulouse, close by which they had their first conventicle, and of the desolation they caused in France. Volumes would not suffice to relate all the destruction caused by Calvin and his followers, not only in France, but in many other countries. I will only then give a sketch of them, to show how much harm one perverse heresiarch may occasion. During the reigns of Francis I. and his son, Henry II., though both zealous Catholics, and ever prosecuting the Calvinists with the utmost rigour, even condemning many of them to the stake, still this heresy was so spread through every province of the kingdom, that there was not a city or town but had its temple or ministers of the new sect. In the year 1559, however, when Henry was succeeded by his son, Francis II., only sixteen years of age, it broke forth like a torrent, and overwhelmed the whole kingdom with errors, sacrileges, sedition, and bloodshed (7). Jeane, Queen of Navarre, was the chief promoter of all this; she used all her endeavours to extinguish the Faith; she encouraged the heretics to take up arms, and when they were worsted, she was always ready to assist them. She encouraged Louis Bourbon, Prince of Conde, too, at his first presentation to her, to take up arms in the cause of the Reformation, and she was the head of the conspiracy of Amboise, which, however, did not succeed according to her wishes (8). The Huguenots, however, are blamed for the death of the young King, Francis II., who, it is said, was poisoned by a Huguenot surgeon, at the age of seventeen, by putting poison into his ear while treating him for an abscess (9).

(7) Van Ranst, Hist. sec. 16, p. 322. (8) Van Ranst, loc. cit. vide Her. t. 2, c. 272.
(9) Spondan. ad an. 1560, n. 7.

77. A royal decree was published in the reign of Charles IX., granting leave to the Calvinists to hold meetings, and preach outside the cities, and on this occasion, nothing could equal the disturbances they caused. The first outbreak took place in Vassey, in Champagne, where seventy Calvinists were killed; the Prince of Conde immediately put himself at the head of the Calvinistic party, and they declared war against their king and country. They took several cities, and destroyed the churches, broke open the tombs of saints, and burned their relics. Many battles were subsequently fought, in which the rebels were beaten, though not conquered. The first was fought in Dreux, in the Venassain, in which Conde was taken prisoner by Francis of Guise, who commanded the Catholics, and Anthony, King of Navarre, who commanded the royal army, was so severely wounded, that he died shortly after, leaving an only son Henry, who was afterwards the famous Henry IV., King of France. In the following year, 1563, while the Duke of Guise, commander of the royal troops, was besieging Orleans, he was treacherously wounded by one John Poltroze, employed by Beza; the wound proved mortal, and the Queen-Mother made a treaty of peace with the heretics, most hurtful to the Catholic interests, but which was subsequently modified by another edict (10).

78. The Calvinists went to war again in 1567, and were again beaten, and in the year 1569, the Catholics gained the battle of Jarnac, in which the Prince of Conde, leader of the Calvinists, was killed (11). In the year 1572, a great number of Calvinists were killed on St. Bartholomew's day, and it is thought that not less than a hundred thousand Calvinists perished in this war; such were the hellish fruits of the doctrines Calvin taught. It is terrifying to read the details of the excesses committed by the Calvinists against the churches, the priests, the sacred images, and especially the Holy Eucharist. It is related in the Annals of France, in the year 1563, (12), that a Huguenot went into the Church of St. Genevieve, and, possessed by a diabolical spirit, snatched the Sacred Host out of the hands of the officiating priest; he paid dearly, however, for the sacrilege, as he was immediately taken, his hand was cut off, he was then hanged, and his body burned. As an atonement for this irreverence, the same month, the king, his mother, the princes of the blood, and the Parliament, went in procession from the Chapel Royal to the Church of St. Genevieve, bearing lighted torches in their hands. About this time, also, the Huguenots burned the body of St. Francis a Paula, which was preserved incorrupt for fifty years, in the Church of St. Gregory of Tours, in the suburbs of Tours. Louis XIV. used every means, by sending preachers

(10) Nat. Alex. *t.* 19, *c.* 11, *art.* 9, *n.* 3, & 4. (11) Nat. Alex. *n.* 5; Hermant, *t.* 2, *c.* 806.   (12) Apud Gotti, *c.* 111, *s.* 4, *n.* 15.

among these sectaries, to convert them, and finally adopted such rigorous measures against them, that a great many returned to the Faith, and those who refused compliance left the kingdom. Innocent XI., in the year 1685, wrote him a letter, praising his zeal (13).

79. Would to God, however, that the plague never spread further than France, and never tainted any other kingdom. The Low Countries were likewise infected by it, and the chief reason of its spreading there was on account of the Lutheran and Calvinistic troops, maintained by the house of Austria to oppose France; both sects rivalled each other in making proselytes there, but Calvin sent many of his disciples to Flanders, and the Calvinists, therefore, remained the most numerous. The Flemings, also, felt themselves aggrieved by the Spanish Governors, and succeeded with Philip II., in obtaining the recall of Cardinal Granville, who had been sent as Counsellor of Mary, Queen of Hungary, and sister of Charles V., Regent of the Low Countries. This was a most fatal blow to the Catholic cause, for this great prelate, by his vigorous measures, and his zealous administration of his Inquisitorial powers, kept the heretics in check, but after his departure, in 1556, they broke out into open insurrection, wrecked the churches of Antwerp, broke the altars and images, and left the monasteries heaps of ruins, and this sedition spread through Brabant and other provinces, already infected with heresy, so that the Regent felt herself obliged to grant them a provisional license for the exercise of their false religion. King Philip refused to ratify this concession, and the heretics again took up arms; the King then sent the Duke of Alva with a powerful army to chastise them, but the Prince of Orange, though under many obligations to the King of Spain, proclaimed himself chief of the rebels and Calvinists, and led an army of thirty thousand Germans into the Low Countries (14). The scale of victory inclined sometimes to one side, sometimes to another, but the whole province was in rebellion against the King of Spain and the authority of the Catholic Church. The best authority to consult regarding this war of the Netherlands is Cardinal Bentivoglio. Although the Calvinists were most numerous in Holland, it is now divided between a thousand sects—Calvinists, Lutherans, Anabaptists, Socinians, Arians, and the like. There are, likewise, a great number of Catholics; and, although they do not enjoy the free exercise of their religion, still they are tolerated, and allowed to have private chapels in the cities, and in the country towns and villages they enjoy greater freedom* (15).

(13) Gotti, loc. cit. *n.* 16, *c.* 17. (14) Varillas, *t.* 2, *l.* 27, dalla *p.* 441, Jovet Storia della Relia, *t.* 1, *p.* 95. (15) Jovet, loc. cit. *p.* 105.

---

* N.B —This was written in 1770. At present the Catholic Hierarchy is re-established.

80. Calvinism spread itself also into Scotland, and totally infected that kingdom. Varillas (16) gives the whole history of its introduction there; we will give a sketch of it. The perversion of this kingdom commenced with John Knox, an apostate priest of dissolute morals, who was at first a Lutheran, but afterwards residing some time in Geneva, and being intimate with Calvin, became one of his followers, and so ardent was he in his new religion, that he promised Calvin that he would risk everything to plant it in Scotland; soon after he quitted Geneva and came to Scotland to put his design into execution. The opportunity was not long wanting. Henry VIII., King of England, strove to induce his nephew, James V., King of Scotland, to follow his example, and establish a schism and separate himself from the Roman Church, and invited him to meet him at some place where they could hold a conference and discuss the matter. King James excused himself under various pretexts, and the upshot of the matter was that Henry went to war with him. James gave the command of his army to a favourite of his, Oliver Sinclair, whom the nobility obeyed with the greatest reluctance, as he was not of noble birth, and the consequence was that the Scots were beaten, and James died of grief (17), leaving an infant, only eight days old, to inherit his throne, Mary Stuart. Now this was exactly what Knox wanted; a long regency was just the thing to give him an opportunity to establish his opinions, and he unfortunately succeeded so well that he substituted Calvinism for Catholicity. The infant Mary, being now Queen of Scotland, Henry VIII. asked her in marriage for his son Edward, afterwards the sixth of that name, and then only five years old. This demand raised two parties in the kingdom. James Hamilton, Earl of Arran, then all-powerful in Scotland, and Governor of the kingdom, favoured Henry's wishes, gained over by Knox, who had already instilled heretical opinions into his mind; and one great reason he alleged was, that it would establish a perpetual peace between the two kingdoms. On the contrary, the Archbishop of St. Andrew's, David Beatoun (18), afterwards Cardinal, and the Catholics, gave it all the opposition in their power, as tending to make Scotland a province of England, but the chief cause of their opposition to it was the injury to religion, for this marriage would draw Scotland into schism.

81. Meanwhile, the Regent, who was a friend of the heretics, permitted the Calvinists to disseminate their doctrines, and gave liberty to every one in private or in public to pray as he liked, or, in other words, to choose whatever religion he pleased. The archbishop opposed this concession, but the Calvinists rose in arms against him, and imprisoned him, and made him promise to favour

(16) Varillas, Hist. Her. *t.* 2, *l.* 28, dalla *p.* 471; Hermant, Histor. de Concil. *t.* 2, c. 265.
(17) Varillas, *p.* 475.   (18) Varillas, loc. cit.

the English alliance. In this, however, they did not succeed, for previous to her departure for England, the cardinal, with consent of the Queen-Mother, Mary of Lorrain, sister to the Prince of Guise, proposed to Francis I., King of France, to marry Mary to the Dauphin, son of Henry II. The King of France was very well pleased with the proposal, and sent a large body of troops into Scotland, which kept the Calvinists in check, and enabled the Queen Regent to send her daughter to France, and so Mary was sent, before she completed her seventh year, to be brought up in the family of Henry II., and in time to be married to his son, Francis II. On the death of Francis I. and Henry II., Mary was married to Francis II., but was soon left a widow, and the marriage was not blessed with children. Queen Mary then returned to Scotland, where she found religious affairs in the greatest confusion. The Calvinists assassinated the archbishop in his very chamber, and afterwards hanged his body out of the window (19).

82. The rebels, likewise, in this sedition, destroyed the churches, and obliged the Queen-Mother to grant them the free exercise of Calvinism. Such was the miserable state of the kingdom when the Queen returned to it from France; and she immediately set about remedying these religious disorders. About the year 1568 she married Henry Darnley (20), who was afterwards assassinated in the King's house by Earl Bothwell, leaving one son, afterwards James VI. (21). Bothwell, blinded with love of the Queen, engaged a body of conspirators, seized her as she was returning from visiting her son at Stirling, brought her to a castle, and obliged her to marry him. On hearing this the Calvinists immediately broke out into rebellion against her, and accused her of being privy to the murder of her former husband, since she married his murderer, but the principal cause of their hatred to her was her religion. Bothwell himself, however, who had to fly to Denmark from this outbreak, declared before his death that the Queen was perfectly innocent of Henry Darnley's murder. The Calvinists, however, glad of a pretext to persecute the Queen, became so bold at last, that they took her prisoner and confined her in a castle, and the perfidious Knox advised that she should be put to death. The rebels did not go so far as that, but they told her that she should consent to be banished either into France or England, and should renounce the crown in favour of her son, and on her refusal they threatened to throw her into the lake, and one of them had the cowardice to hold a dagger to her breast. Under fear of death she then took the pen and signed the deed making over the kingdom to her son, then thirteen months old (22).

83. The poor Queen was still detained in prison, notwithstand-

(19) Varill. *t.* 28, *l.* 2, *p.* 426. (20) Varill. *p.* 479. (21) Varill. *p.* 500.
(22) Varill. *p.* 502, 503.

ing her renunciation, so some of her friends planned and accomplished her liberation, but not knowing where to seek a place of security, she unfortunately sought it in England from Queen Elizabeth, who promised to aid and assist her as a sister Sovereign. Thus she threw herself into the power of the very woman of all others most anxious to deprive her of life and kingdom, for Mary was her only rival, and the greatest difficulty the Pope had in recognizing Elizabeth was, that while Mary lived she was the lawful inheritor of the English throne. When Mary arrived in England, Elizabeth pretended to receive (23) her; but she imprisoned her—first, at Carlisle, and afterwards in Bolton—under pretence that her enemies wished to make away with her. The national pride of the Scotch was raised when they learned their Queen was a prisoner, and they invaded England with six thousand men. Elizabeth, then unprepared for war, had recourse to craft to avert the blow, and she therefore promised Mary that if she used her authority to make the Scotch retire from England, she would assist her to recover her kingdom, but otherwise that there would be no chance of her liberation till the war was at an end. Mary yielded, and ordered the Scotch to disband themselves, under pain of high treason; the chiefs of the party were thus constrained to obey, but she was still kept in prison, and Elizabeth, to have another pretext for detaining her, induced Murray, a natural brother of Mary, and the Countess of Lennox, mother of the murdered Darnley, to accuse her of procuring her husband's murder. Elizabeth appointed a commission to try her, and though many persons of the greatest weight took up her defence, still, after being imprisoned nineteen years, and having changed from prison to prison, sixteen times in England alone, she was condemned to be beheaded. She received the news of her sentence with the greatest courage, and an entire resignation to the divine will. She asked for a pen, and wrote three requests to Elizabeth: First.—That after her death her servants might be at liberty to go where they pleased. Second.—To allow her to be buried in consecrated ground; and, Third.—Not to prosecute any one who wished to follow the Catholic faith.

84. The execution of the sentence was deferred for two months, but on the day appointed, the 18th February, 1587, at the dawn of day, the officers of justice came to conduct her to the place of execution. The Queen asked for a confessor to prepare her for death, but was refused, and a minister was sent to her whom she refused to receive. It is said that she received the holy Communion herself, having, by permission of the Pope, St. Pius V., retained a consecrated particle for that purpose (24). She then dressed herself with all the elegance of a bride, prayed for a short time in her

(23) Varill. *p.* 50, *seq.* (24) Vide P. Suar. *t.* 3, in St. Thom. *c.* 72, *ar.* 8, in fin.

oratory, and went to the scaffold which was prepared in the hall of Fotheringay Castle, the last prison she inhabited. Everything was covered with black, the hall, the scaffold, and the pulpit from which the sentence was read. Mary entered, covered with a long veil, which reached to her feet, a golden cross on her breast, a Rosary pendant at her girdle, and a crucifix in one hand, the Office of the Blessed Virgin in the other. She went forward with a majestic gait, and calling Melvin, her Major-domo, she saluted him with a serene countenance, and said: " My dear Melvin, when I am dead go to my son and tell him that I die in the Catholic religion, and tell him if he loves me or himself to follow no other; let him put his trust in God, and He will help him, and tell him to pardon Elizabeth for my death, which I voluntarily embrace for the Faith." She then requested the Governor to allow the persons composing her suite to be present at her death, that they might certify that she died in the Catholic Faith. She knelt down on a cushion covered with black, and heard the sentence signed by Elizabeth's own hand read, she then laid her head on the block, and the executioner cut it off at the second stroke. Her body was buried near Queen Catherine's, the wife of Henry VIII., and it is said this inscription was put on her tomb, but immediately after removed by order of Elizabeth: " Maria Scotorum Regina virtutibus Regiis et animo Regio ornata, tyrannica crudelitate ornamentum nostri seculi extinguitur." Mary's death filled all Europe with horror and compassion for her fate, and even Elizabeth, when she heard it, could not conceal the effect it had on her, and said it was too precipitate, but for all that she continued to persecute the Catholics more and more, and added many martyrs to the Church (25).

85. James VI., King of Scotland, and the son of Queen Mary, took little heed of his mother's advice or example, for, after Elizabeth's death, being then King of Scotland, he succeeded her, and took the title of James I., King of Great Britain, and the year after his coronation, which took place in 1603, he ordered, under pain of death, that all Catholic priests should quit the kingdom. In the year 1606 he brought out that famous declaration that the King of England was independent of the Roman Church, called the Oath of Supremacy. He died in 1625, the fifty-ninth year of his age, and the twenty-second of his English reign. He was the first King who governed the three kingdoms of England, Ireland, and Scotland, but he lived and died a heretic, while his mother lived forty-two years in almost continual sorrow and persecution, but died the death of the just. This unhappy monarch was succeeded by his son, Charles I., born in the year 1600, and like his father, the Sovereign of three kingdoms; he followed his father's

---

(25) Varillas, sopra, *t.* 2, *l.* 28; Bern. *t.* 4, *s.* 16, *c.* 11; Joves Istoria della Rel. *t.* 2, *p.* 84; Dizion. Port.

errors in religion, and sent succours to the Calvinists in France, to enable them to retain Rochelle then in their possession. He was unfortunate; for both the Scotch and English Parliamentarians took up arms against him, and after several battles he lost the kingdom. He took refuge with the Scotch, but they delivered him up to the English, and they, at Cromwell's instigation, who was then aiming at sovereign power, condemned him to be beheaded, and he died on the scaffold on the 30th of July, 1648, the twenty-fifth of his reign and forty-eighth of his age.

86. He was succeeded by his son, Charles II., born in 1630; at his father's death he went to Scotland, and was proclaimed King of that country and of England and Ireland likewise. Cromwell, who then governed the kingdom, under title of Protector of England, took the field against him, and put his forces to flight, so that Charles had to make his escape in disguise, first to France and afterwards to Cologne and Holland. He was recalled after Cromwell's death, which took place in 1658, and was crowned King of England in 1661, and died in 1685, at the age of sixty-five. He was succeeded by his brother, James II., born in 1633. James was proclaimed King on the day of his brother's death, the 16th of February, 1685, and was soon after proclaimed King of Scotland, though he openly declared himself a Roman Catholic, and forsook the communion of the English Church. Ardently attached to the Faith, he promulgated in 1687 an Edict of Toleration, granting to the Catholics the free exercise of religion, but this lost him his crown, for the English called in William, Prince of Orange, who, though James's son-in-law, took possession of the kingdom, and, in 1689, James had to fly to France. He soon after went over to Ireland, to keep possession of that kingdom at all events, but being again beaten he fled back again to France, and died in St. Germains, in 1701, the sixty-eighth year of his age. As this sovereign did not hesitate to sacrifice his temporal kingdom for the Faith, we have every reason to believe that he received an eternal crown from the Almighty. James II. left one son, James III., who died in the Catholic Faith in Rome.

SEC. III.—THE ERRORS OF CALVIN.

87. Calvin adopts the Errors of Luther. 88. Calvin's Errors regarding the Scriptures. 89. The Trinity. 90. Jesus Christ. 91. The Divine Law. 92. Justification. 93. Good Works and Free Will. 94. That God predestines Man to Sin and to Hell, and Faith alone in Jesus Christ is sufficient for Salvation. 95. The Sacraments, and especially Baptism. 96. Penance. 97. The Eucharist and the Mass. 98. He denies Purgatory and Indulgences; other Errors.

97. CALVIN adopted almost all the principal errors of Luther, who adopted almost all the errors of the ancient heretics, as we shall hereafterwards show in the refutation of Luther and Calvin. Prate-

olus (1) reckons two hundred and seven heretical doctrines, promulgated by Calvin, and another author (2) makes the number amount to fourteen hundred. At present I will only speak of the principal errors of Calvin, and will give in the last part of the work a particular treatise to refute them.

88. As regards the Holy Scriptures, Calvin, in his book against the Council of Trent (3), says the Church has no right to interpret and judge of the true sense of the Scriptures. Second.—He refuses to receive the Canon of the Scriptures as settled by the Council. Third.—He denies the authority of the Vulgate. Fourth.—He denies the Canonicity of the books of Ecclesiasticus, Wisdom, Tobias, Judith, and the Maccabees, and totally rejects Apostolical Traditions (4).

89. Regarding the Persons of the Trinity, he does not like the words Consubstantial, Hypostasis, or even Trinity. "I wish," he says, "all these words were buried in oblivion, and we had this Faith alone, that the Father, Son, and Holy Ghost are one God" (5). The Church, however, has inserted in the Office of the Breviary the Athanasian Creed, in which it is positively laid down that the Father, and the Son, and the Holy Ghost, are not only one God, but also three distinct Persons; for otherwise one might fall into the errors of Sabellius, who said that these were but simple words, and that in the Trinity there is but one Divine Nature, and one Person, and on that account the Holy Fathers made use of the words Hypostatic and Consubstantial to explain both the distinction and the equality of the Divine Persons. Second.—It is a foolish thing, he says, to believe in the continual actual generation of the Son from the Eternal Father (6); but this doctrine is not only the general one among theologians (7), but is proved by the Scriptures: "Thou art my Son, this day have I begotten thee" (Ps. ii. 7). St. Augustin, explaining this text, says: "This day, that is, from all eternity, and in every continuous instant, he begets me according to my Divine Nature, as his Word and his Natural Son."

90. Speaking of Jesus Christ, he says, that he was the mediator of mankind with his Eternal Father before he became man, and before Adam sinned (8). "Not alone," he says in one of his letters, "did Christ discharge the office of a mediator after the fall of Adam, but as the Eternal Word of God." This is a manifest error, for it was when Christ took flesh in the womb of the Virgin Mary that he became the mediator of reconciliation between God and man; as the Apostle says, "for there is one God, and one mediator of God and man, the *man* Christ Jesus" (1 Timothy, ii. 5). He also blasphemously taught, that when Christ descended into hell (and

(1) Præteol. Hær. 13. (2) Francisc. Forfandes. in Theomach. Calv. (3) Calvin, Antid. ad Synod. Trident. ad Sess. IV. (4) Calvin. in Antid. loc. cit. (5) Calvin. Instit. *l.* 1, *c.* 13, *sec.* (6) Calvin. vide loc. cit. (7) Calvin. Epist. ad Stancarum. (8) Calvin, Instit. *l.* 2, *c.* 16

he understands it as the hell of the damned), that he suffered the pains of the damned, and this was the great price he offered to his Eternal Father for our redemption. Cardinal Gotti says (9), that like Nestorius, he recognized two persons in Christ (10).

91. Concerning the Divine law, and the sins of mankind (11), he says it is impossible for us to observe the law imposed on us by God, and that original concupiscence, or that vicious leaning to sin which exists in us, though we do not consent to it, is still sinful, since such desires arise from the wickedness which reigns in us; that there are no venial sins, but that all are mortal; that every work which even the just man performs is sinful; that good works have no merit with God, and that to say the contrary is pride, and proceeds from a wish to depreciate grace (12).

92. Concerning justification, he says that it does not consist in the infusion of sanctifying grace, but in the imposition of the justice of Christ, which reconciles the sinner with God. The sinner, he says in another place, puts on the justice of Christ by Faith, and clothed in that, appears before God not as a sinner, but as one of the just, so that the sinner, though continuing a sinner still, is justified by being clothed with—masked as it were—the justice of Christ, and appears just by that means (13). He also says, that man, in a state of sin, is not justified by contrition, but by Faith alone, believing in the promises and in the merits of Jesus Christ (14). This was the doctrine of the French Calvinists in their celebrated profession of faith: "We believe that we are made participators of this justification by Faith alone, and this so happens because the promises of life offered to us in Christ are applied to our use." He likewise said, that those who are justified should believe with a certainty of Faith that they are in a state of grace, and that this certainty should be understood not only of perseverance, but even of eternal salvation; so that one should consider himself as one of the elect, as St. Paul was by the special revelation he received from God (15). He likewise said, that Faith and justification belong to the elect alone, and that once in possession of them, they cannot be lost, and if any one thinks he lost them, he never had them. The Synod of Dort, however (16), opposed this doctrine, when it decided that in particular instances one may lose the Divine grace. We should not at all be surprised at this disagreement in the same sect, for as the heresiarchs separate from the Church, they cannot blame their disciples for separating from them; as Tertullian says, when each follows his own will, the Valentinians have the same right to their own opinions as Valentine himself (17).

93. He uttered horrible blasphemies when speaking of human

(9) Gotti, Vera Chiesa, *t.* 1, *c.* 8, *sec.* 1, *n.* 9. (10) Calvin. Instit. *l.* 1, *c.* 13, *sec.* 9, *n.* 23, 24. (11) Calv. *l.* 3, *c.* 3, *sec.* 10. (12) Idem. *l.* 3, *c.* 14, *sec.* 4. (13) Idem. *l.* 3, *c.* 11, *sec.* 15, 16. (14) Idem, *l.* 3, *c.* 11, *sec.* 3. (15) Calv. Inst. *l.* 3, *c.* 2, *sec.* 16, & seq. (16) Idem, *l.* 3, *c.* 2, *sec.* 11, 12. (17) Tertull. de Script. Hærat. *c.* 42.

actions as meritorious to salvation or otherwise. The first is, that
man has no free will, and that this word free will is but a name
without the substance (18). The first man alone, he said, had free
will, but he and all his posterity lost it through sin; hence, anything
that man does he does through necessity, for God has so willed it,
and it is God himself moves him to do it, which movement man
cannot resist. But then, it may be said, when man acts without
free will, and through necessity, both when he does what is good,
as well as when he does what is evil, how can he have merit or demerit? Calvin again blasphemously answers this and says, that to
acquire merit, or deserve punishment, it is enough that man should
act spontaneously, without being driven to it by others, though all
the while he acts without liberty and through necessity. But if
God moves the will of man even to commit sin, then God is the
author of sin. "No," says Calvin, "because the author of sin is he
alone who commits it, not he who commands or moves the sinner
to commit it." He does not blush, then, to give utterance to a third
blasphemy, that every sin is committed by the Divine authority and
will; and those, he says, who assert that God merely permits sins,
but does not wish them, or instigate them, oppose the Scriptures.
"They feign that he permits those things which the Scripture pro-
nounces are done, not only by his permission, but of which he is
the author" (19). He bases this falsehood on that text of David (20):
"Whatsoever the Lord pleased he both done in heaven and on
the earth" (Psalms, cxxxiv. 6); but he appears to forget what the
Psalmist says in another place: "Thou art not a God that willeth
iniquity" (Psalms, v. 5). If God, I ask, moves man to commit
sin, how can he avoid it? Calvin not being able to get out of
this difficulty, says, that carnal men as we are, we cannot understand it (21).

94. It is a necessary consequence of this doctrine that the sinner
who is lost is lost by Divine ordinance, and even this horrible blasphemy did not affright Calvin; monstrous as it is he agrees to it,
and concludes that God, knowing beforehand the salvation or reprobation of each person, as he has decreed it, that some men are
predestined to eternal torment by the Almighty, solely by his will,
and not by their evil actions (22). Such, reader, is the fine theology of these new Reformers of the Church—Luther and Calvin,
who make the Almighty a tyrant, a deceiver, unjust and wicked—
a tyrant, because he creates men for the purpose of tormenting them
for all eternity; a deceiver, because he imposes on them a law which
they never can, by any means in 'their power, observe; unjust,
since he condemns men to eternal punishment, while, at the same
time, they are not at liberty to avoid sin, but constrained to commit

---

(18) Calv. Inst. *l.* 3, *c.* 2 *sec.* 16, & seq.   (19) Calv. *l.* 2, c. 3.   (20) Calvin
de Prædest. Dei, æterna.   na.) Calv. Inst. *l.* 3, *c.* 23.   (22) Calv. ibid.

it; and wicked, for he himself first causes a man to sin, and then punishes him for it. Finally, they make God distribute his rewards unjustly, since he gives his grace and heaven to the wicked, merely because they have Faith, that they are justified, though they should not even be sorry for their sins. Calvin says that this is the benefit of the death of Christ; but I answer him thus: If, according to his system, a man may be saved, then good works are no longer necessary, and Christ died to destroy every precept both of the Old and New Law, and to give freedom and confidence to Christians to do whatever they like, and to commit even the most enormous sins, since it is enough to secure their salvation without any cooperation on their part, that they should merely believe firmly that God does not impute to them their sins, but wishes to save them through the merits of Christ, though they do everything in their power to gain hell. This certain faith in our salvation, which he calls *confidence*, God, he says, gives to the elect alone.

95. Speaking of the sacraments, he says that they have effect on the elect alone, so that those who are not predestined to eternal happiness, though they may be in a state of grace, receive not the effect of the sacrament. He also says that the words of the ministers of the sacraments are not consecrating, but only declaratory, intended alone to make us understand the Divine promises (23), and hence he infers, that the sacraments have not the power of conferring grace, but only of exciting our Faith, like the preaching of the Divine Word (24), and he ridicules our theological term, *ex opere operato*, for explaining the power of the sacraments, as an invention of ignorant monks; but in this he only shows his own ignorance, as he understands by *opus operatum*, the good work of the ministers of the sacraments (25). We, Catholics, understand by *opus operatum*, not the act of the minister himself, so much as the power which the Almighty gives to the sacraments (if not hindered by sin), of operating in the soul; that which the sacrament signifies, as Baptism, to wash; Penance, to forgive; the Eucharist, to nourish. He denies that there is any difference between the sacraments of the Old and the New Law (26); but St. Paul says that the former were but weak and needy elements (Gal. iv. 9), and a shadow of things to come (Colos. ii. 17). He ridicules the sacramental character which is impressed by Baptism, Confirmation, and Orders (27), and Christ, he says, only instituted three sacraments—Baptism, the Supper, and Ordination; the first two he positively asserts to be sacraments, and the third he admits. " The imposition of hands," he says, " which is performed in true and lawful Ordinations, I grant to be a sacrament;" but he totally rejects the Sacraments of Confirmation, Penance, Extreme Unction, and Matrimony (28).

(23) Calvin. Instit. *l*. 4, *c*. 14, *s*. 4.   (24) Idem, *l*. 4, *c*. 14, *s*. 11.   (25) Idem, *l*. 4, *c*. 14, *s*. 26.   (26) Idem. *l*. 4, *c*. 14, *s*. 23.   (27) Calvin, Instit. in Antid. Conc. Trid. ad Can. 9, Sess. 7.   (28) Idem, *l*. 4, *c*. 19, *s*. 19, 20.

Though he admits Baptism as a sacrament, he denies that it is necessary for salvation (29), because children, he says, snatched off by death, though they are not baptized, are saved, for they are members of the Church when they are born, for all children of Christians, he says, being born in the alliance of the New Law (30), are all born in grace (31), and he teaches that laymen and women cannot baptize a child, even in danger of death (an error most dangerous to the salvation of these poor innocents), because, though they die without baptism, they are saved (32). Finally, he teaches that the Baptism of John the Baptist was of the same efficacy as the Baptism instituted by Jesus Christ (33).

96. He not alone denies that Penance is a sacrament, but he teaches many errors concerning it; for the sins committed after Baptism, he says, are remitted by the remembrance of Baptism, and do not require the Sacrament of Penance (34); that the absolution of the confessor has no power to remit sins, but is merely an abstraction of the remission God grants us, by the promise made to Christians; that the confession of sins is not of Divine right, but only ordained by Innocent III., in the Council of Lateran; and that it is not necessary to make satisfaction for our sins, because God is not to be pleased with our works, and such satisfaction would be to derogate from that atonement made by Christ for our sins.

97. Regarding the Sacrament of the Eucharist, against which all his malice is directed, as we see in his book, " De Cœna Domini," he says that Transubstantiation, as believed by Catholics, is nothing but a mere invention, and that the Eucharist ought not to be preserved or adored, because it is a sacrament only while it is used, and that the essence of this sacrament is eating by Faith (35). He denies (and this is the error he most furiously defends) the Real Presence of Jesus Christ in the Eucharist. The words of consecration: " This is my body, and this is my blood," are to be taken, he says, not in reality, as we believe them, but figuratively, and that they do not mean the conversion of the bread and wine into the body and blood of Christ, but that the bread and wine in the sacrament are merely figures of the body and blood of our Lord (36), and that in the communion we receive the life and substance of Jesus Christ, but not his proper flesh and blood; then he says, " we do and do not receive Jesus Christ," proving that he did not believe in, or admit, the Real Presence in the Eucharist (37). Nothing, he says, can be more reprehensible than dividing the Supper—in other words, giving communion under one kind. When such is their doctrine, we ought surely be surprised to see the Calvinists in their famous Synod of Charenton, in 1631, deciding that the Lutherans,

(29) Idem, c. 19, s. 31. (30) Idem, l. 4, c. 15, s. 20. (31) Bossuet, Variat. t. 3, l. 14, n. 37. (32) Calvin, l. 4, c. 15, s. 20 & seq. (33) Idem, l. 3, c. 15, s. 3 & 4. (34) Vide loc. cit. (35) Calvin, loc. cit. de Cœna Dom. (36) Calvin, Instit. l. 4, c. 17, s. 32. (37) Idem, loc. cit. s. 33, 34.

who they knew believed in the Real Presence, should be admitted to their communion, because, as they asserted, both believed in the fundamental articles (38). Daille denies (39) that there is anything in this Decree contrary to piety or to the honour of God: but we may ask the Calvinists: Is not idolatry contrary to the honour of God? and are not the Lutherans idolaters, when they adore as God mere bread? Calvin denies, also, that the Mass is a sacrifice instituted by Jesus Christ for the living and the dead (40), and it is, he says, injurious to the Sacrifice of the Cross to say so, and that private Masses are in direct opposition to the institution of Christ.

98. Calvin likewise denies purgatory (41), the value of indulgences (42), the intercession of saints, and the veneration of images (46); and St. Peter, he says, enjoyed among the apostles merely a supremacy of honour, but not of jurisdiction (44), and then he rejects the primacy of St. Peter and the Pope (45). The Church and General Councils, he says, are not infallible in the definition of articles of Faith, or the interpretation of the Scriptures. He entirely renounces ecclesiastical laws, and the rites appertaining to discipline (46), such rites, as he alleges, being pernicious and impious, and he rejects the fast of Lent (47), and the celibacy of the clergy (48); vows to fast or to go on a pilgrimage, and the religious vows, he says, are superstitious (49). Usury, he says, may be permitted, for there is no text of Scripture prohibiting it. Noel Alexander and Cardinal Gotti (50) enumerate many other errors of his, and, in a word, he preached and wrote so many blasphemies, that it was not without reason, at his death, that he cursed his life, his studies, and his writings, and called on the devil to take him, as we read above (N. 70) (51).

SEC. IV.—THE DIFFERENT SECTS OF CALVINISTS.

99. The Sects into which Calvinism was divided.   100. The Puritans.   101. The Independents and Presbyterians.   102. The Difference between these Sects.   103. The Quakers and Tremblers.   104. The Anglo-Calvinists.   105. The Piscatorians.   106. The Arminians and Gomarists.

99. THE sect of Calvin was soon divided into numerous other sects—in fact, we may say that from every sect a thousand others sprung, and that is the case, especially in England, where you can scarcely find the members of the same family believing the same thing. We shall speak of the principal sects described by Noel Alexander and Cardinal Gotti (1). These are the Reformed, who

(38) Calvin, *l.* 4, *c.* 17, *s.* 46–48.   (39) Dallæus, Apol. Eccl. Reform. *p.* 43.   (40) Calvin, Instit. *l.* 4, *c.* 18.   (41) Idem, *l.* 3, *c.* 5, *s.* 6, 10.   (42) Calvin, Inst. Idem, *l.* 3, *c.* 5, *s.* 2.   (43) Idem, *l.* 3, *c.* 20.   (44) Idem, I. *c.* II.   (45) Idem, *l.* 4, *c.* 6.   (46) Idem, *l.* 4, *c.* 9.   (47) Idem, *l.* 4, *c.* 20.   (48) Idem, *l.* 4, *c.* 12, *s.* 19 & 20.   (49) Ibid. *s.* 23.   (50) Idem, *l.* 4, *c.* 13, *s.* 6.   (51) Calvin, Respons. de Usur. inter Epist. *p.* 228; Nat. Alex. *t.* 19, *art.* 13, *s.* 2; Gotti, *t.* 2, *c.* 3, *s.* 5.
(1) Nat. Alex. *t.* 19, *art.* 13, *s.* 3; Gotti, Ver. Rel. *c.* 312, *s.* 1, 2.

are found in France, in the Palatinate, in Switzerland, and Flanders, and these, in general, follow the doctrine of Calvin to the letter. In England and Scotland they are called Puritans, and, besides, we find among his followers others called Independents, Presbyterians, Anglo-Calvinists, Piscatorians, Arminians, and Gomorists.

100. The most rigid of all the Calvinists are the Puritans, who hate all who do not follow their own way of thinking, but abhor the Catholics especially, and do not even like to pray in the churches consecrated by them. They rejected Episcopacy—the rites, and ceremonies, and Liturgy, both of the Catholic and Anglican Churches, not even keeping the Lord's Prayer. They are as exact in the observance of the Sunday as the Jews are of the Sabbath. They are no friends to royalty, and it was through their means that Charles I. was brought to the block (as we have seen above, *N.* 85), in 1649.

101. The Independents and Presbyterians believe much the same as the Puritans, but their system of church government is different. When Oliver Cromwell became Protector of England (*N.* 86), he was an Independent. They believe just what they like, and recognize no superior as invested with the power of teaching them. According to them, that supreme power resides in each sect which they would not allow to the Councils of the Universal Church. They allow no one to preach who does not follow their doctrine. They celebrated the " Supper" on Sundays; but they do not admit to the " Supper," nor to Baptism, only those of their own sect. They celebrated the Supper, with their hats on, without catechism, sermon, or singing; and they were the progenitors of all the other sects that overran England, as the Anabaptists, the Antinomians (who rejected all law, *N.* 35), disciples of John Agricola, and the Anti-Scripturists, who totally rejected the Scriptures, boasting that they had the spirit of the Prophets and Apostles.

102. The Presbyterians are a powerful body in the British islands. They separated themselves from the Independents. Their churches are formed into classes; the classes are subject to Provincial Synods; and these to a National Synod, whose decisions must be obeyed, as if almost of Divine authority. They are called Presbyterians, because they adopt a form of church government by lay elders, and they say that bishops have no more authority than presbyters. Their elders are generally men of years, unless in the case of some specially gifted young person; the name is derived from the Greek word, *Presbuteroi*, which means our elders.

103. There are also Quakers, or, as they were sometimes called, Tremblers, who considered themselves perfect in this life. They imagined they were frequently moved by the Spirit to such a pitch, that they trembled all over, not being able to endure the abun-

dance of the Divine light they enjoyed. They reject not only all ecclesiastical, but even civil ceremonies, for they never uncover for any one. They say no prayers in their meeting-houses; they even look on prayer as useless, for they are justified by their own justice itself. They did believe, though it is supposed they hold those opinions no longer, that Jesus Christ despaired on the cross, and that he had other human defects. They held erroneous opinions even on the first dogmas of Faith, not believing in the Trinity, or the second coming of Christ, or in hell or heaven after this life; many of these opinions, which were held by the first Quakers, are now changed or modified, and it is difficult at present to know exactly what their creed is. Their founder was an Englishman, John Fox, a tailor. There is another sect, called Ranters, who believe that nothing is vile or unlawful which nature desires. Another sect was called Levellers, enemies of all political order; they wished that all men should dress exactly alike, and that no one should be honoured more than another, and they frequently were punished for seditious conduct by the magistrates.

104. The Anglo-Calvinists are different from the Puritans, Independents, and Presbyterians, both in church discipline and doctrine. Unlike all these sects, they have preserved the Episcopal Order, not alone as distinct from other offices, but as superior by Divine right; they retain a sort of form of consecration for bishops; they ordain priests, and confirm those who have received Baptism, and show some honour to the Sign of the Cross, which their cognate sects reject totally. Besides bishops, there are chancellors, archdeacons, deans, and rectors of parishes; they have preserved the cathedrals, and have canons and prebends, who say morning and evening prayers, and the surplice is used as a vestment. They recognize both the orders of priesthood and deaconship. The King, according to the laws of Henry and Elizabeth, is head of the Church, and the fountain of all ecclesiastical authority. The Sovereign, they say, has the power of making new laws, and establishing new rites, with consent of the Metropolitan and Convocation; and his royal tribunal decides all judgments brought before it. He can, with his Council, decide on matters of Faith, publish ordinances and censures. Such are the powers granted to the Sovereign, in the work entitled, "The Policy of the Church of England," published in London, in the year 1683.

105. The Piscatorians were so called, from John Piscator, a Professor of Theology, and pastor, at Herborne, a proud and vain man. He differed in several points with the Calvinists. He divided the justification of Christ into active and passive; the active he acquired by the holiness of his life—the passive, by his sufferings; the active justification was profitable to himself alone—the passive to us, and it is by this we are justified. It is, on the contrary, our doctrine, that Christ, by his labours and sufferings, gained merit

both for himself and us; as the Apostle says: "He humbled himself, being made obedient unto death............For which God exalted him, &c." (Philip. ii. 8, 9). Hence God exalted him, both for the sanctity of his life, and for his passion. He, likewise, taught that the breaking of the bread in the "Supper" was essential; and the Academy of Marpurg embraced this opinion, but the other Calvinists did not. The Mosaic Law, he said, should be observed, as far as the judicial precepts go. He differed almost entirely with Calvin, regarding predestination, the atonement, penance, and other points, and composed a new Catechism. He likewise published a new version of the Bible, filled with a thousand errors. Both himself and his doctrines were unanimously condemned by the Reformers.

106. Two other Calvinistic sects had their origin in Holland, the Arminians and Gomarists. Arminius or Harmensen, and Gomar, were Professors of Theology in the University of Leyden. In 1619, Arminius published a Remonstrance, and, on that account, his followers were called Remonstrants. In this writing, or Catechism, which in several articles comes near to the Catholic doctrine, he rejects eight errors of Calvin. The first error he attacks is, that God gives to the predestined alone, faith, justification, and glory; God, he says, wishes the salvation of all men, and gives all sufficient means of salvation, if they wish to avail themselves of them. He rejects the second error, that God, by an absolute decree, has destined many to hell before he created them; he says, that such reprobation is because of the sins they commit, and die without repenting of. Of the third error, that Christ has redeemed the elect alone, he says that no one is excluded from the fruit of redemption, if he is disposed to receive it as he ought. The fourth error he reproves, is that no one can resist grace; this, he says, is false, for man by malice can, if he like, reject it. The fifth error is, that he who has once received grace cannot again lose it; but he teaches that in this life we may both lose the grace received, and recover it again by repentance. Gomar (2), on the other hand, though a professor in the same University, adopted all the dogmas of Calvin, and opposed Arminius and his Remonstrants with the greatest violence, and his disciples were called Anti-Remonstrants, and they accused the Arminians of Pelagianism. The dispute, at length, became so violent, that the States-General convoked a Synod, at Dort, to terminate it, and invited deputies from England, Scotland, Geneva, and other kingdoms. The Synod was held; but as almost all the deputies who attended were Calvinists, or differed but slightly from the Calvinistic doctrines, the Arminians were condemned, and the Gomarists got the upper hand. The States' Chancellor, Barneveldt, and Hugo Grotius, took the part of Arminius, for which Barneveldt

(2) Nat. Alex. *t.* 19, *c.* 3, *art.* 11, *sec.* 13, *n.* 6.

perished on the scaffold, and Grotius was condemned to perpetual imprisonment, but was saved by a stratagem of his wife, who obtained leave to send him a chest of books, to amuse him in his solitude; after a time, the chest was sent back, and, instead of the books, Grotius was concealed in it, and thus escaped (3).

CHAPTER XII.

HERESIES OF THE SIXTEENTH CENTURY—(CONTINUED).

ARTICLE I.

THE SCHISM OF ENGLAND.

SEC. I.—THE REIGN OF HENRY VIII.

1. Religion of England previous to the Reformation. 2. Henry VIII. marries Catherine of Arragon, but becomes enamoured of Anna Boleyn. 3. The wicked Wolsey suggests the Invalidity of the Marriage. Incontinence of Anna Boleyn; Suspicion that she was the Daughter of Henry. 4. Catherine refuses to have her Cause tried by English Judges; Wolsey is made Prisoner and dies at Leicester. 5. Henry seizes on the Property of the Church, and marries Anna Boleyn. 6. He obliges the Clergy to swear Obedience to him, and Cranmer declares the Marriage of Catherine invalid. 7. The Pope declares Anna Boleyn's Marriage invalid, and excommunicates Henry, who declares himself Head of the Church. 8. He persecutes Pole, and puts More and Fisher to Death. 9. The Pope declares Henry unworthy of the Kingdom; the King puts Anna Boleyn to Death, and marries Jane Seymour. 10. The Parliament decides on six Articles of Faith; the Bones of St. Thomas of Canterbury are burned; Jane Seymour dies in giving Birth to Edward VI. 11. The Pope endeavours to bring Henry to a Sense of his Duty, but does not succeed. 12. He marries Anne of Cleves; Cromwell is put to Death. 13. Henry marries Catherine Howard, whom he afterwards put to Death, and then marries Catherine Parr. 14. His Remorse in his last Sickness. 15. He makes his Will and dies.

1. THE history of England cannot be read without tears when we see that nation, formerly the most zealous in Europe for Catholicity, now become its persecuting enemy. Who will not be touched with sorrow to see a kingdom so attached to the Faith, that it was called the Land of Saints, now buried in heresy? Fifteen English kings, and eleven queens, renounced the world and became religious in different convents. Twelve kings were martyrs, and ten have been placed in the catalogue of the saints. It is said that previous to the schism there was not a village in England which had not a patron saint born on the spot. How dreadful it is to behold this land the abode of schism and heresy (1). England, it is said, received the Faith of Christ in the time of Tiberius Cæsar. Joseph

---

(3) Nat. Alex. loc. cit. Gotti, Ver. Rel. *c.* 12, *sec.* 2, *n.* 40; Dizion. Port. alla parola Grozio.   (1) Jovet. Storia delle Relig. *t.* 2, dal prin.; Gotti Ver. Re. *c.* 113, *s.* 1.

of Arimathea (2), Sanders says, with twelve of his disciples, were the first to introduce Christianity into the country which, in the time of Pope Eleutherius, had spread so much, that, at the request of King Lucius, he sent them Fugacius and Damian, who baptized the King and many of his subjects, and having cast down the idols, consecrated many churches, and established several bishoprics. England remained firm in the Faith in the time of Diocletian, and there were many martyrs there during his reign. Christianity increased very much during the reign of Constantine, and though many fell away into the errors of Arius and Pelagius, they were converted again to the true Faith by the preaching of St. Germain and St. Lupus, who came from France for that purpose. About the year 596 religion was almost lost by the Saxon conquest, but St. Gregory sent over St. Austin and forty Benedictine monks, who converted the whole Anglo-Saxon nation, and they were remarkable for nearly a thousand years after for their zeal for the Faith and their veneration for the Holy See. During all this long period there were no sovereigns in Christendom more obedient to the See of Rome than those of England. In the year 1212, King John and the barons of the kingdom made England feudatory to the Holy See, holding the kingdoms of England and Ireland as fiefs from the Pope, and paying a thousand marks every year on the feast of St. Michael and Peter's Pence, according to the number of hearths in these kingdoms, which was first promised by King Ina, in the year 740, augmented by King Etholf, and paid up to the twenty-fifth year of Henry's reign, when he separated himself from the obedience of the Holy See. Many provincial Councils were held in England during these centuries likewise for the establishment of ecclesiastical discipline, which was always observed till Henry's reign, when, to satisfy a debasing passion for a wicked woman, he plunged himself into a whirlpool of crimes, and involved the nation in his ruin, and thus this unfortunate country, the glory of the Church, became a sink of wickedness and impiety.

12. You shall now hear the cause of England's ruin. In the year 1501, Henry VII. married his eldest son, Arthur, to Catherine of Arragon (3), daughter of his Catholic Majesty Ferdinand, but the prince died before the consummation of the matrimony; she was then married to his second son, Henry VIII., by a dispensation of Julius II., with the intention of preserving the peace with Spain, and had five children by him. Before we proceed, however, it will be right to learn that Henry was so much attached to the Catholic religion that when it was attacked by Luther he persecuted his followers to death, and caused all his books to be burned one day in his presence by the public executioner, and had a sermon

(2) Sand. de Schism. Anglic. in Pro. Conc. c. 166.   (3) Gotti, c. 113, s. 2, n. 1, 2; Herm. Hist.

preached on the occasion by John Fisher, Bishop of Rochester. He then published a work defending the doctrine of Faith in the Seven Sacraments, in opposition to Luther, though some say the book was composed by Fisher of Rochester, and dedicated it to Leo X., who honoured him on the occasion with the title of Defender of the Faith (4). Blind to everything, however, but his love for Anna Boleyn, he began to hold his wife, Queen Catherine, in the greatest aversion, though she was twenty-five years married to him (5). She was five or six years older than Henry, but Anna Boleyn was considered the most beautiful woman in England, and when she saw the impression she made on the king's heart, refused to see him any more unless he married her. She subsequently yielded to his solicitations, and cohabited for three years with him before her marriage.

13. It was England's misfortune at that period to be almost governed by Thomas Wolsey, a man of low birth, but whose intriguing disposition made him such a favourite with Henry, that he was elevated not only to the Archbishopric of York, but was made Lord Chancellor of the kingdom, and Cardinal (6). This unprincipled flatterer, seeing the King disgusted with Catherine, his Queen, advised him to apply for a divorce, and encouraged his scruples (if he had any), telling him his marriage never could be legalized, as Catherine was his brother's wife. This objection, however, never could stand, for Henry had the Pope's dispensation to marry Catherine (7); the case was maturely examined at Rome, and the impediment that existed was not imposed by the Divine Law, but merely a canonical one. That is proved by the Scripture, for we learn from Genesis, xxxviii., that the patriarch Juda made his second son Onan, marry Thamar, the wife of his elder brother, who died without children; and in the Mosaic Law there was a precept obliging the younger brother to take his elder brother's widow to wife, if he had died without leaving children; "When brethren dwell together, and one of them died without children, the wife of the deceased shall not marry to another, but his brother shall take her, and raise up seed for his brother" (Deut. xxv. 5). What, therefore, was not only permitted but commanded by the Old Law, never could be contrary to the law of nature. Neither is the prohibition of Leviticus, xviii. 16, to be taken into account, for that applies only to the case that the deceased brother has left children, and not, as in the former case, where he died childless, for then the brother is commanded to marry the widow, that his dead brother's name should not be lost in Israel. There is, then, not the least doubt but the dispensation of the Pope and the marriage of Henry were both valid. Bossuet, in his History of the Varia-

(4) Gotti, loc. cit. n. 2. (5) Bossuet, Hist. des Variat. t. 2, l. 7, n. 1. (6) Nat. Alex. Hist. t. 19, c. 13, a. 3, n. 1; Gotti, c. 213, s. 2, n. 6. (7) Gotti, s. 2, n. 3.

tions (8), tells us, that Henry having asked the opinion of the Sorbonne as to the validity of his marriage, forty-five doctors gave their opinion that it was valid, and fifty-three were of the contrary opinion, but Molineaux says, that all these votes were purchased on the occasion. Henry even wrote to the Lutheran doctors in Germany, but Melancthon, having consulted others, answered him that the law prohibiting a man to marry his brother's wife could be dispensed with, and that his marriage with Catherine was, therefore, valid. This answer was far from being agreeable to Henry, so he held on to Wolsey's opinion, and determined to marry Anna Boleyn. It has been said that this lady was even Henry's own daughter, and it is said that her father, who was ambassador in France at the time, came post to England (9) when he heard of the affair, and told Henry that his wife confessed to him that Anna was Henry's daughter, but Henry made him, it is said, a rude answer, told him to go back to his place, and hold his tongue, and that he was determined to marry her. Mary Boleyn, her sister, was, however, one of Henry's mistresses. It is also said, that, from the age of fifteen, Anna was of bad character, and that, during her residence in France, her conduct was so depraved that she was called usually by an improper name (10).

4. Henry, fully determined to marry this unfortunate woman(11), sent to Rome to demand of the Pope to appoint Cardinal Campeggio and Cardinal Wolsey to try the case of the divorce. The Pope consented, but the Queen appealed against these prelates as judges, one of them being the King's subject, and the other under obligations to him. Notwithstanding the appeal, the cause was tried in England, and Henry was in the greatest hurry to have it decided, being certain of a favourable issue for himself, as one of the judges was Wolsey, the prime mover of the case. Wolsey, however, was now afraid of the tempest he raised, which portended the ruin of religion, so he and Campeggio tried every means to avoid coming to a decision, seeing the dreadful scandal it would cause if they gave a decision in the King's favour, and dreading his displeasure if they decided against him. The Pope admitted the justice of the Queen's appeal (12), and prohibited the Cardinal Legates from proceeding with the cause, which he transferred to his own tribunal. Henry then sent Cranmer to Rome to look after his interests. This man was a priest, but of immoral life, and had privately embraced the Lutheran doctrines, and he was indebted to Anna Boleyn for the King's favour. Henry likewise endeavoured to draw to his party Reginald Pole and Thomas More; but these were men of too much religion to yield to him.

(8) Boss. al. cit. *l.* 7, *n.* 61. (9) Floremund, *l.* 6, Synop. *c.* 2, *n.* 2; Gotti, *c.* 113, *s.* 2, *n.* 8, 9, 10; Nat. Alex. loc. cit. *n.* 1. (10) Gotti, *n.* 9. (11) Nat. Alex. cit. *n.* 1; Varillas Ist. *t.* 1, *l.* 9, *p.* 412. (12) Nat. Alex. *l.* 19, *art. c. n.* 2.

To frighten the Pope into compliance with his wishes, he prohibited, under the severest penalties, any of his subjects from applying for any favour or grace to Rome, without first obtaining his consent. God made use of Henry as an instrument to punish Wolsey now for his crimes. The King was furious with him, because he did not expedite the sentence in his favour, so he deprived him of the bishopric of Winchester (though this is doubtful), and the chancellorship, and banished him to his See of York. He lived some time at Cawood, in Yorkshire, and made himself very popular in the neighbourhood by his splendid hospitality. Henry gave an order for his arrest, and commanded that he should be brought to London, but he suffered so much on the journey, both in mind and body, that, before he could arrive, he died at Leicester, in the month of December, 1530. A report was sent abroad that he poisoned himself, but the fact is, that when he found he was accused of high treason, his heart broke. "Had I served God," said he, "as faithfully as I served the King, he would not have given me over in my grey hairs" (13).

5. In the meantime, Cranmer wrote from Rome that he found it impossible to get the Pope to consent to the divorce, so he was recalled by Henry (14), and went to Germany, where he married Osiander's sister or niece (15); and on the death of William Warham, Archbishop of Canterbury, was appointed to that See, but with the express condition of doing what the Pope refused—pronouncing a sentence of divorce between Henry and Catherine (16). When Henry found that the ecclesiastics of the kingdom took up Catherine's side, he determined to punish some of them, and prosecuted them on a *præmunire*, for preferring the Legatine to the Royal authority. The clergy, terrified at this proceeding, and having now no one to recur to, offered the King 400,000 crowns to compromise the matter, and admitted his sovereign power in the realm, both over the clergy and laity. Thomas More (17), seeing the ruin of England at hand, resigned the chancellorship to the King, who accepted his resignation, and appointed Thomas Audley, a man of little means, in his place. Pope Clement VII., seeing what imminent danger the kingdom ran, from the blind admiration the King professed for Anna Boleyn, endeavoured to save it, by prohibiting him, under pain of excommunication, from contracting a new marriage till the question of divorce was settled (18). This prohibition only exasperated Henry the more, so, despising both the admonitions and censures of the Pope, he was privately married to Anna Boleyn, before the break of day, in the month of December, 1532, having previously created her

---

(13) Gotti, c. 113, sec. 2, n. 13 in fin. & Nat. Alex. loc. cit. n. 2. (14) Jovet, t. 2, p. 29; Gotti, sec. 2, n. 14. (15) Bossuet, l. 7, n. 9. (16) Nat. Alex. t. 19, c. 13, a. 3, n. 2; Gotti, loc. cit. (17) Gotti, c. 113, sec. 2, n. 15. (18) Nat. Alex. t. 19, c. 13, a. 3, n. 3.

Countess of Pembroke (19). Roland Lee was the officiating priest, and it is believed by some that Henry deceived him, telling him he had the Pope's leave for marrying again.

6. Thomas Cromwell (20), under favour of Queen Anna, was now advanced to the highest honours. He was a man of the greatest cunning, and the most unbounded ambition, and a follower of the Lutheran doctrine. Henry made him Knight of the Garter, Grand Chamberlain of the Kingdom, Keeper of the Privy Seal, and made him also his Vicar-General for Ecclesiastical Affairs (21), which he entirely managed as he pleased, in conjunction with Archbishop Cranmer and the Chancellor Audley. He obliged ecclesiastics to take an oath of obedience in spirituals to the King, paying him the same obedience as they previously did the Pope. Every means was used to induce John Fisher, the Bishop of Rochester, to take this oath, which he at first refused to do, but at last consented, adding, as a condition, "inasmuch as it was not opposed to the Divine Word."* When this pillar of the Church fell, it was not difficult to induce the rest of the clergy to take the oath. Cranmer was now ready to fulfil his part of the agreement made with Henry; he accordingly pronounced his marriage with Catherine opposed to the Divine law, and declared him at liberty to marry any other woman, but we have seen that he was already married privately to his concubine, Anna Boleyn.

7. Pope Clement VII. now saw that there was no longer any use in mild measures, and was determined to act with extreme severity. He, accordingly, declared the marriage with Anna invalid; the issue, either present or future, illegitimate; and restored Queen Catherine to her conjugal and royal rights (23). He likewise declared Henry excommunicated for his disobedience to the Holy See, but this sentence was not to be enforced for a month, to give him time for repentance. So far from showing any signs of change, Henry prohibited, under the severest penalties, any one from giving the title of Queen to Catherine, or styling Mary heiress to the kingdom, though she had been already proclaimed as such by the estates of the realm. He declared her illegitimate, and sent her to live with her mother Catherine, appointing a certain fixed place for their residence, and employing about them a set of spies, or guards, rather than servants (24). In the meantime, Anna Boleyn had a daughter, Elizabeth, born on the 7th of September,

(19) Gotti, sec. 2, n. 16; Varillas, t. 1, l. 9, n. 420.   (20) Gotti, sec. 2, n. 17.
(21) Nat. Alex. loc. cit. n. 8; Gotti, loc. cit.   (22) Nat. Alex. loc. cit.; Gotti, c. 113, sec. 2, n. 11; Bossuet, Variat. l. 7, n. 21.   (23) Nat. Alex. art. 3, n. 4; Gotti, sec. 2, n. 20.   (24) Gotti, loc. cit.

* "Of which Church and clergy (English) we acknowledge his Majesty to be the chief protector, the only and supreme Lord, and *as far as the Law of Christ will allow*, the supreme head."—*Lingard Hist. of England*, vol. 6, c. 3.

seven months after her marriage, and Henry continued his persecution of the Catholics, by sending to prison Bishop Fisher, Sir Thomas More, and two hundred Observantine Friars of the Order of St. Francis; and in the parliament convoked on the 3rd of November, 1534, a bill was passed in both houses, declaring Mary, the daughter of Catherine, excluded from the succession, and recognizing Elizabeth, Anna's daughter, as heiress to the throne. The power of the Pope in England and Ireland was rejected at the same time, and whoever professed to believe in the primacy of the Holy See was declared a rebel. He assumed an authority over the bishops of the kingdom greater than the Pope ever possessed, for he granted them their powers as if they were secular magistrates, only till he wished to revoke them, and it was only by his authority they were allowed to ordain priests or publish censures. Finally, it was decreed that the King was the supreme head of the Church of England; that to him alone it belonged to extirpate heresies and correct abuses, and that to him, by right, belonged all tithes and first-fruits. The name of the Pope was expunged from the Liturgy, and among the petitions of the Litany the following was sacrilegiously inserted: "From the tyranny and detestable enormities of the Bishop of Rome deliver us, O Lord" (25).

8. Henry knew that his assumption of the primacy was condemned, not alone by Catholics, but even by Luther and Calvin, so he gave orders that it should be defended by theologians in their writings, and many complied with this command—some willingly, and others were forced to it. He was desirous that his relative, Reginald Pole, should publish something in favour of it, but he not alone most firmly refused to prostitute his pen to such a purpose, but wrote four books, "De Unione Ecclesiastica," in opposition to the pretended right, which so provoked the tyrant, that he declared him guilty of high treason, and a traitor to his country, and tried to get him into his power to put him to death, and when he could not accomplish his wish, he had his mother, his brother, and his uncle executed, and this noble family was almost destroyed and brought to ruin. He, for the same reason, commenced a most dreadful persecution of the Friars, especially the Franciscans, Carthusians, and Brigittines, many of whom he put to death (26), besides Bishop Fisher and Thomas More, whom he sent to execution in the year 1534 (27). While Bishop Fisher was in prison, he was appointed Cardinal by Paul III., which, when Henry heard, he at once had him condemned to death. It is related of this holy bishop, that when he was about to be brought to the place of execution, he dressed himself in the best clothes he could procure, as that was, he said, the day of his marriage, and as, on account of his

(25) Nat. Alex. *t.* 19, *c.* 13, *a.* 3, *n.* 5; Gotti, *c.* 113, *sec.* 2, *n.* 21. (26) Gotti, *n.* 22; Nat. Alex. loc. cit. *n.* 5. (27) Bossuet, His. *l.* 7, *n.* 11.

age and his sufferings in prison, he was so weak that he was obliged to lean on a staff, when he came in sight of the scaffold he cast it away, and cried out: " Now, my feet, do your duty, you have now but a little way to carry me." When he mounted the scaffold he entoned the *Te Deum*, and thanked the Almighty for permitting him to die for the Faith; he then laid his head on the block. His head was exposed on London Bridge, and, it is said, appeared quite florid, and more like the head of a living than a dead person, so that it was ordered to be taken down again (28). Sir Thomas More also died a glorious death. When he heard that the Bishop of Rochester was condemned to death, he exclaimed: " O Lord, I am unworthy of such glory, but I hope thou wilt render me worthy." His wife came to the prison to induce him to yield to the King's wishes, but he refused, and after fourteen months' confinement he was brought to trial, but never swerved, and was condemned to lose his head. When about to mount the scaffold, he called to a man near him to assist him to climb the steps; " But when I am to come down, my friend," said he, " I will want no one to assist me." On the scaffold he protested before the people that he died for the Catholic Faith. He then most devoutly recited the *Miserere*, and laid his head on the block. His execution spread general grief all over England (29).

9. When Paul III., the successor of Clement, was informed of the turn affairs had taken, he summoned Henry and all his accomplices to his tribunal, and in case of contumacy, fulminated the sentence of excommunication against him, but this was not published at the time, as there appeared still some hope that he would change his conduct; but all was in vain, he only every day involved himself more and more in crime. He now, as head of the Church, issued a commission to Cromwell, a layman, to visit the convents, both male and female, in his dominions, to dismiss all religious who were not twenty-four years of age, and to leave the others at liberty to go or stay, as they wished; this, it is said, though I believe not on sufficient foundation, threw ten thousand religious back again into the world (30). About this time Queen Catherine died; she always bore her affliction with the greatest patience, and just before her death, wrote to the King in terms which would melt the hardest heart (31). The vengeance of the Almighty was now impending over Anna Boleyn, the first cause of so much misery and woe. Henry's affection was now very much cooled towards her, especially as he became enamoured of one of her maids of honour, Jane Seymour. Anna still had some hopes of regaining his affection, by presenting him with a male heir, but in this she was disappointed, the child was still born; then her misfortunes commenced; she was

(28) Sand. *l.* 1, de Schis. Ang. *p.* 135; Gotti, *sec.* 2, *n.* 22.   (29) Sand. & Gotti, loc. cit. *n.* 23.   (30) Gotti, *c.* 113, *s.* 2, *n.* 24; Nat. Alex. *t.* 19, *c.* 13, *art.* 3, *n.* 6. (31) Sanders, *l.* 1, *p.* 107, 112; Gotti, *s.* 3, *n.* 25; Nat. Alex. loc. cit.

accused of incest with her brother, George Boleyn, and of criminal conversation with four other gentlemen of the Court. Henry refused at first to believe the charge, but his jealousy was raised, and his love for Jane Seymour contributing, likewise, to her ruin, she was committed to the Tower at once. Bossuet informs us, that Henry called on Cranmer to declare now, that his marriage with Anna was invalid from the beginning, and Elizabeth, his daughter, illegitimate, since Anna was married to him during the lifetime of Lord Percy, then Earl of Northumberland, between whom and Anna, it was asserted, there was a contract of marriage. But this charge was unfounded; there was not even a promise between them; the only foundation for the assertion was, that Percy was at one time anxious to marry her; for all, she was condemned to death for adultery, and the sentence was, that she should be burned or beheaded, at the King's pleasure. She begged to be allowed to speak to the King, but was refused; all the favour she could obtain was, that she should be beheaded; this sentence was carried into execution, and her brother, likewise, and the four gentlemen accused of being her paramours, underwent the same fate. On the day of her execution, the Lieutenant of the Tower remarked to her, by way of consolation, that she would not suffer much, as the executioner was very expert; she smilingly answered: "My neck is very slender." The day after, Henry married Jane Seymour (32).

10. He again convoked Parliament on the 7th of June, 1536, and had the law passed in favour of Elizabeth, to the exclusion of Mary, daughter of Queen Catherine, repealed, and the six Articles were passed for the regulation of religious affairs in the kingdom. The First was, that the Transubstantiation of the bread into the body of Christ in the Eucharist was an article of Faith. Second.—That Communion should be given under one kind. Third.—That the celibacy of the clergy should be observed. Fourth.—That the vow of chastity was binding. Fifth.—That the celebration of the Mass was in conformity with the Divine law, and that private Masses were not only useful, but necessary. Sixth.—That auricular confession should be strictly practised. All these Articles were confirmed by the King, and both houses, and the penalties imposed on heretics applied to all who would either believe or teach doctrines in opposition to them (33). The primacy of the King, however, was left intact, so Henry, using his new power, appointed Cromwell, though a mere layman, his Vicar-General in Spirituals for the entire kingdom, and ordained that he should preside at all the Synods of the bishops (34). When Paul III. was informed of all these sacrilegious attempts on the integrity of Faith, and especially of the affair of St. Thomas of Canterbury, who was tried and

(32) Varill. *l.* 9, *p.* 423; Gotti, *s.* 2, *n.* 26; Hermant, *c.* 266; Nat. Alex. cit. *n.* 6; Bossuet, Hist. *l.* 7, *n.* 21, 22, 23.   (33) Bossuet, Hist. *l.* 7, *n.* 33; Nat. Alex. *t.* 19, art. 3, *n.* 7; Gotti, *s.* 2, *art.* 27.   (34) Varill. *t.* 1, *l.* 12, *p.* 544.

condemned as a traitor to his country (35), and his sacred body disinterred, burned, and the ashes thrown into the Thames, he published a brief on the 1st of January, 1538, ordering that the sentence before passed against Henry should be published (36). It was, however, delayed on account of the melancholy death of Queen Jane, who died in childbirth, leaving Henry an heir, afterwards Edward VI.. under whom the ruin of England was completed, as in his time heresy was firmly rooted in the country. It is said (but the report does not rest, I believe, on a good foundation), that when Henry found that there was danger of the child being lost, he ordered an operation to be performed on the mother, saying he could get wives enough, but not heirs (37).

11. On the death of Jane Seymour, Henry immediately began to look about for his fourth wife, and Paul III., hoping to bring him to a sense of his duty, wrote him a letter in which he told him of the sentence of excommunication hanging over him, which he did not promulgate, having still hopes that he would be reconciled with the Church; at the same time, he created Reginald Pole a Cardinal, and sent him to France as his Legate, that he might endeavour to arrange a marriage between Henry and Margaret, the daughter of Francis I. of France. Cardinal Pole accordingly went to France, and arranged the matter with Francis, but Henry would not agree to it, and he wrote to Francis, telling him that Pole was a rebel, and requiring Francis to deliver him up to him. This Francis refused to do, but he told the Cardinal the danger he was in, and by his advice he quitted France. Henry, disappointed in his vengeance, laid a price of fifty thousand crowns on his head (38).

12. Cromwell (not Oliver the President) now thought it a good opportunity to induce the King to take a wife on his recommendation, and bring him over to his own religion, which was Lutheran (39). He then proposed as a wife to him Anne, daughter of the Duke of Cleves, head of one of the noblest families in Germany, sister of the Electress of Saxony. Anne had a great many good qualities which would fit her for a crown, but she was, unfortunately, a Lutheran, and her relations were the chiefs of the League of Smalcald. Of this League Henry was anxious to be admitted a member, but the Lutherans had not confidence in him, and he then imagined that by marrying a Lutheran Princess he would remove any difficulties which previously existed to his admission. The marriage was celebrated, to Henry's great joy, on the 3rd of January, 1540, and Cromwell was made High Chancellor on the occasion, and Earl of Essex. Henry was only seven months married when, as usual, he publicly declared himself discontented with his Queen,, especially as she was a heretic, as if he could be called

(35) Varill. *t.* 1, *c.* 11, *p.* 315 ; Nat. Alex. loc. cit. *n.* 8.   (36) Gotti, *s.* 2, *n.* 23.
(37) Varill. *p.* 306 ; Nat. Alex. loc. cit. ; Gotti, *s.* 2, *n.* 2.   (38) Varill. *l.* 11, *p.* 507,
& seq.   (39) Varill. *t.* 1, *l.* 12, *p.* 551.

a Catholic. He now became enamoured of Catherine Howard, niece of the Duke of Norfolk, Earl Marshal of England, and one of the maids of honour to Queen Anne, and seeing no hopes of obtaining her favour unless he married her, he called on Cromwell to assist him now again to get divorced from Anne of Cleves. Cromwell had embarked his fortunes in the same boat with the Queen; he dreaded that her divorce would be the cause of his fall, and endeavoured to prevent it. Henry, displeased with his opposition, eagerly sought an occasion to ruin him, and was not long in finding it. The chiefs of the Protestant League sent their agents to London to conclude with Henry the alliance he was before so desirous of, but as he was now determined to repudiate Anne, he had no longer any wish to league himself with the Lutherans, so he refused to treat with the agents; but Cromwell, confiding in his favour, took on himself to sign the treaty. Some say that Henry was privy to this act, but this is denied by others; however it was, the upshot of the affair was the disgrace of Cromwell, for when the Emperor loudly complained of the alliance, Henry swore that he had no cognizance of it. He sent for Cromwell one day, and in presence of many of the nobility, charged him publicly with signing a treaty for which he had no authority, and ordered him immediately to be conducted to the Tower. Cromwell begged hard for a public trial, to give him an opportunity of justifying his conduct in the affair, but as, independently of that charge, he was convicted of other crimes—heresy, peculation, and illegal impositions—he, who was the cause of so many Catholics being condemned without a hearing, was, by the just judgment of the Almighty, condemned himself, and was decapitated, and his property confiscated (40). Henry now had the Queen informed, that unless she consented to a divorce, he would have the laws against heretics put in force against her, she being a Lutheran. Dreading the fate that awaited her, from his known cruelty, and wishing to avoid also the shame of a public repudiation, she confessed, it is said, that, previous to her marriage with the King, she was promised to another; so Thomas Cranmer, who gave the sentence of divorce in the cases of Catherine, and of Anna Boleyn, now, for the third time, pronounced a similar sentence. The decision was based on the greatest injustice; for the contract of marriage between Anne and the Duke of Lorraine, on which it was founded, took place while they were both children, and was never ratified. How, then, could Henry's solemn marriage be affected by this? But Cranmer—whom Burnet compares to St. Athanasius and St. Cyril—decided that it was null and void, merely to please Henry, who immediately married another. Queen Anne accepted a pension of £3,000 a-year, but never returned to Germany again (41).

(40) Varillas, *t.* 1, *l.* 12, *p.* 53; Nat Alex. c. 23, *a.* 3, *n.* 7; Bossuet, *l.* 7, *n.* 34.
(41) Varill. loc. cit. *p.* 575; Bossuet, loc. cit.

13. Within a week Henry was married to Catherine Howard, who soon met the same fate as Anna Boleyn. She was charged before Parliament with dissolute conduct with two individuals, before her marriage, and with adultery since, and was condemned to be beheaded (42). Henry then got a law passed, the like of which was never before heard of, enacting it high treason for any lady to marry the King, if previously she had ever offended against chastity (43). He then married Catherine Parr, sister to the Earl of Essex (44); she survived him, but having married the brother of the Regent Somerset, Thomas Seymour, Lord High Admiral of England, who suffered death by the sentence of his own brother, she died of a broken heart.

14. Death, at last, was about to put an end to Henry's crimes; he was now fifty-seven years of age, and had grown to such an enormous size that he could not almost pass through the doorway of his palace, and was obliged to be carried by servants up and down stairs (45). A deep-rooted sadness and remorse now seized him; all his crimes, sacrileges, and scandals stared him in the face. To establish the sacrilegious doctrine of his primacy over the English Church he had put to death two cardinals, three archbishops, eighteen bishops and archdeacons, five hundred priests, sixty superiors of religious houses, fifty canons, twenty-nine peers, three hundred and sixty-six knights, and an immense number both of the gentry and people. Ulcers in one of his legs, together with fever, now plainly told him that his end was nigh, and some writers assert that he then spoke to some of the bishops of his intention of being again reconciled to the Church, but not one among them had the courage to tell him plainly the course he should take. All dreaded his anger; and none were willing to brave the danger of death, by plainly telling him that his only chance of salvation was to repent of his evil deeds—to repair the scandal he had given—and humbly return to the Church he had abandoned. No one was courageous enough to tell him this; one alone suggested to him that he ought to convoke Parliament, as he had done when about to make the changes, to set things again to rights. He ordered, it is said, the Secretaries of State to convoke it, but they feared they should be obliged to disgorge the plunder of the Church, and put off the convocation, and thus he left the Church in the greatest confusion; and soon, as we shall see, irreparable ruin overtook it (46).

15. Just before Henry's death he opened a church belonging to the Franciscans, and had Mass again said in it (now Christ Church Hospital), but this was but little reparation for so much mischief. He then made his will, leaving his only son, Edward, heir to the throne, then only nine years of age, appointing sixteen guardians

(42) Gotti, *s.* 2, *n.* 29; Hermant, *t.* 2, *c.* 266; Nat. Alex loc. cit. *n.* 7. (43) Varill. loc. cit. *p.* 575. (44) Varill. *t.* 2, *l.* 13, *n.* 575; Nat. Alex. *a.* 3, *n.* 7. (45) Varill. *t.* 2, *l.* 16, *p.* 98. (46) Varillas, loc. cit. *p.* 99.

to him, ordering that he should be brought up in the Catholic Faith, but never resign the primacy of the English Church, so that he was unchanged even in death. In case that Edward died without issue, he left the crown to Mary, daughter of Queen Catherine, and should she likewise die without issue, to Elizabeth, daughter of Anna Boleyn (47). He caused Mass to be celebrated several times in his chamber, and wished that the Viaticum should be administered to him in the one kind alone. When the Viaticum was brought in he received it kneeling, and when it was told, that, considering the state he was in, that was unnecessary, he said: " If I could bury myself under the earth, I could not show sufficient respect to the God I am about to receive" (48). How could he, however, expect to please the Almighty by such acts of reverence, after trampling on his Church, and dying out of her communion? He endeavoured, by these external acts, to quiet that remorse of conscience he felt, but, withal, he could not recover the Divine grace, nor the peace he sought. He called for some Religious to attend him at his last moments, after banishing them out of the kingdom (49); he next called for something to drink, and having tasted it he said to those around him, in a loud tone, " So this is the end of it, and all is lost for me," and immediately expired. He died on the 1st of February, 1547, at the age of fifty-six, according to Noel Alexander, or in his fifty-seventh year, according to others, and in the thirty-eighth year of his reign (50).

SECT. II.—REIGN OF EDWARD VI.

16. The Duke of Somerset, as Guardian of Edward VI., governs the Kingdom. 17. He declares himself a Heretic, and gives Leave to the Heretics to preach; invites Bucer, Vermigli, and Ochino to England, and abolishes the Roman Catholic Religion. 18. He beheads his Brother, the Lord High-Admiral. 19. He is beheaded himself. 20. Death of Edward; the Earl Warwick makes an Attempt to get Possession of the Kingdom, and is beheaded, but is converted, and dies an edifying Death.

16. EDWARD SEYMOUR, Earl of Hertford, was one of the guardians appointed by Henry to his son; he was maternal uncle to the young King, being brother to Jane Seymour, his mother. Although he passed all along as a Catholic, he was a Zuinglian, and as the majority of Edward's guardians were Catholics, he intrigued with some of the principal nobility of the kingdom, and pointed out how dangerous it would be to their interests that the young King should be left in the hands of those gentlemen; that the consequence would be that they should have, sooner or later, to surrender again the ecclesiastical property given them by Henry; that the suppressed and ruined churches should be again repaired and rebuilt, to the great impoverishing of the Royal treasury; and that the only way

(47) Gotti, s. 2, n. 31; Varillas, t. 2, p. 99. (48) Nat. Alex. a. 3, n. 9; Gotti, s. 2, n. 30; Varillas, loc. cit. (49) Bart. Ist. d'Inghil. l. 1, c. 1, p. 4. (50) Natal. loc. cit.; Varill. p. 100; Bartol. p. 3.

to avoid such evils was that he should be made Governor of the kingdom. He craftily suppressed Henry's will, and substituted another, in which Edward was declared head of the Church of England, and he was appointed Regent; he then got himself created Duke of Somerset, and took the title of Protector of the Kingdom (1).

17. No sooner had he got the supreme power into his hands as Protector than he at once took off the mask, proclaimed himself a Protestant, and appointed preachers to disseminate the heresy. He prohibited the bishops from preaching, or ordaining, without the King's permission, and he then refused permission to any one to preach, unless to the Zuinglian ministers. Among the rest the impious Cranmer, pseudo-Archbishop of Canterbury, now began publicly to preach against the Catholic Church, and published a Catechism filled with the most wicked doctrines against the Faith, and was not ashamed to marry publicly, with the approbation of the Regent, a woman who lived with him as concubine before he was made bishop (2). Hugh Latimer, Bishop of Winchester—but deposed from his See for preaching, in London, against the Real Presence—was now appointed by Somerset principal preacher of the Zuinglian errors. He invited at the same time from Strasbourg three famous ministers of Satan, apostate Religious, well known through all Europe: Martin Bucer, now seventy years of age, and three times married, Peter Martyr, and Bernard Ochin, and appointed them to Professors' Chairs in the Universities of Oxford and Cambridge, to poison the minds of the poor youths studying there, and he banished every Catholic professor out of these colleges. To complete the work of iniquity, he appointed as tutors to the young King, Richard Crock, a priest, who violated his vows by marrying, and John Check, a layman of debauched life—fit instructors for a young prince in vice and heresy (3). He tried by sending Bucer, Peter Martyr, and Ochino, to Mary, to induce her to forsake the Church likewise (4); but she showed such determined opposition that he never tried it again. His next step was to abolish the six Articles of Henry VIII., and on the 5th of November, 1547, he obtained the sanction of Parliament for abolishing the Roman Catholic religion, the Mass, the veneration of sacred images, and for the confiscation of the sacred vessels and ornaments of the altar (5); and thus, under him, the whole plan of religion established by Henry and the Parliament (*N.* 10), six Articles, and all, were done away with. Here we naturally wonder how so many bishops and theologians could establish, in Henry's reign, a form of worship of such little value as to be abolished almost immediately on his

(1) Varillas, Istor. *t.* 2, *p.* 100; Nat. Alex. *t.* 19, *c.* 13, *a.* 4; Hermant, Ist. *t.* 2, *c.* 267; Gotti, Ver. Rel. *c.* 114, *s.* 1, *n.* 1.   (2) Varillas, loc. cit. *p.* 101; Gotti, loc. cit. *n.* 2; Hermant, *c.* 267.   (3) Varillas, *t.* 2, *l.* 17, *p* 105, & seq.; Nat. Alex. *art.* 4. (4) Varillas, *l.* 17, *p.* 116.   (5) Bossuet, *n.* 90.

death. Burnet says, that these theologians were ignorant of the truth. Behold, then, the reformed Faith, called by him "The Work of Light." They sanctioned articles of Faith without having a knowledge of the truth. The Reformation may, indeed, be called a work of darkness, since it upset Faith, Religion, and all Divine and human laws, in England (6). Somerset next ordained, that Communion should be administered under both kinds—that the Scripture should be generally read in the vulgar tongue—and that all bishops, or other ecclesiastics, refusing obedience to this order, should be sent to prison, and deprived of their benefices, and reformers installed in their places (7). In this he followed the advice of Calvin, who wrote him a long letter from Geneva on the subject, advising him to abolish the Catholic religion by persecution; and the prisons of London were accordingly filled with suspected Catholics. At this period, three-fourths of the clergy had shaken off the law of celibacy (8).

18. Such were the crimes of the Duke of Somerset against the Church; but the Divine vengeance soon overtook him, in a most unexpected manner (9). He had raised his brother, Thomas Seymour, to the dignity of Lord High Admiral of the kingdom, and this nobleman had gained the affection of Henry's last Queen, Catherine Parr, and had his consent to the marriage. This was highly displeasing, however, to the Duchess of Somerset, as, in case of his marriage with Catherine, she should resign to her the precedence which she enjoyed, as wife of the Protector, and, though she yielded to the Queen Dowager, she was unwilling to take rank beneath her sister-in-law; and thus a quarrel was commenced between the ladies, in which their husbands were soon engaged. John Dudley, Earl of Warwick, was an enemy to both parties, and bent on their destruction; and, to accomplish it with greater certainty, he pretended to be a mediator, while he dexterously encouraged the strife between them, and succeeded so well, that Somerset engaged Sharington to accuse his brother of high treason. He appeared to be highly displeased when the accusation was first made; but then he alleged that the King's life and honour were more dear to him than his brother's life, and he gave orders to proceed with his trial. The Admiral was condemned, and executed on the 20th of March, 1549. His lady, Queen Catherine, according to some, died of a broken heart; but we believe that she had previously died in childbirth (10).

19. On the death of the Admiral, Earl Warwick was entire master of Somerset's mind; he wound him round as he pleased, and had sufficient interest to appoint friends of his own to several

---

(6) Bossuet, *t.* 2, *l.* 7, *n.* 96.   (7) Gotti, loc. cit. sec. 1, *n.* 3; Nat. Alex. loc. cit.; Bossuet, Hist. *l.* 7, *n.* 86.   (8) Varillas, *l.* 17, *p.* 126.   (9) Varillas, loc. cit. *p.* 126, coll. 2.   (10) Varillas, *l.* 17, *p.* 120.

important places, by which he laid the foundation of the Duke's ruin. He strengthened his party, besides, by the adhesion of the Catholic lords—very numerous still—who were persuaded by him that there was no hope of re-establishing the Catholic religion while Somerset was in power. About the same time, the English lost Boulogne, in the ancient province of Picardy, and the Regent was severely censured, for not having sent reinforcements in time, to save it from the French. Several of the barons and nobility, likewise, had enclosed commonages in different parts of the kingdom, to the great grievance of the people, who looked to the Regent for redress, and not obtaining it, broke out into rebellion, and Warwick got the Parliament convoked. He had a very strong party in both houses, so the Regent was attainted, and sent to the Tower, and was executed on the 22nd of January, 1552, and both Catholics and Protestants rejoiced at his death (11).

20. The Earl of Warwick having now disposed of all his rivals, took the administration of affairs, even during Edward's lifetime, into his own hands, and got another step in the peerage, being created Duke of Northumberland; and not satisfied with all this, prevailed on the King to leave his crown, by will, to his daughter-in-law, Lady Jane Grey, daughter of the Duke of Norfolk, excluding Mary, daughter of Queen Catherine, as she was declared illegitimate in the reign of Henry VIII., and Elizabeth, as daughter of the adultress, Anna Boleyn. Edward died soon after, in the sixteenth year of his age, on the 7th of July, 1553, and Northumberland, it is said, immediately gave orders that Mary should be secured; but his secretary, a Catholic, thought it too bad that the heiress of the crown should be thus deprived of her right, and he escaped from his master, and arrived in Mary's presence two hours sooner than the person the Duke sent to arrest her (12). Mary immediately fled to Norfolk, where the people showed their attachment to her cause, by taking up arms in her defence. She collected an army of fifteen thousand men, and though Northumberland marched against her with thirty thousand, he was deserted by most of them (some say he never had more than six thousand in the beginning), and returned to London; but the citizens would not now admit him, and the fleet, likewise, declared for Mary. When Queen Mary was settled in the government, Northumberland was indicted for high treason, and, as there was no doubt of his guilt, he was condemned and executed. His sons suffered, likewise, and his daughter-in-law, Lady Jane Grey, Henry's niece, who wore the crown for ten days against her will, paid the penalty of her treason on the scaffold. Elizabeth was, likewise, kept in custody on suspicion. Northumberland had embraced Protestantism merely from political motives, but now returned again to the

(11) Varillas, *t.* 2, *l.* 17, *p.* 131, & *l.* 20, *p.* 1.   (12) Varillas, *t.* 2, *l.* 20, *p.* 208.

Faith, confessed to a priest, and declared on the scaffold, that it was merely the ambition of obtaining the crown for his family that caused him to dissemble his Faith, and that he considered his punishment now a grace from God to procure his salvation. His sons and others, executed for the same crime, made a similar declaration. It is melancholy to see in this history so many persons condemned to death for trying to elevate themselves above their sphere, and how England became immediately on her loss of the Faith a field of slaughter for her children (13).

SEC. III.—MARY'S REIGN.

21. Mary refuses the Title of Head of the Church; repeals her Father's and Brother's Laws; Cranmer is condemned to be burned, and dies a Heretic; Mary sends off all Heretics from her Court. 22. Cardinal Pole reconciles England with the Church; her Marriage with Philip II., and Death.

21. THE good Queen Mary, on her accession to the throne, refused to take the impious title of Head of the Church, and immediately sent ambassadors to Rome, to pay obedience to the Pope. She repealed all the decrees of her father and brother, and re-established the public exercise of the Catholic religion (1). She imprisoned Elizabeth, who twice conspired against her, and, it is said, she owed her life to the intercession of King Philip. She opened the prisons, and gave liberty to the bishops and other Catholics who were confined; and on the 5th of October, 1553, the Parliament rescinded the iniquitous sentence of Cranmer, Archbishop of Canterbury, by which he declared the marriage of Catherine and Henry null and void, and he was condemned to be burned as a heretic. When the unfortunate man found that he was condemned to death, he twice retracted his errors; but when all this would not save him from being burned, he cancelled his retractation, and died a Calvinist (2). By the Queen's orders, the remains of Bucer and Fagius, who died heretics, were exhumed and burned; and thirty thousand heretics were banished the kingdom, comprising Lutherans, Calvinists, Zuinglians, Anabaptists, Socinians, Seekers, and such like. The Seekers are those who are seeking the true religion, but have not yet found it, nor ever will out of the Catholic Church alone; because in every other religion, if they trace it up to the author, they will find some impostor, whose imagination furnished a mass of sophisms and errors.

22. Mary, likewise, proclaimed the innocence of Cardinal Pole, and requested Julius III. to send him to England as his Legate *a latere*. He arrived soon after, and, at the request of the Queen, reconciled the kingdom again to the Church, and absolved it from

(13) Varillas, *l.* 20, *p.* 202, *a.* 211; Nat. Alex. *t.* 19, *c.* 13, *art.* 5; Gotti, *c.* 114, *sec.* 1, *n.* 4; Hermant, *c.* 268. (1) Bartol. *l.* 1, *c.* 3; Nat. Alex. loc. cit.; Hermant, *c.* 269; Varillas, *t.* 2, *l.* 20, *p.* 212; Gotti, *c.* 114, *sec.* 2, *a.* 1. (2) Varillas, *l.* 21, *p.* 252; Gotti, ibid. *n.* 4; Hermant, loc. cit.; Bossuet, 1st. *l.* 7, *n.* 103. (3) Nat. Alex. ibid.; Gotti, loc. cit. *n.* 4.

schism, on the Vigil of St. Andrew, 1554. He next restored ecclesiastical discipline, reformed the Universities, and re-established the practices of religion. He absolved all the laymen from the censures they incurred, by laying hands on the property of the Church during the time of the schism, remitted the tithes and first-fruits due to the clergy; confirmed in their sees the Catholic bishops, though installed in the time of the schism, and recognized the new sees established by Henry. All this was subsequently confirmed by Paul IV.; but, unfortunately for England, Mary died on the 15th of November, 1558, in the forty-fourth year of her age, and fifth of her reign. She was married to Philip II., King of Spain, and at first mistook her sickness, which was dropsy, for pregnancy. The Faithful all over the world mourned for her death (4).

SEC. IV.—THE REIGN OF ELIZABETH.

23. Elizabeth proclaimed Queen; the Pope is dissatisfied, and she declares herself a Protestant. 24. She gains over the Parliament, through the Influence of three of the Nobility, and is proclaimed Head of the Church. 25. She establishes the Form of Church Government, and, though her Belief is Calvinistic, she retains Episcopacy, &c. 26. Appropriates Church Property, abolishes the Mass; the Oath of Allegiance; Persecution of the Catholics. 27. Death of Edmund Campion for the Faith. 28. The Pope's Bull against Elizabeth. 29. She dies out of Communion with the Church. 30. Her Successors on the Throne of England; deplorable State of the English Church. 31. The English Reformation refutes itself.

23. MARY died on the 13th of January, 1559, and Elizabeth, daughter of Anna Boleyn, was proclaimed Queen, according to the iniquitous will of Henry VIII. I call it iniquitous, for the crown, by right, appertained to Mary Stuart, Queen of Scots, for Elizabeth's birth was spurious, as she was born during the lifetime of Henry's first Queen and lawful wife, Catherine, and when Clement VIII. and Paul III. had already declared his marriage with Anna Boleyn null and void (1). Elizabeth was then twenty-five years of age, and highly accomplished, and learned both in science and languages. She spoke French, Italian, and Latin. She had, besides, all the natural qualities requisite for a great Queen, but obscured by the Lutheran heresy, of which she was a follower in private. During the lifetime of Mary she pretended to be a Catholic, and, perhaps, would have continued to do so when she came to the throne, or have become a Catholic in reality, if the Pope would recognize her as Queen, for in the beginning she allowed freedom of religion to all, and even took the old Coronation Oath to defend the Catholic Faith, and preserve the liberties of the Church (2). She commanded Sir Edward Cairne, the Ambassador in Rome from her sister Mary, to notify her accession and coronation to Paul IV., and present her duty, and ask his benediction. The Pope, how-

(4) Nat. Alex. *art.* 5, in fin.; Varillas, *l.* 21, *p.* 229; Gotti, *sec.* 2, *n.* 5, ad 7.
(1) Gotti, *c.* 114, *s* 3, *n.* 2; Varillas, *t.* 2, *l.* 22, *p.* 284.   (2) Nat. Alex. *t.* 19, c. 13; Berti, His. *sec.* 16.

ever, answered, that it was not lawful for her to have assumed the government of the kingdom, a fief of the Holy See, without the consent of Rome, that it would be necessary to examine the rights which Queen Mary of Scotland had to the throne also, and therefore that she should place herself altogether in his hands, and that she would experience from him paternal kindness. Elizabeth then saw that it would be difficult to keep herself on the throne, unless by separating from the Roman Church; she therefore tore off the mask, recalled her Ambassador, Cairne, from Rome, and publicly professed the heresy she had previously embraced in private (3).

24. All now she had to do was to get the Parliament to establish the Reformed Religion, and this was easily accomplished. The House of Commons being already gained over, the only difficulty was to get the peers to agree to it. The Upper House was almost entirely led by the Duke of Norfolk, Lord Dudley, and the Earl of Arundel. On each of these Elizabeth exercised her influence, and through them gained over the majority of the peers, especially as the lay peers were more numerous than the bishops, to declare her Head of the Church. All the regulations made in religious affairs during the reign of Edward VI. were re-established, and those of Mary repealed (4). Each of these noblemen expected that Elizabeth, who was a most consummate intriguer, would make him the partner of her crown (5). There were sixteen thousand ecclesiastics in England. Three-fourths, as Burnet writes, immediately joined the Reformers. The greater part of the clergy were married at that period, and this was the reason, as Burnet himself allows, that they changed so easily.

25. Elizabeth, now fortified with parliamentary authority, prohibited most rigorously any of her subjects from obeying the Pope, and commanded all to recognize her as Head of the Church, both in spirituals and temporalities. It was also ordained, at the same time, that to the Crown alone belonged the appointment of bishops, the convocation of Synods, the power of taking cognizance of heresy and abuses, and the punishment of spiritual delinquencies. A system of church government and discipline was also established, and though the doctrine of the Anglican Church is Calvinism, which rejects bishops, together with all the sacred ceremonies of the Roman Church, as well as altars and images, still she wished that the bishops should be continued, but without any other power than what they held from herself. " Nisi ad beneplacitum Reginæ nec aliter nisi per ipsam a Regali Majestate derivatum auctoritatem" (6). Then was seen in the Church what before was unheard of—a woman arrogating to herself the supremacy of the Church. How totally opposed this was to the Scriptures, St. Paul tells us plainly, for he says (1 Cor. xiv. 34); " Let women keep silence

---

(3) Nat. Alex. loc. cit.; Gotti, c. 114; Varillas, t. 2; Hermant, c. 270. (4) Nat. Alex. ar. 6, Gotti, s. 3. (5) Varillas, l. 22. (6) Nat. Alex. loc. cit.; Gotti, cit. n. 3.

in the churches, for it is not permitted to them to speak, but to be subject." She wished that the priesthood, altars, and sacred ceremonies, should be in somewise retained, for the people, she said, required such things (7). Thus it would appear that she looked on the ceremonies of the Church as mere theatrical representations, fit to amuse the vulgar. A new hierarchy and new ceremonies were, accordingly, instituted, and, we may say, a new martyrology, with Wickliffe, Huss, and Cranmer, as its martyrs; and Luther, Peter Martyr, Henry VIII., Edward VI., and Erasmus, its saints.

26. The benefices and the monastic property were now all seized on, and part applied to government purposes, and the rest granted to the nobility. Vicars-General in spirituals were also appointed. All sacred images were removed from the churches, but she kept a Crucifix in her own chamber, placed on an altar, with two candles, but these were never lighted. The Mass was prohibited, together with all the ancient ceremonies used in preaching and administering the Sacraments, and new ceremonies were instituted, and a form of prayers commanded to be read in English, savouring strongly of Calvinism, which she wished should be the leading doctrine of the Anglican Church, but the government and discipline after a plan of her own (8). She then got the sanction of Parliament for all these regulations, and it was ordered that all bishops and ecclesiastics should take the oath of supremacy, under pain of deprivation and imprisonment for the first refusal, and of death for the second. The oath was this: "I, A. B., declare in my conscience that the Queen is the sole and supreme ruler in this kingdom of England, both in spirituals and temporals, and that no foreign prelate or prince has any authority ecclesiastical in this kingdom, and I, therefore, in the plain sense of the words, reject all foreign authority." Elizabeth hoped that an order, enforced under such severe penalties, would be at once obeyed by all; but all the bishops (with the exception of the Bishop of Llandaff) refused, and were degraded and banished, or imprisoned, and their glorious example was followed by the better part of the clergy, by numbers of the religious, of various orders, and by many doctors, and several of the nobility, whose constancy in adhering to the Faith was punished by exile and imprisonment. Soon, however, these punishments were looked on as too mild—many priests, friars, and preachers were put to death for the Faith, and crowned with martyrdom (9). Sanders gives a diary of all the occurrences that took place during this period in England, beginning in 1580.

27. I cannot allow this opportunity to pass without relating the death of Edmund Campion, one of the many martyrs put to death by Elizabeth for the Faith. While in Rome he heard of the

(7) Varillas, *t.* 2, *l.* 22, *n.* 290.   (8) Nat. Alex. *s.* 6, *n.* 2; Gotti, *c.* 144, *s.* 3, *n.* 5; Varill. *t.* 2.   (9) Nat. Alex. *ar.* 6, *n.* 3; Gotti, *c.* 114, *s.* 3, *n.* 6, 7.

dreadful persecution the Catholics, and, above all, the missionaries who came to their assistance, were suffering from Elizabeth. He was a young Englishman, a scholar, and a linguist, and, burning with zeal for the salvation of his countrymen, he determined to go to their assistance. This was a matter of great difficulty, for several spies were on the look-out for him, to take him on his landing, and not only was his person described, but even his likeness was taken; still, disguised as a servant, he escaped all the snares laid for him, and arrived safely in the kingdom. Night and day he laboured, preaching, hearing confessions, and animating the faithful to perseverance; he was continually moving about from one place to another, under different names, and in various disguises, and so escaped, for a long time, the emissaries who were in search of him. He was at last betrayed by an apostate priest, while he was saying Mass, and preaching, in the house of a Catholic. He had not time to escape, the house was surrounded, and the master shut him up in a hiding hole, which was so well contrived, that after a most rigorous search, he could not be discovered. The bailiffs were going away in despair, when, at the bottom of the staircase they accidentally broke through a wall, and discovered him on his knees, offering up his life to God. They put him in prison, and he was then so violently racked, that when brought to trial, and told to raise up his arm to attest his confession, he had not the power of doing so, and it was raised up by an assistant. He was arraigned as a traitor, for thus they indicted the Catholic priests, in those days, to do away with the honour of martyrdom. They put them to death, they said, not for preaching their Faith, but for conspiring against the Queen. When Campion was charged with treason, he confounded his accusers by replying: "How can you charge us with treason, and condemn us for that alone, when all that is requisite to save ourselves is, that we go to your preachings (thus changing their religion); it is, then, because we are Catholics that we are condemned, and not because we are, as you say, rebels." He was condemned to be drawn on a hurdle to the place of execution and hanged. He then declared that he never rebelled against the Queen, that it was for the Faith alone he was put to death. He was disembowelled, his heart torn out and cast into the fire, and his body quartered. Several other priests underwent a like punishment for the Faith during this reign (10).

28. When St. Pius V. learned the cruelties practised by Elizabeth on the Catholics, he published a Bull against her, on the 24th of February, 1570; but this was only adding fuel to the fire, and the persecution became more furious (11). It was then, as we

---

(10) Bartol. Istor. d'Inghil. *l.* 6, *c.* 1. (11) Nat. Alex. *t.* 19, *art.* 3, *s.* 6; Gotti, *c.* 144, *s.* 3, *n.* 8.

have already related, that she, under false pretences, beheaded Mary, Queen of Scots (*Chap.* xi. *art.* iii. *sec.* ii. *n.* 78). She was desirous, if possible, even to destroy Catholicity in all Christian kingdoms, and entered into a league with the Reformers of the Netherlands, and the Calvinists of France, and this league never was interrupted during her lifetime (12), and in the wars waged by these rebels against their Sovereigns, she sent them powerful assistance (13), and she left no stone unturned to advance the Calvinistic Reformation in Scotland (14).

29. The end of her reign and life was now at hand; a Protestant author has said that she died a *happy death*. It is worth while to see what sort of a death it was. I find that after the death of the Earl of Essex, whom she beheaded—though very much attached to him—for the crime of insurrection, she never more enjoyed a day's happiness. As old age came on her, also, she was tormented by fear and jealousy, and doubted the affectionate fidelity of her subjects. She went to Richmond, where the pleasing scenery had no effect in calming her mind; she conceived that all her friends abandoned her, that everything went against her, and complained that she had no sincere attached friend. The death-sickness at last came on her, and she refused all medical aid, and could not, her impatience was so great, bear even the sight of a physician. When she saw death approaching, she declared King James of Scotland her successor, and on the 24th of March, 1603, two hours before midnight, she breathed her last, in the seventieth year of her age, and forty-fourth of her reign. Thus she closed her days in sorrow and anguish, not so much through pain of body, as of mind. She sunk into the grave without any sign of repentance, without Sacraments, without the assistance of a priest; she was attended by some Protestant ecclesiastics, but they only exhorted her to persevere in the heresy she embraced (15). Such was the *happy death* of Queen Elizabeth. It is said that she used to say: "If God gives me forty years to reign, I will give up even heaven itself" (16). Unhappy woman! not alone forty, but nearly forty-five years did she possess the throne. She became head of the Church; she separated the Church of England from the Roman See; she prohibited the exercise of the Catholic religion; how many innocent persons did she doom to all the horrors of exile, of imprisonment, of cruel death! She is now in eternity, and I would like to know, is she satisfied with all the crimes and cruelties she committed during her life. Oh, happy would it be for her had she never sat upon a throne.

30. Elizabeth, before she died, nominated James VI., the son of Mary Stuart, her successor. When he became King of England (*Chap.* xi., *art.* iii., *sec.* ii., *n.* 85), he neglected to comply with the

(12) Varil. *t.* 2, *l.* 26, *p.* 437.   (13) Idem, *l.* 29.   (14) Idem, *l.* 28.   (15) Nat. Alex. *art.* 3; Gotti, *c.* 114, *s*, 3; Bartoli. Istor. d'Inghil, *l.* 6.   (16) Bartoli. Istor. cit.

wishes of his good mother, never to follow any other than the Catholic religion; he leant, therefore, to Lutheranism—was anything but a friend to the Calvinists—and was anxious that Scotland, which kingdom he retained, should follow the Lutheran doctrine also; but in this he was disappointed. His son and successor, Charles I., endeavoured to carry out his father's intentions, and lost his head on the scaffold. He was succeeded by his son, Charles II., who died without issue, and the crown then devolved on his brother, James II. This good Prince declared himself a Catholic, and the consequence was, that he was obliged to fly to France, where he died a holy death in 1701, leaving one son, James III., who lived and died in Rome, in the Catholic Faith. In fine, unhappy England was, and is, separated from the Catholic Church, and groans under the weight of various heresies. Every religion, with the exception of the Catholic, is tolerated, but the faithful are exposed to all the frightful severities of the penal laws, and there are among the sectarians almost as many religions as individuals. In fact, we may say, that in that unhappy country there is no religion at all, for, as St. Augustin says (17): "The true religion was always one, from the beginning, and will always be the same."*

31. I have placed at the end of the historical portion of the Work, the Refutation of the principal Heresies which infected the Church, but it is impossible to take any particular hold of the English schism, for it is not a religion in itself, so much as a mixture composed of every heresy, excluding Catholicity, the only true religion. This is, then, according to Burnet, "The Work of Light," which smooths the way to heaven. What blindness, or rather, what impiety! The Reformation smooths the way to heaven, by allowing every one to live as he pleases, without law or sacraments, and with no restraint. A foreign Protestant author even ridicules Burnet's boast: "The English, by the Reformation," he says, "have become so totally independent, that every one takes whatever road to heaven that pleases himself." Thus the English Reformation refutes itself.

(17) St. Augus. Epis. 102, alias 49, cont. Pagan. *b.* 2, 3.

---

* This was written in the last century, but the reader will praise the Almighty that such a state of things exists no longer. The holy Author can now look down from heaven on a flourishing Church in England, and behold his own children, the Redemptionists, labouring with the other faithful labourers of the Gospel, in extending the kingdom of Christ.

Article II.

THE ANTITRINITARIANS AND SOCINIANS.

SEC. I.—MICHAEL SERVETUS.

32. Character of Servetus; his Studies, Travels, and false Doctrine. 33. He goes to Geneva; disputes with Calvin, who has him burned to Death.

32. MICHAEL SERVETUS, the chief of the Antitrinitarians, was a Spaniard, a native of Saragossa, in Catalonia. He was a man of genius (1), but light-headed, and held such a presumptuous opinion of himself, that, even before he was twenty-five years old, he thought himself the most learned man in the world. He went to Paris to study medicine, and there met some German Lutheran professors, employed by Francis I. to teach in that University, as he wished to have, at all risks, the best professors in Europe. He learned from these doctors, not only Latin, Greek, and Hebrew, but at the same time imbibed their errors. He went to Dauphiny, and, as he commenced disseminating the errors he had learned (2), he was accused of Lutheranism, but cleared himself, and denounced all Lutheran doctrine. He next went to Lyons, then to Germany, and from that to Africa to learn the Alcoran of Mahomet. He next went to Poland, and fixed himself there; and, puffed up with an extraordinary idea of his own learning, he disdained attaching himself to any sect, and formed a religion of his own, composed of the errors of all sects, and then, as Varillas tells us, he changed his name to Revez. With Luther, he condemned all which that Reformer condemned in the Catholic Church; he rejected the baptism of infants, with the Anabaptists; with the Sacramentarians, he said that the Eucharist was only a figure of the body and blood of Jesus Christ. But his most awful errors were those against the Most Holy Trinity, and especially against the Divinity of Jesus Christ and the Holy Ghost. With Sabellius, he denied the distinction of the three Divine Persons; with Arius, that the Word was God; with Macedonius, that the Holy Ghost was God, for he said that in God there was but one nature and one person, and that the Son and the Holy Ghost were only two emanations from the Divine essence, and had a beginning only from the creation of the world. Thus, as Jovet (3) says, Arianism, which was extinct for eight hundred years, was resuscitated by Servetus in 1530. Europe, and the northern nations of it especially, being then all in confusion, overrun by so many heresies, he soon found followers. Besides the errors enumerated, the books of Servetus were filled

---

(1) Jovet, Hist. delle Relig. *t.* 2, *p.* 287; Varil. *t.* 1, *l.* 8, *p.* 370; Nat. Alex. *s.* 19; Gotti, Ver. Rel. *l.* 2, *c.* 115; Van Ranst, *s.* 16, *p.* 325.   (2) Varil. loc. cit.   (3) Jovet, *p.* 288.

with the errors of Apollinares, of Nestorius, and of Eutyches, as the reader can see, by consulting Noel Alexander and Gotti. Another of his opinions was, that man did not commit mortal sin till he passed the age of twenty; that by sin the soul became mortal like the body; that polygamy might be permitted; and to these he added many other blasphemies.

33. Servetus left Germany and Poland, and was coming to Italy to disseminate his doctrine. He arrived in Geneva, where Calvin resided at the time. Calvin was at one time accused of Arianism, and to prove the contrary, wrote some treatises against Servetus. Having him now in his power, he thought it a good opportunity to give a cruel proof of his sincere abhorrence of this heresy, so he had him denounced by one of his servants to the magistrates, and imprisoned (*Chap.* xi, *art.* iii., *sec.* i., *n.* 67). They then had a long disputation. Servetus asserted that the Scriptures alone were sufficient to decide Articles of Faith, without reference either to Fathers or Councils, and, in fact, that was Calvin's own doctrine also, especially in his disputes with the Catholics. He was, therefore, very hard pressed by Servetus, who explained the texts adduced to prove the Trinity and the Divinity of Jesus Christ, after his own fashion, especially as he himself—rejecting Fathers and Councils in the explanation of that text of St. John (x. 30), "The Father and I am one"—said that all were wrong in proving by this the unity of essence between the Father and Son, as it only proved the perfect uniformity of the will of Christ with that of his Father. When he found, therefore, that Servetus obstinately held his Antitrinitarian doctrines, he laid another plan to destroy him. He sent his propositions to the University of the Zuinglian cantons, and, on their condemnation, he caused him to be burned alive on the 27th of October, 1553, as we have already narrated (*Chap.* xi., *art.* iii., *sec.* i., *n.* 67) (4). This cursed sect, however, did not expire with Servetus, for his writings and disciples carried it into Russia, Wallachia, Moravia, and Silesia; it was afterwards split into thirty-two divisions, and in these provinces the Antitrinitarians are more numerous than the Lutherans or Calvinists.

SEC. II.—VALENTINE GENTILIS, GEORGE BLANDRATA, AND BERNARD OCHINO.

34. Valentine Gentilis; his impious Doctrine. 35. He is punished in Geneva, and retracts. 36. Relapses, and is beheaded. 37. George Blandrata perverts the Prince of Transylvania; disputes with the Reformers; is murdered. 38. Bernard Ochino; his Life while a Friar; his Perversion, and Flight to Geneva. 38. He goes to Strasburg, and afterwards to England, with Bucer; his unfortunate Death in Poland.

34. VALENTINE GENTILIS was a native of Cosenza, in Calabria, and a disciple of Servetus. He was astonished, he said (1), that the Reformers would trouble themselves so much in disputing with the

---

(4) Nat. Alex. *t.* 19, *art.* 14; Van Ranst, *p.* 326. (1) Van Ranst, *p.* 326.

Catholics about sacraments, purgatory, fasting, &c., matters of such little importance, and still agree with them in the principal mystery of their Faith, the Trinity. Although he agreed in doctrine with Servetus, he explained it differently (2). Three things, he said, concur in the Trinity—the essence, which was the Father, the Son, and the Holy Ghost. The Father is the one only true God, the *Essenciator;* the Son and the Holy Ghost are the *Essenciati.* He did not call the Father a Person, because, according to his opinion, the essence was in itself true God, and therefore he said, if we admit the Father to be a Person, we have no longer a Trinity, but a Quaternity. He thus denied that there were three Persons in the same essence, as we believe. He recognized in God three external Spirits (3); but of these, two were inferior to the Father, for he had given them a Divinity indeed, but inferior to his own. In the book which he presented to Sigismund Augustus, King of Poland (4), he complains that many monstrous terms have been introduced into the Church, as Persons, Essence, and Trinity, which are, he says, a perversion of the Divine Mysteries. He admitted that there were three holy and eternal essences, as the Athanasian Creed teaches, but in all the rest he says it is " a satanical symbol."

35. Valentine, and some Antitrinitarian friends of his, being in Geneva (5), in 1558, and the magistracy, having a suspicion of his opinions, obliged them to sign a profession of Faith in the Trinity. Valentine subscribed it, and swore to it, but not sincerely, for he immediately after began to teach his errors, so he was taken up and imprisoned for perjury. He presented another Confession of Faith while in prison, but as his heresy appeared through it, Calvin strenuously opposed his release. Fear then drove him to a more ample retractation, and from his prison he presented the following one to the magistrates: " Confiteor Patrem, Filium et Spiritum Sanctum esse unum Deum, id est tres Personas distinctas in una Essentia, Pater non est Filius, nec Filius, et Spiritus Sanctus, sed unaquæque illarum Personarum est integra illa Essentia. Item Filius, et Spiritus Sanctus quantum ad Divinam Naturam sunt unus Deus cum Patre, cui sunt coæquales et coæterni. Hoc sentio, et corde ac ore profiteor. Hæreses autem contrarias damno, et nominatim blasphemias quas descripsi," &c. It would have been well for him had he never changed again this profession; he would not then have made the miserable end he did.

36. Notwithstanding his retractation, the Senate of Geneva, in 1558, condemned him to be brought forth, stripped to his shirt, to kneel with a candle in his hand, and pray to God and the state for pardon for his blasphemies, and then to cast his writings into the fire with his own hands. He was led through the principal streets

(2) Gotti, *c.* 115; Nat. Alex. *t.* 19, *ar.* 14; Jovet, *t.* 1, *p.* 296.   (3) Jovet, loc. cit.
4) Van Ranst, loc. cit.   (5) Gotti, *s.* 2, 3; Nat. Alex. cit.

of the city, and the sentence executed (6). He was prohibited, likewise, from leaving the city; indeed, at first he was kept in prison, but afterwards was allowed out, promising on oath that he would not make his escape. He fled, however, at the first opportunity, and took refuge in the house of a lawyer of Padua, who lived in Savoy, and held the same opinions as himself, and began writing again in opposition to the Trinity. He was again put into prison, and escaped to Lyons, where he published a Treatise against the Athanasian Creed. From Lyons he went to Poland, and when Sigismund banished him from that kingdom, he took up his residence in Bearn. He was here accused by Musculus, in the year 1556, and imprisoned. He refused to retract, and was sentenced to death. Just before laying his head on the block, he said: "Others died martyrs for the Son; I die a martyr for the Father." Unfortunate man! dying an enemy of the Son, he died an enemy of the Father likewise (7).

37. George Blandrata was another of the disciples of Servetus. He was born in Piedmont, and was a physician, and the writings of Servetus having fallen in his way, he embraced his errors. The Inquisition was very strict at that period in Piedmont, so he consulted his safety by flying, first, into Poland, and, afterwards, in 1553, into Transylvania (8). He here succeeded in getting himself appointed physician to the Sovereign, John Sigismund, and to his Prime Minister, Petrowitz, a Lutheran, and by that means endeavoured to make them Arians. There were a great many Lutherans and Calvinists in the country, and they all joined in opposing Blandrata's doctrine, so the Sovereign, to put an end to the dispute, commanded that a public conference (9) should be held in his presence, and acted himself the part of judge. The conference took place in his presence, in Waradin, between the Reformers and Blandrata, and several other Arian friends of his. They began by quoting the various passages of the Scripture used by Arius to impugn the Divinity of Christ. The Reformers answered by quoting the interpretation of these texts by the Council of Nice, and by the Holy Fathers, who explained them in their proper sense. This doctrine, they said, we should hold, otherwise every one might explain away the Scriptures just as he pleased. One of the Arians then stepped forward and cried out: "How is this? When you argue with the Papists, and quote your texts of Scripture to defend your doctrine, and they say that the true meaning of these texts is only to be found in the Decrees of Councils, and the works of the Fathers, you at once say that the Holy Fathers and the Bishops composing the Councils were

(6) Gotti, loc. cit. (7) Spondan. ad Ann. 1561, n. 34; Van Ranst, sec. 16, p. 327; Gotti, c. 115. (8) Jovet, His. Rel. p. 291; Gotti, s. 2, n. 6; Nat. Alex. t. 19, art. 14. (9) Jovet, p. 294.

men subject to be deceived, like any one else—that the Word of God alone is sufficient for understanding the Articles of Faith—that it is clear enough in itself, and requires no explanation; and now you want to make use of the same arms against us which you blame the Catholics for having recourse to." This answer was applauded by the Prince and the majority of the meeting, and the preachers were confounded, and knew not what reply to make. Arianism then became the most numerous sect in Transylvania, and the impious doctrine of Arius was resuscitated after a lapse of nine hundred years. It is worthy of remark, as Jovet (10) tells us, that the first who embraced it were all Lutherans or Calvinists, and that all their chiefs came to an unhappy end. Paul Alciatus, their companion, at last became a Mahometan, as Gotti informs us. Francis David, as Noel Alexander tells us, was killed by a house falling on him; another of them, called Lismaninus, drowned himself in a well, and Blandrata (11) was killed by a relative of his, to rob him.

38. Bernard Ochino was also an Antitrinitarian. He was a Capuchin friar, and the heretics even make him founder of that Institute; but the Capuchin Chronicle, and the majority of writers, deny this and say he was only General of the Capuchins for a while (12). Their real founder was Matthew de Basso, in 1525, and Ochino did not enter the order until 1534, nine years after, when the order already had three hundred professed members. He lived as a Religious for eight years, and threw off the habit in 1542. At first, while a Religious, he led a most exemplary life (13), wore a very poor habit, went always barefooted, had a long beard, and appeared to suffer from sickness and the mortified life he led. Whenever he had occasion, in his journeys, to stop in the houses of the great, he eat most sparingly, and only of one dish, and that the plainest—scarcely drank any wine—and never went to bed, but extending his mantle on the ground, took a short repose. With all this, he was puffed up with vanity, especially as he was a most eloquent preacher, though his discourses were more remarked for ornament of diction than soundness of doctrine, and the churches were always crowded when he preached. The Sacramentarian Valdez, who perverted Peter Martyr (*Chap.* xi. *art.* ii. *sec.* iii. *n.* 57), was also the cause of his fall. He perceived his weakness, he saw he was vain of his preaching, and (14) he used frequently go to hear him, and visit him afterwards, and under the praises he administered to him for his eloquence, conveyed the poison of his sentiments. Ochino had a great opinion of his own merits, and hoped, when he was made General of his Order, that the Pope would raise him to some higher dignity, but when he saw that neither a cardinal's hat,

(10) Jovet, cit. *p.* 300.   (11) Nat. Alex. *s.* 3; Gotti, *s.* 2, *n.* 6; Jovet, cit.
(12) Varill. Hist. *t.* 2, *p* 109; Gotti, 115.   (13) Varill. *p.* 111.   (14) Varill. cit. *p.* 100.

nor even a mitre, fell to his lot, he entertained the most rancorous feeling against the Roman Court, and Valdez made him an easy prey. Being now infected with the poisonous sentiments of Zuinglius and Calvin, he began in the pulpit to speak derogatory of the Pope and the Roman See, and preaching in the archbishoprics of Naples, after Peter Martyr, he began to deride the doctrines of purgatory and indulgences, and sowed the first seeds of that great revolution which afterwards, in 1656, convulsed the city. When the Pope received information of this, he commanded him to come to Rome and account for his doctrine. His friends advised him to go; but, as he felt himself hurt by the order, he was unwilling to obey. While he was thus wavering he went to Bologna, and called on the Cardinal Legate, Contarini, to solicit his protection and interest. The cardinal was then suffering from sickness, of which, in fact, he died soon after; so he received him coldly, hardly spoke to him, and dismissed him. He now suspected that the cardinal knew all, and would have him put in prison, so he threw off the habit, and went to Florence, where he met Peter Martyr, and concerted with him a flight to Geneva, then the general refuge of apostates. In fact, he arrived there even before Peter Martyr himself, and though sixty years old, he brought a young girl of sixteen along with him, and married her there, thus giving a pledge of his perpetual separation from the Catholic Church. He then wrote an apology of his flight, and abused, in the most violent terms, the Order of St. Francis and the Pope, Paul III. The Pope for a while entertained the notion of dissolving the Capuchin Order altogether, but relinquished it on finding that Ochino had made no perverts among that body.

39. Calvin received Ochino most kindly on his arrival in Geneva, but he soon perceived that the Capuchin had no great opinion of him, and leaned more to the doctrines of Luther, and he therefore began to treat him with coolness; so, having no great affection for the doctrines of either one or the other, he determined to establish his fame by founding a new sect. He then took up the opinions of Arius, and published some tracts in Italian, in which he confounded the personality and properties of the Three Divine Persons, so Calvin procured a sentence of banishment to be passed on him by the Senate of Geneva. He then went to Basle, but as he was not safe even there, he went to Strasbourg, to Bucer, who protected heretics of every shade, and received him kindly, appointed him Professor of Theology, and took him, along with himself and Peter Martyr, to England afterwards. They were both banished from that kingdom by Queen Mary, on her accession, together with thirty thousand others, so he went first to Germany and then to Poland Even there he had no rest, for all heretics were banished from that country by the King, Sigismund, and so, broken down by old age, and abandoned by every one, he concealed himself in

the house of a friend, and died of the plague in 1564, leaving two sons and a daughter, their mother having died before. Cardinal Gotti, Moreri, and others, say that he died an apostate and impenitent; but Zachary Boverius, in the Annals of the Capuchins, proves on the authority of other writers, and especially of the Dominican, Paul Grisaldus, and of Theodore Beza himself, that he abjured all his errors, and received the sacraments before his death. Menochius and James Simidei follow the opinion of Boverius. I do not give an opinion either on one side or the other, but, with Spondanus and Graveson, leave the matter between them (15).

SEC. III.—THE SOCINIANS.

40. Perverse Doctrine of Lelius Socinus. 41. Faustus Socinus; his Travels, Writings, and Death. 42. Errors of the Socinians.

40. LELIUS and Faustus Socinus, from whom the Socinians take their name, were born in Sienna. Lelius was the son of Marianus Socinus, a celebrated lawyer, and was born in 1525. His talents were of the first order, and he surpassed all his cotemporaries at the schools; but he, unfortunately, became acquainted with some Protestants, and they perverted him; so, dreading to come under the notice of the Inquisition, then extremely strict in Italy, he left it at the age of twenty-one, and spent four years in travelling through France, England, Flanders, Germany, and Poland, and finally came to Switzerland, and took up his abode in Zurich. He was intimate with Calvin, Beza, Melancthon, and several others of the same sort, as appears from their letters to him; but he attached himself chiefly to the Antitrinitarian doctrines of Servetus. When he learned that Servetus was burned in Geneva, he hid himself, and fled to Poland first, and afterwards to Bohemia, but after a time returned to Zurich, where he died, in the year 1562, at the early age of thirty-seven (1).

41. Faustus Socinus was a nephew of the former; he was born in 1539, and was infected with his uncle's heresy. He was twenty-three years of age when his uncle died. He at once went to Zurich and took possession of all his manuscripts, which he afterwards published, to the great injury of the Church. Next, pretending that he was a true Catholic (2), he returned to Italy, and lived for nine years attached to the service of the Duke of Tuscany, who treated him with honour and respect. Finding it impossible to spread his heresy in Italy as he wished, he went to Basle, and lived

---

(15) Gotti, cit. *sec.* 2, *n.* 8; Varillas, *p.* 112, & seq.; Nat. Alex. *t.* 19, *a.* 14, *sec.* 3; Van Ranst, *sec.* 16, *p.* 328; Bern. *t.* 4, *sec.* 16, *c.* 5; Berti, Brev. Hist. Eccl. *sec.* 6, *c.* 3; Bover. in Ann. Capuccin. 1543; Menoch. Cent. *p.* 2, *c.* 89; Paulus Grisald. Decis. Fid. Cath. in Ind. Error. & Hærat. Simid. Comp. Stor. degli Eresiarchi, *sec.* 16; Graveson, *t.* 4, Hist. Eccl. *coll.* 3. (1) Nat. Alex. *t.* 19, *art.* 14; Gotti, *c.* 116, *sec.* 3, *n.* 1; Van Ranst, *sec.* 16, *p.* 328. (2) Gotti, loc. cit. *n.* 2.

there three years, and published his impious work on theology, in two volumes, and spread his doctrines not only there, but in Poland and Transylvania, both by word and writing. His writings were very voluminous, for not only did he publish his theology, but several treatises besides, especially Commentaries on the fifth and sixth chapters of St. Matthew, on the first chapter of St. John, on the seventh chapter of St. Paul to the Romans, on the first Epistle of St. John, and many more enumerated by Noel Alexander, all of a heretical tendency (3). He was obliged to fly from Cracow (4), in 1598, and went to a village, where he continued to write works of the same tendency, and where, at last, he died in 1604, the sixty-fifth year of his age, leaving one daughter after him.

42. The Socinian errors are very numerous, and Noel Alexander and Cardinal Gotti (5) give them all without curtailment. I will only state the principal ones: They say, first, that the knowledge of God and of Religion could not come from Nature. Second.—That there is no necessity for Christians reading the Old Testament, since they have everything in the New. Third.—They deny Tradition. Fourth.—They assert that in the Divine Essence there is but one Person. Fifth.—That the Son of God is improperly called God. Sixth.—That the Holy Ghost is not a Divine Person, but merely a Divine power. Seventh.—That Jesus Christ is true man, but not a mere man, for he was honoured by the filiation of God, inasmuch as he was formed without the assistance of man; and they also blasphemously assert that he did not exist before the Blessed Virgin. Eighth.—They deny that God assumed human nature in unity of person. Ninth.—That Christ is our Saviour, only because he showed us the way of salvation. Tenth.—Man was not immortal, nor had he original justification before he committed original sin. Eleventh.—Christ did not consummate his sacrifice on the Cross, but only when he went into heaven. Twelfth.—Christ did not rise from the dead by his own power; the body of Christ was annihilated after his Ascension, and it is only a spiritual body that he has in heaven. Thirteenth.—Baptism is not necessary for salvation, nor is grace acquired by it. Fourteenth.—We receive mere bread and wine in the Eucharist, and these symbols are only of use to remind us of the death of Christ. Fifteenth.—The Socinians follow the Pelagians in the matter of Grace, and say that our natural strength alone is sufficient to observe the Law. Sixteenth.—God has not an infallible knowledge of future things which depend on the free will of man. Seventeenth.—The soul does not survive after death; the wicked are annihilated, with the exception of those who will be alive on the day of judgment, and these will be condemned to everlasting fire;

(3) Nat. Alex. loc. cit. n. 1. (4) Gotti, cit. n. 2. (5) Nat. Alex. n. 2; Gotti, n. 3.

but the damned will not suffer for ever. Eighteenth.—They teach, with Luther, that the Church failed, and did not continually exist. Nineteenth—That Antichrist began to exist when the Primacy of the Bishop of Rome was established. (It is remarkable that heretics of every class attack the Primacy of the Pope.) Twentieth.—That the words, " Thou art Peter, and on this rock," &c., were addressed equally to the other Apostles as to Peter. Twenty-first.—That the words, " The gates of hell shall not prevail against it," do not mean that the Church can never fail. Twenty-second.—That the keys given to St. Peter have no other meaning but this: That he had the power of declaring who did or did not belong to the state of those who enjoy the Divine Grace. Twenty-third.—They deny that we should have faith in General Councils. Twenty-fourth.—They deny that it is lawful for Christians to defend their lives by force against unjust aggressors, for it is impossible, they say, that God would permit a pious and religious man to be placed in these circumstances, so that there would be no way of saving himself unless by shedding the blood of another. Besides, they say, that it is even worse to kill an aggressor than an enemy, for he who kills an enemy kills one who has already done him an injury; but he who kills an aggressor kills one who has as yet done him no injury, and only desires to injure him and kill him; and even he cannot be sure that the aggressor intends to kill him at all, as, perhaps, he only intends to terrify him, and rob him then with more ease to himself. Here are the original words of the proposition, as quoted by Noel Alexander, error 39: " Non licere Christianis vitam suam, suorumque contra latrones, et invasores vi opposita defendere, si possint; quia fieri non potest, ut Deus hominem vere pium, ipsique ex animo confidentem, tali involvi patiatur periculo, in quo ipsum servatum velit, sed non aliter, quam sanguinis humani effusione. Homicidium aggressoris pro graviori delicto habendum esse, quam ipsam vindictam. Vindicando enim retribuo injuriam jam acceptam: at hic occido hominem, qui me forsan nondum læserat, nedum occiderat, sed qui voluntatem tantum habuit me lædendi, aut occidendi; imo de quo certo scire non possum, an me animo occidendi, et non potius terrendi tantum, quo tutius me spoliari possit, aggrediatur." Twenty-fifth.—That it is not necessary for Preceptors to have a Mission from the Superiors of the Church, and that the words of St. Paul, " How shall they preach if they be not sent?" are to be understood when they preach doctrines unheard till then, such as the doctrine preached by the Apostles to the Gentiles, and, therefore, a Mission was necessary for them. I omit many other errors of less importance, and refer the reader to Noel Alexander, who treats the subject diffusely. The worst is, that this sect still exists in Holland and Great Britain. Modern Deists may be called followers of Socinus, as appears from the works they are every day publishing.* The Socinians say of their founder, Faustus:

> Toto licet Babylon destruxit tecta Lutherus,
> Muros Calvinus, sed fundamenta Socinus (6).

Well may this be said, for the Socinians deny the most fundamental articles of the faith.

CHAPTER XIII.

HERESIES OF THE SIXTEENTH AND SEVENTEENTH CENTURIES.

ARTICLE I.

ISAAC PERIERES, MARK ANTHONY DE DOMINIS, WILLIAM POSTELLUS, AND BENEDICT SPINOSA.

1. Isaac Perieres, Chief of the Pre-Adamites; abjures his Heresy. 2. Mark Anthony de Dominis; his Errors and Death. 3. William Postellus; his Errors and Conversion; 4. Benedict Spinosa, Author of a new Sort of Atheism. 5. Plan of his impious System; his unhappy Death.

1. ISAAC PERIERES, a native of Aquitaine, lived in this century. He was at first a follower of Calvin, but afterwards founded the sect of the Pre-Adamites, teaching that, previous to the creation of Adam, God had made other men. The Old Testament, he says, speaks only of Adam and Eve, but says nothing of the other men who existed before them, and these, therefore, were not injured by original sin, nor did they suffer from the Flood. He fell into this error because he rejected tradition, and, therefore, his opinion appeared consonant to reason, and not opposed to the Scripture. He published a treatise in Holland on the Pre-Adamites, in 1655. He was convinced of the fallacy of his opinions, both by Catholics and Calvinists, and his life even was in danger from both one and the other, so he at last recognized the authority of constant and universal tradition, and in the Pontificate of Alexander VII. renounced all his heresies, and returned to the Church (1).

2. Mark Anthony de Dominis was another of the remarkable heretics of this century. He joined the Jesuits at first in Verona, but left them, either because he did not like the restraint of discipline, or was dismissed for some fault. He was afterwards elevated,

(6) Gotti, c. 115, sec. 3, n. 15; Van Ranst, p. 308.   (1) Berti, Brev. Hist. t. 2, sec. 17; Bernini, t. 4, sec. 17, c. 5.

---

* N.B.—This was written in 1765, or thereabouts.

we know not how, to the bishopric of Segni, by Clement VIII., and was subsequently translated to the archbishopric of Spalatro by Paul V. He did not hold this diocese long, for he was sued and condemned to pay a pension, charged on the diocese by the Pope with his consent before he was appointed. He was so chagrined with the issue of the case that he resolved to be revenged on the Apostolic See, and went to England in 1616, and there published a pestilent work, " De Republica Christina." In this book he has the temerity to assert that out of the Roman Catholic religion, Calvinism, Lutheranism, and the Anabaptist doctrines, a sound and orthodox religion could be formed, and his mode of doing this—of uniting truth and error in this impossible union—is even more foolish than the thing itself. After residing six years in England, agitated by remorse, he was desirous of changing his life, and returning once more to the Catholic Church, but he was dreadfully agitated, between the desire of repentance and the despair of pardon; he feared he would be lost altogether. In this perplexity he consulted the Spanish ambassador, then resident in England, and he offered his influence with the Holy See, and succeeded so well that Mark Anthony went to Rome, threw himself at the Pope's feet, and the Sovereign Pontiff was so satisfied that his repentance was sincere, that he once more received him into favour. Soon after he published a document in which he solemnly and clearly retracts all that he had ever written against the doctrine of the Church, so that to all appearance he was a sincere penitent and a true Catholic. Still he continued to correspond privately with the Protestants, till God removed him from the world by a sudden death. His writings and papers were then examined, and his heresy was proved. A process was instituted; it was proved that he meditated a new act of apostacy, and so his body and painted effigy were publicly burned by the common hangman in the most public place in Rome—the *Campo de Fiori*, to show the revenge that God will take on the enemies of the Faith (2).

3. William Postellus, or Postell, was born in Barenton, in Lower Normandy; he was a learned philosopher, and Oriental traveller, and was remarkable as a linguist, but fell into errors of Faith. Some even go so far as to say, that in his work, called *Virgo Veneta*, he endeavours to prove that an old maid of Venice, called Mother Johanna of Venice, was the Saviour of the feminine sex. Florimund, however, defends him from this charge, and says he wrote this curious work merely to praise this lady, who was a great friend of his, and frequently afforded him pecuniary assistance. He lived some time also in Rome, and joined the Jesuits, but they soon dismissed him, on account of the extraordinary opinions he professed. He was charged with heresy, and condemned to perpetual impri-

(2) Van Ranst, *sec.* 17, *p.* 525; Bernin, *t.* 4, *sec.* 17, *c.* 1, 2, 3; Berti, loc. cit.

sonment, by the Inquisition; but he escaped to France, and his fame as a linguist procured him a favourable reception from King Charles IX., and the learned of that country. He then wrote several works, filled with the most extravagant errors, as "*De Trinitate*," "*De Matrice Mundi*," "*De Omnibus Sectis salvandis*," "*De futura Nativitate Mediatoris*," and several others of the same stamp. He was reprimanded by the Faculty of Theology, and the magistracy of Paris, for these writings, but as he refused to retract them, he was confined in the monastery of St. Martin des Champes, and there he got the grace of repentance, for he retracted everything he had written, and subjected all to the judgment of the Church. He then led a most religious life in the monastery, and died on the 7th of September, 1581, being nearly a hundred years old. Some time previously he published a very useful book, entitled "*De Orbis Concordia*," in which he defends the Catholic religion against Jews, Gentiles, Mahometans, and heretics of every shade (3).

4. Benedict Spinosa was born in Amsterdam, in 1632. His parents were Jewish merchants, who were expelled from Portugal, and, with numbers of his co-religionists, took refuge in Holland. He preferred the Jewish religion at first; he next became a Christian, at least nominally, for it is said he never was baptized; and he ended by becoming an Atheist. He studied Latin and German under a physician, called Francis Van Dendedit, who was afterwards invited to France, and entering into a conspiracy against the King, ended his life on the scaffold; and it is thought that from this man he imbibed the first seeds of Atheism. In his youth he studied the Rabbinical theology, but, disgusted with the puerilities and nonsense which form the greater part of it, he gave it up, and applied himself to philosophy, so he was excommunicated by the Jews, and was even in danger of his life from them. He, therefore, separated himself altogether from the synagogue, and laid the foundation of his atheistical system. He was a follower of the opinions of Des Cartes, and took his principles as a base on which to establish his own by geometrical dissertations, and he published a treatise to this effect, in 1664. In the following year he published another work, "*De Juribus Ecclesiasticorum*," in which, following the opinion of Hobbes, he endeavours to prove that priests should teach no other religion but that of the state. Not to be interrupted in his studies, he went into retirement altogether, and published a most pestilent work, "Tractatus Theologico-Politicus," which was printed in Amsterdam or Hamburg, and in which he lays down the principles of his atheistical doctrine.

4. In this work he speaks of God as the Infinite, the Eternal, the Creator of all things, while, in fact, he denies his existence,

(4) Gotti, loc. cit.; Van Ranst, sec 17, p. 346.

and does away with the Divinity altogether, for he says that the world is a mere work of nature, which necessarily produced all creatures from all eternity. That which we call God, he says, is nothing else but the power of nature diffused in external objects, which, he says, are all material. The nature of all things, he says, is one substance alone, endowed with extension and mind, and it is *active* and *passive;* passive, as to itself—active, inasmuch as it thinks. Hence he supposes that all creatures are nothing but modifications of this substance; the material ones modifications of the passive substance, and the spiritual ones—that is, what we call spiritual, for he insists that all are material—being modifications of the active substance. Thus, according to his opinion, God is, at the same time, Creator and Creation, active and passive, cause and effect. Several authors, as Thomasius, Moseus, Morus, Buct, Bayle, and several others, Protestants even, combated this impious system by their writings. Even Bayle, though an Atheist himself, like Spinosa, refuted it in his Dictionary. I, also, in my work on the Truth of the Faith (4), have endeavoured to show the incoherence of the principles on which he founds his doctrines, and, therefore, I do not give it a particular refutation in this work. Notwithstanding the monstrosity of his system, Spinosa had followers; and it is even said, that there are some at present in Holland, though they do not publicly profess it, only among themselves. The work itself was translated into several languages, but its sale was prohibited by the States of Holland. Spinosa died at the Hague, on the 23rd of February, 1677, in the 59th year of his age. Some say, that his servants being all at church on a Sunday, found him dead on their return, but others tell that he was dying of consumption, and feeling death approaching, and knowing that it is natural for every one to call on God, or some superhuman power, to assist him, at that awful moment, he, dreading to call on God for assistance, or to let it be seen that he repented of his doctrine, ordered that no one should be allowed into his chamber, and there at last he was found dead (5).

Article II.

THE ERRORS OF MICHAEL BAIUS.

6. Michael Baius disseminates his unsound Doctrine, and is opposed. 7. St. Pius V. condemns seventy-nine Propositions of Baius, and he abjures them. Retractation written by Baius, and confirmed by Pope Urban VIII.

6. MICHAEL BAIUS was born in Malines, in Flanders, in 1513, was made a Doctor of the University of Louvain, in 1550, and subsequently Dean of the same University. He was a man of learning,

(4) Verita della Fede, Par. 1, *c.* 6, *s.* 5.   (5) Gotti, cit. in fin.

and of an exemplary life, but fond of new opinions, which he maintained in his works, published about 1560 (1), and thus he sowed the first seeds of that discord which disturbed the Church in the following century. Some Franciscan Friars thought his doctrines not sound, and submitted them, in eighteen chapters, to the Faculty of Sorbonne, and that learned body judged them worthy of censure. This only added fuel to the fire, and the party of Baius published an Apology in opposition to the censures of the Parisian University. Cardinal Commendon, who was then in the Low Countries, sent by the Pope for some other affairs, thought himself called on to interfere, as Apostolic Legate, and imposed silence on both parties, but in vain, for one of the Superiors of the Franciscans punished some of his subjects for defending the doctrines of Baius, and this proceeding caused a great uproar. At last the Governor of the Low Countries was obliged to interfere to prevent the dispute from going any further (2).

7. Some time after this Baius was sent by Philip II., as his Theologian, to the Council of Trent, together with John Hessel, and Cornelius, Bishop of Ghent (not Cornelius Jansenius, Bishop of Ipres), all Doctors of Louvain. His opinions were not examined in the Council of Trent, though he had already printed his works on Free Will, Justification, and Sacrifice. When he returned from the Council he printed his Treatises on the Merit of Works, the Power of the Wicked, on Sacraments in general, on the Form of Baptism; and hence his opinions were spread more extensively, and disputes grew more violent, so that at last the Holy See was obliged to interfere. St. Pius V. then, in a particular Bull, which begins, " Ex omnibus affectionibus," after a rigorous examination, condemned seventy-nine propositions of Baius (in globo) as heretical, erroneous, suspect, rash, scandalous, and offensive to pious ears, but without specifying them in particular, and with this clause, " that some of them might, in rigour, be sustained, and in the proper sense which the authors had," or as others explain it, " that although some of them might be in some way sustained, still the Pope condemns them in the proper and rigorous sense of the authors." Here are the words of the Bull: " Quas quidem sententias stricto coram nobis examine ponderatas, quamquam nonnullæ aliquo pacto sustineri possent, in rigore et proprio verborum sensu ab assertoribus intento, hæreticas, erroneas, suspectas, temerarias, scandalosas, et in pias aures offensionem immittentes damnamus." The name of Baius was not inserted in the Bull in 1567, nor did Pius command that it should be affixed in the public places, as is customary, but, wishing to act with mildness, consigned it to Cardinal Granvell, Archbishop of Mechlin, then in Rome, telling him to notify it to Baius, and to the University of Louvain, and

(1) Possevin. *t.* 2, in M. Bajum.   (2) Gotti, Ver. Rel. *t.* 2, *c.* 116 ; Bernin. *sec.* 16.

to punish, by censures or other penalties, all who refused to receive it. The Cardinal discharged his commission by his Vicar, Maximilian Mabillon. The Bull was notified to the University, and accepted by the Faculty, who promised not to defend any more the Articles condemned in it, and Baius promised the same, though he complained that opinions were condemned as his which were not his at all, nor could he be pacified, but wrote to the Pope, in 1579, in his defence. The Pope answered him in a Brief, that his cause had already undergone sufficient examination, and exhorted him to submit to the judgment already passed. This Brief was presented to him by Mabillon, who reprimanded him harshly for daring to write to the Pope after the sentence had been once given, and intimated to him, that he incurred an Irregularity by the proceeding. Baius then humbled himself, and prayed to be dispensed from the Irregularity. Mabillon answered that he could not do so till Baius would abjure his errors. He asked to see the Bull, to know what errors he was to abjure. Mabillon said he had not the Bull by him, and prevailed on him there and then to abjure in his hands all his errors. He was then absolved from all censures, without giving any written document, and the matter was private between them (3).

8. After all that, there were not wanting others who defended the opinions of Baius, so after the death of St. Pius V., his successor, Gregory XIII., in his Bull *Provisionis Nostræ*, expedited in 1579, confirmed the Bull of St. Pius, and published it first in Rome, and then had it presented to the Faculty of Louvain, and to Baius himself, by Father Francis Toledo, afterwards raised to the purple by Clement VIII., who prevailed on Baius to submit quietly, and send a written retractation to the Pope, as follows: " Ego Michael de Bajo agnosco, et profiteor, me ex variis colloquiis cum Rev. P. Francisco Toledo ita motum, et perauctum esse, ut plane mihi habeam persuasum, earum sententiarum damnationem jure factum esse. Fateor insuper ex iisdem sententiis in nonnullis libellis a me in lucem editis contineri in eo sensu, in quo reprobantur. Denique declaro ab illis omnibus me recedere, neque posthac illas defendere velle: Lovanii, 24 Mart. 1580." The Faculty of Louvain then passed a law, that no one should be matriculated to the University, unless he first promised to observe the foregoing Bulls. Urban VIII., in the year 1641, in another Bull, which begins, " In eminenti," confirmed the condemnation of Baius, in conformity with the two preceding Bulls, and this Bull was received by the Sorbonne (4). Baius died about the year 1590, and as he was born in 1513, he must have been seventy-seven years of age. The system of Baius and his errors will be seen in the Refutation XII. of this volume.

(3) Gotti, cit. *s.* 3, *n.* 1, 2.   (4) Gotti, Ver. Rel. *c.* 118, *s.* 1, *n.* 1.

Article III.

THE ERRORS OF CORNELIUS JANSENIUS.

9. Cornelius, Bishop of Ghent, and Cornelius, Bishop of Ipres; his Studies and Degrees. 10. Notice of the condemned Work of Jansenius. 11. Urban VIII. condemns the Book of Jansenius in the Bull " In eminenti;" the Bishops of France present the Five Propositions to Innocent X. 12. Innocent condemns them in the Bull "Cum occasione;" Notice of the Propositions. 13. Opposition of the Jansenists; but Alexander VIII. declares that the Five Propositions are extracted from the Book, and condemned in the Sense of Jansenius; Two Propositions of Arnould condemned. 14. Form of Subscription commanded by the Pope to be made. 15. The Religious Silence. 16. The *Case of Conscience* condemned by Clement XI. in the Bull *Vineam Domini*. 16. The Opinion, that the Pontificate of St. Paul was equal to that of St. Peter, condemned.

9. I SHOULD remark, first of all, that there were in Flanders, almost at the same time, two of the name of Cornelius Jansenius, both Doctors and Professors of the renowned University of Louvain. The first was born in Hulst, in the year 1510, and taught theology to the Premonstratentian Monks for twelve years, and during that time composed his celebrated book *Concordia Evangelica*, and added his valuable Commentaries to it. He then returned to Louvain, and was made Doctor. He was next sent to the Council of Trent, by King Philip II., together with Baius, and, on his return, the King appointed him to the Bishopric of Ghent, where, after a holy life, he died in 1576, the sixty-sixth year of his age, leaving, besides his great work, *De Concordia*, several valuable Treatises on the Old Testament (1). The other Jansenius was born in the village of Ackoy, near Leerdam, in Holland, in 1585. He completed his philosophical studies in Utrecht, and his theological in Louvain, and then travelled in France, where he became united in the closest friendship with Jean du Verger de Hauranne, Abbot of St. Cyran. On his return to Louvain he was appointed, at first Professor of Theology, and afterwards of Scripture. His Commentaries on the Pentateuch and Gospels were afterwards printed, and no fault has ever been found with them. He wrote some works of controversy also, in defence of the Catholic Church, against the Ministers of Bois-le-Duc. Twice he went to Spain to arrange some affairs for his University, and at last was appointed Bishop of Ipres, in 1635 (2).

10. Jansenius never printed his work *Augustinus*, the fruit of twenty years' labour, during his lifetime, but charged his executors to put it to press. In this work, at the end of the book *De Gratia Christi*, in the Epilogue, he says that he does not mean to assert that all that he wrote concerning the Grace of Christ should be held as Catholic doctrine, but that it was all taken from the works of St. Augustin; he, however, declares that he himself is a fallible

(1) Bernin. *t.* 4, *sec.* 18, *l.* 3, in fine.   (2) Bernin. cit.

man, subject to err, and that if the obscurity of some passages in the Saint's works deceived him, that he would be happy to be convinced of his error, and, therefore, he submitted it all to the judgment of the Apostolic See—" Ut illum teneam (he says) si tenendum, damnem si damnamdum esse judicaverit" (3). He died on the 6th of May, 1638, and left his book to his chaplain, Reginald Lamée, to be printed, repeating in his will that he did not think there was anything in his book to be corrected, but as it was his intention to die a faithful child of the Roman Church, that he submitted it in everything to the judgment of the Holy See— " Si Sedes Romana aliquid mutari velit, sum obediens filius, et illius Ecclesiæ, in qua semper vixi, usque adhunc lectum mortis obediens sum. Ita mea suprema voluntas" (4). Would to God that the disciples imitated their master in obedience to the Holy See, then the disputes and heartburnings which this book caused would never have had existence.

11. Authors are very much divided regarding the facts which occurred after the death of Jansenius. I will then succinctly state what I can glean from the majority of writers on the subject. It is true he protested, both in the work itself and in his will, that he submitted his book *Augustinus* in everything to the judgment of the Apostolic See; still his executors at once put it into the hands of a printer, and notwithstanding the protest of the author, and the prohibition of the Internuncio and the University of Louvain, it was published in Flanders in 1640, and in Rouen in 1643. It was denounced to the Roman Inquisition, and several theologians composed Theses and Conclusions against it, and publicly sustained them in the University of Louvain. An Apology in favour of the work appeared in the name of the publisher, and soon the press groaned with treatises in favour of, or opposed to, Jansenius, so that all the Netherlands were disturbed by the dispute. The Congregation of the Inquisition then published a decree forbidding the reading of Jansenius's work, and also the Conclusions and Theses of his adversaries, and all publications either in favour of or opposed to him. Still peace was not restored; so Urban VIII., to quiet the matter, published a Bull renewing the constitution of Pius V. and Gregory XIII. In this he prohibited the book of Jansenius, as containing propositions already condemned by his predecessors, Pius V. and Gregory XIII. The Jansenists exclaimed against this Bull; it was, they said, apocryphal, or at all events vitiated. Several propositions extracted from the book were presented to the Faculty of Sorbonne in 1649, to have judgment passed on them, but the Sorbonne refused to interfere, and referred the matter to the judgment of the bishops, and these, assembled in the name of the Gallican

(3) Gotti, *s.* 3, *n.* 5. (4) Pallav. His. Con. Trid. *l.* 15, *c.* 7, *n.* 13; Collet. Cont. Tournel. de Grat. 4, *p.* 1.

clergy in 1653, declined passing any sentence, but referred it altogether to the judgment of the Pope. Eighty-five bishops, in 1650, wrote to Pope Innocent X., the successor of Urban, thus (5): "Beatissime Pater, majores causas ad Sedem Apostolicam referre, solemnus Ecclesiæ mos est quem Fides Patri nunquam deficiens perpetuo retineri pro jure suo postulat." They then lay before the Holy Father the five famous propositions extracted from the book of Jansenius, and beg the judgment of the Apostolic See on them.

12. Innocent committed the examination (6) of these propositions to a congregation of five cardinals and thirteen theologians, and they considered them for more than two years, and held thirty-six Conferences during that time, and the Pope himself assisted at the last ten. Louis de Saint Amour and the other deputies of the Jansenist party were frequently heard, and finally, on the 31st of May, 1563, the Pope, in the Bull *Cum occasione*, declared the five propositions which follow heretical:—

"First.—Some commandments of God are impossible to just men, even when they wish and strive to accomplish them according to their present strength, and grace is wanting to them by which they may be possible to them. This we condemn as rash, impious, blasphemous, branded with anathema, and heretical, and as such we condemn it.

"Second.—We never resist interior grace in the state of corrupt nature. This we declare heretical, and as such condemn it.

"Third.—To render us deserving or otherwise in the state of corrupt nature, liberty, which excludes restraint, is sufficient. This we declare heretical, and as such condemn it.

"Fourth.—The Semipelagians admitted the necessity of interior preventing grace for every act in particular, even for the commencement of the Faith, and in this they were heretics, inasmuch as they wished that this grace was such that the human will could neither resist it nor obey it. We declare this false and heretical, and as such condemn it.

"Fifth.—It is Semipelagianism to say that Jesus Christ died or shed his blood for all men in general. This we declare false, rash, scandalous, and understood in the sense that Christ died for the salvation of the predestined alone, impious, blasphemous, contumelious, derogatory to the Divine goodness, and heretical, and as such we condemn it."

The Bull also prohibits all the faithful to teach or maintain the propositions, otherwise they will incur the penalties of heretics. Here are the original propositions:—

"Primam prædictarum Propositionum—Aliqua Dei præcepta hominibus justis volentibus, et conantibus, secundum præsentes quas habent vires, sunt impossibilia; deest quoque illis gratia, qua possi-

(5) Gotti, loc. cit. c. 118.   (6) Tournell. loc. cit.

bilia fiant: temerariam, impiam, blasphemam, anathemate damnatam, et hæreticam declaramus, et uti talem damnamus.

"Secundam.—Interiori gratiæ in statu naturæ lapsæ nunquam resistitur: hæreticam declaramus, et uti talem damnamus.

"Tertiam.—Ad merendum, et demerendum in statu naturæ lapsæ non requiritur in homine libertas a necessitate, sed sufficit libertas a coactione: hæreticam declaramus, et uti talem damnamus.

"Quartam.—Semipelagiani admittebant prævenientis gratiæ interioris necessitatem ad singulos actus, etiam ad initium Fidei; et in hoc erant hæretici, quod vellent eam gratiam talem esse, cui posset humana voluntas resistere, vel obtemperare: falsam et hæreticam declaramus, et uti talem damnamus.

"Quintam.—Semipelagianum est dicere, Christum pro omnibus omnino hominibus mortuum esse, aut Sanguinem fudisse: falsam, temerariam, scandalosam, et intellectam eo sensu, ut Christus pro salute dumtaxat Prædestinatorum mortuus sit, impiam, blasphemam, contumeliosam, Divinæ pietati derogantem, hæreticam declaramus, et uti talem damnamus (7)."

13. The whole Church accepted the Decree of Innocent, so the partisans of Jansenius made two objections: First.—That the five propositions were not those of Jansenius; and secondly, that they were not condemned in the sense of Jansenius; and hence sprung up the famous distinction of Law and Fact—*Juris* and *Facti*. This sprung entirely from the just condemnation of the five propositions. Clement XI., in his Bull of 1705, "*Vineam Domini Sabaoth*," particularly on that account renews the condemnation of the five propositions. Here are his words: "Inquieti homines docere non sunt veriti: Ad obedientiam præfatis Apostolicis Constitutionibus debitam non requiri, ut quis prædicti Janseniani libri sensum in antedictis quinque propositionibus, sicut præmittitur, damnatum interius, ut hæreticum damnet, sed satis esse, ut ea de re obsequiosum (ut ipsi vocant) silentium teneatur. Quæ quidem assertio quam absurda sit, et animabus fidelium perniciosa, satis apparet, dum fallacis hujus doctrinæ pallio non deponitur error, sed absconditur, vulnus tegitur, non curatur, Ecclesiæ illuditur, non paretur, et data demum filiis inobedientiæ via sternitur ad fovendam silentio hæresim, dum ipsam Jansenii doctrinam, quam ab Apostolica Sede damnatam Ecclesia Universalis exhorruit, adhuc interius abjicere, et corde improbare detrectent," &c. Hence, also, the French bishops, assembled in 1654, by a general vote decided that the five propositions were really and truly in the Book of Jansenius, and that they were condemned in the true and natural sense of Jansenius, and the same was decided in six other assemblies. Afterwards Alexander VII., in the Bull expedited on the 16th of October, 1656, definitively and expressly declared: "Quinque pro-

(7) Tournelly, *p.* 250.

positiones ex libro Cornelii Jansenii excerptas ac in sensu ab eodem Cornelio intento damnatus fuisse." About the same time the Faculty of Paris censured a proposition of Arnauld, who asserted (8), " Duas propositiones nec esse in Jansenio nec ejus sensu damnatas fuisse, adeoque circa partem illam Apostolicæ constitutionis sufficere silentium Religiosum."

14. The Gallican clergy, from 1655 used a Formula as follows: "Quinque propositiones ex libro Jansenii extractas tanquam hæreticas damnatas fuisse in eo ipso sensu quo illas docuit," and prescribed that every one taking Orders should sign it. Several, however, refused obedience, on the plea that unless the Pope commanded them, they could not be obliged to subscribe. A petition was, therefore, sent to Alexander VII., begging him to order it to be done; he consented to the prayer, and issued a Bull on the 15th of February, 1656, sanctioning the formula of an oath to which all should subscribe. Here it is: " Ego N. Constitutioni Alexandri VII., datæ die 16. Octobr. an. 1656, me subjicio, et quinque propositiones ex Jansenni libro, Augustinus, excerptas, et in sensu ab eodem Auctore intento, prout illas sancta Sedes Apostolica damnavit sincero animo damno, ac rejicio, et ita juro, sic me Deus adjuvet, et hæc sancta Evangelia." The King sanctioned it also by royal authority, and severe penalties were imposed on the disobedient (9).

15. This put the Jansenists into a quandary; some of them said that the oath could not be taken without perjury, but others, of a more hardened conscience, said that it might, for it was enough that the person subscribing should have the intention of following the doctrine of St. Augustine, which, they said, was that of Jansenius, and as to the *fact* externally, it was quite enough to keep a reverent silence, and the Bishops of Alet, Pamiers, Angers, and Beauvais were of this opinion; but under Clement XI., the successor of Alexander VII., they gave in, and consented to subscribe themselves, and oblige their subjects to subscribe the condemnation of the five propositions, without any restriction or limitation, and thus peace was re-established (10). The Jansenists, however, would not still yield; the limitation of the religious silence was, they said, inserted in the Verbal Acts of the Diocesan Synods, and they, therefore, demanded that the silence should be approved by the Pope. In this they acted unreasonably, for the four above-mentioned bishops were admitted to peaceable communion, on condition of signing *purely, sincerely, and without any limitation whatever* (11). In 1692 some other disputes arose concerning the subscription of the Formula, and the bishops of Flanders added some other words to it, to remove every means of deception. The Louvanians complained to Innocent XII. of this addition, and he expedited two Briefs, in 1694 and 1696, removing every means of subterfuge (12).

(8) Libell. inscrip. Second Letter de M. Arnauld. (9) Tournelly, *p.* 253. (10) Ibid. 225. (11) Tournelly, ibid. (12) Ibid. *p.* 256.

16. About the year 1702, the Jansenists again raised the point of the religious silence, by the publication of a pamphlet, in which it was said that Sacramental Absolution was denied to a clergyman because he asserted that he condemned the five propositions, as far as the law was concerned (jus), but as to the fact that they were to be found in Jansenius's book, that he considered it was quite enough to preserve a religious silence on that point. This was the famous *Case of Conscience*, on which forty Doctors of Paris decided that absolution could not be refused to the clergyman. The Pope, however, condemned this pretended silence by a formal decree, "Ad perpetuam rei memoriam," on the 12th of January, 1703. Many of the French bishops also condemned it, and more especially Cardinal de Noailles, Archbishop of Paris, who likewise obliged the forty doctors to retract their decision, with the exception of one alone, who refused, and was, on that account, dismissed from the Sorbonne, and that famous Faculty also branded their decision as rash and scandalous, and calculated to renew the doctrines of Jansenius, condemned by the Church. Clement XI. expedited another Bull, *Vineam Domini*, &c., on the 16th of July, 1705, condemning the "Case of Conscience," with various notes. All this was because the distinction of Law and Fact (Juris et Facti) was put forth to elude the just and legitimate condemnation of the five propositions of Jansenius. This is the very reason Clement himself gives for renewing the condemnation. His Bull was accepted by the whole Church, and, first of all, by the assembly of the Gallican Church; thus the Jansenists could no longer cavil at the condemnation of the book of their patron (13). In the Refutation of the errors of Jansenism, we will respond to their subterfuges in particular.

17. We may as well remark here, that about this time an anonymous work appeared, entitled, "De SS. Petri et Pauli Pontificatu," in which the writer endeavoured to prove that St. Paul was, equally with St. Peter, the Head of the Church. The author's intention was not to exalt the dignity of St. Paul, but to depress the primacy of St. Peter, and, consequently, of the Pope. The book was referred to the Congregation of the Index, by Innocent XI., and its doctrine condemned as heretical by a public Decree (14). The author lays great stress on the ancient practice used in Pontifical Decrees, that of painting St. Paul on the right and St. Peter on the left. That, however, is no proof that St. Paul was equally the Head of the Church, and exercised equal authority with St. Peter, for not to him but St. Peter, did Christ say, "Feed my sheep." Hence, St. Thomas says (15), "Apostolus fuit par Petro in executione, authoritatis, non in auctoritate regiminis." Again, if the argument be allowed that, because St. Paul was painted to the right of St. Peter, he was equal to him, would it not prove even that

(13) Jour. 257.   (14) Gotti, c. 118, s. 4.   (15) St. Thom. in cap. ii. ad Galatas.

he was superior? Some say that he was painted so, because, according to the Roman custom, as is the case in the East, the left hand place was more honourable than the right. Others, as St. Thomas (16), give a different explanation. Bellarmine may be consulted on this point (17). The author also quotes in favour of his opinion, the lofty praises given by the holy Fathers to St. Paul; but that is easily answered. He was praised, as St. Thomas says, more than the other Apostles, on account of his special election, and his greater labours and sufferings in preaching the Faith through the whole world (18). Not one of the Fathers, however, makes him superior or equal to St. Peter, for the Church of Rome was not founded by him but by St. Peter.

Article IV.

18. Quesnel is dismissed from the Congregation of the Oratory. 19. He publishes several unsound Works in Brussels. 20. Is imprisoned, escapes to Amsterdam, and dies excommunicated. 21. The Book he wrote. 22. The Bull "Unigenitus," condemning the Book. 23. The Bull is accepted by the King, the Clergy, and the Sorbonne; the Followers of Quesnel appeal to a future Council. 24. Several Bishops also, and Cardinal de Noailles, appeal to a future Council likewise, but the Council of Embrun declares that the Appeal should not be entertained. 25. The Consultation of the Advocates rejected by the Assembly of the Bishops; Cardinal de Noailles retracts, and accepts the Bull; the Bull is declared dogmatical by the Sorbonne and the Bishops. 26. Three Principles of the System of Quesnel.

18. WHILE Clement XI. still sat on the chair of St. Peter, Quesnel published his book, entitled, "The New Testament, with Moral Reflections," &c., which the Pope soon after prohibited by the Bull *Unigenitus*. Quesnel was born in Paris, on the 14th of July, 1634, and in 1657 was received by Cardinal de Berulle into his Congregation of the Oratory. In a General Assembly of the Oratory of France, held in 1678, it was ordained that each member of the Congregation should sign a formula, condemnatory of the doctrine of Baius and Jansenius, but Quesnel refused obedience, and was consequently obliged to quit the Congregation, and left Paris; he then retired to Orleans (1).

19. As he was not in safety in France, he went to Brussels, in 1685, and joined Arnauld, who had fled previously, and was concealed there, and they conjointly published several works, filled with Jansenistic opinions. They were both banished from Brussels, in 1690, and went to Delft, in Holland, first—afterwards, to the Pais de Liege—and then again returned to Brussels. Quesnel, after having administered the last Sacraments, Arnauld changed his dress, adopted a feigned name, and lived concealed in that city, where he was elected by the Jansenists as their chief, and was called by them the "Father Prior." From his hiding-place, he un-

---

(16) St. Thomas in cap. i. ad Gal. *l*. 1.   (17) Bell. de Rom. Pontiff. *c*. 27.   (18) St. Thom. in 2 Cor. *l*. 3, *c. n.*   (1) Tour. Comp. Theol. *t*. 5, *p*. 1, *Diss*. 9, *p*. 396.

ceasingly sent forth various pamphlets, defending and justifying his conduct in opposing the decrees of the Popes, and the Ordinances of the Sovereigns, condemning the appellants. This appears from the sentence passed on his conduct, by the Archbishop of Mechlin (2).

20. The Archbishop of Mechlin, in 1703, determined to extirpate the tares sown by the works of Quesnel, and, empowered by the authority of the King of Spain, his Sovereign, caused a strict search to be made for the author and his faithful friend, Gerberonius, and on the 30th of May, they were both confined in the Archiepiscopal prison. Gerberonius remained there until 1710, when Cardinal de Noailles induced him to retract and sign the formula, and he was liberated, but Quesnel was detained only about three months, having escaped through a small hole made in the wall by his friend (he was a very small man), and taken refuge in Holland, where he continued to write in favour of Jansenism. He was called a *second Paul*, after his escape, by his disciples, and he himself, writing to the Vicar of Mechlin, says, that he was liberated from his prison by an angel like St. Peter. The difference was great, however; St. Peter did not concert the means of escape with his friends outside, by writing with a nail on a plate of lead, and telling them to break a hole at night through a certain part of the wall of his prison, as Quesnel did (3). A process was instituted against him in Brussels, and on the 10th of November, 1704, the Archbishop declared him excommunicated, guilty of Jansenism and Baiism, and condemned him to inclusion in a monastery till the Pope would absolve him (4). Quesnel took no other notice of the sentence than by writing several pamphlets against the Archbishop, and even attacked the Pope himself, for the condemnation of his works. The unfortunate man, obstinate to the last, died under Papal censure, in Amsterdam, on the 2nd of December, 1719, in the eighty-fifth year of his age (5).

21. We should remark concerning the book of Quesnel, " The New Testament with Moral Reflections," &c. (it was published in French), that in 1671, while he still lived in France, he only published, at first, a small work in *duodecimo*, containing the French translation of the Four Gospels, and some very short reflections, extracted principally from a collection of the words of Christ, by Father Jourdan, Superior of the Oratory. By degrees, he added to it, so that sixteen years after the printing of the first edition, in 1687, he published another, in three small volumes, adding other reflections on the whole of the New Testament. In 1693, he published another larger edition in eight volumes, and another again in 1695, with the approbation of Cardinal de Noailles, then

---

(2) Tour. *p.* 397; Gotti, *c.* 119, *s.* 1, *n.* 3.   (3) Tour. *p.* 309; Gotti, *n.* 5.
(4) Tour. *p.* 405.   (5) Tour. *p.* 406.

Bishop of Chalons, first making some slight corrections on the edition of 1693. He published the last edition of all in 1699, but this had not the approbation of the Cardinal. In a word, for twenty-two years, that is, from 1671 to 1693, he laboured to perfect this work, but not correcting, but rather adding to the errors that deformed it; for in the first edition five errors alone were condemned—the twelfth, thirteenth, thirtieth, sixty-second, and sixty-fifth; in the second, more than forty-five were published; and they amounted up to the number of one hundred and one in the later editions, when they were condemned by the Bull *Unigenitus*. We should observe, that it was only the first edition of 1671 that had the approbation of the Bishop of Chalons, and the subsequent editions, containing more than double the matter of the first, were printed with only the approbation given in 1671 (6). The followers of Quesnel boast, that the work was generally approved of by all; but Tournelly (7) shows that the greater part of the Doctors and Bishops of France condemned it. They also boast that Bossuet gave it his approval, but there are several proofs, on the contrary, to show that he condemned it (8).

22. When the complete work appeared in 1693, it was at once censured by theologians, and prohibited by several bishops, and was condemned by a particular Brief of Pope Clement XI., in 1708. Three French bishops prohibited it by a formal condemnation in 1711, and Cardinal de Noailles felt so mortified at seeing these edicts published in Paris, condemning a work marked with his approbation, as heretical, that he condemned the three edicts. This excited a great tempest in France, so the King, with the consent of several bishops, and of Cardinal de Noailles himself, requested Pope Clement XI. to cause a new examination of the work to be made, and, by a solemn Bull, to censure any errors it might contain. The Pope, then, after two years' examination by Cardinals and Theologians, published in 1713, on the 8th of September, the Bull *Unigenitus Dei Filius*, &c., in which he condemned a hundred and ten propositions, extracted from the work, as false, captious, rash, erroneous, approximating to heresy, and in fine, respectively heretical, and recalling the propositions of Jansenius, in the sense in which they were condemned. The Bull, besides, delared that it was not the intention of his Holiness to approve of all else contained in the work, because while marking these hundred and ten propositions, it declares that it contains others of a like nature, and that even the very text of the New Testament itself was vitiated in many parts (9).

23. His Most Christian Majesty, on the reception of the Bull of Clement from the Nuncio, ordered an assembly of the bishops, to

---

(6) Tour. *p.* 409, 310.   (7) Tour. *p.* 412.   (8) Tour. *p.* 419.   (9) Tour. *p.* 426 & seq.; Gotti, 2, *n.* 3, 4.

receive and promulgate it solemnly, and, in fact, after several private conferences, the assembly was held on the 23rd of January, 1714, and the Bull was received, together with the condemnation of the hundred and one propositions, in the same manner as the Pope had condemned them, and a form of acceptation was drawn up for all the bishops of the kingdom, that the Bull might be everywhere promulgated, and also a formula by which the clergy should declare their acceptance of it. The followers of Quesnel said, that the form of acceptation was restricted and conditional, but if we take the trouble of reading the declaration of the assembly, given word for word by Tournelly (*P.* 431), we will clearly see that there is neither restriction nor condition in it. This declaration was subscribed by forty bishops; eight alone refused, and the principal among them was Cardinal de Noailles; they had some difficulty, they said, about some of the condemned propositions, and considered it would be wise to ask an explanation from the Pope on the subject. When the acceptation of the Bull, by the assembly, was notified to Louis XIV., he ordered, on the 14th of the following month of February, that it should be promulgated and put into execution through the whole kingdom. The bishops wrote to the Pope in the name of the assembly, that they had received the Bull with joy, and would use all their endeavours that it should be faithfully observed; and the Pope, in his reply, congratulated them on their vigilance, and complained of those few bishops who refused to conform to the assembly. The Faculty of Paris, also, accepted the Bull on the 5th of March, 1714, imposing a penalty, to be incurred, *ipso facto*, by all members of the University refusing its acceptance. It was received in the same way by the other Universities, native and foreign, as Douay, Ghent, Nantz, Louvain, Alcala, and Salamanca (10). Notwithstanding all, the partisans of Quesnel scattered pamphlets on every side against the Bull. Two of them, especially, made the most noise, the "Hexaplis," and the "Testimony of the Truth of the Church;" these were both condemned by the bishops congregated in 1715, and those who still continued pertinaciously attached to their erroneous opinions had only then recourse to an appeal from the Bull of the Pope to a General Council.

24. Four bishops, to wit, those of Montpelier, Mirepoix, Sens, and Boulogne, appealed on the 1st of March, 1717, from the Bull *Unigenitus*, to a future General Council. These four were soon after joined by twelve others, and soon after that by eighteen dissentients. This was the first time in the Catholic Church, that it was ever known that the bishops of the very Sees where a dogmatical Bull was accepted, appealed against it. The appeal was, therefore, justly rejected, both by the secular and ecclesiastical

(10) Tour. cit.

authorities. In the year 1718, Cardinal de Noailles subscribed to the appeal of the bishops, but still it was annulled by the Pope, and towards the end of the year 1718, about fifty of the bishops of France published pastoral letters to their diocesans, ordering them to yield unreserved obedience to the Bull: " Quippe quæ universalis est Ecclesiæ judicium dogmaticum, a quo omnis appellatio est nulla" (11). The defenders of Quesnel only became more violent in their opposition to the bishops after this, and the press groaned with their pamphlets; so in the year 1727, a Provincial Council was held at Embrun, in which the Bishop of Sens was suspended for refusing to subscribe to the Bull, which was declared to be the dogmatical and unchangeable judgment of the Church, and it decided that the appeal was, *ipso jure*, schismatical, and of no avail. The whole proceeding there received the sanction of the Pope, Benedict XIII., and the King (12).

25. The appellants then had recourse to the lawyers of Paris, and they published a " Consultum," in which they undertook to invalidate the judgment of the Council, on account of several irregularities. They were then joined by twelve bishops, who signed a letter to the King, against the Council, but he strongly censured the production, and ordered that all the bishops should be assembled in Paris in an extraordinary assembly, and record their opinion on the Consultum of the lawyers. On the 5th of May, 1728, the prelates assembled, and made a representation to the King that the Consultum was not only not to the point, but that it smelt of heresy, and was in fact heretical. The King, therefore, published a particular edict, ordering the Consultum to be set aside (13). Soon after this, in the same year, Cardinal de Noailles, now very far advanced in years, yielded to the admonition of Benedict XIII., and revoked his appeal, and sincerely accepted the Bull, prohibiting all his diocesans from reading Quesnel's works. He sent his retractation to the Pope, who was delighted to receive it. In about six months after, he died (14). In the year 1729, the Faculty of the Sorbonne again solemnly accepted the Bull, and revoked as far as was necessary (quantum opus est), the appeal which appeared under the name of the Faculty. The decree was signed by more than six hundred masters, and was confirmed by the other Universities of the kingdom, and by the assembly of the clergy, in 1730. Finally, the whole proceeding was approved by Clement XII. in the same year, and the King ordered, by a solemn edict, that the Bull should be observed as the perpetual law of the Church, and of the kingdom. On the death of Benedict XIII., in 1730, his successors, Clement XII. and Benedict XIV., confirmed the Bull (15).

26. Before we conclude Quesnel's history, we may as well see

(11) Tour. cit.   (12) Tour. cit.   (13) Tour. cit.   (14) Tour. cit.   (15) Tour. cit.

what his system was. It comprised, properly speaking, three condemned systems—those of Baius, of Jansenius, and of Richer. The first condemned propositions of Quesnel agree with Jansenius's system of the two delectations without deliberation, the celestial and the terrestrial, one of which necessarily, by a relative necessity, conquers the other. From this false principle several dreadful consequences follow, such as that it is impossible for those persons to observe the Divine law who have not efficacious grace; that we never can resist efficacious grace; that the *delectatio victrix*, or conquering delectation, drives man of necessity to consent; and several other maxims condemned in the five propositions of Jansenius. Some also, I recollect, savour of the doctrine condemned in the second, ninth, and tenth propositions of Quesnel. In his second proposition he says: " Jesu Christi gratia, principium efficax boni cujuscunque generis, necessaria est ad omne opus bonum; absque illa (here is the error) non solum nihil fit, sed nec fieri potest." Hence he re-establishes the first proposition of Jansenius, that some of the Commandments of God are impossible to those who have not efficacious grace. Arnold, as Tournelly tells us, asserted the same thing, when he says (16) that Peter sinned in denying Jesus Christ, because he wanted grace, and for this he was condemned by the Sorbonne, and his name expunged from the list of Doctors. Quesnel says just the same thing in his ninth proposition: " Gratia Christi est gratia suprema, sine qua confiteri Christum (mark this) nunquam possumus, et cum qua nunquam illum abnegamus;" and in the tenth proposition: " Gratia est operatio manus Omnipotentis Dei, quam nihil impedire potest aut retardare." Here another of the heretical dogmas of Jansenius is renewed: " Interiori gratiæ nunquam resistitur." In fine, if we investigate the doctrines of both, we will find Jansenius and Quesnel perfectly in accordance.

27. Quesnel's propositions also agree with the doctrine of Baius, who says, that between vicious concupiscence and supernatural charity, by which we love God above all things, there is no middle love. Thus the forty-fourth proposition of Quesnel says: " Non sunt nisi duo amores, unde volitiones et actiones omnes nostræ nascuntur: amor Dei, qui omne agit propter Deum, quemque Deus remuneratur, et amor quo nos ipsos, ac mundum diligimus, qui quod ad Deum referendum est, non refert, et propter hoc ipsum sit malus." The impious deductions from this system of Baius the reader will find in the refutation of his heresy (*Conf.* xii.).

28. The last propositions of Quesnel agree with the doctrine of Richer, condemned in the Councils of Sens and Bagneres. See his nineteenth proposition: " Ecclesia auctoritatem excommunicandi habet, ut eam exerceat per primos Pastores, de consensu

(16) Apud Tour. *p.* 745.

saltem præsumpto totius Corporis." As the bishops said in the Assembly, in 1714, this was a most convenient doctrine for the appellants, for as they considered themselves the purest portion of the Church, they never would give their consent to the censures fulminated against them, and, consequently, despised them.

ARTICLE V.

THE ERRORS OF MICHAEL MOLINOS.

29. The unsound Book of Molinos called the "Spiritual Guide." 30. His impious Doctrine, and the Consequences deduced from it. 31. His affected Sanctity; he is found out and imprisoned, with two of his Disciples. 32. He is condemned himself, as well as his Works; he publicly abjures his Errors and dies penitent. 33. Condemnation of the Book entitled "The Maxims of the Saints."

29. THE heresy of the Beghards, of which we have already treated (*Chap.* x. *art.* iv. *n.* 31), was the source of the errors of Molinos. He was born in the diocese of Saragossa, in Arragon, and published his book, with the specious title of " The Spiritual Guide which leads the Soul by an interior way to the acquisition of perfect Contemplation, and the rich treasure of internal Grace." It was first printed in Rome, next in Madrid, then in Saragossa, and finally in Seville, so that in a little time the poison infected Spain, Rome, and almost all Italy. These maxims were so artfully laid down, that they were calculated to deceive not alone persons of lax morality, who are easily led astray, but even the purest souls, given totally to prayer. We ought to remark, also, that the unfortunate man did not, in this book, teach manifest errors, though he opened a door by it for the introduction of the most shocking principles (1).

30. Hence, the consequence was, that those who studied this work were oppressed, as it were, by a mortal lethargy of contemplation and false quietism. Men and women used to meet together in conventicles professing this new sort of contemplation; they used to go to Communion satisfied with their own spirit, without confession or preparation; they frequented the churches like idiots, gazing on vacancy, neither looking to the altar where the Holy Sacrament was kept, nor exciting their devotion by contemplating the sacred images, and neither saying a prayer, nor performing any other act of devotion. It would be all very well if they were satisfied with this idle contemplation and imaginary quietude of spirit, but they constantly fell into gross acts of licentiousness, for they believed that while the soul was united with God it was no harm to allow the body unbridled license in sensuality, all which, they said, proceeded solely from the violence of the devil or the animal pas-

(1) Bernin. Hist. de Heres. *t.* 4, *sec.* 17, *c.* 8; Gotti, Ver. Rel. 120.

sions; and they justified this by that text of Job (xvi. 18): " These things have I suffered without the iniquity of my hand, when I offered pure prayers to God." Molinos, in his forty-ninth proposition, gives an impious explanation to this text; " Job ex violentia Dæmonis se propriis manibus polluebat," &c. (2).

31. This hypocrite lived in Rome unfortunately for twenty-two years, from the year 1665 till 1687, and was courted by all, especially by the nobility, for he was universally esteemed as a holy man, and an excellent guide in the way of spiritual life. His serious countenance, his dress neglected, but always clerical, his long and bushy beard, his venerably old appearance, and his slow gait, all were calculated to inspire devotion, and his holy conversation caused him to be venerated by all who knew him. The Almighty at length took compassion on his Church, and exposed the author of such iniquity. Don Inigo Carracciolo, Cardinal of St. Clement, discovered that the diocese of Naples was infected with the poisonous error, and immediately wrote to the Pope, imploring him to arrest the progress of the heresy by his supreme authority, and several other bishops, not only in Italy, but even in France, wrote to the same effect. When his Holiness was informed of this, he published a circular letter through Italy, pointing out, not so much the remedy as the danger of the doctrine which was extending itself privately. The Roman Inquisitors then, after taking information on the subject, drew up a secret process against Molinos, and ordered his arrest. He was accordingly taken up, with two of his associates, one a priest of the name of Simon Leone, and the other a layman, called Anthony Maria, both natives of the village of Combieglio, near Como, and all three were imprisoned in the Holy Office (3).

32. The Inquisition, on the 24th of November, 1685, prohibited the " Spiritual Guide" of Molinos, and on the 28th of August, 1687, condemned all his works, and especially sixty-eight propositions extracted from his perfidious book " The Guide," and of which he acknowledged himself the author, as we read in Bernini (4). He was condemned himself, together with his doctrine, and after twenty-two months' imprisonment, and the conviction of his errors and crimes, he professed himself prepared to make the act of abjuration. On the 3rd of September, then, in 1687, he was brought to the Church of " the Minerva," before an immense concourse of people, and was placed by the officials in a pulpit, and commenced his abjuration. While the process was read, at the mention of every heretical proposition and every indecent action proved against him, the people cried out with a loud voice, "*fuoco, fuoco*"—" burn him." When the reading of the process was concluded, he was conducted to the feet of the Commissary of the Holy

(2) Gotti, *n.* 2, 3.   (3) Gotti, loc. cit. *n.* 4, 5, 6.   (4) Bernin. loc. cit.

Office, and there solemnly abjured the errors proved against him, received absolution, was clothed with the habit of a penitent, and received the usual strokes of a rod on the shoulders; he was then again conducted back to the prison of the Holy Office by the guards, a small apartment was assigned to him, and he lived for ten years with all the marks of a true penitent, and died with these happy dispositions. Immediately after his abjuration, Pope Innocent XI. published a Bull on the 4th of September, 1687, again condemning the same propositions already condemned by the Holy Inquisition; and on the same day the two brothers, the disciples of Molinos, Anthony Maria and Simon Leone, already mentioned, made their abjuration, and gave signs of sincere repentance (5).

33. About the end of the 17th century there was a certain lady in France, Madame Guion, who, filled with false notions of spiritual life, published several manuscripts, against which Bossuet, the famous Bishop of Meaux, wrote his excellent work, entitled " De Statibus Orationis," to crush the evil in the bud. Many, however, deceived by this lady's writings, took up her defence, and among these was Fenelon, the Archbishop of Cambray, who published another work, with the title of " Explanations of the Maxims of the Saints on Interior Life." This book was at once condemned by Innocent XII., who declared that the doctrine of the work was like that of Molinos. When Fenelon heard that his book was condemned he at once not only obeyed the decision of the Pope, but even published a public edict, commanding all his diocesans to yield obedience to the Pontifical decree (6). The propositions condemned by the Pope in this book were twenty-three in number; they were condemned on the 12th of March, 1699, and Cardinal Gotti gives them without curtailment.

SUPPLEMENTARY CHAPTER.

HERESIES OF THE EIGHTEENTH AND NINETEENTH CENTURIES.

1. Introductory Matter. 2. Rationalists. 3. Hernhutters, or Moravians. 4. Swedenborgians, or New Jerusalemites. 5. Methodism; Wesley. 6, 7. Doctrines and Practices of the Methodists. 8. Johanna Southcott. 9. Mormonism. Table Rapping. Tertullian. 10. German Catholics.

1. THE holy author, as the reader may perceive, concludes his History of Heresies with the account of the famous Bull *Unigenitus*, which gave the death-blow to Jansenism. He brings down the history of this most dangerous of sects and its ramifications to the Pontificate of Benedict XIV. A little more than a century has

---

(5) Bernin. 4, *c.* 8.   (6) Gotti, Ver. Rel. *c.* 5.

elapsed since, and though heresy has produced nothing new—for every heresiarch only reproduces the errors of his predecessors—still it will not, I hope, be ungrateful to the reader to have before him a succinct account of the sectaries who have since appeared, especially the Methodists, the most numerous, and, on many accounts, the most remarkable body of the present day. It is a fact which every close observer must be aware of, that heresy naturally tends to infidelity. When once we lose hold of the anchor of Faith, and set up our own fallible judgments in opposition to the authority of the Church, we are led on from one false consequence to another, till in the end we are inclined to reject Revelation altogether. Such is the case, especially in Germany at the present day, where Rationalism has usurped the place of religion, and infidelity is promulgated from the Theological Chair. It is true that in Catholic countries infidelity has also not alone appeared, but subverted both the throne and altar, and shaken society to its very foundations; but there it is the daughter of indifferentism. Lax morality produces unbelief, and those whose lives are totally opposed to the austere rule of the Gospel, are naturally anxious to persuade themselves that religion is altogether a human invention. This madness, however, passes away after a time. Religion is too deeply rooted in the hearts of a truly Catholic people to be destroyed by it. The storm strips the goodly tree of a great deal of its fruit and foliage, the rotten branches are snapped off, and the dead and withered leaves are borne away, but the vital principle of the trunk remains untouched, and in due season produces again fruit a hundred-fold.

2. That free spirit of inquiry, the boast of Protestantism, which, rejecting all authority, professes to be guided by reason alone, produced Rationalism. Luther and Calvin rejected several of the most important Articles of the Christian Faith. Why should not their followers do the same? They appealed to reason—so did their disciples; one mystery after another was swept away, till Revelation, we may say, totally disappeared, and nothing but the name of religion remained. The philosopher Kant laid down a system, by which *true* and *ecclesiastical* religion were distinguished. True religion is the religion of reason; ecclesiastical, the religion of Revelation, and this is only a vehicle for conveying the truths of natural religion. By this rule, then, the Scriptures were interpreted. Nothing but what reason could measure was admitted; every mystery became a *myth:* miracles were all the effects of natural causes, working on an unenlightened and wonder-loving people. Hetzel, Eichhorn, the Rosenmüllers, promulgated these blasphemies. Strauss, in his "Life of Christ," upsets all Revelation; and Becker teaches that St. John the Baptist and our Lord, with the determination of upsetting the Jewish Hierarchy, whose pride and tyranny they could not bear, plotted together, and agreed that one should play the part of the precursor and the other of the

Messiah. Such is the woeful state of Continental Protestantism, and the worst of it is, that it is a necessary consequence of the fundamental principle of the Reformation, "unrestricted liberty of opinion" (1).

3. In contra-distinction to the Rationalists, we have the Pietists in Germany, who cannot so much be called a sect as a party. They date their origin from Spener, who flourished in Frankfort in the sixteenth century, and caused a great deal of disturbance in the Lutheran Church in that and the following age. They are entitled to our notice here, as from some of their doctrines originated some extraordinary sects. Among these may be ranked the Hernhutters, otherwise called Moravians, and by themselves, "United Brethren." They assert that they are the descendants of the Bohemian and Moravian Hussites of the fifteenth century; but it is only in the last century they appeared as a distinct and organized sect, and now they are not only numerous and wealthy, but have formed establishments—partly of a missionary and partly of a trading character—in many parts of the world, from Labrador to Southern Africa. Their founder was Count Zinzendorf, who, in 1721, on attaining his majority, purchased an estate called Bertholsdorf, in Lusatia, and collected round him a number of followers, enthusiasts in religion, like himself. A carpenter of the name of Christian David came to join him from Moravia, and was followed by many of his countrymen, and they built a new town on the estate, which was at first, from the name of a neighbouring village, called Huthberg, but they changed it to Herren Huth, the Residence of the Lord, and from that the sect took its name. They profess to follow the Confession of Augsburg, but their government is totally different from that of Lutheranism. They have both bishops and elders, but the former have no governing power; they are merely appointed to ordain, and, individually, are but members of the general governing consistory. Zinzendorf himself travelled all over Europe, to disseminate his doctrines, and twice visited America. He died in 1760 (2). The doctrines preached by this enthusiast were of the most revolting and horrible nature. All we read of the abominations of the early Gnostics is nothing, compared to the revolting and blasphemous obscenity to be found in his works. An attempt has been made by some of his followers to defend him, but in vain, and it is truly a melancholy feeling to behold the sacred name of religion prostituted to such vile abominations (3).

4. Emmanuel Swedenborg, the founder of the New Jerusalemites, was another extraordinary fanatic, and his case is most remarkable, since he was a man of profound learning, a civil and military engineer, and the whole tenor of his studies was calculated to banish

---

(1) Perron. de Protes.   (2) Encyc. Brit. Art. Zinzendorf and United Brethren.
(3) Mosheim, Cent. XVIII.

any tendency to mystic fanaticism which might have been interwoven in his nature. He was born in Stockholm, in 1689, and was the son of the Lutheran Bishop of West Gotha. From his earliest days he applied himself to the study of science, under the best masters, and made such progress, that he published some works at the age of twenty. His merit recommended him to his Sovereign, Charles XII., the warrior King of Sweden, and he received an appointment as Assessor of the College of Mines. At the siege of Frederickshall, in 1713, he accomplished an extraordinary work, by the transmission of the siege artillery over the ridge of mountains which separates Sweden from Norway. It was considered one of the boldest attempts of military engineering ever accomplished. His application to study was continual, and from time to time he published works which gave him a European scientific reputation. It would have been well for himself had he never meddled in theological speculations; but his extravagances prove that the strongest minds, when destitute of Faith, fall into the grossest errors. His system was, that there is a spiritual world around us corresponding in everything to the material world we inhabit. He used himself, he assures us, converse with people in the most distant climes, and was in daily communication with those who were dead for ages. When a man dies, he says, he exchanges his *material* body, of which there is no resurrection, for a *substantial* one, and can immediately enjoy all the pleasures of this life, even the most gross, just as if he were still in the flesh. In fact a man frequently does not well know whether he is living or dead. Jesus Christ is God himself, in human form, who existed from all eternity, but became incarnate in time to bring the hells or evil spirits into subjection. He admitted a Trinity of his own, consisting of the Divinity, the Humanity, and the Operation. This Trinity commenced only at the Incarnation. He travelled through a great part of Europe, disseminating his doctrines, and finally died in London, in 1772, and was buried in the Swedish Church, Ratcliffe Highway. His followers have increased since his death, but they still only form small and obscure congregations. They style themselves "the Church of the New Jerusalem."

5. The Patriarch of Methodism was John Wesley, who was born in 1703, at Epworth, in Lincolnshire, of which place his father was rector. At the age of seventeen he was sent to the University of Oxford, and being more seriously inclined than the generality of young men there, applied himself diligently to his studies. One of his favourite books at that period was the famous work of Thomas á Kempis, "The Imitation of Christ." During his long and varied life this golden work was his manual, and he published even an edition of it himself in 1735, but, as should be expected, corrupted and mutilated. His brother Charles, a student like himself, at Oxford, and a few other young men, formed themselves

into a Society for Scripture-reading and practices of piety, and, as the state of morals was peculiarly lax in that seat of learning, they were jeered by their fellow-students, called the Godly Club, and, on account of their methodical manner of living, were nicknamed "Methodists," which afterwards became the general designation of the whole sect or society in all its numerous subdivisions. Wesley was ordained in the Anglican Church, and assisted his father for awhile as curate, till an appointment was offered to him in Georgia. He sailed, accordingly, for America, in company with his brother and two others. He led quite an ascetic life at this period, slept frequently on the bare boards, and continually practised mortification. He remained in America till 1738, and then returned to England. He was disappointed in a matrimonial speculation while there, and had a lawsuit also on hands. Like all Protestant apostles, a comfortable settlement in life appeared to him the first consideration. This is one of the principal causes of the sterility of all their missions; if, however, they do not seek first the kingdom of God, they take care that all other things that the world can afford shall be added to them, as the investigations into the land tenures of New Zealand and the islands of the Pacific bear witness. While in America he associated a great deal with the Moravians, and became imbued, to a great extent, with their peculiar doctrines of grace, the new birth, and justification, and on his return paid a visit to Herrenhutt, to commune with Zinzendorf. He was not at all popular in America; he appears to have been a proud, self-opinionated man, filled up with an extraordinary idea of his own perfections. Indeed, it only requires a glance at his diary, which, it would appear, he compiled, not so much for his own self-examination as for making a display before others, to be convinced that he was a vain, proud man. He was always a determined enemy of Catholicity, and for his bigoted attacks on Popery he received a just castigation from the witty and eloquent Father O'Leary. He dates the origin of Methodism himself from a meeting held in Fetter-lane, London, on the 1st of May, 1738. "The first rise of Methodism," he says, "was in November, 1729, when four of us met together at Oxford; the second was in Savannah, in April, 1736, when twenty or thirty persons met at my house; the last in London, when forty or fifty of us agreed to meet together every Wednesday evening, in order to free conversation, begun and ended with singing and prayer." Whitfield, a fellow-student of Wesley, began to preach at this time to numerous congregations in the open air. He was a man of fervid eloquence, and the people, deserted, in a great measure, by the parsons of the Anglican Church, flocked in crowds to hear him, and as he could not obtain leave to preach in the churches, he adopted the system of field-preaching. His doctrine was thoroughly Calvinistic, and this was, ultimately, the cause of a separation between him and

Wesley. Indeed, it would appear, Wesley could bear no competitor. He ruled his society most absolutely; appointed preachers, and removed them, according to his own will—changed them from one station to another, or dismissed them altogether, just as he pleased. One of the most extraordinary proceedings of his life, however, was his ordaining a bishop for the States of America. Both he and Whitfield planted Methodism in our Colonies in North America, and the people, always desirous of religion, ardently took up with it, since no better was provided for them. When the revolutionary war commenced, Wesley wrote a bitter tract against "the Rebels," and were it not suppressed in time, his name would be branded with infamy by the patriotic party. The fate of war, however, favoured the "Rebels," and our *consistent* preacher immediately veered round. He was now the apologist of insurrection, and besought them to stand fast by the liberty God gave them. What opinion can we hold of the principles of a man who acts thus? But to return to the ordination. Wesley always professed himself not only a member of the Anglican Church, but a faithful observer of its doctrines, articles, and homilies. His followers in America, however, called loudly for ministers or preachers, and then he became convinced that there was no distinction, in fact, between Presbyters and Bishops, and thus with the 23rd and 36th Articles of his Church staring him in the face, he not only ordained priests, as he called them, but actually consecrated Coke a Bishop for the North American congregations. "God," says Coke, "raised up Wesley as a light and guide in his Church; he appointed to all offices, and consequently, had the right of appointing bishops." We would wish, however, to have some proof of the Divine mission of Wesley, such as the apostles gave, when "they went forth and preached everywhere, the Lord working withal, and confirming the Word with the signs that followed" (Mark, xvi. 20). He travelled through England, Scotland, and Ireland, preaching in towns, hamlets, and villages, and, as usual, giving "Popery" a blow, whenever he had an opportunity. He married, when advanced in years, but soon separated from his wife, by whom he had no children. He appears, on the whole, to be a man of most unamiable character, and though God was constantly on his lips, self was always predominant. He died in London, in 1781, in the eighty-eighth year of his age.

6. It is rather difficult to give a precise account of the doctrines of Methodism. Wesley always professed himself a member of the Church of England, and maintained that his doctrine was that of the Anglican Church, but we see how far he deviated from it in the ordination affair. Whitfield was a Calvinist, and some of the first Methodists were Moravians. Salvation by Faith alone, and sudden justification, appear to be the distinguishing marks of the sect. Their doctrines open a wide door for the most dangerous

enthusiasm; the poor people imagine, from the ardour of their feelings, that they are justified, though every Christian should be aware that he knows not whether he is worthy of love or hatred, and this has been productive of the most serious consequences. If only the thousandth part of all we hear of the scenes which take place at a "Revival" in America be true, it should fill us with compassion to see rational beings committing such extravagances in the holy name of religion. I will not sully the page with a description of the "Penitents' pen," the groanings in spirit, the sighs, contortions, howlings, and faintings which accompany the "new birth" at these re-unions. It has been partially attempted in these countries to get up a similar demonstration, but we hope the sense of propriety and decorum is too strongly fixed in the minds of our people ever to permit themselves to be thus fooled.

7. The curse of all heresies, the want of cohesion, has fallen also on the Methodist society. They are now divided into several branches, Primitive Wesleyans, &c. They are governed by Conferences, and there are districts, and other minor divisions, down to classes. The form of worship consists generally of extemporaneous prayer and preaching. Wesley established *bands*, or little companies for self-examination and confession, and it is rather strange that sectaries who reject sacramental confession, where the penitent pours into the ear of the priest his sins and his sorrows, under the most inviolable secrecy, should encourage promiscuous confession of sins, which can be productive of no good, but must necessarily cause a great deal of harm. Hear Wesley's own words on the subject: "*Bands*," he says, "are instituted in order to confess our faults to one another, and pray for one another; we intend to meet once a week at least; to come punctually at the hour appointed; to begin with singing or prayer; to speak to each of us, in order, freely and plainly, the true state of our soul, with the *faults we have committed in thought, word, or deed*, and the temptations we have felt since our last meeting, and to desire some person among us (thence called a leader) to speak his own state first, and then to ask the rest, in order, as *many* and as *searching questions* as may be, concerning their state, sins, and temptations." Such a shocking practice is only calculated to make men hypocrites and liars, for we know that it is not in human nature to confess *freely* and *plainly* all the turpitude of their hearts, before five or six, or more, fellow-mortals; and did such a thing happen, society would be shaken to its foundations, the peace of families destroyed, and mortal hatred usurp the place of brotherly love. The Methodists have another peculiar custom—of holding a *love feast* every quarter. Cake and water is given to each person, and partaken of by all, and each is at liberty to speak of his *religious experience*. There certainly could not be a better nurse of spiritual pride than

a practice of this sort. Every year they have a *watch-night*, that is, they continue in prayer and psalm-singing, till after midnight, on the last night of the year; the new year is then ushered in with a suitable hymn and appropriate service. It is melancholy to see so many people, of really religious dispositions, most of them irreproachably moral, honest, and honourable, led astray by error, buffeted about by every wind of doctrine. Those who are members of the holy Catholic Church are bound to praise God daily for the inestimable blessing conferred on them; and seeing how little in general they correspond to the extraordinary graces they receive by the sacraments, and the holy sacrifice, should be humbled at their own unworthiness, and unceasingly pray to God, that the strayed sheep may be brought into the fold, under the guidance of the one Shepherd. Had Wesley, their founder, been born and disciplined, from his youth, in the doctrines and practices of the Catholic Faith—his self-love and spiritual pride corrected by the holy practice of the confessional—he might have been one of the lights of his age, and, perhaps, have carried the Gospel with effect to the nations still sitting in darkness. But the judgments of God are inscrutable (4).

8. Johanna Southcott. This extraordinary woman was born in Devonshire, in 1750, and is no less remarkable for the extravagance of her tenets, than as a melancholy example of the credulity of her numerous followers. She was, in the early part of her life, only a domestic servant, and scarcely received any education. She joined a Methodist society, and being of an excitable temperament, persuaded herself at first, it is supposed, that she was endowed with extraordinary gifts. She soon found followers, and then commenced as a prophetess, and proclaimed herself the " woman" spoken of in the Book of Revelations. She resided all this time in Exeter, and it is wonderful to find that an ignorant woman could make so many dupes. She had seals manufactured, and sold them as passes to immortal happiness. It was impossible that any one possessed of one of these talismens could be lost. Exeter soon became too confined a sphere for her operations, and, at the expense of an engraver of the name of Sharp, she came to London, where the number of her disciples was considerably increased, and many persons joined her, whom we would be the last to suspect of fanaticism. She frequently denounced unbelievers, and threatened the unfaithful nations with chastisement. She was now sixty years of age, and put the finishing stroke to her delusions. She proclaimed that she was with-child of the Holy Spirit, and that she was about to bring into the world the Shiloh promised to Jacob. This event was to take place on the 19th of October, 1814. This we would

(4) Wesley's Journal; Centenary Report, and Benson's Apology, &c.

imagine would be enough to shake the whole fabric of imposture she had raised, but, on the contrary, her dupes not only believed it, but actually prepared a gorgeous cradle for the Shiloh, and crowded round her residence at the appointed time, in expectation of the joyful event. Midnight passed, and they were told she fell into a trance. She died on the 27th of the following December, declaring that if she was deceived, it must be by some spirit, good or bad, and was buried in Paddington churchyard. A *post mortem* examination showed that she died of dropsy. Among other reveries, she taught the doctrine of the Millennium. The strangest thing of all is that the delusion did not cease at her death; her followers still exist as a sect, though not numerous. They are distinguished by wearing brown coats and long beards, and by other peculiarities. It is supposed they expect the reappearance of their prophetess.

9. A new sect sprung up in the United States of America only a few years since. They were called Mormons, or Latter-Day Saints. It is very generally believed along the sea-board of the States, that the buccaneers of the seventeenth century, and the loyalists in the late revolution, buried large sums of money, and that all traces of the place of concealment were lost by their death. Several idle persons have taken up the trade of exploring for this concealed treasure, and are known by the name of " Money Diggers," calculating, like the alchymists of old, on the avaricious credulity of their dupes. The prophet and founder of Mormonism, Joe Smith, followed this profession. Not he alone, but his whole family, were remarkable for a total absence of every quality which constitutes honest men. Smith was well aware, from his former profession, of the credulity of many of his countrymen, so he gave out that he had a revelation from above, that he was received up into the midst of a blaze of light, and saw two heavenly personages who told him his sins were forgiven, that the world was all in error in religious matters, and that in due season the truth would be revealed through him. It was next revealed to him that the aborigines, the "red men" of America, were a remnant of the tribes of Israel, whose colour was miraculously changed as a punishment for their sins, and whose prophets deposited a book of Divine records, engraved on plates of gold, and buried in a stone chest in a part of the State of New York. Smith searched for the treasure and found it, but was not allowed to remove it until he had learned the Egyptian language in which it was written. In 1827 he was at last allowed to take possession of it, and published an *English version* in 1830. His father and others were partners in the scheme. The rhapsody made a deep impression on the uncultivated minds of many—especially among the lower orders—in the States, and a congregation was formed, usually called Mormonites, from the Book

of Mormon, as Smith called it, or, according to the name by which they designated themselves, "The Church of Jesus Christ of Latter-Day Saints." The book, such as it is, is supposed to have been written by a person of the name of Spaulding as a sort of novel, and offered to a publisher, who declined having anything to do with it, and it eventually fell into the hands of one Rigdon, a friend of Smith, and as it was written something in the style of the Old Testament, and purported to be an account of the adventures of a portion of the tribe of Joseph, who sailed for America under the guidance of a Prophet called Nephi, and became the fathers of the red Indians, they determined to pass it off as a new Revelation. It is evidently the production of a very ignorant person, whose whole knowledge of antiquity was acquired from the English Bible. The sect became so numerous in a little time, that a settlement was made in the State of Missouri; but the sturdy people of the West rose up against them and banished them. They next settled down in Illinois, and founded a city which they called Nauvoo, near the Mississippi. A temple on a magnificent scale was commenced, and a residence for the Prophet, who took especial care that his revelations should all turn to his own profit. He established two orders of priesthood—the order of Melchizedec, consisting of high priests and elders, and the order of Aaron, containing bishops, priests, and deacons; but "my servant, Joseph Smith," was of course the autocrat of the whole system, and the others were but his tools. Not alone from the States, but even from the manufacturing districts of England, did multitudes flock to the land of promise. Disputes, however, arose. The prophet, Joe Smith, was killed by a mob in 1846, at Carthage, in Illinois, and most of his fanatical followers dispersed. Numbers have emigrated to California, and intend forming establishments in that country, and time alone will tell whether the delusion will have any duration. The temple remains unfinished, like the Tower of Babel, a standing monument of human folly. The scattered followers of Smith some time since settled down near the great Salt Lake, in the western territory of the United States, and founded a settlement called Utah. Here they have hitherto been permitted to carry out, to its fullest extent, the last and most complete development of Protestantism. Their proselytes are chiefly recruited from Wales and the manufacturing towns of England, where the population is distinguished for profligacy. Polygamy and divorce are most revoltingly practised, and Mahometanism is pure, and paganism holy, compared with Mormonism, the last offshoot of the "glorious Reformation." The late governor of Utah had, it is said, nineteen wives at one time, and the elders a proportionate number, and frequent divorces and interchanges, "sealing and unsealing," as they call it, have made the modern Sodom a portent of iniquity. We may hope that in a little time the central authority of the United States will be extended over this land of abomination, and the common law enforced against these enemies of God and society.

Spirit-rapping and table-turning are the most melancholy proofs of what the human intellect may come to, when losing the light of Faith. Thousands in the United States believe, that certain persons, called "Mediums," have the power of conversing with the spirits of the departed, who answer the questions put to them by a certain number of raps on a table, and by causing the table to turn when pressed by the fingers. Numbers have become lunatic by believing and practising this superstition. The Mediums are well trained to cause the noises by muscular contractions, and the table-turning is but a clumsy juggle. It is remarkable, however, how errors repeat themselves century after century. Tertullian, in his "Apologeticus pro Christianis," mocks the table-rappers and turners of his day: "Per quos et capræ et *mensæ divinare* consueverunt." (Apol. c. xxiii.); and Virgil, in the second Æneid, appears to allude to it when he says:

"Troia gaza
Incensis erepta adytis, *mensæque* Deorum."

10. The German Catholic Church. Such was the designation adopted by a party raised up within the last few years in Germany; but the reader will perceive what little right it has to such a title, when, at the last meeting, held at Schneidemuhl, they not only rejected the Dogmas and Sacraments, which peculiarly distinguish the Catholic Church from the various Protestant sects, but openly renounced even the Apostles' Creed, denied the Divinity of Christ and of the Holy Spirit, and, in fact, their whole creed now consists, we may say, of one article—to believe in the existence of God. The origin of this party was thus: In the cathedral of Treves, it is piously believed, the seamless garment worn by our Lord is preserved; it is usually called the Holy Robe of Treves. From time to time this is exhibited to the veneration of the people. The Bishop of Treves, Monsigneur Arnoldi, published to the faithful of Germany and the world, that the robe would be exhibited for a few weeks. Hundreds of thousands responded to the pious invitation. From the snowy summits of the Swiss mountains, to the low lands of Holland, the people came in multitudes, to venerate the sacred relic. Ronge, an unquiet, immoral priest, who had been previously suspended by his bishop, imagined that it would be just the time to imitate Luther in his attack on Indulgences, and, accordingly, wrote a letter to the prelate Arnoldi, which was published, not alone in the German papers, but in several other parts of Europe besides. He then declared that he

renounced the Roman Catholic Church altogether, and established what he called the German Catholic Church. He was soon joined by another priest of the same stamp, Czerski; and numbers of the Rationalists of Germany, having no fixed religious principles of any sort, ranked themselves under the banners of the new apostles, not through any love for the new form of faith, but hoping to destroy Catholicity. We have seen, however, at their last Conference, that they have abolished Christianity itself, and the sect, as it is, is already nearly extinct.

END OF THE HISTORY.

REFUTATION OF HERESIES.

REFUTATION I.

THE HERESY OF SABELLIUS, WHO DENIED THE DISTINCTION OF PERSONS IN THE TRINITY.

THE Catholic Church teaches that there are in God one Nature and three distinct Persons. Arius, of whose heresy we shall have to speak in the next chapter, admits the distinction of Persons in the Trinity, but said that the three Persons had three different natures among themselves, or, as the latter Arians said, that the three Persons were of three distinct natures. Sabellius, on the other hand, confessed, that in God there was but one nature; but he denied the distinction of Persons, for God, he said, was distinguished with the name of the Father, or the Son, or the Holy Ghost, by denomination alone, to signify the different effects of the Divinity, but that in himself, as there is but one nature, so there is but one Person. The Sabellian heresy was first taught by Praxeas, who was refuted by Tertullian in a special work. In the year 257, the same heresy was taken up by Sabellius (1), who gave it great extension, especially in Lybia, and he was followed by Paul of Samosata. These denied the distinction of the Persons, and, consequently, the Divinity of Jesus Christ, and, therefore, the Sabellians were called Patro-passionists, as St. Augustin (2) tells us, for as they admitted in God only the Person of the Father alone, they should, consequently, admit that it was the Father who became incarnate, and suffered for the redemption of mankind. The Sabellian heresy, after being a long time defunct, was resuscitated by Socinus, whose arguments we shall also enumerate in this dissertation.

SEC. I.—THE REAL DISTINCTION OF THE THREE DIVINE PERSONS IS PROVED.

2. IN the first place, the plurality and the real distinction of the three Persons in the Divine nature is proved from the words of Genesis: "Let us make man to our own image and likeness" (Gen. i. 26); and in chap. iii., v. 22, it is said: " Behold, Adam is

---

(1) Euseb. His. Eccles. (2) St. Augus. *trac.* 26, in Jo.

become one of us;" and again, in chap. xi., ver. 7: "Come ye, therefore, let us go down, and there confound their tongues." Now these words, "let us do," "let us go down," "let us confound," show the plurality of Persons, and can in no wise be understood of the plurality of natures, for the Scripture itself declares that there is but one God, and if there were several Divine natures, there would be several Gods; the words quoted, therefore, must mean the plurality of Persons. Theodoret (1), with Tertullian, makes a reflection on this, that God spoke in the plural number, " let us make," to denote the plurality of Persons, and then uses the singular, " to our image," not images, to signify the unity of the Divine nature.

3. To this the Socinians object:—First.—That God spoke in the plural number, for the honour of his Person, as kings say "We" when they give any order. But we answer, by saying, that sovereigns speak thus, " *we* ordain," " *we* command," in their ordinances, for then they represent the whole republic, but never when they speak of their private and personal acts; they never say, for example, "*we* are going to sleep," or "*we* are going to walk," nor did God speak in the way of commanding, when he said, " Behold Adam is become as one of us." Secondly.—They object, that God did not thus speak with the other Divine Persons, but with the Angels; but Tertullian, St. Basil, Theodoret, and St. Irenæus, laugh at this foolish objection (2), for the very words, " to our image and likeness," dispose of it, for man is not created to the image of the angels, but of God himself. Thirdly.—They object, that God spoke with himself then, as if exciting himself to create man, as a sculptor might say, " Come, let us make a statue." St. Basil (3), opposing the Jews, disposes of this argument. " Do we ever see a smith," he says, " when sitting down among his tools, say to himself—Come, let us make a sword?" The saint intends by this to prove, that, when God said, " let us make," he could not speak so to himself alone, but to the other Persons: for no one, speaking to himself, says, " let us make." It is clear, therefore, that he spoke with the other Divine Persons.

4. It is proved, also, from the Psalms (ii. 7): "The Lord hath said to me, thou art my Son; this day have I begotten thee." Here mention is made of the Father begetting the Son, and of the Son begotten; and in the same Psalm the promise is made: "I will give thee the Gentiles for thy inheritance, and the utmost parts of the earth for thy possession." Here a clear distinction is drawn between the Person of the Son and the Person of the Father, for we cannot say it is the same Person who begets and is begotten.

---

(1) Theod. *qu.* 19, in Gen.   (2) Tertull. 1. contra Prax. *c.* 12 ; St. Basil, *t.* 1; Hom. 9 in Hexamer.; Theod. *qu.* 19, in Gen.; St. Iræn. *l.* 4, *n.* 37.   (3) St. Basil, loc. cit. *p.* 87.

And St. Paul declares that these words refer to Christ the Son of God: "So Christ also did not glorify himself, that he might be made a high priest, but he that said unto him: *Thou art my son; this day have I begotten thee*" (Heb. v. 5.)

5. It is also proved by the 109th Psalm: "The Lord said to my Lord, sit thou at my right hand;" and it was this very passage that our Saviour made use of to convince the Jews, and make them believe that he was the Son of God. "What think you of Christ, said he? Whose Son is he? They say to him: David's. He saith to them: How, then, doth David in spirit call him Lord, saying, &c. If David then call him Lord, how is he his Son?" (Mat. xxii. 42-45). Christ wished by this to prove that, although the Son of David, he was still his Lord, and God, likewise, as his Eternal Father was Lord.

6. The distinction of the Divine Persons was not expressed more clearly in the Old Law, lest the Jews, like the Egyptians, who adored a plurality of Gods, might imagine that in the three Divine Persons there were three Essential Gods. In the New Testament, however, through which the Gentiles were called to the Faith, the distinction of the three Persons in the Divine Essence is clearly laid down, as is proved, first from St. John, i. 1: "In the beginning was the Word and the Word was with God, and the Word was God." Now, by the expression, "the Word was with God," it is proved that the Word was distinct from the Father, for we cannot say of the same thing, that it is with itself and nigh itself at the same time. Neither can we say that the Word was distinct by Nature, for the text says, "the Word was God;" therefore, the distinction of Persons is clearly proved, as St. Athanasius and Tertullian agree (4). In the same chapter these words occur: "We saw his glory, the glory as it were of the only-begotten of the Father." Here no one can say, that the Son is begotten from himself; the Son, therefore, is really distinct from the Father.

7. It is proved, also, from the command given to the Apostles: "Go, therefore, teach all nations, baptizing them in the name of the Father, and of the Son, and of the Holy Ghost" (Mat. xxviii. 19). Hence the words, *in the name*, denote the unity of Nature, and signify that Baptism is one sole operation of all the three named Persons; and the distinct appellation afterwards given to each Person, clearly proves that they are distinct. And, again, if these three Persons were not God, but only creatures, it would be absurd to imagine that Christ, under the same name, would liken creatures to God.

8. It is proved, also, by that text of St. John: "Philip, he that seeth me seeth the Father also.........I will ask the Father, and he shall give you another Paraclete" (John, xiv. 9, 16). By the

---

(4) Tert. adv. Prax. c. 26; St. Ath. Orat. contr Sab Gregal.

words, " he that seeth me seeth the Father," he proves the unity of the Divine Nature; and by the other expression, " I will ask," &c., the distinction of the Persons, for the same Person cannot be at once the Father, the Son, and the Holy Ghost. This is even more fully explained by the words of St. John, xv. 26: " But the Paraclete, the Holy Ghost, whom the Father shall send in my name."

9. It is also proved by that text of St. John: " There are three who give testimony in heaven—the Father, the Word, and the Holy Ghost, and these three are one" (1 John, v. 7.) Nor is the assertion of the adversaries of the Faith, that the Father, the Word, and the Holy Ghost, are merely different in name, but not in reality, of any avail, for then it would not be three testimonies that are given, but only one alone, which is repugnant to the text. The Socinians labour hard to oppose this text especially, which so clearly expresses the distinction of the three Divine Persons, and they object that this verse is wanting altogether in many manuscripts, or, at all events, is found only in part; but Estius, in his commentaries on this text of St. John, says, that Robert Stephens, in his elegant edition of the New Testament, remarks that, having consulted sixteen ancient copies collected in France, Spain, and Italy, he found that, in seven of them, the words "in heaven" alone were omitted, but that the remainder of the text existed in full. The Doctors of Louvain collected a great number of manuscripts for the edition of the Vulgate brought out in 1580, and they attest that it was in five alone that the whole text was not found (5). It is easy to explain how a copyist might make a mistake in writing this verse, for the seventh and eight verses are so much alike, that a careless copyist might easily mix up one with the other. It is most certain that in many ancient Greek copies, and in all the Latin ones, the seventh verse is either put down entire, or, at least, noted in the margin; and, besides, we find it cited by many of the Fathers, as St. Cyprian, St. Athanasius, St. Epiphanius, St. Fulgentius, Tertullian, St. Jerome, and Victor Vitensis (6). The Council of Trent, above all, in its Decree of the Canonical Scriptures, Sess. IV., obliges us to receive every book of the Vulgate edition, with all its parts, as usually read in the Church: " If any one should not receive as holy and canonical the entire books, with all their parts, as they are accustomed to be read in the Catholic Church, and contained in the old Vulgate edition ..... let him be anathema." The seventh verse quoted is frequently read in the Church, and especially on Low Sunday.

10. The Socinians, however, say that it cannot be proved from

(5) Tournel. Theol. Comp. *t.* 2, *qu.* 3, *p.* 41; Juenin. Theol. *t.* 3, *c.* 2. (6) St. Cypr. *l.* 1, de Unit. Eccl.; St. Ath. *l.* 1. ad Theoph.; St. Epiph. Hær.; St. Fulg. 1. contra Arian.; Tertull. 1. adv. Prax. 25; St. Hier. (aut Auctor) Prol. ad Ep. Canon. Vitens. *l.* 3, de Pers. Afr.

that text of St. John, that there are in God three distinct Persons, and one sole essence, because, say they, the words " these three are one" signify no other union but the union of testimony, as the words of the eighth verse signify, " There are three that give testimony on earth, the spirit, and the water, and the blood, and these three are one." These words prove, according to us, that Christ is truly the Son of God, which is what St. John is speaking about; and this, he says, is testified by the water of Baptism, by the blood shed by Jesus Christ, and by the Holy Spirit, who teaches it by his illuminations, and in this sense St. Augustin, St. Ambrose, and Liranus explain it, and especially Tirinus, who rejects the explanation of an anonymous author, who interprets the water as that which flowed from our Lord's side; the blood, that which flowed from his heart when it was pierced with a spear; and the spirit, the soul of Jesus Christ. To return to the point, however; I cannot conceive any objection more futile than this. So from the words of St. John, " the Father, the Son, and the Holy Ghost," the distinction of the Divine Persons cannot be proved, because these Persons " are one," that is, make one testimony alone, and denote by that, that they are but one essence. But we answer, that we are not here labouring to prove that God is one, that is, one essence, and not three essences; for our adversaries themselves do not call this in doubt, and, besides, it is proved from a thousand other texts of Scripture adduced by themselves, as we shall soon see; so that, granting even that the words " are one" denote nothing else but the unity of testimony, what do they gain by that? The point is this—not whether the unity of the Divine Essence is proved by the text of St. John, but whether the real distinction of the Divine Persons is proved by it, and no one, I think, can deny that it is, when St. John says, "There are three who give testimony in heaven, the Father, the Word, and the Holy Ghost." If three give testimony, it is not one Person, but three distinct Persons, who do so, and that is what we mean to prove. I have found several other answers to this objection in various authors, but this, I think, is the clearest and the most convincing against the Socinians.

11. The real distinction of the Divine Persons is also proved from the traditions of the Fathers, and from their unanimous consent in teaching this truth. To avoid doubtful meanings, however, it is right to premise that in the fourth century, about the year 380, there were great contests in the Church, even among the Holy Fathers themselves, regarding the word *Hypostasis*, and they were split into two parties. Those who adhered to Miletius taught that there are in God three *Hypostases;* and those who followed Paulinus, that there was only one, and so the followers of Miletius called the followers of Paulinus Sabellians, and these retorted by calling the others Arians. The whole dispute, however, arose from the doubtful meaning of the word

Hypostasis, as some of the Fathers, the Paulinians, understood by it the Essence or the Divine Nature, and the others, the Miletians, the Person; and the word *Ousia* was also of doubtful meaning, being taken for Essence or for Person. When the words were, therefore, explained in the Synod of Alexandria, both parties came to an agreement, and from that to this, by the word *Ousia* we understand the Essence, and by the word *Hypostasis*, the Person. The doctrine, therefore, of one Essence and three Persons, really distinct in God, is not taught alone by St. Cyprian, St. Athanasius, St. Epiphanius, St. Basil, St. Jerome, and St. Fulgentius, already cited (*n.* 9), but also by St. Hilary, St. Gregory Nazianzan, St. Gregory of Nyssa, St. Chrysostom, St. Ambrose, St. Augustin, St. John of Damascus, &c. (10). Among the Fathers of the first three centuries we have St. Clement, St. Polycarp, Athenagoras, St. Justin, Tertullian, St. Irenæus, St. Dionisius Alexandrinus, and St. Gregory Thaumaturgus (11). Many General Councils declare and confirm the same truth. It is taught by the Nicene (*in Symb. Fidei*); by the first of Constantinople (*in Symb.*); by that of Ephesus (*act* 6), which confirms the Nicene Symbol; of Chalcedon (*in Symb.*); of the second of Constantinople (*act* 6); third of Constantinople (*act* 17); fourth of Constantinople (*act* 10); fourth of Lateran (*cap.* 1); second of Lyons (*can.* 1); of Florence, in the Decree of Union; and finally, by the Council of Trent, which approved the first of Constantinople, with the addition of the word *Filioque*. It was so well known that the Christians believed this dogma, that the very Gentiles charged them with believing in three Gods, as is proved from the writings of Origen against Celsus, and from the Apology of St. Justin. If the Christians did not firmly believe in the Divinity of the three Divine Persons, they would have answered the Pagans, by saying that they only considered the Father as God, and not the other two Persons; but they, on the contrary, always confessed, without fearing that by doing so they would admit a plurality of Gods, that the Son and the Holy Ghost were God equally with the Father; for although with the Father they were three distinct Persons, they had but one Essence and Nature. This proves clearly that this was the faith of the first ages.

SEC. II.—OBJECTIONS ANSWERED.

12. THE Sabellians bring forward several texts of Scripture, to prove that God is one alone, as "I am the Lord that make all things, that alone stretch out the heavens, that establish the

---

(10) St. Hilar. in 12 lib.; St. Greg. Nazian. in plur. Orat. Nyss. Orat. contra Ennom.; St. Chrys. in 5 Hom.; St. Amb. lib. de Spir. S. St. Augus. *l.* 15; Jo. Dam. *l.* 1, de Fide. (11) St. Clem. Epis. ad Corint.; St. Polycar. Orat. in suo marg. apud Euseb. *l.* 4; His. c. 14; Athenagor. Leg. pro Chris.; St. Iren. in ejus oper.; Tertullian. contra Prax. Diony. Alex. Ep. ad Paul. Samosat.; St. Gregor. Thaum. in Expos. Fid.

earth, and there is none with me" (Isaias, xliv. 24); but to this we answer, that the words "I am the Lord" refer not alone to the Father, but to all the three Persons, who are but one God and one Lord. Again, "I am God, and there is no other" (Isaias, xlv. 22. Hence, we assert that the word *I* does not denote the person of the Father alone, but also the Persons of the Son and of the Holy Ghost, because they are all but one God; and the words "there is no other" signify the exclusion of all other Persons who are not God. But, say they, here is one text, in which it is clearly laid down that the Father alone is God, "yet to us there is but one God the Father, of whom are all things, and we unto him, and one Lord Jesus Christ, by whom are all things, and we by him" (1 Cor. viii. 6). To this we answer, that here the Apostle teaches the faithful to believe one God in three Persons, in opposition to the Gentiles, who, in many Persons, adored many Gods. For as we believe that Christ, called by St. Paul "one Lord," is not Lord alone, to the exclusion of the Father, so, when the Father is called "one Lord," we are not to believe that he is God alone, to the exclusion of Christ and of the Holy Ghost; and when the Apostle speaks of "one God the Father," we are to understand that he speaks of the unity of Nature, and not of Person.

13. Again, they object that our natural reason alone is sufficient to prove to us, that as among men three persons constitute three individual humanities, so in God the three Persons, if they were really distinct, would constitute three distinct Deities. To this we reply, that Divine mysteries are not to be judged according to our stunted human reason; they are infinitely beyond the reach of our intellect. "If," says St. Cyril of Alexandria, "there was no difference between us and God, we might measure Divine things by our own standard; but if there be an incomprehensible distance between us, why should the deficiency of our nature mark out a rule for God?" (12) If, therefore, we cannot arrive at the comprehension of Divine mysteries, we should adore and believe them; and it is enough to know that what we are obliged to believe is not evidently opposed to reason. We cannot comprehend the greatness of God, and so we cannot comprehend the mode of his existence. But, say they, how can we believe that three Persons really distinct are only one God, and not three Gods? The reason assigned by the Holy Fathers is this—because the principle of the Divinity is one, that is, the Father, who proceeds from nothing, while the two other Persons proceed from him, but in such a manner that they cease not to exist in him, as Jesus Christ says: "The Father is in me, and I in the Father" (John, x. 38). And this is the difference between the Divine Persons and human

---

(12) St. Cyril, Alex. *l.* 11, in Jo. *p* 99.

persons—with us three persons constitute three distinct substances, because, though they are of the same species, they are still three individual substances, and they are also three distinct natures, for each person has his own particular nature. In God, however, the Nature or the substance, is not divisible, but is in fact one—one Divinity alone, and, therefore, the Persons, although really distinct, still having the same Nature and the same Divine substance, constitute one Divinity alone, only one God.

14. They next object that rule received by all philosophers: "Things equal to a third are equal to each other." Therefore, say they, if the Divine Persons are the same thing as the Divine Nature, they are also the same among themselves, and cannot be really distinct. We might answer this by saying, as before, that a philosophical axiom like this applies very well to created, but not to Divine things. But we can even give a more distinct answer to it. This axiom answers very well in regard to things which correspond to a third, and correspond also among themselves. But although the Divine Persons correspond in everything to the Divine Essence, and are, therefore, the same among themselves as to the substance, still, because in the personality they do not correspond, on account of their relative opposition, for the Father communicates his Essence to the two other Persons, and they receive it from the Father, therefore, the Person of the Father is really distinct from that of the Son, and of the Holy Ghost who proceeds from the Father and the Son.

15. They object, Fourthly—that as the Divine Presence is infinite, therefore it must be but one, for what is infinite in all perfections, cannot have a second like itself, and that is the great proof of the Unity of God; for if there were many Gods, one could not possess the perfections of the other, and would not, therefore, be infinite, nor be God. To this we answer, that although on account of the infinity of God, there can be no more Gods than one, still from the infinity of the Divine Persons in God, it does not follow that there can be only one Divine Person; for although in God there are three distinct Persons, still each, through the unity of essence, contains all the perfections of the other two. But, say they, the Son has not the perfection of the Father to generate, and the Holy Ghost has not the perfection of the Father and the Son to *spirate*, therefore the Son is not infinite as is the Father, nor has the Holy Ghost the perfections of the Father and the Son. We reply, that the perfection of anything is that which properly belongs to its nature, and hence it is that the perfection of the Father is to generate,—of the Son, to be generated,—and of the Holy Ghost to be spirated. Now, as these perfections are relative, they cannot be the same in each Person, for otherwise, the distinction of Persons would exist no longer, neither would the perfection of the Divine Nature exist any longer,

for that requires that the Persons should be really distinct among themselves, and that the Divine Essence should be common to each. But then, say they, those four expressions, the Essence, the Father, the Son, and the Holy Ghost, are not synonymous; they, therefore, mean four distinct things, and that would prove not alone a Trinity, but a Quaternity in God. The answer to this frivolous objection is very simple. We freely admit that these four words are not synonymous, but for all that, the Essence is not distinct from the Persons; the Divine Essence is an absolute thing, but common to all the three Persons, but the three Persons, though distinct among themselves, are not distinct from the Essence, for that is in each of the three Persons, as the Fourth Council of Lateran (*can.* 2) declares: " In Deo Trinitas est non quaternitas quia qualibet trium personarum, est illa res videlicet essentia, sive natura Divina quæ sola est universorum principium præter quod aliud inveniri non potest."

16. The Socinians object—Fifthly.—The Father generated the Son, either existing or not existing; if he generated him already existing, he cannot be said to be generated at all, and if the Son was not existing, then there was a time when the Son was not, therefore they conclude that there are not in God Three Persons of the same essence. To this we reply, that the Father has always generated the Son, and that the Son is always existing, for he was generated from all eternity, and will be generated for ever, and therefore we read in the Psalms: "To-day I have begotten thee" (Psalms, ii. 7), because in eternity there is no succession of time, and all is equally present to God. Neither is there any use in saying that the Father has generated the Son in vain, as the Son already existed always, for the Divine generation is eternal, and as the Father generating is eternal, so the Son is eternally generated; both are eternal, but the Father has been always the *principium* in the Divine nature.

17. Finally, they object that the primitive Christians did not believe the mystery of the Trinity, for if they did, the Gentiles would have attacked them on the great difficulties with which this mystery, humanly speaking, was encompassed; at all events, they would have tried to prove from that that they believed in a plurality of Gods, but we find no such charge made against the Christians by the Gentiles, nor do we find a word about it in the Apologies written by the early Fathers in defence of the Faith. To this we answer: First.—That even in these early days the pastors of the Church taught the Catechumens the Apostles' Creed, which contains the mystery of the Trinity, but they did not speak openly of it to the Gentiles, who, when their understanding could not comprehend Divine things, only mocked them. Secondly.—Many of the writings of the Gentiles have been lost in the lapse of centuries, and through the prohibitory decrees of the Christian Emperors, and many of the Apologies were lost in like manner. Praxeas, how-

ever, who denied the Trinity, uses this very argument against the Catholics: "If you admit three Persons in God," says he, "you admit a plurality of Gods like the Gentiles." Besides, in the first Apology of St. Justin, we read that the idolaters objected to the Christians, that they adored Christ as the Son of God. The pagan Celsus, as we find in Origen (13), argued that the Christians, by their belief in the Trinity, should admit a plurality of Gods, but Origen answers him that the Trinity does not constitute three Gods, but only one, for the Father, the Son, and the Holy Ghost, though three Persons, are still only one and the same essence. The acts of the martyrs prove in a thousand places that the Christians believed that Jesus Christ was the true Son of God, and they could not believe this unless they believed at the same time that there were three Persons in God.

REFUTATION II.

THE HERESY OF ARIUS, WHO DENIED THE DIVINITY OF THE WORD.

SEC. I.—THE DIVINITY OF THE WORD PROVED FROM THE SCRIPTURES.

1. THE Dogma of the Catholic Church is, that the Divine Word, that is, the Person of the Son of God, is, by his nature, God, as the Father is God, and in all things is equal to the Father, is perfect and eternal, like the Father, and is consubstantial with the Father. Arius, on the contrary, blasphemously asserted that the Word was neither God, nor eternal, nor consubstantial, nor like unto the Father; but a mere creature, created in time, but of higher excellence than all other creatures; so that even by him, as by an instrument, God created all other things. Several of the followers of Arius softened down his doctrine; some said that the Word was like the Father, others, that he was created from eternity, but none of them would ever admit that he was consubstantial with the Father. When we prove the Catholic doctrine, however, expressed in the proposition at the beginning of this chapter, we shall have refuted, not alone the Arians, Anomeans, Eunomians, and Aerians, who followed in everything the doctrine of Arius, but also the Basilians, who were Semi-Arians. Those in the Council of Antioch, in 341, and in the Council of Ancyra, in 358, admitted that the Word was *Omoiousion Patri*, that is, like unto the Father, in substance, but would not agree to the term, *Omousion*, or of the same substance as the Father. The Acacians, who held a middle place between the Arians and Semi-Arians, and admitted that the Son was *Omoion Patri*, like to the Father, but not of the same substance, will all be refuted. All these will be proved to be in error,

(13) Origen, lib. Con. Celsum.

when we show that the Word in all things, not only like unto the Father, but consubstantial to the Father, that is of the very same substance as the Father, as likewise the Simonians, Corinthians, Ebionites, Paulinists, and Photinians, who laid the foundations of this heresy, by teaching that Christ was only a mere man, born like all others, from Joseph and Mary, and having no existence before his birth. By proving the Catholic truth, that the Word is true God, like the Father, all these heretics will be put down, for as the Word in Christ assumed human nature in one person, as St. John says: "The Word was made flesh;" if we prove that the Word is true God, it is manifest that Christ is not a mere man, but man and God.

2. There are many texts of Scripture to prove this, which may be divided into three classes. In the first class are included all those texts in which the Word is called God, not by grace or predestination, as the Socinians say, but true God in nature and substance. In the Gospel of St. John we read: "In the beginning was the Word, and the Word was with God, and the Word was God. The same was in the beginning with God. All things were made by him, and without him was made nothing that was made" (John, i.) St. Hilary looked on this passage as proving so clearly the Divinity of the Word, that he says (1), " When I hear *the Word was God*, I hear it not only said but proved that the Word is God. Here the thing signified is a substance where it is said *was God*. For to be, to exist, is not accidental, but substantial." The holy doctor had previously met the objection of those who said that even Moses was called God by Pharoe (Exod. viii.) and that judges were called Gods in the 81st Psalm, by saying: It is one thing to be, as it were, appointed a God, another to be God himself; in Pharoe's case a God was appointed as it were (that is Moses), but neither in name or nature was he a God, as the just are also called God: "I said—you are Gods." Now the expression " I said," refers more to the person speaking than to the name of the thing itself; it is, then, the person who speaks who imposes the name, but it is not *naturally* the name of the thing itself. But here he says the Word is God, the thing itself exists, in the Word, the substance of the Word is announced in the very name: " Verbi enim appellatio in Dei Filio de Sacramento nativitatis est." Thus, says the Saint, the name of God given to Pharoe and the Judges mentioned by David in the 81st Psalm was only given them by the Lord as a mark of their authority, but was not their proper name; but when St. John speaks of the Word, he does not say that he was *called* God, but that he was in reality God: " The Word was God."

3. The Socinians next object that the text of St. John should

---

(1) Hilar. *l*. 7, de Trinit.

not be read with the same punctuation as we read it, but thus: "In the beginning was the Word, and the Word was with God, and the Word was. God the same was in the beginning," &c., but this travestie of the text is totally opposed to all the copies of the Scriptures we know, to the sense of all the Councils, and to all antiquity. We never find the text cut up in this way; it always was written "The Word was God." Besides, if we allowed this Socinian reading of the text, the whole sense would be lost, it would be, in fact, ridiculous, as if St. John wanted to assert that God existed, after saying already that the Word was with God. There are, however, many other texts in which the Word is called God, and the learned Socinians themselves are so convinced of the weakness of this argument, as calculated only to make their cause ridiculous, that they tried other means of invalidating it, but, as we shall presently see, without succeeding.

4. It is astonishing to see how numerous are the cavils of the Arians. The Word, they say, is called God, not the God the fountain of all nature, whose name is always written in Greek with the article (o Theos), such, however, is not the case in the text; but we may remark that in this very chapter, St. John, speaking of the supreme God, "there was a man sent from God, whose name was John," does not use the article, neither is it used in the 12th, 13th, or 18th verses. In many other parts of the Scriptures, where the name of God is mentioned, the article is omitted, as in St. Matthew, xiv. 33, and xxvii. 43; in St. Paul's 1st Epistle to the Corinthians, viii. 4, 6; to the Romans, i. 7; to the Ephesians, iv. 6; and on the other hand we see that in the Acts of the Apostles, vii. 43; in the 2nd Epistle to the Corinthians, iv. 4, and in that to the Galatians, iv. 8, they speak of an idol as God, and use the article, and it is most certain that neither St. Luke nor St. Paul ever intended to speak of an idol as the supreme God. Besides, as St. John Chrysostom teaches (2), from whom this whole answer, we may say, is taken, the Word is called God, sometimes even with the addition of that article, on whose omission in St. John they lay such stress, as is the case in the original of that text of St. Paul, Romans, ix. 5: "Christ, according to the flesh, who is over all things, God blessed for ever." St. Thomas remarks, that in the first cited passage the article is omitted in the name of God, as the name there stands in the position not of a *subject*, but a *predicate:* "Ratio autem quare Evangelista non apposuit articulum hinc nomini Deus.......... est quod Deus ponitur hic in *prædicato* et tenetur formaliter, consuetum erat autem quod nominibus in prædicato positis non ponitur articulus cum discretionem importet" (3).

5. They object, fourthly, that in the text of St. John the Word is called God, not because he is so by nature and substance, but

(2) St. Jo. Chry. in Jo.   (3) St. Thom. in cap. 1, Joan. lec. 2.

only by dignity and authority, just as they say the name of God is given in the Scriptures to the angels and to judges. We have already answered this objection by St. Hilary (*N.* 2), that it is one thing to give to an object the name of God, another to say that he is God. But there is, besides, another answer. It is not true that the name of God is an appellative name, so that it can be positively and absolutely applied to one who is not God by nature; for although some creatures are called Gods, it never happened that any one of them was called " God," absolutely, or was called true God, or the highest God, or singularly God, as Jesus Christ is called by St. John: " And we know that the Son of God is come, and he hath given us understanding, that we may know the *true God*, and may be in his true Son" (1 John, v. 20). And St. Paul says, " Looking for the blessed hope and the coming of the glory of the *great God*, and our Saviour, Jesus Christ" (Epis. to Titus, ii. 13), and to the Romans, ix. 5: " Of whom is Christ, according to the flesh, who is *over all things God*, blessed for ever." We likewise read in St. Luke, that Zachary, prophesying regarding his Son, says, " And thou, child, shalt be called the prophet of the *Highest*, for thou shalt go before the face of the Lord to prepare his ways" (Luke, i. 76); and again, ver. 78: " Through the bowels of the mercy of *our God*, in which the Orient from on high has visited us."

6. Another most convincing proof of the Divinity of the Word is deduced from the 1st chapter of St. John, already quoted. In it these words occur: " All things were made by him, and without him was made nothing that was made." Now any one denying the Divinity of the Word must admit from these words that either the Word was eternal, or that the Word was made by himself. It is evidently repugnant to reason to say the Word made himself, *nemo dat quod non habet*. Therefore, we must admit that the Word was not made, otherwise St. John would be stating a falsehood when he says, " Without him was made nothing that was made." This is the argument of St. Augustin (4), and from these words he clearly proves that the Word is of the same substance as the Father: " Neque enim dicit omnia, nisi quæ facta sunt, idest omnem creaturam; unde liquido apparet, si facta substantia est, ipsum factum non esse, per quem facta sunt omnia. Et si factum non est, creatura non est; si autem creatura non est, ejusdem cum Patre substantiæ cujus Pater, ergo facta substantia, quæ Deus non est, creatura est; et quæ creatura non est, Deus est. Et si non est Filius ejusdem substantiæ cujus Pater, ergo facta substantia est: non omnia per ipsum facta sunt; et omnia per ipsum facta sunt. Ut unius igitur ejusdemque cum Patre substantiæ est, et ideo non tantum Deus, sed et verus Deus." Such are the words of the Holy Father; the passage is rather long, but most convincing.

(4) St. Aug. *l. n.* de Trinit. cap. 6.

7. We shall now investigate the passages of the second class, in which the Divine Nature and the very substance of the Father is attributed to the Word. First, the Incarnate Word, himself, says: " I and the Father are one" (John, x. 30). The Arians say that Christ here does not speak of the unity of nature but of will, and Calvin, though he professes not to be an Arian, explains it in the same manner. " The ancients," he says, " abused this passage, in order to prove that Christ is *omousion*, consubstantial with the Father, for here Christ does not dispute of the unity of substance, but of the consent he had with the Father." The Holy Fathers, however. more deserving of credit than Calvin and the Arians, always understood it of the unity of substance. Here are the words of St. Athanasius (5): " If the two are one they must be so according to the Divinity, inasmuch as the Son is consubstantial to the Father....they are, therefore, two, as Father and Son, but only one as God is one." Hear, also, St. Cyprian (6): " The Lord says, I and the Father are one, and again it is written of the Father, and the Son, and the Holy Ghost, and these three are one." St. Ambrose takes it in the same sense as do St. Augustine and St. John Chrysostom, as we shall see presently; why the very Jews took it in this sense, for they took up stones to stone him, as St. John relates (x. 32): "Many good works I have shown you from my Father; for which of those works do you stone me? The Jews answered him: For a good work we stone thee not, but for blasphemy, and because thou, being a man, makest thyself God." "See," says St. Augustine (7), " how the Jews understood what the Arians will not understand, for they are vexed to find that these words—*I and the Father are one*, cannot be understood, unless the equality of the Son with the Father be admitted." St. John Chrysostom here remarks, that if the Jews erred in believing that our Saviour wished to announce himself as equal in power to the Father, he could immediately have explained the mistake, but he did not do so (8), but, quite the contrary, he confirms what he before said the more he is pressed; he does not excuse himself, but reprehends them; he again says he is equal to the Father: " If I do not the works of my Father," he says, " believe me not; but if I do, though you will not believe me, believe the works, that you may know and believe that the Father is in me, and I in the Father" (John, x. 37, 38). We have seen that Christ expressly declared in the Council of Caiphas, that he was the true Son of God: " Again the High Priest asked him and said to him: Art thou the Christ, the Son of the Blessed God? and Jesus said to him, I am" (Mark, xiv. 61, 62). Who shall then dare to say that Jesus Christ is not the Son of God, when he himself has said so?

(5) St. Athan. Orat. con. Arian. *n.* 9.   (6) St. Cyprian, de Unit. Eccles.   (7) St. Aug. Tract. 48 in Joan.   (8) St. Joan. Chrysos. Hom. 6 in Jo.

8. Again, say the Arians, when our Saviour prayed to his Father for all his disciples, he said: And the glory thou hast given me I have given to them, that they may be one, as we also are one" (John, xvii. 22). Now in this passage, say they, Christ certainly speaks of the unity of will, and not of the unity of substance. But we reply: It is one thing to say that " I and the Father are one," quite another thing " that they may be one, as we are also one;" just as it is one thing to say, " your heavenly Father is perfect," and another to say, " Be ye, therefore, perfect, as your heavenly Father is perfect" (Matthew, v. 48). For the particle *as* (sicut) denotes, as St. Athanasius (9) says, likeness or imitation, but not equality of conjunction. So, as our Lord here exhorts us to imitate the Divine perfection as far as we can, he prays that his disciples may be united with God as far as they can, which surely cannot be understood except as a union of the will. When he says, however: " I and the Father are one," there is no allusion to imitation; he there speaks of a union of substance; he there positively and absolutely asserts that he is one and the same with the Father: " We are one."

9. There are, besides, many other texts which most clearly corroborate this. Our Lord says in St. John, xvi. 15, and xvii. 10: " All things whatsoever the Father hath are mine." " And all my things are thine, and thine are mine." Now, as these expressions are used by him without any limitation, they evidently prove his consubstantiality with the Father, for when he asserts that he has everything the Father has, who will dare to say that the Father has something more than the Son? And if we denied to the Son the same substance as the Father, we would deny him everything, for then he would be infinitely less than the Father; but Jesus says that he has all the Father has, without exception, consequently he is in everything equal to the Father: " He has nothing less than the Father," says St. Augustin, " when he says that, *All things whatsoever the Father hath are mine*, he is, therefore his equal" (10).

10. St. Paul proves the same when he says, " Who, being in the form of God, thought it not robbery to be equal with God, but emptied himself, taking the form of a servant" (Phil. ii. 6). Now, here the Apostle says Christ humbled himself—" emptied himself, taking the form of a servant," and that can only be understood of the two Natures, in which Christ was, for he humbled himself to take the nature of a servant, being already in the Divine Nature, as is proved from the antecedent expressions, " who, being in the form of God, thought it not robbery to be equal to God." If Christ usurped nothing by declaring himself equal to God, it cannot be denied that he is of the same substance with God, for otherwise it would be a " robbery" to say that he was equal to God.

(9) St. Athan. Orat. 4 ad Arian.   (10) St. August. lib. 1, con. Maxim. cap. 24.

St. Augustin, also, explaining that passage of St. John, xiv. 28, "The Father is greater than I," says, that he is less than the Father, according to the form of a servant, which he took by becoming man, but that, according to the form of God, which he had by Nature, and which he did not lose by becoming man, he was not less than the Father, but his co-equal. "To be equal to God in the form of God," says the Saint, "was not a robbery, but Nature. He, therefore," says the Father, "is greater, because he humbled himself, taking the form of a servant, but not losing the form of God" (11).

11. Another proof is what our Saviour himself says: "For what things soever he (the Father) doth, these the Son also doth in like manner" (John, v. 19). Hence, St. Hilary concludes that the Son of God is true God, like the Father—"Filius est, quia abs se nihil potest; Deus est, quia quæcunque Pater facit, et ipse eadem facit; unum sunt, quia eadem facit, non alia" (12). He could not have the same individual operation with the Father, unless he was consubstantial with the Father, for in God there is no distinction between operation and substance.

12. The third class of texts are those in which attributes are attributed to the Word, which cannot apply unless to God by Nature, of the same substance as the Father. First.—The Word is eternal according to the 1st verse of the Gospel of St. John: "In the beginning was the Word." The verb *was* denotes that the Word has always been, and even, as St. Ambrose remarks (13), the Evangelist mentions the word "was" four times—"Ecce quater erat ubi impius invenit quod non erat." Besides the word "was," the other words, "in the beginning," confirm the truth of the eternity of the Word: "In the beginning was the Word," that is to say, the Word existed before all other things. It is on this very text that the First Council of Nice founded the condemnation of that proposition of the Arians, "There was a time once when the Word had no existence."

13. The Arians, however, say that St. Augustin (14) interpreted the expression "in the beginning," by saying it meant the Father himself, and according to this interpretation, they say, that the Word might exist in God previous to all created things, but not be eternal at the same time. To this we reply that though we might admit this interpretation, and that "in the beginning" meant in the Father; still if we admit that the Word was before all created things, it follows that the Word was eternal, and never made, because as "by him all things were made," if the Word was not eternal, but created, he should have created himself, an impossibility, based on the general maxim admitted by all, and quoted

(11) St. August. Ep. 66. *l.* 1, de Fide ad Gratian, *c.* 5.   (12) St. Hilar. *l.* 7, de Trin. *n.* 21.   (13) St. Amb.
(14) St. Aug. *l.* 6, de Trinit. *c.* 5.

before: "Nemo dat quod non habet"—No one can give what he has not.

14. They assert, secondly, that the words "in the beginning" must be understood in the same way as in the passage in the 1st chapter of Genesis; "In the beginning, God created the heavens and the earth;" and as these were created in the beginning, so also the Word was created. The answer to this is, that Moses says: "In the beginning God *created;*" but St. John does not say in the beginning the Word was created, but the Word *was*, and that by him all things were made.

15. They object, in the third place, that by the expression, "the Word," is not understood a person distinct from the Father, but the internal wisdom of the Father distinct from him, and by which all things were made. This explanation, however, cannot stand, for St. John, speaking of the Word, says: "By him all things were made," and towards the end of the chapter: "The Word was made flesh and dwelt amongst us;" now we cannot understand these expressions as referring to the internal wisdom of the Father, but indubitably to the Word, by whom all things were made, and who, being the Son of God, became flesh, as is declared in the same place: "And we saw his glory, the glory as it were of the only-begotten of the Father." This is confirmed by the Apostle, when he says, that by the Son (called by St. John the Word) the world was created. "In these days hath spoken to us by his Son, whom he hath appointed heir of all things, by whom also he made the world" (Heb. i. 2). Besides, the eternity of the Word is proved by the text of the Apocalypse (i. 8): "I am Alpha and Omega, the beginning and the end, who is, and who was, and who is to come;" and by the Epistle to the Hebrews (xiii. 8), "Jesus Christ, yesterday, and to-day, and the same for ever."

16. Arius always denied that the Word was eternal, but some of his latter followers, convinced by the Scriptures, admitted that he was eternal, but an eternal creature, and not a Divine Person. The answer given by many theologians to this newly invented error is, that the very existence of an eternal creature is an impossibility. That a creature, they say, should be said to be created, it is necessary that it should be produced out of nothing, so that from a state of non-existence, it passes to a state of existence, so that we must suppose a time in which this creature did not exist. But this reply is not sufficient to prove the fallacy of the argument, for St. Thomas (15) teaches, and the doctrine is most probable, that in order to assert that a thing is created, it is not necessary to suppose a time in which it was not, so that its non-existence preceded its existence; but it is quite enough to suppose a creature, as nothing

---

(15) St. Thomas, *quæs.* Disp. de Potentia, *art.* 14, ad 7.

by its own nature, or by itself, but as having its existence altogether from God. "It is enough," says the Saint, "to say that a thing has come from nothing, that its non-existence should precede its existence, not in duration, but nature, inasmuch, as, if left to itself, it never would have been anything, and it altogether derives its existence from another." Supposing then that it is unnecessary to look for a time in which the thing did not exist, to call it a creature, God, who is eternal, might give to a creature existence from all eternity, which by its own nature it never could have had. It appears to me, then, that the fit and proper reply to this argument is, that the Word being (as has been already proved) eternal, never could be called a creature, for it is an article of Faith, as all the Holy Fathers teach (16), that there never existed, in fact, an eternal creature, since all creatures were created in time, in the beginning, when, as Moses says, God created the world: "In the beginning, God created the heavens and the earth." The creation of heaven and earth, according to the doctrine of all Fathers and theologians, comprises the creation of all beings, both material and spiritual. The Word, on the contrary, had existence before there was any creature, as we see in the book of Proverbs, where Wisdom, that is the Word, thus speaks: "The Lord possessed me in the beginning of his ways, before he made anything from the beginning" (Prov. viii. 22). The Word, therefore, is not a created being, since he existed before God had made anything.

17. The materialists of modern times, however, cannot infer from this that matter is eternal of itself, for although we admit that matter might exist from eternity, inasmuch as God could, from all eternity, give to it existence which it had not of itself (though he did not do so in fact); still, as we have proved in our book on the "Truth of the Faith," it could not exist from itself, it should have existence from God, for, according to the axiom so frequently repeated, *Nemo dat quod non habet*, it could not give to itself that (existence) which it had not to give. From St. John's expression regarding the Word, "by him all things were made," not alone his eternity is proved, but the power of creating likewise, which can belong to none but God; for, in order to create, an infinite power is necessary, which, as all theologians say, God could not communicate to a creature. Returning, however, to the subject of the eternity of the Word, we say, that if the Father should, by the necessity of the Divine nature (*necessitate naturæ*), generate the Son, the Father being eternal, the Son should also be eternal, keeping always in mind the Father the generator, the Son as the generated. Thus the error of the modern materialists, the basis of whose system is, that matter is eternal, falls to the ground.

(16) St. Thomas, 1. *part. quæs.* 46, *art.* 2, 3.

18. Now, it being admitted that by the Word all things were made, it is a necessary consequence that the Word was not made by himself, for otherwise there would exist a being made, but not made by the Word, and this is opposed to the text of St. John, who says that " by him all things were made." This is the great argument of St. Augustin against the Arians, when they assert that the Word was made: " How," says the Saint (17), " can it be possible that the Word is made, when God by the Word made all things? If the Word of God himself was made, by what other Word was he made? If you say it was by the Word of the Word, that, I say, is the only Son of God; but, if you say it is not by the Word of the Word, then you must admit that that Word, by whom all things were made, was not made himself, for he could not, who made all things, be made by himself.

19. The Arians, too much pressed by this argument to answer it, endeavour to do so by a quibble—St. John, say they, does not tell us that all things were made by *Him* (ab ipso), but rather *through Him* (per ipsum), and hence they infer that the Word was not the principal cause of the creation of the world, but only an instrument the Father made use of in creating it, and therefore they agree that the Word is not God. But we answer, that the creation of the world, as described by David and St. Paul, is attributed to the Son of God. " In the beginning, O Lord," says David, " thou foundedst the earth, and the heavens are the works of thy hands" (Psalm ci. 26); and St. Paul, writing to the Hebrews, dictates almost a whole chapter to prove the same thing; see these passages: " But to the Son, thy throne, O God, is for ever and ever" (i. 8); and again, verse 13, " But to which of his angels said he at any time, sit on my right hand till I make thy enemies thy footstool." Here St. Paul declares that that Son of God called by St. John " the Word" has created the heavens and the earth, and is really God, and as God, was not a simple instrument, but the Creator-in-Chief of the world. Neither will the quibble of the Arians on the words *per ipsum* and *ab ipso* avail, for in many places of the Scriptures we find the word *per* conjoined with the principal cause: *Possedi hominem per Deum* (Gen. iv.); *Per me Reges regnant* (Prov. viii.); *Paulus vocatus Apostolus Jesu Christi per voluntatem Dei* (1 Cor. i.)

20. There is another proof of the Divinity of the Word in the 5th chapter of St John, where the Father wills that all honour should be given to the Son the same as to himself: " But he hath given all judgment to the Son, that all may honour the Son as they honour the Father" (John, v. 22, 23). The Divinity of the Word and of the Holy Ghost is also proved by the precept given to the Apostles: " Go ye, therefore, teach all nations, baptizing them in

---

(17) St. Augus. Trac. in Joan.

the name of the Father, and of the Son, and of the Holy Ghost" (Matt. xxviii. 19). The Holy Fathers, St. Athanasius, St. Hilary, St. Fulgentius, and several others, made use of this text to convince the Arians, for baptism being ordained in the name of the three Divine Persons, it is clear that they have equal power and authority, and are God; for if the Son and the Holy Ghost were creatures we would be baptized in the name of the Father, who is God, and of two creatures; but St. Paul, writing to the Corinthians, states that this is opposed to our Faith, " Lest any should say that you are baptized in my name" (1 Cor. i. 15).

21. Finally, there are two powerful arguments, to prove the Divinity of the Word. The first is taken from the power manifested by the Word in the fact related in the fifth chapter of St. Luke, where Christ, in healing the man sick of the palsy, pardoned him his sins, saying: " Man, thy sins are forgiven thee" (Luke, v. 20). Now, God alone has the power of forgiving sins, and the very Pharisees knew this, for they said: " Who is this who speaketh blasphemies ? who can forgive sins but God alone?" (Luke, v. 21).

22. The second proof is taken from the very words of Christ himself, in which he declares himself to be the Son of God. He several times spoke in this manner, but most especially when he asked his disciples what they thought of him: " Jesus saith to them, Whom do you think I am? Simon Peter answered and said: Thou art the Christ, the Son of the living God. And Jesus answering, said to him: Blessed art thou, Simon Barjona, because flesh and blood hath not revealed it to thee, but my Father who is in heaven" (Matt. xvi. 15, 17). He also declared it as we have seen above, when Caiphas asked him, " Art thou Christ, the Son of the Blessed God? And Jesus said to him, I am" (Mark, xiv. 61). See now the argument. The Arians say that Christ is not the true Son of God, but they never said he was a liar; on the contrary, they praise him, as the most excellent of all men and enriched, above all others, with virtues and divine gifts. Now, if this man (according to them) called himself the Son of God, when he was but a mere creature, or if he even permitted that others should consider him the Son of God, and that so many should be scandalized in hearing him called the Son of God, when he was not so in reality, he ought at least declare the truth, otherwise he was the most impious of men. But no; he never said a word, though the Jews were under the impression that he was guilty of blasphemy, and allowed himself to be condemned and crucified on that charge, for this was the great crime he was accused of before Pilate, " according to the Law he ought to die, because he made himself the Son of God" (John, xix. 7). In fine, we reply to all opponents, after Jesus Christ expressly declared himself the Son of God, as we remarked in St. Mark's Gospel, chap. xiv. 62, " I am," though this

declaration was what cost him his life, who will dare to deny, after it, that Jesus Christ is the Son of God?

SEC. II.—THE DIVINITY OF THE WORD PROVED BY THE AUTHORITY OF HOLY FATHERS AND COUNCILS.

23. THE unceasing opposition of the Arians to the Council of Nice was on account of the *consubstantiality* attributed to the Word. This term, *consubstantiality*, was never used, they said, by the ancient Fathers of the Church; but St. Athanasius, St. Gregory of Nyssa, St. Hilary, and St. Augustin, attest that the Nicene Fathers took this word from the constant tradition of the first Doctors of the Church. Besides, the learned remark, that many works of the Fathers, cited by Saint Athanasius, St. Basil, and even by Eusebius, were lost, through the lapse of ages. We should also remember that the ancient Fathers who wrote previous to the existence of heresy, did not always write with the same caution as the Fathers who succeeded them, when the truths of the Faith were confirmed by the decrees of Councils. The doubts stirred up by our enemies, says St. Augustin, have caused us to investigate more closely, and to establish the dogmas which we are bound to believe. "Ab adversario mota quæstio discendi existit occasio"(1). The Socinians do not deny that all the Fathers posterior to the Council of Nice held the sentence of that Council, in admitting the consubstantiality of the Son with the Father, but they say that those who wrote previous to the Council held quite another opinion. In order, therefore, to prove that the Socinians in this are totally astray, we will confine our quotations to the works of the Fathers who preceded the Council, who, if they have not made use of the very word *consubstantial*, or of the same *substance* as the Father, have still clearly expressed the same thing in equivalent terms.

24. The Martyr St. Ignatius, the successor of St. Peter in the See of Antioch, who died in the year 108, attests, in several places, the Divinity of Christ. In his Epistle ad Trallianos, he writes: "Who was truly born of God and the Virgin, but not in the same manner;" and afterwards; "The true God, the Word born of the Virgin, he who in himself contains all mankind, was truly begotten in the womb." Again, in his Epistle to the Ephesians: "There is one carnal and spiritual physician, made and not made, God in man, true life in death, and both from Mary and from God;" and again, in his Epistle to the Magnesians: "Jesus Christ, who was with the Father before all ages, at length appeared," and immediately after, he says: "There is but one God, who made himself manifest by Jesus Christ, his Son, who is his eternal Word."

25. St. Polycarp was a disciple of St. John, and Bishop of Smyrna; he lived in the year 167. Eusebius (2) quotes a celebrated

---

(1) St. Aug. *l.* 16, de Civ. *c.* 2. (2) Euseb. His. *l.* 4, *c.* 13.

Epistle written by the Church of Smyrna to that of Pontus, giving an account of his martyrdom, and in it we read, that just before his death he thus expressed himself; " Wherefore in all things I praise Thee, I bless Thee, I glorify Thee, by the eternal Pontiff, Jesus Christ, thy beloved Son, through whom, to Thee, with him, in the Holy Ghost, be glory, now and for evermore. Amen." First, therefore, St. Polycarp calls Christ the eternal Pontiff, but nothing but God alone is eternal. Second.—He glorifies the Son, together with the Father, giving him equal glory, which he would not have done unless he believed that the Son was God equal to the Father. In his letter to the Philippians he ascribes equally to the Son and to the Father the power of giving grace and salvation. "May God the Father," he says...." and Jesus Christ, sanctify you in faith and truth.... and give you lot and part among his Saints."

26. St. Justin, the philosopher and martyr, who died about the year 161, clearly speaks of the Divinity of Christ. He says in his first Apology: " Christ, the Son of God the Father, who alone is properly called his Son and his Word, because with Him before all creatures he existed and is begotten." Mark how the Saint calls Christ properly the Son and the Word, existing with the Father before all creatures, and generated by him; the Word, therefore, is the proper Son of God, existing with the Father before all creatures, and is not, therefore, a creature himself. In his second Apology he says: " When the Word is the first-born of God, he is also God." In his Dialogue with Triphon, he proves that Christ in the Old Testament was called the Lord of Hosts, the God of Israel, and he then concludes by addressing the Jews: " If," says he, " you understood the prophets, you would not deny that he is God, the Son of the only and self-existing God." I omit many other passages of the same tenor, and I pass on to answer the objections of the Socinians. St. Justin, they say, in his Dialogue with Triphon, and in his Apology, asserts that the Father is the cause of the Word, and existed before the Word. To this we answer: the Father is called the cause of the Son, not as creator, but as generator, and the Father is said to be before the Son, not in time, but in origin, and, therefore, some Fathers have called the Father the cause of the Son, as being the principle of the Son. They also object that St. Justin calls the Son the Minister of God—" Administrum esse Deo." We reply he is God's Minister as man, that is, according to human nature. They make many other captious objections of this sort, which are refuted in Juenin's Theology (3), but the few words of the Saint already quoted: " Cum Verbum Deus etiam est"—When the Word is also God, are quite enough to answer them all.

27. St. Iræneus, a disciple of St. Polycarp, and Bishop of Lyons, who died in the beginning of the second century, says (4) that the

(3) Juenin. Theol. t. 3, c. 1, s. 1.   (4) St. Iræn. ad Hær. l. 3, c. 6.

Son is true God, like the Father. "Neither," he says, "the Lord (the Father) nor the Holy Ghost would have absolutely called him God, if he was not true God." And again (5), he says, "the Father is the measure, and he is infinite, and the Son containing him must be infinite likewise." They object that St. Iræneus has said that the day of judgment is known to the Father alone, and that the Father is greater than the Son; but this has been already answered (vide *n.* 10); and again, in another place, where the Saint says, "Christ, with the Father, is the God of the living" (6).

28. Athenagoras, a Christian philosopher of Athens, in his Apology for the Christians, writes to the Emperors Antoninus and Commodus, that the reason why we say that all things were made by the Son is this: "Whereas," he says, "the Father and the Son are one and the same, and the Son is in the Father, and the Father in the Son, by the unity and power of the Spirit, the Mind and Word is the Son of God." In these words: "Whereas the Father and the Son are one," he explains the unity of nature of the Son with the Father; and in the other, "the Son is in the Father, and the Father in the Son," that peculiarity of the Trinity called by theologians *Circuminsession*, by which one Person is in the others. He immediately adds: "We assert that the Son the Word is God, as is also the Holy Ghost united in power."

29. Theophilus, Bishop of Antioch, under the Emperor Marcus Aurelius, says (7): "We ought to know that our Lord Christ is true God and true man—God from God the Father—man from Mary, his human Mother." Clement of Alexandria (8) writes: "Now the Word himself has appeared to man, who alone is both at the same time God and man." And again he says (9): "God hates nothing, nor neither does the Word, for both are one, to wit, God, for he has said, *In the beginning was the Word, and the Word was with God, and the Word was God.*" Origen (10) wrote against Celsus, who objected to the Christians, that they adored Jesus Christ as God, though he was dead, and he thus expresses himself: "Be it known to our accusers that we believe this Jesus to be God and the Son of God." And again he says (11), that although Christ suffered as man, the Word who was God did not suffer. "We distinguish," he says, "between the nature of the Divine Word, which is God, and the soul of Jesus." I do not quote the passage which follows, as it is on that theologians found their doubts of the faith of Origen, as the reader may see by consulting Nat. Alexander (12), but there can be no doubt, from the passage already quoted, that Origen confessed that Jesus was God and the Son of God.

(5) St. Iræn. ad Hær. *l.* 4, c. 8. (6) Idem, *l.* 3, c. 11. (7) Theoph. *l.* 5; Allegor. in Evang. (8) Clem. Alex. in Admon. ad Græcos. (9) Idem, *l.* 1; Pædagog. c. 8. (10) Origen, *l.* 3, cont. Celsum. (11) Idem, *l.* 4, cont. Celsum. (12) Nat. Alex. *sec.* 3, *Diss.* 16, *art.* 2.

30. Dionysius Alexandrinus, towards the end of the third century, was accused (13) of denying the consubstantiality of the Word with the Father, but he says: "I have shown that they falsely charge me with saying that Christ is not consubstantial with God." St. Gregory Thaumaturgus, one of Origen's scholars, Bishop of Pontus, and one of the accusers of Paul of Samosata in the Synod of Antioch, says, in his Confession of Faith (14): "There is one God, the Father of the living Word, the perfect Father of the perfect, the Father of the only-begotten Son (solus ex solo), God of God. And there is one Holy Ghost from God having existence." St. Methodius, as St. Jerome informs us (15), Bishop of Tyre, who suffered martyrdom under Diocletian, thus speaks of the Word in his book entitled *De Martyribus*, quoted by Theodoret (16): "The Lord and the Son of God, who thought it no robbery to be equal to God."

31. We now come to the Latin Fathers of the Western Church. St. Cyprian, Bishop of Carthage (17), proves the Divinity of the Word with the very texts we have already quoted. "The Lord says: I and the Father are one." And again, it is written of the Father, and the Son, and the Holy Ghost, "and these three are one." In another place he says (18), "God is mingled with man; this is our God—this is Christ." I omit the authority of St. Dionisius Romanus, of St. Athanasius, of Arnobius, of Lactantius, of Minutius Felix, of Zeno, and of other eminent writers, who forcibly defend the Divinity of the Word. I will merely here quote a few passages from Tertullian, whose authority the Socinians abuse. In one part he says, speaking of the Word (19), "Him have we learned as produced from God (prolatum), and so generated, and therefore he is said to be God, and the Son of God, from the unity of substance.... He is, therefore, Spirit from Spirit, God from God, and light from light." Again he says (20): "I and the Father are one, in the unity of substance, and not in the singularity of number." From these passages it clearly appears that Tertullian held that the Word was God, like the Father, and consubstantial with the Father. Our adversaries adduce some obscure passages from the most obscure part of his works, which they imagine favour their opinion; but our authors have demolished all their quibbles, and can consult them (21).

32. It is, however, certain, on the authority of the Fathers of the first three centuries, that the Faith of the Church in the Divinity and consubstantiality of the Word with the Father has been un-

---

(13) Dionys. Alex. apud St. Athan. *t.* 1, *p.* 561.   (14) St. Greg. Thaum. *p.* 1, Oper. apud Greg. Nyssen. in Vita Greg. Thaum.   (15) St. Hier. de Scrip. Eccles. *c.* 34. (16) Theodoret, Dial. 1, *p.* 37.   (17) St. Cyprian, de lib. Unit. Eccles.   (18) Idem, *l.* de Idol. vanit.   (19) Tertull. Apol. *c.* 21.   (20) Idem, lib. con. Praxeam, *c.* 25. (21) Vide Juvenin. *t.* 3, *q.* 2, *c.* 1, *a* 1, *sec.* 2; Tournelly, *t.* 2, *q.* 4, *art.* 3, *sec.* 2; Antoin. Theol. Trac. de Trin. *c.* 1, *art.* 3.

changeable, and even Socinus himself is obliged to confess this (22). Guided by this tradition, the three hundred and eighteen Fathers of the General Council of Nice, held in the year 325, thus defined the Faith: " We believe in one Lord Jesus Christ, the Son of God, the only-begotten Son from the Father, that is, from the substance of the Father; God of God, light of lights, true God of true God, consubstantial to the Father, by whom all things were made." This self-same profession of Faith has been from that always preserved in the subsequent General Councils, and in the whole Church.

SEC. III.—OBJECTIONS ANSWERED.

33. Before commencing, it would be well to remember, as St. Ambrose (1) remarks, that the texts of Scripture adduced by our adversaries are not always to be taken in the same sense, as some of them refer to Christ as God, and more as man; but the heretics confuse one with the other, applying those which refer to him as man, as if they referred to him as God. " The pious mind," the Saint says, " will distinguish between those which apply to him, according to the flesh, and according to the Divinity; but the sacrilegious mind will confound them, and distort, as injurious to the Divinity, whatever is written according to the humility of the flesh." Now, this is exactly how the Arians proceed, in impugning the Divinity of the Word; they always fasten on those texts, in which Christ is said to be less than the Father. To upset most of their arguments, therefore, it will always be sufficient to explain, that Jesus, as man, is less than the Father, but as God, by the Word, to which his humanity is united, he is equal to the Father. When we speak, therefore, of Jesus Christ, as man, we can lawfully say that he is created, that he was made, that he obeys the Father, is subject to the Father, and soforth.

34. We shall now review the captious objections of our opponents: First.—They object to us that text of St. John (iv. 28): " The Father is greater than I am." But, before quoting this passage, they ought to reflect that Christ, before speaking thus, said: " If you loved me, you would, indeed, be glad, because I go to the Father, for the Father is greater than I." Here, then, Jesus calls the Father greater than himself, inasmuch as he, as man, was going to the Father in heaven; but mark how, afterwards, speaking of himself, according to the Divine nature, he says, " The Father and I are one;" and all the other texts already quoted (*Sec.* I), are of the same tenor, and clearly prove the Divinity of the Word, and of Christ. Second.—They object that Christ says: " I came

---

(22) Socinus, Epist. ad Radoc. in *t.* 1, suor. Oper. *c.* 8, *n.* 115. (1) St. Ambrose, *l.* 5, de Fide,

down from heaven, not to do my own will, but the will of him that sent me" (John, vi. 38); and also that passage of St. Paul: " And when all things shall be subdued unto him, then the Son also himself shall be subject unto him, that put all things under him" (1 Corinth. xv. 28). The Son, therefore, obeys, and is subject to the Father, and, therefore, is not God. In regard to the first text, we answer that Jesus Christ then explained the two wills, according to the two natures he had—to wit, the human will, by which he was to obey the Father, and the Divine will, which was common both to him and the Father. As far as the second text goes, St. Paul only says, that the Son, as man, will be always subject to the Father; and that we do not deny. How, then, can it interfere with our belief in his Divinity? Third.—They object that passage of the Acts of the Apostles (iii. 13): " The God of Abraham, and the God of Isaac, and the God of Jacob, the God of our fathers, hath glorified his Son Jesus, whom you, indeed, delivered up," &c. See here, they say, how a distinction is made between the Son and between the Father, who is called God. We answer, that this refers to Christ as man, and not as God; for the words, " he glorified his Son," are to be understood, as referring to Christ in his human nature. St. Ambrose, besides, gives another answer, when he says, " that if the Father is understood by the name of God alone, it is because from him is all authority."

35. The following objections are just of the same character as the preceding. They object, fourthly, that text of the Proverbs: " The Lord possessed me in the beginning of his ways, before he made anything from the beginning" (Prov. viii. 22). This is the text, according to the Vulgate, and the Hebrew original is just the same; but in the Greek Septuagint it is thus read: " The Lord created me in the beginning of his ways." Therefore, the Arians say, the Divine Wisdom which is here spoken of was created, and they strengthen their argument, by quoting from Ecclesiasticus (xxiv. 14): " From the beginning, and before all ages, I was created." We answer, first of all, the true reading is that of the Vulgate, and that alone, according to the Decree of the Council of Trent, we are bound to obey; but though we even take the Greek, it is of no consequence, as the word *created* (here used in the text of Proverbs and Ecclesiasticus), as St. Jerome and St. Augustin (2) teach us, does not exactly mean *creation*, for the Greeks promiscuously used the words *created* and *begotten*, to signify sometimes creation, sometimes generation, as appears from Deuteronomy (xxxii. 16): " Thou hast forsaken the God that *begot* thee, and hast forgotten the Lord that *created* thee." Hence generation is taken for creation. There is a passage also in the Book of Proverbs, which, if we consider the text, can only be understood of the

---

(2) St. Hieron. in Cap. 4 ; Ep. ad Eph. St. August. lib. de Fi l. & Simb.

generation of the Divine Wisdom: " I was set up from eternity, and of old, before the earth was made....... Before the hills I was brought forth" (Proverbs, viii. 23). We should remark here the expression, "*I was set up from eternity.*" That shows how we ought to understand the word *created* is to be understood in the former quotation. We might also answer, with St. Hilary, that the word *created* refers to the human nature the Word assumed, and the words, *brought forth*, to the eternal generation of the Word (3). Wisdom here is spoken of as created, and, immediately after, as begotten; but creation is to be referred, not to the immutable nature of God, but to the human generation. "Sapientia itaque quæ se dixit creatam, eadem in consequenti se dixit genitam: creationem referens ad Parentis inde mutabilem naturam, quæ extra humani partus speciem, et consuetudinem, sine imminutione aliqua, ac diminutione sui creavit ex seipsa quod genuit." In the text of Ecclesiasticus, cited immediately after, it is clear that the Incarnate Wisdom is spoken of: " He that made me rested in my tabernacle ;" for this by the Incarnation was verified. God, who "*created*" Jesus Christ according to his humanity, "*rested in his tabernacle*"—that is, reposed in that created humanity. The following passage is even, if possible, clearer: " Let thy dwelling be in Jacob, and thy inheritance in Israel, and take root in my elect." All this surely refers to the Incarnate Wisdom, who came from the stock of Israel and Jacob, and was then the root of all the elect. Read on this subject St. Augustin, St. Fulgentius, and, above all, St. Athanasius (4).

36. They object, fifthly, that St. Paul says of Christ, in his Epistle to the Colossians (i. 15): " Who is the image of the invisible God, the first-born of every creature." Hence, they infer that Christ is the most excellent of creatures, but still only a creature. We may here reply, that the Apostle speaks of Christ in this text, according to his human nature, as St. Cyril explains it (5). But it is generally interpreted of the Divine Nature, and he is called the first-born of all creatures, because by him all creatures were made, as St. Basil explains it (6): " Since in him were made all things in heaven and on earth." In the same manner, he is called, in the Apocalypse, " the first-born of the dead " (Apoc. i. 5); because, as St. Basil again explains it, he was the cause of the resurrection of the dead. Or he may be called the first-born, because he was generated before all things, as Tertullian (7) explains it: " The first-born, because he was born before all things; the only-begotten, as the only begotten of God." St. Ambrose (8) says the same thing. We read the first-born—we read the only-begotten ; the

---

(3) St. Hilar. lib. de Synod. *c.* 5. (4) St. Aug. *l.* 5, de Trin. *c.* 12; St. Fulgent. lib. contra serm. fastid. Arian. St. Athanas. Orat. contra Arian. (5) St. Cyril, *l.* 25; Thesaur. (6) St. Basil, *l.* 4, con. Eunom. (7) Tertul. con. Prax. *c.* 7. (8) St. Ambrose, *l.* 1, de Fide.

first-born, because there was none before him—the only-begotten, because there was none after him.

37. They object, sixthly, that expression of St. John the Baptist (John, i. 15) : " He that shall come after me is preferred before me" (ante me factus est); therefore, say they, the Word was created. St. Ambrose (9) answers, that all that St. John meant by the expression, "was made before me" (ante me factus est), was, that he was preferred or placed before him, for he immediately assigns the reason: " Because he was before me," that is, because he preceded him for all eternity, and he was, therefore, not even worthy to " unloose the latchet of his shoe." The same answer meets the passage of St. Paul : "Being made so much better than the angels" (Heb. i. 4), that is, he was honoured so much more than the angels.

38. They object, seventhly, that text of St. John (xvii. 3) : " Now this is eternal life, that they may know thee the only true God, and Jesus Christ, whom thou hast sent." Hence it is declared, say they, that the Father *only* is true God; but we answer, that the word " *only* " does not exclude from the Divinity, unless creatures alone, as St. Matthew says: " No one knoweth the Son but the Father, nor the Father but the Son" (Matt. xi. 27). Now, it would be a false conclusion to deduce from this that the Father does not know himself ; and, therefore, the word " *only*," in the former text, is to be taken, as in the twelfth verse of the thirty-second chapter of Deuteronomy: " The Lord alone was his leader, and there was no strange God with him." Another proof is that text of St. John (xvi. 32): " And shall leave me alone." Here the word *alone* (solum) does not mean that he is excluded from the Father, for he immediately adds: " And yet I am not alone, for the Father is with me." And thus, likewise, must we understand that text of St. Paul: " We know that an idol is nothing in the world, and that there is no God but one; for although there be that are called gods, either in heaven or on earth, yet to us there is but one God, the Father, of whom are all things, and we unto him, and one Lord Jesus Christ, by whom are all things, and we by him " (1 Cor. viii. 5, 6). Here the expression, " One God, the Father," is meant to exclude the false gods, but not the Divinity of Jesus Christ, no more than saying " Our Lord Jesus Christ," excludes the Father from being still our Lord.

39. They also adduce the sixth verse of the fifth chapter of the Epistle to the Ephesians: " One God, and Father of all, who is above all, and through all, and in us all." We answer that the words: " One God, and Father of all," do not exclude the Divinity of the other two Persons; for the word, Father, is not here taken in its strict sense, as denoting the Person of the Father alone, but in that essential sense by which the word, Father, is applied to the

(9) St. Ambrose, *l.* 3, de Fide.

whole Trinity, which we invoke when we say: "Our Father, who art in heaven." We thus, also, answer the other text adduced from St. Paul to Timothy: "For there is one God and one Mediator of God and man, the man, Christ Jesus (1 Tim. ii. 5). The expression, "one God," does not exclude the Divinity of Jesus Christ; but, as St. Augustin remarks, the words which immediately follow, "one Mediator of God and man," prove that Jesus Christ is both God and man. "God alone," the Saint says, "could not feel death, nor man alone could not subdue it."

40. They object, eighthly, the text: "But of that day or time, no man knoweth, neither the angels in heaven, nor the Son, but the Father" (Mark, xiii. 32). So, say they, the Son is not omniscient. Some have answered this, by saying, that the Son did not know the day of judgment as man, but only as God; but this does not meet the objection, since we know from the Scriptures, that to Christ, even as man, the fulness of knowledge was given: "And we saw the glory, the glory as it were of the only-begotten of the Father, full of grace and truth" (John, i. 14); and again: "In whom are hid all the treasures of wisdom and knowledge" (Colos. ii. 3). And St. Ambrose (10), treating of this point, says: "How could he be ignorant of the day of judgment, who told the hour, and the place, and the signs, and the causes of judgment." The African Church, therefore, obliged Leporius to retract, when he said, that Christ, as man, did not know the day of judgment, and he at once obeyed. We, therefore, answer, that it is said the Son did not know the day of judgment, as it would be of no use, nor fit that men should know it. This is the way in which St. Augustin explains it. We are, therefore, to conclude that the Father did not wish that the Son should make known the day, and the Son, as his Father's Legate, said in his name, he did not know it, not having received a commission from his Father to make it known.

41. They object, ninthly, that the Father alone is called good, to the exclusion of the Son: "And Jesus said to him: Why callest thou me good? None is good but one, that is God" (Mark, x. 18). Christ, therefore, they say, confesses that he is not God. St. Ambrose (11) answers this. Christ, he says, wished to reprove the young man, who called him good, and still would not believe he was God, whereas, God alone is essentially good; it is, says the Saint, as if our Lord should say: "Either do not call me good, or believe me to be God."

42. They object, tenthly, that Christ has not full power over all creatures, since he said to the mother of St. James and St. John: "To sit on my right or left hand, is not mine to give you" (Matt. xx. 23). We answer, it cannot be denied, according to the Scriptures, that Christ received all power from his Father: "Knowing

---

(10) St. Ambrose, *l.* 5, de Fide, *c.* 16, *n.* 204.   (11) St Ambrose, *l.* 2, de Fide, *c.* 1.

that the Father had given him all things into his hands" (John, xiii. 3); " All things are delivered to me by my Father" (Matt. xi. 27); " All power is given to me in heaven, and on earth" (Matt. xxviii. 18). How, then, are we to understand his inability to give places to the sons of Zebedee? We have the answer from our Lord himself: " It is not mine," he says, " to give to you, but to them for whom it is prepared by my Father." See, then, the answer: " It is not mine to give you;" not because he had not the power of giving it, but I cannot give it *to you*, who think you have a right to heaven, because you are related to me; for heaven is the portion of those only for whom it has been prepared by my Father; to them, Christ, as being equal to the Father, can give it. "As all things," says St. Augustin (12), " which the Father has, are mine, this is also mine, and I have prepared it with the Father."

43. They object, eleventhly, that text: " The Son cannot do anything from himself, but what he sees the Father doing" (John, v. 19). St. Thomas (13) answers this. " When it said that the Son cannot do anything for himself, no power is taken from the Son, which the Father has, for it is immediately added: " For what things soever he doth, these the Son also doth, in like manner;" but it is there that the Son has the power, from his Father, from whom he also has his Nature." Hence, Hilary (14) says: " This is the Unity of the Divine Nature; *ut ita per se agat Filius quod non agat a se*." The same reply will meet all the other texts they adduce, as: " My doctrine is not mine" (John, vii. 16); " The Father loves the Son, and shows him all things" (John, v. 20); " All things are delivered to me by my Father" (Matt. xi. 27). All these texts, prove, they say, that the Son cannot be God by Nature and Substance. But we answer, that the Son, being generated by the Father, receives everything from him by communication, and the Father, generating, communicates to him all he has, except the Paternity; and this is the distinction between him and the Son, for the power, the wisdom, and the will, are all the same in the Father, the Son, and the Holy Ghost. The Arians adduce several other texts, but the reader will find no especial difficulty in answering them, by merely referring to what he has already read.

REFUTATION III.

OF THE HERESY OF MACEDONIUS WHO DENIED THE DIVINITY OF THE HOLY GHOST.

1. Though Arius did not deny the Divinity of the Holy Ghost, still it was a necessary consequence of his principles, for, denying

(12) St. Augus. *l.* 1, de Trin. *c.* 12.   (13) St. Thomas, 1, *p.* 9, 42, *a.* 6, ad 1.
(14) Hilar. de Trin. *l.* 9.

the Son to be God, the Holy Ghost, who proceeds from the Father and the Son, could not be God. However, Aezius, Eunomius, Eudoxius, and all those followers of his, who blasphemously taught that the Son was not like unto the Father, attacked also the Divinity of the Holy Ghost, and the chief defender and propagator of this heresy was Macedonius. In the refutation of the heresy of Sabellius, we will prove, in opposition to the Socinians, that the Holy Ghost is the Third Person of the Trinity, subsisting and really distinct from the Father and the Son; here we will prove that the Holy Ghost is true God, equal and consubstantial to the Father and the Son.

SECT. I.—THE DIVINITY OF THE HOLY GHOST PROVED FROM SCRIPTURES, FROM THE TRADITIONS OF THE FATHERS, AND FROM GENERAL COUNCILS.

2. WE begin with the Scriptures. To prove that this is an article of Faith, I do not myself think any more is necessary than to quote the text of St. Matthew, in which is related the commission given by Christ to his Apostles: " Go, ye, therefore, teach all nations, baptizing them in the name of the Father, and of the Son, and of the Holy Ghost" (Matt. xxviii. 19). It is in this belief we profess the Christian religion, which is founded on the mystery of the Trinity, the principal one of our Faith; it is by these words the character of a Christian is impressed on every one entering into the Church by Baptism; this is the formula approved by all the Holy Fathers, and used from the earliest ages of the Church: " I baptize thee in the name of the Father, and of the Son, and of the Holy Ghost." As the three Persons are named consecutively, and without any difference, the equality of the authority and power belonging to them is declared, and as we say, "in the name," and not " in the names," we profess the unity of essence in them. By using the article " *and* in the name of his Father, *and* of the Son, *and* of the Holy Ghost," we proclaim the real distinction that exists between them! for if we said, in the name of the Father, Son, *and* Holy Ghost, the latter expression, Holy Ghost, might be understood, not as a substantive, as the proper name of one of the Divine Persons, but as an epithet and adjective applied to the Father and the Son. It is for this reason, Tertullian says (15), that our Lord has commanded to make an ablution, in the administration of baptism, at the name of each of the Divine Persons, that we may firmly believe that there are three distinct Persons in the Trinity. " Mandavit ut tingerent in Patrem et Filium, et Spiritum Sanctum; non in unum nec semel sed ter ad singula nomina in personas singulas tingimur."

3. St. Athanasius, in his celebrated Epistle to Serapion, says, that we join the name of the Holy Ghost with the Father and the Son in baptism, because, if we omitted it, the Sacrament would

---

(15) Tertullian, con. Praxeam, *c.* 26.

be invalid: " He who curtails the Trinity, and baptizes in the name of the Father alone, or in the name of the Son alone, or omitting the Holy Ghost, with the Father and Son, performs nothing, for initiation consists in the whole Trinity being named." The Saint says that if we omit the name of the Holy Ghost the baptism is invalid, because baptism is the Sacrament in which we profess the Faith, and this Faith requires a belief in all the three Divine Persons united in one essence, so that he who denies one of the Persons denies God altogether. "And so," follows on St. Athanasius, "Baptism would be invalid, when administered in the belief that the Son or the Holy Ghost were mere creatures." He who divides the Son from the Father, or lowers the Spirit to the condition of a mere creature, has neither the Son nor the Father, and justly, for, as it is one baptism which is conferred in the Father, and the Son, and the Holy Ghost and it is one Faith in Him, as the Apostle says, so the Holy Trinity, existing in itself, and united in itself, has, in itself, nothing of created things. Thus, as the Trinity is one and undivided, so is the Faith of three Persons united in it, one and undivided. We, therefore, are bound to believe that the name of the Holy Ghost, that is, the name of the Third Person expressed by these two words, so frequently used in the Scriptures, is not an imaginary name, or casually invented, but the name of the Third Person, God, like the Father and the Son. We should remember, likewise, that the expression, Holy Ghost, is, properly speaking, but one word, for either of its component parts might be applied to the Father or the Son, for both are Holy, both are Spirit, but this word is the proper name of the Third Person of the Trinity. "Why would Jesus Christ," adds St. Athanasius, "join the name of the Holy Ghost with those of the Father and the Son, if he were a mere creature? is it to render the three Divine Persons unlike each other? was there anything wanting to God that he should assume a different substance, to render it glorious like unto himself?"

4. Besides this text of St. Matthew, already quoted, in which our Lord not only orders his disciples to baptize in the name of the three Persons, but to teach the Faith: " Teach all nations, baptizing them in the name of the Father," &c., we have that text of St. John: " There are three who give testimony in heaven, the Father, and the Son, and the Holy Ghost, and these three are one" (1 John, v. 7). These words (as we have already explained in the Refutation of Sabellianism, *n.* 9), evidently prove the unity of nature, and the distinction of the three Divine Persons (16). The text says, " These three are one;" if the three testimonies are one and the same, then each of them has the same Divinity, the same substance, for otherwise how, as St. Isidore (17) says, could the text of St. John be verified? " Nam cum tria sunt unum sunt."

---

(16) St. Athan. Epis. ad Serapion, *n.* 6.   (17) St. Isidore, *l.* 7; Etymol. *c.* 4.

St. Paul says the same, in sending his blessing to his disciples in Corinth: "The grace of our Lord Jesus Christ, and the charity of God, and the communication of the Holy Ghost be with you all" (2 Cor. xiii. 13).

5. We find the same expressions used in those passages of the Scriptures which speak of the sending of the Holy Ghost to the Church, as in St. John (xiv. 16): "I will ask the Father, and he will give you another Paraclete, that he may abide with you for ever." Remark how our Lord uses the words, "another Paraclete," to mark the equality existing between himself and the Holy Ghost. Again, he says, in the same Gospel (xv. 26): "When the Paraclete cometh, whom I will send you from the Father, the Spirit of Truth, who proceedeth from the Father, he shall give testimony of me." Here Jesus says, "he will send" the Spirit of Truth; now this Spirit which he will send is not his own Spirit, for his own Spirit he could communicate or give, but not "send," for sending means the transmission of something distinct from the person who sends. He adds, "Who proceeds from the Father;" and "procession," in respect of the Divine Persons, implies equality; and it is this very argument the Fathers availed themselves of against the Arians, to prove the Divinity of the Word, as we may see in the writings of St. Ambrose (18). The reason is this: the procession from another is to receive the same existence from the principle from which the procession is made, and, therefore, if the Holy Ghost proceeds from the Father, he receives the Divinity from the Father in the same manner as the Father himself has it.

6. Another great proof is, that we see the Holy Ghost called God in the Scriptures, like the Father, without any addition, restriction, or inequality. Thus Isaias, in the beginning of his 6th chapter, thus speaks of the Supreme God: "I saw the Lord sitting upon a throne high and elevated; ...... upon it stood the seraphim, ... and they cried to one another, Holy, Holy, Holy, the Lord God of Hosts, all the earth is full of his glory; ...... and I heard the voice of the Lord saying, ... Go, and thou shalt say to this people, hearing, hear and understand not. .... Blind the heart of this people, and make their ears heavy." Now, St. Paul informs us that this Supreme God, of whom the Prophet speaks, is the Holy Ghost. Here are his words: "Well did the Holy Ghost speak to our fathers by Isaias the Prophet, saying: *Go to this people, and say to them, with the ear you shall hear,*" &c. (Acts, xxviii. 25, 26). So we here see that the Holy Ghost is that same God called by Isaias the Lord God of Hosts. St. Basil (19) makes a beautiful reflection regarding this expression, the Lord God of Hosts. Isaias, in the prayer quoted, refers it to the Father. St. John (*cap.* 12), applies it to the Son, as is manifest from the 37th and the following verse,

(18) St. Ambrose, *l.* 1, de Spir. S. *c.* 4.   (19) St. Basil, *l.* 5, con. Eunom.

where this text is referred to, and St. Paul applies it to the Holy Ghost: "The Prophet," says the Saint, "mentions the Person of the Father, in whom the Jews believed, the Evangelist the Son, Paul the Holy Spirit"—" Propheta inducit Patris in quem Judei credebant personam Evangelista Filii, Paulus Spiritus, illum ipsum qui visus fuerat unum Dominum Sabaoth communiter nominantes. Sermonem quem de hypostasi instituerunt distruxere indistincta manente in eis de uno Deo sententia." How beautifully the Holy Doctor shows that the Father, the Son, and the Holy Ghost are three distinct Persons, but still the one and the same God, speaking by the mouth of his Prophets. St. Paul, also, speaking of that passage in the Psalms (xciv. 9), " Your fathers tempted me," says, that the God the Hebrews then tempted was the Holy Ghost; " therefore," says the Apostle, " as the Holy Ghost saith .... *your fathers tempted me*" (Heb. iii. 7, 9).

7. St. Peter confirms this doctrine (Acts, i. 16), when he says that the God who spoke by the mouth of the Prophets is the Holy Ghost himself: " The Scripture must be fulfilled, which the Holy Ghost spoke before by the mouth of David." And in the second Epistle (i. 21), he says: " For prophecy came not by the will of man at any time, but the holy men of God spoke, inspired by the Holy Ghost." St. Peter, likewise, calls the Holy Ghost God, in contradistinction to creatures. When charging Ananias with a lie, he says: " Why hath Satan tempted thy heart, that thou shouldst lie to the Holy Ghost,......thou hast not lied to man, but to God" (Acts, v. 4). It is most certain that St. Peter, in this passage, intended to say that the Third Person of the Trinity was God, and thus St. Basil, St. Ambrose, St. Gregory Nazianzen (20), and several other Fathers, together with St. Augustin (21), understood it so. St. Augustin says: " Showing that the Holy Ghost is God, you have not lied," he says, " to man, but to God."

8. Another strong proof of the Divinity of the Holy Ghost is, that the Scriptures attribute to him qualities which belong alone by nature to God: First.—Immensity, which fills the world: " Do not I fill the heaven and the earth, saith the Lord?" (Jer. xxiii. 24). And the Scripture then says that the Holy Ghost fills the world: " For the Spirit of the Lord hath filled the whole world" (Wisdom, i. 7). Therefore the Holy Ghost is God. St. Ambrose says (22): " Of what creature can it be said what is written of the Holy Ghost, that he filled all things? I will pour forth my Spirit over all flesh, &c., for it is the Lord alone can fill all things, who says, I fill the heaven and the earth." Besides, we read in the Acts (ii. 4), " They were all filled with the Holy Ghost." " Do we ever hear," says Didimus, " the Scriptures say, filled by a

---

(20) St. Basil, *l.* 1, con. Eunom. et lib. de Sp. S. *c.* 16 ; St. Ambro. *l.* 1, de Spir. S. *c.* 4 ; St. Gregor. Nazianz. Orat. 37. (21) St. Augus. *l.* 2, con. Maximin. *c.* 21. (22) St. Ambrose, *l.* 1, de S. S. *c.* 7.

creature? The Scriptures never speak in this way." They were, therefore, filled with God, and this God was the Holy Spirit.

9. Secondly.—God alone knows the Divine secrets. As St. Ambrose says, the inferior knows not the secrets of his superior. Now, St. Paul says, "The Spirit searcheth all things, yea, the deep things of God, for what man knoweth the things of a man, but the spirit of a man that is in him? So the things also that are of God no man knoweth but the Spirit of God" (1 Cor. ii. 10, 11). The Holy Ghost is, therefore, God; for, as Paschasius remarks, if none but God can know the heart of man, "the searcher of hearts and reins is God" (Ps. vii. 10). Much more so must it be God alone who knows the secrets of God. This, then, he says, is a proof of the Divinity of the Holy Spirit. St. Athanasius proves the consubstantiality of the Holy Ghost with the Father and the Son from this same passage, for as the Spirit of man, which knows the secrets of man, is nothing foreign from him, but is of the very substance of man, so the Holy Ghost, who knows the secrets of God, is not different from God, but must be one and the same substance with God. "Would it not be the height of impiety to say that the Spirit who is in God, and who searches the hidden things of God, is a creature? He who holds that opinion will be obliged to admit that the spirit of man is something different from man himself" (23).

10. Thirdly.—God alone is omnipotent, and this attribute belongs to the Holy Ghost. "By the word of the Lord the heavens were established, and all the power of them by the Spirit of his mouth" (Psalms, xxxii. 7). And St. Luke is even clearer on this point, for when the Blessed Virgin asked the Archangel how she could become the mother of our Saviour, having consecrated her virginity to God, the Archangel answered: "The Holy Ghost shall come upon thee, and the power of the Most High shall overshadow thee.... because no word shall be impossible with God." Hence we see the Holy Ghost is all-powerful, that to him there is nothing impossible. To the Holy Ghost, likewise, is attributed the creation of the universe: "Send forth thy Spirit, and they shall be created" (Psalms, ciii. 30). And in Job we read: "His Spirit has adorned the heavens" (Job, xxvi. 13). The power of creation belongs to the Divine Omnipotence alone. Hence, concludes St. Athanasius (24), when we find this written, it is certain that the Spirit is not a created, but a creator. The Father creates all things by the Word in the Spirit, inasmuch as when the Word is there, the Spirit is, and all things created by the Word have, from the Spirit, by the Son the power of existing. For it is thus written in the 32nd Psalm: "By the Word of the Lord the heavens were established, and all the power of them by the Spirit of his mouth." There can,

---

(23) St. Athanas. Epis. 1, ad Serapion, n. 22.   (24) St. Athanas. ibid.

therefore, be no doubt but that the Spirit is undivided from the Son.

11. Fourthly.—It is certain that the grace of God is not given unless by God himself: " The Lord will give grace and glory" (Psalms, lxxxiii. 12). Thus, also, it is God alone who can grant justification. It is God "that justifieth the wicked"(Prov. xvii. 15). Now both these attributes appertain to the Holy Ghost. " The charity of God is poured forth in our hearts by the Holy Ghost, who is given to us" (Romans, v. 5). Didimus (25) makes a reflection on this: The very expression, he says, "poured out," proves the uncreated substance of the Holy Ghost; for whenever God sends forth an angel, he does not say, I will " pour out" my angel. As to justification, we hear Jesus say to his disciples: " Receive ye the Holy Ghost; whose sins you shall forgive, they are forgiven" (John, xx. 22, 23). If the power of forgiving sins comes from the Holy Ghost, he must be God. The Apostle also says that it is God who operates in us the good we do; "the same God who worketh all in all" (1 Cor. xii. 6). And then in the 11th verse of the same chapter he says that this God is the Holy Ghost: " But all those things one and the same Spirit worketh, dividing to every one according as he will." Here, then, says St. Athanasius, the Scripture proves that the operation of God is the operation of the Holy Ghost.

12. Fifthly.—St. Paul tells us that we are the temples of God. " Know you not that you are the temple of God" (1 Cor. iii. 16). And then further on in the same epistle he says that our body is the temple of the Holy Ghost: " Or know you not that your members are the temple of the Holy Ghost, who is in you" (vi. 19). If, therefore, we are the temples of God and of the Holy Ghost, we must confess that the Holy Ghost is God, for if the Holy Ghost were a creature, we would be forced to admit that the very temple of God was the temple of a creature. Here are St. Augustin's (26) words on the subject: " If the Holy Ghost be not God, he would not have us as his temple....for if we would build a temple to some saint or angel, we would be cut off from the truth of Christ and the Church of God, since we would be exhibiting to a creature that service which we owe to God alone. If, therefore, we would be guilty of sacrilege, by erecting a temple to any creature, surely he must be true God to whom we not only erect a temple, but even are ourselves his temple." Hence, also, St. Fulgentius (27), in his remarks on the same subject, justly reproves those who deny the Divinity of the Holy Ghost: " Do you mean to tell me," says the Saint, " that he who is not God could establish the power of the heavens—that he who is not God could sanctify us by the regene-

(25) Didim. *l.* de St. San. (26) St. Augus. in 1 Cor. *c.* 6 ; Coll. eum Maximin. in Arian. (27) St. Fulgentius, *l.* 3 ad Trasimund *c.* 35.

ration of Baptism—that he who is not God could give us charity—that he who is not God could give us grace—that he could have as his temples the members of Christ, and still be not God? You must agree to all this, if you deny that the Holy Ghost is true God. If any creature could do all these things attributed to the Holy Ghost, then he may justly be called a creature; but if all these things are impossible to a creature, and are attributed to the Holy Ghost, things which belong to God alone, we should not say that he is naturally different from the Father and the Son, when we can find no difference in his power of operating." We must then conclude, with St. Fulgentius, that where there is a unity of power, there is a unity of nature, and the Divinity of the Holy Ghost follows as a necessary consequence.

13. In addition to these Scripture proofs, we have the constant tradition of the Church, in which the Faith of the Divinity of the Holy Ghost, and his consubstantiality with the Father and the Son, has been always preserved, both in the formula of administering Baptism, and in the prayers in which he is conjointly invoked with the Father and the Son, especially in that prayer said at the conclusion of all the psalms and hymns: " Glory be to the Father and to the Son and to the Holy Ghost," or, " Glory to the Father, by the Son, in the Holy Ghost," or, " Glory to the Father with the Son, and the Holy Ghost," all three *formulæ* having been practised by the Church. St. Athanasius, St. Basil, St. Ambrose, St. Hilary, Didimus, Theodoret, St. Augustin, and the other Fathers, laid great stress on this argument when opposing the Macedonians. St. Basil (28) remarks that the formula, " Glory be to the Father, and to the Son, and to the Holy Ghost," was rarely used in his time in the Church, but generally " Glory be to the Father, and to the Son, with the Holy Ghost." However, it all amounts to the same thing, for it is a general rule, in speaking of the Trinity, to use the words "from whom," " by whom," " in whom" (as when we say of the Father, " from whom are all things;" of the Son, " by whom are all things;" of the Holy Ghost, " in whom are all things"), in the same sense. There is no inequality of Persons marked by these expressions, since St. Paul, speaking of God himself, says: " For of him, and by him, and in him, are all things; to him be glory for ever. Amen" (Rom. xi. 36).

14. This constant faith of the Church has been preserved by the Holy Fathers in their writings from the earliest ages. St. Basil, one of the most strenuous defenders of the Divinity of the Holy Ghost (29), cites a passage of St. Clement of Rome, Pope: " The ancient Clement," he says, " thus spoke: 'The Father lives,' he says, ' and the Lord Jesus Christ, and the Holy Ghost.' " Thus, St. Clement attributes the same life to the three Divine Persons

---

(28) St. Basil, *l.* 1, de S. Sancto, *c.* 25.   (29) St. Basil, *l.* de S. Sancto, *c.* 29.

equally, and therefore believed them all three to be truly and substantially God. What makes this stronger is, that St. Clement is contrasting the three Divine Persons with the gods of the Gentiles, who had no life, while God in the Scriptures is called "the living God." It is of no importance either, that the words quoted are not found in the two Epistles of St. Clement, for we have only some fragments of the Second Epistle, and we may, therefore, believe for certain, that St. Basil had the whole Epistle before him, of which we have only a part.

15. St. Justin, in his second Apology, says: "We adore and venerate, with truth and reason, himself (the Father), and he who comes from him.........the Son and the Holy Ghost." Thus St. Justin pays the same adoration to the Son and the Holy Ghost as to the Father. Athenagoras, in his Apology, says: "We believe in God, and his Son, the Word, and the Holy Ghost, united in power.........For the Son is the mind, the word, and the wisdom of the Father, and the Spirit is as the light flowing from fire." St. Iræneus (30) teaches that God, the Father, has created and now governs all things, both by the Word and by the Holy Ghost. "For nothing," he says, "is wanting to God, who makes, and disposes, and governs all things, by the Word and by the Holy Ghost." We here see, according to St. Iræneus, that God has no need of anything; and he afterwards says, that he does all things by the Word and by the Holy Ghost. The Holy Ghost is, therefore, God, the same as the Father. He tells us, in another part of his works (31), that the Holy Ghost is a creator, and eternal, unlike a created spirit. "For that which is made is," he says, "different from the maker; what is made is made in time, but the Spirit is eternal." St. Lucian, who lived about the year 160, says, in a Dialogue, entitled Philopatris, attributed to him, addressing a Gentile who interrogates him: "What, then, shall I swear for you?" Triphon, the Defender of the Faith, answers: "God reigning on high.........the Son of the Father, the Spirit proceeding from the Father, one from three, and three from one." This passage is so clear that it requires no explanation. Clement of Alexandria says (32): "The Father of all is one; the Word of all is also one; and the Holy Ghost is one, who is also everywhere." In another passage he clearly explains the Divinity and Consubstantiality of the Holy Ghost with the Father and the Son (33): "We return thanks to the Father alone, and to the Son, together with the Holy Ghost, in all things one, in whom are all things, by whom all things are in one, by whom that is which always is." See here how he explains that the three Persons are equal in fact, and that they are but one in essence.

(30) St. Iræn *l.* 1, ad Hæres. *c.* 19.   (31) St. Iræn. *l.* 5, c. 12.   (32) Clem. Alex. Padag. *l.* 1, *c.* 6.   (33) Idem, *l.* 3, c. 7.

Tertullian (34) professes his belief in the " Trinity of one Divinity, the Father, the Son, and the Holy Ghost;" and in another place (35), he says: " We define, indeed, two, the Father and the Son, nay, three, with the Holy Ghost; but we never profess to believe in two Gods, although the Father is God, the Son God, and the Holy Ghost God, and each one is God," &c. St. Cyprian (36), speaking of the Trinity, says: " When the three are one, how could the Holy Ghost be agreeable to him, if he were the enemy of the Father or the Son?" And, in the same Epistle, he proves that Baptism administered in the name of Christ alone is of no avail, for " Christ," he says, " orders that the Gentiles should be baptized in the full and united Trinity." St. Dionisius Romanus, in his Epistle against Sabellius, says: " The admirable and Divine unity is not, therefore, to be divided into three Deities; but we are bound to believe in God, the Father Almighty, and in Christ Jesus, his Son, and in the Holy Ghost." I omit the innumerable testimonies of the Fathers of the following centuries; but I here merely note some of those who have purposely attacked the heresy of Macedonius, and these are—St. Athanasius, St. Basil, St. Gregory Nazianzen, St. Gregory of Nyssa, St. Epiphanius, Didimus, St. Cyril of Jerusalem, St. Cyril of Alexandria, and St. Hilary (37). These Fathers, immediately on the appearance of the Macedonian heresy, all joined in condemning it—a clear proof that it was contrary to the Faith of the Universal Church.

16. This heresy was condemned, besides, by several Councils, both general and particular. First.—It was condemned (two years after Macedonius had broached it) by the Council of Alexandria, celebrated by St. Athanasius, in the year 372, in which it was decided that the Holy Ghost was consubstantial in the Trinity. In the year 377, it was condemned by the Holy See, in the Synod of Illiricum; and about the same time, as Theodoret (38) informs us, it was condemned in two other Roman Synods, by the Pope, St. Damasus. Finally, in the year 381, it was condemned in the first Council of Constantinople, under St. Damasus; and this Article was annexed to the symbol of the Faith: " We believe in the Holy Ghost, the Lord and Giver of life, proceeding from the Father, and with the Father and the Son to be adored and glorified, who spoke by the Prophets." He to whom the same worship is to be given as to the Father and the Son, is surely God. Besides, this Council has been always held as ecumenical by the whole Church, for though composed of only one hundred and fifty Oriental bishops, still, as the Western bishops, about the same time, defined the same

(34) Tertul. de Pudic. c. 21.   (35) Idem, con. Praxeam, c. 3.   (36) St. Cyp. Ep. ad Juba.   (37) St. Athan. Ep. ad Serap.; St. Basil, l. 3, 5, cont. Eunom. & l. de Spi. S.; St. Greg. Naz. l. 5, de Theol.; St. Greg. Nys. l. ad Eust.; St. Epiphan. Hier. 74; Didimus, l. de S. San.; St. Cyril, Hieros. cat. 16, 17; St. Cyril, Alex. l. 7, de Trin. & l. S. Sanc.; St. Hil. de Trinit.   (38) Theodoret, l. 2, Hist. c. 22.

Article of the Divinity of the Holy Ghost, under St. Damasus, this decision has been always considered as the decision of the Universal Church; and the subsequent General Councils—that is, the Council of Chalcedon, the second and third of Constantinople, and the second of Nice—confirmed the same symbol. Nay more, the fourth Council of Constantinople pronounced an anathema against Macedonius, and defined that the Holy Ghost is consubstantial to the Father and to the Son. Finally, the fourth Council of Lateran thus concludes: " We define that there is but one true God alone, the Father, and the Son, and the Holy Ghost, three Persons indeed, but only one essence, substance, or simple nature . . . . . And that all these Persons are consubstantial, omnipotent, and co-eternal, the one beginning of all things."

SEC. II.—ANSWER TO OBJECTIONS.

17. First, the Socinians, who have revived the ancient heresies, adduce a negative argument. They say that the Holy Ghost is never called God in the Scriptures, nor is ever proposed to us to be adored and invoked. But St. Augustin (1) thus answers this argument, addressing the Macedonian Maximinus: " When have you read that the Father was not born, but self-existing? and still it is no less true," &c. The Saint means to say that many things in the Scriptures are stated, not in express terms, but in equivalent ones, which prove the truth of what is stated, just as forcibly; and, for a proof of that, the reader can refer to N. 4 and 6, where the Divinity of the Holy Ghost is incontestibly proved, if not in express, in equivalent terms.

18. Secondly, they object that St. Paul, in his first Epistle to the Corinthians, speaking of the benefits conferred by God on mankind, mentions the Father and the Son, but not the Holy Ghost. We answer, that it is not necessary, in speaking of God, that we should always expressly name the three Divine Persons, for, when we speak of one, we speak of the three, especially in speaking of the operations, *ad extra*, to which the three Divine Persons concur in the same manner. " Whosoever is blessed in Christ," says St. Ambrose (2), " is blessed in the name of the Father, and of the Son, and of the Holy Ghost, because there is one name and one power; thus, likewise, when the operation of the Holy Ghost is pointed out, it is referred, not only to the Holy Ghost, but also to the Father and the Son."

19. They object, thirdly, that the primitive Christians knew nothing of the Holy Ghost, as we learn from the Acts of the Apostles, when St. Paul asked some newly-baptized, if they had received the Holy Ghost, they answered: " We have not so much as heard

---

(1) St. Augus. *l.* 2, alias 3, cont. Maxim. *c.* 3.   (2) St. Amb. *l.* 1, de Sanc. *c.* 3.

if there be a Holy Ghost" (Acts, xix. 2). We reply that the answer to this is furnished by the very passage itself, for, St. Paul hearing that they knew nothing of the Holy Ghost, asked them: " In what, then, were you baptized?" and they answered, "in John's Baptism." No wonder, then, that they knew nothing of the Holy Ghost, when they were not even as yet baptized with the Baptism instituted by Christ.

20. They object, fourthly, that the Council of Constantinople, speaking of the Holy Ghost, does not call him God. We answer that the Council does call him God, when it says he is the Lord and giver of life, who proceeds from the Father, and who, with the Father and the Son, should be adored and glorified. And the same answer will apply, when they object that St. Basil (or any other Father) has not called the Holy Ghost God, for they have defended his Divinity, and condemned those who called him a creature. Besides, if St. Basil, in his sermons, does not speak of the Holy Ghost as God, it was only an act of prudence in those calamitous times, when the heretics sought every occasion to chase the Catholic Bishops from their Sees, and intrude wolves into their places. St. Basil, on the other hand, defends the Divinity of the Holy Ghost in a thousand passages. Just take one for all, where he says, in his Fifth Book against Eunomius, tit. 1: " What is common to the Father and the Son is likewise so to the Holy Ghost, for wherever we find the Father and the Son designated as God in the Scripture, the Holy Ghost is designated as God likewise."

21. Fifthly, they found objections on some passages of the Scripture, but they are either equivocal or rather confirmatory of the Divinity of the Holy Ghost. They lay great stress especially on that text of St. John: " But when the Paraclete cometh, whom I will send you from the Father, the Spirit of Truth who proceedeth from the Father" (John, xv. 26). Now, they say, when the Holy Spirit is sent, it is a sign that he is inferior, and in a state of subjection, or dependence; therefore, he is not God. To this we answer, that the Holy Ghost is not sent by a command, but sent solely by a procession from the Father, and the Son, for from these he proceeds. Mission, or being sent, means nothing more *in Divinis*, than this, the presence of the Divine Person, manifested by any sensible effect, which is specially ascribed to the Person sent. This, for example, was the mission of the Holy Ghost, when he descended into the Cenaculum on the Apostles, to make them worthy to found the Church, just as the eternal Word was sent by the Father to take flesh for the salvation of mankind. In the same way we explain that text of St. John: " He shall not speak of himself, but what things soever he shall hear, he shall speak . . . . . . he shall glorify me, because he shall receive of mine" (John, xvi. 14, 15). The Holy Ghost takes from the Father and the Son the knowledge of all things, not by learning them, but proceeding from

them without any dependence, as a necessary requirement of his Divine Nature. And this is the very meaning of the words: "He shall receive of mine;" since, through the Son, the Father communicates to the Holy Ghost, together with the Divine Essence, wisdom, and all the attributes of the Son. "He will hear from him," says St. Augustin (3), "from whom he proceeds. To him, to hear is to know, to know is to exist. Because, therefore, he is not from himself, but from him from whom he proceeds, from whom he has his essence, from him he has his knowledge. Ab illo igitur audientia, quod nihil est aliud, quam scientia." St. Ambrose expresses the same sentiments (4).

22. They object, sixthly, that St. Paul says: "The Spirit himself asketh for us with unspeakable groanings" (Rom. viii. 26). Therefore, the Holy Ghost groans and prays, as an inferior. But St. Augustin thus explains the text: "He asketh with groanings that we should understand that he causes us to ask with groanings" (5). Thus St. Paul wishes to instruct us, that by the grace we receive, we become compunctious and groaning, making us pray with "unspeakable groanings," just as God makes us triumph, when he says that Jesus Christ triumphs in us: "Thanks be to God, who always makes us triumph in Christ Jesus" (2 Cor. ii. 14).

23. They object, seventhly, another passage of St. Paul: "The Spirit searcheth all things, yea, the deep things of God" (1 Cor. ii. 10); and they then say that the word, "searcheth," shows that the Holy Ghost is ignorant of the Divine secrets; but we answer, that this expression does not mean seeking or inquiring, but the simple comprehension which the Holy Ghost has of the whole of the Divine Essence, and of all things, as it is said of God: "That he searcheth the heart and the reins" (Psalms, vii. 10); which means that God comprehends all the thoughts and affections of mankind. Hence, St. Ambrose (6) concludes: "The Holy Ghost is a searcher like the Father, he is a searcher like the Son, and this expression is used to show that there is nothing which he does not know."

24. They object, eighthly, that passage of St. John: "All things were made by him, and without him was made nothing that was made" (John, i. 3); therefore, the Holy Ghost was made by him, and is consequently a creature. We answer, that in this sense, it cannot be said that all things were made by the Word, for in that case, even the Father would be made by him. The Holy Ghost is not made, but proceeds from the Father and the Son, as from one principle, by the absolute necessity of the Divine Nature, and without any dependence.

(3) St. Augus. Trac. 99, in Joan. (4) St. Ambrose, *l.* 2, de Sp. San. *c.* 12. (5) St. Augus. Coll. cum Maxim. (6) St. Ambrose, *l.* de Sp. San. *c.* 11.

REFUTATION IV.

THE HERESY OF THE GREEKS, WHO ASSERT THAT THE HOLY GHOST PROCEEDS FROM THE FATHER ALONE, AND NOT FROM THE FATHER AND THE SON.

1. It is necessary to remark here, in order not to confuse the matter, that the heresy of the schismatical Greeks consists in denying the procession of the Holy Ghost from the Father and the Son; they contend that he proceeds from the Father alone, and this is the difference between the Greek and Latin Churches. The learned have not yet agreed on the author of this heresy. Some say it was Theodoret, in his refutation of the ninth anathematism of St. Cyril, against Nestorius, but others again defend him (as well as several others quoted by the schismatics), and explain that passage of his works which gave rise to this opinion, by saying that he only meant to prove that the Holy Ghost was not a creature, as the Arians and Macedonians asserted. There can be no doubt but that passages from the works both of Theodoret and the other Fathers, which the writers intended as refutations of the errors of the Arians and Macedonians, taken in a wrong sense by the schismatics, have confirmed them in holding on to this error. This heresy, up to the time of Photius, was only held by a few persons, but on his intrusion into the See of Constantinople, in 858, and especially in 863, when he was condemned by Pope Nicholas I., he constituted himself, not alone the chief of the schism, which for so many years has separated the Greek and Latin Churches, but induced the whole Greek Church to embrace this heresy—that the Holy Ghost proceeds from the Father alone, and not from the Son. Fourteen times, Osius writes (1), up to the time of the Council of Florence, held in 1439, the Greeks renounced this error, and united themselves to the Latin Church, but always relapsed again. In the Council of Florence, they themselves agreed in defining that the Holy Ghost proceeds from the Father and the Son, and it was thought that the union would be everlasting, but such was not the case, for after they left the Council, they again (*ch.* ix. *n.* 31) returned to their vomit, at the instigation of Mark of Ephesus. I now speak of these Greeks who were under the obedience of the Eastern Patriarchs, for the others who were not subject to them remained united in Faith to the Roman Church.

SEC. I.—IT IS PROVED THAT THE HOLY GHOST PROCEEDS FROM THE FATHER AND THE SON.

2. It is proved by the words of St. John: "When the Paraclete cometh, whom I will send you from the Father, the Spirit of Truth who proceedeth from the Father" (John, xv. 16). This

---

(1) Osius, *l.* de Sac. Conjng.

text not only proves the dogma decided by the Council of Constantinople against the Arians and Macedonians, that the Holy Ghost proceeds from the Father ("And in the Holy Ghost the Lord and Giver of life, who proceeds from the Father"); but also that the Holy Ghost proceeds from the Son, as is shown by the words: "Whom I will send you;" and the same expression is repeated in St. John in other places: "For if I go not, the Paraclete will not come to you, but if I go, I will send him to you" (John, xvi. 7). "But the Paraclete, the Holy Ghost, whom the Father will send in my name" (John, xiv. 26). In the Divinity, a Person is not spoken of as sent, unless by another Person from whom he proceeds. The Father, as he is the origin of the Divinity, is never spoken of in the Scriptures as being sent. The Son, as he proceeds from the Father alone, is said to be sent, but it is never thus said of the Holy Ghost: "As the Father living, sent me, &c., God sent his Son, made from a woman, &c." When, therefore, the Holy Ghost is said to be sent from the Father and the Son, he proceeds from the Son as well as from the Father; especially as this mission of one Divine Person from another cannot be understood either in the way of command or instruction, or any other way, for in the Divine Persons both authority and wisdom are equal. We, therefore, understand one Person as sent by another, according to the origin, and according to the procession of one Person from the other, this procession implying neither inequality nor dependence. If, therefore, the Holy Ghost is said to be sent by the Son, he proceeds from the Son. "He is sent by him," says St. Augustin (1), "from whence he emanates," and he adds, "the Father is not said to be sent, for he has not from whom to be, or from whom to proceed."

3. The Greeks say that the Son does not send the Person of the Holy Ghost, but only his gifts of grace, which are attributed to the Holy Spirit. But we answer that this interpretation is wrong, for in the passage of St. John, just quoted, it is said that this Spirit of Truth, sent by the Son, proceeds from the Father; therefore, the Son does not send the gifts of the Holy Ghost, but the Spirit of Truth himself, who proceeds from the Father.

4. This dogma is proved from all those texts, in which the Holy Ghost is called the Spirit of the Son—"God has sent the Spirit of his Son into your hearts" (Gal. iv. 6)—just as, in another place, the Holy Ghost is called the Spirit of the Father; "For it is not you that speak, but the Spirit of your Father that speaketh in you" (Mat. x. 20). If, therefore, the Holy Ghost is called the Spirit of the Father, merely because he proceeds from the Father, he also proceeds from the Son, when he is called the Spirit of the Son. This is what St. Augustin says (2): "Why should we not believe that the Holy Ghost proceeds also from the Son,

---

(1) St. Augus. *l.* 4, de Trinit. *c.* 20.   (2) St. Augus. Trac. 99, in Joan.

when he is the Spirit of the Son?" And the reason is evident, since he could not be called the Holy Ghost of the Son, because the Person of the Holy Ghost is consubstantial to the Son, as the Greeks said: for otherwise the Son might be called the Spirit of the Holy Ghost, as he is also consubstantial to the Holy Ghost. Neither can he be called the Spirit of the Son, because he is the instrument of the Son, or because he is the extrinsic holiness of the Son, for we cannot speak thus of the Divine Persons; therefore, he is called the Spirit of the Son, because he proceeds from him. Jesus Christ explained this himself, when, after his Resurrection, he appeared to his disciples, and "breathed on them, and said to them, Receive ye the Holy Ghost," &c. (John, xx. 22). Remark the words, "he breathed on them, and said," to show that, as the breath proceeds from the mouth, so the Holy Ghost proceeds from him. Hear how beautifully St. Augustin (3) explains this passage: "We cannot say that the Holy Ghost does not proceed from the Son also, for it is not without a reason that he is called the Spirit both of the Father and of the Son. I cannot see what other meaning he had when he breathed in the face of his disciples, and said, Receive the Holy Ghost. For that corporeal breathing was not, indeed......the substance of the Holy Ghost, but a demonstration, by a congruous signification, that the Holy Ghost did not proceed from the Father alone, but from the Son likewise."

5. It is proved, thirdly, from all those passages of the Holy Scripture, in which it is said that the Son has all that the Father has, and that the Holy Ghost receives from the Son. Hear what St. John says: "But when he, the Spirit of Truth, is come, he will teach you all truth. For he shall not speak of himself; but what things soever he shall hear, he shall speak, and the things that are to come he shall show you. He shall glorify me; because he shall receive of mine, and shall show it to you. All things whatsoever the Father hath are mine. Therefore, I said, that he shall receive of mine, and show it to you" (John, xvi. 13, &c.) It is expressly laid down in this passage, that the Holy Ghost receives of the Son, "shall receive of mine;" and when we speak of the Divine Persons, we can never say that one receives from the other in any other sense but this, that the Person proceeds from the Person he receives from. To receive and to proceed is just the same thing, for it would be repugnant to sense, to say that the Holy Ghost, who is God equal to the Son, and of the same Nature as the Son, receives from him either knowledge or doctrine. It is said, therefore, that he receives from the Son, because he proceeds from him, and from him receives, by communication, the Nature and all the attributes of the Son.

(3) St. Augus. *l.* 4, de Trin. *c.* 20.

6. The Greeks make a feeble reply to this. Christ, in this passage, they say, does not say that the Holy Ghost receives *from me*, but "*of mine*," that is, of my Father. This reply carries no weight with it, for Christ himself explains the text in the next passage: "All things whatsoever the Father hath are mine; therefore, I said, that he shall receive of mine." Now, these words prove that the Holy Ghost receives from the Father and the Son, because he proceeds from the Father and the Son. The reason is plain; for if the Son has all that the Father hath (except Paternity relatively opposed to Filiation), and the Father is the *principium esse* of the Holy Ghost, the Son must be so likewise, for otherwise he would not have all that the Father has. This is exactly what Eugenius IV. says, in his Epistle of the Union: " Since all things which belong to the Father he gave to his only-begotten Son, in begetting him, with the exception that he did not make him the Father—for this the Son, from all eternity, is in possession of—that the Holy Ghost proceeds from him, from whom he was eternally begotten." Before Eugenius's time, St. Augustin said just the same thing (4): " Therefore, he is the Son of the Father, from whom he is begotten, and the Spirit is the Spirit of both, since he proceeds from both. But when the Son speaks of him, he says, therefore, ' he proceeds from the Father,' since the Father is the author of his procession, who begot such a Son, and begetting him, gave unto him that the Spirit should also proceed from him." The holy Father, in this passage, forestalls the objection of Mark of Ephesus, who said that the Scriptures teach that the Holy Ghost " proceeds from the Father," but do not mention the Son, " for," says St. Augustin, " although in the Scripture it is said only that the Holy Ghost proceeds from the Father, still the Father, by generating the Son, communicated to him also to be the *principium* of the Holy Ghost, " gignendo ei dedit, ut etiam de ipso procederet Spiritus Sanctus."

7. St. Anselm (5) confirms this by that principle embraced by all theologians, that all things are one in the Divinity: " In Divinis omnia sunt unum, et omnia unum, et idem, ubi non obviat relationis oppositio." Thus in God these things alone are really distinguished, among which there is a relative opposition of the producing and the produced. The first producing cannot produce himself, for otherwise he would be at the same time existent and non-existent—existent, because he produces himself—non-existent, because he had no existence till after he was produced. This is a manifest absurdity. That axiom, that no one can give what he has not—" Nemo dat, quod non habet," proves the same thing; for if the producer gave existence to himself before he was produced, he would give that which he had not. But is not God self-existing? Most certainly; but that does not mean that he gave existence

---

(4) St. August. *l.* 2 (alias 3), cent. Maxim. *c.* 14. (5) St. Ansel. *l.* de Proc. Spi. S. *c.* 7.

to himself. God exists of necessity; he is a necessary Being that always did and always will exist; he gives existence to all other creatures; if he ceased to exist, all other things, likewise, would cease to exist. Let us return to the point. The Father is the principle (*principium*) of the Divinity, and is distinguished from the Son by the opposition that exists between the producer and produced. On the other hand, those things in God, which have no relative opposition among themselves, are in nowise distinguished, but are one and the same thing. The Father, therefore, is the same with the Son, in all that in which he is not opposed relatively to the Son. And as the Father is not relatively opposed to the Son, nor the Son to the Father, by both one and the other being the principle in the spiration of the Holy Ghost, therefore, the Holy Ghost is spirated, and proceeds from the Father and the Son; and it is an Article of Faith, defined both by the Second General Council of Lyons, and by that of Florence, that the Holy Ghost proceeds from one principle and from one spiration, and not from two principles nor from two spirations. "We condemn and reprobate all," say the Fathers of Lyons, "who rashly dare to assert that the Holy Ghost proceeds from the Father and the Son, as from two principles, and that he does not proceed from them as from one principle." The Fathers of the Council of Florence "define that the Holy Ghost proceeds from the Father and the Son eternally, as from one principle, and by one spiration." The reason is this (6): "Because the power of spirating the Holy Ghost is found in the Son as well as in the Father, without any relative opposition. Hence, as the world was created by the Father, and the Son, and the Holy Ghost, still, because the power of creating appertains equally to the three Persons, we say, God the Creator; so, because the power of spirating the Holy Ghost is equally in the Father and in the Son, therefore, we say that the principle is one, and that the spiration of the Holy Ghost is one. We now pass on to other proofs of the principal point, that the Holy Ghost proceeds from the Father and the Son.

8. The procession of the Holy Ghost from the Father and the Son is proved, fourthly, by the following argument used by the Latins against the Greeks, in the Council of Florence. If the Holy Ghost did not proceed from the Son also, there would be no distinction; the reason is, because, as we have already said, there is no real distinction in God between those things between which there is not a relative opposition of the producer and the produced. If the Holy Ghost did not proceed also from the Son, there would be no relative opposition between him and the Son, and, consequently, there would be no real distinction; one person would not be distinct from the other. To this convincing argument the Greeks replied that even in this case there would be a distinction,

---

(6) St. Greg. Nyss. *l. ad Ablav.*

because the Son would proceed from the Father by the intellect, and the Holy Ghost by the will. But the Latins answered, justly, that this would not be enough to form a real distinction between the Son and the Holy Ghost, because, at the most, it would be only a virtual distinction such as that which exists in God between the understanding and the will, but the Catholic Faith teaches us that the three Divine Persons, though they are of the same nature and substance, are still really distinct among themselves. It is true that some of the Fathers, as St. Augustin and St. Anselm, have said that the Son and the Holy Ghost are also distinct, because they have a different mode of procession, one from the will and the other from the understanding; but when they speak thus they only mean the remote cause of this distinction, for they themselves have most clearly expressed, on the other hand, that the proximate and formal cause of the real distinction of the Son and the Holy Ghost is the relative opposition in the procession of the Holy Ghost from the Son. Hear what St. Gregory of Nyssa (7) says: " The Spirit is distinguished from the Son, because it is by him he is." And St Augustin himself, whom the Greeks consider as favouring their party (8), says: " Hoc solo numerum insinuant, quod ad invicem sunt." And St. John of Damascus (9) also says, that it is merely in the properties of Paternity, Filiation and Procession, that we see the difference, according to the cause and the effect: " In solis autem proprietatibus, nimirum, Paternitatis Filiationis, et Processionis secundum causam, et causatam discrimen advertimus." The Eleventh Council of Toledo (*Cap.* I.) says: " In relatione Personarum numerus cernitur; hoc solo numerum insinuat, quod ad invicem sunt."

9. Finally, it is proved by the tradition of all ages, as is manifest from the text of those Greek Fathers whom the Greeks themselves consider an authority, and of some Latin Fathers who wrote before the Greek schism. St. Epiphanius, in the Anchoratum, thus speaks: " Christ is believed from the Father, God of God, and the Spirit from Christ, or from both;" and in the Heresia he says: " But the Holy Ghost is from both, a Spirit from a Spirit." St Cyril (10) writes: " The Son, according to nature, is indeed from God (for he is begotten of God and of the Father), but the Spirit is properly his, and in him, and from him;" and again (11): " The Spirit is of the essence of the Father and the Son, who proceeds from the Father and the Son." St. Athanasius explains (12) the procession of the Holy Ghost from the Son in equivalent expressions. " The Spirit," he says, " does not unite the Word with the Father, but the Spirit receives from the Word......whatsoever the Spirit has he has from the Word." St. Basil (13),

(7) St. Greg. Nyss. *l.* ad Ablavium. (8) St. Augus. *trac.* 39, in Jo. (9) Jo. Damasc. *l.* 1, de Fide, *c.* 11. (10) St. Cyril. in Joelem, *c.* 2. (11) Idem, *l.* 14, Thesaur. (12) St. Athan. Orat. 3, cont. Arian. *n.* 24. (13) St. Basil, *l.* 5, cont. Eunom.

replying to a heretic, who asks him why the Holy Ghost is not called the Son of the Son, says, he is not called so, "not because he is not from God through the Son, but lest it might be imagined that the Trinity consists of an infinite multitude of Persons, if Sons would follow from Sons, as in mankind." Among the Latin Fathers, Tertullian (14) writes: " The Son is deduced from the Father, the Spirit from the Father by the Son." St. Hilary (15) says: " There is no necessity to speak of Him who is to be confessed as coming from the Father and the Son." St. Ambrose says (16), that "the Holy Ghost proceeds from the Father and the Son," and in another place (17), " the Holy Ghost, truly a Spirit, proceeding from the Father and the Son, not the Son himself."

10. I omit the authorities of the other Fathers, both Greek and Latin, collected by the Theologian John, in his disputation with Mark of Ephesus, in the Council of Florence, where he clearly refuted all the cavils of that prelate. It is of more importance to cite the decisions of the General Councils, which have finally decided on this dogma, as the Council of Ephesus, the Council of Chalcedon, the Second and Third Councils of Constantinople, by approving the Synodical Epistle of St. Cyril of Alexandria, in which this doctrine of the procession of the Holy Ghost from the Father and the Son is expressed in these terms: " The Spirit is called the Spirit of Truth, and Christ is the Truth, so that he proceeds from him as he does from the Father." In the Fourth Council of Lateran, celebrated in the year 1215, under Innocent III., both Greeks and Latins united in defining (*cap.* 153), " that the Father was from none, the Son from the Father alone, and the Holy Ghost equally from both, always without beginning and without end." In the Second Council of Lyons, held in 1274, under Gregory X., when the Greeks again became united with the Latins, it was again agreed on by both that the Holy Ghost proceeds from the Father and the Son: " With a faithful and devout confession we declare that the Holy Ghost proceeds from the Father and the Son, not as from two principles, but as from one principle—not by two spirations, but by one spiration."

11. Finally, in the Council of Florence, held under Eugenius IV., in the year 1438, in which both Greeks and Latins were again united, it was decided unanimously, "that this truth of Faith should be believed and held by all Christians, and that all should then profess that the Holy Ghost eternally proceeds from the Father and the Son, as from one principle, and by one spiration; we also define, explaining the word " *Filioque*" (and from the Son), that it has been lawfully and rationally introduced into the Creed, for the sake of declaring the truth, and because there was a necessity for doing so

---

(14) Tertul. *l.* cont. Praxeam, *c.* 4.   (15) St. Hilar. *l.* 2, de Trin.   (16) St. Ambrose, *l.* 1, de S. S. c. 11, *art.* 10.   (17) Idem. de Symb. ap. *c.* 30.

at the time." Now, all those Councils in which the Greeks joined with the Latins in defining the procession of the Holy Ghost from the Father and the Son, supply an invincible argument to prove that the schismatics uphold a heresy, for otherwise we should admit that the whole united Church, both Latin and Greek, has defined an error in three General Councils.

12. As to theological reasons, we have already given the two principal ones: the first is, that the Son has all that the Father has, with the exception of the Paternity alone, which is impossible, on account of the Filiation. " All things whatsoever the Father hath are mine"(John, xvi. 15); therefore, if the Father has the power of spirating the Holy Ghost, the same power belongs also to the Son, since there is no relative opposition between the Filiation and the active spiration. The second reason is, that if the Holy Ghost did not proceed from the Son, he would not be really distinct from the Son, for then there would be no relative opposition or real distinction between them, and, consequently, the mystery of the Trinity would be destroyed. The other arguments adduced by theologians can either be reduced to these, or are arguments *a congruentia*, and, therefore, we omit them.

SEC. II.—OBJECTIONS ANSWERED.

13. THEY object, first, that the Scripture speaks of the procession of the Holy Ghost from the Father alone, and not from the Son, but we have already answered this (*N*. 6), and we remind the reader that though the Scripture does not express it in formal, it does in equivalent terms, as has been already proved. But, besides, remember that the Greeks recognized, equally with the Latins, the authority of tradition, and that teaches that the Holy Ghost proceeds from the Father and the Son.

14. They object, secondly, that in the First Council of Constantinople, in which the Divinity of the Holy Ghost was defined, it was not defined that he proceeded from the Father and the Son, but from the Father alone; but to this we reply, that this Council did not declare it, because this was not the point that the Macedonians controverted. The Council, therefore, defined the procession from the Father alone, because the Macedonians and Eunomians denied the procession from the Father, and, consequently, the Divinity of the Holy Ghost. The Church does not draw up definitions of Faith until errors spring up, and, on that account, we see, that in several General Councils afterwards, the Church defined the procession of the Holy Ghost as well from the Son as from the Father.

15. They object, thirdly, that when, in the Council of Ephesus, the priest Carisius publicly read a Symbol, composed by Nestorius, in which it was asserted that the Holy Ghost was not from the Son,

nor that he had not his substance through the Son, that the Fathers did not reject the doctrine. We reply, First.—That this can be easily explained, by supposing that Nestorius properly denied, in a Catholic sense, that the Holy Ghost was from the Son, in opposition to the Macedonians, who said that he was a creature of the Son, and had received existence from the Son, just like any other creature. Secondly.—We should not forget that in the Council of Ephesus it was not of the procession of the Holy Ghost that they were treating at all, and, therefore, they left it undecided, as it is always the practice of Councils, as we have stated already, not to turn aside to decide on incidental questions, but merely to apply themselves to the condemnation of those errors alone on which they are then deciding.

16. They object, fourthly, some passages of the Holy Fathers which appear to deny the procession from the Son. St. Dionisius (1) says, that the Father alone is the consubstantial fountain of the Divinity: " Solum Patrem esse Divinitatis fontem consubstantialem." St. Athanasius (2) says, that he is the cause of both Persons: " Solum Patrem esse causam duorum." St. Maximus says (3), that the Fathers never allowed the Son to be the cause, that is, the principle, of the Holy Ghost: " Patres concedere Filium esse causam, id est principium, Spiritus Sancti." St. John of Damascus says (4), We believe the Holy Ghost to be from the Father, and we call him the Spirit of the Father: " Spiritum Sanctum et ex Patre esse statuimus, et Patris Spiritum appellamus." They also quote certain passages of Theodoret, and, finally, they adduce that fact which we read of in the life of Pope Leo III., who commanded that the word " *Filioque*" (and from the Son), added by the Latins to the Symbol of Constantinople, should be expunged, and that the Symbol, with that word omitted, should be engraved on a table of silver, for perpetual remembrance of the fact. We answer that the preceding authorities quoted from the Holy Fathers prove nothing for the Greeks. St. Dionisius calls the Father alone the fountain of the Divinity, because the Father alone is the first fountain, or the first principle, without a beginning, or without derivation from any other Person of the Trinity. To St. Dionisius we can add St. Gregory of Nazianzen (5), who says, " *Quidquid habet Pater, idem Filii est, excepta causa.*" But all that the Saint means to say is, that the Father is the first principle, and for this special reason he is called the cause of the Son and the Holy Ghost, and this reason of the first principle cannot be applied to the Son in this way, for he has his origin from the Father; but by this the Son is not excluded from being, together with the Father, the principle of the Holy Ghost, as St. Basil, St. John Chrysostom, and several others,

(1) St. Dionys. *l.* 1, de Divin. nom. *c.* 2. (2) St. Athan. Quæs. de Nat. Dei. (3) St. Maxim. Ep. ad Marin. (4) St. Damas. *l.* 1, de Fide Orth. *c.* 11. (5) St. Greg. Nazian. Orat. 24, ad. Episcop.

with St. Athanasius (quoted in *N.* 9), attest. The same answer will apply to the quotation of St. Maximus, especially as the learned Petavius remarks (6), as the word principle, or "principium," among the Greeks means the first fountain, or first origin, which applies to the Father alone.

17. We can reply to the argument adduced from the quotation from St. John of Damascus, by remarking that the Saint here speaks guardedly, to oppose the Macedonians, who taught that the Holy Ghost was a creature of the Son, as he uses the same caution in not allowing that the Blessed Virgin should be called the Mother of Christ—*Christiparam Virginem Sanctam non dicimus*—to avoid the error of Nestorius, who called her the Mother of Christ, to argue that there were two persons in Christ. Cardinal Bessarion, however, in the Council of Florence (7), answered this objection most clearly. The Saint, he says, used the preposition *ex* to denote the principle without a beginning, as is the Father alone. St. John of Damascus himself, however, teaches the procession of the Holy Ghost from the Son, both in the place quoted, where he calls him the Spirit of the Son, as also in the subsequent part of the same chapter, in which he compares the Father to the sun, the Son to the rays, and the Holy Ghost to the light, thus showing that as the light or splendour proceeds from the sun and the rays, so the Holy Ghost proceeds from the Father and the Son: "Quemadmodum videlicet ex sole est radius, et splendor; ipse enim (Pater), et radii, et splendoris fons est; per radium autem splendor nobis communicatur, atque ipse est, qui nos collustrat, et a nobis percipitur."

18. To the objection from Theodoret we answer, that the authority of Theodoret on this point is of no weight, because here he is opposed to St. Cyril, or we may suppose also that he was opposing the Macedonians, who taught that the Holy Ghost was a creature of the Son. Finally, as to the fact related of Leo III., we answer, that the Holy Father did not disapprove of the Catholic dogma of the procession of the Holy Ghost from the Son, since he agreed on this point with the Legates of the Gallican Church, and of Charlemagne, as we see by the acts of the Legation (*Vol.* II.); but he disapproved of the addition of the word *Filioque* to the Symbol, without absolute necessity, and without the authority of the whole Church, and this addition was afterwards made by subsequent General Councils, when it was found necessary to do so, on account of the Greeks, who so frequently relapsed, and it was thus confirmed by the authority of the universal Church.

19. The last objection made by the Greeks is founded on these reasons: If the Holy Ghost proceeded from the Father and the Son, he would proceed not from one, but from two principles, for he would be produced by two Persons. We have already answered

---

(6) Petavius, *l.* 7, de Trin. *c.* 17, *n.* 12.   (7) Bessar. Orat. pro. Unit.

this in proving the dogma (*N*. 6), but we will explain it more clearly. Although the Father and the Son are two Persons, really distinct, still they neither are, nor can be, called two principles of the Holy Ghost, but only one principle, for the power by which the Holy Ghost is produced is but one alone, and is the same in the Father as in the Son. Neither is the Father the principle of the Holy Ghost by paternity, nor the Son by filiation, so that they might be two principles; but the Father and the Son are the principle of the Holy Ghost by active spiration, which, as it is one alone, and is common to both, and undivided in the Father and the Son, therefore the Father and the Son cannot be called two principles, or two spirators, because they are but one spirator of the Holy Ghost, and although both Persons spirate, still the spiration is but one. All this has been expressly laid down in the Definition of the Council of Florence.

REFUTATION V.

REFUTATION OF THE HERESY OF PELAGIUS.

1. It is not my intention here to refute all the errors of Pelagius concerning Original Sin and Free Will, but only those concerning grace. In the historical part of the work (*Chap.* v. *art.* ii. *n.* 5), I have said that the principal heresy of Pelagius was, that he denied the necessity of grace to avoid evil, or to do good, and I there mentioned the various subterfuges he had recourse to, to avoid the brand of heresy, at one time saying that grace and free-will itself was given us by God; again, that it is the law teaching us how to live; now, that it is the good example of Jesus Christ; now, that it is the pardon of sins; again, that it is an internal illustration, but on the part of the intellect alone, in knowing good and evil, though Julian, his disciple, admitted grace of the will also; but neither Pelagius nor his followers ever admitted the necessity of grace, and have even scarcely allowed that grace was necessary to do what is right more easily, and they always denied that this grace was gratuitous, but said it was given us according to our natural merits. We have, therefore, two points to establish; first, the *necessity*, and next, the *gratuity* of grace.

SECT. I.—OF THE NECESSITY OF GRACE.

2. It is first proved from that saying of Jesus Christ: "No man can come to me, except the Father who hath sent me draw him" (John, vi. 44). From these words alone it is clear that no one can perform any good action in order to eternal life without internal grace. That is confirmed by another text: "I am the vine, you

the branches: he that abideth in me, and I in him, the same beareth much fruit; for without me you can do nothing" (John, xv. 5). Therefore, Jesus Christ teaches that of ourselves we can do nothing available to salvation, and, therefore, grace is absolutely necessary for every good work, for otherwise, as St. Augustin says, we can acquire no merit for eternal life: "Ne quisquam putaret parvum aliquem fructum posse a semetipso palmitem ferre, cum dixisset hic, *fert fructum multum*, non ait, sine me parum, potestis facere: sed, *nihil potestis facere:* sive ergo parum, sive multum, sine illo fieri non potest, sine quo nihil fieri potest." It is proved, secondly, from St. Paul (called by the Fathers the Preacher of grace), who says, writing to the Philippians: " With fear and trembling work out your salvation, for it is God who worketh in you both to will and to accomplish according to his good-will" (Phil. ii. 12, 13). In the previous part of the same chapter he exhorts them to humility: " In humility let each esteem others better than themselves," as Christ, who, he says, " humbled himself, becoming obedient unto death;" and then he tells them that it is God who works all good in them. He confirms in that what St. Peter says: " God resisteth the proud, but to the humble he giveth grace" (1 Peter, v. 5). In fine, St. Paul wishes to show us the necessity of grace to desire or to put in practice every good action, and shows that for that we should be humble, otherwise we render ourselves unworthy of it. And lest the Pelagians may reply, that here the Apostle does not speak of the absolute necessity of grace, but of the necessity of having it to do good more easily, which is all the necessity they would admit, see what he says in another text: " No man can say, the Lord Jesus, but by the Holy Ghost" (1 Cor. xii. 3). If, therefore, we cannot even mention the name of Jesus with profit to our souls, without the grace of the Holy Ghost, much less can we hope to work out our salvation without grace.

3. Secondly.—St. Paul teaches us that the grace alone of the law given to us is not, as Pelagius said, sufficient, for actual grace is absolutely necessary to observe the law effectually: " For if justice be by the law, then Christ died in vain" (Gal. ii. 21). By justice is understood the observance of the Commandments, as St. John tells us: " He that doth justice is just" (1 John, iii. 7). The meaning of the Apostle, therefore, is this: If man, by the aid of the law alone, could observe the law, then Jesus Christ died in vain; but such is not the case. We stand in need of grace, which Christ procured for us by his death. Nay, so far is the law alone sufficient for the observance of the commandments, that, as the Apostle says, the very law itself is the cause of our transgressing the law, because it is by sin that concupiscence enters into us: " But sin taking occasion by the commandment, wrought in me all manner of concupiscence. For without the law sin was dead. And I lived some time without the law, but when the commandment came, sin

revived" (Rom. vii. 8, 9). St. Augustin, explaining how it is that
the knowledge of the law sooner renders us guilty than innocent,
says that this happens (1), because such is the condition of our
corrupt will, that, loving liberty, it is carried on with more vehe-
mence to what is prohibited than to what is permitted. Grace is,
therefore, that which causes us to love and to do what we know we
ought to do, as the second Council of Carthage declares: " Ut
quod faciendum cognovimus, per gratiam præstatur, etiam facere
dirigamus, atque valeamus." Who, without grace, could fulfil the
first and most important of all precepts, to love God? " Charity is
from God" (1 John, iv. 9). "The charity of God is poured forth into
our hearts by the Holy Ghost, who is given to us" (Rom. v. 5).
Holy charity is a pure gift of God, and we cannot obtain it by our
own strength. " Amor Dei, quo pervenitur ad Deum, non est nisi a
Deo," as St. Augustin says (2). Without grace how could we conquer temptations, especially grievous ones? Hear what David says:
"Being pushed, I was overturned, that I might fall, but the Lord
supported me" (Psalms, cxvii. 13). And Solomon says: "No one
can be continent (that is, resist temptations to concupiscence), except
God gave it" (Wisdom, viii. 21). Hence, the Apostle, speaking of
the temptations which assault us, says: " But in all these things we
overcome, because of him that hath loved us" (Rom. viii. 37). And
again, " Thanks be to God, who always maketh us to triumph in
Christ" (2 Cor. ii. 14). St. Paul, therefore, thanks God for the
victory over temptations, acknowledging that he conquers them
by the power of grace. St. Augustin (3) says, that this gratitude
would be in vain if the victory was not a gift of God: " Irrisoria
est enim illa actio gratiarum, si ob hoc gratiæ aguntur Deo, quod
non donavit ipse, nec fecit." All this proves how necessary grace
is to us, either to do good or avoid evil.

4. Let us consider the theological reason for the necessity of
grace. The means should always be proportioned to the end.
Now, our eternal salvation consists in enjoying God face to face,
which is, without doubt, a supernatural end; therefore, the means
which conduce to this end should be of a supernatural order, likewise. Now, everything which conduces to salvation is a means
of salvation; and, consequently, our natural strength is not sufficient
to make us do anything, in order to eternal salvation, unless it is
elevated by grace, for nature cannot do what is beyond its
strength, and an action of a supernatural order is so. Besides
our weak natural powers, which are not able to accomplish
supernatural acts, we have the corruption of our nature, occasioned
by sin, which even is a stronger proof to us of the necessity of
grace.

(1) St. Augus. *l.* de Spir. S. et litt.   (2) St. Augus. *l.* 4, con. Julian. *c.* 3.   (4) St.
Augus. loc. cit. ad Corinth.

SEC. II.—OF THE GRATUITY OF GRACE.

5. THE Apostle shows in several places that the Divine grace is, in everything, gratuitous, and comes from the mercy of God alone, independent of our natural merits. In one place he says: "For unto you it is given for Christ, not only to believe in him, but also to suffer for him" (Phil. i. 29). Therefore, as St. Augustin reflects (1), it is a gift of God, through the merits of Jesus Christ, not alone to suffer for love of him, but even to believe in him, and, if it is a gift of God, it cannot be given us through our merits. "Utrumque ostendit Dei donum, quia utrumque dixit esse donatum; nec ait, ut plenius, et perfectius credatis, sed ut credatis in eum." The Apostle writes similarly to the Corinthians, that "he had obtained mercy of the Lord, to be faithful" (1 Cor. vii. 25). It is not through any merit of ours, therefore, that we are faithful to the mercy of God. "Non ait," says St. Augustin, in the same place already quoted, "quia fidelis eram; fideli ergo datur quidem, sed datum est etiam, ut esset fidelis."

6. St. Paul next shows most clearly, that, whenever we receive light from God, or strength to act, it is not by our own merits, but a gratuitous gift from God. "For who distinguisheth thee," says the Apostle, "or what hast thou, that thou hast not received; and if thou hast received, why dost thou glory, as if thou hast not received it" (1 Cor. iv. 7)? If grace was given according to our natural merits, derived solely from the strength of our free will, then there would be something to distinguish a man who works out his salvation from one who does not do so. St. Augustin even says, that if God would give us only free will—that is, a will, free and indifferent either to good or evil, according as we use it—in case the good will would come from ourselves, and not from God, then what came from ourselves would be better than what comes from God: "Nam si nobis libera quædam voluntas ex Deo, quæ adhuc potest esse vel bona, vel mala; bono vero voluntas ex nobis est, melius est id quod a nobis, quam quod ab illo est" (2). But it is not so; for the Apostle tells us, that whatever we have from God is all gratuitously given to us, and, therefore, we should not pride ourselves on it.

7. Finally, the gratuity of grace is strongly confirmed by St. Paul, in his Epistle to the Romans (xi. 5, 6): "Even so then at this present time also, there is a remnant saved according to the election of grace. (The Apostle means, by "the remnant," those few Jews who were faithful among the multitude of unbelievers.) And if by grace, it is not now by works; otherwise grace is no more grace." Now, the Apostle could not express in stronger terms the

---

(1) St. Aug. *l.* 2, de Præd. S. S. *c.* 2.   (2) St. Aug. *l.* 2, de Pec. mer. *c.* 18.

Catholic truth, that grace is a gratuitous gift of God, and depends not on the merits of our free will, but on the mere liberality of the Lord.

SEC. III.—THE NECESSITY AND THE GRATUITY OF GRACE IS PROVED BY TRADITION; CONFIRMED BY THE DECREES OF COUNCILS AND POPES.

8. St. Cyprian (1) lays it down as a fundamental maxim in this matter, that we should not glorify ourselves, as we have nothing of ourselves: " In nullo gloriandum, quando nostrum nihil est." St. Ambrose says (2) just the same thing: " Ubique Domini virtus studiis cooperatur humanis, ut nemo possit ædificare sine Domino, nemo custodire sine Domino, nemo quicquam incipere sine Domino." And St. John Chrysostom expresses the same sentiments in several parts of his works, and in one passage, in particular, says (3): " Gratia Dei semper in beneficiis priores sibi partes vindicat." And again (4): " Quia in nostra voluntate totum post gratiam Dei relictum est, ideo et peccantibus supplicia proposita sunt, et bene operantibus retributiones." He is even clearer in another passage (5), saying, that *all* we have is not from ourselves, but merely a gift gratuitously given us: " Igitur quod accepisti, habes, neque hoc tantum, aut illud, sed quidquid habes; non enim merita tua hæc sunt, sed Dei gratia; quamvis fidem adducas, quamvis dona, quamvis doctrinæ sermonem, quamvis virtutem, omnia tibi inde provenerunt. Quid igitur habes quæso, quod acceptum non habeas? Num ipse per te recte operatus es? Non sane, sed accepisti......... Propterea cohibearis oportet, non enim tuum ad munus est, sed largientis." St. Jerome (6) says, that God assists and sustains us in all our works, and that, without the assistance of God, we can do nothing: " Dominum gratia sua nos in singulis operibus juvare, atque sustentare." And again (7): " Velle, et nolle nostrum est; ipsumque quod nostrum est, sine Dei miseratione nostrum non est." And in another place (8): " Velle, et currere meum est, sed ipsum meum, sine Dei semper auxilio non erit meum." I omit innumerable other quotations from the Fathers, which prove the same thing, and pass on to the Synodical Decrees.

9. I will not here quote all the Decrees of particular Synods against Pelagius, but only those of some particular Councils, approved of by the Apostolic See, and received by the whole Church. Among these is the Synod of Carthage, of all Africa, approved of by St. Prosper (9), which says, that the grace of God, through Jesus Christ, is not only necessary to know what is right and to practise it, but that, without it, we can neither think, say, or do anything conducive to salvation: " Cum 214.—Sacerdotibus

(1) St. Cypri. *l*. 3, ad Quir. *c*. 4.   (2) St. Amb. *l*. 7, in Luc. *c*. 3.   (3) St. Chrysos. Hom. 13, in Jean.   (4) Idem, Hom. 22, in Gen.   (5) St. Chrysos. Hom. in cap. 4, 1, ad Cor.   (6) St. Hieron. *l*. 3, con. Pelag.   (7) Idem, Ep. ad Demetri.   (8) Idem, Ep. ad Ctesiphon.   (9) St. Prosp. Resp. ad *c*. 8, Gallor.

quorum constitutionem contra inimicos gratiæ Dei totus mundus amplexus est, veraci professione, quemadmodum ipsorum habet sermo, dicamus gratiam Dei per Jesum Christum Dominum, non solum ad cognoscendam, verum ad faciendam justitiam, nos per actus singulos adjuvari; ita sine illa nihil veræ sanctæque pietatis habere, cogitare, dicere, agere valeamus."

10. The Second Synod of Orange (*cap.* vii.) teaches, that it is heretical to say that, by the power of nature, we can do anything for eternal life: " Si quis per naturæ vigorem bonum aliquod, quod ad salutem pertinet vitæ æternæ, cogitare, aut eligere posse confirmet, absque illuminatione, et inspiratione Spiritus Sancti hæretico falliter spiritu." And again it defines: " Si quis sicut augmentum, ita etiam initium Fidei, ipsumque credulitatis affectum, quo in eum credimus, qui judicat impium, et ad generationem sacri Baptismatis pervenimus, non per gratiæ donum, idest per inspirationem Spiritus Sancti corrigentem voluntatem nostram ab infidelitate ad Fidem, ab impietate ad pietatem, sed naturaliter nobis inesse dicit, Apostolicis documentis adversarius approbatur."

11. Besides the Councils, we have the authority of the Popes, who approved of several particular Synods celebrated to oppose the Pelagian errors. Innocent I., in his Epistle to the Council of Milevis, approving the Faith they professed, in opposition to Pelagius and Celestius, says that the whole Scriptures prove the necessity of grace: " Cum in omnibus Divinis paginis voluntati liberæ, non nisi adjutorium Dei legimus esse nectendum, eamque nihil posse Cœlestibus præsidiis destitutam, quonam modo huic soli possibilitatem hanc, pertinaciter defendentes, sibimet, imo plurimis Pelagius Celestiusque persuadent." Besides, Pope Zosimus, in his Encyclical Letter to all the bishops of the world, quoted by Celestine I., in his Epistle to the bishops of Paul, says much the same: " In omnibus causis, cogitationibus, motibus adjutor et protector orandus est. Superbum est enim ut quisquam sibi humana natura præsumat." In the end of the Epistle we have quoted of Celestine I., there are several chapters, taken from the definitions of other Popes, and from the Councils of Africa, concerning grace, all proving the same thing. The fifth chapter says: "Quod omnia studia, et omnia opera; ac merita sanctorum ad Dei gloriam, laudemque referenda sunt; quia non aliunde ei placet, nisi ex eo quod ipse donaverit." And in the sixth chapter it says: " Quod ita Deus in cordibus hominum, atque in ipso libero operatur, arbitrio ut sancta cogitatio, pium consilium, omnisque motus bona voluntatio ex Deo sit, quia per illum aliquid boni possumus, sine quo nihil possumus."

12. The Pelagians were formally condemned in the General Council of Ephesus, as Cardinal Orsi tells us (10). Nestorius received the Pelagian bishops, who came to Constantinople, most

---

(10) C. Orsi; Ir. Ecc. *t.* 13, *l.* 29, *n.* 52, cum. St. Prosp. *l.* con. Collat. *c.* 21.

graciously, for he agreed with Pelagius in this, that grace is given to us by God, not gratuitously, but according to our merits. This erroneous doctrine was agreeable to Nestorius, as it favoured his system, that the Word had chosen the Person of Christ as the temple of his habitation, on account of his virtues, and therefore the Fathers of the Council of Ephesus, knowing the obstinacy of those Pelagian bishops, condemned them as heretics. Finally, the Council of Trent (*Sess.* vi. *de Justif.*) defines the same doctrine in two Canons. The second Canon says: " Si quis dixerit Divinam gratiam ad hoc solum dari, ut facilius homo juste vivere, ac ad vitam æternam promoveri possit, quasi per liberum arbitrium sine gratia utrumque, sed ægre tamen et difficulter possit; anathema sit." And in the third Canon the Council says: " Si quis dixerit, sine præveniente Spiritus Sanctus inspiratione, atque ejus adjutoriis hominem credere, sperare, diligere, aut pœnitere posse sicut oportet, ut ei justificationis gratia conferatur; anathema sit."

SEC. IV.—OBJECTIONS ANSWERED.

13. THE Pelagians object, firstly, if you admit that grace is absolutely necessary to perform any act conducive to salvation, you must confess that man has no liberty, and free will is destroyed altogether. We answer, with St. Augustin, that man, after the fall, is undoubtedly no longer free without grace, either to begin or bring to perfection any act conducive to eternal life, but by the grace of God he recovers this liberty, for the strength which he is in need of to do what is good is subministered to him by grace, through the merits of Jesus Christ; this grace restores his liberty to him, and gives him strength to work out his eternal salvation, without, however, compelling him to do so: " Peccato Adæ arbitrium liberum de hominum natura perisse, non dicimus, sed ad peccandum valere in homine subdito diabolo. Ad bene autem, pieque vivendum non valere, nisi ipsa voluntas hominis Dei gratia fuerit liberata, et ad omne bonum actionis, sermonis cogitationis adjuta." Such are St. Augustin's sentiments (1).

14. They object, secondly, that God said to Cyrus: " Who say to Cyrus, thou art my shepherd, and thou shalt perform all my pleasure" (Isaias, xliv. 28); and, in *chap.* xlvi. *v.* 11, he calls him, " a man of his will." Now, say the Pelagians, Cyrus was an idolater, and, therefore, deprived of the grace which is given by Jesus Christ, and still, according to the text of the Prophet, he observed all the natural precepts; therefore without grace a man may observe all the precepts of the law of nature. We answer, that in order to understand this, we should distinguish, with theologians, between the will of *Beneplacitum* and the will called of *Signum*. The *Bene-*

---

(1) St. Augus. *l.* 2, con. 2, Epis. Pelag. *c.* 5.

placitum is that established by God by an absolute decree, and which God wills should be infallibly followed by us. This is always fulfilled by the wicked. But the other will (voluntas signi) is that which regards the Divine commandments signified to us; but for the fulfilment of this Divine will our co-operation is required, and this we cannot apply of ourselves, but require the assistance of the Divine grace to do so; this will the wicked do not always fulfil. Now the Lord in Isaias does not speak of this will (*Signum*), in respect of Cyrus, but of the other will (*Beneplacitum*), that is, that Cyrus should free the Jews from captivity, and permit them to rebuild the city and temple; that was all that was required then from him, but, on the other hand, he was an idolater, and a sanguinary invader of the neighbouring kingdoms, and, therefore, he did not fulfil the precepts of the natural law.

15. They object, thirdly, that fact related by St. Mark, of the man who was exhorted by our Redeemer to observe the commandments, and he answered: " Master, all these things I have observed from my youth," and the Evangelist proves that he spoke the truth, for " Jesus, looking on him, loved him"(Mark, x. 20, 21). See here, say the Pelagians, is a man who, without grace, and who had not even as yet believed in Christ, observed all the natural precepts. We answer, first, this man was a Jew, and, as such, believed in God, and also implicitly in Christ, and there was, therefore, nothing to prevent him from having grace to observe the commandments of the Decalogue. Secondly—We answer, that when he said, " All these things I have observed from my youth," we are not to understand that he observed all the Commandments, but only those which Christ mentioned to him: " Do not commit adultery, do not kill, do not steal," &c. Even the Gospel itself proves that he was not ardent in the observance of the precept to love God above all things, for when Christ told him to leave his wealth and follow him, he refused to obey, and, therefore, our Lord tacitly reproved him, when he said: " How hardly shall they who have riches enter into the kingdom of God"(*ver.* 23).

16. They object, fourthly, that St. Paul, while still under the law, and not having yet received grace, observed all the law, as he himself attests: " According to the justice that is in the law, conversing without blame" (Phil. iii. 6). We answer, that the Apostle, at that time, observed the law externally, but not internally, by loving God above all things, as he himself says: " For we ourselves, also, were some time unwise, incredulous, erring, slaves to divers desires and pleasures, living in malice and envy, hating one another" (Tit. iii. 3).

17. They object, fifthly, all the precepts of the Decalogue are either possible or impossible; if they are possible, we can observe them by the strength of our free will alone, but if they are impossible, no one is bound to observe them, for no one is obliged to do im-

possibilities. We answer, that all these precepts are impossible to us without grace, but are quite possible with the assistance of grace. This is the answer of St. Thomas (2): " Illud quod possumus cum auxilio Divino, non est nobis omnino impossibile...... Unde Hieronymus confitetur, sic nostrum esse liberum arbitrium, ut dicamus nos semper indigere Dei auxilio." Therefore, as the observance of the Commandments is quite possible to us with the assistance of the Divine grace, we are bound to observe them. We will answer the other objections of the Pelagians in the next chapter, the Refutation of the Semi-Pelagian heresy.

REFUTATION VI.

OF THE SEMPELAGIAN HERESY.

1. THE Semipelagians admit that the strength of the will of man has been weakened by Original Sin, and, therefore, allow that grace is requisite to do what is right; but they deny that it is necessary for the beginning of Faith, or for the desire of eternal salvation; for they say that as the belief of sick people in the utility of medicine, and the wish to recover their health, are not works for which medicine is necessary, so the commencement of belief—or call it an affection for the Faith—and the desire of eternal salvation, are not works for which grace is necessary. But we are bound to believe with the Catholic Church, that every beginning of Faith, and every good desire we entertain, is a working of grace in us.

SEC. I.—THE COMMENCEMENT OF FAITH AND EVERY GOOD DESIRE IS NOT FROM OURSELVES, BUT FROM GOD.

2. FIRST, that it is clearly proved from St. Paul: " Not that we are sufficient to think anything of ourselves, as of ourselves; but our sufficiency is from God" (2 Cor. iii. 5). Thus the beginning of believing—that is, not that beginning of Faith arising from the intellect, which naturally sees the truth of the Faith, but that pious desire of Faith, which is not yet formal faith, for it is no more than a thought, of wishing to believe, and which, as St. Augustin says, precedes belief—this good thought, according to St. Paul, comes from God alone. Such is the explanation St. Augustin gives of the text: " Attendant hic, et verba ista perpendant, qui putant ex nobis esse Fidei cœptum, et ex Deo esse Fidei supplementum. Quis enim non videt, prius esse cogitare quam credere? Nullus quippe credit aliquid, nisi prius crediderit esse credendum. Quamvis enim rapte, quamvis celerrime credendi voluntatem quædam

(2) St Thom. 1, 2, 9, 109, *a.* 4, *ad.* 2.

cogitationes antevolent, moxque illa ita sequatar, ut quasi conjunctissima comitetur; necesse est tamen, ut omnia quæ credentur, præveniente cogitatione credantur.......Quod ergo pertinet ad religionem et pietatem (de qua loquebatur Apostolus), si non sumus idonei cogitare aliquid quasi ex nobismetipsis, quod sine cogitatione non possumus, sed sufficientia nostra, ex Deo est; profecto non sumus idonei credere aliquid quasi ex nobismetipsis, quod sine cogitatione non possumus, sed sufficientia nostra, qua credere incipiamus, ex Deo est"(1).

3. It is proved, secondly, by another text of St. Paul, in which he shows the reason of our proposition. He says: "For who distinguisheth thee? or what hast thou that thou hast not received?" (1 Cor. iv. 7). If the beginning of that good will, which disposes us to receive the Faith from God, or any other gift of grace, came from ourselves, that would *distinguish* us from others who had not this commencement of a wish for eternal life. But St. Paul says, that all that we have, in which is comprised every first desire of Faith or salvation, is received from God: "What hast thou that thou hast not received?" St. Augustin was of opinion, for a time, that Faith in God was not from God, but from ourselves, and that by that we obtain afterwards from God, the grace to lead a good life; but this text of the Apostle chiefly induced him to retract this sentiment afterwards, as he himself confesses (2): " Quo præcipue testimonio etiam ipse convictus sum, cum similiter errarem: putans Fidem, qua in Deum credimus, non esse donum Dei, sed a nobis esse in nobis, et per illam nos impetrare Dei dona, quibus temperanter et juste, et pie vivamus in hoc sæculo."

4. That is confirmed by what the Apostle says in another place: " For by grace you are saved, through faith, and that not of yourselves, for it is the gift of God. Not of works that no man man may glory" (Ephes. ii. 8, 9). St. Augustin (3) says that Pelagius himself, to escape condemnation from the Synod of Palestine, condemned (though only apparently) the proposition that " grace is given to us according to our merits." Hence, the Saint says: "Quis autem, dicat eum, qui jam cœpit credere, ab illo inquam credidit, nihil mereri? Unde sit, ut jam merenti cetera dicantur addi retributione Divina: ac per hoc gratiam Dei secundum merita nostra dari: quod objectum sibi Pelagius, ne damnaretur, ipse damnavit."

5. Our proposition is proved, thirdly, from the words of the Incarnate Wisdom himself: "No man can come to me, except the Father, who hath sent me, draw him" (John, vi. 44). And in another place he says: "Without me you can do nothing" (John, xv. 5). From this it is manifest that we cannot, with our own strength, even dispose ourselves to receive from God the actual graces which conduce to life everlasting, for actual grace is of a

1) St. Aug. *l.* de Praed. S. S. *c.* 2.   (3) St. Aug. Ibid. *c.* 1.   (2) Ibid. *c.* 3.

supernatural order, and, therefore, a disposition morally natural cannot dispose us to receive a supernatural grace. "If by grace it is not now by works," says St. Paul, "otherwise grace is no more grace" (Rom. xi. 6). It is certain, therefore, that grace is given to us by God, not according to our natural merits, but according to his Divine liberality. God who makes perfect in us every good work, He also commenced it: " He who began a good work in you will perfect it unto the day of Christ Jesus" (Phil. i. 6). And in another place the Apostle says that every good wish has its beginning from God, and is brought to a conclusion by Him. "For it is God who worketh in you, both to will and to accomplish, according to his good will" (Phil. ii. 13). And here we are called on to advert to another error of the Semipelagians, who asserted that grace was necessary to do what was good, but not necessary for perseverance in goodness. But this error was condemned by the Council of Trent (*Sess.* vi. *cap.* 13), which teaches that the gift of perseverance can only be obtained from God, who alone gives it: "Similiter de perseverantiæ munere........quod quidem aliunde haberi non potest nisi ab eo, qui potens est eum qui stat statuere, ut perseveranter stet."

SEC. II.—OBJECTIONS ANSWERED.

6. THE Semipelagians object, first, some passages of the Scripture, from which it would appear, that a good will and the beginning of good works are attributed to us, and the perfection of them only to God. In the first book of Kings (vii. 3), we read: "Prepare your hearts for the Lord;" and in St. Luke (iii. 4): "Prepare ye the way of the Lord, make straight his paths." We also see in Zachary: "Be converted to me.......and I will be converted to you;" and St. Paul speaks even plainer to the Romans (vii. 18), for he says: "For to will is present with me; but to accomplish that which is good I find not." It would appear also, from the Acts of the Apostles (xvii. 7), that the Faith which Cornelius received was to be attributed to his prayers. To these and to similar texts we answer, that the prevenent (*preveniens*) internal grace of the Holy Ghost is not excluded by them, but they suppose it, and we are exhorted to correspond to this grace, to remove the impediments to the greater graces, which God has prepared for those who correspond to him. Thus when the Scripture says, "Prepare your hearts," "Be converted to me," &c., it does not attribute to our free will the beginning of Faith or of conversion, without preventing or prevenent grace (*gratia preveniens*), but admonishes us to correspond to it, and teaches us that this preventing grace leaves us at liberty either to choose or reject what is good for us. Thus, on the other hand, when the Scripture says, "The will is prepared by the Lord," and when

we say, "Convert us, O God our Saviour" (Psalms, lxxxiv, 5), we are admonished that grace prepares us to do what is good, but does not deprive us of liberty, if we refuse to do so. This is precisely what the Council of Trent says: "Cum dicitur: *Convertimini ad me, et ego convertar ad vos*, libertatis nostræ admonemur. Cum respondemus: *Converte ad vos nos Domine, et convertemur*, Dei nos gratia præveniri confitemur." The same answer applies to that text of St. Paul: "For to will is present with me, but to accomplish that which is good I find not" (Romans, vii. 18). The meaning of the Apostle is this, that he, being then justified, had the grace to desire what was good, but to perfect it was not his work, but the work of God; but he does not say that he had from himself the desire of doing good. The same answer applies to what is said of Cornelius, because, although he obtained his conversion to the Faith by his prayers, still these prayers were accompanied by preventing grace.

7. They object, secondly, what Christ says in St. Mark (xvi. 16): "He that believeth and is baptized shall be saved." Here they say one thing is required, that is Faith; another is promised, salvation. Therefore, what is required is in the power of man; what is promised is in the power of God. We answer with St. Augustin (1): "St. Paul," says the holy Doctor, "writes: 'If by the Spirit you mortify the deeds of the flesh, you are saved'" (Rom. viii. 13). Here one thing is required, the mortification of the flesh; another thing is promised, that is, eternal life. Now, if the argument of the Semipelagians was worth anything, that what is required is in our power, without the assistance of grace, it would follow, that without grace we have it in our power to conquer our passions; but this, the Saint says, "is the damnable error of the Pelagians." He then gives a direct answer to the Semipelagians, and tells them that it is not in our power to give what is required of us, without grace, but with grace it is, and he then concludes: "Sicut ergo, quamvis donum Dei sit facta carnis mortificare, exigitur tamen a nobis proposito præmio vitæ; ita donum Dei est Fides, quamvis et ipsa, dum dicitur, *si credideris, salvus eris*, proposito præmio salutis exigatur a nobis. Ideo enim hæc et nobis præcipiuntur, et dona Dei esse monstrantur, ut intelligatur, quod et nos ea faciamus, et Deus facit ut illa faciamus."

8. They object, thirdly, that God, in a thousand passages in the Scriptures, exhorts us to pray and seek, if we wish to receive grace; therefore, they say it is in our power to pray at all events, and if the working out of our salvation and faith is not in our own hands, still the desire of believing and being saved is in our power. St. Augustin (2) also answers this argument. It is not the fact, he says, that prayer (such as it ought to be) is in our own unaided power. The gift of prayer comes from grace, as the Apostle says;

(1) St. Aug. *l.* de Dono. Persev. *c.* 23.   (2) St. Aug. de Nat. & Gratia, *c.* 44.

"Likewise, the Spirit also helpeth our infirmity. For we know not what we should pray for as we ought, but the Spirit himself asketh for us" (Rom. viii. 26). Hence, St. Augustin says (3): " Quid est, ipse Spiritus interpellat, nisi interpellare facit;" and he adds: " Attendant quomodo falluntur, qui putant esse a nobis, non dari nobis, ut petamus, quæramus, pulsemus, et hoc esse dicunt, quod gratia præceditur merito nostro..... Nec volunt intelligere, etiam hoc Divini muneris esse, ut oremus, hoc est petamus, quæramus, atque pulsemus; accepimus enim Spiritum adoptionis, in quo clamamus Abba Pater." The same holy doctor teaches us that God gives to all the grace to pray, and through prayer the means of obtaining grace to fulfil the commandments; for otherwise, if one had not the efficacious grace to fulfil the commandments, and had not the grace to obtain this efficacious grace, through means of prayer either, he would be bound to observe a law which to him was impossible. But such, St. Augustin says, is not the case. Our Lord admonishes us to pray with the grace of prayer, which he gives to all, so that by praying we may obtain efficacious grace to observe the commandments. He says: " Eo ipso quo firmissime creditur, Deum impossibilia non præcipere, hinc admonemur et in facilibus (that is, in prayer) quid agamus, et in difficilibus (that is, observing the commandments) quid petamus." This is what the Council of Trent afterwards decreed on the same subject (*Sess.* vi. *c.* xi.), following the remarkable expressions of the great Doctor: " Deus impossibilia non jubet, sed jubendo monet, et facere quod possis, et petere quod non possis, et adjuvat ut possis" (4). Thus by prayer we obtain strength to do what we cannot do of ourselves; but we cannot even boast of praying, for our very prayer is a gift from God.

9. That God gives generally to all the grace of praying, St. Augustin (independently of the passages already quoted) teaches in almost every page of his works. In one place he says: " Nulli enim homini ablatum est scire utilitur quærere" (5). And again: " Quid ergo aliud ostenditur nobis, nisi quia et petere et quærere. Ille concedit, qui ut hæc faciamus, jubet" (6). In another place, speaking of those who do not know what to do to obtain salvation, he says, they should make use of what they have received, that is, of the grace of prayer, and that thus they will obtain salvation (7): " Sed hoc quoque accipiet, si hoc quod accipit bene usus fuerit; accepit autem, ut pie et diligenter quærat, si volet." Besides, in another passage (8), he explains all this more diffusely, for he says it is for this reason that God commands us to pray, that by prayer we may obtain his gifts, and that he would invite us in vain to pray, unless he first gave us grace to be able to pray, and by prayer to obtain grace to fulfil what we are commanded: " Pre-

---

(3) St. Aug. Ibid. (4) Ibid. (5) St. Aug. *l.* de Lib. Arb. *c.* 19, *n.* 58.
(6) Idem, *l.* 1, ad Simp. *q.* 2. (7) Idem, Trac. 26, in Joan. *c.* 22, *n.* 65.
(8) St. Aug. de Grat. & Lib. Arb. *c.* 18.

cepto admonitum est liberum arbitrium, ut quæreret Dei donum; at quidem sine suo fructu admoneretur, nisi prius acciperet aliquid dilectionis, ut addi sibi quæreret, unde quod jubebatur, impleret." Mark how the words, " aliquid dilectionis," that is, the grace by which man prays, if he wishes, and by prayer obtains the actual grace to observe the Commandments. And thus, on the day of judgment, no one can complain that he is lost for want of grace to co-operate to his salvation, because if he had not actual grace to work out his salvation, at all events he had grace to pray, which is denied to no one, and if he prayed, he would obtain salvation according to the promises of our Lord: " Ask, and it shall be given unto you; seek, and you shall find" (Matt. vii. 7).

10. They object, fourthly, and say: If even for the beginning of Faith preventing grace is necessary, then the infidels, who do not believe, are excusable, because the Gospel was never preached to them, and they, therefore, never refused to hear it. Jansenius (9) says that these are not excused, but are condemned, without having had any sufficient grace, either proximate or remote, to become converted to the Faith, and that is, he says, in punishment of original sin, which has deprived them of all help. And those theologians, he says, who in general teach that these infidels have sufficient grace for salvation, some way or other have adopted this opinion from the Semipelagians. This sentiment of Jansenius, however, is not in accordance with the Scripture, which says that God " will have all men to be saved, and come to the knowledge of the truth" (1 Tim. ii. 4); " He was the true light, which enlighteneth every man that cometh into the world" (John, i. 9); " Who is the Saviour of all men, especially the faithful" (1 Tim. iv. 10); " And he is the propitiation for our sins, and not for ours only, but also for those of the whole world" (1 John, ii. 2); " Who gave himself a redemption for all" (1 Tim. ii. 6). From these texts Bellarmin (10) remarks, that St. Chrysostom, St. Augustin, and St. Prosper conclude that God never fails to give to all men sufficient assistance to work out their salvation, if they desire it. And St. Augustin (11), especially, and St. Prosper (12), express this doctrine in several parts of their works. Besides, this sentiment of Jansenius is in direct opposition to the condemnation pronounced by Alexander VIII., in 1690, on that proposition, that Pagans, Jews, &c., have no sufficient grace: " Pagani, Judæi, Hæretici, aliique hujus generis nullum omnino accipiunt a Jesu Christo influxum: adeoque hinc recte inferes, in illis esse voluntatem nudam et inermem sine omni gratia sufficiente." Neither does it agree with the condemnation pronounced by Clement XI. on two propositions of Quesnel (26, 29): " That there are no graces unless by Faith," and that " no grace is granted outside the Church."

(9) Jansen. *l.* 3, de Grat. Christ. *c.* 11.   (10) Bellar. *l.* 2, de Grat. & Lib. Arb. *c.* 3.
(11) St. Aug. *l.* de Spir.. & lit. *c.* 33, & in Ps. 11, *n.* 7.   (12) St. Pros. de Voc. Gent. *l.* 2, *c.* 5.

11. Still we answer the Semipelagians, and say, that infidels who arrive at the use of reason, and are not converted to the Faith, cannot be excused, because though they do not receive sufficient proximate grace, still they are not deprived of remote grace, as a means of becoming converted. But what is this remote grace? St. Thomas (13) explains it, when he says, that if any one was brought up in the wilds, or even among brute beasts, and if he followed the law of natural reason, to desire what is good, and to avoid what is wicked, we should certainly believe either that God, by an internal inspiration, would reveal to him what he should believe, or would send some one to preach the Faith to him, as he sent Peter to Cornelius. Thus, then, according to the Angelic Doctor, God, at least remotely, gives to the infidels, who have the use of reason, sufficient grace to obtain salvation, and this grace consists in a certain instruction of the mind, and in a movement of the will, to observe the natural law; and if the infidel co-operates with this movement, observing the precepts of the law of nature, and abstaining from grievous sins, he will certainly receive, through the merits of Jesus Christ, the grace proximately sufficient to embrace the Faith, and save his soul.

REFUTATION VII.

REFUTATION OF THE HERESY OF NESTORIUS, WHO TAUGHT THAT IN CHRIST THERE ARE TWO PERSONS.

1. NESTORIUS is not charged with any errors regarding the mystery of the Trinity. Among the other heresies which he combated in his sermons, and to punish which he implored the Emperor Theodosius, was that of the Arians, who denied that the Word was consubstantial to the Father. We, therefore, have no reason to doubt that he acknowledged the Divinity of the Word, and his consubstantiality with the Father. His heresy particularly attacked the mystery of the Incarnation of the Divine Word, for he denied the hypostatic or personal union of the Word with the humanity. He maintained that the Word was only united with the humanity of Jesus Christ, just in the same way as with the saints, only in a more perfect manner, and from the first moment of his conception. In his writings he explains this point over and over in different ways, but always only as a simple moral and accidental union between the Person of the Word and the humanity of Jesus Christ, but he never admits a hypostatic or personal union. At one time he said it was an union of *habitation*, that is, that the Word inha-

---

(13) St. Thom. Quæs. 14, de Verit. *art.* 11, *ad.* 1.

bited the humanity of Christ, as his temple; next it was, he said, an union of *affection*, such as exists between two friends. He then said it was an union of *operation*, inasmuch as the Word availed himself of the humanity of Christ as an instrument to work miracles, and other supernatural operations. Then that it was an union of *grace*, because the Word, by means of sanctifying grace and other Divine gifts, is united with Christ. Finally, he teaches that this union consists in a moral communication, by which the Word communicates his dignity and excellence to the humanity, and on this account the humanity of Christ should, he said, be adored and honoured, as we honour the purple of the Sovereign, or the throne on which he sits. He always denied with the most determined obstinacy, that the Son of God was made man, was born, suffered, or died for the redemption of man. Finally, he denied the communication of the *Idioms*, which follows from the Incarnation of the Word, and, consequently, he denied that the Blessed Virgin was truly and properly the Mother of God, blasphemously teaching that she only conceived and brought forth a mere man.

2. This heresy saps the very foundation of the Christian religion, by denying the mystery of the Incarnation, and we will attack it on its two principal points, the first of which consists in denying the *hypostatic union*, that is, the union of the Person of the Word with human nature, and, consequently, admits that there are two Persons in Christ—the Person of the Word, which dwells in the humanity as in a temple, and the person of man, purely human, and which does not ascend to a higher degree than mere humanity. The second point consists in denying that the Blessed Virgin is truly and properly the Mother of God. These two points we will refute in the two following paragraphs.

SEC. I.—IN JESUS CHRIST THERE IS BUT THE ONE PERSON OF THE WORD ALONE, WHICH TERMINATES THE TWO NATURES, DIVINE AND HUMAN, WHICH BOTH SUBSIST IN THE SAME PERSON OF THE WORD, AND, THEREFORE, THIS ONE PERSON IS, AT THE SAME TIME, TRUE GOD AND TRUE MAN.

3. Our first proof is taken from all those passages in the Scripture, in which it is said that God was made flesh, that God was born of a Virgin, that God emptied himself, taking the form of a servant, that God has redeemed us with his blood, that God died for us on the cross. Every one knows that God could not be conceived, nor born, nor suffer, nor die, in his Divine nature, which is eternal, impassible, and immortal; therefore, if the Scripture teaches us that God was born, and suffered, and died, we should understand it according to his human nature, which had a beginning, and was passible and mortal. And, therefore, if the person in which the human nature subsists was not the Divine Word, St. Matthew would state what is false when he says that God was conceived and born of a Virgin: " Now all this was done that it might

be fulfilled which the Lord spoke by the Prophet, saying: Behold a Virgin shall be with child and bring forth a Son, and they shall call his name Emmanuel, which being interpreted, is God with us" (Matt. i. 22, 23). St. John expressly says the same thing: "The Word was made flesh and dwelt among us, and we saw his glory, the glory as it were of the only begotten of the Father, full of grace and truth" (John, i. 14). The Apostle also would have stated a falsehood in saying that God humbled himself, taking the form of a servant: "For let this mind be in you, which was also in Christ Jesus. Who, being in the form of God, thought it not robbery to be equal with God, but emptied himself, taking the form of a servant, being made in the likeness of men and in habit found as a man" (Phil. ii. 5-7). St. John would also state what is not the fact, when he says that God died for us: "In this we have known the charity of God, because he hath laid down his life for us" (1 John, iii. 6); and St. Paul says: "The Holy Ghost placed you bishops to rule the Church of God, which he has purchased with his own blood" (Acts, xx. 18); and speaking of the death of our Redeemer, he says: "For if they had known it, they never would have crucified the Lord of glory" (1 Cor. ii. 8).

4. Now it would be false to speak of God in that manner, if God only inhabited the humanity of Jesus Christ accidentally, as a temple, or morally, through affection, or was not united hypostatically or personally, just as it would be false to say that God was born of St. Elizabeth, when she brought forth the Baptist, in whom God inhabited before his birth, by sanctifying grace, and it would be false to say that God died stoned when St. Stephen was stoned to death, or that he died beheaded when St. Paul was beheaded, because he was united to these saints through the medium of love, and of the many heavenly gifts he bestowed on them, so that between them and God there existed a true moral union. When, therefore, it is said that God was born and died, the reason is because the person sustaining and terminating the assumed humanity is truly God, that is the eternal Word. There is, therefore, in Christ but one Person, in which two natures subsist, and in the unity of the Person of the Word, which terminates the two natures, consists the hypostatic union.

5. This truth is also proved, secondly, from those passages of the Scriptures in which Christ-Man is called God, the Son of God, the only begotten Son, the proper Son of God, for a man cannot be called God or Son of God, unless the person who terminates the human nature is truly God. Now Christ-Man is called the supreme God by St. Paul: "And of whom is Christ according to the flesh, who is over all things God blessed for ever" (Rom. xix. 5). We read in St. Matthew that Christ himself, after calling himself the Son of Man, asked his disciples whom do they believe him to be, and St. Peter answers that he is the Son of the living God: "Jesus

saith to them, but whom do you say that I am? Simon Peter answered and said: Thou art Christ, the Son of the living God. And Jesus answering, said to him: Blessed art thou, Simon Barjona, because flesh and blood hath not revealed it to thee, but my Father who is in heaven" (Matt. xvi. 15-17). Then Jesus himself, at the very time that he calls himself man, approves of Peter's answer, who calls him the Son of God, and says that this answer was revealed to him by his eternal Father. Besides, we read in St. Matthew (iii. 17), St. Luke (ix. 13), and St. Mark (i. 11), that Christ, while he was actually receiving Baptism as man from St. John, was called by God his beloved Son: "This is my beloved Son, in whom I am well pleased." St. Peter tells us that in Mount Thabor the Eternal Father spoke the same words: " For, he received from God the Father, honour and glory; this voice coming down to him from the excellent glory: This is my beloved Son, in whom I have pleased myself, hear ye him" (2 Pet. i. 17). Christ, as man, is called the only begotten Son of the Eternal Father, by St. John: " The only begotten Son, who is in the bosom of the Father, he hath declared him" (John, i. 18). As man alone, he is called God's own Son: " He spared not his own Son, but delivered him up for us all" (Rom. viii. 32). After so many proofs from the Holy Scriptures, who will be rash enough to deny that the man Christ is truly God?

6. The Divinity of Jesus Christ is proved from all these passages of the Scriptures, in which that which can only be attributed to God is attributed to the Person of Christ-Man, and from thence we conclude that this Person, in which the two natures subsist, is true God. Jesus, speaking of himself, says: " I and the Father are one " (John, x. 30); and in the same place he says: " The Father is in me, and I in the Father" (*ver.* 38). In another passage we read that St. Philip, one day speaking with Jesus Christ, said: " Lord, show us the Father," and our Lord answered: " So long a time have I been with thee, and have you not known me? Philip, he that seeth me seeth the Father also. Believe you not that I am in the Father and the Father in me?" (John, xiv. 8, 11). By these words Christ showed he was the same God as the Father. Christ himself said to the Jews that he was eternal: " Amen, amen, I say unto you, before Abraham was I am " (John, vii. 58); and he says, also, that he works the same as the Father: " My Father worketh until now, and I work..... for what things soever he doth, these the Son also doth in like manner " (John, v. 17). He also says: " All things whatsoever the Father hath are mine " (John, xvi. 15). Now, if Christ was not true God all these sayings would be blasphemous, attributing to himself what belongs to God alone.

7. The Divinity of Christ-Man is proved from those other passages of the Scriptures, in which it is said that the Word, or the

Son of God, became incarnate: "The Word was made flesh and dwelt among us" (John, i. 14); "For God so loved the world as to give his only begotten Son" (John, iii. 16); "He spared not his own Son, but delivered him up for all of us" (Rom. viii. 32). Now, if the Person of the Word was not hypostatically united—that is, in one Person with the humanity of Christ—it could not be said that the Word was incarnate, and was sent by the Father to redeem the world, because if this personal union did not exist between the Word and the humanity of Christ, there would be only a moral union of habitation, or affection, or grace, or gifts, or operation, and in this sense we might say that the Father and the Holy Ghost became incarnate also, for all these sorts of unions are not peculiar to the Person of the Word alone, but to the Father and the Holy Ghost, likewise, for God is united in this manner with the Angels and Saints. God has frequently sent Angels as his ambassadors; but as St. Paul says, our Lord has never taken the nature of angels: "For nowhere doth he take hold of the angels, but of the seed of Abraham he taketh hold" (Heb. ii. 16). Thus, if Nestorius means to assert that unions of this sort are sufficient to enable us to say that the Word was incarnate, we should also say that the Father was incarnate, for the Father, by his graces and his heavenly gifts, was united with, and morally dwelt in, Jesus Christ, according to what our Lord himself says: "The Father is in me...... the Father remaining in me" (John, xiv. 10). We should also admit that the Holy Ghost became incarnate, for Isaias, speaking of the Messiah, says: "The Spirit of the Lord shall rest upon him, the Spirit of wisdom and understanding" (Isaias, xi. 2). And in St. Luke it is said, that "Jesus was full of the Holy Ghost" Luke, iv. 1). In fine, according to this explanation, every Saint or holy person who loves God could be called the Incarnate Word, for our Saviour says: "If any one love me...... my Father will love him, and we will come to him, and will make our abode with him" (John, xiv. 23). Thus Nestorius should admit, either that the Word is not incarnate, or that the Father and the Holy Ghost are incarnate. This was the unanswerable argument of St. Cyril (1): "Quod unus sit Christus, ejusmodi in habitatione Verbum non fieret caro, sed potius hominis incola; et conveniens fuerit illum non hominem, sed humanum vocare, quemadmodum et qui Nazareth inhabitavit, Nazarenus dictus est, non Nazareth. Quinimo nihil prorsus obstiterit......hominem vocari una cum Filio etiam Patrem, et Spiritum Sanctum, habitavit enim in nobis."

8. I might here add all those texts of Scripture in which Christ is spoken of as only one Person subsisting in two natures, as in St. Paul: "One Lord Jesus Christ, by whom are all things," &c. (1 Cor. viii. 6), and several other texts of like import. If Nestorius

---

(1) St. Cyril, Dial. 9.

insisted that there were two Persons in Christ, he makes out not *one*, but *two* Lords—one, the Person of the Word which dwells in Christ, and the other the human Person. I will not detain the reader, however, by quoting more Scriptural authorities, for every proof of the Incarnation upsets the whole structure of Nestorianism.

9. We now come to Tradition, which has always taught the Faith of the unity of the Person of Jesus Christ in the Incarnation of the Word. In the Apostles' Creed, taught by the Apostles themselves, we say, we believe " in Jesus Christ, his only Son, our Lord, who was conceived of the Holy Ghost, born of the Virgin Mary." Now, the same Jesus Christ who was conceived, born, and died, is the only Son of God, our Lord; but that would not be the case, if in Christ, as Nestorius taught, there was not only a Divine, but a human Person, because he who was born and died would not have been the only Son of God, but a mere man.

10. This profession of Faith is laid down more amply in the Nicene Creed, in which the Fathers defined the Divinity of Jesus Christ, and his consubstantiality with the Father, and thus condemned the heresy of Nestorius, even before it sprung up: " We believe," say the Fathers, " in one Lord Jesus Christ the Son of God, the only begotten Son of the Father, that is, of the substance of the Father, God of God, light of light, true God of true God, born, not made, consubstantial to the Father, by whom all things were made, both those in heaven and those on the earth, who for us men, and for our salvation, descended and was incarnate, and was made man; he suffered and arose the third day," &c. Behold, therefore, how Jesus Christ alone, who is called God, the only begotten of the Father, and consubstantial to the Father, is called man, who was born, died, and rose again. This same Symbol was approved of by the second General Council, that is, the first of Constantinople, which was also held before Nestorius promulgated his blasphemies; and according to the same Symbol of Nice, he was condemned in the third General Council, that of Ephesus, which was held against his errors. In the Symbol attributed to St. Athanasius, the dogma is thus established in opposition to Nestorianism: " Our Lord Jesus Christ is God and man..... equal to the Father, according to his Divinity; less than the Father, according to his humanity; who, although he is God and man, these are not two, but one Christ..... one altogether not by the confusion of substance, but by ' Unity of the Person.' "

11. Besides those Symbols, we have the authority of the holy Fathers who wrote before the rise of this heresy. St. Ignatius the Martyr (2) says: " Singuli communiter omnes ex gratia nominatim convenientes in una Fide, et uno Jesu Christo, secundum carnem ex genere Davidis, Filio hominis, et Filio Dei." See here how he

---

(2) St. Ignat. Epis. ad Eph. *n*. 20.

mentions *one* Jesus Christ, the Son of man and the Son of God. St. Irænus says (3): " Unum et eundem esse Verbum Dei, et hunc esse unigenitum, et hunc incarnatum pro salute nostra Jesum Christum." St. Dionisius of Alexandria, in a Synodical Epistle, refutes Paul of Samosata, who said that in Christ there were two Persons and two Sons; the one the Son of God, born before all ages; the other the Son of David, called Christ. St. Athanasius (4) says: " Homo una Persona, et unum animal est ex spiritu et carne compositum, ad cujus similitudinem intelligendum est, Christum unam esse Personam, et non duas"—that, as soul and body make but one person in man, so the Divine and human nature constitute but one Person in Christ. St. Gregory of Nazianzen (5) says: " Id quod non erat assumpsit, non quo factus, sed unum ex duobus fieri substinens; Deus enim ambo sunt id quod assumpsit, et quod est assumptum, naturæ duæ in unum concurrentes, non duo Filii." St. John Chrysostom (6) thus writes: " Etsi enim (*in Christo*) duplex natura; verumtamen indivisibilis unio in una filiationis Persona, et substantia." St. Ambrose (7) tersely explains: " Non alter ex Patre, alter ex Virgine, sed item aliter ex Patre, aliter ex Virgine." St. Jerome, opposing Elvidius, says, that " we believe that God was born of a Virgin;" and in another place he says (8): " Anima et caro Christo cum Verbo Dei una Persona est, unus Christus."

12. It would extend the work too much to quote more from the holy Fathers, so I will pass on to the Decrees of Councils. The Council of Ephesus (9), after a mature examination of the Catholic dogma, by Scripture and Tradition, condemned Nestorius, and deposed him from the See of Constantinople. Here are the words of the Decree: " Dominus noster Jesu Christus quem suis ille blasphemis vocibus impetivit per Ss. hunc Synodum eundem Nestorium Episcopali dignitate privatum, et ab universo sacerdotum consortio, et cœtu alienum esse definit." The fourth General Council, that of Chalcedon, defined the same thing (*Act.* 5): " Sequentes igitur Ss. Patres, unum, eumdemque confiteri Filium, et Dominum nostrum Jesum Christum consonanter omnes docemus, eundem perfectum in Deitate, et eundem perfectum in humanitate, Deum verum, et hominem verum..... non in duas personas partitum, aut divisum, sed unum eundemque Filium, et unigenitum Deum Verbum, Dominum Jesum Christum." The third Council of Constantinople— that is, the sixth General Council—defined the same doctrine in the last *Action;* and the seventh General Council, that is, the second of Nice, did the same in the seventh *Action.*

(3) St. Iræn. *l.* 3, *c.* 26, *al.* 18, *n.* 2. (4) St. Athan. *l.* de Inc. Verb. *n.* 2. (5) St. Greg. Naz. Orat. 31. (6) St. Joan. Chry. Ep. ad Cæsar. (7) St. Amb. de Incar. *c.* 5. (8) St. Hieron. *trac.* 49, in Joan. (9) Concil. Ephes. *t.* 3; Con. *p.* 115, & seq.

OBJECTIONS ANSWERED.

13. They object, first, certain passages of the Scripture, in which the humanity of Christ is called the temple and habitation of God: "Destroy this temple, and in three days I will raise it up .... But he spoke of the temple of his body" (John, ii. 19-21). In another place it is said: "For in him dwelleth all the fulness of the Godhead corporeally" (Col. ii. 9). We answer, that in these texts the personal union of the Word with the human nature is not denied, but it is even more strongly confirmed. Why should we be surprised that the body of Christ, hypostatically united with his soul to the Divine Word, should be called a temple? Why, even our body united to the soul is called a house and tabernacle: "For we know if our earthly house of this habitation be dissolved" (2 Cor. v. 1). And again (ver. 4): "For we also who are in this tabernacle do groan, being burthened." As, therefore, it is no argument against the personal union of the body and soul, to call the body a house and tabernacle, so calling the body of Christ a temple does not prove anything against the hypostatic union of the Word with the humanity of Christ; on the contrary, our Saviour even expresses this union himself in the words which follow: "In three days I will raise it up;" for by that he shows that he was not only man, but God. The Divinity of Christ is also clearly proved by the other text, in which St. Paul says that the followers of the Divinity dwelt bodily in him, thus declaring him to be at the same time true God and true man, according to the words of St. John: "The Word was made flesh, and dwelt among us."

14. They object, secondly, that text of the Epistle: "Being made in the likeness of man, and in habit formed as a man" (Phil. ii. 7). According to that, they say that Christ was a man like unto all other men. We answer that in the previous part of the text the Apostle already answers this, for he shows that Christ was God and equal to God: "Who being in the form of God thought it not robbery to be equal with God." Therefore the words quoted only prove that the Divine Word being God was made man like unto other men, but that he was not a mere man like all other men.

15. They object, thirdly, that everything in nature ought to have its own peculiar *subsistentia*, but the subsistentia of human nature is a human person, therefore if in Christ there was not a human person he was not true man. We reply that this is not necessary, if there be a higher or more noble *subsistentia*, as was the case in Christ, where the Word sustained both natures, and, therefore, though in Christ there was only the Divine person of the Word, still he was true man, because the human nature subsisted in the Word itself.

16. They object, fourthly, if the humanity of Christ consisted of both soul and body, it was complete and perfect; there was, there-

fore, in him a human Person, besides the Divine person. We answer that the humanity of Christ was complete by reason of nature, for it wanted nothing, but not by reason of the Person, because the Person in which the nature subsisted and was comprised was not a human but a Divine Person, and, therefore, we cannot say that there were two Persons in Christ, for one Person alone, that of the Word, sustains and comprises both the Divine and human nature.

17. They object, fifthly, that St. Gregory of Nyssa and St. Athanasius have sometimes called the humanity of Christ the house, the domicile, and the temple of God the Word. Besides that, St. Athanasius, Eusebius of Ceserea, and St. Cyril himself, have spoken of it as the instrument of the Divinity. St. Basil calls Christ "Deiferous," the bearer of God. St. Epiphanius and St. Augustin, "Hominem Dominicum," and St. Ambrose and St. Augustin, in the "Te Deum," say that the Word assumed man. We answer, that the Fathers, as we have already seen, have clearly expressed that Christ is true God and true man, so that if there be any obscure passage in these words it is easily cleared up by many others. St. Basil calls Christ the God-bearing man, not because he admits a human person in Christ, but to quash the error of Apollinares, who denied that Christ had a rational soul, and the holy Father only intended, therefore, to show by this expression that the Word assumed both a body and soul; when St. Ambrose and St. Augustin say that the Word assumed man, " assumpsit hominem," they only use the word " hominem" for human nature.

18. We may as well also here refute the errors of the Bishops Felix and Elipandus, who taught (*ch.* v. *n.* 39), that Jesus Christ as man was not the natural, but only the adopted Son of God. This opinion was condemned by several Councils, and also by the Popes Adrian and Leo X. The learned Petavius (1) says that it is not actually heretical, but at all events it is rash, and approaching to error, for it is more or less opposed to the unity of the Person of Christ, who, even as man, should be called the natural, and not the adopted Son of God, lest we might be drawn in to admit that in Christ there were two Sons, one natural, and the other adopted. There are, however, two reasons to prove that Christ as man should be called the natural Son of God; the more simple one is found in that passage of the Scriptures, in which the Father speaks of the eternal and continual generation of the Son: " Thou art my Son, this day have I begotten thee" (Psalms, ii. 7). Hence, as the Divine Son was generated previous to his Incarnation, without being personally united to human nature by the flesh, so when he took flesh he was generated, and is always generated, with human nature, hypostatically united to the Divine Person; and hence the Apostle, speaking of Christ as man, applies to him the text of

---

(1) Petav. *l.* 7, *c.* 4, *n.* 11. et *c.* 5, *n.* 8.

David now quoted: "So Christ also did not glorify himself, that he might be made a high priest, but he that said unto him, Thou art my Son, this day have I begotten thee" (Heb. v. 5). Jesus Christ, therefore, even according to his humanity, is the true Natural Son of God (2).

SEC. II.—MARY IS THE REAL AND TRUE MOTHER OF GOD.

19. THE truth of this dogma is a necessary consequence of what we have already said on the subject of the two natures; for if Christ as man is true God, and if Mary be truly the Mother of Christ as man, it necessarily follows that she must be also truly the Mother of God. We will explain it even more clearly by Scripture and tradition. In the first place the Scripture assures us that a Virgin (that is the Virgin Mary) has conceived and brought forth God, as we see in Isaias (vii. 14): "Behold a Virgin shall conceive and shall bring forth a Son, and his name shall be called Emmanuel, which is interpreted (says St. Matthew), God with us." St. Luke, relating what the angel said to Mary, proves the same truth: "Behold thou shalt conceive in the womb, and shalt bring forth a Son, and thou shalt call his name Jesus. He shall be great, and shall be called the Son of the Most High...... and the Holy which shall be born of thee shall be called the Son of God" (Luke, i. 31-35). Mark the words: "shall be called the Son of the Most High," "shall be called the Son of God," that is, shall be celebrated and recognized by the whole world as the Son of God.

20. St. Paul proves the same truth when he says: "Which he had promised before by his prophets in the Holy Scriptures. Concerning the Son who was made to him in the seed of David, according to the flesh" (Rom. i. 2, 3); and, writing to the Galatians, he says: "When the fulness of time was come God sent his Son made of a woman made under the law" (Gal. iv. 4). This Son, promised by God through the Prophets, and sent in the fulness of time, is God equal to the Father, as has been already proved, and this same God, sprang from the seed of David, according to the flesh, was born of Mary; she is, therefore, the true Mother of this God.

21. Besides, St. Elizabeth, filled with the Holy Ghost, called Mary the Mother of her Lord: "And whence is this to me that the Mother of my Lord should come to me?" (Luke, i. 43). Who was the Lord of St. Elizabeth, unless God? Jesus Christ himself, also, as often as he called Mary his Mother, called himself the Son of Man, and still the Scriptures attest that, without the operation of man, he was born of a Virgin. He once asked his disciples: "Whence do men say that the Son of Man is?" (Matt. xvi. 13),

---

(2) Vide Tournelly, Comp. Theol. *t.* 4, *p.* 2, Incarn. *c.* 3, *ar.* 7, *p.* 800, signanter, *p* 817, vers. ter.

and St. Peter answered: " Thou art Christ, the Son of the living God;" and our Saviour answered: " Blessed art thou, Simon Barjona, because flesh and blood hath not revealed it to thee, but my Father who is heaven." Therefore, the Son of Man is the true Son of God, and, consequently, Mary is the Mother of God.

22. In the second place this truth is proved from tradition. The Symbols or Creeds already quoted against Nestorius, proving that Jesus Christ is true God, also prove that Mary is the true Mother of God, since they teach, " That he was conceived of the Holy Ghost from the Virgin Mary, and was made man." The decree of the Second Council of Nice (*Act.* VII.) even declares, if possible, more clearly, that Mary is the true Mother of God: " Confitemur autem et Dominam nostram sanctam Mariam proprie et veraciter (properly and truly) Dei Genitricem, quoniam peperit carne unum ex S. Trinitate Christum Deum nostrum; secundum quod et Ephesinum prius dogmatizavit Concilium, quod impium Nestorium cum Collegis suis tanquam personalem dualitatem introducentes ab Ecclesia pepulit."

23. Mary has been called the Mother of God by all the Fathers. I will merely quote from a few who wrote in the early ages previous to Nestorius. St. Ignatius the martyr (1) says: " Deus noster Jesus Christus ex Maria genitus est." St. Justin (2): " Verbum formatum est, et homo factus est ex Virgine;" and again: " Ex virginali utero Primogenitum omnium rerum conditarum carne factum vere puerum nasci, id præoccupans per Spiritum Sanctum." St. Iræneus (3) says: " Verbum existens ex Maria, quæ adhuc erat Virgo, recte accipiebat generationem Adæ recapitulationis." St. Dionisius of Alexandria writes (4): " Quomodo ais tu, hominem esse eximium Christum, et non revera Deum, et ab omni creatura cum Patre, et Spiritu Sancto adorandum, incarnatum ex Virgine Deipara Maria?" And he adds: " Una sola Virgo filia vitæ genuit Verbum vivens, et per se subsistens increatum, et Creatorem." St. Athanasiuss (5) ays: " Hunc scopum, et characterem sanctæ Scripturæ esse, nempe ut duo de Salvatore demonstret: illum scilicet Deum semper fuisse, et Filium esse .... ipsumque postea propter nos carne ex Virgine Deipara Maria assumpta, hominem factum esse." St. Gregory of Nazianzen (6) says: " Si quis sanctam Mariam Deiparam non credit, extra Divinitatem est." St. John Chrysostom says (7): " Admodum stupendum est audire Deum ineffabilem, inerrabilem, incomprehensibilem, Patri æqualem per virgineam venisse vulvam, et ex muliere nasci dignatum esse." Among the Latin Fathers we will quote a few. Tertullian says (8): " Ante omnia commendanda erit ratio quæ præfuit, ut Dei Filius de Virgine nasceretur."

---

(1) St. Ignat. Ep. ad Ephe. *a.* 14. (2) St. Justin, Apol. & Dialog. cum Triphon *n.* 44. (3) Iræn. *l.* 3, c. 21, *al.* 31, *n.* 10. (4) St. Dionis. Ep. & Paul, Samos (5) St. Athan. Orat. 3, *a.* 4, con. Arian. (6) St. Greg. Nazian. Orat. 51 (7) St. Chrys. Hom. 2, in Matth. *n.* 2. (8) Tertul. *l.* de Cor. Chris. c. 17.

St. Ambrose says 9 : " Filium coæternum Patri suscepisse carnem natum de Spiritu Sancto ex Virgine Maria." St. Jerome says (10), "Natum Deum ex Virgine credimus, quia legimus." St. Augustin (11) says: " Invenisse apud Deum gratiam dicitur (Maria) ut Domini sui, imo omnium Domini Mater esset."

24. I omit other authorities, and will confine myself to only one, that of John, Bishop of Antioch, who wrote to Nestorius in the name of Theodoret, and several other friends of his, on the name of the Mother of God: " Nomen quod a multis sæpe Patribus usurpatum, ac pronunciatum est, adjungere ne graveris; neque vocabulum, quod piam rectamque notionem animi exprimit, refutare pergas; etenim nomen hoc Theotocos nullus unquam Ecclesiasticorum Doctorum repudiavit. Qui enim illo usi sunt, et multi reperiuntur, et apprime celebres; qui vero illud non usurparunt, nunquam erroris alicujus eos insimularunt, qui illo usi sunt.... Etenim si ad quod nominis significatione offertur, non recipimus, restat ut in gravissimum errorem prolabamur, imo vero ut inexplicabilem illam unigeniti Filii Dei œconomiam abnegemus. Quandoquidem nomine hoc sublato vel hujus potius nominis notione repudiata, sequitur mox illum non esse Deum, qui admirabilem illam dispensationem nostræ salutis causa suscepit, tum Dei Verbum neque sese exinanivisse," &c. We may as well mention that St. Cyril wrote to Pope St. Celestine, informing him, that so deeply implanted was this belief in the hearts of the people of Constantinople, that when they heard Dorotheus, by order of Nestorius, pronounce an anathema against those who asserted that she was the Mother of God, they all rose up as one man, refused to hold any more communication with Nestorius, and from that out would not go to the church, a clear proof of what the universal belief of the Church was in those days.

25. The Fathers adduced several reasons to convince Nestorius. I will only state two: First.—It cannot be denied that she is the Mother of God, who conceived and brought forth a Son, who, at the time of his conception, was God. But both Scripture and tradition prove that our Blessed Lady brought forth this Son of God; she is, therefore, truly the Mother of God. " Si Deus est," says St. Cyril, " Dominus noster Jesus Christus, quomodo Dei Genetrix non est, quæ illum genuit, Sancta Virgo" (12)? Here is the second reason: If Mary be not the Mother of God, then the Son whom she brought forth is not God, and, consequently, the Son of God and the Son of Mary are not the same. Now Jesus Christ, as we have already seen, has proclaimed himself the Son of God, and he is the Son of Mary; therefore, the Nestorians must admit, either that Jesus Christ is not the Son of Mary, or that Mary, being the Mother of Jesus Christ, is truly the Mother of God.

(9) St. Amb. Ep. 63.   (10) St. Hier. *l.* con. Elvid.   (11) St. Aug. in Enchir. *cap.* 36.   (12) St. Cyril, Ep 1 ad Success.

THE OBJECTIONS OF THE NESTORIANS ANSWERED.

26. First, they object that the word Deipara, or Mother of God, is not used either in the Scriptures or in the Symbols of the Councils; but we answer, that neither in Scripture or Symbols do we find the word Christotocos, Mother of Christ; therefore, according to that argument, she should not be called the Mother of Christ, as Nestorius himself calls her. But we will give even a more direct answer. It is just the same thing to say that Mary is the Mother of God, as to say that she conceived and brought forth God; but both Scripture and Councils say that she brought forth a God, they, therefore, proclaim her, in equivalent terms, the Mother of God. Besides, the Fathers of the first centuries, as we have quoted, constantly called her the Mother of God, and the Scripture itself calls her Mother of our Lord, as Elizabeth, when filled with the Holy Ghost, said: " Whence is this to me, that the Mother of my Lord should come to me?"

27. They object, secondly, that Mary did not generate the Divinity, and, consequently, she cannot be called the Mother of God. We answer, that she should be called the Mother of God, because she was the mother of a man, who was at the same time true God and true man, just as we say that a woman is the mother of a man composed both of soul and body, though she only produces the body, and not the soul, which is created by God alone. Therefore, as Mary, though she has not generated the Divinity, still, as she brought forth a man, according to the flesh, who was, at the same time, God and man, she should be called the Mother of God.

28. They object, thirdly, that the Mother ought to be consubstantial to the Son; but the Virgin is not consubstantial to God, therefore, she ought not to be called the Mother of God. We answer, that Mary is not consubstantial to Christ as to the Divinity, but merely in humanity alone, and because her Son is both man and God, she is called the Mother of God. They say, besides, that if we persist in calling her the Mother of God, we may induce the simple to believe that she is a Goddess herself; but we answer, that the simple are taught by us that she is only a mere creature, but that she brought forth Christ, God and man. Besides, if Nestorius was so scrupulous about calling her the Mother of God, lest the simple might be led to believe that she was a Goddess, he ought to have a greater scruple in denying her that title, lest the simple might be led to believe, that as she was not the Mother of God, consequently Christ was not God.

REFUTATION VIII.

REFUTATION OF THE HERESY OF EUTYCHES, WHO ASSERTED THAT THERE WAS ONLY ONE NATURE IN CHRIST.

1. The Eutychian heresy is totally opposed to the Nestorian. Nestorius taught that there were two persons and two natures in Christ. Eutyches, on the contrary, admitted that there was but one Person, but he asserted that there was but one nature, likewise, for the Divine nature, he said, absorbed the human nature. Hence, Nestorius denied the Divinity of Christ, Eutyches his humanity; so both one and the other destroyed the mystery of the incarnation and of the redemption of man. We do not exactly know how Eutyches explained his doctrine of only one nature in Christ. In the Council held by St. Flavian he merely explained it in these terms: " That our Lord was of two natures before the union, but after the union only of one nature." And when the Fathers pressed him to explain more clearly, he only answered, that he came not to dispute, but only to suggest to his Holiness what his opinion was (1). Now, in these few words Eutyches uttered two blasphemies: First.—That after the incarnation there was only one nature in Christ, that is, the Divine nature, as he understood it; and, secondly—That before the incarnation of the Word there were two natures, the Divine and the human nature. As St. Leo says, writing to St. Flavian: " Cum tam impie duarum naturarum ante incarnationem Unigenitus Dei Filius fuisse dicatur, quam nefarie postquam Verbum caro factum est, natura in eo singularis asseritur."

2. Returning, however, to the principal error, that the two natures became one after the incarnation, that might be asserted to have happened in four ways: First.—That one of the natures was changed into the other. Second.—That both natures were mixed up and confused, and so only formed one. Third.—That without this mixing up, the two natures in their union formed a third. And, fourth.—That the human was absorbed by the Divine nature, and this is, most probably, the opinion of the Eutychians. Now, the Catholic dogma is totally opposed to this unity of the natures in Christ, no matter in what sense the Eutychians understood it. This is what we are going to prove.

SEC. I.—IN CHRIST THERE ARE TWO NATURES—THE DIVINE AND THE HUMAN NATURE—DISTINCT, UNMIXED, UNCONFUSED, AND ENTIRE, SUBSISTING INSEPARABLY IN THE ONE HYPOSTASIS, OR PERSON OF THE WORD.

3. This dogma is proved from the passages of Scripture already quoted against Arius and Nestorius, in which Christ is proved to be both God and man; for, as he could not be called God, if he

(1) Tom. 4; Conc.l. Labbæi, p. 223, 226.

had not perfect Divine nature, so he could not be called man, if he had not perfect human nature. We will, however, set the matter in a clearer light. In the Gospel of St. John (*Chap.* i.) after saying that the Word is God—" In the beginning was the Word, and the Word was with God, and the Word was God"—it is stated in the 14th verse, that human nature was assumed by the Word: " The Word was made flesh, and dwelt among us." Hence, St. Leo, in his celebrated Epistle to St. Flavian, says: " Unus idemque (quod sæpe dicendum est) vere Dei Filius, et vere hominis Filius. Deus per id quod in principio erat Verbum, et Verbum erat apud Deum: Homo per id quod Verbum caro factum est, et habitavit in nobis. Deus per id quod omnia per ipsum facta sunt, et sine ipso factum est nihil: Homo per id quod factus est ex muliere, factus sub lege."

4. The two natures in Christ are also most clearly proved by that celebrated text of St. Paul (Philip. ii. 6), which we have so frequently quoted: " For let this mind be in you which was also in Christ Jesus, who being in the form of God, thought it not robbery to be equal with God, but emptied himself, taking the form of a servant, being made in the likeness of man, and in habit formed as a man." Here the Apostle allows in Christ the form of God, according to which he is equal to God, and the form of a servant, according to which he emptied himself, and was made like unto men. Now, the form of God and the form of a servant cannot be the same form, nor the same nature; because, if it was the same human nature, we could not say that Christ is equal to God; and, on the contrary, if it was the same Divine nature, Christ could not be said to have emptied himself, and made himself like unto man. We must, therefore, admit that there are two natures in Christ, the Divine nature, by which he is equal to God, and the human nature, by which he is made like unto man.

5. Besides, this text proves that the two natures in Christ are unmingled and unconfused, each retaining its own properties, because, if the Divine nature was changed in him, he would no longer be God when he became man; but that would contradict what St. Paul says (Rom. ix. 5): " Of whom is Christ according to the flesh, who is over all things God blessed for ever." Thus Christ is, at the same time, God and man, according to the flesh. If the human was absorbed by the Divine nature, or even changed into a Divine substance, as the Eutychians say, as we learn from Theodoret in his Dialogue *Inconfusus*, where Eranistes, an Eutychian, says: " Ego dico mansisse Divinitatem, ab hac vero absorptam esse humanitatem......ut mare mellis guttam si accipiat, statim enim gutta illa evanescit maris aquæ permixta.......Non dicimus delatam esse naturam, quæ assumpta est, sed mutatam esse in substantiam Divinitatis." Thus the human nature, according to them, was absorbed in the Divine nature, like a drop of

honey in the ocean. But supposing that to be the fact, Christ could no longer be called man as he is in the Gospels, and all the New Testament, and as St. Paul calls him in the text already quoted, and again, in his 1st Epistle to Timothy (ii. 6): "The man Christ Jesus, who gave himself in redemption for all." Neither could we say that he emptied himself in human nature, if it was changed into the Divinity. If the human nature, therefore, was thus mixed up with the Divine nature, Christ would no longer be either true God or true man, but some third sort of Person, which is contrary to the whole teaching of the Scriptures. We are bound, therefore, to conclude that the two natures in Christ are unmingled and unconfused, and that each nature retains its own properties.

6. All those other passages of the Scriptures which affirm that Christ had a true body and a true soul united to that body, confirm the truth of this dogma, for from this it is manifest that the human nature remained entire and unmixed in Christ, and was not confused with the Divine nature, which remained entire also. That Christ had a real body is proved by St. John, against Simon Magus, Menander, Saturninus, and others, who asserted that his body was not a true, but only an apparent one. Hear the words of St. John: "Every spirit that confesseth that Jesus Christ is come in the flesh is of God, and every spirit that dissolveth Jesus Christ (in the Greek version *who does not confess that Jesus is come in the flesh*) is not of God, and this is Antichrist" (1 Epis. iv. 2, 3). St. Peter (1 Epis. ii. 24) says: "Who of his ownself bore our sins in his body on the tree;" and St. Paul, writing to the Colossians (i. 22), says: "He hath reconciled in the body of his flesh through death;" and again, writing to the Hebrews (x. 5), he puts into the mouth of Jesus these words of the thirty-ninth Psalm: "Sacrifice and oblation thou wouldst not, but a body thou hast fitted to me." I omit many other passages in which the body of Christ is mentioned. Our Lord himself speaks of his soul in St. John (x. 15), when he says, "I lay down my life (*animam*) for my sheep;" and again (*ver*. 17): "I lay down my life (*animam*) that I may take it again. No man taketh it away from me, but I lay it down of myself." In St. Matthew he says (xxvi. 38): "My soul is sorrowful unto death." It was his blessed soul that was separated from his body at his death, when St. John says (xix. 30), that, "bowing his head, he gave up the ghost." Christ, therefore, had a true body and a true soul united to each other, and he was, therefore, a true man, and that this body and this soul existed whole and entire after the hypostatic union, is clear from the passages quoted, all of which refer to Christ, after this union had taken place. There is no foundation, therefore, for asserting that his human nature was absorbed into the Divinity, or changed into it.

7. A confirmatory proof is given by those texts in which matters are attributed to Christ which belong to the human nature alone, and not to the Divine nature, and others, which properly belong to the Divine nature alone, and not to the human nature. As regards the human nature it is certain that the Divine nature could not be conceived, could not be born, or grow up to manhood, or suffer hunger or thirst, or weakness, or sorrow, or torments, or death, for it is independent, impassible, and immortal; these feelings belong to human nature alone. Now Jesus Christ was conceived and born of the Virgin Mary (Matt. i.). He grew up to manhood: " he advanced in wisdom and in age, and grace with God and man" (Luke, ii. 52); he fasted and was hungry: "When he had fasted forty days and forty nights, afterwards he was hungry" (Matt. iv. 2); he was wearied: " Jesus therefore being weary with his journey, sat thus on the well" (John, iv. 6); he wept: " Seeing the city he wept over it" (Luke, xix. 41); he suffered death: " He was made obedient unto death, even to the death of the Cross" (Phil. ii. 8); and " saying this, he gave up the ghost" (Luke, xxiii. 45); " And crying out with a loud voice he gave up the ghost" (Matt. xxvii. 50). It does not belong, either, to the Divine nature to pray, to obey, to offer sacrifice, to humble himself, and such like actions, all of which the Scriptures attribute to Jesus Christ. All these actions, therefore, belong to Jesus as man, and, consequently, after the Incarnation he was true man.

8. As to the second part, it is certain that human nature cannot be consubstantial to the Father, nor have all that the Father has, nor operate all that the Father operates; it cannot be eternal, nor omnipotent, nor omniscient, nor immutable, and still all these attributes are properly applied to Jesus Christ, as we have proved against Arius and Nestorius; therefore in Jesus Christ there is not alone the human, but also the Divine nature. St. Leo, in his Epistle to St. Flavian, states this so forcibly that I cannot omit quoting the original: " Nativitas carnis manifestatio est humanæ naturæ: partus Virginis Divinæ est virtutis indicium: infantia Parvuli ostenditur humilitate cunaram: magnitudo Altissimi declaratur vocibus Angelorum. Similis est redimentis homines, quem Herodes impius moliter occidere; sed Dominus est omnium, quem Magi gaudentes veniunt suppliciter adorare. Cum ad Præcursoris sui baptismum venit, ne lateret, quod carnis velamine Divinitas operiatur, vox Patris de Cœlo intonans dixit: ' Hic est Filius meus dilectus, in quo mihi bene complacui.' Sicut hominem diabolica tentat astutia, sic Deo Angelica famulantur officia. Esurire, sitire, lassescere, atque dormire, evidenter humanum est: quinque panibus quinque millia hominum satiare, largiri Samaritanæ aquam vivam, &c., sine ambiguitate dicendum est. Non ejusdem naturæ est flere miserationis affectu, amicum mortuum, et eundem quatriduanæ aggere sepulturæ ad vocis imperium excitare redivivum:

aut in ligno pendere, et in noctem luce conversa omnia elementa tremefacere: aut clavis transfixum esse, et Paradisi portas fidei Latroni aperire. Non ejusdem naturæ est dicere: Ego et Pater unum sumus, et dicere: Pater major me est."

9. Besides the Scripture, tradition has constantly preserved the faith of the two natures in Christ. In the Apostles' Creed we see this marked down most clearly: " I believe in Jesus Christ, his only Son, our Lord"—here is the Divine nature—" who was conceived of the Holy Ghost, born of the Virgin Mary, suffered under Pontius Pilate, was crucified, dead, and buried"—here is the human nature. In the Creeds of Nice and Constantinople the Divine nature is thus explained: " And in our Lord Jesus Christ, the Son of God......true God of true God, born, not made, consubstantial to the Father, by whom all things were made." Then the human nature is explained: " Who, for us man, and for our salvation, came down from heaven, and was incarnate of the Holy Ghost by the Virgin Mary, and was made man: he suffered, was crucified, died, and arose the third day."

10. Even before the Eutychian heresy sprung up at all, it was condemned by the first Council of Constantinople, in which the Fathers, in their Synodical Epistle to Pope St. Damasus, thus write: " Se agnoscere Verbum Dei ante secula omnino perfectum et perfectum hominem in novissimis diebus pro nostra salute factum esse." And St. Damasus, in the Roman Synod (1), had already defined against Apollinares that in Christ there was both a body and an intelligent and rational soul, and that he had not suffered in the Divinity, only in the humanity. In the Council of Ephesus the Second Epistle of St. Cyril to Nestorius, in which the dogma of two natures distinct and unmixed in Christ is expressed, was approved. Here are the words: " Neque enim dicimus Verbi naturam per sui mutationem carnem esse factam, sed neque in totum hominem transformatam ex anima, et corpore constitutam. Asserimus autem Verbum, unita sibi secundum hypostasim carne animata, rationali anima, inexplicabili, incomprehensibilique modo hominem factum, et hominis Filium extitisse.....Et quamvis naturæ sint diversæ, veram tamen unionem coeuntes, unum nobis Christum, et Filium effecerunt. Non quod naturarum differentia propter unionem sublata sit, verum quorum Divinitas, et humanitas secreta quadam ineffabilique conjunctione in una persona unum nobis Jesum Christum, et Filium constituerint."

11. Besides the Councils we have the authority of the Holy Fathers, likewise, who wrote previous to the Eutychian heresy. These were quoted in the *Actio* II. of the Council of Chalcedon, and Petavius (2) collected a great number, but I will only call the attention of the reader to a few. St. Ignatius the Martyr (3) thus

(1) Vide *t.* 2, Concil. *p.* 900, 964.   (2) Petav. *l.* 3, de Incar. *c.* 6, 7.   (3) St. Ignat. Ep. Eph. 7.

expresses the doctrine of the two natures: " Medicus unus est et carnalis, et spiritualis, genitus et ingenitus, seu factus et non factus, in homine existens Deus, in morte vita vera, et ex Maria et ex Deo, primum passibilis, et tunc impassibilis, Jesus Christus Dominus noster." St. Athanasius wrote two books against Apollinares, the predecessor of Eutyches. St. Hilary says (4): " Nescit plane vitam suam, nescit qui Christum Jesum ut verum Deum, ita et verum hominem ignorat." St. Gregory of Nazianzen says (5): " Missus est quidem, sed ut homo; duplex enim erat in eo natura." St. Amphilochius, quoted by Theodoret in the dialogue *Inconfusus*, writes thus: " Discerne naturas, unam Dei, alteram hominis; neque enim ex Deo excidens homo factus est, neque proficiscens ex homine Deus." St. Ambrose says (6): " Servemus distinctionem Divinitatis, et carnis, unus in utraque loquitur Dei Filius, qui in eodem utraque natura est. St. John Chrysostom says (7): " Neque enim (Propheta) carnem dividit a Divinitate, neque Divinitatem a carne; non substantias confundens, absit, sed unionem ostendens..... Quando dico eum fuisse humiliatum, non dico mutationem, sed humanæ susceptæ naturæ demissionem." St. Augustin writes (8): " Neque enim illa susceptione alterum eorum in alterum conversum, atque mutatum est; nec Divinitas quippe in creaturam mutata est. ut desisteret esse Divinitas; nec creatura in Divinitatem, ut desisteret esse creatura."

12. I omit a great number of authorities of other holy Fathers taken into account by the Council of Chalcedon, consisting of nearly six hundred Fathers, in which Eutyches was condemned, and which thus defined the doctrine of the Church (*Act.* V.): " Sequentes igitur Ss. Patres unum eundem confiteri Filium et Dominum nostrum Jesum Christum consonanter omnes docemur, eundem perfectum in Deitate, et eundem perfectum in humanitate, Deum verum, et hominem verum; eundem ex anima rationali, et corpore; consubstantialem Patri secundum Deitatem, consubstantialem nobiscum secundum humanitatem ante secula quidem de Patre genitum secundum Deitatem, in novissimis autem diebus eundem propter nos, et propter nostram salutem ex Maria Virgine Dei Genitrice secundum humanitatem, unum eundem Christum, Filium, Dominum, unigenitum in duabus naturis inconfuse, immutabiliter, indivise, inseparabiliter agnoscendum; nusquam sublata differentia naturarum propter unitionem, magisque salva proprietate utriusque naturæ, et in unam Personam, atque substantiam concurrentes." It is related that the Fathers, after hearing the dogmatical Epistle of St. Leo to St. Flavian, read in the Council, all cried out as with one voice: " This is the faith of the Fathers and of the Apostles; we and all orthodox believers hold this faith; anathema to him who believes otherwise. Peter has spoken through Leo."

---

(4) St. Hil. *l.* 9. de Trin.   (5) St. Greg. Nazian. Orat. de Nat.   (6) St. Ambrose, *l.* 2, de Fide, *c.* 9, alias 4, *n.* 79.   (7) St. Chrysos. in Psalm xliv. *n.* 4.   (8) St. Aug *l.* 1, de Trin. *c.* 7, *n.* 14.

The following Councils confirmed the same doctrine, especially the second Council of Constantinople, which, in the eighth Canon, thus decreed: " Si quis ex duabus naturis Deitatis, et humanitatis confitens unitatem factam esse, vel unam naturam Dei Verbi incarnatam dicens, non sic eam excipit, sicut Patres docuerunt, quod ex Divina natura et humana, unione secundum substantiam facta, unus Christus effectus est, sed ex talibus vocibus unam naturam, sive substantiam Deitatis, et carnis Christi introducere conatur; talis anathema sit." The third Council of Constantinople, in the definition of Faith, repeats the words of the Council of Chalcedon and of the second Council of Nice: " Duas naturas confitemur ejus, qui incarnatus est propter nos ex intemerata Dei genitrice semper Virgine Maria, perfectum eum Deum, et perfectum hominem cognoscentes."

14. We may as well give two theological reasons for the dogma. The first is this: if the human nature Christ assumed was, after the Incarnation, absorbed into the Divinity, as the Eutychians believe, there would be an end to the mystery of the Redemption, for in that case we should either deny the Passion and death of Jesus Christ altogether, or admit that the Divinity suffered and died, a supposition from which our very nature shrinks with horror.

15. This is the second reason: if, after the Incarnation, but one nature alone remained in Christ, this must have come to pass, either because one of the two natures was changed into the other, or because both were so mixed up and confused that they formed but one alone, or at least because, being united together without confusion of any sort they formed a third nature, just as the union of soul and body in man forms human nature. But so it is that not one of those things could take place in the Incarnation, consequently both natures, the Divine and the human, remained entire in Jesus Christ, with all the properties of each.

16. It is impossible that one of the two natures could be changed into the other, for in that case the Divine would be changed into the human nature, and that is totally repugnant not only to Faith but to reason itself, for we cannot imagine it even possible that the Divinity should be subject to the slightest change. Then if the human nature was absorbed and changed into the Divine nature, we should admit that the Divinity was born in Christ, suffered, died, and rose again, which is equally repugnant to Faith and reason, as the Divinity is eternal, impassible, immortal, and unchangeable. Besides, if the Divinity suffered and died, then the Father and the Holy Ghost suffered and died also, for the Father, and the Son, and the Holy Ghost are together one Divinity. Again, if the Divinity was conceived and was born, then the Blessed Virgin did not conceive and bring forth Christ according to the one nature consubstantial to herself, and therefore she is not the Mother of God. Finally, if the humanity was absorbed into the Divinity in

Christ, then he could not be our Redeemer, Mediator, and Pontiff of the New Testament, as faith teaches us he is, for these offices required prayers, sacrifice, and humiliations which the Divinity could not fulfil.

17. Therefore it cannot be asserted, First.—That human nature in Christ was changed into the Divine nature, and much less that the Divine was changed into human nature. Second.—It never could happen that the two natures were mixed up with each other and confused, and so formed one nature alone in Christ, for in that case the Divinity would be changed, and would become something else; in Christ there would exist neither Divinity nor humanity, but a nature neither Divine nor human, so that he would be neither true God nor true man. Third.—It never could have happened that the two natures which existed without confusion, and totally distinct from each other, could, by uniting together, form a third nature, common to both, because this common nature must, in that case, have been produced by the two parts, which, uniting together, must be reciprocally perfect, for otherwise, if one part receives nothing from the other, but loses some of its own properties in the union, it will certainly not be as perfect as it was before. Now, in Christ the Divine nature has received no perfection from the human nature, and it could not lose anything itself, therefore it must have remained as it was before, and consequently could never form with the humanity a third nature, common to both. Besides, a common nature only springs out of several parts, which naturally require a reciprocal union, as is the case in the union of the soul with the body; but that is not the case in Christ, in whom it is not naturally requisite that human nature should be united with the Word, nor is it necessary that the Word should be united with human nature.

OBJECTIONS ANSWERED.

18. First the Eutychians quote certain texts of Scripture, by which it would appear that one nature is changed into the other, as that of St. John (i. 14): "The Word was made flesh;" therefore the Word was changed into flesh. Also that passage of St. Paul, in which it is said, that "Christ emptied himself, taking the form of a servant" (Phil. ii. 7); therefore, the Divine nature is changed. We reply to the first objection, that the Word was not changed into flesh, but was made flesh by assuming humanity in the unity of the Person, without suffering any change in the union. Thus it is said also of Jesus Christ (Gal. iii. 13), that "he was made a curse for us," inasmuch as he took on himself the malediction which we deserved, to free us from it. St. John Chrysostom says, that the very words which follow the text they lay so much stress on explain the difference of the two natures: "The Word was made flesh,

and dwelt among us, and we have seen his glory, the glory as it were of the only begotten of the Father." Now, here the Word is said to have dwelt among us, which is a proof that he is different from us, for that which dwells is different from that which is dwelt in. Here are his words (1): " Quid enim subjicit? ' Et habitavit in nobis.' Non enim mutationem illam incommutabilis illius naturæ significavit, sed habitationem, et commemorationem; porro id quod habitat, non est idem cum eo quod habitatur, sed diversum." And here we may remark, that these expressions of St. John give a death blow, at the same time, to the Eutychian and Nestorian heresies, for when Nestorius says that the Word dwells in the humanity of Christ alone, because the Evangelist says, "he dwelt among us," he is refuted by the antecedent part of the sentence, " the Word was made flesh," which proves not alone a mere inhabitation, but a union with human nature in one Person; and, on the other hand, when Eutyches says that the Word is said to be turned into flesh, he is refuted by the subsequent expression, "and dwelt among us," which proves that the Word is not changed into flesh (even after the union of the flesh), but remains God the same as before, without confounding the Divine nature with the human nature he assumed.

19. We should not be startled, either, at the expression, " made flesh," for this is but a manner of expressing a thing, and does not at all times mean the conversion of one thing into another, but frequently that one thing was superadded to another, as in Genesis we read that Adam " became (was made into, *factus est*) a living soul" (ii. 7). Now, the obvious meaning of this is, not that the body of Adam, which was already created, was converted into a soul, but that the soul was created and joined to the body. St. Cyril makes a very pertinent remark on this in his dialogue, " De Incarnatione Unigeniti." He says: " At si Verbum inquiunt, factum est caro, jam non amplius mansit Verbum, sed potius desiit esse quod erat. Atqui hoc merum delirium, et dementia est, nihilque aliud quam mentis erratæ ludibrium. Censent enim, ut videtur, per hoc, *factum est*, necessaria quadam ratione mutationem, alterationemque significari. Ergo cum psallunt quidam, et *factus est nihilominus in refugium; et rursus, Domine refugium factus est nobis*, quid respondebunt? Anne Deus, qui hic decantatur, desinens esse Deus, mutatus est in refugium, et translatus est naturaliter in aliud, quod ab initio non erat? Cum itaque Dei mentio fit, si ab alio dicatur illud *factus est*, quo pacto non absurdum, atque adeo vehementer absurdum existimare mutationem aliquam per id significari, et non potius conari id aliqua ratione intelligere, pudenterque ad id quod Deo maxime convenit accommodari?" St. Augustin also explains how the Word was made flesh without any change (2): " Neque

---

(1) St. John Chrys. Hom. 11, in Joan.   (2) St. August. Ser. 187, & al. 77, de Tempore.

enim, quia dictum est, *Deus erat Verbum, et Verbum caro factum,* sic Verbum caro factum est, ut esse desineret Deus, quando in ipsa carne, quod Verbum caro factum est, Emmanuel natum est nobiscum Deus. Sicut Verbum, quod corde gestamus, sit vox, cum id ore proferimus, non tamen illud in hanc commutatur, sed illo integro, ista in qua procedat, assumitur, ut et intus maneat, quod intelligatur, et foris sonet, quod audiatur. Hoc idem tamen profertur in sono, quod ante sonuerat in silentio. Atque ita in Verbum, cum sit vox, non mutatur in vocem, sed manens in mentis luce, et assumpta carnis voce procedit ad audientem, ut non deferat cogitantem."

20. As to the second objection, taken from the words, "he emptied himself," the answer is very clear, from what we have said already; for the Word " emptied himself," not by losing what he was, but by assuming what he was not, for he, being God, equal to the Father in his Divine nature, " took the form of a servant," thereby making himself less than the Father in his assumed nature, and humbling himself in it even to the death of the Cross: " He humbled himself, being made obedient unto death, even to the death of the Cross;" but, notwithstanding, he retained his Divinity, and was, therefore, equal to the Father.

21. It was not, however, the Eutychians, properly speaking, who made use of these objections, for they did not assert that the Divine was changed into the human nature, but that the human was changed into the Divine nature, and they quoted some passages of the Holy Fathers, which they did not understand in their true sense, in their favour. Firstly.—They say that St. Justin, in his Second Apology, writes, that in the Eucharist the bread is converted into the body of Christ, as the Word was into flesh. But Catholics answer, that the Saint only wished, by this expression, to say that the real and true body of Christ is in the Eucharist, just as the Word in reality assumed and retained human flesh; and the context, if read, shows that this is the true meaning of the passage. The argument is this: that as, in the Incarnation, the Word was made flesh, so, in the Eucharist, the bread is made the body of Christ; but if he intended to teach, as the Eutychians assert, that in the Incarnation of the Word the humanity was absorbed into the Divinity, he never could have said that in the Eucharist the true body of our Lord exists.

22. Secondly.—They found an objection on that passage of the Athanasian Creed: " As a rational soul and flesh is one man, so God and man is one Christ." Hence, they argue the two natures are but one. To this we reply, that these words denote an unity of Person, and not of Nature, in Christ, and that is manifest from the words, " one Christ," for by Christ is properly understood the Person, and not the Nature.

23. They object, thirdly, that St. Irænous, Tertullian, St.

Cyprian, St. Gregory of Nyssa, St. Augustin, and St. Leo (3), call the union of the two natures a mixture or fusion, and compare it to the mixture of two fluids one with the other. We answer with St. Augustin (as quoted), that these Fathers did not make use of these expressions, because they believed that the two natures were confounded, but to explain how close the union was, and that the Divine was united to the human nature as closely and intimately as the colouring poured into a liquid unites with every portion of it. This is St. Augustin's explanation: "Sicut in unitate Personæ anima unitur corpori, ut homo sit: ita in unitate Personæ Deus unitur homini, ut Christus sit. In illa ergo persona mixtura est animæ et corporis; in hac Persona mixtura est Dei et hominis: si tamen recedat auditor a consuetudine corporum, qua solent duo liquores ita commisceri, ut neuter servet integritatem, suam, quamquam et in ipsis corporibus aeri lux incorrupta misceatur." Tertullian previously gave the same explanation.

24. They object, fourthly. the authority of Pope Julius in his Epistle to Dionisius, Bishop of Corinth, in which he blames those who believed that there were two natures in Christ, and also one expression of St. Gregory Thaumaturgus, quoted by Photius, who says that there are not two Persons, nor two natures, for then we should be adoring four. But we answer, with Leontius (4), that these Epistles are falsely attributed to these Holy Fathers, for the Epistle attributed to Julius in supposed to have been the production of Apollinares, since St. Gregory of Nyssa quotes several passages from it, as written by Apollinares, and refutes them. We have the same reply to make to the quotation from St. Gregory Thaumaturgus, for it is universally supposed to have been written by the Apollinarists, or Eutychians.

They object, fifthly, that St. Gregory of Nyssa says, in his Fourth Oration against Eunomius, that human nature was united with the Divine Word; but we answer, that notwithstanding this union, each nature retained its own properties, as St. Gregory himself says: "Nihilominus in utraque, quod cuique proprium est, intuetur." Finally, they say, if there were two natures in Christ, there would be also two Persons; but we have already disposed of that objection in our Refutation of Nestorianism (*Ref.* vii. *n.* 16), in which we have shown that there is nothing repugnant in the existence of two natures, distinct and unmixed, in the sole Person of Christ.

(3) St. Iren. *l.* 2, ad. Hær. *c.* 21; Tertull. Apol. *c.* 21; St. Cyprian, de Van. Idol; St. Greg. Nyss. Catech. *c.* 25; St. Augus. Ep. 137, al. 3, ad Volusian.; St. Leo, Ser. 3, in die Natal. (4) Leon. de Sect. *art.* 4.

REFUTATION IX.

OF THE MONOTHELITE HERESY, THAT THERE IS BUT ONE NATURE AND ONE OPERATION ONLY IN CHRIST.

1. THOSE heretics who believe that there is only one will in Christ are called Monothelites, and the name is derived from two Greek words, *Monos*, one, and *Thelema*, will, and on that account many of the Arians, who asserted that Christ had no soul, but that the Word took the place of it, can be called Monothelites, as may, in like manner, many Apollinarists, who admitted that Christ had a soul, but without mind, and consequently, without will. The true Monothelites, however, formed themselves into a sect, in the reign of the Emperor Heraclius, about the year 626. The chief author of this sect was Athanasius, Patriarch of the Jacobites, as remarked in the History (*Chap.* vii. *n.* 4), and his first followers were the Patriarchs who succeeded him, Sergius, Cirus, Macarius, Pirrus, and Paul. These admitted two natures in Christ, the Divine and the human, but denied the two wills, and the two operations belonging to each nature, asserting that he had but one will, that is, the Divine will, and one operation, the Divine one also; this they called *Theandric*, or belonging to the Man-God, but not in the Catholic sense, in which the operations of Christ in his humanity are called Theandric, as being the operation of the Man-God, and are attributed to the Person of the Word, which sustains and is the term of this humanity, but in a heretical sense, for they believed that the Divine will alone moved the faculties of his human nature, and used them as a mere passive and inanimate instrument. Some of the Monothelites called this operation *Deodecibilem*, or fitted to God, and this expression gives more clearly the peculiar meaning of their heretical tenets. It was a debated question among the ancients, whether the Monothelites, by the word "will," meant the faculty of wishing, or the act of volition itself. Patavius thinks it most probable (1) that they understood by it, not the act of volition itself, but the power of wishing at all, which they say the humanity of Christ did not possess. The Catholic dogma, however, rejects it in both senses, and teaches that as in Christ there were two natures, so there were Divine will and volition with the Divine operation, and human will and volition with the human operation.

SEC. I.—IT IS PROVED THAT THERE ARE TWO DISTINCT WILLS IN CHRIST, DIVINE AND HUMAN, ACCORDING TO THE TWO NATURES, AND TWO OPERATIONS, ACCORDING TO THE TWO WILLS.

2. IT is proved, in the first place, by the Scriptures, that Christ has a Divine will, for every text that proves his Divinity, proves

(1) Petav. *l.* 8, de Incar *c.* 4, et seq.

that, as the will cannot be separated from the Divinity. We have already quoted all these texts against the Nestorians and Eutychians, so there is no necessity of repeating them here, especially as the Monothelites do not deny the Divine, but only the human will, in Christ. There are, however, numberless texts to prove that our Redeemer had a human will likewise. St. Paul, in his Epistle to the Hebrews (x. 5), applies to Christ the words of the 39th Psalm (ver. 8, 9): " Wherefore, when he cometh into the world he said ...... Behold, I come; in the head of the book it is written of me, that I should do the will of God." In the 39th Psalm, also, we find: " In the head of the book it is written of me, that I should do thy will, O my God; I have desired it, and thy law in the midst of my heart" (ver. 9). Now, here both wills are distinctly marked—the Divine, " that I may do thy will, O God;" and the human will, subject to the Divine will, " O my God, I have desired it." Christ himself draws the same distinction in many places; thus in John (v. 30), he says: " I seek not my own will, but the will of him who sent me." And again: " I came down from heaven, not to do my own will, but the will of him who sent me" (vi. 38). St. Leo explains this in his Epistle to the Emperor, for he says, that according to the form of a servant, " secundum formam servi," that is, as man, he came not to do his own will, but the will of him who sent him.

3. Christ, who says in St. Matthew (xxvi. 39): " My Father, if it is possible, let this chalice pass from me, nevertheless, not as I will, but as thou wilt." And in St. Mark (xiv. 36): " Abba, Father, all things are possible to thee, remove this chalice from me, but not what I will, but what thou wilt." Now, the two texts clearly show the Divine will which Christ had, in common with the Father, and the human will which he subjected to the will of his Father. Hence, St. Athanasius, writing against Apollinares, says: " Duas voluntates hic ostendit, humanam quidem quæ est carnis, alteram vero Divinam. Humana enim propter carnis imbecillitatem recusat passionem, Divina autem ejus voluntas est promta." And St. Augustin says (1): " In eo quod ait, *non quod ego volo*, aliud se ostendit voluisse, quam Pater, quod nisi humano corde non potest; nunquam enim posset immutabilis illa natura quidquam aliud velle, quam Pater."

4. The Catholic dogma is proved also by all those texts in which Christ is said to have obeyed his Father. In St. John (xii. 49), we read: " For I have not spoken of myself, but the Father who sent me, he gave commandment what I should say, and what I should speak." And again: " As the Father giveth me commandment, so do I" (xiv. 31). And St. Paul, writing to the Philippians, says, " that he was made obedient unto death, even unto the death of the cross." Many other texts are of the same tenor. All this proves

(1) St. Augus. *l.* 2, adv. Maximin. *c.* 20.

that there must be a human will, for he who has no will can neither obey nor be commanded. It is most certain that the Divine will cannot be commanded, as it recognizes no will superior to itself. The obedience of Christ, therefore, to his Father, proves that he must have had a human will: " Qua," says Pope Agatho, " a lumine veritatis se adeo separavit, ut audeat dicere, Dominum nostrum Jesum Christum voluntate suæ Divinitatis Patri obedisse, cui est æqualis in omnibus, et vult ipse quoque in omnibus, quod Pater?"

5. We pass over other Scripture arguments, and come to Tradition, and first of all, we shall see what the Fathers who lived before the rise of the heresy said on the subject. St. Ambrose says (2): "Quod autem ait: *Non mea voluntas, sed tua fiat, suam,* ad hominem retulit; *Patris,* ad Divinitatem: voluntas enim hominis, temporalis; voluntas Divinitatis, æterna." St. Leo, in his Epistle 24 (*a.* 10, *c.* 4), to St. Flavian, against Eutyches, thus writes: " Qui verus est Deus, idem verus est homo; et nullam est in hac unitate mendacium, dum invicem sunt, et humilitas hominis, et altitudo Deitatis...... Agit enim utraque forma cum alterius communione, quod proprium est; Verbo scilicet operante, quod Verbi est, et carne exequente, quod carnis est" I omit many other authorities from St. Chrysostom, St. Cyril of Alexandria, St. Jerome, and others referred to by Petavius (3). Sophronius compiled two whole books of them against Sergius, as we find from the petition of Stephen Duresius to the Council of Lateran, under Martin I., in 649. It is proved also by the Creeds, in which it is professed that Christ is at the same time true God and true man, perfect in both natures. If Christ had not human will, one of the natural faculties of the soul, he would not be a perfect man, no more than he would be perfect God, if he had not Divine will. The Councils whose Decrees we have already quoted against Nestorius, have defined that there are two natures in Christ, distinct and perfect in all their properties, and that could not be the fact, unless each of the two natures had its proper natural will and natural operation. A Portuguese writer, Hippolitus, in his Fragments against Vero, from the distinction of the different operations in Christ, argued that there was a distinction of the two natures, because if there was but one will and one operation in Christ, there would be but one nature: " Quæ sunt inter se ejusdem operationis, et cognitionis, et omnino idem patiuntur, nullam naturæ differentiam recipiunt."

6. All these things being taken into consideration, in the Third General Council of Constantinople, under Pope Agatho, it was thought proper to condemn, in one Decree (*Act.* 18), all the heresies against the incarnation condemned in the five preceding General Councils. Here is the Decree, in the very words: " Assequti quoque sancta quinque universalia Concilia, et sanctos atque probabiles Patres, consonanterque confiteri definientes, D. N. Jesum

---

(2) St. Ambros. *l.* 20, in Luc. *n.* 59 & 60.   (3) Petav. *l.* 3, de Incarn. *c.* 8 & 9.

Christum verum Deum nostrum, unum de sancta, et consubstantiali, et vitæ originem præbente Trinitate, perfectum in Deitate, et perfectum eundem in humanitate, Deum vere, et hominem vere, eundem ex anima rationali et corpore, consubstantialem Patri secundum Deitatem, et consubstantialem nobis secundum humanitatem, per omnia similem nobis absque peccato; ante secula quidem ex Patre genitum secundum Deitatem, in ultimis diebus autem eundem propter nos et propter nostram salutem de Spiritu Sancto, et Maria Virgine proprie, et veraciter Dei Genitrice secundum humanitatem, unum eundemque Christum Filium Dei unigenitum in duabus naturis inconfuse, inconvertibiliter, inseparabiliter, indivise cognoscendum, nusquam extincta harum naturarum differentia propter unitatem, salvataque magis proprietate utriusque naturæ, et in unam Personam, et in unam subsistentiam concurrente, non in duas Personas partitam, vel divisam, sed unum eundemque unigenitum Filium Dei, Verbum D. N. Jesum Christum; et duas naturales voluntates in eo, et duas naturales operationes indivise, inconvertibiliter, inseparabiliter, inconfuse secundum Ss. Patrum doctrinam, adeoque prædicamus; et duas naturales voluntates, non contrarias, absit, juxta quod impii asseruerunt Hæretici, sed sequentem ejus humanam voluntatem, et non resistentem, vel reluctantem, sed potius, et subjectam Divinæ ejus, atque omnipotenti voluntati...... His igitur cum omni undique cautela, atque diligentia a nobis formatis, definimus aliam Fidem nulli licere proferre, aut conscribere, componere, aut fovere, vel etiam aliter docere."

7. The principal proofs from reason alone against this heresy have been already previously given. First.—Because Christ having a perfect human nature, he must have, besides, a human will, without which his humanity would be imperfect, being deprived of one of its natural powers. Secondly.—Because Christ obeyed, prayed, merited, and satisfied for us, and all this could not be done without a created human will, for it would be absurd to attribute it to the Divine will. Thirdly.—We prove it from that principle of St. Gregory of Nazianzen, adopted by the other Fathers, that what the Word assumed he healed, and hence St. John of Damascus (3) concludes that as he healed human will he must have had it: " Si non assumsit humanam voluntatem, remedium ei non attulit, quod primum sauciatum erat; quod enim assumtum non est, nec est curatum, ut ait Gregorius Theologus. Ecquid enim offenderat, nisi voluntas?"

SEC. II.—OBJECTIONS ANSWERED.

8. THE Monothelites object, first, that prayer of St. Dionisius in his Epistle to Caius: " Deo viro facto unam quandum Theandricam,

(3) St. Joan. Damas. Ora. de duab. Chris. Volunt.

seu Deivirilem operationem expressit in vita;" that is, that in the God made man there is one Theandric or human-divine operation. We answer, with Sophronius, that this passage was corrupted by the Monothelites, by changing the word, "novam quandam" into "unam quandam," or a *new sort* of Theandric operation, into *some one* Theandric operation. This was noticed in the Third Council of Lateran, in which St. Martin commanded the Notary Paschasias to read the Greek copy that was preserved, and the words were found to be *novam quandam*, &c., and not *unam*, &c., and this was in no wise opposed to the Catholic doctrine, and can be explained two ways in an orthodox sense. First.—As St. John of Damascus says, every operation (1) performed by Christ by the Divine and human nature is Theandric, or human-divine, because it is the operation of a Man-God, and is attributed to the Person of Christ, the term, at the same time, of both the Divine and human nature. The second sense, as Sophronius and St. Maximus lay down, is this, that the new Theandric operation St. Dionisius speaks of should be restricted to those operations of Christ alone, in which the Divine and human natures concur, and, therefore, there are three distinct operations to be noted in him: first, those which peculiarly belong to human nature alone, as walking, eating, sitting, and so forth; secondly, those which belong purely to the Divine nature, as remitting sins, working miracles, and the like; and, thirdly, those which proceed from both natures, as healing the sick by touching them, raising the dead by calling them, &c.; and it is of operations of this sort that the passage of St. Dionisius is to be explained.

9. Secondly.—They object that St. Athanasius (2) admits the Divine Will only, "*voluntatem Deitatis tantum;*" but we answer that this does not exclude human will, but only that opposing will which springs from sin, as the context proves. Thirdly.—They object that St. Gregory of Nazianzen (3) says that the will of Christ was not opposed to God, as it was *totally* Deified: "*Christi velle non fuisse Deo contrarium, utpote Deificatum totum.*" We answer, with St. Maximus and St. Agatho, that there is not the least doubt but that St. Gregory admitted two wills, and the whole meaning of this expression is that the human will of Christ was never opposed to the Divine will. They object, fourthly, that St. Gregory of Nyssa, writing against Eunomius, says, that the Deity worked out the salvation of man; the suffering, he says, was of the flesh, but the operation was of God: "Operatur vere Deitas per corpus, quod circa ipsam est omnium salutem, ut sit carnis quidem passio, Dei autem operatio." This objection was answered in the Sixth Council, for the Saint having said that the humanity of Christ suffered, admitted by that that Christ operated by the

---

(1) St. Jo. Damas. *l.* 3, de Fide Orthodox. *c.* 19.   (2) St. Athanas. in *l.* de Adv. Chri.   (3) St. Greg. Naz. Orat. 2 de Filio.

humanity. All that St. Gregory in fact wanted to prove against Eunomius was, that the sufferings and the operations of Christ received a supreme value from the Person of the Word who sustains his humanity, and therefore he attributed these operations to the Word. They object, fifthly, that St. Cyril of Alexandria (4) says that Christ showed some *cognate* operation, " *quandam cognatam operationem*." We reply, that from the context it is manifest that the Saint speaks of the miracles of Christ in which his Divine nature operated by his omnipotence, and his human nature by the contact, commanded by his human will; and thus this operation is called by the Saint an associated one. Sixthly, they object that many of the Fathers called the human nature of Christ the instrument of the Divinity. We answer, that these Fathers never understood the humanity to have been an inanimate instrument, which operated nothing of itself, as the Monothelites say, but their meaning was that the Word being united with the humanity, governed it as its own, and operated through its powers and faculties. Finally, they oppose to us some passages of Pope Julius, of St. Gregory Thaumaturgus, and some writings of Menna to Vigilius, and of Vigilius to Menna; but our reply to this is that these passages are not authentic, but were foisted into the works of the Fathers by the Apollinarists and Eutychians. It was proved in the Sixth Council (*Act*. XIV.), that the writings attributed to Menna and Vigilius were forged by the Monothelites.

10. The Monothelites endeavour to prop up their opinions by several other reasons. If you admit two wills in Christ, they say, you must also admit an opposition between them. But we, Catholics, say that this supposition is totally false; the human will of Christ never could oppose the Divine will, for he took our nature, and was made in all things like us, but with the exception of sin; as St. Paul says (Heb. iv. 15), he was " one tempted in all things like as we are, without sin." He never, therefore, had those movements we have to violate the Divine law, but his will was always conformable to the Divine will. The Fathers make a distinction between the natural and arbitrary will; the natural will is the power itself of wishing, the arbitrary will is the power of wishing anything, either good or bad. Christ had the natural human will, but not the arbitrary human will, for he always wished, and could only wish what was most conformable to the Divine will, and hence he says: " I do always the things that please him"(John, viii. 29). It is because the Monothelites have not made this distinction of the will that they deny altogether to Christ human will: " Sicut origo erroris Nestorianorum et Eutychianorum fuit, quod non satis distinguerent personam, et naturam; sic et Monothelitis, et quod nescirent quia inter voluntatem *Naturalem* et *Personalem*,

---

(4) St. Cyril, Alex. *l*. 4, in Joan.

sive *Arbitrarium* discriminis interesset, hoc in causa fuisse, ut unam in Christo dicerent voluntatem"(5).

11. They say, secondly, that there being only one Person there must be only one will, because, the Mover being but one, the faculty by which he moves the inferior powers must be but one likewise. We answer, that where there is but one Person and one nature there can be only one will and one operation, but where there is one Person and two natures, as the Divine and human nature in Christ, we must admit two wills and two distinct operations, corresponding to the two natures. They say, very properly, that the will and the operations are not multiplied according as the Persons are multiplied, for in the case where one nature is the term of several Persons, as is the case in the Most Holy Trinity, then in this nature there is only one will and one operation alone, common to all the Persons included in the term of the nature. Here the Monothelites have reason on their side, for the Mover is but one. But it is quite otherwise when the Person is one of the two natures, for then the Mover, although but one, has to move two natures, by which he operates, and, consequently, he must have two wills and two operations.

12. They make a third objection. The operations, they say, belong to two Persons, and, consequently, when the Person is but one, the operation must be but one likewise. We answer, that it is not always the case that when there is but one Person that there is but one operating faculty, but when there are more Persons than one, then there must be more than one operating faculty. There are three Persons in God, but only one operation common to all three, because the Divine nature is one and indivisible in God. But as in Jesus Christ there are two distinct natures, there are, therefore, two wills, by which he operates, and two operations corresponding to each nature; and, although all the operations, both of the Divine and human nature are attributed to the Word, which terminates and sustains the two natures, still the will and operations of the Divine nature should not be confounded with those of the human nature; neither are the two natures confused because the Person is one.

REFUTATION X.

THE HERESY OF BERENGARIUS, AND THE PRETENDED REFORMERS, CONCERNING THE MOST HOLY SACRAMENT OF THE EUCHARIST.

1. MOSHEIM, the Protestant ecclesiastical historian, asserts (1) that in the ninth century, the exact nature of the faith of the body

---

(5) St. Joan. Dames Orat. de 2 Christ. Volent. (1) Mosh. His. *t.* 3, Cent. IX. *c.* 3, *p.* 1175.

and blood of Jesus Christ in the Eucharist was not established, and that, therefore, Pascasius Radbertus laid down in a book he wrote two principal points concerning it; first, that after the consecration nothing remained of the substance of the bread and wine; and, secondly, that in the consecrated Host is the very body of Jesus Christ, which was born of Mary, died on the cross, and arose from the sepulchre, and this, he said, is " what the whole world believes and professes." This work was opposed by Retramn, and perhaps others, and hence Mosheim concludes that the dogma was not then established. In this, however, he is astray, for, as Selvaggi writes (*note* 79, *vol.* iii.), there was no controversy at all about the dogma, in which Retramn was agreed with Radbert; he only attacked some expressions in his work. The truth of the Real Presence of Christ in the Sacrament of the Altar has been always established and universally embraced by the whole Church, as Vincent of Lerins says, in 434: " Mos iste semper in Ecclesia viguit, ut quo quisque forte religiosior, eo promtius novellis adinventionibus contrairet." Up to the ninth century the Sacrament of the Eucharist never was impugned, till John Scotus Erigena, an Irishman, first published to the world the unheard-of heresy that the body and blood of Christ were not in reality in the Holy Eucharist, which, he said, was only a figure of Jesus Christ.

2. Berengarius, or Berenger, taught the same heresy in the year 1050, taking his opinions from the works of Scotus Erigena, and in the twelfth century we find the Petrobrussians and Henricians, who said that the Eucharist was only a mere sign of the body and blood of our Lord. The Albigenses held the same error in the thirteenth century, and finally, in the sixteenth century the modern Reformers all joined in attacking this holy Sacrament. Zuingle and Carlostad said that the Eucharist was a signification of the body and blood of Jesus Christ, and Ecolampadius joined them afterwards, and Bucer, also, partially. Luther admitted the Real Presence of Christ in the Eucharist, but said that the substance of the bread remained there also. Calvin several times changed his opinion on the matter; he said, in order to deceive the Catholics, that the Eucharist was not a mere sign, or naked figure of Christ, but was filled with his Divine Virtue, and sometimes he even admitted that the very substance of the body of Christ was there, but his general opinion was that the presence of Christ was not real but figurative, by the power placed there by our Lord. Hence Bossuet says in his " Variations," he never wished to admit that the sinner, in communicating, receives the body of Christ, for then he should admit the Real Presence. The Council of Trent (*Sess.* xiii. *c.* 1) teaches, " that Jesus Christ, God and man, is really, truly, and substantially contained under the appearance of those sensible things in the Sacrament of the Eucharist, after the consecration of the bread and wine."

3. Before we prove the Real Presence of Christ in the Eucharist; we must know that it is a true Sacrament, as the Council of Florence declares in its decree or instruction for the Armenians, and the Council of Trent (*Sess.* vii. *c.* 1), in opposition to the Socinians, who say that it is not a Sacrament, but merely a remembrance of the death of our Saviour. It is, however, an article of Faith that the Eucharist is a true Sacrament; for, First, we have the sensible sign, the appearance of bread and wine. Secondly, there is the institution of Christ: " Do this in commemoration of me" (Luke, xxii.) Thirdly, there is the promise of grace: " Who eats my flesh....hath eternal life." We now have to inquire what in the Eucharist constitutes a Sacrament. The Lutherans say that it is in the use, with all the actions that Christ did, at the last Supper, that the Sacrament consists, as St. Matthew tells us: " Jesus took bread, blessed it, broke it, and gave it to his disciples" (Matt. xxvi). The Calvinists, on the other hand, say that it is in the actual eating that the Sacrament consists. We Catholics believe that the consecration is not the Sacrament, because that is a transitory action, and the Eucharist is a permanent Sacrament, as we shall show hereafter (*sec.* 3), nor the use or communion, for this regards the effect of the Sacrament, which is a Sacrament before it is received at all, nor in the species alone, for these do not confer grace, nor the body of Jesus Christ alone, because it is not there in a sensible manner; but the sacramental species, together with the body of Christ, form the Sacrament, inasmuch as they contain the body of our Lord.

SEC. I.—OF THE REAL PRESENCE OF THE BODY AND BLOOD OF JESUS CHRIST IN THE EUCHARIST.

4. WE have already said that the Council of Trent (*Sess.* xiii. *c.* 3) teaches that Jesus Christ is contained in the sacramental species, *truly, really,* and *substantially:—truly,* rejecting the figurative presence, for the figure is opposed to truth; *really,* rejecting the imaginary presence which Faith makes us aware of, as the Sacramentarians assert; and *substantially,* rejecting the doctrine of Calvin, who said that in the Eucharist it was not the body of Christ, but his virtue or power, that was present, by which he communicates himself to us; but in this he erred, for the whole substance of Jesus Christ is in the Eucharist. Hence, the Council of Trent (*Can.* 1) condemns those who assert that Christ is in the sacrament as a sign, or figure, *signo vel figura, aut virtute.*

5. The Real Presence is proved, first, by the words of Christ himself: " Take and eat, this is my body," words which are quoted by St. Matthew (xxvi. 26); St. Mark (xiv. 22); St. Luke (xxii. 19); and St. Paul (1 Cor. xi. 24). It is a certain rule, says St. Augustin (1), and is commonly followed by the Holy Fathers, to take the

(1) St. Aug *l.* 3, de Doct. Chris. *c.* 10.

words of Scripture in their proper literal sense, unless some absurdity would result from doing so; for if it were allowed to explain everything in a mystic sense, it would be impossible to prove any article of Faith from the Scripture, and it would only become the source of a thousand errors, as every one would give it whatever sense he pleased. Therefore, says the Council (*Cap.* 1), it is an enormous wickedness to distort the words of Christ by feigned figurative explanations, when three of the Evangelists and St. Paul give them just as he expressed them: " Quæ verba a sanctis Evangelistis commemorata, et a D. Paulo repetita cum propriam illam significationem præ se ferant...... indignissimum flagitium est ea ad fictitios tropos contra universum Ecclesiæ sensum detorqueri." Who will dare to doubt that it is his body and blood, says St. Cyril of Jerusalem, when Christ has said so (2)? " Cum ipse de pane pronunciaverit, Hoc est corpus meum, quis audebit deinceps ambigere? Et cum idem ipse dixerit, Hic est sanguis meus, quis dicet non esse ejus sanguinem?" We put this question to the heretics: Could Jesus Christ turn the bread into his body or not? We believe not one of them will deny that he could, for every Christian knows that God is all-powerful, " because no word shall be impossible with God" (Luke, i. 37). But they will answer, perhaps: We do not deny that he could, but perhaps he did not wish to do it. Did not wish to do it, perhaps? But tell me, if he did wish to do so, could he have possibly declared more clearly what his will was, than by saying: " This is my body?" When he was asked by Caiphas: " Art thou the Christ, the Son of the blessed God? And Jesus said to him: I am" (Mark, xiv. 61, 62), we should say, according to their mode of explanation, that he spoke figuratively also. Besides, if you allow, with the Sacramentarians, that the words of Christ: " This is my body," are to be taken figuratively, why, then, do you object to the Socinians, who say that the words of Christ, quoted by St. John (x. 30): " I and the Father are one," ought to be taken not literally, but merely showing that between Christ and the Father there existed a moral union of the will, but not a union of substance, and, consequently, denied his Divinity. We now pass on to the other proofs.

6. The Real Presence is proved, secondly, by that text of St. John where Christ says: " The bread that I will give is my flesh for the life of the world" (John, vi. 52). Our adversaries explain away this text, by saying, that here our Redeemer does not in this chapter speak of the Eucharist, but of the Incarnation of the Word. We do not say that in the beginning of the chapter it is the Incarnation that is spoken of; but there cannot be the least doubt but that from the 52nd verse out it is the Eucharist, as even Calvin admits (3); and it was thus the Fathers and Councils always un-

(2) St Cyril, Hieros. Cath. Mystagog. 4.   (3) Calvin. Instit. *l.* 4, *c.* 17, *s.* 1.

derstood it, as the Council of Trent, which (*Cap.* 2, *Sess.* xiii. and *Cap.* 1, *Sess.* xxii.) quotes several passages from that chapter to confirm the Real Presence; and the Second Council of Nice (*Act.* 6) quotes the 54th verse of the same chapter: " Unless you eat the flesh of the Son of Man," &c., to prove that the true body of Christ is offered up in the sacrifice of the Mass. It is in this chapter, also, that our Saviour promises to give to the faithful, at a future time, his own flesh as food: " The bread that I will give is my flesh, for the life of the world" (*ver.* 52), and here he sets totally aside the false explanation of the sectarians, who say that he only speaks of the spiritual manducation by means of faith, in believing the Incarnation of the Word; for if that was our Lord's meaning, he would not say: " The bread which *will* give," but " the bread which I *have* given," for the Word was already incarnate, and his disciples might then spiritually feed on Jesus Christ; therefore he said: " *I will give*," for he had not as yet instituted the Sacrament, but only promised to do so, and as St. Thomas (4) remarks, he says, " the bread which I will give is my flesh, for the life of the world;" he did not say, it means my flesh (as the Zuinglians afterwards explained it), but it is my flesh, because it is truly the body of Christ which is received. Our Lord next says: " My flesh is meat indeed, and my blood is drink indeed" (John, vi. 56); and, therefore, St. Hilary (5) says he leaves us no room to doubt of the truth of his body and blood. In fact, if the real body and blood of Christ were not in the Eucharist, this passage would be a downright falsehood. We should not forget, also, that the distinction between meat and drink can only be understood as referring to the eating of the true body, and drinking the true blood of Christ, and not of spiritual eating by faith, as the Reformers assert; for, as that is totally internal, the meat and the drink would be only one and the same thing, and not two distinct things.

7. We have another strong proof in the same chapter of St. John (*chap.* vi.); for the people of Caphernaum, hearing Christ speak thus, said: " How can this man give us his flesh to eat?" (*ver.* 53); and they even thought it so unreasonable, that " after this many of his disciples went back, and walked no more with him" (*ver.* 67). Now, if the flesh of Christ was not really in the Eucharist, he could remove the scandal from them at once, by saying that it was only spiritually they were called on to eat his flesh by faith; but, instead of that, he only confirmed more strongly what he said before, for he said: " Except you eat the flesh of the Son of Man, and drink his blood, you shall not have life in you" (*ver.* 54). And he then turned to the twelve disciples, who remained with him, and said: " Will you also go away? And

---

(4) St. Thom. Lec. 9, in Joan.   (5) St. Hilar. *l.* 8, de Trin. *n.* 13.

Peter answered him: Lord, to whom shall we go? thou hast the words of eternal life, and we have believed and have known that thou art the Christ the Son of God" (*ver.* 69, 70).

8. The Real Presence of Christ in the Eucharist is proved also from the words of St. Paul: "For let a man prove himself...... for he that eateth and drinketh unworthily, eateth and drinketh judgment to himself, not discerning the body of the Lord" (1 Cor. xi. 28, 29). Now, mark these words, "the body of the Lord." Does not that prove how erroneously the sectarians act, in saying that in the Eucharist we venerate, by faith, the figure alone of the body of Christ; for if that was the case, the Apostle would not say that they who received in sin were deserving of eternal condemnation; but he clearly states that one who communicates unworthily is so, for he does not distinguish the body of the Lord from the common earthly food.

9. Fourthly, it is proved again from St. Paul, for speaking of the use of this Holy Sacrament, he says: "The chalice of benediction which we bless, is it not the communion of the blood of Christ? and the bread which we break, is it not the partaking of the body of the Lord?" (1 Cor. x. 16). Mark the words, "the bread which we break;" that which is first offered to God on the altar, and afterwards distributed to the people, is it not the partaking of the body of the Lord? Do not, in a word, those who receive it partake of the true body of Christ?

10. Fifthly, it is proved by the Decrees of Councils. We find it first mentioned in the Council of Alexandria, which was afterwards approved of by the first Council of Constantinople. Next, the Council of Ephesus sanctioned the twelve anathematisms of St. Cyril against Nestorius, and in this the Real Presence of Christ in the Eucharist is taught. The second Council of Nice (*Act.* 6) condemns, as an error against Faith, the assertion that the figure alone, and not the true body of Christ, is in the Eucharist; for, says the Council, Christ said, take and eat, this is my body, but he did not say, take and eat, this is the image of my body. In the Roman Council, under Gregory VII., in 1079, Berengarius, in the Profession of Faith which he made, confesses that the bread and wine are, by the consecration, substantially converted into the body and blood of Christ. The Fourth Council of Lateran, under Innocent III., in the year 1215 (*chap.* 1), says: "We believe that the body and blood of Christ are contained under the species of bread and wine, the bread being transubstantiated into the body, and the wine into the blood." In the Council of Constance the propositions of Wickliffe and Huss were condemned, which said that (in the Eucharist) the bread was present in reality, and the body figuratively, and that the expression "this is my body" is a figure of speech, just like the expression, "John is Elias"......

The Council of Florence, in the Decree of Union for the Greeks, decrees, "that the body of Christ is truly consecrated (*veraciter confici*) in bread of wheat, either leavened or unleavened."

11. It is proved, sixthly, by the perpetual and uniform tradition of the Holy Fathers. St. Ignatius the Martyr (6) says: "Eucharistiam non admittunt, quod non confiteantur Eucharistiam esse carnem Salvatoris nostri Jesu Christi." St. Irænus (7): "Panis percipiens invocationem Dei jam non communis panis est sed Eucharistia." And in another place he says (8): "Eum, panem in quo gratiæ sunt actæ, corpus esse Christi, et calicem sanguinis ejus." St. Justin, Martyr, writes (9): "Non hunc ut communem panem sumimus, sed quemadmodum per verbum Dei caro factum est J. C. carnem habuit," &c. He, therefore, says, that the same flesh which the Word assumed is in the Eucharist. Tertullian (10) says: "Caro corpore et sanguine Christi vescitur, ut et anima de Deo saginetur." Origen writes (11): "Quando vitæ pane et poculo frueris, manducas et bibis, corpus et sanguinem Domini." Hear St. Ambrose (12): "Panis iste panis est ante verba Sacramentorum; ubi accesserit consecratio, de pane fit caro Christi." St. Chrysostom says (13): "Quot nunc dicunt vellem ipsius formam aspicere...... Ecce eum vides, Ipsum tangis, Ipsum manducas." St. Athanasius, St. Basil, and St. Gregory of Nazianzen, express the same sentiments (14). St. Augustin says (15): "Sicut mediatorem Dei et hominum, hominem Christum Jesum, carnem suam nobis manducandam, bibendumque sanguinem dantem fidei corde suspicimus." St. Remigius (16) says: "Licet panis videatur, in veritate corpus Christi est." St. Gregory the Great writes (17): "Quid sit sanguis agni non jam audiendo sed libendo didicistis qui sanguis super utrumque postem ponitur quando non solum ore corporis, sed etiam ore cordis hauritur." St. John of Damascus (18) writes: "Panis, ac vinum, et aqua qua per Spiritus Sancti invocationem et adventum mirabili modo in Christi corpus et sanguinem vertuntur." Thus we see an uninterrupted series of Fathers for the first seven centuries proclaiming, in the clearest and most forcible language, the doctrine of the Real Presence of Jesus Christ in the Most Holy Sacrament of the Eucharist.

12. By this we see how false is the interpretation which Zuinglius put on that text, "This is my body," when he said that the word *is* means *signifies*, founding his heresy on a verse of Exodus (xii. 11): "For it is the phase (that is the passage) of the Lord." Now, said he, the eating of the paschal lamb was not itself the

---

(6) St. Ignat. Ep. ad Smirn. ap. Theodor. Dial. 3.   (7) St. Iræn. *l.* ad Hær. *c.* 18, al 34.   (8) Idem, *l.* 4, *c.* 34.   (9) St. Justin. Apol. 2.   (10) Tertul. *l.* Resur. *c.* 8.   (11) Orig. Hom. 5, in divers.   (12) St. Amb. *l.* 4, de Sacram. *c.* 4.   (13) St. Chrys. Hom. ad Pop. Antioch.   (14) Apud. Antoin. de Euch. Theol. Univer. *c.* 4, 1.   (15) St. Aug. *l.* 2, con. adver. legis. *c.* 9.   (16) St. Remig. in Ep. ad Cor. *c.* 10.   (17) St. Greg. Hom. 22, in Evang.   (18) St. Joan. Damas. *l.* 4, Orthodox. *c.* 14.

passage of the Lord; it only meant it, or signified it. The Zuinglians alone follow this interpretation, for we never can take the sense of the word *is* for the word *means* or *signifies*, unless in cases where reason itself shows that the word *is* has a figurative meaning; but in this case the Zuinglian explanation is contrary to the proper literal sense in which we should always understand the Scriptures, when that sense is not repugnant to reason. The Zuinglian explanation is also opposed to St. Paul, relating to us the very words of Christ: "This is my body, which shall be delivered up for you" (1 Cor. xi. 24). Our Lord, we see, did not deliver up, in his Passion, the sign or signification of his body, but his real and true body. The Zuinglians say, besides, that in the Syro-Chaldaic or Hebrew, in which our Redeemer spoke, when instituting the Eucharist, there is no word corresponding in meaning to our word *signify*, and hence, in the Old Testament, we always find the word *is* used instead of it, and, therefore, the words of Christ, "This *is* my body," should be understood, as if he said, "This *signifies* my body." We answer: First.—It is not the fact that the word *signifies* is never found in the Old Testament, for we find in Exodus: "Man-hu! which *signifieth* What is this" (Exod. xvi. 15); and in Judges (xiv. 15): "Persuade him to tell thee what the riddle *meaneth;*" and in Ezechiel (xvii. 12): "Know you not what these things *mean*." Secondly.—Although the words *mean* or *signify* are not found in the Hebrew or Syro-Chaldaic, still the word *is* must not always be taken for it, only in case that the context should show that such is the intention of the speaker; but in this case the word has surely its own signification, as we learn, especially from the Greek version; this language has both words, and still the Greek text says, "This *is* my body," and not "This *means* my body."

13. The opinion of those sectarians, who say that in the Eucharist only a figure exists, and not the body of Christ in reality, is also refuted by these words of our Lord, already quoted: "This is my body, which shall be delivered up for you" (1 Cor. xi. 24); for Jesus Christ delivered up his body to death, and not the figure of his body. And, speaking of his sacred blood, he says (St. Matt. xxvi. 28): "For this is my blood of the New Testament which shall be shed for many unto remission of sins." Christ, then, shed his real blood, and not the figure of his blood; for the figure is expressed by speech, or writing, or painting, but the figure is not shed. Piceninus (19) objects that St. Augustin, speaking of that passage of St John, "Unless you eat the flesh of the Son of Man," says that the flesh of our Lord is a figure, bringing to our mind the memory of his passion: "Figura est præcipiens Passione Dominica esse communicandum." We answer, that we do not deny that our Redeemer instituted the Holy Eucharist in memory of his death, as

(19) St. Aug. *l*. 3, de Doct. Christian. *c*. 16.

we learn from St. Paul (1 Cor. xi. 26): "For as often as you shall eat this bread, and drink this chalice, you shall show the death of the Lord until he come;" but still we assert, that in the Eucharist there is the true body of Christ, and there is, at the same time, a figure, commemorative of his death; and this is St. Augustin's meaning, for he never doubted that the body and blood of Christ were in the Eucharist really and truly, as he elsewhere expresses it (20): "Panis quem videtis in Altari, sanctificatus per verbum Dei, Corpus est Christi."

14. There is, I should say, no necessity of refuting Calvin's opinions on the Real Presence, for he constantly refutes himself, changing his opinion a thousand times, and always cloaking it in ambiguous terms. Bossuet and Du Hamel (21) may be consulted on this point. They treat the subject extensively, and quote Calvin's opinion, who says, at one time, that the true substance of the body of Christ is in the Eucharist, and then again (22), that Christ is united to us by Faith; so that, by the presence of Christ, he understands a presence of power or virtue in the Sacrament; and this is confirmed by him in another part of his works, where he says that Christ is just as much present to us in the Eucharist as he is in baptism. At one time he says the Sacrament of the Altar is a miracle, and then again (23), the whole miracle, he says, consists in this, that the faithful are vivified by the flesh of Christ, since a virtue so powerful descends from heaven on earth. Again, he says, that even the unworthy receive in the Supper the body of Christ, and then, in another place (24), he says that he is received by the elect alone. In fine, we see Calvin struggling, in the explanation of this dogma, not to appear a heretic with the Zuinglians, nor a Catholic with the Roman Catholics. Here is the Profession of Faith which the Calvinist ministers presented to the prelates, at the Conference of Poissy, as Bossuet gives it (25): "We believe that the body and blood are really united to the bread and wine, but in a sacramental manner—that is, not according to the natural position of bodies, but inasmuch as they signify that God gives his body and blood to those who truly receive him by Faith." It was remarkable in that Conference, that Theodore Beza, the first disciple of Calvin, and who had hardly time to have imbibed all his errors, said publicly, as De Thou (26) relates, " that Jesus Christ was as far from the Supper as the heavens were from the earth." The French prelates then drew up a true Confession of Faith, totally opposed to the Calvinists: "We believe," said they, " that in the Sacrament of the Altar there is really and transubstantially the true body and blood of Jesus Christ, under the appearance of bread and wine, by the power of the Divine Word pronounced by the priest," &c.

(20) St. Aug. Ser. 83, de Div. n 27. (21) Bossuet, His. des Variat. t. 2, l. 9; Du Hamel, Theol. de Euch. (22) Calvin, Inst. l. 4, c. 11. (23) Idem. (24) Idem. (25) Bossuet, t. 2, l. 9. (26) Thuan. l. 28, c. 48.

OBJECTIONS AGAINST THE REAL PRESENCE ANSWERED.

15. THEY object, first, the words of Christ: "It is the Spirit that quickeneth, the flesh profiteth nothing. These words that I have spoken to you are spirit and life" (John, vi. 64). See there, they say, the words which you make use of to prove the Real Presence of Christ in the Eucharist are figurative expressions, which signify the celestial food of life, which we receive by faith. We answer, with St. John Chrysostom (1), that when Christ says the flesh profiteth nothing, he spoke not of his own flesh, God forbid! but of those who carnally receive it, as the Apostle says: "The sensual man perceiveth not those things that are of the Spirit of God" (1 Cor. ii. 14), and those who carnally speak of the Divine Mysteries; and to this St. John refers when he says: "The words I have spoken to you are spirit and life" (John, vi. 64), meaning that these words refer not to carnal and perishable things, but to spiritual things and to eternal life. But even supposing these words to refer to the flesh of Christ itself, they only mean, as St. Athanasius and St. Augustin explain them, that the flesh of Christ, given to us as food, sanctifies us by the Spirit, or the Divinity united to it, but that the flesh alone would be of no avail. These are St. Augustin's words (2): "Non prodest quidquam (caro), sed quomodo; illi intellexerunt, carnem quippe sic intellexerunt, quomodo in cadavere dilaniatur, aut in macello venditur, non quomodo spiritu vegetatur. Caro non prodest quidquam, sed sola caro; accedat spiritus ad carnem, et prodest plurimum."

16. They object, secondly, that when Jesus Christ said: "This is my body," the word *this* in the sentence has reference to the bread alone, which he then held in his hand, but bread is only a figure of the body of Christ, but not the body itself. We answer that if we do not consider the proposition "This is my body" as complete in itself, that might be the case if he said, for example, *this is*, and did not say any more, then the word *this* would have reference to the bread alone, which he held in his hand; but taking the whole sentence together, there can be no doubt but that the word *this* refers to the body of Christ. When our Lord changed water into wine, if he had said, *this is wine*, every one would understand that the word *this* referred not to the water but to the wine, and in the same way in the Eucharist the word *this*, in the complete sense of the sentence, refers to the body, because the change is made when the whole sentence is completed. In fact the word *this* in the sentence has no meaning at all, till the latter part is pronounced, *is my body*—then alone the sense is complete.

17. They object, thirdly, that the sentence, "This is my body," is just as figurative as other passages in the Scriptures, as for example,

(1) St. John Chrysos. Hom. in Joan.   (2) St. Aug. Tract. 27 in Joan.

when Christ says: " I am the true vine," " I am the gate," or when it is said he is the Rock. We reply that it is a matter of course that these propositions should be taken figuratively, for that Christ should be literally a vine, a door, or a rock is repugnant to common sense, and the words " I am," therefore, are figurative. In the words of consecration, however, there is nothing repugnant to reason in joining the predicate with the subject, because, as we have remarked already, Christ did not say This bread is my body, but " This is my body;" *this*, that is what is contained under the appearance of this bread, is my body; here there is nothing repugnant to reason.

18. They object, fourthly, that the Real Presence is opposed to the words of Christ himself, for he said (John, xii. 8): " The poor you have always with you, but me you have not always." Our Saviour, therefore, after his ascension, is no longer on earth. Our Lord, we reply, then spoke of his visible presence as man receiving honour from Magdalen. When Judas, therefore, murmured against the waste of the ointment, our Lord reproves him, saying, you have not me always with you, that is, in the visible and natural form of man, but there is here nothing to prove that after his ascension into heaven he does not remain on earth in the Eucharist, under the appearance of bread and wine, invisibly, and in a supernatural manner. In this sense we must understand also all similar passages, as, " I leave the world and go to my Father" (John, xvi. 18): " He was taken up into heaven, and sits at the right hand of God" (Mark, xvi. 19).

19. They object, fifthly, these words of the Apostle: " Our fathers were all under the cloud..... and did all eat the same spiritual food" (1 Cor. x. 1-3); therefore, they say, we only receive Christ in the Eucharist by Faith, just as the Hebrews received him. We answer, that the sense of the words is, that the Hebrews received spiritual food, the Manna, of which St. Paul speaks, the figure of the Eucharist, but did not receive the body of Christ in reality, as we receive it. The Hebrews received the figure, but we receive the real body, already prefigured.

20. Sixthly, they object that Christ said: " I will not drink from henceforth of this fruit of the vine, until that day when I shall drink it with you new, in the kingdom of my Father" (Matt. xxvi. 29), and these words he expressed, after having previously said, " This is my blood of the New Testament, which shall be shed for many for the remission of sins" (*ver.* 28). Now, say they, take notice of the words, *fruit of the vine*, that is a proof that the wine remains after the consecration. We answer, first, that Christ might have called it wine, even after the consecration, not because the substance, but because the form of wine was retained, just as St. Paul calls the Eucharist bread after the consecration: " Whosoever shall eat this bread, or drink the chalice of the Lord unworthily,

shall be guilty of the body and the blood of the Lord" (*ver.* 29). Secondly, we reply, with St. Fulgentius (3), who supposes that Christ took two chalices, one the Paschal chalice, according to the Jewish rite, the other according to the Sacramental rite. Our Lord then, he says, when using the words they found the objection on, spoke of the first chalice, and not of the second, and that he did so is clear from the words of another of the Evangelists, St. Luke (xxii. 17), who says that "having taken the chalice, he gave thanks, and said: Take and divide it among you. For I say to you that I will not drink of the fruit of the vine, till the kingdom of God come." Now, if we read on to the 20th verse of the same chapter, we find that Jesus took the chalice of wine and consecrated it: "In like manner the chalice also, after he had supped, saying: This is the chalice, the New Testament, in my blood which shall be shed for you." Hence it is manifest that the words, "I will not drink of the fruit of the vine," were expressed by our Redeemer previous to the consecration of the chalice.

21. They object, seventhly, that the doctrine of the Real Presence cannot be true, for it is opposed to all our senses. But to this we reply, with the Apostle, that matters of faith are not manifest to the senses, for "Faith....is the evidence of things that appear not" (Heb. xi. 1). And we have another text, also, which disposes of this feeble argument: "The sensual man perceiveth not the things that are of the Spirit of God, for it is foolishness to him" (1 Cor. ii. 14). All this will be answered more extensively farther on (*sec.* 3).

SEC. II. — TRANSUBSTANTIATION, THAT IS, THE CONVERSION OF THE SUBSTANCE OF THE BREAD AND OF THE WINE INTO THE SUBSTANCE OF THE BODY AND BLOOD OF JESUS CHRIST.

22. LUTHER at first left it as a matter of choice to each person, either to believe in Transubstantiation or not, but he changed his opinion afterwards, and in 1522, in the book which he wrote against Henry VIII., he says: "I now wish to transubstantiate my own opinion. I thought it better before to say nothing about the belief in Transubstantiation, but now I declare, that if any one holds this doctrine, he is an impious blasphemer" (1), and he concludes by saying, that in the Eucharist, along with the body and blood of Christ, remains the substance of the bread and wine: "that the body of Christ is in the bread, with the bread, and under the bread, just as fire is in a red-hot iron." He, therefore, called the Real Presence "Impanation," or "Consubstantiation," that is, the association of the substance of bread and wine with the substance of the body and blood of Jesus Christ.

23. The Council of Trent, however, teaches that the whole

(3) St Fulgen. ad Ferrand. Dial. de Zuing. quæst. ix. 5.   (1) Luther, lib. con. Reg. Angliæ.

substance of the bread and wine is changed into the body and blood of Christ. It issued a decree to that effect (*Cap.* 4, *Sess.* xiii.), and says, that the Church most aptly calls this change Transubstantiation. Here are the words of the Second Can.: " Si quis dixerit in sacrosancto Eucharistiæ sacramento remanere substantiam panis et vini una cum corpore et sanguine D. N. J. C., negaveritque mirabilem illam, et singularem conversionem totius substantiæ panis in corpus, et totius substantiæ vini in sanguinem, manentibus dumtaxat speciebus panis et vini, quam quidem conversionem Catholica Ecclesia aptissime Transubstantiationem appellat, anathema sit." Remark the words, *mirabilem illum, et singularem conversionem totius substantiæ*, the wonderful and singular conversion of the whole substance. It is called *wonderful*, for it is a mystery hidden from us, and which we never can comprehend. It is *singular*, because in all nature there is not another case of a similar change; and it is called a *conversion*, because it is not a simple union with the body of Christ, such as was the hypostatic union by which the Divine and human natures were united in the sole person of Christ. Such is not the case, then, in the Eucharist, for the substance of the bread and wine is not united with, but is totally changed and converted into, the body and blood of Jesus Christ. We say a conversion of the *whole substance*, to distinguish it from other conversions or changes, such as the change of food into the body of the person who partakes of it, or the change of water into wine by our Redeemer at Cana, and the change of the rod of Moses into a serpent, for in all these changes the substance remained, and it was the form alone that was changed; but in the Eucharist the matter and form of the bread and wine is changed, and the species alone remain, that is, the appearance alone, as the Council explains it, " remanentibus dumtaxat speciebus panis et vini."

24. The general opinion is, that this conversion is not performed by the creation of the body of Christ, for creation is the production of a thing out of nothing; but this is the conversion of the substance of the bread into the substance of the body of Christ. It does not take place either by the annihilation of the matter of the bread and wine, because annihilation means the total destruction of a thing, and the body of Christ, then, would be changed, we may say, from nothing; but in the Eucharist the substance of the bread passes into the substance of Christ, so that it is not from nothing. Neither does it take place by the transmutation of the form alone (as a certain author endeavours to prove), the same matter still remaining, as happened when the water was changed into wine, and the rod into a serpent. Scotus says that Transubstantiation is an act adducing the body of Christ into the Eucharist (*actio adductiva*); but this opinion is not followed by others, for adduction does not mean conversion by the passage of one substance into the other. It cannot be called, either, a unitive action, for that

supposes two extremes in the point of union. Hence, we say, with St. Thomas, that the consecration operates in such a manner, that if the body of Christ was not in heaven, it would commence to exist in the Eucharist. The consecration really, and *in instanti*, as the same Doctor says (2), reproduces the body of Christ under the present species of bread, for as this is a sacramental action, it is requisite that there should be an external sign, in which the rationale of a Sacrament consists.

25. The Council of Trent has declared (*Sess.* xiii. *cap.* 3), that *vi verborum* the body of Christ alone is under the appearance of bread, and the blood alone under the appearance of wine; that by natural and proximate concomitance the soul of our Saviour is under both species, with his body and his blood; by supernatural and remote concomitance the Divinity of the Word is present, by the hypostatic union of the Word with the body and soul of Christ; and that the Father and the Holy Ghost are present, by the identity of the essence of the Father and the Holy Ghost with the Word. Here are the words of the Council: "Semper hæc fides in Ecclesia Dei fuit, statim post consecrationem verum Domini nostri corpus, vetumque ejus sanguinem sub panis, et vini specie, una cum ipsius anima, et Divinitate existere; sed corpus quidem sub specie panis, et sanguinem sub vini specie ex vi verborum; ipsum autem corpus sub specie vini, et sanguinem sub specie panis, animamque sub utraque vi naturalis illius connexionis, et concomitantiæ, qua partes Christi Domini, qui jam ex mortuis resurrexit, non amplius moriturus, inter se copulantur: Divinitatem porro propter admirabilem illam ejus cum corpore, et anima hypostaticam unionem."

26. Transubstantiation is proved by the very words of Christ himself: " This is my body." The word *this*, according to the Lutherans themselves, proves that Christ's body was really present. If the body of Christ was there, therefore the substance of the bread was not there; for if the bread was there, and if by the word *this* our Lord meant the bread, the proposition would be false, taking it in this sense, This is my body, that is, this bread is my body, for it is not true that the bread was the body of Christ. But perhaps they will then say, before our Lord expressed the word *body*, what did the word *this* refer to? We answer, as we have done already, that it does not refer either to the bread or to the body, but has its own natural meaning, which is this: This which is contained under the appearance of bread, is not bread, but is my body. St. Cyril of Jerusalem says (3): "Aquam aliquando (*Christus*) mutavit in vinum in Cana Galilææ sola voluntate, et non erit dignus cui credamus, quod vinum in sanguinem transmutasset." St. Gregory of Nyssa (4) says: "Panis

(2) St. Thom. *p.* 3, *qu.* 75, *art.* 7. (3) St. Cyril, Hieros. Cath. Mystagog. (4) St. Greg. Nyssa. Orat. Cath. *c.* 37.

statim per verbum transmutatur, sicut dictum est a Verbo: *Hoc est corpus meum.*" St. Ambrose writes thus (5): " Quantis utimur exemplis, ut probemus non hoc esse quod natura formavit, sed quod benedictio consecravit; majoremque vim esse benedictionis, quam naturæ, quia benedictione etiam natura ipsa mutatur." St. John of Damascus (6): " Panis, ac vinum et aqua per Sancti Spiritus invocationem, et adventum mirabili modo in Christi corpus et sanguinem vertuntur." Tertullian, St. Chrysostom, and St. Hilary used the same language (7).

27. Transubstantiation is also proved by the authority of Councils, and especially, first, by the Roman Council, under Gregory VII., in which Berengarius made his profession of Faith, and said: " Panem et vinum, quæ ponuntur in Altari, in veram et propriam ac vivificatricem carnem et sanguinem Jesu Christi substantialiter converti per verba consecratoria." Secondly.—By the Fourth Council of Lateran (*cap.* 1), which says: " Idem ipse Sacerdos et Sacrificium Jesus Christus, cumcorpus et sanguis in Sacramento Altaris sub speciebus panis et vini veraciter continetur, transubstantiatis pane in corpus, et vino in sanguinem potestate Divina," &c. Thirdly.—By the Council of Trent (*Sess.* xiii. *can.* 2), which condemns all who deny this doctrine: " Mirabilem illam conversionem totius substantiæ panis in corpus, et vini in sanguinem......quam conversionem Catholica Ecclesia aptissime Transubstantionem appellat."

OBJECTIONS AGAINST TRANSUBSTANTIATION ANSWERED.

28. THE Lutherans say, first, that the body of Christ is *locally* in the bread as in a vessel, and, as we say, showing a bottle in which wine is contained, " This is the wine," so, say they, Christ, showing the bread, said: " This is my body;" and hence, both the body of Christ and the bread are, at the same time, present in the Eucharist. We answer, that, according to the common mode of speech, a bottle is a fit and proper thing to show that wine is there, because wine is usually kept in bottles, but it is not the case with bread, which is not a fit and proper thing to designate or point out a human body, for it is only by a miracle that a human body could be contained in bread.

29. Just to confound one heresy by another, we will quote the argument of the Zuinglians (1) against the Impanation or Consubstantiation of the bread and the body of Christ, invented by the Lutherans. If, say they, the words " This is my body " are to be taken in a literal sense, as Luther says they are, then the Transubstantiation of the Catholics is true. And this is certainly the case.

---

(5) St. Ambrose de Initiand. *c.* 9. (6) St. Jo. Damas. *l.* 4, Orthod. Fidei, *c.* 14.
(7) Tertul. contra Marcion, *l.* 4, *c.* 4; Chrysos. Hom. 4, in una cor. St. Hil. *l.* 8, de Trinit. (1) Bossuet. Variat. *t.* 1, *l.* 2, *n.* 31; Ospinian. ann. 1527, *p.* 49.

Christ did not say, this bread is my body, or here is my body, but *this* thing is my body. Hence, say they, when Luther rejects the figurative meaning, that it is only the signification of the body of Christ, as they hold, and wishes to explain the words " this is my body" after his own fashion, that is, this bread is really my body, and not the frame of my body, this doctrine falls to the ground of itself, for if our Saviour intended to teach us that the bread was his body, and that the bread was there still, it would be a contradiction in itself. The true sense of the words " This is my body," however, is that the word *this* is to be thus understood: this, which I hold in my hands, is my body. Hence the Zuinglians concluded that the conversion of the substance of the bread into the substance of the body of Christ should be taken either totally figuratively or totally in substance, and this was Beza's opinion in the Conference of Monbeliard, held with the Lutherans. Here, then, is, according to the true dogma, the conclusion we should come to in opposition to Luther. When our Lord says, " This is my body," he intended that of that bread should be formed either the substance, or the figure of his body; if the substance of the bread, therefore, be not the mere simple figure of Christ's body, as Luther says, then it must become the whole substance of the body of Jesus Christ.

30. They object, secondly, that in the Scripture the Eucharist is called bread, even after the consecration: " One body .... who all partake of one bread" (1 Cor. x. 17); " Whosoever shall eat this bread, or drink the Chalice of the Lord unworthily," &c., (1 Cor. xi. 27); the bread, therefore, remains. Such, however, is not the case; it is called bread, not because it retains the substance of bread, but because the body of Christ is made from the bread. In the Scriptures we find that those things which are miraculously changed into other things are still called by the name of the thing from which they were changed, as the water which was changed into wine, by St. John, at the marriage of Cana in Galilee, was still called water, even after the change: " When the chief stewart had tasted the water made wine " (John, ii. 9); and in Exodus also we read that the rod of Moses changed into a serpent was still called a rod: " Aaron's rod devoured their rods " (Exod. vii. 12). In like manner, then, the Eucharist is called bread after the consecration, because it was bread before, and still retains the appearance of bread. Besides, as the Eucharist is the food of the soul, it may be justly called bread, as the Manna made by the angels is called bread, that is, spiritual bread: " Man eat the bread of angels " (Psalms, lxxvii. 25). The sectarians, however, say, the body of Christ cannot be broken, it is the bread alone that is broken, and still St. Paul says: " And the bread which we break is it not the partaking of the body of the Lord?" (1 Cor. x. 16.) We answer, that the breaking is understood to refer to the species of the bread which remain, but not to the body of the Lord, which, being

present in a sacramental manner, cannot be either broken or injured.

31. They object, thirdly, that Christ says, in St. John: "I am the bread of life" (John, vi. 48); still he was not changed into bread. The very text, however, answers the objection itself. Our Lord says: "I am the bread of life:" now the word "life" shows that the expression must be taken not in a natural but a metaphorical sense. The words "This is my body" must, however, be taken in quite another way; in order that this proposition should be true, it was necessary that the bread should be changed into the body of Christ, and this is Transubstantiation, which is an article of our Faith, and which consists in the conversion of the substance of the bread into the substance of the body of Christ, so that in the very instant in which the words of consecration are concluded, the bread has no longer the substance of bread, but under its species exists the body of the Lord. The conversion, then, has two terms, in one of which it ceases to be, and in the other commences to be, for otherwise, if the bread was first annihilated, and the body then produced, it would not be a true conversion or Transubstantiation. It is of no consequence to say that the word Transubstantiation is new, and not found in the Scriptures, when the thing signified, that is, the Eucharist, really exists. The Church has always adopted new expressions, to explain more clearly the truths of the Faith when attacked by heretics, as she adopted the word Consubstantial to combat the heresy of Arius.

SEC. III.—OF THE MANNER IN WHICH JESUS CHRIST IS IN THE EUCHARIST. THE PHILOSOPHICAL OBJECTIONS OF THE SACRAMENTARIANS ANSWERED.

32. BEFORE we reply in detail to the philosophical objections of the Sacramentarians relative to the manner in which the body of Jesus Christ is in the Sacrament, we should reflect that the Holy Fathers in matters of faith do not depend on philosophical principles, but on the authority of the Scriptures and the Church, knowing well that God can do many things which our weak reason cannot comprehend. We never will be able to understand the secrets of nature in created things; how, then, can we comprehend how far the power of the Almighty, the Creator of nature, itself, extends? We now come to their objections. First, they say that, although God is omnipotent, he cannot do anything which is repugnant in itself, but it is repugnant, they say, that Christ should be in heaven and on earth, at the same time, really and truly, as he is according to our belief, and not alone in one, but in many places, at the same time. Hear what the Council of Trent says on this subject (*Sess.* xiii. *c.* 1): "Nec enim hæc inter se pugnant, ut ipse Salvator noster semper ad dexteram Patris in cœlis assideat juxta modum existendi naturalem; et ut multis nihilominus aliis in

locis sacramentaliter præsens sua substantia nobis adsit, ex existendi ratione; quam etsi verbis exprimere vix possumus, possibilem tamen esse Deo, cogitatione per fidem illustrata, assequi possumus, et constantissime credere debemus." The Council, therefore, teaches that the body of Jesus Christ is in heaven in a natural manner, but that it is on earth in a sacramental or supernatural manner, which our limited understanding cannot comprehend, no more than we can understand how the three Divine Persons in the Trinity are the same essence, or how, in the Incarnation of the Word in Jesus Christ, there is but one Divine Person and two natures, the Divine and human.

33. It is impossible, they say also, for a human body to be in several places at once. We believe, however, that the body of Christ is not multiplied in the Eucharist, for our Lord is not there present *definitively*, or circumscribed to that place and to no other, but sacramentally, under the appearance of bread and wine, so that wherever the species of the consecrated bread and wine are, there Jesus Christ is present. The multiplicity of the presence of Christ, therefore, does not proceed from the multiplication of his body in many places, but from the multiplicity of the consecrations of the bread and wine, performed by the priests in different places. But how is it possible, say they, that the body of Christ can be in several places at once, unless it is multiplied? We answer, that before our adversaries can prove this to be impossible, they should have a perfect knowledge of place and of glorified bodies; they should know distinctly what place is, and what existence glorified bodies have. When such knowledge, however, surpasses our weak understandings, who shall have the hardihood to deny, that the body of our Lord can be in several places at once, since God has revealed in the Holy Scriptures that Jesus Christ really exists in every consecrated Host? But, they reply, we cannot understand this. We answer again, that the Eucharist is a mystery of Faith, since our understanding cannot comprehend it, and as we never can do so, it is rashness to say that it cannot be, when God has revealed it, and when we know we cannot decide by reason what is beyond the power of reason.

34. They assert, besides, that it is repugnant to reason to say that the body of Jesus Christ exists under the species, without extension or quantity, for both extension and quantity are essential qualities of bodies, and God himself cannot deprive things of their essences, therefore, say they, the body of Christ cannot exist without filling a space corresponding to its quantity, and, therefore, it cannot be in a small Host, and in every particle of the Host, as Catholics believe. We reply to this, that although God cannot deprive things of their essence, still he can deprive them of the property of their essence; he cannot take away from fire the essence of fire, but he can deprive fire of the essential quality of burning,

as he did in the case of Daniel and his companions, who were unharmed in the furnace. Thus, in like manner, though God cannot make a body to exist without extension and quantity, still he can make it, so that it will not occupy space, and that it will be entire in every part of the sensible species which contain it as a substance; the body of Christ, therefore, into which the substance of the bread is changed, does not occupy place, and is whole and entire in every part of the species. Here is how St. Thomas explains it (1): "Tota substantia corporis Christi continetur in hoc Sacramento post consecrationem, sicut ante consecrationem continebatur ibi tota substantia panis. Propria autem totalitas substantiæ continetur indifferenter in pauca vel magna quantitate, unde et tota substantia corporis et sanguinis Christi continetur in hoc sacramento."

35. That being the case, it is not the fact that the body of Christ in the Eucharist exists without quantity; the whole quantity is there, but in a supernatural not a natural manner. It does not exist, then, *circumscriptive*, that is, according to the measure of the proper quantity corresponding to the quantity of space; but it exists *sacramentaliter*—sacramentally, after the manner of a substance. Hence it is that Jesus Christ, in the Sacrament, does not exercise any action dependent on the senses; and although he exercises the acts of the intellect and of the will, he does not exercise the corporal acts of the sensitive life, which require a certain sensible and external extension in the organs of the body.

36. Neither is it true that Jesus Christ exists in the Sacrament without extension. His body is there, and it has extension; but this extension is not external, or sensible and local, but internal, *in ordine ad se*, so that although all the parts are in the same place, still one part is not confused with the other. Thus Jesus Christ exists in the Sacrament with internal extension; but as to external and local extension, he is inextended, and indivisible, and whole, and entire, in each particle of the Host, as a substance, as has been already said, without occupying space. Hence it is, that as the body of our Lord does not occupy space, it cannot be moved from one place to another, but is moved only *per accidens*, when the species are moved under which it is contained, just as happens to ourselves, that when our bodies are moved from one place to another, our souls are also moved, *per accidens*, though the soul is incapable of occupying any space. In fine, the Eucharist is a Sacrament of Faith, *mysterium Fidei*, and as we cannot comprehend all the matters of Faith, so we should not pretend to understand all that Faith, through the Church, teaches us concerning this Sacrament.

37. But how, say they, can the accidents of bread and wine exist without their substance, or *subject*, as it is called? We answer—the question whether accidents are distinct from matter

---

(1) St. Thom. *p.* 3, *q.* 76, *a.* 1.

has been already mooted; the most general opinion is in the affirmative; the Councils of Lateran, Florence, and Trent, however, keeping clear of the controversy altogether, call the accidents species. In the ordinary course of things these accidents, or species, cannot exist without the subject, but they can in a supernatural and extraordinary manner. In the ordinary course of things, humanity cannot exist without its proper subsistence (*subsistentia*); but notwithstanding, Faith teaches us that the humanity of Christ had not human, but Divine subsistence, that is, the Person of the Word. As the humanity of Christ, therefore, united to the Word hypostatically, subsists without the human person, so, in the Eucharist, the species can exist without the subject, that is, without the substance of bread, because their substance is changed into the body of Christ. These species, therefore, have nothing of reality, but by Divine power they represent their former subject, and appear still to retain the substance of bread and wine, and may even become corrupted, and worms may be generated in them, but, then, it is from a new matter, created by the Almighty, that these worms spring, and Jesus Christ is no longer present, as St. Thomas teaches (2). As far as the sensations of our organs go, the body of Christ in the Eucharist is neither seen nor touched by us immediately in itself, but only through the medium of those species under which it is contained, and it is thus we should understand the words of St. John Chrysostom (3): "Ecce eum vides, Ipsum tangis, Ipsum manducas."

38. It is, then, an article of faith, that Jesus Christ is permanently in the Eucharist, and not alone in the use of the communion, as the Lutherans say, and this is the doctrine of the Council of Trent, which also assigns the reason: " In Eucharistia ipse auctor ante usum est, nondum enim Eucharistiam de manu Domini Apostoli susceperant, cum vere tamen ipse affirmavit corpus suum esse, quod præbebat" (*Sess.* xiii. *Cap.* 3). And as Jesus Christ is present before the use of the Sacrament, so he is also present after it, as the Fourth Canon expresses it: " Si quis dixerit......in Hostiis, seu particulus consecratis, quæ post communionem reservantur, vel supersunt, non remanere verum corpus Domini; anathema sit."

39. This is proved, not alone by reason and authority, but by the ancient practice of the Church, likewise; for in the early ages, on account of the persecution, the Holy Communion was given in private houses and in caverns, as Tertullian testifies (4): " Non sciet Maritus, quid secreto ante omnem cibum gustes: et si sciverit panem, non illum esse credat, qui dicitur." St. Cyprian (5) tells us, that in his time the faithful used to bring home the Eucharist to their houses, to communicate at the proper time. St. Basil (6),

(2) St. Thom. 3, *p. qu.* 76, *a.* 5, *ad.* 3. (3) St. Chrysost. Hom. 60, ad Pap. (4) Tertul. *l.* 2, ad Uxor. *c.* 5. (5) St. Cypri. Tract. de Lapsis. (6) St. Basil, Ep. 289 ad Cesar. Patriciam.

writing to the Patrician Cesaria, exhorts her, that as she could not, on account of the persecution, attend the public communion, she should carry it along with her, to communicate in case of danger. St. Justin, Martyr (7), mentions that the deacons used to carry the communion to the absent. St. Iræneus (8) laments to Pope Victor, that having omitted to celebrate the Pasch, he deprived several priests of the communion on that account, who could not come to the public meetings, and he therefore sent the Eucharist in sign of peace to those who were prevented from attending: " Cum tamen qui te præcesserunt, Presbyteris, quamvis id minime observarent, Eucharistiam transmiserunt."   St. Gregory of Nazianzen (9) relates that her sister Orgonia, standing with great faith nigh to the Sacrament, which was concealed, was freed from a disease under which she was labouring; and St. Ambrose (10) tells us that St. Satirus, having the Eucharist suspended round his neck, escaped shipwreck.

40. Father Agnus Cirillo, in his work entitled " Ragguagli Teologici" (*p.* 353), adduces several other examples to the same effect, and proves that an anonymous author, who lately taught that it was not lawful to give communion with particles previously consecrated, and preserved in the tabernacle, is totally wrong. The learned Mabillon (11) shows that the practice of giving communion when Mass was not celebrated had its origin in the Church of Jerusalem, and existed in the days of St. Cyril, as it was not possible to say Mass each time that the numerous pilgrims frequenting the Holy City required communion. From the Eastern this custom was introduced into the Western Church, and Gregory XIII., in 1584, laid down in his Ritual the mode to be observed by the priest in the administration of the holy communion, when Mass was not said. This Ritual was confirmed, subsequently, by Paul V., in 1614, and in the chapter *de Sac. Eucharis.*, it is ordered that " Sacerdos curare debet, ut perpetuo aliquot particulæ consecratæ eo numero, quæ usui infirmorum, *et aliorum* (mark this) *Fidelium* communioni satis esse possint, conserventur in pixide." Benedict XIV., in his Encyclical Letter of the 12th November, 1742, approves of giving communion when Mass is not celebrated: " De eodem Sacrificio participant, præter eos quibus a sacerdote celebrante tribuitur in ipsa Missa portio Victimæ a se oblatæ, ii etiam quibus sacerdos Eucharistiam præservari solitam ministrat."

41. We may as well remark here, that a certain decree of the Congregation of Rites, dated 2nd September, 1741, was circulated, by which it was prohibited to give communion to the people at the Masses for the dead, with pre-consecrated particles, and taking the pixis from the tabernacle, because the usual benediction cannot be

---

(7) St. Justin. Apol. 2, *p.* 97.   (8) St. Iren. Ep. ad Vic. Pon.   (9) St. Greg. Nazian. Orat. 11.   (10) St. Ambr. Orat. de obitu fratris Satyri.   (11) Mabill. Liturg. Gallic. *l.* 2, c. 9, *n.* 26.

given in black vestments to those who communicate; but Father Cirillo (*p.* 368) says that this decree is not obligatory, as it was not sanctioned by the reigning Pope, Benedict XIV. There is, certainly, one very strong argument in his favour, and it is this, that Benedict, while Archbishop of Bologna, in his work on the Sacrifice of the Mass, approved of the opinion of the learned Merati, that communion might be given, at the Masses for the dead, with pre-consecrated particles, and when he was afterwards Pope, and re-composed the same treatise on the Sacrifice of the Mass, he never thought of retracting his opinion, which he would have done had he considered the decree we mentioned valid, and he would have given it his approbation, as published during his Pontificate. Father Cirillo adds, that one of the consultors of the congregation told him that, although the decree was drawn up, yet several of the consultors refused to sign it, and thus it was held in abeyance, and never published.

42. To come back to the sectaries who deny the Real Presence of Jesus Christ, unless in the use alone, I know not how they can answer the First Council of Nice, which ordains (*Can.* 13), that communion should be administered to the dying at all times, and it would be impossible to do that if the Eucharist was not preserved. The Fourth Council of Lateran expressly ordains the same thing (*Can.* 20): " Statuimus quod in singulis Ecclesiis Chrisma, et Eucharistia sub fideli custodia conserventur;" and this was confirmed by the Council of Trent (*Sess.* xiii. *c.* 6). From the earliest ages the Greeks preserved the Eucharist in silver ciboriums, made in the form of a dove, or of a little tower, and suspended over the altar, as is proved from the life of St. Basil, and the testament of Perpetuus, Bishop of Durs (12).

43. Our adversaries object that Nicephorus (13) relates, that in the Greek Church it was the custom to give the children the fragments that remained after communion; therefore, they say, the Eucharist was not preserved. We answer, that this was not done every day, only on Wednesdays and Fridays, when the pixis was purified; and it was, therefore, preserved on the other days, and, besides, particles were always preserved for the sick. They object, besides, that the words, " This is my body," were not pronounced by Christ before the manducation, but after it, as appears from St. Matthew (xxvi. 26): " Jesus took bread, and blessed, and broke; and gave to his disciples, and said: Take ye, and eat: This is my body." We answer, with Bellarmin, that in this text the order of the words is not to be regarded, for the order is different with each of the Evangelists. St. Mark, speaking of the consecration of the chalice, says (xiv. 23, 24): " Having taken the chalice......they all drank of it. And he said to them: This is my blood." Now,

(12) Tournelly, *t.* 2, de Euch. *p.* 165, *n.* 5.   (13) Niceph. Histor. *l.* 17, *c.* 25.

it would appear from this, also, that the words, "This is my blood," were said after the *sumption* of the chalice; but the context of all the Evangelists shows that both "This is my body," and "This is my blood," was said by our Lord before he gave them the species of bread and wine.

SEC. IV.—THE MATTER AND FORM OF THE SACRAMENT OF THE EUCHARIST.

44. As to the matter of the Eucharist, there is no doubt but that we should use that alone which was used by Jesus Christ—that is, bread of wheat, and wine of the vine, as we learn from St. Matthew (xxv. 26), St. Mark (xiv. 12), St. Luke (xxii. 19), and St. Paul (1 Cor. xi. 27). This is what the Catholic Church has always done, and condemned those who dared to make use of any other matter, as is proved in the third Council of Carthage (*c.* 27), which was held in the year 397. Estius (1) says that consecration can be performed with any sort of bread—wheaten, barley, oaten, or millet; but St. Thomas (2) writes, that it is with bread of wheat alone it can be done, but still that bread made of a sort of rye, which grows from wheat sown in poor soil, is also matter for the consecration: "Et ideo si qua frumenta sunt, quæ ex semine tritici generari possunt, sicut ex grano tritici seminato malis terris nascitur siligo, ex tali frumento panis confectus potest esse materia hujus Sacramenti." He, therefore, rejected all other bread, and this is the only opinion we can follow in practice. Doctors have disputed, as we may see in the works of Mabillon, Sirmond, Cardinal Bona, and others, whether unleavened bread, such as the Latins use, or leavened bread, as used by the Greeks, is the proper matter for the Sacrament. There is not the least doubt but that the consecration is valid in either one or the other; but, at present, the Latins are prohibited from consecrating in leavened, and the Greeks in unleavened bread, according to a Decree of the Council of Florence, in 1429: "Definimus in azimo, sive in fermentato pane triticeo Corpus Christi veraciter confici, Sacerdotesque in alterutro ipsum Domini Corpus conficere debent, unumquenque scilicet juxta suæ Ecclesiæ Occidentalis, sive Orientalis consuetudinem." The matter of the consecration of the blood should be common wine, pressed from ripe grapes; and, therefore, the liquor expressed from unripe grapes, boiled wine, or that which has become vinegar, cannot be used. Must, however, or the unfermented juice of the grape, will answer; but it should not be used without necessity.

45. As to the quantity of bread and wine to be consecrated, it is quite sufficient that it be apparent to the senses, be it ever so little; it must, however, be certain, and of a known quantity, and morally present. According to the intention of the Church, and as St.

---

(1) Æstius, in 4, *dist.* 8, *c.* 6.   (2) St. Thom. *q.* 74, *art.* 3, ad 2.

Thomas teaches (3), a greater number of particles should not be consecrated than is sufficient to give communion to that number of people who are expected to receive within the time that the species would keep without corrupting. From this Peter de Marca concludes (4), that it is not in the power of a priest to consecrate all the bread in a shop, for example; the consecration in this case, he says, would be invalid, though others assert it would only be illicit. Theologians also dispute of the validity of consecration, when performed for the purposes of witchcraft, or to expose the Host to the insult of unbelievers.

46. We now have to treat of the form of the Eucharist. Luther (5) says, that the words of Christ alone, " This is my body," are not sufficient to consecrate, but that the whole liturgy must be recited. Calvin (6) said, that the words were not necessary at all for consecration, but only to excite faith. Some Greek schismatics, Arcudius (7) informs us, said that the words, " This is," &c., being once expressed by Christ, were sufficient in themselves to consecrate all the Hosts offered up ever after.

47. Some Catholics taught that Christ consecrated the Eucharist by his occult benediction, without any words at all, by the excellence of his power; but ordained the form, at the same time, for man to use in consecration. This opinion was held by Durandus (8), Innocent III. (9), and especially by Catherinus (10), but as Cardinal Gotti (11) informs us, it is now not held by any one, and some even say it was branded as rashness to hold it. The true and general doctrine is, as St. Thomas teaches (12), that Jesus Christ consecrated, when he expressed the words, "This is my body, this is my blood," and that the priest, at the present day, consecrates in the same manner, expressing the same words, in the person of Christ, and this not historically *narrative*, but significantly *significative*—that is, by applying this meaning to the matter before him, as the generality of Doctors teach with St. Thomas (13).

48. Catherinus says, also, that besides the words of our Lord, it is necessary, in order to consecrate, to add the prayers which, in the Latin Church, precede, and in the Greek, follow, the act; and the learned Oratorian, Father Le Brun (14), follows this opinion, likewise. The general opinion of theologians agreeing with St. Thomas (15), is, that Christ consecrated with the very same words as priests do at present, and that the prayers of the Canon of the Mass are obligatory, but not necessary for consecration, so that it would be valid without them. The Council of Trent (*Sess.* xiii. *c.* 1) declares that our Saviour, " Post panis vinique benedictionem se

---

(3) St. Thom. 3, *p. q.* 73, *art.* 2.   (4) Petr. de Marca Diss. posthuma de Sacrif. Missa.
(5) Luther, *l.* de Abrog. Missa.   (6) Calvin, Inst. *l.* 4, *c.* 17, *sec.* 39.   (7) Arcud.
l. 3, *c.* 28.   (8) Durand. *l.* 4, de Div. Offic. *c.* 41, *n.* 13.   (9) Innoc. III. *l.* 4,
Myst. *c.* 6.   (10) Ap. Tournelly Comp. de Euch. qu. 4, *a.* 6, *p.* 184.   (11) Gotti,
Theol. de Euch. *qu.* 2, *sec.* 1, *n.* 2.   (12) St. Thom. 3, *p. q.* 78, *a.* 1.   (13) St. Thom.
loc. cit. *a.* 5.   (14) Le Brun, *t.* 3, rer. Liturg. *p.* 212.   (15) St. Thom. 3,
p. q. 78, *a.* 5.

suum ipsius corpus illis præbere, ac suum sanguinem disertis ac perspicuis verbis testatus est; quæ verba a sanctis Evangelistis commemorata, et a D. Paulo postea repetita, cum propriam illam et apertissimam significationem præ se ferant, secundum quam a Patribus intellecta sunt," &c. Were not the words, "Take and eat; this is my body," as the Evangelists inform us, clearly demonstrative that Christ gave his disciples his body to eat? It was by these words, then, and no other, that he converted the bread into his body, as St. Ambrose writes (16): " Consecratio igitur quibus verbis est, et cujus sermonibus? Domini Jesu. Nam reliqua omnia, quæ dicuntur, laudem Deo deferunt; oratio præmittitur pro Populo pro Regibus, pro ceteris; ubi venitur ut conficiatur venerabile Sacramentum, jam non suis sermonibus Sacerdos, sed utitur sermonibus Christi." St. John Chrysostom (17), speaking of the same words, says: " Hoc verbum Christi transformat ea, quæ proposita sunt." And St. John of Damascus says: " Dixit pariter Deus, *Hoc est corpus meum*, ideoque omnipotenti ejus præcepto, donec veniat, efficitur."

49. The same Council (*Cap.* 3) says: " Et semper hæc fides in Ecclesia Dei fuit, statim post consecrationem verum Domini nostri Corpus, verumque ejus sanguinem sub panis et vini specie...... existere......ex vi verborum." Therefore, by the power of the words—that is, the words mentioned by the Evangelist—instantly after the consecration, the bread is converted into the body, and the wine into the blood of Jesus Christ. There is a great difference between the two sentences, "This is my body," and " We beseech thee that the body of Jesus Christ may be made for us," or, as the Greeks say, " Make this bread the body of Christ;" for the first shows that the body of Christ is present at the very moment in which the sentence is expressed, but the second is only a simple prayer, beseeching that the oblation may be made the body, not in a determinative, but a suspended and expectative sense. The Council says that the conversion of the bread and wine into the body and blood of Christ takes place *vi verborum*, not *vi orationum*, by the power of the words, and not by the power of the prayers. St. Justin says (18): " Eucharistiam confici per preces ab ipso Verbo Dei profectas;" and he afterwards explains that these prayers are: " This is my body;" but the prayer in the Canon was not pronounced by the Word of God himself. St. Iræneus (19) says, also: " Quando mixtus calix et factus panis percipit verbum Dei, fit Eucharistia corporis Christi." We do not find that Christ, in consecrating, used any other words but those: " This is my body, and this is my blood." Taking all this into consideration, we must decide that the opinion of Le Brun has not a sound foundation of probability.

(16) St. Ambrose, de Sacramen. *l*. 4, c. 4.   (17) St. Chrysost. Hom. 1 de Prod. Judæ.
(18) St. Justin, Apol. 2.   (19) St. Iræn. *l*. 5, c. 2.

50 Several Fathers (say the supporters of this opinion) teach that the Eucharist is consecrated both by prayer and by the words of Christ. We answer, that by the word prayer they mean the very expression "This is my body," used by Christ, as St. Justin (20) expressly states, that the prayer by which the Eucharist is consecrated is the words, "This is my body," &c. St. Iræneus had previously said the same (21), that the Divine invocation by which the Eucharist is made is the Divine Word St. Augustin (22) says that the mystic prayer (23) by which the Eucharist is made consists in the words of Christ, "This is my body," &c., as the forms of the other Sacraments are called prayers, because they are holy words which have the power of obtaining from God the effect of the Sacraments. They object to us, also, some Liturgies, as those of St. James, St. Mark, St. Clement, St. Basil, and St. John Chrysostom, which would make it appear that besides the words of Christ other prayers are requisite for consecration, as we have in the Canon: "Quæsumus......ut nobis corpus, et sanguis fiat delectissimi Filii tui," &c. The same prayer is also used in the Greek Mass, but, as Bellarmin writes (24), when the Greeks were asked by Eugenius IV. what was the reason that they used the prayer "that this may become the body," &c., after having already expressed the words of consecration, "This is my body," &c., they answered that they added this prayer, not to confirm the consecration, but that the Sacrament might assist the salvation of the souls of those who received it.

51. Theologians (25) say, notwithstanding, that it is not an article of Faith that Christ did consecrate with these words, and ordained that with these words alone priests should consecrate, for although this is the general opinion, and most consonant with the sentiments of the Council of Trent, still it is not anywhere declared to be an article of Faith by the Canon of the Church; and although the Holy Fathers have given it the weight of their authority, they have never laid it down as a matter of Faith. Salmeron mentions (loc. cit.) that the Council of Trent being entreated to explain the form with which Christ consecrated this Sacrament, the Fathers judged it better not to define anything on the subject. Tournelly (26) replies to all the objections made by those who wish to make it a matter of Faith. If it is not a matter of Faith, however, still, as St. Thomas teaches, it is morally certain (27), and we cannot even say that the contrary opinion is probable. The priest, then, would commit a most grievous sin, if he omitted the preceding prayers, but still his consecration would be valid.

(20) St. Justin Apol. 2.　　(21) St. Iren. *l.* 4, c. 24, & *l.* 3, c. 2.　　(22) St. Aug. Serm. 28, de Verb. Do.　　(23) Idem, de Trinit. *c.* 4.　　(24) Bellar. *l.* 4, de Euchar. *c.* 19.　　(25) Salmeron. *t.* 9, trac. 13, *p.* 88; Tournell. de Euchar. 9, 4, *a.* 6, vers. Quær.　　(26) Tournell. loc. cit. *p.* 191, v. Dices. 1.　　(27) St. Thom. 3, p. 9, 78, *a.* 1, ad 4.

It is debated among authors, whether any words unless these, "This is the Chalice of my blood," though the remainder is laid down in the Missal, are essentially necessary for the consecration of the blood. In our Moral Theology (28) the reader will find the point discussed. Several hold the affirmative opinion, and quote St. Thomas in their favour, who says (29): "Et ideo illa quæ sequuntur sunt essentialia sanguini, prout in hoc Sacramento consecratur, et ideo oportet, quod sint de substantia Formæ:" the opposite opinion, however, is more generally followed, and those who hold it deny that it is opposed to the doctrine of St. Thomas, for he says that the subsequent words appertain to the substance but not to the essence of the form, and hence they conclude that these words do not belong to the essence, but only to the integrity of the form, so that the priest who would omit them would commit a grievous sin undoubtedly, but still would validly consecrate.

52. We should remark here that the Council of Trent (*Sess.* xxii.) condemned in nine Canons nine errors of the Reformers concerning the Sacrifice of the Mass, as follows: First.—that the Mass is not a true Sacrifice, and that it is only offered up to administer the Eucharist to the Faithful. Second.—That by these words, "Do this in commemoration of me," Christ did not institute the Apostles priests, or ordain that the priests should offer up his body and blood. Third.—That the Mass is only a thanksgiving or remembrance of the Sacrifice of the Cross, but not a propitiatory Sacrifice, or that it is useful only to those who communicate at it. Fourth.—That this Sacrifice is derogatory to the Sacrifice of the Cross. Fifth.—That it is an imposture to celebrate Mass in honour of the Saints, and to obtain their intercession. Sixth.—That there are errors in the Canon. Seventh.—That the ceremonies, vestments, and signs used in the Catholic Church are incentives to impiety. Eighth.—That private Masses, in which the priest alone communicates, are unlawful. Ninth.—That the practice of saying part of the Canon in a low voice should be condemned; that it all ought to be said in the vulgar tongue, and that the mixture of water with the wine in the Chalice should also be condemned. All these errors I have refuted in my work against the Reformers.

---

(28) Liguor. Theol. Moral. *t.* 2, dub. 6, de Euch., &c. q. 2, *ar.* 2, q. 2.   (29) St. Thom. in 4 Dist. 8,

REFUTATION XI.

ERRORS OF LUTHER AND CALVIN.

SUMMARY OF THE PRINCIPAL POINTS.

1. Free Will exists. 2. The Divine Law is not impossible. 3. Works are necessary 4. Faith alone does not justify us. 5. Of the Uncertainty of Justification, Perseverance, and eternal Salvation. 6. God is not the Author of Sin. 7. God predestines no one to Hell. 8. Infallibility of General Conncils.

SEC. I.—OF FREE WILL.

1. I HAVE already stated in this work (1), that the errors of Luther, Calvin, and their disciples, who have added error to error, are almost innumerable; and in particular, as Prateolus remarks, in the Calvinistic heresy alone two hundred and seven errors against Faith are enumerated, and another author brings them up even to fourteen hundred. I, however, refute only the principal errors of Luther, Calvin, and the other Reformers, for the refutation of their other erroneous opinions will be found in Bellarmin, Gotti, and several other authors. One of Calvin's chief heresies was, that Adam alone had free will, but that by his sin not alone he, but all his posterity, lost it, so that free will is only *titulus sine re*. This error was specially condemned by the Council of Trent (*Sess.* vi. *c.* 5): "Si quis hominis arbitrium post Adæ peccatum amissum et extinctum esse dixerit, aut rem esse de solo titulo, imo titulum sine re, figmentum denique a Satana invectum in Ecclesiam, anathema sit."

2. Free will consists of two sorts of liberty, *Contradictionis*, by which we can either do anything or let it alone, and *Contrarietatis*, by which we have the power of doing anything, and also doing the opposite, as of doing what is good and doing what is bad. Man has retained both species of free will, as the Scriptures prove. First.—As to the liberty of *Contradiction*, to do or not to do what is right, we have several texts to prove it. For example, in Ecclesiasticus (xv. 14, 16): "God made man from the beginning, and left him in the hands of his own counsel. He added his commandments and precepts. If thou wilt keep the commandments.... for ever,..... they shall preserve thee;" "It shall depend on the will of her husband whether she shall do it or do it not" (Numb. xxx. 14; "He could have transgressed, and hath not transgressed, and could do evil things and hath not done them" (Eccles. xxxi. 10); "Whilst it remained did it not remain to thee, and after it was sold was it not in thy power?" (Acts, v. 4); "The lust thereof shall be unto thee, and thou shalt have dominion over it" (Gen.

(1) Cap. xi. Cent. xvi. *ar.* 3.

iv. 7). Many texts, likewise, prove the liberty of *Contrariety:* "I have set before you life and death, blessing and cursing" (Deut. xxx. 19); " Before man is life and death, good and evil; that which he shall choose shall be given unto him" (Eccl. xv. 18). And lest our adversaries should say that those texts apply to man only in a state of innocence, we will quote others, which speak of him without doubt after the fall: "But if it seem evil to you to serve the Lord, you have your choice; choose this day whom you would rather serve, whether the Gods," &c., (Jos. xxiv. 15); " If any man will come after me, let him deny himself, and take up his cross, and follow me" (Luke, ix. 23); " For he hath determined, being steadfast in his heart, having no necessity, but having power of his own will" (1 Cor. vii. 37); " And I gave her a time, that she might do penance, and she will not repent" (Apoc. ii. 21); " If any man shall hear my voice, and open to me the door, I will come in to him" (Apoc. iii. 20). There are many other texts of a like nature, but these are sufficient to prove that man has preserved his free will after the fall. Luther objects that text of Isaias (xli. 23): " Do also good or evil, if you can," but he ought to remember that in the text the Prophet is speaking not of man, but of idols, which, as David said, could do nothing: " They have mouths and speak not, they have eyes and see not" (Psalms, cxiii. 5).

3. That being the case, it is not enough, as Luther, Calvin, and the Jansenists say, to have the liberty *coactionis*, that is, freedom from restraint, that our actions may be meritorious or otherwise. This is exactly the third proposition of Jansenius, condemned as heretical: " Ad merendum, et demerendum in statu naturæ lapsæ non requiritur in homine libertas a *necessitate*, sed sufficit libertas a *coactione*." In this manner we might say that even the beasts have free will, since, without any violence, they are carried on spontaneously (after their way) to seek the pleasures of sense. It is necessary, however, for the true liberty of man, that he should have the liberty *necessitatis*, so that he may choose whatever he pleases, as St. Paul (1 Cor. vii. 37) says, " having no necessity, but having the power of his own will," and it is this will that is required both for merit and demerit. St. Augustin, speaking of sin (2), says: " Peccatum usque adeo voluntarium (that is free, as he afterwards explains it) malum est, ut nullo modo sit peccatum si non sit voluntarium." And the reason is, says the saint, that God judged that his servants would be better if they served him freely; " Servos suos meliores esse Deus judicavit, si ei servirent liberaliter, quod nullo modo fieri posset, si non voluntate, sed necessitate servirent."

4. They say that it is God who operates in us all the good which we perform, as the Scriptures teach (1 Cor. xii. 6): " The same God who worketh all in all;" " Thou hast wrought all our works

---

(2) St. Aug. *l.* de Ver. Rel. *c.* 11.

for us" (Isaias, xxvi. 12); "And I will cause you to walk in my commandments" (Ezechiel, xxxvi. 27). We answer, that there is no doubt but that free will after the fall was not, indeed, extinguished, but still was weakened, and inclined to evil, as the Council of Trent teaches: "Tametsi in eis liberum arbitrium minime extinctum esset, viribus licet attenuatum, et inclinatum" (*Sess.* vi. *cap.* 1). There is no doubt that God operates everything good in us; but, at the same time, he does along with us, as St. Paul (1 Cor. xv. 10) says: "By the grace of God I am what I am.... but the grace of God with me." Mark this—"the grace of God with me." God excites us to do what is good by his preventing grace, and helps us to bring it to perfection by his assisting grace; but he wishes that we should unite our endeavours to his grace, and, therefore, exhorts us to co-operate as much as we can : "Be converted to me" (Zach. i. 3); "Make unto yourselves a new heart" (Ezech. xviii. 31); "Mortify, therefore, your members...... stripping yourselves of the old man with his deeds, and putting on the new" (Col. iii. 5, &c.) He also reproves those who refuse to obey his call: "I called, and you refused" (Prov. i. 24); "How often would I have gathered together thy children.... and thou wouldst not (Matt. xxiii. 37); "You always resist the Holy Ghost" (Acts, vii. 51). All these Divine calls and reprovals would be vain and unjust if God did everything regarding our eternal salvation, without any co-operation on our part; but such is not the case. God does all, and whatever good we do, the greater part belongs to him; but still it is his will that we labour a little ourselves, as far as we can, and hence, St. Paul says: "I have laboured more abundantly than all they, yet not I, but the grace of God with me" (1 Cor. xv. 10). By this Divine grace, therefore, we are not to understand that habitual grace which sanctifies the soul, but the actual preventing and helping grace which enables us to perform what is right, and when this grace is efficacious, it not only gives us strength to do so, in the same manner as sufficient grace does, but more—it makes us actually do what is right. From this first error, then, that free will is extinguished in man by sin, the Innovators deduce other erroneous doctrines—that it is impossible for us to observe the laws of the Decalogue; that works are not necessary for salvation, but only faith alone; that our co-operation is not required for the justification of the sinner, for that is done by the merits of Christ alone, although man should still continue in sin. We shall treat of those errors immediately.

SECT. II.—THAT IT IS NOT IMPOSSIBLE TO OBSERVE THE DIVINE LAW.

5. Man having lost his free will, the sectarians say that it is impossible for him to observe the precepts of the Decalogue, and especially the first and tenth commandments. Speaking of the tenth

commandment, "Thou shalt not covet," &c., *non concupisces*, they say it is quite impossible to observe it, and they found the impossibility on a fallacy. Concupiscence, they say, is itself a sin, and hence, they assert that not alone motions of concupiscence, *in actu secundo*, which precede consent, are sinful, but also movements in *actu primo*, which precede reason, or advertence itself. Catholics, however, teach, that movements of concupiscence, in *actu primo*, which precede advertence, are neither mortal nor venial sins, but only natural defects proceeding from our corrupt nature, and for which God will not blame us. The movements which precede consent are at most only venial sins, when we are careless about banishing them from our minds after we perceive them, as Gerson and the Salmanticenses, following St. Thomas, teach, for in that case the danger of consenting to the evil desired, by not positively resisting and banishing that motion of concupiscence, is only remote, and not proximate. Doctors, however, usually except movements of carnal delectation, for then it is not enough to remain passive, *negative se habere*, as theologians say, but we should make a positive resistance, for, otherwise, if they are any way violent, there is great danger of consenting to them. Speaking of other matters, however, the consenting alone (as we have said) to the desire of a grievous evil is a mortal sin. Now, taking the commandment in this sense, no one can deny that with the assistance of Divine grace, which never fails us, it is impossible to observe it. If one advertently consents to a wicked desire, or takes morose delectation in thinking on it, he is then guilty of a grievous, or, at all events, of a light fault, for our Lord himself says: " Follow not in thy strength the desires of thy heart" (Eccl. v. 2); " Go not after thy lusts" (Eccl. xviii. 30); " Let not sin, therefore, reign in your mortal body, so as to obey the lusts thereof" (Rom. vi. 12). I have used the expression *a light fault*, because the delectation of a bad object is one thing; the thought of a bad object another: this delectation of thought is not mortally sinful in itself, but only venially so; and even if there be a just cause, it is no sin at all. This, however, must be understood to be the case only when we abominate the evil object, and besides, that the consideration of it should be of some utility to us, and that the consideration of it should not lead us to take pleasure in the evil object, because if there was a proximate danger of this, the delectation would, in that case, be grievously sinful. When then, on the other hand, concupiscence assaults us against our will, then there is no sin, for God only obliges us to do what is in our power. Man is composed of the flesh and the spirit, which are always naturally at war with each other; and hence, it is not in our power not to feel many times movements opposed to reason. Would not that master be a tyrant who would command his servant not to feel thirst or cold? In the law of Moses punishment was imposed only on actual external crimes, and hence the

Scribes and Pharisees drew a false conclusion, that internal sins were not prohibited; but in the New Law our Redeemer has explained that even wicked desires are forbidden: "You have heard that it was said to them of old: Thou shalt not commit adultery; but I say to you, that whosoever shall look on a woman to lust after her, hath already committed adultery with her in his heart" (Matt. v. 27, 28). This stands to reason, for if we do not reject evil desires, it would be very difficult to avoid actual external sins; but when these desires are rejected, they are a matter of merit to us, instead of deserving of punishment. St. Paul deplored that he was tormented with carnal temptations, and prayed to God to free him from them, but was answered that his grace alone was sufficient: "There was given to me a sting of my flesh, an angel of Satan to buffet me, which thing thrice I besought the Lord that it might depart from me, and he said to me: My grace is sufficient for thee, for power is made perfect in infirmity" (2 Cor. xii. 7, &c.) Mark here, "power is made perfect," which proves that when evil desires are rejected, they increase, instead of weakening our virtue. Here we should also take occasion to remark, that the Apostle says that God does not permit that we should be tempted beyond our strength: "God is faithful, who will not suffer you to be tempted above that which you are able" (1 Cor. x. 12).

6. They also assert that it is impossible to observe the first commandment: "Thou shalt love the Lord with all thy heart." How is it possible, says Calvin, for us, living in a state of corruption, to keep our hearts continually occupied with the Divine love? Calvin understands the commandment in this way, but St. Augustin (1) does not, for he counsels us that we cannot observe it as to the words, but we can as to the obligation. We fulfil this commandment by loving God above all things, that is, by preferring the Divine grace to everything created. The angelic Doctor, St. Thomas (2) teaches the same. We observe, he says, the precept of loving God with all our hearts, when we love him above everything else: "Cum mandatur, quod Deum ex toto corde diligamus, datur intelligi, quod Deum super omnia debemus diligere." The substance of the first commandment, then, consists in the obligation of preferring God above all things else, and, therefore, Jesus says that "he who loves father or mother more than me... is not worthy of me" (Matt. x. 37). And St. Paul, confiding in the Divine grace, says that he is certain that nothing created could separate him from the love of God: "For I am sure that neither death, nor life, nor angels, nor principalities... nor any other creature, shall be able to separate us from the love of God" (Rom. viii. 38, 39). Calvin (3) not alone taught the impossibility of observing the first and tenth

---

(1) St. Aug. *l.* de Sp. & Lit. *c.* 1, & *l.* de Perf. just. Resp. (2) St. Thom. 2, 2 *qu.* 44, *art.* 8, *ad* 2. (3) Calvin in Antid. Con. Trid. *Sess.* vi. *c.* 12.

commandments, but even that the observance of any of the others was impossible.

7. They object, first, that St. Peter said, in the Council of Jerusalem: " Now, therefore, why tempt you God to put a yoke upon the necks of the disciples, which neither our fathers nor we have been able to bear" (Acts, xv. 10). Here the Apostle himself declares that the observance of the law is impossible. We answer, that St. Peter here does not speak of the moral, but of the ceremonial law, which should not be imposed on Christians, since the Hebrews themselves found it so difficult, that very few of them observed it, though several, however, did so, as St. Luke tells us that St. Zachary and St. Elizabeth did: " They were both just before God, walking in all the commandments and justifications of the Lord, without blame" (Luke, i. 6).

8. They object, secondly, that text of the Apostle: " For I know that there dwelleth not in me, that is to say, in my flesh, that which is good. For to will, is present with me; but to accomplish that which is good, I find not" (Romans, vii. 18). Now, when he says " that there dwelleth not in me that which is good" he tells us that the law cannot be observed; but we should not separate that passage from what follows: " that is to say, in my flesh." What St. Paul means to say is, that the flesh is opposed to the spirit, and no matter how good our will may be, we never can be exempt from every movement of concupiscence; but these movements, as we have already said, do not prevent us from observing the law.

9. They object, thirdly, that St. John says: " If we say we have no sin, we deceive ourselves, and the truth is not in us" (1 John, i. 8). We answer that the Apostle does not mean by that, that it is impossible for us to observe the commandments, so that no one can escape falling into mortal sin, but that on account of the present weakness of corrupt nature, no one is exempt from venial sins, as the Council of Trent declared (*Sess.* vi. *cap.* 11): " Licet enim in hac mortali vita quantumvis sancti, et justi in levia saltem, et quotidiana, quæ etiam venialia dicuntur peccata, quandoque cadant, non propterea desinunt esse justi."

10. They object, fourthly, that St. Paul says: " Christ has redeemed us from the curse of the law being made a curse for us" (Gal. iii. 13). Therefore, say our adversaries, Christ, by the merits of his death, has exempted us from the obligation of observing the law. We answer: It is quite a different thing to say that Christ has freed us from the malediction of the law, since his grace gives us strength to observe, and thus avoid the malediction fulminated by the law against its transgressors, and to assert that he has freed us from the observance of the law, which is totally false.

11. They object, fifthly, that the Apostle says, in another place: " Knowing this, that the law is not made for the just man, but for the unjust and disobedient, for the ungodly and for sinners "

(1 Tim. i. 9). Joining this passage with the other just quoted, they say that our Redeemer has freed us from the obligation of observing the commandments, and that when he told the young man (Matt. xix. 17), "If you wish to enter into eternal life, keep the commandments," he only spoke ironically, as much as to say, "Keep them if you can," knowing that it was quite impossible for a child of Adam to observe them. We answer, with St. Thomas (4), that the law, as to the directive power, is given both to the just and to the unjust, to direct all men as to what they ought to do; but as to the co-active power, the law is not imposed on those who voluntarily observe it without being constrained to observe it, but on the wicked who wish to withdraw themselves from it, for it is these alone should be constrained to observe it. The explanation of the text, "Keep the commandments," given by the Reformers, that Christ spoke ironically, is not only heretical, but totally opposed to common sense and Scripture, and is not worth an answer. The true doctrine in this matter is that of the Council of Trent (5): "Deus impossibilia non jubet, sed jubendo monet, et facere quod possis, et petere quod non possis, et adjuvat ut possis" (*Sess.* vi. *c.* 13). He, therefore, gives to every one the ordinary grace to observe the commandments, and whenever a more abundant grace is required, if we pray to him for it, we are sure of obtaining it.

12. This was the answer of St. Augustin to the Adrometines, who objected to him, that if God does not give us sufficient grace to observe the law, he should not chastise us for violating it: "Cur me corripis? et non potius Ipsum rogas, ut in me operetur et velle" (6). And the Saint answers: "Qui corrigi non vult, et dicit, Ora potius pro me; ideo corripiendus est, ut faciat (id est oret) etiam ipse pro se." Therefore, says St. Augustin, although man does not receive efficacious grace from God to fulfil the law, still he should be punished, and commits a sin by violating it, because, having it in his power to pray, and by prayer obtain more abundant assistance to enable him to observe it, he neglects to pray, and thus does not observe the law. It would be quite otherwise, if it were not granted to all to pray, and, by prayer, obtain strength to do what is right. But another efficacious grace is necessary to pray, and, in my opinion, St. Augustin would not have answered the Adrometines rationally, that man should be punished if he did not pray for himself, for they might in that case answer him, how can he pray, if he have not efficacious grace to pray?

SEC. III.—THAT GOOD WORKS ARE NECESSARY FOR SALVATION, AND THAT FAITH ALONE IS NOT SUFFICIENT.

13. LUTHER said that, not alone the works of infidels and sinners

---

(4) St. Thom. 1, 2, *qu.* 96, *art.* 5.   (5) Ap. St. Aug. de Corrept. et Grat. *t.* 10, *c.* 4, *n.* 6, in fine.   (6) St. Aug. ibid. *c.* 5, *n.* 7.

were of no use, but that even works performed by the just are mere sins, or, at all events, vitiated by sin. Here are his words: "In omni opere bono justus peccat (1). Opus bonum, optime factum, est mortale peccatum secundum judicium Dei (2). Justus in bono opere peccat mortaliter" (3). Becanus (4) says that Calvin taught the same, that the works of the just are nothing but iniquity. O, my God, how blind is the human understanding, when it loses the light of Faith! This blasphemy of Luther and Calvin was properly condemned by the Council of Trent (*Sess.* vi. *Can.* 22): "Si quis in quodlibet bono opere justum saltem venialiter peccare dixerit, aut quod intolerabilius est, mortaliter, atque ideo pœnas æternas mereri; tantumque ob id non damnari, quia Deus ea opera non imputet ad damnationem; anathema sit." They quote Isaias, however, who says (lxiv. 6): "And we have all become as one unclean, and all our justices," &c. But, as St. Cyril explains this text, the Prophet here is not speaking of the works of the just, but of the iniquity of the Jews of that day. How could good works possibly be sinful, when Christ exhorts us to perform them: "Let your light shine before men, that they may see your good works" (Matt. v. 16). They are not sins; but, on the contrary, God delights in them, and without them we cannot obtain salvation. Nothing can be clearer than the Scripture on this point: "Not every one that saith to me, Lord, Lord, shall enter into the kingdom of heaven; but he that doth the will of my Father" (Matt. vii. 21). To do the will of God is to do good works: "If thou wilt enter into life, keep the commandments" (Matt. xix. 17). When God shall condemn the wicked, he shall say to them: "Go from me, ye accursed." And why? "For I was hungry, and you gave me not to eat; I was thirsty, and you gave me not to drink" (Matt. xxv. 42). "Patience is necessary for you: that, doing the will of God, you may receive the promise" (Heb. x. 36). "What shall it profit, my brethren, if a man say he hath faith, but hath not works? Shall Faith be able to save him?" (James, ii. 14). Here it is proved that works are necessary for salvation, and that Faith is not alone sufficient. We will treat this subject more extensively by-and-by.

14. Our adversaries object, that St. Paul, writing to Titus (iii. 5-7), says: "Not by the works of justice, which we have done, but according to his mercy he saved us, by the laver of regeneration, and renovation of the Holy Ghost. Whom he hath poured forth upon us abundantly, through Jesus Christ our Saviour: That being justified by his grace, we may be heirs, according to hope of life everlasting." Therefore, they say that no work of ours, though a work of justice, is available to salvation; but that we should rest

---

(1) Luther, in Assert. *art.* 31.   (2) Idem. *art.* 33.   (3) Idem. *art.* 36.
(4) Becan. Man. contr. *l.* 1, *c.* 18, ex Calv. Inst. *l.* 2, *t.* 1, *sec.* 9, &c.

all our hopes of grace and salvation in Jesus Christ, who, by his merits, has obtained both grace and salvation for us. To answer this argument clearly, we must make several distinctions. We can deserve grace and eternal salvation in two ways—*de condigno* and *de congruo*. To deserve it *de condigno*, it is necessary that the remunerator should be obliged to reward us, as a debt of justice; but to deserve it, *de congruo*, the remunerator has no obligation to reward us—it is fit that he should do so, but it is totally an act of liberality on his part. Now, as far as human merit is with God as a matter of justice, several conditions are requisite. The act itself must be good; it is requisite that he who performs it be in a state of grace, and, on the part of the Almighty it is necessary that he should have promised to reward us, for he, as man's supreme Lord, might require all service from him, without any reward at all. To make it a debt of justice, therefore, it is necessary that a gratuitous Divine promise should have been already given, by which God himself gratuitously makes himself a debtor for the reward promised. It is after this manner that St. Paul could say that he expected, in justice, eternal life, as the reward of his good works: "I have fought the good fight; I have finished my course; I have kept the Faith. As to the next, there is laid up for me a crown of justice, which the Lord, the just judge, will render to me in that day" (2 Tim. iv. 7, 8). And here St. Augustin (5) says: " Debitorem Dominus ipse se fecit, non accipiendo, sed promittendo. Non ei dicimus: Redde quod accepisti, sed redde quod promisisti."

15. Here, then, is what the Catholic Church teaches. No man can merit actual justifying grace *de condigno*, but only *de congruo*, and Melancthon stated a falsehood in his Apology of the Confession of Augsburg (*p.* 137), when he asserted that we believe we can merit justification by our works. The Council of Trent has declared, and this is our faith, and no other, that sinners are justified gratuitously by God, and that no work of theirs preceding their justification can deserve it. But the Council has also said that man justified, although he cannot *de condigno* merit final perseverance (*Sess.* vi. c. 13), still can merit *de condigno*, by the good works he does, assisted by Divine grace, and the merits of Christ, the augmentation of grace and eternal life. The Council fulminates its anathema against all who deny this doctrine, in the Sixth Session (*Can.* 33): " Si quis dixerit hominis justificati bona opera ita esse dona Dei, ut non sint etiam bona ipsius justificati merita; aut ipsum justificatum bonis operibus, quæ ab eo per Dei gratiam, et per Jesu Christi meritum, cujus vivum membrum est, fiunt, non vere mereri augmentum gratiæ, vitam æternam, et ipsius vitæ æternæ (si tamen in gratia decesserit) consecutionem, atque etiam

(5) St. Augus. in Psalm, 83.

gloriæ augmentum: anathema sit." All, therefore, that we receive from God, we get through his mercy, and through the merits of Jesus Christ: but, through his goodness, he has so disposed that, with the good words we perform, by the power of his grace, we can deserve eternal life, on account of the gratuitous promise made by him to those who do what is right. Hear again the words of the Council: "Justificatis, sive acceptam gratiam conservaverint sive amissam recupaverint, proponenda est vita æterna, et tanquam gratia, filiis Dei per Christum Jesum promissa et tanquam merces ex ipsius Dei promissione ipsorum meritis reddenda" (*Sess.* vi. *cap.* 16). Therefore, say the heretics, he who is saved can glorify himself that he is saved through his own works. No; for the Council says: "Licet bonis operibus merces tribuatur........absit tamen, ut Christianus in se ipso vel confidat, vel glorietur, et non in Domino: cujus tanta est erga homines bonitas, ut eorum velit esse merita, quæ sunt ipsius dona."

16. Our adversaries may thus see how unjustly the Calvinists charge us with insulting the mercy of God and the merits of Jesus Christ by attributing to our own merits the acquisition of eternal salvation. We assert that we can do nothing good, unless in virtue of the grace communicated to us by God, through the merits of Jesus Christ, and hence all our merits are the gift of God, and if he gives us glory as a reward of our merits, he does not do so because he is obliged to give it, but because (to encourage us in his service, and make us more certain of eternal salvation if we are faithful) it is his wish, merely through his own goodness, gratuitously to bind himself by a promise to give eternal life to those who serve them. That being the case, what have we to glorify ourselves in, since all that is given to us we receive through the mercy of God, and by the merits of Jesus Christ communicated to us?

17. The Scriptures most clearly prove that eternal glory in the next life is given as a reward for good works, and this glory is called a reward, a debt, a crown of justice, and a payment: "Every man shall receive his own reward according to his own labour" (1 Cor. iii. 8); "Now to him that worketh, the reward is not reckoned according to grace, but according to debt" (Rom. iv. 4). Mark the words "according to debt." "As to the rest there is laid up for me a crown of justice" (2 Tim. iv. 8); "And having agreed with the labourers for a penny a day, he sent them into his vineyard" (Matt. xx. 2); "That you may be counted worthy of the kingdom of God, for which you suffer" (2 Thess. i. 5); Because thou hast been faithful over a few things, I will place thee over many things, enter thou into the joy of thy Lord" (Matt. xxv. 21); "Blessed is the man that endureth temptations, for when he hath been proved he shall receive the crown of life, which God hath promised to them that love him" (James, i. 12). All these texts

prove that the merit of the just man is a merit of justice, *de condigno*.

18. The Holy Fathers prove the same doctrines. St. Cyprian says (6): "Justitiæ opus ..... ut accipiant merita nostra mercedem." St. John Chrysostom, in a long passage which I abridge, says (7): "Nunquam profecto, cum justus sit Deus, bonos hic cruciatibus affici sinerit, si non in futuro seculo mercedem pro meritis parasset." St. Augustin says (8): "Non est injustus Deus, qui justos fraudet mercede justitiæ." And again (9): "Nullane sunt merita justorum? sunt plane, sed ut justi fierent; merita non fuerunt;" as they are not just by their own merits, but by the Divine Grace. Again, the same Saint says: "Deus cum coronat nostra merita, quid aliud coronat quam sua dona?" The Fathers of the Second Council of Oranges decided that, "Debetur merces bonis operibus, si fiant; sed gratiæ Dei, quæ non debetur, præcedit ut fiant." In conclusion, therefore, all our merits depend on the assistance of grace, without which we cannot have any, and the reward of salvation due to our good works is founded in the promise gratuitously made to us by God through the merits of Jesus Christ."

19. They object that text of St. Paul (Rom. vi. 23): "The grace of God life everlasting in Christ Jesus our Lord." Eternal life, therefore, say they, is a grace of the Divine Mercy, and not a reward due to our good works. We reply, that eternal life is justly to be attributed to the mercy of God, for he, by his mercy, has promised it to our good works. The Apostle, therefore, with good reason, calls eternal life a grace, since it is by the grace of God alone that he has constituted himself a debtor of eternal life to all who perform good works.

20. They object, secondly, that eternal life is called an inheritance, "Knowing that you shall receive of the Lord the reward of inheritance" (Col. iii. 24). Inheritance, they say, then, is not the right of Christians, as being children of God by merit, but solely on account of his gratuitous adoption. We answer, that to infants glory is given, solely on the title of inheritance; but adults obtain it as an inheritance, as they are the adopted children of God, and also as a reward for their good works, since God has promised them the inheritance if they observe the law; so that this inheritance is, at the same time, a gift and a retribution due to them for their merits, and this is what the Apostle means when he says: "You shall receive of the Lord the reward of inheritance."

21. They object, thirdly, that our Lord wishes that no matter how carefully we fulfil the commandments, we should call ourselves unprofitable servants: "So you also, when you shall have done all these things that are commanded you, say, we are unprofitable ser-

---

(6) St. Cyprian de Unit. (7) St. Chrys-os. *t.* 5, *l.* 1, de Prav. (8) St. Aug. *l.* de Nat. et Grat. *c.* 2. (9) Idem. Epis. 165.

vants, we have done that which we ought to do" (Luke, xvii. 10). If then, say they, we are unprofitable servants, how can we merit eternal life by our works? We answer, that our works of themselves, without grace, have no merit, but being performed with grace, they, with justice, merit eternal life, in regard of the promise made by God to those who perform them.

22. They object, fourthly, that our works are due to God by obedience, as our supreme Lord, and, hence, they cannot merit eternal life, as justly due to them. We answer, however, that God, through his goodness, laying on one side every other title by which he might justly require all the services we can pay him, has bound himself by a promise to give us eternal glory, as the reward of our good works. But they still say, when every good work is from God, what reward can we expect? We answer, every good work is all from God, but not totally from God, in the same manner as every good work is all our own, but not totally our own, because God works with us, and we with him, and it is to this co-operation of ours that it has pleased God to promise, gratuitously, the reward of eternal life.

23. They object, fifthly, that although the good work might be deserving of glory, still there should be some proportion between the labour and the reward; but what proportion, say they, can be found between our works and eternal glory? "The sufferings of this time are not worthy to be compared with the glory to come that shall be revealed in us" (Rom. viii. 18). We answer, that our works in themselves, and unconnected with Divine grace, are, without doubt, unworthy of eternal glory, but rendered valuable by grace, they are worthy of it, and a proportion then exists between them, as the same Apostle says: "For that which is at present momentary and light of our tribulation, worketh for us above measure exceedingly an eternal weight of glory"(2 Cor. iv. 17).

24. They object, sixthly, that St. Paul says: "For by grace you are saved through faith, and not of yourselves, for it is the gift of God, not of works, that no man may glory" (Ephes. ii. 8, 9). Here, then, say they, it is clear that it is grace that saves us, by means of faith in Jesus Christ. The Apostle, however, is not here speaking of eternal life, but of grace itself, which, undoubtedly, we never can merit by our works; but, as we have already proved, God wishes that those who fulfil his precepts should, on account of the promise made by him, acquire eternal glory. Then, they reply, if our works are necessary for salvation, the merits of Christ alone are not sufficient to save us. No, in truth they are not enough, but our works are also requisite, for the benefit of Jesus Christ is, that he obtained for us the power of applying his merits with our own works. Neither is there anything in that out of which we can pride ourselves, because whatever power we have to merit heaven, we have solely through the merits of Christ; and, therefore, all the

glory is his, as when the vine branches produce fruit, the whole is due to the vine which sends sap to the branches. When the just man, then, obtains eternal life he does not glory in his own works, but in the Divine grace which, by the merits of Christ, gave him the power of meriting it. According to the doctrine of our adversaries, however, almost every means of salvation is taken from us, for if our works are of no avail to us for salvation, and God does everything, then it is no matter whether our morals are good or bad, we need no preparation to receive the sacraments; and prayer inculcated in so many passages of the Scripture, is totally useless to us. What worse doctrine than this could the devil himself invent to lead souls to perdition?

25. This leads us on to another point, following from the former one—that Faith alone is sufficient to save us, as Luther and Calvin said, who, on this anchor alone, trusted their eternal salvation, and therefore despised all law and judgment, cared nothing for righteousness, prayers, or sacraments, and considered all things, no matter how wicked, lawful. They asserted that the Faith by which we firmly believe that God will save us by the merits of Jesus Christ and the promises made by him, is alone sufficient, without works, to obtain salvation for us from God, and this faith they called *Fiducia*, confidence, it being a hope founded on the promise of Jesus Christ. They quote Scripture, too, in favour of this opinion; " Who believes in the Son, hath eternal life" (John, iii. 36); "That he himself may be just, and the justifier of him who is of the Faith of Jesus Christ" (Romans, iii. 26); " In him every one that believeth is justified" (Acts, xiii. 39); " Whoever believeth in him shall not be confounded" (Rom. x. 11); "The just man liveth by Faith" (Gal. iii. 11); " The justice of God, by Faith of Jesus Christ, unto all, and upon all them that believe in him" (Rom. iii. 22).

26. If Faith alone, however, justifies us, how is that the very same Scriptures declare, that it is of no use without works? " What shall it profit, my brethren, if a man say he hath faith but hath not works? Shall faith be able to save him?"(James, ii. 14); and immediately after he says (*ver.* 17): " So Faith also, if it have not works, is dead in itself." Luther, to be sure, says, that this Epistle is not canonical, but we believe rather the authority of the Church, which includes it in her Canon. But there are numberless other passages to prove that Faith alone is not sufficient to save us, but that it is necessary also that we fulfil the commandments. St. Paul says: " If I should have all faith, so that I could remove mountains, and have not charity, I am nothing" (1 Cor. xiii. 2). Jesus Christ commanded his disciples: " Go teach all nations . . . to observe all things whatever I commanded you" (Mark, xxviii.19,20). And he said to the young man: " If thou wilt enter into eternal life, observe the commandments" (Matt. xix. 17), and there are many other texts of a like nature. The texts, therefore, adduced

by our adversaries, must be understood to refer to that Faith, which, as St. Paul teaches, operates by charity: "For in Christ Jesus, neither circumcision availeth anything, nor uncircumcision, but faith, that worketh by charity" (Gal. v. 6); and hence St. Augustin (10) says, that Faith may exist without charity, but it availeth nothing. Hence, when we find it said in the Scriptures, that Faith saves us, we are to understand that living Faith, that is, that Faith which saves us by good works, which are the vital operations of Faith, for if these are wanting it is a sign that the Faith is dead, and that which is dead cannot give life. Hence it is that the Lutherans themselves, as Lomer, Gerard, the Doctors of Strasbourg, and the greater part of the sect, as a certain author states (11), forsaking the doctrine of their master, insist on the necessity of good works for salvation. Bossuet (12) tells us that the Lutherans of the University of Wittemberg, in the confession they presented to the Council of Trent, said "that good works ought of necessity be practised, and that they deserve, by the gratuitous goodness of God, recompense both corporal and spiritual."

27. The Council of Trent (*Sess.* vi. *Can.* 19) says: "Si quis dixerit, nihil præceptum esse in Evangelio præter fidem, cetera esse indifferentia, neque prohibita, sed libera; aut decem præcepta nihil pertinere ad Christianos: anathema sit;" and in Can. 20: " Si quis hominem justificatum, et quantumlibet perfectum, dixerit non teneri ad observantiam mandatorum Dei, et Ecclesiæ, sed tantum ad credendum; quasi vero Evangelium sit nuda, et absoluta promissio vitæ æternæ, sine conditione observationis mandatorum: anathema sit."

SEC. IV.—THE SINNER IS NOT JUSTIFIED BY FAITH ALONE.

28. THE sectarians say, that the sinner, by means of Faith, or *confidence* in the promises of Jesus Christ, and believing, with an infallible certainty, that he is justified, becomes so, for the justice of Jesus Christ is extrinsically imputed to him, by which his sins are not indeed concealed, but covered, and are thus not imputed to him, and they found this dogma on the words of David: "Blessed are they whose iniquities are forgiven, and whose sins are covered. Blessed is the man to whom the Lord hath not imputed sin, and in whose spirit there is no guile" (Psalm xxxi. 1, 2).

29 The Catholic Church, however, condemns and anathematizes the doctrine, that as man is absolved from his sins, by Faith alone, that he is justified. Hear the Council of Trent on this subject (*Sess.* vi. *Can.* 14): " Si quis dixerit, hominem a peccatis absolvi, ac justificari ex eo quod se absolvi ac justificari certo credat; aut

---

(10) St. Aug. *l.* 15 de Trin. c. 18. (11) Pich. Theol. Pol. par. post. *ar* 6.
(12) Bossuet, Variat. *l.* 8, *n.* 30 in fine.

neminem vere esse justificatum, nisi qui credat se esse justificatum, et hac sola fide absolutionem, et justificationem perfici; anathema sit." The Church, besides, teaches, that in order that the sinner should become justified, it is necessary that he be disposed to receive grace. Faith is necessary for this disposition, but Faith alone is not sufficient. The Council of Trent (*Sess.* vi. *cap.* 6), says, that acts of hope, of love, of sorrow, and a purpose of amendment are also necessary, and God then finding the sinner thus disposed, gives him gratuitously his grace, or intrinsic justice (*ibid. cap.* 7), which remits to him his sins, and sanctifies him.

30. We shall now examine the points on which the supposition of our adversaries rests. In the first place, they say, that by means of faith in the merits and promises of Jesus Christ, our sins are not taken away, but are covered. This supposition is, however, totally opposed to the Scriptures, which teach that the sins are not alone covered, but are taken away and cancelled in a justified soul: " Behold the lamb of God, behold him who taketh away the sins of the world" (John, i. 29); " Be penitent, therefore, and be converted, that your sins may be blotted out" (Acts, iii. 19); " He will cast all our sins into the bottom of the sea" (Michaes, vii. 19); " So also Christ was offered once, to exhaust the sins of many" (Heb. ix. 28). Now that which is taken away, which is blotted out, which is annihilated, we cannot say exists any longer. We are also taught that the justified soul is cleansed and delivered from its sins: " Thou shall sprinkle me with hyssop, and I shall be cleansed, thou shalt wash me, and I shall be whiter than snow" (Psalm i. 9); " You shall be cleansed from all your filthiness" (Ezech. xxxvi. 25); " And such some of you were, but you are washed, but you are sanctified, but you are justified" (1 Cor. vi. 11); " But now being made free from sin, and become servants to God, you have your fruit unto sanctification" (Rom. vi. 22). It is on this account that Baptism, by which sin is remitted, is called regeneration and renovation: " He saved us by the laws of regeneration and renovation of the Holy Ghost" (Tit. iii. 5); " Unless a man be born again, he cannot see the kingdom of God" (John, iii. 3). The sinner, therefore, when he is justified, is generated again, and re-born to grace, so that he is changed in all, and renovated from what he was before.

31. How is it, then, that David says our sins are covered? " Blessed are they whose sins are covered." St. Augustin, explaining this Psalm, says, that wounds may be covered both by the sufferer and the physician; the sufferer himself only covers them, but the physician both covers them with a plaister and heals them: " Si tu tegere volueris erubescens (says the Saint) Medicus non sanabit; Medicus tegat, et curet." Our sins, by the infusion of grace, are covered at the same time and healed, but the heretical opinion is, that they are covered, but not healed; they are covered only inasmuch as God does not impute them to the sinner. If sins

remained in the soul as far as the fault was concerned should not God impute them to us? God judges according to truth: "For we know the judgment of God is according to truth" (Rom. ii. 2); but how could God judge according to the truth, judging that man not to be culpable, who is in reality culpable? These are truly some of Calvin's mysteries which surpass our comprehension. The Scripture says, "To God the wicked and his wickedness are equal alike" (Wisdom, xiv. 9). If God hates the sinner on account of the sin that reigns in him, how can he love him as a child, because he is covered with the justice of Christ, while he is still a sinner all the while? Sin, by its very nature, is contrary to God, so it is impossible that God should not hate it as long as it is not taken away, and he must also hate the sinner as long as he retains it. David says: "Blessed is the man to whom the Lord hath not imputed sin." We understand by this not that God does not impute sin by leaving sin in the soul, and not pretending to see it, but that he does not impute it because he cancels and remits it, and hence David says, in the very same passage, "Blessed are they whose iniquities are forgiven." The sins that are forgiven to us are not imputed to us.

32. They say, in the second place, that in the justification of a sinner intrinsic justice is not infused into him, but the justice of Christ alone is imputed to him, so that the wicked man does not become just, but remains wicked still, and is reputed just alone by the intrinsic justice of Christ which is imputed to him. This is, however, an evident error, for the sinner cannot become a friend of God if he does not receive justice of his own, which will renovate him internally, and change him from being a sinner to become one of the just, and as he was previously hateful in the eyes of God, now having acquired this justice, he is agreeable to him. Hence St. Paul exhorts the Ephesians to become renewed in spirit, "And be renewed in the spirit of your mind" (Eph. iv. 23). And hence the Council of Trent says that by the merits of Christ internal justice is communicated to us: "Qua renovamur spiritus mentis nostræ, et non modo reputamur, sed vere etiam justi nominamur, et sumus" (*Sess.* vi. *cap.* 7). The Apostle says in another place, that the sinner, by justification, "is renewed unto knowledge according to the image of him who created him" (Col. iii. 10); so that the sinner, by the merits of Christ, returns back to that state from which he fell by sin, and becomes sanctified as a temple in which God dwells, and hence the Apostle, admonishing his disciples, says: "Fly fornication ...... know you not that your members are the temple of the Holy Ghost" (1 Cor. vi. 18, 19). What is more surprising than all is, that Calvin himself knew that man never can be reconciled with God unless internal and inherent justice is given to him: "Nunquam reconciliamur Deo, quin simul donemur inhærente

justitia" (1). These are his own words, and how can he afterwards say that through faith alone we are justified with the imputative justice of Christ, which is not ours, nor is in us, neither does it belong to us, and is totally extern to us, and is merely intrinsically imputed to us, so that it does not make us just, only to be reputed just? This has been justly condemned by the Council of Trent (*Sess.* v. *Can.* 10): " Si quis dixerit, homines sine Christi justitia, per quam nobis meruit, justificari; aut per eam ipsam formaliter justos esse; anathema sit." (*Can.* 11): " Si quis dixerit homines justificari vel sola imputatione justitiæ Christi, vel sola peccatorum remissione, exclusa gratia, et caritate, quæ in illis inhæreat ...... anathema sit."

33. They object, first, the text (Rom. iv. 5): " But to him that worketh not, yet believeth in him that justifieth the ungodly, his faith is reputed to justice." We answer, briefly, that here the Apostle says that faith should be imputed to justice, to teach us that the sinner is justified, not by his own works, but by his faith in the merits of Christ; but he does not say, that in virtue of this faith the justice of Christ is intrinsically imputed to the sinner who, without being just, is reputed so.

34. They object, secondly, that St. Paul says to Titus: " Not by the works of justice which we have done, but according to his mercy, he saved us by the labour of regeneration and renovation of the Holy Ghost, whom he hath poured forth upon us abundantly, through Jesus Christ our Saviour" (Tit. iii. 5, 6). Therefore, they say, God justifies us by his mercy, and not by the works which, we allege, are necessary for justification. We reply, that our works, as hope, charity, and repentance, with a purpose of amendment, are necessary to render us disposed to receive grace from God; but when the Almighty gives it to us, he does so not for our works, but through his mercy alone, and the merits of Jesus Christ. Let them particularly remark the words " renovation of the Holy Ghost, whom he hath poured forth abundantly upon us, through Jesus Christ our Saviour;" so that when God justifies us, he infuses upon us, not away from us, the Holy Ghost, who renews us, changing us from sinners unto saints.

35. They object, thirdly, another text of St. Paul: " But of him are you in Christ Jesus, who of God is made unto us wisdom, and justice, and sanctification, and redemption" (1 Cor. i. 30). Behold, they exclaim, how Jesus Christ is made our justice. We do not deny that the justice of Jesus Christ is the cause of our justice; but we deny that the justice of Christ is our justice itself, no more than we can say that our wisdom is the wisdom of Christ; and as we do not become wise because of the wisdom of Christ imputed to us,

(1) Calvin, *l.* de vera rat. Reform. Eccles.

neither do we become just because his justice is imputed to us, as the sectarians teach: "He is made unto us wisdom, and justice, and sanctification." All this is to be understood, not imputatively, but effectively, that is, that Jesus Christ, by his wisdom, and justice, and sanctity, has made us become effectively wise, and just, and holy. It is in the same sense we say to God: "I will love thee, O Lord, my strength" (Psalm xvii. 1); "For thou art my patience, O Lord" (Psalm lxx. 5); "The Lord is my light and my salvation" (Psalm xxvi. 1). How is God our strength, our patience, our light? is it imputatively alone? By no means; he is effectively so, for it is he who strengthens, enlightens, and renders us patient; and who saves us.

36. They object, fourthly, that the Apostle says: "Put on the new man, who according to God is created in justice and holiness of truth" (Ephes. iv. 24). Here, say they, it is plain that we, in the justification of faith, clothe ourselves with the justice of Christ as with a garment, which is extrinsic to us. Behold how all heretics boast of not following anything but the pure Scriptures, and will not listen to Tradition, nor the definitions of Councils, nor the authority of the Church. The Scripture, they cry, is our only rule of faith; and why so? Because they distort it, and explain it each after his own fashion, and thus render the Book of Truth a fountain of error and falsehood. In answer to the objection, however, we reply, St. Paul, in that passage, does not speak of extrinsic, but intrinsic justice, and he therefore says: "Be renewed in the spirit of your mind, and put on the new man," &c. (Ephes. iv. 23.) He means that clothing ourselves with Jesus Christ, we should renew ourselves internally in spirit with intrinsic and inherent justice, as Calvin himself admitted; for, otherwise, remaining sinners, we could not renew ourselves. He says: "Put on the new man," because, as a garment is not properly a thing belonging to the body itself, or part of it, so grace or justice does not properly belong to the sinner, but is gratuitously given to him by the mercy of God alone. The Apostle says in another place: "Put on bowels of mercy" (Col. iii. 13). Now, as in this passage he does not speak of extrinsic and apparent mercy, but of that which is real and intrinsic, so when he says, "Put on the new man," he means that we should strip ourselves of the old vicious and graceless man, and put on the new man enriched not with the imputative justice of Jesus Christ, but with intrinsic justice belonging to ourselves, though given us through the merits of Jesus Christ.

SEC. V.—FAITH ALONE CANNOT RENDER US SECURE OF JUSTICE, OR PERSEVERANCE, OR ETERNAL LIFE.

37. It was one of Luther's doctrines, in which he was closely followed by Calvin, that man, after being once justified by Faith, should no longer have either fear or doubt, but that all his sins

were forgiven him, and hence he says (1): "Believe firmly that you are absolved, and you will be so, no matter what contrition you may have;" and he props up this opinion by a text of St. Paul: "Try your ownselves if you be in the faith: prove ye yourselves. Know you not your ownselves, that Christ Jesus is in you, unless perhaps you be reprobated?" (2 Cor. xiii. 6). From this text Luther deduces that a man may be certain of his Faith, and hence he concludes, that being certain of his Faith, he is also certain of the remission of sins. But what sort of conclusion is this? A man is certain of his Faith; but when he knows, at the same time, that he is a sinner, how can he be certain of pardon, unless he is also certain of contrition. Luther himself had previously said (2): "No one can be sure of the truth of his contrition, and much less of pardon." This is the way with all heretics; they are continually contradicting themselves. Besides, in this passage the Apostle is not speaking of justification, but of the miracles which the Corinthians should believe were wrought by God.

38. The Council of Trent (*Sess.* vi. *cap.* 9), teaches, that although every one ought to be certain of the Divine Mercy, of the merits of Christ, and of the power of the sacraments, still no one can be certain of the remission of his sins as a matter of Faith, and in the 13th Canon condemns all who assert the contrary: "Si quis dixerit, omni homini ad remissionem peccatorum assequendam necessarium esse, ut credat certo, et absque ulla hæsitatione propriæ infirmitatis, et indispositionis peccata sibi esse remissa: anathema sit." And this is proved by the Scriptures likewise: "Man knoweth not whether he be worthy of love or hatred, but all things are kept uncertain for the time to come" (Eccles. ix. 1, 2). Calvin (3) objects that this text does not allude to the state of a soul in grace or anger with God, but to the prosperous or adverse circumstances which happen in this life, as by those temporal accidents we cannot know whether God loves or hates us, since prosperity and adversity are the portions of good and bad alike; but, on the other hand, he says man can very well know whether he is just or unjust, if he knows that he has or has not faith. But we answer, that this text does not speak of temporal things, but of the love or hatred with which God looks on the state of the soul, and, therefore, it says, "all things are kept uncertain for the time to come." If, therefore, in this life all things are "kept uncertain," then what our adversaries say cannot be the fact, that man, by the knowledge of his faith, can be certain that he is in a state of grace.

39. God, besides, admonishes us that we should be afraid even of the sin forgiven already: "Be not without fear about sin forgiven" (Eccles. v. 5). The innovators quote the Greek text here, which

---

(1) Luther, Serm. de Indulg. *t.* 1, *p.* 59.   (2) Luther Serm. de Indulg. *t.* 1, *p.* 30.
3) Calvin, Instit. *l.* 3, *c.* 2, *s.* 38.

says not *forgiven*, but *forgiveness*, and that, they say, means that we should not presume that the sins not yet committed will be forgiven. This interpretation, however, is false, because the Greek expression comprehends both past and future sins, and the Greek text is explained in the Latin translation by past sins. St. Paul surely had a knowledge of his Faith, and although he did not feel his conscience laden with any sin, and saw himself favoured by God with revelations and extraordinary gifts, still he did not consider himself with certainty justified. God alone, he says, knew in truth whether he was or not: " I am not conscious to myself of anything, yet I am not hereby justified, but he that judgeth me is the Lord" (1 Cor. iv. 4).

40. Our adversaries object, that the Apostle says: " The Spirit himself giveth testimony of our Spirit, that we are the sons of God"(Rom. viii. 16). Hence Calvin concludes that it is Faith which assures us of being the children of God. We answer that, although the testimony of the Holy Ghost is infallible in itself, still as far as we are concerned, and know anything about it, we can only have a conjectural certainty of being in a state of grace, but never can be infallibly certain of it, unless by a special revelation from God. And, moreover, as far as our knowledge goes, we cannot know if that Spirit be surely from God, for many times the angel of darkness transforms himself into an angel of light, to deceive us.

41. Luther said, that a faithful man, by means of justifying Faith, though he may be in sin at the time, ought to believe, with an infallible certainty, that he is justified by reason of the justice of Christ, imputed to him; but he afterwards said that this justice might be lost by any new sin. Calvin (4), on the contrary, made an addition to this heresy, for he insisted on the *inadmissibility* of this imputative justice. If we could suppose Luther's false principle of justifying Faith to be true, we should admit that Calvin had more reason at his side than he. He said, if any one of the Faithful is sure of his justification, when he prays for it, and believes with confidence that God, by the merits of Christ, justifies him, this petition then, and this certainty of Faith, regard no less the remission of sins committed, than the future perseverance in grace, and, consequently, eternal salvation. Calvin adds (5), that when the faithful man relapses into sin, though his justifying Faith is oppressed by it, it is not, however, lost, for the soul always would have retained possession of it. Such were the specious doctrines of Calvin, and this was the doctrine professed by the Elector Count Palatine, in his Confession of Faith: " I believe," said he, " that I am a living member of the Catholic Church for evermore, since God, appeased by the satisfaction of Jesus Christ, will not remember either the past or future sins of my life " (6).

(4) Bossuet, Var. *t.* 3, *l.* 14, *n.* 16. (5) Calv. Ant. ad Con. Trid. *s.* 6, c. 13.
(6) Recuil. de Genevre, *part* 2, *p.* 169.

42. The whole gist of the matter is this, that the principle of Luther, as we have already seen, is false, in the first place, for, in order to obtain justification, it is not enough to have Faith alone that we are justified by the merits of Christ; but it is necessary, also, that the sinner should have contrition for his faults, so as to dispose himself to receive the remission which God grants him, according to the promise he has made, to pardon those who repent, through the merits of Jesus Christ. Hence, if the justified man relapses into sin, he again loses grace.

43. If the doctrine of Luther, regarding the certainty of justification, is false, the doctrine of Calvin, regarding the certainty of perseverance and eternal salvation, is equally so. St. Paul tells us: "Wherefore he that thinketh himself to stand, let him take heed lest he fall" (1 Cor. x. 12). And, again, he tells us: "With fear and trembling, work out your salvation" (Phil. ii. 12.) How, then, can Calvin say that it is a temptation of the devil, to have any fear about our perseverance? When St. Paul, then, tells us to live in fear, does he mean that we should second the temptations of the devil? But, say they, what is the use of this fear? If what Calvin asserts was true, that having once received justice and the Holy Ghost, we can never lose them, because, according to him, justifying Faith is never lost, and to him who has Faith, God does not impute his sins—if all this, I say, were true, then, indeed, it would be useless to dread the loss of Divine grace. But can any one imagine that God will give his friendship and eternal glory to one who tramples on the Divine law, and commits all sorts of wickedness; and all this because he believes, forsooth, that through the merits of Jesus Christ, the crimes he commits will not be imputed to him? Such, then, is the gratitude these Reformers show to Jesus Christ. They avail themselves for the death he suffered for love of us, to involve themselves more and more in crime, trusting that, through his merits, God will not impute their sins to them. So Jesus Christ, then, has died, that men may have leave to do whatever they please, without fear of punishment. If such, however, was the fact, why did God promulgate his laws—make so many promises to those who observe them—and threaten those who violate them? God, however, never deceives us when he speaks to us; he wishes that the commandments he imposes on us should be exactly observed—"Thou hast commanded thy commandments to be kept most diligently" (Psalm cxviii. 4)—and condemns those who offend against his laws—"Thou hast despised all those that fall off from thy judgments (Psalm cxviii. 118). It is thus that fear is useful: the fear of losing the Divine grace, which makes us cautiously avoid the occasions of sin, and adopt the means of perseverance in a good life, such as frequenting the sacraments, and praying continually.

44. Calvin says that, according to St. Paul, the gifts of God are

irrevocable, and given to us without penance: "The gifts and calling of God are without repentance" (Romans, xi. 29). Whosoever, therefore, he says, has received the Faith, and with the Faith, Grace, to which eternal salvation is united, as these are perpetual gifts, they never can be lost; and thus the faithful man, though he may fall into sin, will always be in possession of that justice, which is given him by Faith. Here, however, we ask a question. David surely had Faith—he fell into the sins of murder and adultery; now, I ask, when David was in sin, before his repentance, was he a sinner or a just man? if he died in that state would he be damned or not? No one, I believe, will be bold enough to assert, that he could be saved in that state. In that state, then, he was no longer just, as he himself, after his conversion, confessed—"I know my iniquity;" and, therefore he prayed to God, to cancel his sins—"Blot out my iniquity" (Psalm l. 2). It will not do to say that he who is predestined may consider himself just in the meantime, since he will do penance for his sins before he dies; that will not do, I assert, because future penance cannot make the sinner just, when he is in a state of sin at the time. Bossuet (7) says that the difficulty of accounting for this, according to Calvin's doctrine, caused many of his followers to return to the bosom of the Church.

45. Before we conclude this subject, we may as well review the Scripture texts on which Calvin founds his doctrine. The Apostle St. James, he says, tells us that we should pray to God for graces—and that of perseverance is the principal of all others—without having any doubt of obtaining them: "Let him ask in Faith, nothing wavering" (James, i. 6); and our Lord himself says: "All things whatsoever you ask when ye pray, believe that you shall receive: and they shall come unto you" (Mark, xi. 24). Therefore, says Calvin, whosoever seeks perseverance from God, and believes that he obtains it, never can want it, as we have the Divine promise for it. We answer that, although the promise of God, to hear him who prays to him, can never fail, still that is to be understood, when we pray for grace, with all the requisite conditions, and one of the conditions of beseeching prayer is perseverance; but if we cannot be certain that in future we will persevere in prayer, how can we be sure at the present time that we will persevere in grace? Calvin, besides, objects that St. Paul says: "I am sure that neither death nor life, &c......shall be able to separate us from the love of God" (Rom. viii. 38, 39). But we reply to this, that the Apostle does not here speak of an infallible certainty of Faith, but only of a simple moral certainty, founded on the Divine Mercy, and on that good will which God gave him, to suffer everything, sooner than be separated from his love.

(7) Bossuet, Variat. *t.* 3, *l.* 14, *n.* 16.

46. Leave Calvin aside, and hear what the Council of Trent teaches, concerning perseverance and predestination. Speaking of perseverance, it says: "Si quis magnum illud usque in finem perseverantiæ donum se certo habiturum, absoluta et infallibili certitudine dixerit, nisi hoc ex speciali revelatione didicerit: anathema sit" (*Sess.* vi. *Can.* 16). And, regarding predestination: "Si quis dixerit, hominem renatum, et justificatum teneri ex fide ad credendum, se certo esse in numero prædestinatorum: anathema sit" (*Sess.* vi. *Can.* 15). Behold, then, how clearly and distinctly the Council defines all the dogmas of Faith, opposed to the errors of modern innovators. I make this remark for the instruction of those who assert that the Council gave only ambiguous decisions in their controversies, and that it only increased disputes, instead of putting an end to them. The Fathers of the Council said over and over, that it was never their intention to give any decision regarding the questions debated in Catholic schools, but solely to define matters of Faith, and condemn the errors of the pretended Reformers, who were endeavouring, not to reform morals, but to subvert the ancient and true doctrines of the Catholic Church. The Council, therefore, speaks ambiguously of scholastic questions, and gives no decision on them; but in matters of Faith, contested by Protestants, it always speaks with the greatest clearness, and without any ambiguity. Those alone find the definitions of the Council doubtful who refuse to yield obedience to them. To come back to the subject. The Council teaches that no one can be sure that he is predestined; and, in fact, how can any one be sure of predestination, when he is not sure that he will persevere in goodness. But, says Calvin, St. John teaches that "You have eternal life, you who believe in the name of the Son of God" (1 John, v. 13). Therefore, says he, whoever has faith in Jesus Christ has eternal life. We answer, he who believes in Jesus Christ with true Faith, enlivened by charity, has eternal life, not in possession, but in hope, as St. Paul says: "For we are saved by hope" (Rom. viii. 24). Perseverance is necessary to obtain eternal life—"He that shall persevere to the end, he shall be saved" (Matt. x. 22)—but as long as we are uncertain of perseverance, we are never sure of eternal life.

47. The sectarians object that the uncertainty of eternal salvation makes us doubt of the Divine promises, to be saved by the merits of Jesus Christ. We answer that the Divine promises never can fail, so, on God's part, we never can doubt that he will be wanting, by denying what he promised us. The doubt and fear is on our side, for we may be found wanting, by transgressing his Divine commandments, and thus losing his grace. God in that case is not obliged to fulfil the promises made to us, but rather punish our infidelity; and, therefore, St. Paul exhorts us to work out our salvation with fear and trembling (Phil. ii. 12). We are, therefore,

certain of salvation, if we remain faithful to God; but, on the other hand, should dread our perdition, if we are unfaithful. But, they add, this fear and uncertainty destroys peace of conscience. We answer, that peace of conscience in this life does not consist in a certain belief that we will be saved, for this is not what God promises us, but it consists in the hope that he will save us, through the merits of Jesus Christ, if we strive to live well, and endeavour, by prayer, to obtain the Divine assistance to persevere in a holy life. This it is which is so hurtful to these heretics; for, trusting to this Faith alone for salvation, they pay little attention to the observance of the Divine commandments, and much less to prayer, and, not praying, they are deprived of the Divine assistance necessary for a good life, and thus they are lost. Surrounded as we are by dangers and temptations, we have need of a continual assistance from grace, which, without prayer, we cannot obtain; and, for that reason, God tells us we should pray continually: "We ought always to pray and not to faint" (Luke, xviii. 1). He, however, who believes that he is sure of salvation, and believes that prayer is not necessary for this object, scarcely prays at all, and then is lost. He, on the contrary, who is not sure of his salvation, and fears to fall into sin, and be lost, will surely pray continually to God to succour him, and thus hopes to obtain perseverance and salvation, and this is the only peace of conscience we can have in the present life. No matter how the Calvinists may strive to obtain perfect peace, by believing their salvation certain, they never can accomplish it in this way; and we even see the Synod of Dort, the great exponent of their doctrine (*Art.* 12), declare that the gift of Faith (which, according to them, includes past and future justification) is not granted by God unless to his elect alone. How, then, can a Calvinist be sure that he is among the number of the elect, when he knows nothing about his election? This alone would, we think, be sufficient to show them that they cannot be certain of their salvation.

SEC. VI.—GOD CANNOT BE THE AUTHOR OF SIN.

48. DEAR reader, you will be horrified to hear the blasphemies which those sectarians, and especially Calvin, vomited forth, concerning sin. They are not afraid to say that God ordains all the sins committed on this earth. Here are Calvin's own words (1): "Nec absurdum videri debet, quod dico, Deum non modo primi hominis casum, et in eo posteriorum ruinam prævidisse, sed arbitrio quoque suo dispensasse." And again he says (2): "Ex de ordi-

---

(1) Calvin, Inst. *l.* 3, *c.* 23, *sec.* 7, infra.

natione reprobis injicitur peccandi necessitas." He says, in the second place (3), that God pushes on the devil to tempt man to sin: " Dicitur et Deus suo modo agere, quod Satan ipse (instrumentum cum sit iræ ejus) pro ejus nutu, atque imperio se inflectit ad exequendo ejus justa justitia." And again (*Sec.* 5), he says: " Porro Satanæ ministerium intercedere ad reprobos, instigandos, quoties huc atque illuc Dominus providentia sua eos destinat." He says, thirdly (4), that God instigates man to sin: " Homo justo Dei impulsu agit, quod sibi non licet." In the fourth place (5), he says, that God himself operates sin in us and with us, and makes use of men as instruments for the execution of his judgments: " Concedo fures, homicidas, &c., Divinæ esse providentiæ instrumenta, quibus Dominis ad exequenda sua judicia utitur." In this respect, Calvin's doctrine approaches Luther's and Zuinglius's. Luther says: " Mala opera in impiis Deus operatur." And Zuinglius (6) writes: " Quando facimus adulterium, homicidium, Dei opus est auctoris." In fine, Calvin (7) is not ashamed to say that God is the author of all sin: " Et jam satis aperte ostendi, Deum vocari omnium eorum (peccatorum) auctorem, quæ isti Censores volunt tantum ejus permissu contingere." Soothed by such doctrines, the sectarians flatter themselves that their vices are excusable; for, if they sin, they do it through necessity, and if they are damned, it is by necessity also, for all the damned are destined to be so by God, even before their creation. This monstrous doctrine will be refuted in the next section.

49. Calvin maintains this horrible opinion by the following reasons: God never, he says, could have had the foreknowledge of the eternal happiness or misery of any of us, if he had not ordained by his decree the good or bad works we perform during our lives: " Decretum quidem horribile fateor, inficiari tamen nemo poterit, quin præsciverit Deus, quem exitum esset habiturus homo; et ideo præsciverit, quia decreto suo sic ordinaverat." We answer, that there is a great difference between forseeing and predestining the sins of mankind. There is not the least doubt but that God, by his infinite intelligence, knows and comprehends everything that will come to pass, and, among the rest, all the sins which each one will commit; but some things he foresees according to his positive decree; others according to his permission; but neither the Divine decree nor the permission are opposed to man's free will, for when God foresees our good or evil works, he foresees them all performed freely. The sectaries argue thus: If God has foreseen Peter's sin, for example, he cannot be mistaken as to his knowledge of what will happen when the time foreseen arrives; therefore Peter must

(2) Idem, ibid. *sec.* 39.   (3) Idem, *l.* 3, *c* 4, *sec.* 3.   (4) Calvin, Inst. *l.* 1, *c.* 18, *sec.* 4.   (5) Idem, *l.* 1, *c.* 17, *sec.* 5.   (6) Zuing. Serm. de Provid. *c.* 6.   (7) Calv. *l.* 1, *c.* 1, *sec.* 3.

necessarily sin. Here they are in error, however, when they say *necessarily;* he will infallibly sin, because God has foreseen it, and cannot err in his foresight; but he will not necessarily sin, because, if he wishes to sin, he will do so of his own free will, by his own malice, and God will permit him to do so, solely not to deprive him of that free will which he gave him.

50. We shall now see how many absurd consequences proceed from this sectarian doctrine. First absurdity.—They say that God, for his own just ends, ordains and wills the sins committed by mankind. But nothing can be clearer than the Scriptures on this point, which tell us that God not only does not wish sins, but looks on them with horror, and wishes nothing so much as our sanctification: " Thou art not a God that willest iniquity" (Psalm, v. 5); " To God the wicked and his wickedness are hateful alike" (Wisdom, xiv. 9); " Thy eyes are too pure to behold evil, and thou canst not look on iniquity" (Habak. i. 13). Now, when God protests that he does not wish sin, but hates and prohibits it, how can the sectarians say, that, contradicting himself, he wishes it and predestines it? Calvin himself (8) takes notice of this difficulty: " Objiciunt," he says, "si nihil eveniat, nisi volente Deo, duas esse in eo contrarias voluntates, quia occulto consilio decernat, quæ lege sua palam vetuit, facile diluitur." How does he get out of the difficulty? merely by saying, " We cannot understand it." The true answer, however, is, that his supposition is totally false, for God can never wish that which he hates and forbids. Melancthon, even in the Augsburg Confession, says: " Causa peccati est voluntas impiorum, quæ avertit se a Deo." The will of the wicked turned away from God is the cause of sin.

51. The second absurdity is this.—God, they say, incites the devil to tempt us, and he himself even tempts man, and drives him on to sin. How can that be, however, when God prohibits us from following our evil inclinations: " Go not after thy lusts" (Eccles. xviii. 30); and to fly from sin as from a serpent: " Flee from sin as from the face of a serpent" (Eccles. xxi. 2)? St. Paul tells us to clothe ourselves with the armour of God, that is prayer, against temptations: " Put on the armour of God, that you may be able to stand against the deceits of the devil" (Ephes. vi. 11). St. Stephen reproaches the Jews, that they resisted the Holy Ghost; but if it were true that God moved them to sin, they might answer, we do not resist the Holy Ghost, by any means, but do what he inspires us, and on that account we stone you. Jesus Christ teaches us to pray to God not to permit us to be tempted by those dangerous occasions, which may lead to our fall: " Lead us not into temptation." Now, if God urges on the devil to tempt us, and even tempts us himself, and moves us to sin, and decrees that we

(8) Calvin, Inst. *l.* 1, *c.* 16, *sec.* 3.

sin, how can he command us to fly from sin and resist it, and to pray that we may be free from temptations. If God has decreed that Peter, for example, should have a certain temptation, and succumb to it, how can he command this same Peter to pray that he may free him from this temptation, and change his own decree? God never urges the devil to tempt us, but merely permits him to do so to prove us. When the devil tempts us, he commits a wickedness, and God cannot command him to do this: "He hath commanded no man to do wickedly, and he hath given no man license to sin" (Eccles. xv. 21). Our Lord himself promises, even, that whenever we are tempted he will assist us, and give us sufficient grace to resist, and declares that he will never allow us to be tempted beyond our strength: "God is faithful, who will not suffer you to be tempted above that which you are able" (1 Cor. x. 13). But they still insist God, as we read in the Scriptures, several times tempted man: "God hath tried them" (Wisdom, iii. 5). "After these things God tempted Abraham" (Gen. xxii. 1). We must here draw a distinction: the devil tempts men to make them fall into sin, but God tempts them solely to prove their fidelity, as he did in Abraham's case, and does continually, with his faithful servants: "God hath tried them, and found them worthy of himself" (Wisdom, iii. 5); but he never tempts man to fall into sin, as the devil does: "For God is not a tempter of evils, and he tempteth no man" (James, i. 13).

52. The third absurdity is this.—God says: "Believe not every spirit, but try the spirits if they be of God" (1 John, iv. 1). Hence, we Catholics are bound to examine the resolutions we take, as well as the counsels we receive from others, even when at first they appear good and holy, because frequently what we believe to be an inspiration from God is nothing but a snare of the devil. According to Calvin's doctrine, however, we are not obliged to make this examination, and see whether the spirit is good or bad, because whether it be one or the other, it is all from God, who wills that we should put in practice whatever he inspires us to do, whether it be good or bad. According to this, then, the reformer's own maxim —of understanding the Scriptures, according to our private judgment—falls to the ground, for no matter what we do, or what erroneous or heretical interpretation we may give to the Holy Writ, it is all an inspiration from God.

53. The fourth absurdity.—The whole Scriptures teach us that God leans much more to mercy and pardon than to justice and punishment: "All the ways of the Lord are mercy and truth" (Psalm, xxiv. 10); "The earth is full of the mercy of the Lord. His tender mercies are above all his works" (Psalm, cxliv. 9); "Mercy exalteth itself above judgment" (James, ii. 13). The Almighty, therefore, superabounds in mercy, not alone to the just, but to sinners. The great desire he has to make us live well, and

work out our salvation, is manifest from that passage so frequently repeated in the Gospel: "Ask and ye shall receive (John, xvi. 24); "Ask and it shall be given to you" (Matt. vii. 7); "Every one that asketh receiveth" (Luke, xi. 10). To all he offers the treasures of enlightenment, of Divine love, of efficacious grace, of final perseverance, and of eternal salvation, if we only pray for them. He is faithful, and cannot fail in his promises, and so, whoever is lost, is solely through his own fault. Calvin says the elect are few; these are Beza and his own disciples; and all others are reprobates, on whom God exercises his justice alone, since he has predestined them to hell, and therefore deprives them of all grace, and incites them to sin. According to Calvin's doctrine, then, we should imagine the Almighty not as a God of mercy, but the most unjust and cruel of tyrants, since he wishes us to sin that he may torment us for all eternity. God, says Calvin, only acts thus to exercise his justice, but this is what all cruel tyrants do; they wish others to commit crimes, that by punishing them they may gratify their own cruel dispositions.

54. *The fifth absurdity.*—As man is obliged to sin, for God wishes that he should, and pushes him on, it is unjust to punish him, for as he is forced to sin he has no freedom, and therefore commits no sin; nay, more, as he does the will of God, who wishes him to sin, he ought to be rewarded for conforming to the Divine will; how, then, can God punish him in justice? Beza says, the Apostle tells us that God "worketh all things according to the counsel of his will" (Ephes. i. 11). If everything is done, then, by the will of God, sins, also, he says, are committed by his will. Beza, here, however, is in error; everything except sin is done by the will of God. God does not wish sin, nor that any one should be lost through sin: "Is it my will that a sinner should die, saith the Lord?" (Ezech. xviii. 23); "Not willing that any should perish, but that all should rather do penance" (2 Peter, iii. 5). The Almighty wishes that we should all become saints: "For it is the will of God your sanctification" (1 Thess. iv. 3).

55. *The sixth absurdity.*—These sectarians say that God himself operates sins with us, and uses us as instruments for the accomplishment of sin, and hence Calvin, as we have already remarked, calls God the author of sin. This is condemned by the Council of Trent (*Sess.* vi. *can.* 6): "Si quis dixerit, non esse in potestate hominis vias suas malas facere, sed mala opera, ita ut bona, Deum operari; non permissive solum, sed etiam proprie, et per se, adeo ut sit proprium ejus opus, non minus proditio Judæ, quam vocatio Pauli; anathema sit." If God, then, be the author of sin, since he wishes it, and urges us on to commit it, and operates it with us, how is it that man sins, and God does not sin? When this difficulty was put to Zuinglius, he only answered: "Ask God himself; I am not one of his counsellors." When Calvin himself was asked: How is

it that God condemns men for executing sin, when he himself operates it through their means; in every wicked work it is not the instrument but the operator who is culpable? and hence, if man sins alone as the instrument of God, it is not he but God who is culpable? he answered, that "our carnal minds could not understand it" (9). Some sectaries answer this by saying, that God does not sin by operating the sin, but man alone, for man does it for an evil end, but God for a good end, to wit, exercising his justice by punishing the sinner for his crime. But this answer will not excuse God, because, according to Calvin, the Almighty decrees and predestines man not alone to do the work of sin, but to do it with an evil end, for otherwise he could not punish him. Hence God is the true author of sin, and truly sins. Zuinglius gives another answer (10): Man, he says, sins because he acts against the law, but God does not sin, because he has no law; but this ridiculous answer is rejected by Calvin himself (11), who says, " we cannot suppose God without a law." And it stands to reason, for though no one can give a law to God, still his own goodness and justice are a law to him. Hence as sin is contrary to the law of nature, it is also opposed to the goodness of God, and he, therefore, never can will sin. Now, as Calvinists assert, that whatever a man does, good or bad, he does through necessity, for it is all the work of God, I would like to see, if one broke another's head, and he asked him, Why do you strike me? and the other would answer, It is not I who strike you, but God who makes me, and forces me to do so, would his co-religionist be satisfied with the excuse? What God are you talking about? he would say; away with such nonsense, it is you have done it, and I will punish you for it. Poor people! We hope they are not wilfully blind, for really it would appear that those who entertain such extravagant opinions must be so.

56. The sectarians adduce several portions of Scripture to prove that God wishes, commands, and operates sins. He says, in Isaias, " I make peace, and create evil" (Isaias, xlv. 7); but Tertullian answers, that there are two sorts of evil crimes and punishments. God performs punishments, but not crimes, for the crimes of the wicked, he says, belong to the devil, the punishments to God. When Absalom rebelled against his father, David, God wished the chastisement of David, but not the sin of Absalom. But, say they, we read in 2 Kings, xvi. 10, that the Lord bid Semei "curse David;" and in Ezech. xiv. 9, " I, the Lord, have deceived that Prophet;" in the 104th Psalm, ver. 25: " He turned their heart to hate his people;" and in St. Paul (2 Thess. ii. 10): " God shall send them the operation of error to believe lying." Behold then, say they, how God commands and operates sins. They do not, however, in these

(9) Calvin, Inst. *l.* 1, *c.* 18, *s.* 1.   (10) Zuing. Serm. de Provident. *c.* 5.   (11) Calv. *l.* 3, *c.* 23, *s.* 2.

texts distinguish between the will of God and his permission. God, for his own just ends, permits that man may deceive or sin, either for the punishment of the wicked or for the advantage of the just, but he neither wishes nor operates sin. Tertullian (12) says, God is not the author nor the actor of sin, though he undoubtedly permits it. St. Ambrose (13) says he does what is good, but not what is evil, and St. Augustin (14) writes: He (God) knows how to condemn iniquity, but not to do it.

SEC. VII.—GOD NEVER PREDESTINED ANY ONE TO ETERNAL DAMNATION WITHOUT REGARD TO HIS SINS.

57. CALVIN teaches that God has predestined many to eternal damnation, not because of their sins, but merely for his own pleasure. Here are his words (1): " Aliis vita æterna, aliis damnatio æterna præordinatur; itaque prout in alterutrum finem quisque conditus est, ita vel ad vitam, vel ad mortem prædestinatum dicimus," and the only reason he assigns for this predestination is the will of God (2): "Neque in aliis reprobandis aliud habebimus, quam ejus voluntatem." I can understand very well how the heretics embrace this doctrine, for they argue thus: I may commit whatever sins I please, without fear or remorse; for, if I am predestined to heaven, I will, notwithstanding, be infallibly saved, no matter what wickedness I commit; if I am among the reprobate I will be damned, no matter how virtuously I live. Cesarius tells a story of a certain physician who gave a very good answer to this argument, if it can be called one. A man of the name of Louis Landgrave got a mortal fit of sickness, and sent for this physician, who called on him, and asked him what he wanted with him. "I hope," said the sick man, "you will be able to restore me to health." "Oh," said the physician, "what can I do for you? If your hour is come you will die, no matter what remedies I may give you, but if not, you will recover, without any assistance from me." Remember this was the same answer the sick man had previously given to a person who reprimanded him in presence of the physician, for his wicked life. "If I am to be saved," said he, "I will be so, no matter how wicked I may be; and if I am to be damned, it will happen, no matter how good I am." "Oh," said the sick man, "do what you can for me, perhaps your skill will restore me, but if you do nothing for me I will surely die." The physician, then, who was both a pious and prudent man, said to him: "If, then, you think that you can recover your bodily health with the assistance of medicine, why do not you try and restore your soul to health by a good confession?" The argument hit hard, the man sent immediately for a confessor, and became a true penitent.

(12) Tertull. le cont. Hermog. (13) St. Ambr. i. de Par. c. 15. (14) St. Augus. *l.* 105, ad Sixtum. (1) Calvin, Inst. *l.* 1, c. 21, *sec.* 5. (5) Calvin, Inst. *l.* 1, c. 21, *s.* 5.

58. We shall, however, give Calvin a direct answer. If you are predestined to eternal life, it is because you will be saved by the good works you perform, at least that your predestination may be carried out, but if you are destined to hell it is on account of your sins, and not through the mere will of God, as you blasphemously assert. Forsake, then, your evil ways; do what is just, and you will be saved. Nothing can be more false than the supposition of Calvin, that God created many men for hell alone. Numberless passages in the Scriptures prove most clearly that it is his will that all should be saved. St. Paul most expressly says (1 Tim. ii. 4), that he will " have all men to be saved, and come to the knowledge of the truth;" and, as St. Prosper says, speaking of this passage, nothing can be clearer than that it is the will of God that all should be saved: " Sacrificium credendum atque profitendum est Dominum velle omnes homines salvos fieri, siquidem Apostolus (cujus hæc sententia est) sollicite præcipit ut Deo pro omnibus supplicetur " (3). This is clear from the context, for the Apostle says: " I desire first of all that supplications ..... be made for all men ..... for this is good and acceptable in the sight of God our Saviour, who will have all men to be saved," &c. So we see the Apostle tells us to pray for all, since God wishes to save all. St. John Chrysostom argues in the same manner on the same text (4): " Si omnes Ille vult salvos fieri, merito pro omnibus oportet orare. Si omnes ipse salvos fieri cupit, Illius et tu concorda voluntate." St. Paul, speaking of our Saviour, also says: " Christ Jesus, who gave himself a redemption for all " (1 Tim. ii. 6). If then, Jesus Christ wished to redeem all men, then he wills that all men should be saved.

59. But, says Calvin, God certainly foresees the good and bad actions of every man: he has, therefore, decreed to send some to hell on account of their sins, and how, then, can it be said that he wills that all should be saved? We answer, with St. John of Damascus, St. Thomas of Aquin, and the great body of Catholic Doctors, that with regard to the reprobation of sinners, it is necessary to distinguish between the priority of time and the priority of order, or, if we may say, of reason. In priority of time, the Divine Decree is anterior to man's sin; but in priority of order, sin is anterior to the Divine Decree; for God has decreed many sinners to hell, inasmuch as he has foreseen their sins. Hence we may see that God, with that antecedent will which regards his goodness, truly wills that all should be saved, but by that consequent will which regards the sins of the reprobate, he wishes their damnation. Hear the words of St. John of Damascus on the subject (5): " Deus precedenter vult omnes salvari, ut efficiat nos

---

(3) St. Prosper. resp. ad 2. Object. Vin.   (4) St. Chrysos. in 1 Tim. 2, Hom. 7.
(5) St. Joan. Damas. l. 2, de Fide Orthod. c. 2.

bonitatis suæ participes ut bonus; peccantes autem puniri vult ut justus;" and St. Thomas says: "Voluntas antecedens est, qua (Deus) omnes homines salvos fieri vult...... Consideratis autem omnibus circumstantiis personæ, sic non invenitur de omnibus bonum esse quod salventur; bonum enim est eum qui se præparat, et consentit, salvari; non vero nolentem, et resistentem .... Et hæc dicitur voluntas consequens, eo quod præsupponit præscientiam operum, non tanquam causam voluntatis, sed quasi rationem voliti " (6).

60. There are many other texts to prove that God wills the salvation of all. I will quote at least a few. Christ says: " Come to me, all you that labour and are burthened, and I will refresh you" (Matt. xi. 28). Come, he says, all you burthened with your sins, and I will repair the ruin you yourselves have occasioned. When, therefore, he invites all to accept a remedy, he wishes that all should be saved. In another place St. Peter says, the Lord " dealeth patiently for your sake, not willing that any should perish, but that all should return to penance" (2 Peter, iii. 9). Mark this, " that all should return to penance." God does not wish that any one should be damned, even sinners, while in this life, but that all should repent of their sins, and be saved. Again, in another place, David says: " For wrath is in his indignation, and life in his *good* will" (Psalm, xxix. 6). St. Basil, explaining this passage, says, that it proves that God wishes all men to be saved: " Et vita in voluntate ejus, quid ergo dicit? nimirum quod vult Deus omnes vitæ fieri participes." Although we offend God by our sins, he does not wish our death, but that we should live. In the book of Wisdom (xi. 25), we read: " Thou lovest all things that are, and hatest none of the things thou hast made...... thou sparest all, because they are thine, O Lord, who lovest souls." If, therefore, God loves all his creatures, and especially the souls he created, and is always ready to pardon those who repent of their sins, how can we imagine, for a moment, that he creates souls solely for the purpose of tormenting them eternally in hell? No; God does not wish to see them lost, but saved, and when he sees that we are hurrying to eternal torments, by our sins, he almost implores us to retrace our steps, and avoid destruction: " Turn ye, turn ye from your evil ways, and why will you die, O house of Israel" (Ezech. xxxiii. 11). Poor sinners, he says, why will you persevere in damning yourselves? return to me, and you will find again the life which you lost. Hence it was, that our Saviour, viewing Jerusalem, and considering the destruction the Jews were bringing on it, by the crime of putting him to death, " wept over it" (Luke, xix. 41). In another place he declares that he does not wish the death of the sinner, and even swears so: " As I live, saith the

(6) St. Thom cap. 6, Joan. lec. 4.

Lord God, I desire not the death of the wicked, but that the wicked turn from his evil way, and live" (Ezech. xxxiii. 11).

61. Now, taking into account so many Scripture proofs, by which God tells us that he wishes to save all mankind, it is, as the learned Petavius says, an insult to the Divine Mercy, and a mockery of the Faith, to say that God does not wish that it should be so: "Quod si ista Scripturæ loca, quibus hanc suam voluntatem tam illustribus, ac sæpe repetitis sententiis, imo lacrymis, ac jurejurando testatus est Deus, calumniari licet, et in contrarium detorquere sensum, ut præter paucos genus humanum omne perdere statuerit, nec eorum servandorum voluntatem habuerit, quid est adeo disertum in Fidei decretis, quod simili ab injuria, et cavillatione tutum esse possit"(7). Cardinal Sfrondati adds, that to assert the contrary, that God wishes only some few to be saved, and has absolutely decreed that all the rest should be damned, when he has so often manifested that he wishes all to be saved, is only making him an actor, who says one thing, and wishes and performs another: "Plane qui aliter sentiunt, nescio an ex Deo vero Deum scenicum faciant"(8). All the Fathers, both Greek and Latin, are agreed in this, that God sincerely wishes that all should be saved. Petavius cites St. Justin, St. Basil, St. Gregory, St. Cyril, St. Chrysostom, and St. Methodius, on the subject. Hear what the Latin Fathers say—St. Jerome: "Vult (Deus) salvare omnes, sed quia nullus absque propria voluntate salvatur, vult nos bonum velle, ut cum voluerimus, velit in nobis et Ipse suum implere consilium"(9). St. Hilary says (10): "Omnes homines Deus salvos fieri vult, et non eos tantum qui ad Sanctorum numerum pertinebunt, sed omnes omnino, ut nullus habeat exceptionem." St. Paulinus (11) thus writes: "Omnibus dicit Christus, venite ad me, &c., omnem enim quantum in ipso est, hominem salvum fieri vult, qui fecit omnes." St. Ambrose says (12): "Etiam circa impios suam ostendere debuit voluntatem, et ideo nec proditorem debuit præterire, ut adverterent omnes, quod in electione etiam proditoris sui salvandorum omnium prætendit . . . . . et quod in Deo fuit, ostendit omnibus, quod omnes voluit liberare." I omit all other proofs from the Fathers, as they are too numerous, but as Petrocoresius well remarks, the Divine precept of hope assures us that God truly on his part wishes all to be saved; for if we were not certain that God wishes all to be saved, our hope would not be secure and firm, as St. Paul tells us, "an anchor of the soul sure and firm"(Heb. vi. 18, 19), but weak and doubtful: "Qua fiducia," he says, "Divinam misericordiam sperare poterunt homines, si certum non sit quod Deus salutem omnium eorum velit"(13). I have expounded this argument in my Work on Prayer (14).

(7) Petav. Theol. *t.* 1, *l.* 10, *c.* 15, *n.* 5.   (8) Nodus Præd. Par. 1.   (9) St. Hier. Comment. in *c.* 1, ad Ephesios.   (10) St. Hilar. Ep. ad Aug.   (11) St. Paulin. Ep. 24, ad Sever. *n.* 9.   (12) St. Ambr. de Libro Parad. *c.* 8.   (13) Petrocor. Theol. *t.* 1, *c.* 3, *q.* 4.   (14) Mezzo della Preghiera Par. 2, *c.* 4.

62. Calvin, however, says that, by the sin of Adam, the whole human race became a "condemned mass;" and hence God does no injury to mankind, if he only saves a few, and allows the rest to be damned, if not for their own sins, at all events for the sin of Adam. But we answer, that it is this very "condemned mass" itself, that Jesus Christ came to save by his death: "For the Son of Man is come to save that which was lost" (Matt. xviii. 11). He offered up his death, not alone for those who were to be saved, but for all, without exception: "He gave himself a redemption for all" (1 Tim. ii. 6); "Christ died for all" (1 Cor. v. 15); "We hope in the living God, who is the Saviour of all men, especially of the faithful" (1 Tim. iv. 10). And even St. Paul, to show that we were all dead by sin, says that Christ died for all: "The charity of Christ presseth us...... if one died for all, then all were dead" (2 Cor. v. 14). Hence, St. Thomas says, Christ is the mediator, not of some, but of all: "Christus Jesus est mediator Dei, et hominum, non quorundam, sed inter Deum et omnes homines et hoc non esset, nisi vellet omnes salvare" (15).

63. If, God, however, wishes that all should be saved, and Christ died for all, how then is it, St. Chrysostom asks, that all are not saved? He answers the question himself: Because all will not act in conformity with the will of God, who wishes that all should be saved, but, at the same time, will not force any one's will: "Cur igitur non omnes salvi fiunt, si vult (Deus) omnes salvos esse? quoniam non omnium voluntas Illius voluntatem sequitur, porro ipse neminem cogit (16). And St. Augustin (17) says: "Bonus est Deus, justus est Deus; potest aliquos sine bonis meritis liberare, quia bonus est, non potest quenquam sine malis meritis damnare, quia justus est." Even the Lutheran Centuriators of Magdeburg, speaking of the reprobate, confess that the Holy Fathers have taught that God does not predestine sinners to hell, but condemns them, on account of the foreknowledge he has of their sins: "Patres nec prædestinationem in eo Dei, sed præscientiam solum admiserunt" (18). But, says Calvin, God, although he predestines many to eternal death, still does not insist on the punishment until after they have sinned; and therefore, he first predestines the reprobates to sin, that he may, in justice, condemn them afterwards. But if it would be an act of injustice to send the innocent to hell, would it not be much more so to predestine them first to sin, that they may be subsequently damned. "Major vero injustitia," says St. Fulgentius, "si lapso Deus retribuit pœnam, quam stantem prædestinasse dicitur ad ruinam" (19).

64. The truth is, that those who are lost are so through their

---

(15) St. Thom. ad 1 Tim. ii. *lect.* 1. (16) St. Chrysos. Hom. 43, de Longitud. prem.   (17) St. Augus. *l.* 3, contra Julian, *c.* 18.   (18) Centuriat. 102, *c.* 4. (19) St. Fulgent. *l.* 1, ad Monim. *c.* 24.

own negligence, since, as St. Thomas writes, our Lord gives to all the necessary grace for salvation: " Hoc ad Divinam providentiam pertinet, ut cuilibet provideat de necessariis ad salutem" (20). And in another place, explaining the text of St. Paul, that God wishes all men to be saved, he says: " Et ideo gratia nulli deest, sed omnibus (quantam in se est) se communicat" (21). God himself has said the self-same thing, by the mouth of the Prophet Osee, that, if we are lost, it is altogether through our own fault, for he gives us sufficient assistance to work out our salvation: " Destruction is thine own, O Israel; thy help is only in me" (Osee, xiii. 9); and, therefore, it is that the Apostle says, that God will not allow us to be tempted beyond our strength: " God is faithful, who will not suffer you to be tempted above that which you are able" (1 Cor. x. 13). It would, indeed, be both wicked and cruel of God, as St. Thomas and St. Augustin say, if he, as Calvin teaches, obliged men to observe commandments which he knew they could not: " Peccati reum," says St. Augustin, " tenere quenquam, quia non fecit quod facere non potuit, summa iniquitas est" (22). And St. Thomas says: " Homini imputatur ad crudelitatem, si obliget aliquem per præceptum ad id quod implere non possit; ergo de Deo nullatenus est æstimandum" (23). It is quite otherwise, however, the Saint says, when the sinner, on account of his own negligence, has not grace to observe the commandments (24). This negligence is carelessness in availing ourselves of, at least, the remote grace of prayer, by which we may obtain proximate grace to observe the commandments, as the Council of Trent teaches: " Deus impossibilia non jubet, sed jubendo monet, et facere quod possis, et petere quod non possis et adjuvat ut possis" (*Sess.* vi. *c.* 13).

65. Hence, we conclude, with St. Ambrose, our Saviour has manifested to us most clearly that, although all men are infirm and guilty, still he has provided a sufficient remedy for their salvation: " Omnibus opem sanitatis detulit.......ut Christi manifesta in omnes prædicetur misericordia qui omnes homines vult salvos fieri" (25). What greater felicity can a sick man have, says St. Augustin, than to have his life in his own hands, having always a remedy to heal himself whenever he pleases? " Quid enim te beatius quam ut tanquam in manu tua vitam, sic in voluntate tua sanitatem habeas" (26)? Hence, St. Ambrose again says, that he who is lost is guilty of his own death, since he will not make use of the remedy prepared for him: " Quicumque perierit mortis suæ causam sibi adscribat qui curari noluit cum remedium haberet." For, as St. Augustin says, our Lord heals all, and heals them

(20) St. Thom. *quæst* 14, de Verit. *art.* 11, ad 1. (21) Idem in Epist. ad Hebr. c. 12, *lect.* 3. (22) St. Aug. de Anima, *l.* 2, *c.* 12, *n.* 17. (23) St. Thom. in 2, Sent. Dist. 28, *qu.* 1, *a.* 3. (24) Idem, *ques.* 24, de Verit. *a.* 14, *ad* 2. (25) Ambro. *l.* 2, de Abel. *c.* 3. (26) St. Augus. *trac.* 12, in Joan, cir. fin.

perfectly, as far as he is concerned, but will not heal him who refuses to be healed: "Quantum in medico est sanare venit ægrotum.......Sanat omnino, Ille sed non sanat invitum" (27). Finally, says St. Isidore of Pelusium, God wishes, by every means, to assist sinners to save themselves, and, therefore, in the day of judgment, they will find no excuse for their condemnation: "Etenim serio et modis omnibus (Deus) vult eos adjuvare qui in vitio volutantur ut omnem eis excusationem eripiat" (28).

66. Calvin, however, objects to all this, first, several texts of Scripture, in which it is said that God himself hardens the hearts of sinners, and blinds them, so that they cannot see the way of salvation: "I shall harden his heart" (Exod. iv. 21); "Blind the heart of this people" (Isaias, vi. 10). But St. Augustin explains these and similar texts, by saying that God hardens the hearts of the obstinate, by not dispensing to them that grace, of which they have rendered themselves unworthy, but not by infusing wickedness into them, as Calvin teaches: "Indurat subtrahendo gratiam non impendendo malitiam" (29); and it is thus, also, he blinds them: "Excecat Deus deserendo non adjuvando" (30). It is one thing to harden and blind men, but quite another thing to permit them, as God does, for just reasons, to become blind and obstinate. We give the same answer to that saying of St. Peter to the Jews, when he reproached them for putting Christ to death: "This same being, delivered up by the determined counsel and foreknowledge of God, you, by the hands of wicked men, have crucified and slain" (Acts, ii. 23). When they say, therefore, that it was by the counsel of God that the Jews put our Saviour to death, we answer, that God, indeed, decreed the death of Christ, for the salvation of the world, but he merely permitted the sin of the Jews.

67. Calvin objects, in the second place, these expressions of the Apostle (Rom. ix. 11, &c.): "For when the children were not yet born, nor had done any good or evil (that the purpose of God according to election might stand), not of works, but of him that calleth, it was said to her: *The elder shall serve the younger.* As it is written: *Jacob I have loved, but Esau I have hated.*" And then he quotes, further on in the same chapter: "So then it is not of him that willeth, nor of him that runneth, but of God that showeth mercy." And again: "Therefore, he hath mercy on whom he will; and whom he will he hardeneth." And, finally: "Hath not the potter power over the clay, of the same lump, to make one vessel unto honour, and another unto dishonour?" I cannot, understand, however, how these passages favour Calvin's doctrines. The text of St. Paul says, "Jacob I have loved, but Esau I have hated," after having first said that they had not yet done any good or evil. How, then, could God hate Esau before

---

(27) St. Augus. *trac.* 12, in Joan. cir. fin.　　(28) St. Isid. Pelus. *l.* 2, Ep. 270.
(29) St. Augus. Ep. 194, ad Sixtum.　　(30) Idem, Tract. in Joan.

he had done anything wicked? St. Augustin (31) answers: " God did not hate Esau as a man, but as a sinner. No one can deny that it does not depend on our will, but on the goodness of God, to obtain the Divine Mercy, and that God leaves some sinners hardened in their sins, and makes them vessels of dishonour, and uses mercy towards others, and makes them vessels of honour. No sinner can glorify himself, if God uses mercy towards him, nor complain of the Almighty, if he does not give him the same grace as he gives to others. " Auxilium," says St. Augustin, " quibuscumque datur, misericordia datur; quibus autem non datur, ex justitia non datur" (32). In all that, we must only adore the Divine Judgments, and say, with the Apostle: " O, the depth of the riches, of the wisdom, and of the knowledge of God. How incomprehensible are his judgments, and how unsearchable his ways" (Rom. xi. 33). But all that does not, in the least, strengthen Calvin's position, for he says that God predestines man to hell, and that he first predestines him to sin; but this is not the case, as St. Fulgentius (33) says: " Potuit Deus prædestinare quosdam ad gloriam, quosdam ad pœnam, sed quos prædestinavit ad gloriam, predestinavit ad justitiam; quos predestinavit ad pœnam, non prædestinavit ad culpam." Some charged St. Augustin with the same error, and, therefore, Calvin says: " Non dubitabo cum Augustino fateri, voluntatem Dei esse rerum necessitatem"—that is, the necessity a man has to perform what is either good or bad (34). St. Prosper, however, clears his venerable master from this charge: " Prædestinationem Dei sive ad bonum, sive ad malum in hominibus operari, ineptissime dicitur" (35). The Fathers of the Council of Oranges also defended St. Augustin: " Aliquos ad malum Divina potestate prædestinatos esse, non solum non credimus, sed etiam si sint qui tantum malum credere velint, cum omni detestatione illis anathema dicimus."

68. *Calvin objects, in the third place.*—Do not you Catholics teach that God, by the supreme dominion he has over all creatures, can exclude, by a positive act, some from eternal life: is not this the " Negative Reprobation" defended by your theologians? We answer, that it is quite one thing to exclude some from eternal life, and another to condemn them to everlasting death, as it is one thing for a Sovereign to exclude some of his subjects from his table, and another to condemn them to prison; and, besides, all our theologians do not teach this opinion—the greater part reject it. Indeed, for my own part, I cannot understand how this positive exclusion from everlasting life can be in conformity with the Scripture, which says: " Thou lovest all things that are, and hatest none of the things which thou hast made" (Wisdom, xi. 25); " Destruc-

(31) St. Augus. Ep. 194, ad Sixtum. (32) St. Aug. *l.* de Corrept. et Grat. *c.* 5 & 6, ad 1. (33) St. Fulgen. *l.* 1, ad Monim. *c.* 15. (34) Calvin, *l.* 3, *c.* 21, *sec.* 7. (35) St. Prosp. in libell. ad Capit. Gallor. *c.* 6.

tion is thy own, O Israel: thy help is only in me" (Osee, xiii. 9); " Is it my will that a sinner should die, saith the Lord God, and not that he should be converted from his ways, and live" (Ezech. xviii. 23). And in another place our Lord even swears that he does not wish the death, but the life of the sinner: " As I live, saith the Lord God, I desire not the death of the wicked, but that the wicked turn from his way and live" (Ezech. xxxiii. 11); " For the Son of man is come to save that which was lost" (Matt. xviii. 11); " Who wishes all men to be saved" (1 Tim. ii. 4); " Who gave himself a redemption for all" (*ver.* 6).

69. Now, when our Lord declares in so many places that he wishes the salvation of all, and even of the wicked, how can it be said, that by a positive decree he excludes many from glory, not because of their crimes, but merely for his own pleasure, when this positive exclusion necessarily involves, at least *necessitate consequentiæ*, positive damnation; for, according to the order established by God, there is no medium between exclusion from eternal life and condemnation to everlasting death. Neither will it serve to say, that all men, by original sin, have become a condemned mass; and God, therefore, determines that some should remain in their perdition, and others be saved; for although we know that all are born children of wrath, still we are also aware that God, by an antecedent will, really wishes that all should, through means of Jesus Christ, be saved. Those who are baptized, and in a state of grace, have even a greater claim, for in them, as St. Paul says, there is found nothing worthy of damnation: " There is now, therefore, no condemnation to them that are in Christ Jesus" (Rom. viii. 1.) And the Council of Trent teaches, that in such God finds nothing to hate: " In renatis enim nihil odit Deus" (*Sess.* V., *Decret. de Pec. Orig. n.* 5). Those who die, then, after baptism, free from actual sin, go at once to the joys of heaven: " Nihil prorsus eos ab ingressu cœli removetur" (*Ibid.*) Now, if God entirely remits original sin to those who are baptized, how can it be asserted, that, on account of it, he afterwards excludes some of them from eternal life? That God, however, may wish to free from eternal and deserved damnation some of those who voluntarily have lost their baptismal grace by mortal sin, and leave others to their fate, is a matter which entirely depends on his own will, and his just judgments. But even of these, St. Peter says God does not wish, as long as they are in this life, that one should perish, but should repent of his wickedness, and be saved: " He dealeth patiently for your sake, not willing that any should perish, but that all should return to penance" (2 Peter, iii. 9). Finally, St. Prosper says, that those who die in sin are not necessarily lost, because they are not predestined; but they were not predestined, inasmuch as God foresaw that they wished to die obstinately in sin: " Quod hujusmodi in hæc prolapsi mala, sine correctione pœnitentiæ defecerunt, non ex eo necessitatem habuerunt, quia prædestinati non sunt, sed

ideo prædestinati non sunt; quia tales futuri ex voluntaria prævaricatione præsciti sunt" (36).

70. From all we have already written on the subject, we see how confused are all heretics, but especially the pretended Reformers, with the dogmas of Faith. They are all united in opposing the dogmas taught by the Catholic Church, but they afterwards contradict each other in a thousand points of belief among themselves, and it is difficult to find one who believes the same as another. They say that they are only seeking for and following the truth; but how can they find the truth, if they cast away the rule of truth? The truths of the Faith were not manifested of themselves to all men, so that if every one was bound to believe that which pleased his own judgment best, there would be no end to disputes. Hence, our Lord, to remove all confusion regarding the dogmas of Faith, has given us an infallible judge to put an end to all disputes, and as there is but one God, so there is but one Faith: "One faith, one baptism, one God" (Ephes. iv. 5).

71. Who, then, is this judge who puts an end to all controversies regarding Faith, and tells us what we are to believe? It is the Church established by God, as the pillar and the ground of truth: "That thou mayest know how thou ought to behave thyself in the house of God, which is the Church of the living God, the pillar and the ground of the truth." The voice of the Church, then, it is which teaches the truth, and distinguishes the Catholic from the heretic, as our Lord says, speaking of him who contemns the correction of his pastor: "If he will not hear the Church, let him be to thee as the heathen and the publican" (Matt. xviii. 17). Perhaps, however, some will say: Among the many churches in the world, which is the true one—which is it we are to believe? I briefly answer—having treated the subject at length in my Work on the Truth of the Faith, and also in the Dogmatic part of this Work—that the only true Church is the Roman Catholic, for this is the first founded by Jesus Christ. It is certain that our Redeemer founded the Church in which the faithful may find salvation; he it was who taught us what we should believe and practise to obtain eternal life. After his death, he committed to the Apostles, and their successors, the government of his Church, promising to assist them, and to be with them all time, "even to the consummation of the world" (Matt. xxviii. 20). He also promised that the gates of hell should never prevail against it: "Thou art Peter, and on this rock I will build my Church, and the gates of hell shall not prevail against it" (Matt. xvi. 18). Now, every heresiarch, in founding his Church, separated himself from this first Church founded by Jesus Christ; and if this was the true Church of our Saviour, all the others are, necessarily, false and heretical.

72. It will not do to say, as the Donatists did of old, and the Protestants in later times, that they have separated themselves from

(36) St. Prosper, Res. 3 ad Capit. Gallor.

the Church, because although in the beginning it was the true one, still, through the fault of those who governed it, the doctrine preached by Jesus Christ became corrupted, for he, as we have seen, has promised that the gates of hell should never prevail against the Church he founded. Neither will it avail them to say that it was only the visible, and not the invisible Church that failed, on account of the wickedness of the shepherds, for it is necessary that there should always be a visible and infallible judge, in the Church, to decide all doubts, that disputes may be quashed, and the dogmas of Faith be secure and certain. I wish every Protestant would consider this, and see how he can be certain then, of his salvation outside the Holy Catholic Church.

SEC. VIII.—THE AUTHORITY OF GENERAL COUNCILS.

73. THERE can be only one Faith, for as Faith and truth are indivisibly united, and as truth is one, so Faith must be one likewise. Hence, we conclude, as we have already shown, that in all controversies regarding the dogmas of Faith, it has always been, and is always necessary to have, an infallible judge, whose decisions all should obey. The reason of this is manifest, for if the judgment of every one of the faithful was to be taken on this matter, as the sectaries expect, it would not be alone opposed to the Scriptures, as we shall see, but to reason itself, for it would be quite impossible to unite the opinions of all the faithful, and give from them a distinct and definitive judgment in dogmas of Faith, and there would be endless disputes, and, instead of unity of Faith, there would be as many creeds as persons. Neither is the Scripture alone sufficient to assure us of the truth of what we should believe, for several passages of it can be interpreted in different senses, both true and false, so that the Bible will be, for those who take it in a perverse sense, not a rule of Faith, but a fountain of errors; the Gospel, as St. Jerome says, will become, not the Gospel of Christ, but the Gospel of man, or of the devil: " Non putemus in verbis Scripturarum esse Evangelium sed in sensu, interpretatione enim perversa de Evangelio Christi fit hominis Evangelium aut diaboli." Where, in fact, can we look for the true sense of the Scriptures, only in the judgment of the Church, the pillar and the ground of truth, as the Apostle calls it?

74. That the Roman Catholic Church is the only true one, and that the others who have separated from it are false, is manifest from what we have already seen; for, as the sectaries themselves admit, the Roman Catholic Church has been certainly first founded by Jesus Christ. He promised to assist it to the end of time, and the gates of hell, that is, as St. Epiphanius explains it, heretics and founders of heresies, will never prevail against it, as was promised to St. Peter. Hence, in all doubts of Faith, we should bow to the decisions of this Church, subjecting our judgment to her judgment,

in obedience to Christ, who, as St. Paul tells us, commands us to obey the Church: " Bring into captivity every understanding unto the obedience of Christ" (2 Cor. x. 5).

75. The Church, then, teaches us through General Councils, and hence, the perpetual tradition of all the faithful has always held as infallible the definitions of General Councils, and considered as heretics those who refused obedience to them. Such have been the Lutherans and Calvinists, who have denied the infallibility of General Councils. Here are Luther's own words, taken from the thirtieth article of the forty-one condemned by Leo X. (1): " Via nobis facta est enervandi auctoritatem Conciliorum, et judicandi eorum Decreta, et confidenter confitendi quidquid verum videtur, sive prolatum fuerit, sive reprobatum a quocunque Concilio." Calvin said the same thing, and the followers of both heresiarchs have adopted their opinion. We know, especially, that Calvin and Beza both said, that no matter how holy a Council might be, still it may err in matters appertaining to Faith (2). The Faculty of Paris, however, censuring the thirtieth article of Luther, declared the contrary: " Certum est, Concilium Generale legitime congregatum in Fidei et morum determinationibus errare non posse." How, in fact, can we deny infallibility to General Councils, when we know that they represent the whole Church? for, if they could err in matters of Faith, the whole Church could err, and the infidels might say, then, that God had not provided sufficiently for the unity of Faith, as he was bound to do, when he wished that all should profess the same Faith.

76. Hence, we are bound to believe, that in matters relating to the dogmas of Faith, and to moral precepts, General Councils cannot err, and this is proved, in the first place, from Scripture. Christ says: " Where there are two or three gathered together in my name, there am I in the midst of them" (Matt. xviii. 20). But then, says Calvin, according to that a Council of two persons assembled in the name of God cannot err. The Council of Chalcedon, however (*Act* 3, *in fine*), in the Epistle to Pope St. Leo, and the Sixth Synod (*Act* 17), had previously disposed of this objection, by explaining that the words, " in my name," show that this cannot be applied to a meeting of private persons assembled to discuss matters regarding their own private interests, but a meeting of persons congregated to decide on points regarding the whole society of Christendom. It is proved, secondly, by the words of St. John: " When he, the Spirit of Truth, is come, he will teach you all truth" (John, xvi. 13). And previously, in the 14th chap. 16th verse, he says: " I will ask the Father, and he shall give you another Paraclete, that he may abide with you for ever: the Spirit of Truth." Now the expression, " that he may abide with you for

(1) Luther, lib. de Concil. ar. 28, 29.   (2) Joan Vysembogard. Ep. ad Lud. Colin.

ever," clearly shows that the Holy Ghost continually abides in the Church, to teach the truths of the Faith, not alone to the Apostles, who, being mortal, could not remain always with us, but to the bishops, their successors. Unless, then, in this congregation of bishops, we do not know where the Holy Ghost teaches these truths.

77. It is proved, also, from the promises made by our Saviour always to assist his Church, that it may not err: "Behold, I am with you all days, even to the consummation of the world" (Matt. xxviii. 20); "And I say to thee, thou art Peter, and upon this rock I will build my Church, and the gates of hell shall not prevail against it" (Matt. xvi. 18). A General Council, as has been said already, and as the eighth Synod (*Act* 5) declared, represents the universal Church; and, hence, this interrogatory was put to all suspected of heresy in the Council of Constance: "An non credunt Concilium Generale universam Ecclesiam repræsentare?" And St. Athanasius, St. Epiphanius, St. Cyprian, St. Augustin, and St. Gregory, teach the same thing (3). If, therefore, the Church, as it has been proved, cannot err, neither can the Council which represents the Church fall into error. It is proved, besides, from those texts, in which the faithful are commanded to obey the prelates of the Church: "Obey your prelates, and be subject to them" (Heb. xiii. 17); "Who hears you, hears me" (Luke, x. 16); "Go, therefore, teach all nations" (Matt. xxviii. 19). These prelates, separately, may fall into error, and frequently disagree with each other on controverted points, and, therefore, we should receive what they tell us as infallible, and as coming from Christ himself, when they are united in Council. On this account the Holy Fathers have always considered as heretics those who contradicted the dogmas defined by General Councils, as the reader may see, by consulting St. Gregory of Nazianzen, St. Basil, St. Cyril, St. Ambrose, St. Athanasius, St. Augustin, and St. Leo(4).

78. Besides all these proofs, there is another, that if General Councils could err, there would be no established tribunal in the Church, to terminate disputes about points of dogma, and to preserve the unity of the Faith, and if they were not infallible in their judgments, no heresy could be condemned, nor could we say it was a heresy at all. We could not be certain either of the canonicity of several books of the Scripture, as the Epistle of St. Paul to the Hebrews, the Second Epistle of St. Peter, the Third Epistle of St. John, the Epistles of St. James and St. Jude, and the Apocalypse of St. John; for, although the Calvinists receive all these, still they

---

(3) St. Athanas. Ep. de Synod. Arim. St. Epiphan. An. at. in fin.; St. Cyprian. *l.* 4, Ep. 9; St. Augus. *l.* 1 contra at *c.* 18, St. Greg. Ep. 24 ad Patriarch. (4) St. Greg. Nazian. Ep. ad Cledon.; St. Basil, Ep. 78; St. Cyril. de Trinit.; St. Ambr. Ep. 32; St. Athan. Ep. ad Episc. Afric.; St. Aug. *l.* 1, de Bapt. *c.* 18; St. Leo, Ep. 77, ad Anatol.

are considered doubtful by others, because they were not declared canonical by the Fourth Council. Finally, we may add, that if Councils could err, they committed an intolerable error in proposing, as Articles of Faith, matters, which they could not assert were true or false; and thus the Creeds of Nice, of Constantinople, of Ephesus, and of Chalcedon, would fall to the ground, in which several dogmas were declared, which before were not held as such, and still these four General Councils are received as Rules of Faith by the Innovators themselves. We have now to consider their numerous and importunate objections.

79. First, Calvin objects (5) several passages of the Scriptures, in which the prophets, priests, and pastors, are called ignorant and liars: " From the prophet to the priest, all deal deceitfully" (Jer. viii. 10); " His watchmen are all blind.........the shepherds themselves know no understanding" (Isaias, lvi. 10, 11). We answer, that frequently in the Scriptures, because some are wicked, all are reprimanded, as St. Augustin (6) says, explaining that passage (Phil. ii. 21): " All seek the things that are their own, and not the things that are Jesus Christ's." But the Apostles surely did not seek the things which were their own; they sought solely the glory of God, and, therefore, St. Paul calls on the Philippians, and tells them: " Be followers of me, brethren, and observe them who walk, so as you have our model" (Phil. iii. 17). We should, besides, remember that the texts quoted speak of priests and prophets divided among themselves, and deceiving the people, and not of those who speak to us, assembled in the name of God. Besides, the Church of the New Testament has received surer promises than did the Synagogue of old, which was never called " The Church of the living God, the pillar and the firmament of truth" (1 Tim. iii. 15). Calvin, however, says (7), that even in the New Law there are many false prophets and deceivers, as St. Matthew (xxiv. 11) tells us: " Many false prophets shall arise, and seduce many." This is also true; but he ought to apply this text to himself, and Luther, and Zuinglius, and not to the Ecumenical Councils of bishops, to whom the assistance of the Holy Ghost is promised, and who can say: " It hath seemed good to the Holy Ghost and to us" (Acts, xv. 28).

80. Calvin objects, secondly, the iniquity of the Council of Caiphas, which, withal, was a General one, composed of the Princes and Priests, and still condemned Jesus Christ as guilty of death (Matt. xxvi. 66). Therefore, he says, even General Councils are fallible. We reply, that we call infallible those legitimate General Councils alone, at which the Holy Ghost assists; but how can we call that council either legitimate, or assisted by the Holy Ghost,

---

(5) Calv. Inst. *l.* 4, *c.* 9, *sec.* 3.   (6) St. Aug. de Unit. Eccl. *c.* 11.   (7) Calvin, loc. cit. *sec.* 4.

in which Christ was condemned as a blasphemer, for attesting that he was the Son of God, after so many proofs given by him that he was really so—whose proceedings were all based on false testimony, suborned for the purpose, and which was governed by envy alone, as even Pilate knew: "For he knew that for envy they had delivered him" (Matt. xxvii. 18.)

81. Luther objects, thirdly, (in *art.* 29), that, in the Council of Jerusalem, St. James changed the sentence given by St. Peter, who decided that the Gentiles were not bound to the observance of the precepts of the Law; but St. James said that they should abstain from meats offered to idols, from things suffocated, and from blood, and this was forcing them to a Jewish observance. We answer, with St. Augustin and St. Jerome (8), that this prohibition does not subvert the decision of St. Peter; nor, properly speaking, was it an imposition of the precepts of the Old Law, but a mere temporary precept of discipline, to satisfy the Jews, who could not bear just then, at the beginning of Christianity, to see the Gentiles eating blood and meats abhorred by them. It was, however, only a simple command, which fell into disuse, when the time passed away it was intended for, as St. Augustin remarks (9).

82. They object, fourthly, that in the Council of Neocesarea, received by the First Council of Nice, as the Council of Florence attests, second marriages were condemned: "Presbyterum convivio secundarum nuptiarum interesse non debere." But how, say they, could such a prohibition be given, when St. Paul says: " If her husband should die, she is at liberty; let her marry to whom she will, only in the Lord" (1 Cor. vii. 39). We answer that, in the Council of Neocesarea, second marriages are not forbidden, but only the solemn celebration of them, and the banquets which were usual at first marriages alone; and, therefore, it was forbidden to the priests to attend, not at the marriage, but at the banquets, which were a part of the solemnity. Fifthly, Luther objects that the Council of Nice prohibited the profession of arms, although St. John the Baptist (Luke, iii. 14) held it as lawful. We answer, that the Council did not prohibit the profession of arms, but forbid the soldiers to sacrifice to idols, to obtain the belt, or military distinction, which, as Ruffinus (10) tells us, was only given to those who offered sacrifice; and it is these alone the Council condemned in the Second Canon. Sixthly, Luther objects that this same Council ordained that the Paulinians should be re-baptized, while another Council, which St. Augustin calls Plenary, and which is believed to have been the Council celebrated by the whole French Church in Arles, prohibited the re-baptism of heretics, as the Pope St. Stephen commanded, in opposition to St. Cyprian. We answer, that the Council

---

(8) St. Augus. *l.* 32, contra Faust, *c.* 13; St. Hier. Ep. ad Aug. quæ est 11 inter Epist. August. (9) St. Aug. loc. cit. (10) Ruffin. Histor. *l.* 10, *c.* 32.

commanded that the Paulinians should be re-baptized, for those heretics, believing Christ to be but a mere man, corrupted the form of Baptism, and did not baptize in the name of the three Persons, and, therefore, their Baptism was null and void. But this was not the case with other heretics, who baptized in the name of the Trinity, though they did not believe that the three Persons were equally God.

83. The innovators object, eighthly, that in the Third Council of Carthage (*Can.* 47), the books of Tobias, Judith, Baruch, Wisdom, Ecclesiasticus, and the Maccabees, were received as Canonical, and the Council of Laodicea (*cap. ult.*) rejected them. We reply, first, that neither of these Councils were Ecumenical. One was a Provincial Council, composed of twenty-two bishops; and that of Carthage was a national one, of forty-four prelates, and this was confirmed by Pope Leo IV. (as may be seen, *Can. de libellis, Dist.* 20), and was later than that of Laodicea, which, therefore, may be said to have amended the preceding one. Secondly, we answer, that the Council of Laodicea did not reject these books, but only omitted their insertion in the Canon of the Scriptures, as their authority was, at that time, doubtful; but the matter being made more clear, in the Council of Carthage, afterwards, they were, at once, admitted as authentic. They object, ninthly, that several errors were decided in the sixth Council, such as that heretics should be re-baptized, and that the marriages between Catholics and heretics were invalid. We answer, with Bellarmin (11), that these Canons were foisted in by the heretics; and, in the seventh Council (*Act* 4), it was declared, that these Canons did not belong to the sixth Council, but were promulgated by an illegitimate Council, many years after, in the time of Julian II., and, as Venerable Bede tells us (12), this Council was rejected by the Pope. They object, tenthly, that the seventh Council—the second of Nice—was opposed to the Council of Constantinople, celebrated under the Emperor Copronimus, regarding the veneration of images, which the Constantinopolitan Council prohibited. We answer that this Council was neither a lawful nor a General one; it was held by only a few bishops, without the intervention of the Pope's Legates, or of the three Patriarchs of Antioch, Alexandria, and Jerusalem, who should, according to the discipline of those times, be present.

84. They object, eleventhly, that the Second Council of Nice was rejected by the Council of Frankfort. But we reply, with Bellarmin, that this was all by mistake, for the Frankfort Council supposed that it was decided in the Nicene Council, that images should receive supreme worship (*Cultus Latriæ*), and that it was held without the Pope's consent; but both these suppositions were incorrect, as appears from the Acts of the Nicene Council itself.

(11) Bellar. de Conc. *l.* 2, *c.* 8 *r.* 13.   (12) Beda, lib. de sex ætatib.

They object, twelfthly, that, in the fourth Council of Lateran, the transubstantiation of the bread and wine into the body and blood of Christ was defined as an Article of Faith, while an anathema was fulminated by the Council of Ephesus against all who would promulgate any other Symbol besides that established by the first Council of Nice. We answer, first, that the Lateran Council did not compose any new Symbol, but merely defined the question then debated. Secondly, that the Council of Ephesus anathematized any one publishing a Symbol opposed to the Nicean one, but not a new Symbol declaratory of some point not previously defined. They object, thirteenthly, that as in Councils the points of Faith are defined by the majority of votes, it might so happen that one vote might incline the scale to the side of error, and thus the better part be put down by the major part of the Synod. We answer that, in purely secular affairs, such might be the case, that the majority might, in a worldly meeting, put down the more worthy; but, as the Holy Ghost presides in General Councils, and as Jesus Christ has promised, and does not fail to assist his Church, such can never be the case.

85. They object, fourteenthly, that it is the business of the Council merely to seek the truth; but the Scripture must decide it, and hence, then, the decision does not depend on the majority of votes, but on that judgment which is most in conformity with the Scripture, and hence, say they, every one has a right to examine and see for himself, whether the decrees of Councils are in conformity with the Scriptures. This is the doctrine of Luther, Calvin (13), and all Protestants. We answer, that in Canonical Councils it is the bishops who give an infallible decision on dogmas, and this all should obey without examination. This is proved from Deuteronomy (vii. 12), in which our Lord commands that all should obey the priest, who decides doubts, presiding at the Council, and those who refuse should be punished with death: "He who will be proud, and refuse to obey the commandment of the priest, who ministereth at the time to the Lord thy God, and the decree of the judge, that man shall die, and them that take away the evil from Israel." It is also proved most clearly from the Gospel, which says: "If he will not hear the Church, let him be unto you as a heathen and a publican" (Matt. xviii. 17). A General Council represents the Church, as understood by all, and, therefore, should be obeyed. Recollect, also, that in the Council of Jerusalem (*Act* 15, 16), the question of legal observances was decided, not by the Scriptures, but by the votes of the Apostles, and all were obliged to obey their decision. Therefore, reply the sectarians, the authority of Councils is superior to that of the Scriptures. What a blasphemy, exclaims Calvin (14)! We an-

(13) Luther de Conc. *art.* 29, & Calvin, Inst. *l.* 4, *c.* 9, *sec.* 8   (14) Calvin, Inst. *l.* 4, *c.* 9, *sec.* 14.

swer that the Word of God, both written and unwritten, or Scripture and Tradition, is certainly to be preferred to any Council; but Councils do not make the Word of God, but merely declare what true Scripture is, and true Tradition is, and what is their true sense; they do not, therefore, give themselves the authority of infallibility, but merely declare that which they already possess, deducing it from the Scripture itself, and thus they define the dogmas the faithful should believe. It was thus the Council of Nice declared that the Word was God, and not a creature, and the Council of Trent, that the real body of Christ, and not the figure, was in the Eucharist.

86. But then, the heretics say, the Church is not composed of Bishops alone, but of all the faithful, both Clergy and laity, and why, then, are Councils held by the Bishops alone? Therefore, says Luther, all Christians, no matter of what degree, should be judges in the Councils. The Protestants maintained this doctrine in the time of the Council of Trent, and sought to have a decisive voice in decreeing the dogmas of the Faith. This they required, when they were invited to attend the Council, to explain themselves on all controverted points, and when a safe conduct was given them, promising them security while in Trent, perfect liberty of conferring, as often as they pleased, with the Fathers, and no hindrance to leave whenever they wished to go. Their ambassadors came, and at first said that they did not consider the safeguard sufficient, since the Council of Constance said that no faith was to be kept with public heretics. The Fathers of Trent, however, replied, that the safe conduct from the Council of Constance to Huss was not given by the Council itself, but by the Emperor Sigismund, so that the Council had then full jurisdiction over him. Besides, as we have already explained in *Chap.* X., *art.* v. *n.* 43, of this History, the safe conduct given to Huss was for other crimes with which he was charged, but not for errors against Faith, and, when Huss was charged with this, he knew not what defence to make. The Tridentine Fathers, at all events, explained to those delegates that the safe conduct given by them was as secure as the Council could make it, and different from that given by the Council of Constance to Huss. The delegates then made three requisitions, in case the Lutheran Doctors came to Trent, none of which could be agreed to (15): First.—That questions of Faith should be decided by the Scriptures alone. This could not be granted, since the Council had already decreed in the Fourth Session, that the same veneration was to be paid to traditions preserved in the Catholic Church as to the Scriptures. Secondly.—They required that all Articles already decided on by the Council should be debated over again; but this could not be granted, because it would be just the same

(15) Vedi Pallavic. Istor. del Conc. di Trento, *t.* 2, *c.* 15, *n.* 9.

thing as to declare that the Council was not infallible when it had made the Decrees, and that would be to give a triumph to the Protestants, even before the battle commenced. Thirdly.—They demanded that their Doctors should have a seat in the Council as judges, for the decision of dogmatical points, just as the Bishops had.

87. We answer, that the Church is a body, as St. Paul writes, in which our Lord has assigned the duties and obligations of each individual: "Now you are the body of Christ, and members of member. And God indeed hath set some in the Church: first, apostles; secondly, prophets; thirdly, doctors" (1 Cor. xii. 27, 28). And in another place he says: "And other same pastors and doctors" (Ephes. iv. 11). And he adds, afterwards: "Are all doctors" (1 Cor. xii. 29). God, therefore, has appointed some pastors in his Church to govern the flock; others, doctors, to teach the true doctrine, and he charges others, again, not to allow themselves to be led astray by new doctrines: "Be not led away with various and strange doctrines" (Heb. xiii. 9); but to be obedient and submissive to the masters appointed to them: "Obey your prelates, and be subject to them, for they watch, as being to render an account of your souls" (Heb. xiii. 17). Who, then, are these masters whom our Lord has promised to assist to the end of time? They were, in the first place, the Apostles, to whom he said: "Behold, I am with you all days, even to the consummation of the world" (Matt. xxviii. 20). He promised them the Holy Ghost, who would remain always with them, to teach them all truth: "I will ask the Father, and he shall give you another Paraclete, that he may abide with you for ever" (John, xiv. 6). And when he, the "Spirit of Truth, is come, he will teach you all truth" (John, xvi. 13). The Apostles, however, being mortal, should soon leave this world, and how, then, could we understand the promise that the Holy Ghost would perpetually remain with them, to instruct them in all truth, that they might afterwards communicate it to others? It must be understood, therefore, that they would have successors, who, with the Divine assistance, would teach the faithful people, and the Bishops are exactly these successors, appointed by God to govern the flock of Christ, as the Apostle says: "Take heed to yourselves, and to the whole flock, wherein the Holy Ghost hath placed you bishops to rule the Church of God, which he hath purchased with his own blood" (Acts, xx. 28). Estius (16), commenting on this passage, says: "Illud, in quo vos Spiritus Sanctus posuit, &c............de iis qui proprii Episcopi sunt, intellexit." And, hence, the Council of Trent (*Sess.* xxiii. *Cap.* 4) declared: "Delarat præter ceteros Ecclesiasticos gradus, Episcopus, qui in Apostolorum locum successerunt........positos a Spiritu

---

(16) Estius, in 20 *Act. v.* 12.

Sancto regere Ecclesiam Dei, eosque Presbyteris superiores esse." Hence, the Bishops in Council are the witnesses and judges of the Faith, and say, as the Apostles did in the Council of Jerusalem: " It hath seemed well to the Holy Ghost and to us" (Acts, xv. 18).

88. St. Cyprian, therefore, says (17) : " Ecclesia est in Episcopo;" and St. Ignatius the Martyr (18) had previously said: " Episcopus omnem principatum et potestatem ultra omnes obtinet." The Council of Chalcedon (19) decided " Synodus Episcoporum est, non Clericorum, superfluos foras mittite;" and although, in the Council of Constance, the Theologians, Canonists, and Ambassadors of the Sovereigns were allowed to vote, still it was declared that this was permitted merely in the affair of the schism, to put an end to it, but was not allowed when dogmas of Faith were concerned. In the Assembly of the Clergy of France, in 1656, the Parish Clergy of Paris signed a public protest against any other judges in matters of Faith but the Bishops alone. The Archbishop of Spalatro, Mark Anthony de Dominis, whose Faith was justly suspected, said that the consent of the whole Church to any article required not alone that of the Prelates, but of the laity, likewise: " Consensus totius Ecclesiæ in aliquo articulo non minus intelligitur in Laicis, quam etiam in Prælatis; sunt enim etiam Laici in Ecclesia, imo majorem partem constituunt." But the Sorbonne condemned his doctrine as heretical: " Hæc propositio est hæretica, quatenus ad Fidei propositiones statuendas consensum Laicorum requirit."

89. It is usual to allow the Generals of Religious Orders and Abbots to give a decisive vote in Ecumenical Councils; but this is only by privilege and custom, for, by the ordinary law, the Bishops alone are judges, according to the Tradition of the Fathers, as St. Cyprian, St. Hilary, St. Ambrose, St. Jerome, Osius, St. Augustin, St. Leo the Great, and others testify (20). But they say that, in the Council of Jerusalem, not alone the Apostles, but the Elders had a place: " The apostles and ancients assembled" (Acts, xv. 6), and gave their opinion; " then it pleased the apostles and ancients" (ver. 22). We answer, that some consider the " Ancients" to have been Bishops, already consecrated by the Apostles; but others think that they were convoked, not as judges, but as advisers, to give their opinions, and thus more easily quiet the people. It will not avail our adversaries either, to say that many of the Bishops are men of prejudiced minds, or lax morality, who cannot expect, consequently, the Divine assistance, or that they are ignorant, and not sufficiently instructed in religious knowledge; for as God promised infallibility to his Church, and, consequently, to the Council which

---

(17) St Cypr. Ep. ad Papinum.   (18) St. Ignat. Ep. ad Trallian.   (19) Tom. 4, Conc. p. 111.   (20) St. Cypr. Ep. ad Jubajan; St. Hilar. de Synod.; St. Ambr. Ep. 22; St Hieron. Apol. 2 contra Ruffin., Osius ap. St. Athanas. Ep. ad Solit.; St. Leo Magnus Ep. 16.

represents it, he so disposes everything that, in the definition of the dogmas of the Faith, all the means requisite are supplied. Hence, whenever there is not a manifest defect in any decision, by the omission of some requisite absolutely necessary, every one of the Faithful should bow down with submission to the decrees of the Council.

90. With regard to the other errors promulgated by these sectarians againgst Tradition, the Sacraments, the Mass, Communion under one kind, the Invocation of Saints, Feast Days, Relics, Images, Purgatory, Indulgences, and the Celibacy of the Clergy, I omit their refutation here, for I have done so already in my Dogmatic Work against the Reformers, on the Council of Trent (*Sess.* xxiii. *sec.* 1 & 2). But that the reader may form an opinion of the spirit of these new matters of the Faith, I will just quote one of Luther's sentiments, from one of his public sermons to the people (21). He was highly indignant with some who rebelled against his authority, and, to terrify them into compliance with his sentiments, he said: " I will revoke all I have written and taught, and make my recantation." Behold the Faith this new Church Reformer teaches —a Faith, which he threatens to revoke, when he is not respected as he considers he should be. The Faith of all other sectaries is just the same; they never can be stable in their belief, when once they leave the true Church, the only Ark of Salvation.

REFUTATION XII.

THE ERRORS OF MICHAEL BAIUS.

IN order to refute the false system of Michael Baius, it is necessary to transcribe his seventy-nine condemned propositions, for it is out of them we must find out his system. Here, then, are the propositions, condemned by Pope St. Pius V., in the year 1564, in his Bull, which commences, " Ex omnibus afflictionibus," &c.: —" 1. Nec Angeli, nec primi hominis adhuc integri merita recte vocantur gratia. 2. Sicut opus malum ex natura sua est mortis æternæ meritorium, sic bonum opus ex natura sua est vitæ æternæ meritorium. 3. Et bonis Angelis, et primo homini, si in statu illo permansissent usque ad ultimum vitæ, felicitas esset merces, et non gratia. 4. Vita æterna homini integro, et Angelo promissa fuit intuitu bonorum operum : et bona opera ex lege naturæ ad illam consequendam per se sufficiunt. 5. In promissione facta Angelo, et primo homini, continetur naturalis justitiæ constitutio, quæ pro bonis operibus sine alio respectu, vita æterna justis promittitur. 6. Naturali lege constitutum fuit homini, ut si obedientia perse-

---

(21) Luther. Ser. in Abus. *t.* 7, *p.* 275.

veraret, ad eam vitam pertransiret, in qua mori non posset. 7. Primi hominis integri merita fuerunt primæ creationis munera: sed juxta modum loquendi Scripturæ Sacræ, non recte vocantur gratiæ; quo fit ut tantum merita, non etiam gratiæ debeant nuncupari. 8. In redemptis per gratiam Christi nullum inveniri potest bonum meritum, quod non sit gratis indigno collatum. 9. Dona concessa homini integro, et Angelo, forsitan, non improbanda ratione, possunt dici gratia: sed quia secundum usum Scripturæ nomine gratiæ tantum ea munera intelliguntur, quæ per Jesum male merentibus et indignis conferuntur, ideo neque merita, nec merces quæ illis redditur, gratia dici debet. 10. Solutionem pœnæ temporalis, quæ peccato dimisso sæpe manet, et corporis resurrectionem, proprie nonnisi meritis Christi adscribendam esse. 11. Quod pie et juste in hac vita mortali usque in finem conversati vitam consequimur æternam, id non proprie gratiæ Dei, sed ordinationi naturali statim initio creationis constitutæ, justo Dei judicio deputandum est. 12. Nec in hac retributione bonorum ad Christi meritum respicitur, sed tantum ad primam constitutionem generis humani, in qua lege naturali institutum est, ut justo Dei judicio obedientiæ mandatorum vita æterna reddatur. 13. Pelagii sententia est, opus bonum citra gratiam adoptionis factum non esse Regni Cœletis meritorium. 14. Opera bona a filiis adoptionis facta non accipiunt rationem meriti ex eo quod fiunt per spiritum adoptionis inhabitantem corda filiorum Dei, sed tantum ex eo quod sunt conformia Legi, quodque per ea præstatur obedientia Legi. 15. Opera bona justorum non accipient in die Judicii extremi ampliorem mercedem, quam justo Dei judicio merentur accipere. 16. Ratio meriti non consistit in eo quod qui bene operatur, habeat gratiam et inhabitantem Spiritum Sanctum, sed in eo solum quod obedit divinæ Legi. 17. Non est vera Legis obedientia, quæ fit sine caritate. 18. Sentiunt cum Pelagio, qui dicunt esse necesarium ad rationem meriti, ut homo per gratiam adoptionis sublimetur ad statum Deificum. 19. Opera Catechumenorum, ut Fides, et Pœnitentia, ante remissionem peccatorum facta sunt vitæ æternæ merita; quam ii non consequentur, nisi prius præcedentium delictorum impedimenta tollantur. 20. Opera justitiæ, et temperantiæ, quæ Christus fecit, ex dignitate Personæ operantis non traxerunt majorem valorem. 21. Nullum est peccatum ex natura sua veniale, sed omne peccatum meretur pœnam æternam. 22. Humanæ naturæ sublimatio et exaltatio in consortium Divinæ naturæ debita fuit integritati primæ conditionis; ac proinde naturalis dicenda est, non supernaturalis. 23. Cum Pelagio sentiunt, qui textum Apostoli ad Romanos secundo: *Gentes quæ legem non habent, naturaliter quæ legis sunt faciunt;* intelligunt de Gentilibus fidem non habentibus. 24. Absurda est eorum sententia, qui dicunt, hominem ab initio dono quodam supernaturali, et gratuito supra conditionem naturæ fuisse exaltatum, ut fide, spe, caritate Deum supernaturaliter coleret. 25. A vanis, et otiosis hominibus secundum insipientiam Philosophorum excogitata est sententia hominem ab initio sic constitutum, ut per dona naturæ superaddita fuerit largitate Conditoris sublimatis, et in Dei filium adoptatus, et ad Pelagianismum rejicienda est illa sententia. 26. Omnia opera Infidelium sunt peccata, et Philosophorum virtutes sunt vitia. 27. Integritas prima creationis non fuit indebita humanæ naturæ exaltatio, sed naturalis ejus conditio. 28. Liberum arbitrium sine gratiæ Dei adjutorio nonnisi ad peccandum valet. 29. Pelagianus est error dicere, quod liberum arbitrium valet ad ullum peccatum vitandum. 30. Non solum fures ii sunt et latrones, qui Christum viam, et ostium veritatis et vitæ negant; sed etiam quicunque aliunde quam per Christum in viam justitiæ, hoc est, ad aliquam justitiam conscendi posse dicunt; aut tentationi ulli sine gratiæ ipsius adjutorio resistere hominem posse, sic ut in eam non inducatur, aut ab ea superetur. 31. Caritas perfecta et sincera, quæ est ex corde puro et conscientia bona, et fide non ficta, tam in Catechumenis, quam in Pœnitentibus potest esse sine remissione peccatorum. 32. Caritas illa quæ est plenitudo Legis, non est semper conjuncta cum remissione peccatorum. 33. Catechumenus juste, recte, et sancte vivit, et mandata Dei observat, ac Legem implet per caritatem, ante obtentam remissionem peccatorum, quæ in Baptismi lavacre demum percipitur. 34. Distinctio illa duplicis amoris, naturalis videlicet, quo Deus amatur ut auctor naturæ, et gratuiti, quo Deus amatur ut beatificator, vana est et commentitia, et ad illudendum Sacris Litteris, et plurimis Veterum testimoniis excogitata. 35. Omne quod agit peccator, vel servus peccati peccatum est. 36. Amor naturalis, qui ex viribus naturæ exoritur, et sola Philosophia per elationem præsumptionis humanæ, cum injuria Crucis Christi defenditur a nonnullis Doctoribus. 37. Cum Pelagio sentit, qui boni aliquid naturalis, hoc est, quod ex naturæ solis viribus ortum ducit, agnoscit. 38. Omnis amor creaturæ naturalis, aut vitiosa est cupiditas, qua mundus diligitur, quæ a Joanne prohibetur: aut laudabilis illa caritas, qua per Spiritum Sanctum in corde diffusa Deus amatur. 39. Quod voluntarie fit, etiamsi in necessitate fiat, libere tamen fit. 40. In omnibus suis actibus peccator servit dominanti cupiditati. 41. Is libertatis modus, qui est a necessitate, sub libertatis nomine non reperitur in scripturis, sed solum libertatis a peccato? 42. Justitia, qua justificatur, per fidem impius, consistit formaliter in obedientia mandatorum, quæ est operum justitia, non autem in gratia aliqua animæ infusa, qua adoptatur homo in filium Dei, et secundum interiorem hominem renovatur, et Divinæ naturæ consors efficitur, ut sic per Spiritum Sanctum renovatus, deinceps bene vivere, et Dei mandatis obedire possit. 43. In hominibus pœnitentibus, ante Sacramentum absolutionis, et in Catechumenis ante Baptismum est vera justificatio, et separata tamen a remissione peccatorum. 44. Operibus plerisque, quæ a fidelibus fiunt, solum ut Dei mandatis pareant, cujusmodi sunt obedire parentibus, depositum reddere, ab homicidio, a furto, a fornicatione abstinere, justificantur quidem homines, quia sunt legis obedientia, et vera legis justitia; non tamen iis obtinent incrementa virtutum. 45. Sacrificium Missæ non alia ratione est Sacrificium, quam generali illa, qua omne opus quod fit, ut sancta societate Deo homo inhæreat. 46. Ad rationem, et definitionem peccati non pertinet voluntarium nec definitionis quæstio est, sed causæ, et originis, utrum omne peccatum debeat esse voluntarium. 47. Unde peccatum originis vere habet rationem peccati, sine ulla relatione, ac respectu ad voluntatem, a qua originem habuit. 48. Peccatum originis est habituali parvuli voluntate voluntarium, et habitualiter dominatur parvulos, eo quod non gerit contrarium voluntatis arbitrium. 49. Et ex habituali voluntate dominante fit ut parvulus decedens sine regenerationis Sacramento, quando usum rationis consequens erit, actualiter Deum odio habeat, Deum blasphemet, et Legi Dei repugnet. 50. Prava desideria, quibus ratio non consentit, et quæ homo invitus patitur, sunt prohibita præcepto: *Non concupisces.* 51. Concupiscentia, sive lex membrorum, et prava ejus desideria, quæ inviti sentiunt homines, sunt vera legis inobedientia. 52. Omne scelus est ejus conditionis, ut suum auctorem, et omnes posteros eo modo inficere possit, quo infecit prima transgressio. 53. Quantum est ex vi transgressionis, tantum meritorum malorum a generante contrahunt, qui cum minoribus nascuntur vitiis, quam qui cum majoribus. 54. Definitiva hæc sententia, Deum homini nihil impossibile præcepisse, falso tribuitur Augustino, cum Pelagii sit. 55. Deus non potuisset ab initio talem creare hominem, qualis nunc nascitur. 56. In peccato duo sunt, actus, et renatus; transeunte autem actu nihil manet, nisi reatus, sive obligatio ad pœnam. 57. Unde in Sacramento Baptismi, aut Sacerdotis absolutione proprie reatus peccati dumtaxat tollitur; et ministerium Sacerdotum solum liberat a reatu. 58. Peccatur pœnitens non vivificatur ministerio Sacerdotis absolventis, sed a solo Deo, qui pœnitentiam suggerens, et inspirans vivificat eum, et resuscitat; ministerio autem Sacerdotis solum reatus tollitur. 59. Quando per eleemosynas aliaque pœnitentiæ opera Deo satisfacimus pro pœnis temporalibus, non dignum pretium Deo pro peccatis nostris offerimus, sicut quidem errantes autumant (nam alioqui essemus saltem aliqua ex parte redemptores), sed aliquid facimus, cujus intuitu Christi satisfactio nobis applicatur, et communicatur. 60. Per passiones Sanctorum in indulgentiis communicatas non proprie redimuntur nostra delicta, sed per communionem caritatis nobis eorum passiones impartiuntur, et ut digni simus, qui pretio Sanguinis Christi a pœnis pro peccatis debitis liberemur. 61. Celebris illa Doctorum distinctio, divinæ legis mandata bifariam impleri, altero modo quantum ad præceptorum operum substantiam tantum, altero quantum ad certum quendam modum, videlicet, secundum quem valeant operantem perducere ad regnum (hoc est ad modum meritorum) commentitia est, et explodenda. 62. Illa quoque opus dicitur bifariam bonum, vel quia ex objecto, et omnibus circumstantiis rectum est, et bonum (quod moraliter bonum appellare consueverunt), vel qui est meritorium Regni, æterni, eo quod sit a vivo Christi membro per spiritum caritatis, rejicienda est. 63. Sed et illa distinctio duplicis justitiæ alterius, quæ fit per spiritum caritatis inhabitantem, alterius, quæ fit ex inspiratione quidem Spiritus Sancti cor ad penitiam excitantis, sed nondum cor habitantis, et in eo caritatem diffundentis, qua Divinæ legis justificatio impleatur, similiter rejicitur. 64. Item et illa distinctio duplicis vificationis, alterius, qua vivificatur peccatur, dum ei pœnitentiæ, et vitæ novæ propositum, et inchoatio per Dei gratiam inspiratur; alterius, qua vivificatur, qui vere justificatur, et palmes vivus in vite Christo efficitur; pariter commentitia est, et Scripturis minime congruens. 65. Nonnisi Pelagiano errore admitti potest usus aliquis liberi arbitrii bonus, sive non malus, et gratiæ Christi injuriam facit, qui ita sentit, et docet. 66. Sola violentia repugnat libertati hominis naturali. 67. Homo peccat, etiam damnabiliter; in eo quod necessario facit. 68. Infidelitas pure negativa in his, in quibus Christus non est prædicatus, peccatum est. 69. Justificatio impii fit formaliter per obedientiam Legis, non autem per occultam communicationem, et inspirationem gratiæ, quæ per eam justificatos faciat implere legem. 70. Homo existens in peccato mortali, sive in reatu æternæ damnationis, potest habere veram caritatem; et caritas, etiam perfecta, potest consistere cum reatu æternæ damnationis. 71. Per contritionem, etiam cum caritate perfecta, et cum voto suscipiendi Sacramentum conjunctam, non remittitur crimen, extra causam necessitatis, aut Martyrii, sine actuali susceptione Sacramenti. 72. Omnes omnino justorum afflictionis sunt ultiones peccatorum ipsorum; unde et Job, et Martyres, quæ passi sunt, propter peccata sua passi sunt. 73. Nemo, præter Christum est absque peccato originali, hinc Virgo mortua est propter peccatum ex Adam contractum, omnesque ejus afflictiones in hoc vita, sicut et aliorum justorum, fuerunt ultiones peccati actualis, vel originalis. 74. Concupiscentia in renatis relapsis in peccatum mortale, in quibus jam dominatur, peccatum est, sicut et alii habitus pravi. 75. Motus pravi concupiscentiæ sunt pro statu hominis vitiati prohibiti præcepto, *Non concupisces;* Unde homo eos sentiens, et non consentiens, transgreditur præceptum, *Non concupisces;* quamvis transgressio in peccatum non deputetur. 76. Quandiu aliquid concupiscentiæ carnalis in diligente est, non facit præceptum, *Diliges Dominum Deum tuum ex toto corde tuo.* 77. Satisfactiones laboriosæ justificatorum non valent expiare de condigno pœnam temporalem restantem post culpam conditionatam. 78. Immortalitas primi hominis non erat gratiæ beneficium, sed naturalis conditio. 79. Falsa est Doctorum sententia, primum hominem potuisse a Deo creari, et institui sine justitia naturali."

1. I should remark here that several of these propositions are taken word for word from the writings of Baius—others only according to their meaning—and others again belong to his companion, Esselius, or other supporters of his; but as they were almost all taught by him, they are all generally attributed to him, and from them his system can be clearly deduced. He distinguishes three states of human nature—Innocent, Fallen, and Restored or Redeemed.

2. Regarding nature in a state of innocence, he says: First.—That God, as a matter of justice, and by that right which the creature has, ought to create both angels and men for eternal beatitude. This opinion is deduced from eight articles, condemned in the Bull—the twenty-first, twenty-third, twenty-fourth, twenty-sixth, twenty-seventh, fifty-fifth, seventy-second, and seventy-ninth. Secondly.—That sanctifying grace was due, as a matter of right, to nature in a state of innocence. This proposition follows, as a necessary consequence, from the former one. Thirdly.—That the gifts granted to the angels and to Adam were not gratuitous and supernatural, but were natural, and due to them by right, as the twenty-first and twenty-seventh articles assert. Fourthly.—That the grace granted to Adam and to the angels did not produce supernatural and Divine merits, but merely natural and human ones, according to the first, seventh, and ninth articles. And, in fact, if merits follow from grace, and the benefits of grace were due by right, and naturally belonged to nature, in a state of innocence, the same should be said of merits, which are the fruit of this grace. Fifthly.—That beatitude would be, not a grace but a mere natural reward, if we had persevered in a state of innocence, as the third, fourth, fifth, and sixth articles say; and this is also a consequence of the antecedent propositions, for if it were true that merits, in a state of innocence, were merely human and natural, then beatitude would be no longer a grace, but a reward due to us.

3. Secondly.—Baius taught, regarding *fallen* nature, that when Adam sinned he lost all gifts of grace, so that he was incapable of doing anything good, even in a natural sense, and could only do evil. Hence, he deduces, first, that in those who are not baptized, or have fallen into sin after Baptism, concupiscence, or the *fomes* of sensitive pleasure, which is contrary to reason, though without any consent of the will, is truly and properly a sin, which is imputed to them by reason of the will of mankind included in the will of Adam, as is explained in the seventy-fourth proposition. Nay, more, he says, in the seventy-fifth proposition, that the evil movements of our senses, though not consented to, are transgressions even in the just, though God does not impute it to them. Secondly, he deduces, that all that the sinner does is intrinsically a sin (see the thirty-fifth proposition). He deduces, thirdly, that for merit or demerit violence alone is repugnant to the liberty of man; so that

when he does any voluntary bad action, though he does it of necessity, he sins, as the thirty-ninth and sixty-seventh propositions teach. In the third place, with regard to redeemed nature, Baius supposes that every good work, by its very nature, and of itself, merits eternal life, independently, altogether, of the Divine arrangement, the merits of Jesus Christ, and the knowledge of the person who performs it. The second, eleventh, and fifteenth propositions show this. From this false supposition he draws four false consequences: First.—That man's justification does not consist in the infusion of grace, but in obedience to the Commandments (see propositions forty-two and sixty-nine). Second.—That perfect charity is not always conjoined with the remission of sins. Third.—That in the Sacraments of Baptism and Penance the penalty of the punishment alone is remittted, and not the fault, for God alone can take away that (see the fifty-seventh and fifty-eighth propositions). Fourth.—That every sin deserves eternal punishment, and that there are no venial sins (proposition twenty-one). We see, then, that Baius taught, by his system, the errors of Pelagius, when he treats of innocent nature—man's nature before the fall; for, with that heresiarch, he teaches that grace is not gratuitous, or supernatural, but as natural, and belongs to nature, of right. With regard to fallen nature, he teaches the errors of Luther and Calvin, for he asserts that man is, of necessity, obliged to do good or evil according to the movements of the two delectations which he may receive, heavenly or worldly. With regard to the state of redeemed nature, the errors which he teaches concerning justification, the efficacy of the Sacraments, and merit, are so clearly condemned by the Council of Trent, that if we did not read them in his works, we never could believe that he published them, after having personally attended that Council.

4. He says, in the forty-second and sixty-ninth propositions, that the justification of the sinner does not consist in the infusion of grace, but in obedience to the Commandments; but the Council teaches (*Sess.* vi. *cap.* 7), that no one can become just, unless the merits of Jesus Christ are communicated to him; for it is by these the grace which justifies is infused into him: "Nemo potest esse justus, nisi cui merita passionis D. N. Jesu Christi communicantur." And this is what St. Paul says: "Being justified freely by his grace, through the redemption that is in Christ Jesus" (Rom. iii. 24). He says that perfect charity is not conjoined with the remission of sins (propositions thirty-one and thirty-two); but the Council, speaking specially of the Sacrament of Penance, declares (*Sess.* xiv. *c.* 4), that contrition, united with perfect charity, justifies the sinner before he receives the Sacrament. He says that by the Sacraments of Baptism and Penance the penalty of punishment, but not of the fault, is remitted (propositions fifty-seven and fifty-eight). But the Council, speaking of Baptism (*Sess.* v. *Can.* 5), teaches that

by Baptism the penalty of original sin, and everything else which has the rationale of sin, is remitted: " Per Jesu Christi gratiam, quæ in Baptismate confertur, reatum originalis peccati remitti, et tolli totum id quod veram, et propriam peccati rationem habet, illudque non tantum radi, aut non imputari." Speaking of the Sacrament of Penance, the Council diffusely explains (*Sess.* xiv. *c*. 1), that it is a truth of Faith, that our Lord has left to priests the power to remit sins in this Sacrament, and condemns anew the error of the Novatians, who denied it. Baius says that concupiscence, or every evil motion of concupiscence, in those who are not baptized, or who, after Baptism, have fallen, is a real sin, because they then transgress the Commandment, " Thou shalt not covet," &c. (propositions seventy-four and seventy-five); but the Council teaches that concupiscence is not a sin, and that it does no harm to those who do not give consent to it: " Concupiscentia, cum ad agonem relicta sit, nocere non consentientibus non valet .... Hanc concupiscentiam Ecclesiam nunquam intellexisse peccatum appellari, quod vere peccatum sit, sed quia ex peccato est, et ad peccatum inclinas" (*Sess.* v. *cap.* 5).

5. In fine, all that Baius taught regarding the three states of nature is a necessary consequence of one sole principle of his, that is, that there are but two authors, either theological charity, by which we love God above all things, as the last end; or concupiscence, by which we love the creature as the last end, and that between these two loves there is no medium. He says, then God being just, could not, in opposition to the right which an intelligent creature has, create man subject to concupiscence alone; and therefore, as leaving concupiscence out of the question, there is no other proper love but supernatural love alone, when he created Adam he must have given him, in the first instance of his creation, this supernatural love, the essential end of which is the beatific vision of God. Charity, therefore, was not a supernatural and gratuitous gift, but a natural one, which was the right of human nature, and, therefore, the merits of this charity were natural, and beatitude was our due, and not a grace. From this, then, he drew another consequence, which was, that free will being, after the fall, deprived of grace, which was, as it were, a supplement of nature, was of no use, only to cause us to sin. We answer, however, that this principle is evidently false, and, therefore, every consequence deduced from it is false, likewise. There is evidence to prove, in opposition to the principle of Baius, that the intelligent creature has no positive right to existence, and, consequently, has no innate right to exist in one way more than another. Besides, several learned theologians, whose opinions I follow, teach, with very good reason, that God could, if it pleased him, create man in a state of pure nature, so that he would be born without any supernatural gift, and without sin, but with all the perfections and imperfections which belong

to this state of nature; so that the object of pure nature might be natural, and all the miseries of human life, as concupiscence, ignorance, death, and all other calamities, might belong of right to mere human nature itself, just as now in the state of fallen nature they are the effects and punishments of sin; and, therefore, in our present state, concupiscence inclines us much more to sin than it would do in a state of pure nature, since by sin the understanding of man is more obscured, and his will wounded.

6. It was undoubtedly one of the errors of Pelagius, that God had in fact created man in a state of pure nature. On the other hand, it was one of Luther's errors to assert that the state of pure nature is repugnant to the right which man has to grace; but this error was already taken up by Baius, because surely it was not necessary by right of nature that man should be created in a state of original justice; but God might create him without sin, and without original justice, taking into account the right of human nature. This is proved, first, from the Bulls already quoted, of St. Pius V., Gregory XIII., and Urban VIII., which confirm the Bull of St. Pius, in which the assertion, that the *consortium* of the Divine nature was due to, and even natural to, the nature of man, as Baius said—" Humanæ naturæ sublimatio, et exaltatio in consortium Divinæ naturæ debita fuit integritati primæ conditionis, et proinde naturalis dicenda est, et non supernaturalis"—was condemned (proposition twenty-two). He says the same in the fifty-fifth proposition: " Deus non potuisset ab initio talem creare hominem, qualis nunc nascitur;" that is, exclusive of sin we understand. In the seventy-ninth proposition, again he says: " Falsa est Doctorum sententia, primum hominem et potuisse a Deo creari, et institui sine justitia naturali." Jansenius, though a strong partisan of the doctrine of Baius, confesses that those Decrees of the Pope made him very uneasy: " Hæreo, fateor" (1).

7. The disciples of Baius and Jansenius, however, say they have a doubt whether the Bull of Urban VIII., " In eminenti," should be obeyed; but Tournelly (2) answers them, and shows that the Bull being a dogmatic law of the Apostolic See, whose authority, Jansenius himself says, all Catholics, as children of obedience, should venerate, and being accepted in the places where the controversy was agitated, and by the most celebrated churches in the world, and tacitly admitted by all others, should be held as an infallible judgment of the Church, which all should hold by; and even Quesnel himself admits that.

8. Our adversaries also speak of the way the Bull of St. Pius should be understood, and say, first, that we cannot believe that the Apostolic See ever intended to condemn in Baius the doctrine of

---

(1) Jansen. *l.* 9, *d.* Statu. nat. pur. *c.* ult.   (2) Comp. Theol. *t.* 5, *p.* 1, Disp. 5, *art.* 3, *s.* 2.

St. Augustine, who, as they suppose, taught that the state of pure nature was an impossibility. This supposition of theirs, however, is totally unfounded, for the majority of theologians assert, that the Holy Doctor in many places teaches the contrary, especially in his writings against the Manicheans (3), and distinguishes four modes in which God might create the souls of men blameless, and, among them, the second mode would be, if, previously to any sin being committed, these created souls were infused into their bodies subject to ignorance, concupiscence, and all the miseries of this life; by this mode, the possibility of pure nature is certainly established. Consult Tournelly (4) on this point, where he answers all objections, and you will see also how Jansenius treats it.

9. They say, likewise, that the propositions of Baius were not condemned in the Bull of St. Pius in the sense the author understood them. The words of the Bull are: "Quas quidem sententias stricto coram nobis examine ponderatas, quanquam nonnullæ aliquo pacto sustineri possent, in rigore, et proprio verborum sensu ab assertoribus intento hæreticas. erroneas, temerarias, &c., respective damnamus," &c. They then say that between the word *possent*, and the following ones, *in rigore, et proprio verborum sensu*, there was no comma, but that it was placed after the words *ab assertoribus intento;* so that the sentence being read thus: "quanquam nonnullæ aliquo pacto sustineri possent in rigore et proprio verborum sensu ab assertoribus intento," the proposition could be sustained in this proper and intended sense, as the Bull declares. According to this interpretation, however, the Bull would contradict itself, condemning opinions which, in their proper sense, and that intended by the author, could be sustained. If they could be sustained in the proper sense, why were they condemned, and why was Baius expressly called on to retract them? It would be a grievous injustice to condemn these propositions, and oblige the author to retract them, if in the proper and plain sense they could be defended. Besides, though in the Bull of St. Pius the comma may be wanted after the word *possent*, still no one has ever denied or doubted but that it was inserted in the subsequent Bulls of Gregory XIII. and Urban VIII. There cannot be the least doubt that the opinions of Baius were condemned by these Pontifical Bulls.

10. They say, thirdly, that the propositions were condemned, having regard to the Divine Omnipotence, according to which the state of pure nature was possible. but not in regard to the wisdom and goodness of God. The theologians already quoted answer, that in that case the Apostolic See has condemned not a real, but only an apparent, error, since, in reality, the doctrine of Baius, in regard to the wisdom and goodness of God, is not condemnable. It is false, however, to suppose that the state of pure nature is only

(3) St. August. *l.* 3, de lib. arb. *c.* 20.   (4) Tourn. *t.* 5, *p.* 2, *c.* 7, *p.* 67.

possible according to the Omnipotence of God, and not according to his other attributes. That which is repugnant or not agreeable to any of the attributes of God is, in fact, impossible, for " He cannot deny himself" (2 Tim. ii. 13). St. Anselm says (5): " In Deo quantumlibet parvum inconveniens sequitur impossibilitas." Besides, if that principle of our adversaries themselves were true, that there is no middle love between vicious cupidity and laudable charity, then the state of pure nature, even in regard to the Divine Omnipotence, as they suppose, would be an impossibility, since it would, in fact, be repugnant to God to produce a creature contrary to himself, with the necessity of sinning, as, according to their supposition of possibility, this creature would be.

11. In fact, I think no truth can be more evident, than that the state of pure nature is not an impossibility, a state in which man would be created without grace and without sin, and subject to all the miseries of this life. I say this with all reverence for the Augustinian school, which holds the contrary opinion. There are two very evident reasons for this doctrine: First.—Man could very well have been created without any supernatural gift, but merely with those qualities which are adapted to human nature. Therefore, that grace which was supernatural, and was given to Adam, was not his due, for then, as St. Paul says (Rom. xi 6): " Grace is no more grace." Now, as man might be created without grace, God might also create him without sin—in fact, he could not create him with sin, for then he would be the author of sin. Then he might likewise create him subject to concupiscence, to disease, and to death, for these defects, as St. Augustin explains, belong to man's very nature, and are a part of his constitution. Concupiscence proceeds from the union of the soul with the body, and, therefore, the soul is desirous of that sensitive pleasure which the body likes. Diseases, and all the other miseries of human life, proceed from the influence of natural causes, which, in a state of pure nature, would be just as powerful as at present, and death naturally follows from the continual disagreement of the elements of which the body is composed.

12. The second reason is, that it is not repugnant to any of the Divine attributes to create man without grace and without sin. Jansenius himself admits that it is not opposed to his Omnipotence; neither is it to any other attribute, for in that state, as St. Augustin (6) teaches, all that is due by right to man's natural condition, as reason, liberty, and the other faculties necessary for his preservation, and the accomplishment of the object for which he was created, would be given to him by God. Besides, all theologians, as Jansenius himself confesses in those works in which he speaks of pure nature, are agreed in admitting the possibility of this state, that is consi-

---

(5) St. Anselm, *l.* 1, Cum Deus homo, c. 1.   (6) St. August. *l.* 3, de lib. arb. c. 20, 22, 23.

dering the right of the creature alone, and this is precisely the doctrine of the Prince of Schoolmen, St. Thomas. He teaches (7), that man might be created without consideration to the Beatific Vision. He says: " Carentia Divino visionis competeret ei qui in solis naturalibus esset etiam absque peccato." He likewise, in another passage (8), teaches that man might be created with that concupiscence which rebels against reason: " Illa subjectio inferiorum virium ad rationem non erat naturalis." Several theologians, therefore, admit the possibility of the state of pure nature, as Estius, Ferrarensis, the Salmanticenses, Vega, and several others. Bellarmin (9), especially, says he does not know how any one can doubt of this opinion.

13. We have now to answer the objections of our adversaries. The first objection is on the score of " Beatitude." St. Augustin, according to Jansenius, teaches in several places that God could not, without injustice, deny eternal glory to man in a state of innocence: " Qua justitia quæso a Regno Dei alienatur imago Dei in nullo transgressu legem Dei." These are St Augustin's words(10) We answer that the Holy Father in this passage was opposing the Pelagians, according to man's present state, that is, supposing the gratuitous ordination of man to a supernatural end: according to that supposition, he said that it would be unjust to deprive man of the kingdom of God if he had not sinned. Neither is it of any consequence that St. Thomas (11) says that man's desires can find no rest except in the vision of God: " Non quiescit naturale desiderium in ipsis, nisi etiam ipsius Dei substantiam videant;" and as this appetite is naturally implanted in man, he could not have been created unless in order to this end. We answer, that St. Thomas (12), in several places, and especially in his book of Disputed Questions, teaches that by nature we are not inclined in particular to the vision of God, but only to beatitude in general: " Homini inditus est appetitus ultimi sui finis in communi, ut scilicet appetat se esse completum in bonitate; sed in quo ista completio consistat non est determinatum a natura." Therefore, according to the Holy Doctor, there is not in man an innate tendency to the beatific vision, but only to beatitude in general. He confirms this in another place (13): " Quamvis ex naturali inclinatione voluntas habeat, ut in beatitudinem feratur, tamen quod feratur in beatitudinem talem, vel talem, hoc non est ex inclinatione naturæ." But they will still say that it is only in the vision of God that man can have perfect happiness, as David says (Psalm, xvi. 15): "I shall be satisfied when thy glory shall appear." To this we reply, that this refers to man in his present state, since

---

(7) St. Thom. *qu.* 4, de Malo. *a.* 1.   (8) Idem in Summa. 1, *p. q.* 95, *art* 1.
(9) Bellarm. *l* de Grat. primi. hom. *cap.* 5.   (10) St. August. *l.* 3, contra. Julian, *cap.* 12.   (11) St. Thom. 1. 4, contra Gentes, *c.* 50.   (12) St. Thom. *q.* 22, de Verit.
(13) Idem, 4, Sent. Dist. 49, *q.* 1, *art.* 3.

he has been created in order to eternal life, but never would be the case in another state, that of pure nature, for example.

14. The second objection is on the score of "Concupiscence." God, they say, could never be the author of concupiscence, since we read in St. John (1st Epis. ii. 16), that "it is not of the Father, but is of the world;" and St. Paul says: "Now, then, it is no more I that do it, but sin (*that is concupiscence*), that dwelleth in me" (Rom. vii. 17). We answer the text of St. John, by saying that the concupiscence of the flesh is not from the Father, in our present state of existence, for in that it springs from sin, and inclines to sin, as the Council of Trent (*Sess.* v. *Can.* 5) declares: "Quia est a peccato, et ad peccatum inclinat." In our present state even, it influences us more powerfully than it would in a state of pure nature; but even in this state it would not proceed formally from the Father, considered as an imperfection, but would come from him as one of the conditions of human nature. We answer the text of St. Paul in like manner, that concupiscence is called sin, because, in our present state, it springs from sin, since man was created in grace; but in a state of pure nature it would not come from sin, but from the very condition itself, in which human nature would have been created.

15. They say, secondly, that God could not create a rational being with anything which would incline him to sin, as concupiscence would. We answer, that God could not create man with anything which, in itself, *in se*, would incline him to sin, as with a vicious habit, for example, which of itself inclines and induces one to sin; but he might create man with that which accidentally, *per accidens*, inclines him to sin, for in this is the condition of his nature only accomplished, for otherwise God should create man impeccable, for it is a defect to be peccable. Concupiscence, of itself, does not incline man to sin, but solely to that happiness adapted to human nature, and for the preservation of nature itself, which is composed of soul and body; so that it is not of itself, but only accidentally, and through the deficiency of the condition of human nature itself, that it sometimes inclines us to sin. God, surely, was not obliged, when he produced his creatures, to give them greater perfections than those adapted to their natures. Because he has not given sensation to plants, or reason to brutes, we cannot say that the defect is his; it belongs to the nature itself of these creatures, and so if, in the state of pure nature, God did not exempt man from concupiscence, which might accidentally incline him to evil, it would not be a defect of God himself, but of the condition itself of human nature.

16. The third objection is on the score of the "Miseries" of human nature. St. Augustin, they say, when opposing the Pelagians, frequently deduced the existence of original sin from the miseries of this life. We briefly answer, that the Holy Doctor

speaks of the misery of man in his present state, remembering the original holiness in which he was created, and knowing, from the Scriptures, that Adam was created free from death and from all the penalties of this life. On this principle, God could not, with justice, deprive him of the gifts granted to him, without some positive fault on his side; and, hence, the Saint inferred that Adam sinned, from the calamities which we endure in this life. He would say quite the contrary, however, if he were speaking of the state of pure nature, in which the miseries of life would spring from the condition itself of human nature, and especially as in the state of lapsed nature our miseries are, by many degrees, greater than they would be in a state of pure nature. From the grievous miseries, then, of our present state, original sin can be proved; but it could not be so from the lesser miseries which man would suffer in a state of pure nature.

REFUTATION XIII.

THE ERRORS OF CORNELIUS JANSENIUS.

1. IN order to refute the errors of Jansenius, it is quite sufficient to refute his system, which, in substance, consists in supposing that our will is forced by necessity to do either what is good or bad, according to the impulse it receives from the greater or less degree of celestial or terrestrial delectation, which predominates in us, and which we cannot resist, since this delectation, as he says, precedes our consent, and even forces us to yield consent to it. This error he founded on that well-known expression of St. Augustin: " Quod amplius delectat, id nos operemur, necessum est." Here are his words: " Gratia est delectatio et suavitas, qua Anima in bonum appetendum delectabiliter trahitur; ac pariter delectationem concupiscentiæ esse desiderium illicitum, quo animus etiam repugnans in peccatum inhiat" (1). And again, in the same book (*cap*. 9), he says: " Utraque delectatio invicem pugnat, earumque conflictus sopiri non potest, nisi alteram altera delectando superaverit, et eo totum animæ pondus vergat, ita ut vigente delectatione carnali impossibile sit, quod virtutis, et honestatis consideratio prævaleat."

2. Jansenius says that in that state of justice, in which man was created—" God made man right" (Eccles. vii. 30)—being then inclined to rectitude, he could with his own will easily perform what was right, with the Divine assistance alone, called *sine quo*—that is, sufficient grace (which gives him the power, but not the will); so that, with the ordinary assistance alone, he could then agree to,

(1) Jansen. *l*. 4, de Grat. Christ. *c*. 11.

and follow grace, but when his will was weakened by sin, and inclined to forbidden pleasures, it then could not, with sufficient grace alone, do what is right, but required that assistance called, theologically, *Quo*—that is, efficacious grace (which is his conquering delectation, in relation to the superiority of degrees), which pushes him on, and determines him to perform what is good, otherwise he never could resist the opposing carnal delectation: " Gratia sanæ voluntatis in ejus libero relinquebatur arbitrio, ut eam, si vellet desereret; aut si vellet uteretur; gratia vero lapsæ ægrotæque voluntatis nullo modo in ejus relinquitur arbitrio, ut eam deserat, et arripiat si voluerit" (2). During the period that the carnal delectation predominates, then, says Jansenius, it is impossible that virtue should prevail: " Vigente delectatione carnali, impossibile est, ut virtutis et honestatis consideratio prævaleat" (3). He says, besides, that this superior delectation has such power over the will, that it obliges it necessarily either to wish or reject, according as it moves it: " Delectatio, seu delectabilis objecti complacentia, est id quod tantam in liberum arbitrium potestatem habet, ut eum faciat velle vel nolle, seu ut ea præsente actus volendi sit reipsa in ejus potestate, absente non sit" (4).

3. In another passage he says, that if the celestial delectation is less than the terrestrial one, it will only give rise to some inefficacious and impotent desires in the soul, but will never lead us on to embrace what is good: " Delectatio victrix, quæ Augustino est efficax adjutorium, relativa est; tunc enim est victrix, quando alteram superat. Quod si contingat alteram ardentiorem esse, in solis inefficacibus desideriis hærebit animus, nec efficaciter unquam volet, quod volendum est" (5). Again, he says that as the faculty of vision not only causes us to see, but gives us the power of seeing, so the predominant delectation not only causes us to act, but gives us the power of acting: " Tantæ necessitatis est, ut sine illa effectus fieri non possit . . . . . . dat enim simul et posse, et operari" (6). He says, besides, that it is just as impossible to resist this superior delectation, as for a blind man to see, a deaf one to hear, or a bird deprived of its wings to fly (7). Finally, he concludes that this delectation, " delectatio victrix," be it heavenly or earthly, so binds down our free will, that it loses all power when opposed to it: " Justitiæ vel peccati delectatio est illud vinculum, quo liberum arbitrium ita firmiter ligatur, ut quamdiu isto stabiliter constringitur, actus, oppositus sit extra ejus potestatem" (8). These passages alone, I think, are quite sufficient to show how false is Jansenius's system of relative conquering delectation, to which the will is always obliged, of necessity, to yield obedience.

(2) Jansen. de lib. arb. *l*. 2, *c*. 4.   (3) Jansen. *l*. 7, de Grat. Chr. *c*. 3, vide etiam, *c*. 50.   (4) Idem. eod. tit. *l*. 7, c 3.   (5) Idem. eod. tit. *l*. 8, *c*. 2.   (6) Jansen. *l*. 2, *c*. 4.   (7) Jans. de Grat. Christ. *l*. 4, *c*. 7, & *l*. 7, *c*. 5.   (8) Ibid. *l*. 7, *c*. 5.

2 o

4. From this system, then, spring his five propositions, condemned by Innocent X., as we have seen in the Historical Part of the Work (9). It is necessary to repeat them here again. The first proposition is: " Some commandments of God are impossible to just men, even when they wish and strive to accomplish them, according to their present strength, and grace is wanting to them, by which they may be possible to them." The censure passed on this was—It was rash, impious, blasphemous, branded with anathema, and heretical; and, as such, condemned. The Jansenists made many objections to the condemnation of this proposition, as well as of the other four. Their two principal objections, however, were the following: First, that the propositions quoted in the Bull of Innocent were not in the book of Jansenius at all; and, secondly, that these propositions were not condemned in the sense intended by Jansenius. These two objections, however, were quashed by Alexander VII., in his Bull, promulgated in 1656, in which he expressly declares that the five propositions were taken from the book of Jansenius, and in the sense intended by him: " Quinque propositiones ex libro Cornelii Jansenii excerptas, ac in sensu ab eodem Cornelio intento damnatas fuisse." This was, in reality, the fact, and so to refute, first of all, these most dangerous and most general objections (for by and by we will have occasion to attack others), I will quote the passages transcribed from the book of Jansenius himself, in which the reader will see that though the words are not the same, the substance is, and, taken in their natural and obvious sense, prove that this was the meaning intended by the author.

5. To begin with the first proposition, it is expressed in Jansenius's book almost in the same words: " Hæc igitur omnia plenissime planissimeque demonstrant, nihil esse in St. Augustini doctrina certius ac fundatius, quam *esse præcepta quædam, quæ hominibus* non tantum infidelibus, excæcatis, obscuratis, sed fidelibus quoque, et *justis volentibus, et conantibus secundum præsentes quas habent vires, sunt impossibilia, deesse quoque gratiam, qua possibilia fiant"* (10). He then immediately, as an example, quotes the fall of St. Peter, and says: " Hoc enim St. Petri exemplo, aliisque multis quotidie manifestum esse, qui tentantur ultra quam possint substinere." Listen to this. St. Paul says, that God will not permit us to be tempted beyond our strength: " God is faithful, who will not suffer you to be tempted above that which you are able" (1 Cor. x. 13); and Jansenius says that many are tempted beyond their strength. Towards the end of the same chapter, he labours to prove that the grace of prayer sometimes fails the just, or at least that they have not that grace of prayer, which is sufficient to obtain efficacious assistance to observe the commandments, and, consequently, that they have not power to fulfil them. In fine, the sense

(9) *Chap.* 12, *art.* 3.   (10) Jansen. *l.* 3, de Grat. Christi, *c.* 13.

of this first proposition of his is, that some precepts are impossible even to the just, on account of the strength of earthly delectations, for then they want that grace by which these commandments could be observed. He says: " Secundum præsentes quas habent vires;" by which he understands that these precepts, as to observance, are not absolutely impossible, but only relatively so, according to that stronger grace, which would be necessary for them, and which they then want to enable them to observe them.

6. This proposition, then, as we have already remarked, was condemned, first, as "rash," since it is opposed to Scripture: "This commandment........is not above thee" (Deut. xxx. 11); "My yoke is easy and my burthen light" (Matt. xi. 30). The Council of Trent had already branded this same proposition as rash (*Sess.* vi. *c.* 11), when it was previously taught by Luther and Calvin: " Nemo temeraria illa, et a Patribus sub anathemate prohibita voce uti, Dei præcepta homini justificato ad observandum esse impossibilia." It was also condemned in the fifty-fourth proposition of Baius: " Definitiva hæc sententia: Deum homini nihil impossibile præcepisse, falso tribuitur Augustino, cum Pelagii sit." Secondly, it was condemned as "impious;" for it makes of God an unjust tyrant, who obliges men to impossibilities and then condemns them for not performing them. Jansenius prides himself in having adopted all the doctrines of St. Augustin, and did not blush to entitle his book " Augustinus," though Anti-Augustinus would have been a more appropriate name, since the Saint, in his works, expressly opposes his impious opinions. St. Augustin taught (11) that God does not desert those once justified by his grace, unless previously deserted by them; and Jansenius held up the Almighty void of all pity, since he says: " He deprives the just of grace without which they cannot escape sin, and so abandons them before they abandon him." Besides, St. Augustin writes, in opposition to this sentiment of Jansenius: " Quis non clamet stultum esse præcepta dare ei, cui liberum non est quod præcipitur facere? et iniquam esse eum damnare, cui non fuit potestas jussa complere" (12); and, above all, we have that celebrated Decree of the Council of Trent (*Sess.* vi. *c.* 11): " Deus impossibilia non jubet, sed jubendo monet et facere quod possis, et petere quod non possis, et adjuvat ut possis"(13). Thirdly, it was condemned as " blasphemous;" for it makes out God to be without either faith or truth, since he has promised that he will not allow us to be tempted beyond our strength—" God is faithful who will not suffer you to be tempted above that which you are able" (1 Cor. x. 13)—and afterwards commands us to do what is not in our power. St. Augustin himself, from whom Jansenius falsely asserted he had learned

---

(11) St. August. lib. de Nat. et Grat. *c.* 26. (12) Idem. de Fide contra Manich. *l.* 10. (13) St. August. lib. de Nat. et Grat. *c.* 43.

this doctrine, calls it a blasphemy: "Execramur blasphemiam eorum, qui dicunt, impossibile aliquid a Deo esse præceptum" (14). Finally, it was condemned as "heretical," being as we have seen opposed to the Holy Scriptures and to the definitions of the Church.

7. The Jansenists still, however, made objections. First.—That passage of St. Augustin, they say—"Deus sua gratia non deserit, nisi prius deseratur"—which is adopted by the Council of Trent (*Sess.* vi. *cap.* 11), is thus to be understood: That God does not deprive those who are justified of his habitual grace before they fall into actual sin, but often deprives them of actual grace before they sin. We reply, however, with St. Augustin himself, that our Lord, in justifying the sinner, not only gives him the grace of remission, but also assistance to avoid sin in future; and this, says the Saint, is the virtue of the grace of Jesus Christ: "Sanat Deus, non solum ut deleat quod peccavimus, sed ut præstet etiam ne peccemus (15). If God, previous to sin, denied to man sufficient assistance not to fall into sin, he would not heal him, but rather abandon him, before he sinned. Secondly.—They say that the text of St. Paul, already quoted—"God is faithful, who will not suffer you to be tempted above that which you are able"—does not apply to all the faithful, but only to the predestined. But the text itself already shows that here all the faithful are spoken of, and it says: "But will make also with temptation issue, that you may be able to bear it" (1 Cor. x. 13). That is, that God permits his faithful servants to be tempted, that the temptation may be an occasion of merit and profit to them. We should not forget either, that St. Paul was writing to all the faithful of Corinth, and we are not aware that all the faithful of that city were predestined. St. Thomas, therefore, properly understands it as referring to all in general, and God, he says, would not be faithful if he did not grant them (as far as he himself was concerned) the necessary grace to work out their salvation: "Non autem videretur esse fidelis, si nobis denegaret (in quantum in ipso est) ea per quæ pervenire ad Eum possemus" (16).

8. The second condemned proposition originates from the same principle of Jansenius, the "delectatio victrix" which necessitates the consent of his will: "Interior grace in the state of corrupt nature is never resisted." This, says the sentence, we declare heretical, and as such condemn it. Hear what Jansenius says in one place: "Dominante suavitate spiritus, voluntas Deum diligit, ut peccare non possit" (17). And again: "Gratiam Dei Augustinus ita victricem statuit supra voluntatis arbitrium, ut non raro dicat hominem operanti Deo per gratiam non posse resistere" (18). St. Augustin, however, in many passages, declares the contrary, and

(14) Idem. Serm. 191, de Temp. (15) St. August. lib. de Nat. & Grat. *c.* 26.
(16) St. Thom. Lect. 1, in cap. 1, Epist. 1 ad Cor. (17) Janser. *l.* 4, de Grat. Christ. *c.* 9. (18) Jansen. eod. tit. *l.* 2, *c.* 24.

especially in one (19), in which, reproving the sinner, he says: "Cum per Dei adjutorium in potestate tua sit, utrum consentias Diabolo; quare non magis Deo, quam ipsi obtemperare deliberas." And, hence, the proposition was justly condemned as heretical, being, in fact, opposed to the Scripture: "You always resist the Holy Ghost" (Acts, vii. 51). It is also opposed to Councils—to that of Sens, celebrated in Paris, against the Lutherans, in 1528 (*p.* 1, *c.* 15), and to the Council of Trent (*Sess.* vi. *can.* 4), which fulminates an anathema against those who assert that we cannot go contrary to grace: "Si quis dixerit, liberum hominis arbitrium a Deo motum et excitatum.....neque posse dissentire, si velit."

9. The third proposition is: "To render us deserving or otherwise, in a state of corrupt nature, liberty, which excludes constraint, is sufficient." This has been declared heretical, and as such condemned. Jansenius, in several places, expresses this proposition. In one passage he says: "Duplex necessitas Augustino, coactionis, et simplex, seu voluntaria; illa, non hæc, repugnat libertati" (20) And again: "Necessitatem simplicem voluntatis non repugnare libertati" (21). And in another place, he says, that our theologians teach a paradox, when they say, "quod actus voluntatis propterea liber sit, quia ab illo desistere voluntas, et non agere potest;" that it is the liberty of indifference which is required for us to have merit or otherwise. His third proposition springs also from the supposed predominant delectation invented by him, which, according to him, forces the will to consent, and deprives it of the power of resistance. This, he asserts, is the doctrine of St. Augustin; but the Saint (22) denies that there can be sin where there is no liberty: "Unde non est liberum abstinere;" and, on the contrary, in another place he says (23), that it is false that man, in this life, cannot resist grace. Therefore, according to St. Augustin, man can at all times resist grace, and always resist concupiscence, likewise, and it is only thus he can acquire merit or otherwise.

10. The fourth proposition says: "That the Pelagians admitted the necessity of interior preventing grace for every act in particular, even for the commencement of the Faith, and in this they were heretics, inasmuch as they wished that the human will could either resist it or obey it." This proposition consists of two parts—the first false, the second heretical. In the first part Jansenius says that the Semipelagians admitted the necessity of internal and actual grace for the beginning of Faith. Here are his words: "Massiliensium opinionibus, et Augustini doctrina quam diligentissime ponderata, certum esse debere sentio, quod Massilienses præter prædicationem, atque naturam, veram etiam, et internam, et actualem gratiam ad ipsam etiam Fidem, quam humanæ voluntatis ac

---

(19) St. August. Hom. 12, inter 50.   (20) St. Aug. *l.* 6, de Grat. Chr. *c.* 6.
(21) Idem, eod. tit. *c.* 24.   (22) Idem, *l.* 3, de lib. arb. *c.* 3.   (23) St. Aug. de Nat. & Grat. *c.* 67.

libertatis adscribunt viribus, necessariam esse fateantur" (24). This is false, then, for St. Augustin always taught as a dogma, that grace was necessary for the commencement of Faith; but the Semipelagians, for the most part, denied it, as the Holy Doctor himself attests (25). In the second place, Jansenius says that the Semipelagians were heretics, in teaching that grace was of such a nature that man could either use or reject it; hence, he called them, " Gratiæ medicinalis destructores, et liberi arbitrii præsumptores." In this, however, not the Massilians, but Jansenius himself, was heretical, in saying that free will had not the power of agreeing to or dissenting from grace, contrary to the definition of the Council of Trent (*Sess.* vi. *can.* 4), which says: " Si quis dixerit liberum hominis arbitrium a Deo motum et excitatum non posse dissentire si velit..... anathema sit." With good reason, then, the proposition was branded as heretical.

11. The fifth proposition says: " That it is Semipelagianism to say that Jesus Christ died or shed his blood for all men in general;" and this has been condemned as false, rash, and scandalous, and, understood in the sense that Christ died for the predestined alone, impious, blasphemous, contumelious, derogatory to the Divine goodness, and heretical. Therefore, if we are to understand the proposition in the sense that Jesus Christ died for the predestined alone, it is impious and heretical; and yet in this sense it is published in several places by Jansenius. In one passage he says: "Omnibus illis pro quibus Christus sanguinem fudit, etiam sufficiens auxilium donari, quo non solum possint, sed etiam velint, et faciant id quod ab iis volendum, et faciendum esse decrevit" (26). Therefore, according to Jansenius, Jesus Christ offered up his blood solely for those whom he selected both to will and to perform good works, understanding by the *sufficiens auxilium* the assistance, *Quo* (as explained already), that is, efficacious grace, which, according to him, necessarily obliges them to perform what is good. Immediately after he explains it even more clearly; for, speaking of St. Augustin, he says: " Nullo modo principiis ejus consentaneum est, ut Christus vel pro Infidelium, vel pro Justorum non perseverantium æterna salute mortuus esse sentiatur." See, then, how Jansenius explains how it is that our Saviour did not die for the just not predestined. When his proposition was, then, understood in this sense, it was justly censured as heretical, as opposed both to Scripture and Councils—as to the first Council of Nice, for example, in which, in the Symbol, or Profession of Faith (27), then promulgated, and afterwards confirmed by several other General Councils, it was decreed as follows: " Credimus in unum Deum Patrem......et in unum Dom. Jesum Christum Filium Dei......

(24) St. Aug. *l.* 2 de Peccator. merit. *c.* 17.   (25) Idem de Prædest. Ss. *c.* 3 in Ep. 227 ad Vital. *n.* 9.   (26) Jansen. *l.* 3 de Grat. Christ. *c.* 21.   (27) *Chap.* 4, *art.* 1, *n* 16.

Qui propter nos homines; et propter nostram salutem descendit, et incarnatus est, et homo factus; passus est, et resurrexit," &c.

12. Let us consider the proposition in general, that Christ did not die for all. Jansenius said it was an error against Faith to assert that he did: "Nec enim juxta doctrinam Antiquorum pro omnibus omnino Christus mortuus est, cum hoc potius tanquam errorem a Fide Catholica abhorrentem doceant esse respuendum" (28). And this opinion, he adds, was an invention of the Semipelagians. Understanding it in this sense, it was *false* and *rash*, as not in accordance with the Scripture, or the sentiments of the Holy Fathers. As Jesus Christ died for every individual in particular of the human race, some theologians teach that he prepared the price for the redemption of all; and, therefore, say he is the Redeemer of all, solely *sufficientia pretii*. But the opinion more generally followed is, that he is the Redeemer *sufficientia voluntatis*, also—that is, that he desired, with a sincere will, to offer up his death to his Father, in order to obtain for all mankind the helps necessary for salvation.

13. We do not agree in opinion with those who say that Jesus Christ died with equal affection for all, distributing to each individual the same grace; for there can be no doubt that he died with special affection for the Faithful, and more especially for the elect, as he himself declared, previous to his Ascension: "I pray not for the world, but for them whom thou hast given me" (John, xvii. 9). And St. Paul says he is "the Saviour of all men, especially of the faithful" (1 Tim. iv. 10). Neither can we agree with others, who say that, for a great number, Christ has done nothing more than prepare the price sufficient to redeem them, but without offering it up for their salvation. This opinion, I think, is not in conformity with the Scripture, which says: "If one died for all, then all were dead; and Christ died for all," &c. (2 Cor. v. 14, 15). Therefore, as all were dead, through original sin, so Christ died for all. By his death he cancelled the general decree of death, which descended from Adam to all his posterity; "Blotting out the hand-writing of the decree which was against us, which was contrary to us; and he hath taken the same out of the way, fastening it to the cross" (Col. ii. 14). Osee, speaking in the person of Christ, before his coming, says that he will, by his death, destroy that death which was produced by the sin of Adam: "I will be thy death, O death" (Osee, xiii. 14). And the Apostle St. Paul afterwards speaks to the same effect: "O death, where is thy victory" (1 Cor. xv. 15); meaning by that, that our Saviour, by his death, killed and destroyed the death brought among men by sin. Again, St. Paul says: "Jesus Christ, who gave himself a redemption for all" (1 Tim. ii. 5, 6); "Who is the Saviour of all

---

(28) Jansen *l.* 3, de Grat. Christ. c. 3.

men, especially of the faithful" (iv. 10); and St. John says that he " is the propitiation for our sins, and not for ours only, but also for those of the world" (1 John, ii. 2). When I see the Scripture speak thus so plainly, I do not know how any one can say that Jesus Christ, by his death, has only prepared a sufficient price for the redemption of all, but has not offered it to the Father for the redemption of all. Taken in that sense, we might say that Christ shed his blood even for the devils themselves, for there is no doubt but that this sacred blood would have been a price sufficient even to save them.

14. This opinion is most clearly opposed, likewise, by many of the Holy Fathers, who say that Christ has not alone prepared the ransom, but, likewise, offered it to his Father for the salvation of all. St. Ambrose says: " Si quis autem non credit in Christum, generali beneficio ipse se fraudat; ut si quis clausis fenestris solis radios excludat, non ideo sol non est ortus omnibus" (29). The sun not alone prepares light for all, but offers its light likewise to all, if they wish to avail themselves of it, and do not close their windows against it; and, in another place, the same Saint says, in the clearest manner: "Ipse pro omnibus mortem suam obtulit"(30). St. Jerome says just the same: " Christus pro nobis mortuus est, solus inventus est, qui pro omnibus, qui erant in peccatis mortui, offerretur" (31). St. Prosper says: " Salvator noster......dedit pro mundo sanguinem suum (remark dedit, he *gave*, not paravit), et mundus redimi noluit, quia lucem tenebræ non receperunt" (32). St. Anselm says: " Dedit redemptionem semetipsum pro omnibus, nullum excipiens, qui vellet redimi ad salvandum......et ideo qui non salvantur, non de Deo, vel Mediatore possent conqueri, sed de seipsis, qui redemptionem quam Mediator dedit, noluerunt accipere" (33). And St. Augustin, explaining these words of St. John, " God sent not his Son into the world to judge the world, but that the world should be saved by him" (John, iii. 17), says: " Ergo, quantum in Medico est, sanare venit ægrotum. Ipse se interimit, qui præcepta Medici servare non vult. Sanat omnino Ille, sed non sanat invitum"(34). Remark the words, " quantum in Medico est, sanare venit ægrotum;" this shows that he did not alone come to prepare the price as the remedy of our evils, but that he offers it to every one sick, and willing to be healed.

15. Then (perhaps those who hold the contrary opinion will say) God gives to the infidels who do not believe in him at all, the same sufficient grace which he gives to the faithful. I do not mean to say that he gives them the same grace; but I hold, with St. Prosper, that he gives them at all events a lesser grace;—call it a remote grace; and if they correspond to this they will be exalted by the

(29) St. Ambrose, in Ps. 118, *t.* 1, *p.* 1077. (30) Idem, *l.* de Joseph, *c.* 7. (31) St. Hier. in Ep. 2, ad Cor. *c.* 5. (32) St. Prosp. ad object. 9, Gallor. (33) St. Anselm. in *c* 2, Ep 1, ad Tim. (84) St. Aug. Tract. 12, in Joan. circa fin.

reception of a more abundant grace which will save them. Here are the Saint's words: "Adhibita semper est universis hominibus quædam supernæ mensura doctrinæ, quæ et si parcioris gratiæ fuit, sufficit tamen quibusdam ad remedium, omnibus ad testimonium"(35). A remedy to those who correspond to it, a testimony to those who do not. Hence it is that among the thirty-one propositions, condemned by Alexander VIII., on the 7th of December, 1690, the fifth was that "Pagans, Jews, Heretics, and such like, receive no influx from Jesus Christ, and had nothing but a naked and powerless will without any sufficient grace:"—"Pagani, Judæi, Hæretici, aliique hujus generis nullum omnino accipiunt a Jesu Christo influxum; adeoque hinc recte inferes, in illis esse voluntatem nudam et inermem, sine omni gratia sufficienti." Finally, God does not blame us for ignorance alone, but only for culpable ignorance, which, in some sort, must be wilful; he does not punish the sick, but only those who refuse to be healed: "Non tibi deputatur ad culpam, quod invitus ignoras, sed quod negligis quærere quod ignoras. Nec quod vulnerata membra non colligis, sed quod volentem sanare contemnis" (36). There can be no doubt, then, but that Jesus Christ died for all, though, as the Council of Trent teaches, the benefit of his death does not avail all: "Verum, et si ille pro omnibus mortuus est, non omnes tamen mortis ejus beneficium recipiunt, sed ii dumtaxat quibus meritum passionis ejus communicatur" (*Sess.* vi. c. 3). This must be understood, as applying solely to infidels, who, being deprived of the Faith, do not in effect participate in the merits of the Redeemer, as the faithful do, by means of the Faith and Sacraments, though, through their own fault, all the faithful even do not participate in the complete benefit of eternal salvation. The renowned Bossuet says that every one of the faithful is bound to believe, with a firm faith, that Jesus Christ died for his salvation; and this, he says, is the ancient tradition of the Catholic Church. And, in truth, every one of the faithful is bound to believe that Jesus Christ died for us and for our salvation, according to the Symbol drawn up in the First General Council. [See the historical part of the work (37), which says: "We believe in one God Almighty ...... and one Lord Jesus Christ, the Son of God ...... who, for us men, and for our salvation, descended, and was made flesh, and suffered," &c.] Now, when Jesus Christ died for us all who profess the Christian Faith, how can one say that he has not died for those who are not predestined, and that he does not wish them to be saved?

15. We should, therefore, with a firm faith, believe that Jesus Christ died for the salvation of all the faithful. Every one of the faithful, says Bossuet, should believe with a firm faith that God wishes to save him, and that Jesus Christ has shed every drop of

---

(35) St. Prosp. de Vocat. Gent. *c.* 4.   (36) St. August. *l.* 3, de lib. arb. *c.* 19, *n.* 53.
(37) *Chap.* 4, *art.* 2, *n.* 16.

his blood for his salvation (38). The Council of Valence (*Can.* 4) had previously published the same doctrine: "Fideliter tenendum juxta Evangelicam, et Apostolicam veritatem, quod pro illis hoc datum pretium (sanguinis Christi) teneamus, de quibus Dominus noster dicit ...... Ita exaltari oportet Filium hominis, ut omnis, qui credit in ipsum, non pereat, sed habeat vitam æternam" (39). The Church of Lyons, also, in its Book of the Truth of the Scripture, says: "Fides Catholica tenet, et Scripturæ sanctæ veritas docet, quod pro omnibus credentibus, et regeneratis vere Salvator noster sit passus" (40). Antoine in his Scholastic and Dogmatic Theology (41) says: "Est Fidei Dogma Christum mortuum esse pro salute æterna omnium omnino Fidelium." Tournelly (42) teaches the same, and quotes the Body of Doctrine, published by Cardinal de Noailles, in 1720, and signed by ninety bishops, which says, " that every one of the faithful is bound by firm faith to believe that Jesus Christ shed his whole blood for his salvation." And the Assembly of the Gallican clergy, in 1714, declared that all the faithful, both just and sinners, are bound to believe that Jesus Christ has died for their salvation.

17. Now, when the Jansenists held that our Redeemer did not die for all the faithful, but only for the elect, they say, then, he had no love for us. One of the principal motives which induces us to love our Saviour and his Eternal Father, who has given him to us, is the great work of redemption, by which we know that for love of us the Son of God sacrificed himself on the Cross: " He loved us, and delivered himself up for us" (Ephes. v. 2). It was this same love that inclined the Eternal Father to give up his only begotten Son: "God so loved the world as to give up his only begotten Son" (John, iii. 16). This was the chief incentive St. Augustin made use of to inflame Christians with the love of Jesus: "Ipsum dilige; qui ad hoc descendit, ut pro tua salute sufferet" (43). When the Jansenists, then, believe that Christ solely died for the elect, how can they have for him an ardent affection, as having died for love of them, when they cannot be sure that they are among the number of the predestined? They must, consequently, be in doubt that Christ died for love of them.

18. This belief of theirs, that Christ did not die for all the faithful, is also totally destructive of Christian hope. Christian hope, as St. Thomas defines it, is an expected certainty of eternal life: "Spes est expectatio certa beatitudinis" (44). We are, therefore, bound to hope that God will surely save us, trusting to the promises of salvation, through the merits of Jesus Christ, who died to save us, if we correspond to his grace. This is what Bossuet states, also,

(38) Bossuet, lib. Justisic. des Reflex. &c. *sec.* 16, *p.* 100.   (39) Syn. Valent. com. Concil. *p.* 136.   (40) Eccl. Lugdun. *l.* de ten. ver. &c. c. 5.   (41) Antoine Theol. univers. *t.* 2, de Grat. *c.* 1, *a.* 6, ad Prop. 6.   (42) Tourn. Theol. *t.* 1, *q.* 8, *art.* 10, Concl. 2.   (43) St. August. Tract. 2, in Ep. 1, Jo.   (44) St. Thom. 2, 2, *q.* 18, *a.* 4.

in the Catechism which he composed for his Diocese of Meaux: Q. Why do you say that you hope for the eternal life which God has promised? A. Because the promise of God is the foundation of our hope (45).

19. A modern writer, in a work entitled "Christian Confidence," says that we should not found the certainty of our hope on the general promise made by God to all believers, that he will give them eternal life, if they faithfully correspond to his grace, although our Lord in several places makes this promise: "If any man keep my word, he shall not taste death for ever" (John, viii. 52); "If thou wilt enter into life, keep the commandments" (Matt. xix. 17). This general promise, says this writer, made to all Christians who observe the Divine commandments, is not enough to give a certain hope of salvation; for, as it is subject to a condition which may not be fulfilled, that is, that we should correspond to it, it only gives us an uncertain hope. Hence, he says, we ought to found our hope on that particular promise of salvation given to the elect; for, as this promise is absolute, it is the foundation of a certain hope. Hence, he concludes, that our hope consists in appropriating to ourselves the promise made to the elect by considering ourselves enrolled among the number of the predestined. The opinion, however, I imagine, does not square with the doctrine of the Council of Trent (*Sess.* vi. *c.* 16), which says: "In Dei auxilio firmissimam spem collocare omnes debent, Deus enim, nisi ipsi illius gratiæ defuerint, sicut cœpit opus bonum, ita perficiet." And, therefore, though we should fear on our part that we may lose our salvation, by abusing grace, still we should have a most firm hope, on the part of God, that he will save us by his Divine assistance: "In Deo auxilio (says the Council) firmissimum spem collocare omnes debent." All should hope, the Council says; for even those who are buried in sin frequently receive from God the gift of Christian hope, expecting that our Lord, through the merits of Jesus Christ, will show them his mercy; and hence the same Council says, speaking of sinners: "Ad considerandam Dei misericordiam se convertendo, in spem eriguntur, fidentes Deum sibi propter Christum propitium fore." St. Thomas says to those who are in a state of grace, that the dread of falling away from it should not weaken the certainty of this hope, which is founded on the Divine power and mercy, which cannot fail: "Dicendum quod hoc quod aliqui habentes spem deficiant a consecutione beatitudinis, contigit ex defectu liberi arbitrii ponentis obstaculum peccati, non autem ex defectu potentiæ, vel misericordiæ, cui spes innitur; unde hoc non præjudicat certitudini spei"(46). Our hope is, therefore, made certain, not by regarding ourselves as written among the number of the elect, by being based on the power and

(45) Bossuet, Catech. Meldens. 3, *p.* 161, *n.* 117.   (46) St. Thom. 2, 2, *qu* 18, *art.* 4 ad 3.

mercy of God; nor should the uncertainty of our correspondence with grace prevent us from having this certain hope of salvation, founded on the power, and mercy, and faithfulness of God, who has promised it to us through the merits of Jesus Christ, since this promise never can fail, if we fail not to correspond to it.

20. Besides, if our hope, as this writer says, was to be founded on the promise alone made to the elect, it would be uncertain not only as far as concerned ourselves, but with regard to God, likewise; for as we are not sure that we are enrolled among the number of the predestined, neither could we be sure of the Divine assistance promised to us to work out our salvation; and as the number of the reprobate is much greater than that of the elect, we would have greater reason to despair of than to hope for salvation. The writer has taken notice of this difficulty, and admits it to be a most important one. The number of the elect, he says, is, without comparison, much smaller than the reprobate, even among those called. One will then ask himself in this difficulty: Why should I imagine myself to belong to the lesser, instead of the greater number? And, on the other hand, I am commanded to hope; but how can I think that I am separated from the number of the reprobate in the decrees of the Almighty, when he commands the reprobates as well as me? Let us see how he extricates himself out of this difficulty. It is, he says, a mystery which we cannot understand; and, as we are bound to believe the articles of Faith, though we cannot comprehend them, because God commands to do so; so, in like manner, and for the same reason, we should hope, though our reason cannot explain the difficulty we encounter. The true answer, however, is that the writer, to uphold his system, imagines a mystery in the commandment to hope which does not exist in reality. In Faith there are mysteries which we are bound to believe, without being able to comprehend, as the Trinity, Incarnation, &c.; these are beyond our reason; but in the Commandment to hope there is no mystery, for this precept merely regards eternal life, and the motive we have in hoping for it, the promise of God to save us through the merits of Christ, if we correspond to his grace, and all this is clear to us and no mystery. On the other hand, when it is most true that all the faithful should have a most firm hope of salvation by the assistance of God, as the Council, St. Thomas, and all theologians teach, how can we most firmly and most surely hope for this salvation, by hoping that we are among the number of the elect, when we do not know for certain, nor have we any certain argument in Scripture, to prove that we are comprised in that number?

21. There are, to be sure, powerful arguments in the Scriptures to induce us to hope for eternal life,—confidence, and prayer; for God tells us that "No one hoped in the Lord and hath been confounded" (Eccles. ii. 11); and our Redeemer says: "Amen, I say to

you, if you ask the Father anything in my name he will give it to you" (John, xvi. 23). But if, as this writer said, the certainty of our hope consisted in considering ourselves among the number of the elect, where would we find a foundation in Scripture for believing that we belong to that number? We would rather find proofs to the contrary, as that the elect were but few in comparison with the reprobate: "Many are called, but few chosen" (Matt. xx. 16); "Fear not, little flock," &c. (Luke, xii. 32). To conclude the subject, however, I will quote the words of the Council of Trent: "In Dei auxilio firmissimam spem collocare omnes debent," &c. Now God having commanded all to repose in his assistance a certain hope of salvation, he ought to give a sure foundation for this hope. The promise made to the elect is a sure foundation for them, but not for us individually, since we do not know that we are of the elect. The certain foundation, then, that each of us has to hope for salvation, is not the particular promise made to the elect, but the general promise of assistance made to all the faithful to save them if they correspond to grace. To make the matter more brief: If all the faithful are obliged to hope with certainty for salvation in the Divine assistance, and this assistance being promised not to the elect alone but to all the faithful, it is on this, then, that every one of the faithful should base his hope.

22. To return to Jansenius. He wants us to believe that Christ did not die for all men, not even for all the faithful, but only for the predestined. If that were the case Christian hope would exist no longer, for, as St. Thomas says, hope is a sure foundation on the part of God, and this foundation is in fact the promise made by God to give, through the merits of Christ, eternal life to all who observe his law. Hence St. Augustin said that the certainty of his hope was in the blood of Christ, shed for our salvation: " Omnis spes, et totius fiduciæ certitudo mihi est in pretioso Sanguine ejus, qui effusus est propter nos, et propter nostram salutem" (47). The death of Christ, then, as the Apostle tells us, is the sure and firm anchor of our hope: " We may have the strongest comfort who have fled for refuge to hold fast the hope set before us, which we have as an anchor of the soul, sure and firm" (Heb. vi. 18, 19). St. Paul had previously, in the same chapter, explained what this hope was which was proposed to us—the promise made to Abraham to send Jesus Christ to redeem mankind. If Jesus Christ had not died, then, at least for all the faithful, the anchor St. Paul speaks of would not be secure or firm, but weak and doubtful, not having that sure foundation, the blood of Jesus Christ shed for our salvation. See, then, how the doctrine of Jansenius destroys Christian hope. Let us, then, leave their opinions to the Jansenists, and warmly excite in our hearts a confidence of salvation, through the death of Jesus

(47) St. Augus. Medis. 50, cap. 14.

Christ, but still let us never cease to fear and tremble, as the Apostle says: "With fear and trembling work out your salvation" (Phil. ii. 12). Notwithstanding the death of Christ, we may be lost through our own fault. Thus, during our whole lives, we should fear and hope, but hope should predominate, for we have stronger reasons to hope in God than to fear him.

23. Some people give themselves a great deal of trouble by seeking to penetrate the order of God's Divine judgments, and the great mystery of Predestination. These mysterious secrets of the Most High our weak intellects can never arrive at. Let us then leave these secrets which God keeps to himself, since we have so many things to learn which he has revealed for our instruction. First, he wishes us to know that he ardently desires that all should be saved, and that none should perish: "Who will have all men to be saved" (1 Tim. ii. 4); "Not willing that any should perish, but that all should return to penance" (2 Pet. iii. 9). Secondly, he wishes us to know that Jesus Christ died for all: "Christ died for all, that they also who live may not now live to themselves but unto him who died for them, and rose again" (2 Cor. v. 15). Thirdly, he wishes us to know that he who is lost is so through his own fault, since he provides all the requisite means for his salvation: "Destruction is thy own, O Israel, thy help is only in me" (Osee, xiii. 9). It will not avail sinners in the day of judgment to excuse themselves by saying that they could not resist temptation, for the Apostle teaches that God is faithful, and will suffer no one to be tempted beyond his strength: "God is faithful, who will not suffer you to be tempted beyond what you are able" (1 Cor. x. 13). If we require more strength to resist we have only to ask the Almighty, and he will give it to us, for with his assistance we can subdue all carnal and infernal temptations: "Ask and it shall be given unto you" (Matt. vii. 7); "Every one that asketh receiveth" (Luke, ii. 10). St. Paul shows that he is most bountiful to those who invoke him: "Rich unto all that call upon him, for whosoever shall call upon the name of the Lord shall be saved" (Rom. x. 12, 13).

24. Behold, then, the sure means of obtaining salvation. We should pray to God for light and strength to accomplish his will, but we should also pray with humility, confidence, and perseverance, which are the three requisites for prayer to be heard. We should labour to co-operate to our salvation as much as we can, without waiting for God to do everything while we do nothing. Let the order of predestination be as it will, and let heretics say what they like, one thing is certain, that if we are to be saved, it is our good works that will save us, and if we are to be damned it is our own sins that will damn us. Let us place, however, all our hopes of salvation, not in our own works, but in the Divine mercy, and in the merits of Jesus Christ, and we shall be surely saved.

If we are saved, then, it will be solely by the grace of God, for even our good works are but gifts of his grace, and if we are lost it is solely through our own sins. It is this truth that preachers should frequently hold up to the people, and not go into the pulpit to make subtle theological disquisitions, uttering opinions not taught by the Fathers, and Doctors, and Martyrs of the Church, and explaining things in a way only calculated to make their hearers uneasy.

REFUTATION XIV.

THE HERESY OF MICHAEL MOLINOS.

1. This heresiarch preached two impious maxims; one did away with everything good, the other admitted everything evil. His first maxim was that the contemplative soul should fly from and banish all sensible acts of the will and understanding, which, according to him, impede contemplation, and thus deprive man of all those means which God has given him to acquire salvation. When the soul, he said, had given itself entirely up to God, and annihilated its will, resigning itself entirely into his hands, it becomes perfectly united with God, it should then have no further care for its salvation, no longer occupy itself with meditations, thanksgivings, prayers, devotion to Holy Images, or even to the Most Holy Humanity of Jesus Christ: it should avoid all devout affections of hope, of self sacrifice, of love for God, and in fine, drive away all good thoughts and avoid all good actions, for all these are opposed to contemplation, and to the perfection of the soul.

2. That we may perceive how poisoning this maxim is, we should know what is meditation and what contemplation. In meditation we labour to seek God by reasoning and by good acts, but in contemplation we behold him without labour, already found. In meditation the mind labours operating with its powers, but in contemplation it is God himself who operates, and the soul merely receives the infused gifts of his grace, *anima potitur*. Hence, when the soul is by passive contemplation absorbed in God, it should not strain itself to make acts and reflections, because then God supports it in an union of love with himself. " Then," says St. Theresa, " God occupies with his light the understanding, and prevents it from thinking of anything else." " When God," says the Saint, " wishes that our understanding should cease to reason, he occupies it, and gives us a knowledge superior to that which we can arrive at, and keeps the intellect suspended." But then she also remarks that the gift of contemplation and suspension of the intellectual powers, when it comes from God, produces good effects, but when it is procured by ourselves only makes the soul more dry than before.

Sometimes in prayer, she says, we have a beginning of devotion which comes from God, and we wish to pass of ourselves into this quietude of will, but if it is procured by ourselves it is of no effect, it is soon over, and leaves nothing but dryness behind. This is the defect which St. Bernard noticed in those who wish to pass from the foot to the mouth, alluding to that passage in the Canticle of Canticles, which refers to holy contemplation: " Let him kiss me with the kiss of his mouth" (Cant. i. 1). "Longus saltus," says the Saint, " et arduus de pede ad os."

3. It may be objected to us, however, that our Lord says by David: " Be still, and see that I am God" (Psalm, xlv. 11). The word " be still," however, does not mean that the soul should remain in a total state of quiescence in prayer, without meditating, offering up affections, or imploring grace. " Be still" means that in order to know God, and the immensity of his goodness, it is sufficient to abstain from vices, to remove ourselves from the cares of the world, to suppress the desires of self-love, and to detach ourselves from the goods of this life. That great mistress of prayer, St. Theresa, says: " It is necessary on our part to prepare ourselves for prayer; when God elevates us higher, to Him alone be the glory. When, therefore, in prayer, God elevates us to contemplation, and makes us feel that he wishes to speak to us, and does not wish that we should address him, we should not try to do anything then ourselves, lest we impede the Divine operation in us; we should only apply our loving attention to the voice of God, and say: 'Speak, Lord, for thy servant heareth.' When God, however, does not speak to us, then we should address him in prayer, making acts of contrition, acts of love, purposes of advancement in perfection, and not lose our time doing nothing." St. Thomas says: " Contemplatio diu durare non potest, licet quantum ad alios contemplationis actus, possint diu durare" (1). True contemplation, in which the soul is absorbed in God, can operate nothing, and does not last long; the effects of it, however, last, and so, when the soul returns to the active state, it ought to return also to labour, to preserve the fruit received in contemplation, by reading, reflecting, offering up pious affections, and performing similar acts of devotion, because, as St. Augustin confesses, he always felt himself, after being exalted to some unusual union with God, drawn back again as it were by a weight, to the miseries of this life, so that he felt obliged again to assist himself by acts of the will and the understanding, to an union with God. He says: " Aliquando, intromittis me in affectum inusitatum..... sed recido in hæc ærumnosis ponderibus, et resorbeor solitis" (2).

4. We have now to examine the pernicious propositions of Molinos, of which I will merely quote the principal ones, which will clearly show the impiety of his system. In his first proposi-

---

(1) St. Thomas, 2, 2, *q.* 180, *a.* 8, ad 2.   (2) St. Aug. Conf. *l.* 10, *c.* 40.

tion he says: "Oportet hominem suas potentias annihilare, et hæc est via interna;" in the second: " Velle operari active, est Deum offendere, qui vult esse Ipse solus agens; et ideo opus est seipsum in Deo totum, et totaliter delinquere, et postea permanere velut corpus exanime." Thus he wished, that, abandoning all to God, man should do nothing, but remain like a dead body, and that the wish to perform any good act of the intellect or the will was an offence against God, who wishes to do everything by himself; this, he said, was the annihilation of the powers of the soul, which renders it divine, and transfuses it in God, as he said in his fifth proposition: "Nihil operando anima se annihilat, et ad suum principium redit, et ad suam originem, quæ est essentia Dei, in quem transformata remanet, ac divinizata....... et tunc non sunt amplius duæ res unitæ, sed una tantum." See what a number of errors in few words.

5. Hence, also, he prohibited his disciples from having any care about, or even taking any heed of, their salvation, for the perfect soul, said he, should think neither of hell nor paradise: " Qui suum liberum arbitrium Deo donavit, de nulla re debet curam habere, nec de Inferno, nec de Paradiso; nec desiderium propriæ perfectionis, nec propriæ salutis, cujus *spem purgare* debet." Remark the words " spem purgare." To hope for our salvation, then, or make acts of hope, is a defect; to meditate on death and judgment, hell and heaven, shows a want of perfection, although our Lord says that the meditation on them is the greatest safeguard against sin: " In all thy works remember thy last end, and thou shalt never sin" (Eccles. vii. 40). He also taught that we should make no acts of love towards the Saints, the Divine Majesty, or even Jesus Christ himself, for we should banish all sensible objects from our soul. See his thirty-fifth proposition: " Nec debent elicere actus amoris erga B. Virginem, Sanctos, aut humanitatem Christi; quia, cum ista objecta sensibilia sint, talis est amor erga illa." Good God! to prohibit acts of love towards Jesus Christ, because he is a sensible object, and prohibits our union with God! But, as St Augustin says, when we approach Jesus Christ, is it not God himself we approach, for he is both God and man? How even can we approach God, unless through Jesus Christ? " Quo imus nisi ad Jesum, et qua imus, nisi per Ipsum?"

6. This is exactly what St. Paul says: " For by him we have access both in one spirit to the Father" (Ephes. ii. 18). And our Saviour himself says in St. John: " I am the door. By me if any man enter in, he shall be saved, and he shall go in and go out, and shall find pastures" (John, x. 9). " He shall go in and go out," that is, as an author quoted by Cornelius Lapide explains it: " Ingredietur ad Divinitatem meam, et egredietur ad humanitatem, et in utriusque contemplatione mira pascua inveniet." Thus, whether the soul contemplates Jesus either as God or man, it will

always find pastures. St. Theresa having once read in one of these condemned mystical books, that stopping in the contemplation of Christ prevented the soul from passing on to God, began to adopt this evil practice, but she constantly afterwards grieved for having done so. "Is it possible, my Lord," she says, "that you could be an impediment to me for greater good? Whence does all good come to me, if not from you alone?" She afterwards says: "I have seen that in order to please God, and that we may obtain great graces from him, he wishes that everything should pass through the hands of this Most Holy Humanity, in which he has declared that he is well pleased."

7. Molinos, in prohibiting us from thinking of Jesus Christ, consequently prevented us from meditating on his passion, though all the saints have done nothing else during their lives than meditate on the ignominy and sufferings of our loving Saviour. St. Augustin says: "Nihil tam salutiferum quam quotidie cogitare, quanta pro nobis pertulit Deus homo;" and St. Bonaventure: "Nihil enim in anima ita operatur universalem sanctificationem, sicut meditatio Passionis Christi." St. Paul said he wished to know nothing but Christ crucified: "For I judged not myself to know anything among you but Jesus Christ, and him crucified" (Cor. ii. 2). And withal, Molinos says we ought not to think on the humanity of Jesus Christ.

8. He also had the impiety to teach, that we should ask nothing from God, for petitioning is a defect of our own will. Here is his fourteenth proposition: "Qui Divinæ voluntati resignatus est, non convenit ut a Deo rem aliquam petat; quia petere est imperfectio, cum sit actus propriæ voluntatis. Illud autem *Petite* et *accipietis*, non est dictum a Christo pro animabus internis," &c. He thus deprives the soul of the most efficacious means of obtaining perseverance in a good life, and arriving at the grace of perfection. Jesus Christ himself, in the Gospel, tells us to pray unceasingly. "We ought always to pray, and not to faint" (Luke, xviii. 1); "Watch ye, therefore, praying at all times" (Luke, xxi. 36); and St. Paul says: "Pray without ceasing" (1 Thes. v. 17); and "Be instant in prayer" (Col. iv. 2.) And still Molinos will tell us not to pray, and that prayer is an imperfection. St. Thomas (3) says that continual prayer is necessary for us till our salvation is secured; for though our sins may have been remitted, still the world and the devil will never cease to attack us till the last hour of our lives: "Licet remittantur peccata, remanet tamen fomes peccati nos impugnant interius, et mundus et Dæmones, qui impugnant exterius." In this battle we cannot conquer without the Divine assistance, and this is only to be acquired by prayer, as St. Augustin teaches us, that except the first grace, that is, the voca-

(3) St. Thom. 3, *p. q.* 1, 39, *a*. 5.

tion to grace or penance, every other grace, especially that of perseverance, is only given to those who pray for it: "Deus nobis dat aliqua non orantibus, ut initium Fidei, alia nonnisi orantibus præparavit, sicut perseverantiam."

9. We have now to examine his second maxim, which, as we said in the commencement, allows evil to be innocent. When the soul, he says, is given up to God, whatever happens in the body is of no harm, even though we perceive that it is something unlawful; for the will, as he said, being then given to God, whatever happens in the flesh is to be attributed to the violence of the devil and of passion; so that, in that case, we should only make a negative resistance, and permit our nature to be disturbed, and the devil to operate. Here is his seventeenth proposition: "Traditio Deo libero arbitrio, non est amplius habenda ratio tentationum, nec eis alia resistentia fieri debet nisi negativa, nulla adhibita industria; et si natura commovetur, oportet sinere ut commoveatur, quia est natura." And in the forty-seventh proposition, also, he says: "Cum hujusmodi violentiæ occurrunt, sinere oportet, ut Satanas operetur......etiamsi sequantur pollutiones, et pejora..... et non opus est hæc confiteri."

10. Thus this deceiver led people astray, though our Lord tells us, through St. James: "Resist the devil, and he will fly from you" (James, iv. 7). It is not sufficient, then, to take no active part, *negative se habere*, we are not to allow the devil to operate in us, and our concupiscence to be gratified, for God commands us to resist him with all our strength. Nothing can be more false than what he says in his forty-first proposition: "Deus permittit, et vult ad nos humiliandos......quod Dæmon violentiam inferat corporibus, et actus carnales committere faciat," &c. Nay, it is most false, for St. Paul teaches us that God will not allow us to be tempted above our strength: "God is faithful, who will not suffer you to be tempted above that which you are able; but will make also with temptation issue, that you may be able to bear it" (1 Cor. x. 13). The meaning of the Apostle is this: that God will not fail to give us sufficient assistance in time of temptation to resist with our will, and by this resistance our temptations will be advantageous to us. He allows the devil to tempt us to sin; "but, as St. Jerome says, he will not permit him to force us: "Persuadere potest, præcipitare non potest." And St. Augustin (4) says that he is like a chained dog, who can bark at us, but not bite us, unless we put ourselves in his power. No matter how violent the temptation may be, if we call on God we will never fail: "Call on me in the day of trouble......I will deliver you" (Psalm, xlix. 15); "Praising I will call upon the Lord, and I will be saved from my enemies" (Psalm, xvii. 4). It is on this account that St. Bernard says (5) that prayer

---

(4) St. August. *l.* 5, de Civ. *c.* 20.   (5) St. Bern. Serm. 49, de Modo bene viv. *ar.* 7.

prevails over the devil, and St. Chrysostom, that nothing is more powerful than the prayer of a man.

11. In his forty-fifth proposition Molinos says that St. Paul suffered violence in his body from the devil, for the Saint says: "The good I will, I do not; but the evil which I will not, that I do." But we reply, that by the words " that I do," the Apostle only intends to say that he could not avoid involuntary motions of concupiscence; and, therefore, he says again: "Now that is no more I that do it, but sin that dwelleth in me" (Rom. viii. 17). In his forty-ninth proposition, also, he adduces the example of Job: " Job ex violentia Dæmonis se propriis manibus polluebat eodem tempore, *quo mundas habebat ad Deum preces.*" What a shocking perversion of the Scripture! Job says (*chap.* xvi.): " These things I have suffered without the iniquity of my hand, when I offered pure prayers to God." Now, is there any allusion to indecency in this text? In the Hebrew, and the version of the Septuagint, as Du Hamel informs us, the text is: " I have not neglected God nor injured any one." Therefore, by the words " these things I have suffered without the iniquity of my hand," Job meant to say that he never injured his neighbour; as Menochius explains it: " I raised up my hands to God, unstained by plunder or by any other crime." In his fifty-first proposition, also, he quotes in his defence the example of Sampson: " In sacra Scriptura multa sunt exempla violentiarum ad actus externos peccaminosos, ut illud Sampsonis, qui per violentiam seipsum occidit, cum Philistæi," &c. We reply, however, with St. Augustin, that this self-destruction of Sampson was accomplished by the pure inspiration of the Holy Ghost, and that is proved by the restoration to him, at the time, of his miraculous strength by the Almighty, who employed him as an instrument for the chastisement of the Philistines; for he having repented of his sins before he grasped the pillar which supported the building, prayed to the Lord to restore him his original strength: "But he called upon the Lord, saying: O Lord God, remember me, and restore me now to my former strength." And hence, St. Paul places him among the Saints: " Sampson, Jeptha, David, Samuel, and the Prophets, who, by Faith, conquered kingdoms, wrought justice," &c. (Heb. xi. 32, 33). Behold, then, the impiety of the system of this filthy impostor. He had good reason to thank the Almighty for his mercies, in giving him grace to die repentant, after his imprisonment of several years (*Hist. c.* 13, *ar.* 5, *n.* 32).

REFUTATION XIV.

BERRUYER'S ERRORS.

The abstruse matters treated of in this Chapter will not, perhaps, be interesting to the general reader; but several will be desirous to study profoundly the mysteries of the Faith, and to them this will be highly interesting and instructive.

SUMMARY OF THESE ERRORS.

Sec. I.—Jesus Christ was created in time, by an operation *ad extra*, natural Son of God, of one God, subsisting in three Persons, who united the Humanity of Christ with a Divine Person.

Sec. II.—Jesus Christ, during the three days he was in the sepulchre, as he ceased to be a living man, consequently ceased to be the Son of God, and when God raised him again from the dead, he again begot him, and caused him to be again the Son of God.

Sec. III.—It was the Humanity alone of Christ which obeyed, prayed, and suffered; and his oblations, prayers, and meditations were not operations, produced from the Word, as from a physical and efficient principle, but, in this sense, were mere actions of his Humanity.

Sec. IV.—The miracles performed by Jesus Christ were not done by his own power, but only obtained by him from the Father by his prayers.

Sec. V.—The Holy Ghost was not sent to the Apostles by Jesus Christ, but by the Father alone, through the prayers of Jesus Christ.

Sec. VI.—Several other errors of his on various subjects.

1. Reading in the Bullarium of Benedict XIV. a Brief, which begins " *Cum ad Congregationem,*" &c., published on the 17th of April, 1758, I see there prohibited and condemned the second part of a work (the first having been condemned in 1734), entitled the " History of the People of God, according to the New Testament," written by Father Isaac Berruyer; and all translations of the work into any language whatever are also condemned and prohibited. The whole of Berruyer's work, then, and the Latin Dissertations annexed, and the Defence, printed along with the Italian edition, are all condemned, as containing propositions false, rash, scandalous, favouring and approaching to heresy, and foreign to the common sense of the Fathers and the Church in the interpretation of Scripture. This condemnation was renewed by Pope Clement XIII.,

on the 2nd of December, 1758, and the literal Paraphrase of the Epistles of the Apostles, after the Commentaries of Hardouin, was included in it: " Quod quidem Opus ob doctrinæ fallaciam, et contortas Sacrarum Litterarum interpretationes .... scandali mensuram implevit." With difficulty, I procured a copy of the work, and I took care also to read the various essays and pamphlets in which it was opposed. It went, however, through several editions, though the author himself gave it up, and submitted to the sentence of the Archbishop of Paris, who, with the other bishops of France, condemned it. Besides the Pontifical and Episcopal condemnation, it was prohibited, likewise, by the Inquisition, and burned by the common hangman, by order of the Parliament of Paris. Father Zacchary, in his Literary History, says that he rejects the work, likewise, and that the General of the Jesuits, whose subject Father Berruyer was, declared that the Society did not recognize it.

2. I find in the treatises written to oppose Berruyer's work, that the writers always quote the errors of the author in his own words, and these errors are both numerous and pernicious, especially those regarding the Mysteries of the Trinity, and the Incarnation of the Eternal Word, against which especially the devil has always worked, through so many heresies; for these Mysteries are the foundation of our Faith and salvation, as Jesus Christ, the Son of God, is God made man, the fountain of all graces, and of all hope for us; and hence, St. Peter says that, unless in Jesus, there is no salvation: " Neither is there salvation in any other" (Acts, iv. 12).

3. I was just concluding this work, when I heard of Berruyer's work, and the writings opposing it; and, to tell the truth, I was anxious to conclude this work of mine, and rest myself a little after the many years of labour it cost me; but the magnitude and danger of his errors induced me to refute his book as briefly as I could. Remember that, though the work itself was condemned by Benedict XIV. and Clement XIII., the author was not, since he at once bowed to the decision of the Church, following the advice of St Augustin, who says that no one can be branded as a heretic, who is not pertinaciously attached to, and defends his errors: " Qui sententiam suam, quamvis falsam, atque perversam, nulla pertinaci animositate defendunt ...... corrigi parati cum invenerint, nequaquam sunt inter Hæreticos deputandi."

4. Before we commence the examination of Berruyer's errors, I will give a sketch of his system, that the reader may clearly understand it. His system is founded principally on two Capital Propositions, both as false as can be. I say Capital ones, for all the other errors he published depend on them. The first and chief proposition is this, that Jesus Christ is the natural Son of one God, but of God *subsisting in three Persons;* that is to say, that Jesus Christ is Son, but not Son of the Father, as principal, and first Person of the Trinity, but Son of the Father subsisting in three

Persons, and, therefore, he is, properly speaking, the Son of the Trinity. The second proposition, which comes from the first, and is also what I call a Capital one, is this, that all the operations of Jesus Christ, both corporal and spiritual, are not the operations of the Word, but only of his humanity, and from this, then, he deduced many false and damnable consequences. Although, as we have already seen, Berruyer himself was not condemned, still his book is a sink of extravagancies, follies, novelties, confusion, and pernicious errors, which, as Clement XIII. says, in his Brief, obscure the principal Articles of our Faith, so that Arians, Nestorians, Sabellians, Socinians, and Pelagians, will all find, some more, some less, something to please them in this work. There are mixed up with all this many truly Catholic sentiments, but these rather confuse than enlighten the mind of the reader. We shall now examine his false doctrine, and especially the first proposition, the parent, we may say, of all the rest.

SEC. I.—BERRUYER SAYS THAT JESUS CHRIST WAS MADE IN TIME, BY AN OPERATION *ad extra*, THE NATURAL SON OF GOD, ONE SUBSISTING IN THREE PERSONS, WHO UNITED THE HUMANITY OF CHRIST WITH A DIVINE PERSON.

5. HE says, first: " Jesus Christus D. N. vere dici potest et debet naturalis Dei Filius; Dei, inquam, ut vox illa Deus supponit pro Deo uno et vero subsistente in tribus personis, agente ad extra, et per actionem transeuntem et liberam uniente humanitatem Christi cum Persona Divina in unitatem Personæ"(1). And he briefly repeats the same afterwards: " Filius factus in tempore Deo in tribus Personis subsistenti" (2). And again: " Non repugnat Deo in tribus Personis subsistenti, fieri in tempore, et esse Patrem Filii naturalis, et veri." Jesus Christ, then, he says, should be called the natural Son of God, not because (as Councils, Fathers, and all Theologians say) the Word assumed the humanity of Christ in unity of Person; and thus our Saviour was true God and true man —true man, because he had a human soul and body, and true God because the Eternal Word, the true Son of God, true God generated from the Father, from all eternity, sustained and terminated the two natures of Christ, Divine and human, but because, according to Berruyer, God, *subsisting in Three Persons*, united the Word to the humanity of Christ, and thus Jesus Christ is the natural Son of God, not because he is the Word, born of the Father, but because he was made the Son of God in time, by God subsisting in three Persons, " uniente humanitatem Christi cum Persona Divina." Again, he repeats the same thing, in another place: " Rigorose loquendo per ipsam formaliter actionem unientem Jesus Christus constituitur tantum Filius Dei naturalis." The natural Son, according to Hardouin's and Berruyer's idea; because the real

(1) Berruyer, *t.* 8, *p.* 59.   (2) Idem. ibid. *p.* 60.

natural Son of God was the only begotten Son, begotten from the substance of the Father; and hence, the Son that Berruyer speaks of, produced from the three Persons, is Son in name only. It is not repugnant, he says, to God to become a Father in time, and to be the Father of a true and natural Son, and he always explains this of God, subsisting in three Divine Persons.

6. Berruyer adopted this error from his master, John Hardouin, whose Commentary on the New Testament was condemned by Benedict XIV., on the 28th of July, 1743. He it was who first promulgated the proposition, that Jesus Christ was not the Son of God as the Word, but only as man, united to the Person of the Word. Commenting on that passage of St. John, "In the beginning was the Word," he says: "Aliud esse Verbum, aliud esse Filium Dei, intelligi voluit Evangelista Joannes. Verbum est secunda Ss. Trinitatis Persona; Filius Dei, ipsa per se quidem, sed tamen ut eidem Verbo hypostatice unita Christi humanitas." Hardouin, therefore, says that the Person of the Word was united to the humanity of Christ, but that Jesus Christ then became the Son of God, when the humanity was hypostatically united to the Word; and, on this account, he says, he is called the Word, in the Gospel of St. John, up to the time of the Incarnation, but, after that, he is no longer called the Word, only the Only-begotten, and the Son of God: "Quamobrem in hoc Joannis Evangelio Verbum appellatur usque ad Incarnationem. Postquam autem caro factum est, non tam Verbum, sed Unigenitus, et Filius Dei est."

7. Nothing can be more false than this, however, since all the Fathers, Councils, and even the Scriptures, as we shall presently see, clearly declare that the Word himself was the only-begotten Son of God, who became incarnate. Hear what St. Paul says: " For let this mind be in you, which was also in Christ Jesus, who, being in the form of God, thought it not robbery to be equal with God, but emptied himself, taking the form of a servant" (Phil. ii. 5, &c.) So that the Apostle says, that Christ, being equal to God, emptied himself, taking the form of a servant. The Divine Person, which was united with Christ, and was equal to God, could not be the only-begotten Son of God, according to Hardouin, but must be understood to be the Word himself, for, otherwise, it would not be the fact that He who was equal to God emptied himself, taking the form of a servant. St. John, besides, in his First Epistle (v. 20), says: "We know that the Son of God is come." He says, "is come;" it is not, therefore, true that this Son of God became the Son, only when he came, for we see he was the Son of God before he came. The Council of Chalcedon (*Act.* v.) says, speaking of Jesus Christ: " Ante sæcula quidem de Patre genitum secundum Deitatem, et in novissimis autem diebus propter nos et propter nostram salutem ex Maria Virgine Dei Genitrice secundum humanitatem . . . . . non in duas personas partitum, sed unum eundemque

Filium, et unigenitum Deum Verbum." Thus we see it there declared, that Jesus Christ, according to the Divinity, was generated by the Father before all ages, and afterwards became incarnate in the fulness of time, and that he is one and the same, the Son of God and of the Word. In the Third Canon of the Fifth General Council it is declared: " Si quis dixerit unam naturam Dei Verbi incarnatam dicens, non sic ea excipit, sicut Patres docuerunt, quod ex Divina natura et humana, unione secundum subsistentiam facta, unus Christus effectus..... talis anathema sit." We see here there is no doubt expressed that the Word was incarnate, and became Christ, but it was prohibited to say absolutely that the Incarnate nature of the Word was one. We say, in the Symbol at Mass, that we believe in one God, Jesus Christ, the only-begotten Son of God, born of the Father, before all ages. Jesus Christ is not, therefore, the Son of God, merely because he was made the Son in time, or because his humanity was united to the Word, as Hardouin says, but because his humanity was assumed by the Word, who was already the Son of God, born of the Father before all ages.

8. All the Fathers teach that the Son of God who was made man is the very Person of the Word. St. Iræneus (3) says: " Unus et idem, et ipse Deus Christus Verbum est Dei." St. Athanasius (4) reproves those who say: " Alium Christum, alium rursum esse Dei Verbum, quod ante Mariam, et sæcula erat Filius Patris." St. Cyril says (5): " Licet (Nestorius) duas naturas esse dicat carnis et Verbi Dei, differentiam significans........ attamen unionem non confitetur; nos enim illas adunantes unum Christum; unum eundem Filium dicimus." St. John Chrysostom (6), reproving Nestorius for his blasphemy, in teaching that in Jesus Christ there were two Sons, says: " Non alterum et alterum, absit, sed unum et eundem Dom. Jesum Deum Verbum carne nostra amictum," &c. St. Basil writes (7): " Verbum hoc quod erat in principio, nec humanum erat, nec Angelorum, sed ipse Unigenitus qui dicitur Verbum; quia impassibiliter natus, et Generantis imago est." St. Gregory Thaumaturgus (8) says: " Unus est Deus Pater Verbi viventis..... perfectus perfecti Genitor, Pater Filii unigeniti." St. Augustin says (9): " Et Verbum Dei, forma quædam non formata, sed forma omnium formarum existens in omnibus. Quærunt vero, quomodo nasci potuerit Filius coævus Patri: nonne si ignis æternus esset, coævus esset splendor?" And in another passage he says (10): " Christus Jesus Dei Filius est, et Deus, et Homo; Deus ante omnia secula, Homo in nostro seculo. Deus, quia Dei Verbum: Homo autem, quia in unitatem personæ accessit Verbo anima rationalis, et caro." Eusebius of Ceserea says (11), not like Hardouin: " Non

(3) St. Iræneus. *l.* 17, adv. Hæres. (4) St. Athan. Epist. ad Epictetum. (5) St. Cyril. in Commonitor. ad Eulogium. (6) St. Chrysost. Hom. 3, ad c. 1, Ep. ad Cæsar. (7) St. Basil Hom. in Princ. Johann. (8) St. Greg. Thaumat. in Vita St. Greg. Nyss. (9) St. August. Serm. 38, de Verb. Dom. (10) St. August. in Euchirid. c. 35. (11) Euseb. Ces. *l.* 1, de Fide.

cum apparuit, tunc et Filius: non cum nobiscum, tunc et apud Deum: sed quemadmodum in principio erat Verbum, in principio erat ..... in principio erat Verbum, de Filio dicit." We would imagine that Eusebius intended to answer Hardouin, by saying that the Word, not alone when he became incarnate and dwelt amongst us, was then the Son of God, and with God, but as in the beginning he was the Word, so, in like manner, he was the Son; and hence, when St. John says: " In the beginning was the Word," he meant to apply it to the Son. It is in this sense all the Fathers and schoolmen take it, likewise, as even Hardouin himself admits, and still he is not ashamed to sustain, that we should not understand that it is the Word, the Son of God, who became incarnate, though both doctors and schoolmen thus understand it. Here are his words: " Non Filius stilo quidem Scripturarum sacrarum, quamquam in scriptis Patrum, et in Schola etiam Filius."

9. This doctrine has been taken up, defended, and diffusely explained, by Berruyer; and to strengthen his position, even that Jesus Christ is not the Son of the Father, as the first Person of the Trinity, but of one God, *as subsisting in the three Divine Persons*, he lays down a general rule, by which he says all texts of the New Testament in which God is called the Father of Christ, and the Son is called the Son of God, should be understood of the Father subsisting in three Persons, and the Son of God subsisting in three Persons. Here are his words: " Omnes Novi Testamenti textus, in quibus aut Deus dicitur Pater Christi, aut Filius dicitur Filius Dei, vel inducitur Deus Christum sub nomine Filii, aut Christus Deum sub nomine Patris interpretans: vel aliquid de Deo ut Christi Patre, aut de Christo ut Dei Filio narratur, intelligendi sunt de Filio facto in tempore secundum carnem Deo uni et vero in tribus Personis subsistenti." And this rule, he says, is necessary for the proper and literal understanding of the New Testament: " Hæc notio prorsus necessaria est ad litteralem et germanam intelligentiam Librorum Novi Testamenti" (12). He previously said that all the writers of the Old Testament who prophesied the coming of the Messiah should be understood in the same sense: " Cum et idem omnino censendum est de omnibus Vet. Testamenti Scriptoribus, quoties de futuro Messia Jesu Christo prophetant" (13). Whenever God the Father, or the first Person, he says, is called the Father of Jesus Christ, it must be understood that he is not called so in reality, but by appropriation, on account of the omnipotence attributed to the Person of the Father: " Recte quidem, sed per appropriationem Deus Pater, sive Persona prima, dicitur Pater Jesu Christi, quia actio uniens, sicut et actio creans, actio est omnipotentiæ, cujus attributi actiones Patri, sive primæ Personæ, per appropriationem tribuuntur" (14).

(12) P. Berruyer, *t.* 8, *p.* 89 & 98. (13) Berruyer, *t.* 8, *p.* 3. (14) Berruyer, *t.* 8, *p.* 83.

10. This false notion of the Filiation of Jesus Christ Berruyer founds on that text of St. Paul (Rom. i. 3, 4): "Concerning his Son, who was made to him of the seed of David, according to the flesh, who was predestined the Son of God in power," &c. Now, these words, "his Son, who was made to him according to the flesh," he says, prove that Jesus Christ was the Son of God made in time according to the flesh. We reply, however, to this, that St. Paul, in this passage, speaks of Jesus Christ not as Son of God, but as Son of man: he does not say that Jesus Christ was made his Son according to the flesh, but "concerning his Son, who was made to him of the seed of David, according to the flesh;" that is, the Word, his Son, was made according to the flesh, or, in other words, was made flesh—was made man as St. John says: "The Word was made flesh." We are not, then, to understand with Berruyer, that Christ, as man, was made the Son of God; for as we cannot say that Christ, being man, was made God, neither can we say that he was made the Son of God; but we are to understand that the Word being the only Son of God, was made man from the stock of David. When we hear it said, then, that the humanity of Jesus Christ was raised to the dignity of Son of God, that is, understood to have taken place by the communication of the idioms founded on the unity of Person: for the Word having united human nature to his Person, and as it is one Person which sustains the two natures, Divine and human, the propriety of the Divine Nature is then justly affirmed of man, and the propriety of God, of the human nature be assumed. How, then, is this expression, "who was predestined the Son of God in power," to be taken? Berruyer endeavours to explain it by a most false supposition, which we will presently notice. It is, he says, to be understood of the new filiation which God made in the resurrection of Jesus Christ, for when our Lord died, as his soul was separated from his body, he ceased to be a living man, and was then no longer, he said, the Son of God; but when he rose again from the dead, God again made him his Son, and it is of this new filiation St. Paul, he says, speaks in these words: "Who was predestinated the Son of God in power, according to the spirit of sanctification, by the resurrection of our Lord Jesus Christ from the dead" (Rom. i. 4). Commentators and Holy Fathers give different interpretations to this text, but the most generally received is that of St. Augustin, St. Anselm, Estius, and some others, who say that Christ was from all eternity destined to be united in time, according to the flesh, to the Son of God, by the operation of the Holy Ghost, who united this man to the Word, who afterwards wrought miracles, and raised him from the dead.

11. To return to Berruyer. In his system he lays it down for a certainty, that Jesus Christ is the natural Son of one God, subsisting in three Persons. Is Christ, then, the Son of the Trinity? an

opinion which shocked St. Fulgentius (15), who says that our Saviour, according to the flesh, might be called the work of the Trinity; but, according to his birth, both eternal and in time, is the Son of God the Father alone: " Quis unquam tantæ reperiri possit insaniæ, qui auderet Jesum Christum totius Trinitatis Filium prædicare?...... Jesus Christus secundum carnem quidem opus est totius Trinitatis; secundum vero utramque Nativitatem solus Dei Patris est Filius." But Berruyer's partisans may say that he does not teach that Jesus Christ is the Son of the Trinity; but granting that he allows two filiations—one eternal, the filiation of the Word, and the other in time, when Christ was made the Son of God, subsisting in three Persons—he must then, of necessity, admit that this Son made in time was the Son of the Trinity. He will not have Jesus Christ to be the Word, that is, the Son generated from the Father, the first Person of the Trinity from all eternity. If he is not the Son of the Father, whose Son is he if not the Son of the Trinity? Had he any Father at all? There is no use in wasting words on the matter, for every one knows that in substance it is just the same to say the Son of one God subsisting in three Persons, as to say the Son of the Trinity. This, however, is what never can be admitted; for if we said Christ was the Son of the three Persons, it would be' the same, as we shall prove, as to say that he was a mere creature; but when we say he is the Son, we mean that he was produced from the substance of the Father, or that he was of the same substance as the Father, as St. Athanasius teaches (16): " Omnis filius ejusdem essentiæ est proprii parentis, alioquin impossibile est, ipsum verum esse filium." St. Augustin says that Christ cannot be called the Son of the Holy Ghost, though it was by the operation of the Holy Spirit the Incarnation took place. How, then, can he be the Son of the three Persons? St. Thomas (17) teaches that Christ cannot be called the Son of God, unless by the eternal generation, as he has been generated by the Father alone; but Berruyer wants us to believe that he is not the Son, generated by the Father, but made by one God, subsisting in three Persons.

12. To carry out this proposition, if he understands that Jesus Christ is the Son, consubstantial to the Father, who subsists in three Persons, he must admit four Persons in God, that is, three in which God subsists, and the fourth Jesus Christ, made the Son of the most Holy Trinity; or, in other words, of God subsisting in three Persons. If, on the other hand, he considers the Father of Jesus Christ as one Person alone, then he falls into Sabellianism, recognizing in God not three distinct Persons, but one alone under three different names. He is accused of Arianism by others, and, in my opinion, his error leads to Nestorianism. He lays down as a principle, that

(15) St. Fulgent. Fragm. 32, l. 9.   (16) St. Athan. Epist. 2, ad Serapion.   (17) St. Thom. 3. p. qu. 32, art. 3.

there are two generations in God—one eternal, the other in time—one of necessity, *ad intra*—the other voluntary, *ad extra*. In all this he is quite correct; but then, speaking of the generation *in time*, he says that Jesus Christ was not the natural Son of God the Father, as the first Person of the Trinity, but the Son of God, as subsisting in three Persons.

13. Admitting this, then, to be the case, it follows that Jesus Christ had two Fathers, and that in Jesus Christ there are two Sons—one the Son of God, as the Father, the First Person of the Trinity, who generated him from all eternity—the other, the Son made in time by God, but by God subsisting in three Persons, who, uniting the humanity of Jesus Christ (or, as Berruyer says, uniting that man, *hominem illum*) to the Divine Word, made him his natural Son. If we admit this, however, then we must say that Jesus Christ is not true God, but only a creature, and that for two reasons, first—because Faith teaches us that there are only two internal operations (*ad intra*) in God, the generation of the Word and the spiration of the Holy Ghost; every other operation in God is external (*ad extra*), and external operations produce only creatures, and not a Divine Person. The second reason is—because if Jesus Christ were the natural Son of God, subsisting in three Persons, he would be the Son of the Trinity, as we have already stated, and that would lead us to admit two grievous absurdities—first, the Trinity, that is, the three Divine Persons, would produce a Son of God; but as we have already shown, the Trinity, with the exception of the production of the Word and the Holy Ghost, *ad intra*, only produces creatures, and not Sons of God. The second absurdity is, that if Jesus Christ was made the natural Son of God by the Trinity, he would generate or produce himself (unless we exclude the Son from the Trinity altogether), and this would be a most irrational error, such as Tertullian charged Praxeas with: "Ipse se Filium sibi fecit" (18). Therefore we see, according to Berruyer's system, that Jesus Christ, for all these reasons, would not be true God, but a mere creature, and the Blessed Virgin would be, as Nestorius asserted, only the Mother of Christ, and not, as the Council decided, and Faith teaches, the Mother of God, for Jesus Christ is true God, seeing that his humanity had only the Person of the Word alone to terminate it, for it was the Word alone which sustained the two natures, human and Divine.

14. Berruyer's friend, however, says that he does not admit the existence of two natural Sons—one from eternity, the other in time. But then, I say, if he does not admit it, where is the use of torturing his mind by trying to make out this second filiation of Jesus Christ, made in time the natural Son of God, subsisting in three Persons. He ought to say, as the Church teaches, and all Catholics

---

(18) Tertull. adv. Praxeam. *n.* 50.

believe, that it is the same Word who was from all eternity the natural Son of God, generated from the substance of the Father, who assumed human nature, and thus redeemed mankind. But Berruyer wished to enlighten the Church with the knowledge of this new natural Son of God, about whom we know nothing before, telling us that this Son was made in time, not from the Father, but by all the three Divine Persons, because he was united to, or, as he expressed it, had the honour of the *Consortium* of the Word, who was the Son of God from all eternity. We knew nothing of all this till Berruyer and his master, Hardouin, came to enlighten us.

15. Berruyer, however, was grievously astray in asserting that Jesus Christ was the natural Son of one God, subsisting in three Persons. In this he has all Theologians, Catechisms, Fathers, Councils, and Scripture, opposed to him. We do not deny that the Incarnation of the Word was the work of the three Divine Persons; but neither can it be denied that the Person who became incarnate was the only Son, the second Person of the Trinity, who was, without doubt, the Word himself, generated from all eternity by the Father, who, assuming human nature, and uniting it to himself in unity of Person, wished by this means to redeem the human race. Hear what the Catechisms and the Symbols of the Church say; they teach that Jesus Christ is not the Son of God made in time by the Trinity, as Berruyer imagines, but the eternal Word, born of the Father, the principal and first Person of the Most Holy Trinity. This is what the Roman Catechism teaches: " Filium Dei esse (Jesum) et verum Deum, sicut Pater est, qui eum ab æterno genuit" (19). And again (*N.* 9), Berruyer's opinion is directly impugned: " Et quamquam duplicem ejus nativitatem agnoscamus, unum tamen Filium esse credimus; una enim Persona est, in quam Divina et humana natura convenit." The Athanasian Creed says that the Son is from the Father alone, not made nor created, but begotten; and speaking of Jesus Christ, it says that he is God, of the substance of the Father, begotten before all ages, and man, of the substance of his Mother, born in time, who, though he is God and man, still is not two, but one Christ—one, not by the conversion of the Divinity into flesh, but by the assumption of the humanity into God. As Jesus Christ, therefore, received his humanity from the substance of his Mother alone, so he had his Divinity from the substance of his Father alone.

16. In the Apostles' Creed we say: " I believe in God, the Father Almighty ...... and in Jesus Christ, his only Son..... born of the Virgin Mary, suffered," &c. Remark, Jesus Christ, his Son, of the Father, the first Person, who is first named, not of the three Persons; and his only Son, that is one Son, not two. In the Symbol of the Council of Florence, which is said at Mass, and which com-

(19) Catech. Rom. *c.* 3, *art.* 2, *n.* 11.

prises all the other Symbols previously promulgated by the other General Councils, we perceive several remarkable expressions. It says: "I believe in one God, the Father Almighty.... and in one Lord Jesus Christ, the only begotten Son of God, and born of the Father before all ages (see, then, this only begotten Son is the same who was born of the Father before all ages), consubstantial to the Father, by whom all things were made, who for us men, and for our salvation, came down from heaven, and became incarnate," &c. The Son of God, then, who wrought the redemption of mankind, is not he whom Berruyer supposes made in time on this earth, but the eternal Son of God, by whom all things were made, who came down from heaven, and was born and suffered for our salvation. Berruyer, then, is totally wrong in recognizing two natural Sons of God, one born in time of God, subsisting in three Persons, and the other generated by God from all eternity.

17. But, says Berruyer, then Jesus Christ, inasmuch as he was made a man in time, is not the real, natural Son of God, but merely his adopted Son, as Felix and Elipandus taught, and for which they were condemned? But this we deny, and we hold for certain that Jesus Christ, even as man, is the true Son of God (*See Refutation* vii. *n.* 18), but that does not prove that there are two natural Sons of God, one eternal and the other made in time, because, as we have proved in this work, as quoted above, Jesus Christ, even as man, is called the natural Son of God, inasmuch as God the Father continually generates the Word from all eternity, as David writes: "The Lord hath said to me, Thou art my Son, this day have I begotten thee" (Psalm, ii. 7). Hence it is that as the Son, previous to the Incarnation, was generated from all eternity, without flesh, so from the time he assumed humanity he was generated by the Father, and will for ever be generated, hypostatically united to his humanity. But it is necessary to understand that this man, the natural Son of God created in time, is the very Person of the Son, generated from all eternity, that is the Word, who assumed the humanity of Jesus Christ, and united it to itself. It cannot be said, then, that there are two natural Sons of God, one, man, made in time, the other, God, produced from all eternity, for there is only one natural Son of God, that is the Word, who, uniting human nature to himself in time, is both God and man, and is, as the Athanasian Creed declares, one Christ: "For as the rational soul and flesh is one man, so God and man is one Christ. And as every man, though consisting of soul and body, is still only one man, one person, so in Jesus Christ, though there is the Word and the humanity, there is but one Person and natural Son of God."

18. Berruyer's opinion also is opposed to the First Chapter of the Gospel of St. John, for there we read: "In the beginning was the Word, and the Word was with God, and the Word was God;" and then it is said that it was this same Word which was made

flesh: "And the Word was made flesh." Being made flesh does not mean that the Word was united to the human person of Jesus Christ, already existing, but it shows that the Word assumed humanity in the very instant in which it was created, so that from that very instant the soul of Jesus Christ and his human flesh became his own proper soul and his own proper flesh, sustained and governed by one sole Divine Person alone, which is the Word, which terminates and sustains the two natures, Divine and human, and it is thus the Word was made man. Just pause for a moment! St. John affirms that the Word, the Son, generated from the Father from all eternity, is made man, and Berruyer says that this man is not the Word, the Son of the eternal God, but another Son of God, made in time by all the three Divine Persons. When, however, the Evangelist has said: "The Word was made flesh," if you say and understand that the Word is not made flesh, are you not doing just what the Sacramentarians did, explaining the Eucharistic words, "This is my body," that the body of Jesus Christ was not his body, but only the figure, sign, or virtue of his body? This is what the Council of Trent reprobates so much in the heretics, distorting the words of Scripture to their own meaning. To return, however, to the Gospel of St. John. The Evangelist says, he dwelt among us. It was the eternal Word, then, which was made man, and worked out man's redemption, and, therefore, the Gospel again says: "The Word was made flesh....... and we saw his glory, as it were the glory of the only-begotten of the Father." This Word, then, who was made man in time, is the only-begotten, and, consequently, the only natural Son of God, generated by the Father from all eternity. St. John (1 Epis. iv. 9), again repeats it: "By this has the charity of God appeared towards us, because God hath sent his only-begotten Son into the world, that we may live by him." In this text we must remark that the Apostle uses the word "hath sent." Berruyer then asserts what is false, in saying that Jesus Christ is the Son of God, made in time, for St. John says that he existed before he "was sent," for in fact it was the eternal Son of the Father that was sent by God, who came down from heaven, and brought salvation to the world. We should also recollect that St. Thomas says (20), that speaking of God, whenever one Person is said to be sent by another, he is said to be sent, inasmuch as he proceeds from the other, and therefore the Son is said to be sent by the Father to take human flesh, inasmuch as he proceeds from the Person of the Father alone. Christ himself declared this in the resurrection of Lazarus, for though he could have raised him himself, still he prayed to his Father that they might know he was his true Son, "That they may believe that thou hast sent me" (John, xi. 42);

(20) St. Thomas, *p.* 1, *q.* 4, *ar.* 1.

and hence St. Hilary says (21): " Non prece eguit, pro nobis oravit, ne Filius ignoraretur."

19. Along with all this we have the tradition of the Fathers generally opposed to Berruyer's system. St. Gregory of Nazianzen (22) says: " Id quod non erat assumpsit, non duo factus, sed unum ex duobus fieri subsistens; Deus enim ambo sunt, id quod assumpsit, et quod est assumptum, naturæ duæ in unum concurrentes, non duo Filii." St. John Chrysostom (23) writes: " Unum Filium unigenitum, non dividens eum in Filiorum dualitatem, portantem tamen in semetipso indivisarum duarum naturarum inconvertibiliter proprietates;" and again, " Etsi enim duplex natura, verumtamen indivisibilis unio in una filiationis confitenda Persona, et una subsistentia." St. Jerome says (24): " Anima et caro Christi cum Verbo Dei una Persona est, unus Christus." St. Dionisius of Alexandria wrote a Synodical Epistle to refute Paul of Samosata, who taught a doctrine like Berruyer; " Duas esse Personas unius, et solius Christi; et duos Filios, unum natura Filium Dei, qui fuit ante sæcula, et unum homonyma Christum Filium David." St. Augustin says (25): " Christus Jesus Dei Filius est Deus et Homo: Deus quia Dei Verbum: Homo autem, quia in unitatem Personæ necessit Verbo Anima rationalis et caro." I omit the quotations from many other Fathers, but those who are curious in the matter will find them in the Clypeum of Gonet and in the writings of Petavius, Gotti, and others.

20. Another reflection occurs to my mind. Besides the other errors published by Berruyer, and which follow from his opinions, which we will immediately refute, if the reader goes back to *N*. 9, he will perceive that the faith of Baptism, as taught by all Christians and Councils, is jeopardized. According to this system, all passages in the New Testament in which God is called the Father of Christ, or the Son is called the Son of God, or where anything is mentioned about God, as Father of Christ, the Son of God, must be understood to apply to the Son of God made in time, according to the flesh, and made by that God, subsisting in three Persons. On the other hand, it is certain that Baptism is administered in the Church in the name of the three Persons, expressly and individually named, as Jesus Christ commanded his Apostles to do: " Go ye, therefore, and teach all nations, baptizing them in the name of the Father, and of the Son, and of the Holy Ghost" (Matt. xxviii. 19). But if the general rule laid down by Berruyer, as we have explained it, should be observed, then the Baptism administered in the Church would be no longer Baptism in the sense we take it, because the Father who is named would not be the first Person of

---

(21) St. Hilar. *l*. 10, de Trin.   (22) St. Greg. Nazian. Orat. 31.   (23) St. John Chrysos. Ep. ad Cæsar. et Hom. 3, ad cap. I.   (24) St. Hieron. Tract 49, in Jo. (25) St. August. in Enchirid. *cap*. 33.

the Trinity, as is generally understood, but the Father Berruyer imagined, a Father subsisting in three Divine Persons—in a word, the whole Trinity. The Son would not be the Word, generated by the Father, the Principle of the Trinity, from all eternity, but the Son, made in time by all the three Persons, who, being an external work of God, *ad extra*, would be a mere creature, as we have seen already. The Holy Ghost would not be the third Person, such as we believe him, that is, proceeding from the Father, the first Person of the Trinity, and from the Son, the second Person, that is, the Word, generated from all eternity by the Father. Finally, according to Berruyer, the Father, the Son, and the Holy Ghost would not be what they are in reality, and what the whole Church believes them to be, the real Father, the real Son, and the real Holy Ghost, in opposition to what that great theologian, St. Gregory of Nazianzen teaches: " Quis Catholicorum ignorat Patrem vere esse Patrem, Filium vere esse Filium, et Spiritum Sanctum vere esse Spiritum Sanctum, sicut ipse Dominus ad Apostolos dicit: Euntes docete, &c. Hæc est perfecta Trinitas," &c. (26). Read, however, further on the Refutation of the third error, and you will find this fiction more diffusely and clearly refuted. We now pass on to the other errors of this writer, which flow from this first one.

SEC. II.—BERRUYER SAYS THAT JESUS CHRIST, DURING THE THREE DAYS HE WAS IN THE SEPULCHRE, CEASED TO BE A LIVING MAN, AND, CONSEQUENTLY, WAS NO LONGER THE SON OF GOD. AND WHEN GOD AGAIN RAISED HIM FROM THE DEAD, HE ONCE MORE GENERATED HIM, AND AGAIN MADE HIM THE SON OF GOD.

21. ONE must have a great deal of patience to wade through all these extravagant falsehoods. Christ, he says, during the three days he was in the sepulchre, ceased to be the natural Son of God: " Factum est morte Christi, ut homo Christus Jesus, cum jam non esset homo vivens, atque adeo pro triduo quo corpus ab Anima separatum jacuit in sepulchro, fieret Christus incapax illius appellationis, Filius Dei (1); and he repeats the same thing in another part of his work, in different words: " Actione Dei unius, Filium suum Jesum suscitantis, factum est, ut Jesus qui desierat esse homo vivens, et consequenter Filius Dei, iterum viveret deinceps non moriturus." This error springs from that false supposition we have already examined, for supposing that Jesus Christ was the Son of God subsisting in three Persons, that is the Son of the Trinity by an operation *ad extra*, he was then a mere man, and as by death he ceased to be a living man, he also ceased to be the Son of God subsisting in three Persons; because if Jesus Christ were the Son of God, as first Person of the Trinity, then in him was the Word, which, being hypostatically united to his soul and

(26) St. Greg. Nazian. in Orat. de Fide, post init.   (1) Berruyer, *t.* 8, *p.* 63.

body, could never be separated from him, even when his soul was by death separated from his body.

22. Supposing, then, that Jesus Christ, dying, ceased to be the Son of God, Berruyer must admit that in those three days in which our Lord's body was separated from his soul, the Divinity was separated from his body and soul. Let us narrow the proposition. Christ, he says, was made the Son of God, not because the Word assumed his humanity, but because the Word was united to his humanity, and hence, he says, as in the sepulchre he ceased to be a living man, his soul being separated from his body, he was no longer the Son of God, and, therefore, the Word ceased to be united with his humanity. Nothing, however, can be more false than this, for the Word assumed and hypostatically and inseparably united to himself in unity of Person the soul and body of Jesus Christ, and hence when our Lord died, and his most holy body was laid in the tomb, the Divinity of the Word could not be separated either from the body or the soul. This truth has been taught by St. Athanasius (2): " Cum Deitas neque Corpus in sepulchro desereret, neque ab Anima in inferno separaretur." St. Gregory of Nyssa writes (3): " Deus qui totum hominem per suam cum illo conjunctionem in naturam Divinam mutaverat, mortis tempore a neutra illius, quam semel assumpserat, parte recessit;" and St. Augustin says (4): " Cum credimus Dei Filium, qui sepultus est, profecto Filium Dei dicimus et Carnem, quæ sola sepulta est."

23. St. John of Damascus tells us the reason the soul of Christ had not a different subsistence from his body, as it was the one Person alone which sustained both: " Neque enim unquam aut Anima, aut Corpus peculiarem atque a Verbi subsistentia diversam subsistentiam habuit" (5). On that account, he says, as it was one Person which sustained the soul and body of Christ, although the soul was separated from the body, still the Person of the Word could not be separated from them: " Corpus, et Anima simul ab initio in Verbi Persona existentiam habuerant, ac licet in morte divulsa fuerint, utrumque tamen eorum unam Verbi, qua subsisteret, semper habuit." As, therefore, when Jesus descended into hell, the Word descended, likewise, with his soul, so, while his body was in the sepulchre, the Word was present, likewise; and, therefore, the body of Christ was free from corruption, as David foretold: " Nor wilt thou give thy holy One to see corruption" (Psalm, xv. 10). And St. Peter, as we read in the Acts (ii. 27), shows that this text was applied to our Lord lying in his tomb. It is true, St. Hilary (6) says, that, when Christ died, the Divinity

---

(1) St. Athanasius, contra Apollinar. *l.* 1, *n.* 15.   (3) St. Greg. Nyss. Orat. 1 in Christ. Resur.   (4) St. Aug. Tract. 78, in Joan, *n.* 2.   (5) St. Jo. Damasc. *l.* 3, de Fide, *c.* 27.   (6) St. Hilar. *c.* 33, in Matth.

left his body; but St. Ambrose (7) explains this, and says, that all the Holy Doctor meant to say was, that, in the Passion, the Divinity abandoned the humanity of Christ to that great desolation, which caused him to cry out: "My God, my God, why hast thou forsaken me?" (Matt. xxvii. 46). In his death, therefore, the Word abandoned his body, inasmuch as the Word did not preserve his life, but never ceased to be hypostatically united with him. Christ never, then, could cease to be the Son of God in the sepulchre, as Berruyer teaches; for it is one of the axioms of all Catholic schools (10): "Quod semel Verbum assumpsit, nunquam misit" —The Word, having once assumed human nature, never gives it up again. But when Berruyer admits, then, that the Word was united in the beginning in unity of Person with the body and soul of Jesus Christ, how can he afterwards say that, when the soul was separated from the body, the Word was no longer united with the body? This is a doctrine which, surely, neither he nor any one else can understand.

24. When Berruyer says that Jesus Christ, at his death, ceased to be the natural Son of God, because he was no longer a living man, he must, consequently, hold that the humanity, previous to his death, was not sustained by the Person of the Word, but by its own proper human subsistence, and was a Person distinct from the Person of the Word. But, then, how can he escape being considered a Nestorian, admitting two distinct Persons in Jesus Christ. Both Nestorius and Berruyer are expressly condemned by the Symbol promulgated in the Council of Constantinople, which says, that we are bound to believe in one God, the Father Almighty, and in one only-begotten Son of God, born of the Father before all ages, and consubstantial to the Father, who, for our salvation, came down from heaven, and became incarnate of the Virgin Mary, suffered, was buried, and rose again the third day. It is, therefore, the only-begotten Son of God the Father, generated by the Father from all eternity, and who came down from heaven, that was made man, died, and was buried. But, how could God die and be buried? you will say. By assuming human flesh, as the Council teaches. As another General Council, the Fourth of Lateran, says (9), as God could not die, nor suffer, by becoming man he became mortal and passible: "Qui cum secundum Divinitatem sit immortalis et impassibilis, idem ipse secundum humanitatem factus est mortalis et passibilis."

25. As one error is always the parent of another, so Berruyer having said that Jesus Christ in the sepulchre ceased to be the natural Son of God, said, likewise, that when God raised Christman again from the dead, he again generated him, and made him

---

(7) St. Ambrose. *l.* 10, in Luc. *c.* 13. (8) Cont. Tournely, de Incarn. *t.* 4, *part* 2, *pag.* 487. (9) Cont. Lat. in cap. Fermiter, de Summ. Trin. &c.

Man-God, because, by raising him again, he caused him to be his Son, who, dying, ceased to be his Son. We have already (*N.* 18) alluded to this falsehood. He says: " Actione Dei unius, Filium suum Jesum suscitantis, factum est, ut Jesus, qui desierat esse homo vivens, et consequenter Filius Dei, iterum viveret deinceps non moriturus." He says the same thing, in other words, in another place: "Deus Christum hominem resuscitans, hominem Deum iterato generat, dum facit resuscitando, ut Filius sit, qui moriendo Filius esse desierat"(10). We should, indeed, be rejoiced to hear of this new dogma, never before heard of, that the Son of God twice became incarnate, and was made man—first, when he was conceived in the holy womb of the Virgin, and, again, when he arose from the tomb. We should, indeed, feel obliged to Berruyer, for enlightening us on a point never before heard of in the Church. Another consequence of this doctrine is, that the Blessed Virgin must have been twice made the Mother of God; for, as Jesus ceased to be the Son of God while in the tomb, so she ceased also to be the Mother of God at the same time, and then, after his resurrection, her Divine maternity was again restored to her. In the next paragraph we will examine even a more brainless error than this. I use the expression, " brainless," for I think the man's head was more in fault than his conscience. A writer, who attacked Berruyer's errors, said that he fell into all these extravagancies, because he would not follow the Tradition of the Fathers, and the method they employed in the interpretation of the Scriptures, and the announcement of the unwritten Word of God, preserved in the works of these doctors and pastors. It is on this account, as the prelate, the author of " The Essay," remarks, that Berruyer, in his entire work, does not cite one authority either from Fathers or theologians, although the Council of Trent (*Sess.* iv. *Dec. de Scrip. S.*) expressly prohibits the interpretation of the Sacred Writings, in a sense contrary to the generality of the Fathers. We now pass on to the examination of the next error— a most pernicious and enormous one.

SEC. III.—BERRUYER SAYS THAT IT WAS THE HUMANITY ALONE OF CHRIST THAT OBEYED, PRAYED, AND SUFFERED, AND THAT HIS OBLATIONS, PRAYERS, AND MEDITATIONS, WERE NOT OPERATIONS PROCEEDING FROM THE WORD, AS A PHYSICAL AND EFFICIENT PRINCIPLE, BUT THAT, IN THIS SENSE, THEY WERE ACTIONS MERELY OF HIS HUMANITY.

26. BERRUYER says that the operations of Jesus Christ were not produced by the Word, but merely by his humanity, and that the hypostatic union in no wise tended to render the human nature of Christ a complete principle of the actions physically and supernaturally performed by him. Here are his words: " Non sunt operationes a Verbo elicitæ . . . . sunt operationes totius humani-

---

(10) Berruyer, *t.* 8, *p.* 66.

tatis" (1). He had already written (2): " Ad complementum autem naturæ Christi humanæ, in ratione principii agentis, et actiones suas physice sive supernaturaliter producentis, unio hypostatica nihil omnino contulit." In another passage he says that all the propositions regarding Christ, in the Scriptures, and especially in the New Testament, are directly and primarily verified in the Man-God, or, in other words, in the humanity of Christ, united to the Divinity, and completed by the Word in the unity of Person, and this, he says, is the natural interpretation of Scripture: " Dico insuper, omnes et singulas ejusdem propositiones, quæ sunt de Christo Jesu in Scripturis sanctis, præsertim Novi Testamenti, semper et ubique verificari directe et primo in homine Deo, sive in humanitate Christi, Divinitati unita et Verbo, completa in unitate personæ . . . . . Atque hæc est simplex obvia, et naturalis, Scripturas interpretandi methodus," &c. (3).

27. In fine, he deduces from this, that it was the humanity alone of Christ that obeyed, and prayed, and suffered—that alone was endowed with all the gifts necessary for operating freely and meritoriously, by the Divine natural and supernatural cohesion (*concursus*) : " Humanitas sola obedivit Patri, sola oravit, sola passa est, sola ornata fuit donis et dotibus omnibus necessariis ad agendum libere et meritorie (4). Jesu Christi oblatio, oratio, et mediatio non sunt operationis a Verbo elicitæ tamquam a principio physico et efficiente, sed in eo sensu sunt operationes solius humanitatis Christi in agendo, et merendo per concursum Dei naturalem et supernaturalem completæ" (5). By this Berruyer deprives God of the infinite honour he received from Jesus Christ, who, being God, equal to the Father, became a servant, and sacrificed himself. He also deprives the merits of Jesus Christ of their infinite value, as they were the operations of his humanity alone, according to him, and not performed by the Person of the Word, and, consequently, he destroys that hope which we have in those infinite merits. Besides, he does away with the strongest motive we have to love our Redeemer, which is the consideration that he, being God, and it being impossible that he could suffer as God, took human flesh, that he might die and suffer for us, and thus satisfy the Divine justice for our faults, and obtain for us grace and life everlasting. But what is more important even, as the Roman Censor says, if it was the humanity of Christ alone which obeyed, prayed, and suffered, and if the oblations, prayers, and mediation of Christ were not the operations of the Word, but of his humanity alone, it follows that the humanity of Christ had subsistence of its own, and, consequently, the human Person of Christ was distinct from the Word, and that would make two Persons.

(1) Berruyer, *t.* 8, *p.* 53.   (2) Idem. *p.* 22.   (3) Idem. *p.* 18, 19.   (4) Berruyer, *t.* 8, *p.* 20, 21, & 23.   (5) Idem. *p.* 53.

28. Berruyer concludes the passage last quoted, " Humanitas sola obedivit," &c., by these words: " Ille (inquam) homo, qui hæc omnia egit, et passus est libere et sancte, et cujus humanitas in Verbo subsistebat, objectum est in recto immediatum omnium, quæ de Christo sunt, narrationem" (6). It was the man, then, in Christ, and not the Word, that operated: " Ille homo qui hæc omnia egit." Nor is that cleared up by what he says immediately after: " Cujus humanitas in Verbo subsistebat;" for he never gives up his system, but constantly repeats it in his Dissertations, and clothes it in so many curious and involved expressions, that it would be sufficient to turn a person's brain to study it. His system, as we have previously explained it, is, that Christ is not the Eternal Word, the Son, born of God the Father, but the Son, made in time by one God, subsisting in three Persons, who made him his Son by uniting him to the Divine Person; so that, rigorously speaking, he says he was formally constituted the Son of God, merely by that action which united him with the Divine Person: " Rigorose loquendo, per ipsam formaliter actionem unientem cum Persona Divina." He, therefore, says that God, by the action of uniting the humanity of Christ with the Word, formed the second filiation, and caused Christ-Man to become the Son of God, so that, according to his opinion, the union of the Word with the humanity of Christ was, as it were, a means to make Christ become the Son of God. All this, however, is false, for when we speak of Jesus Christ, we cannot say that that man, on account of being united with a Divine Person, was made by the Trinity the Son of God in time; but we are bound to profess that God, the Eternal Word, is the Son, born of the Father from all eternity, born of the substance of the Father, as the Athanasian Creed says, " God, of the substance of the Father, born before all ages," for, otherwise, he never could be called the natural Son of God. He it is who, uniting to himself humanity in unity of Person, has always sustained it, and he it is who performed all operations, who, notwithstanding that he was equal to God, emptied himself, and humbled himself to die on a cross in that flesh which he assumed.

29. Berruyer's whole error consists in supposing the humanity of Christ to be a subject subsisting in itself, to which the Word was subsequently united. Faith and reason, however, would both teach him that the humanity of Christ was accessary to the Word which assumed it, as St. Augustin (7) explains: " Homo autem, quia in unitatem personæ accessit Verbo Anima et Caro." Berruyer, however, on the contrary, says that the Divinity of the Word was accessary to the humanity; but he should have known, as Councils and Fathers teach, that the humanity of Jesus Christ did not exist until the Word came to take flesh. The Sixth Council (*Act* 11) reproved Paul of Samosata, for teaching, with

(6) Berruyer, *t.* 8, *p.* 53 & 95.   (7) St. Augus. in Euchirid. *c.* 35.

Nestorius, that the humanity of Christ existed previous to the Incarnation. Hence, the Council declared: "Simul enim caro, simul Dei Verbi caro fuit; simul animata rationabiliter, simul Dei Verbi caro animata rationabiliter." St. Cyril (8), in his Epistle to Nestorius, which was approved of by the Council of Ephesus, writes: " Non enim primum vulgaris quispiam homo ex Virgine ortus est, in quem Dei Verbum deinde Se dimiserit; sed in ipso utero carni unitum secundum carnem progenitum dicitur, utpote suæ carnis generationem sibi ut propriam vindicans." St. Leo the Great (9), reprobating the doctrine of Eutyches, that Jesus Christ alone, previous to the Incarnation, was in two natures, says: " Sed hoc Catholicæ mentes auresque non tolerant..........natura quippe nostra non sic assumpta est, ut prius creata postea sumeretur sed ut ipsa assumptione crearetur." St. Augustin, speaking of the glorious union of the humanity of Christ with the Divinity, says: " Ex quo esse Homo cœpit, non aliud cœpit esse Homo, quam Dei Filius" (10). And St. John of Damascus (11) says: "Non quemadmodum quidam falso prædicant, mens ante carnem ex Virgine assumptam Deo Verbo copulata est, et tum Christi nomen accepit."

30. Berruyer, however, does not agree with Councils or Fathers, for all the passages of Scripture, he says, which speak of Jesus Christ are directly verified in his humanity united to the Divinity: " Dico insupere omnes propositiones quæ sunt de Christo in Scripturis......verificari directe et primo in homine Deo, sive in humanitate Christi Divinitati unita," &c. (12). So that the primary object of all that is said regarding Christ is, according to him, Man-God, and not God-Man: ." Homo-Deus, non similiter Deus-homò objectum primarium," &c. ; and again, as we have already seen that Jesus Christ was formally constituted the natural Son of God, solely by that act which united him to the Word: " Per ipsam formaliter actionem unientem Jesus Christus constituitur tantum Filius Dei naturalis." This, however, is totally false, for Jesus Christ is the natural Son of God, not on account of the act which united him to the Word, but because the Word, who is the natural Son of God, as generated by the Father from all eternity, assumed the humanity of Christ, and united it to himself in the unity of Person. Berruyer then imagines that the humanity was the primary object *in recto*, and self-subsisting, to whom the Word was united, and that by this union Christ-Man was subsequently made the Son of God in time. Hence, he says, that the humanity alone obeyed, prayed, and suffered: and it was that man (Christ), he says, who did all those things: " Ille (inquam) homo qui hæc omnia egit.....objectum est in recto immediatum eorum, quæ de Christo sunt," &c. In this, however, he is wrong. Faith

(8) St. Cyril. Ep. 2, ad Nestor. (9) St. Leo, Ep. ad Julian. (10) St. Aug. in Euchir. c. 36. (11) St. Jo. Dam. *l.* 4 Fide orth. *c.* 6. (12) Berruyer, *t.* 8, *p.* 18.

tells us that we ought to regard as the primary object, the Eternal Word, who assumed the humanity of Christ, and united it to himself hypostatically in one Person, and thus the soul and body of Jesus Christ became the proper soul and body of the Word. When the Word, St. Cyril says, assumed a human body, that body was no longer strange to the Word, but was made his own: " Non est alienum a Verbo corpus suum" (13). This is what is meant by the words of the Creed; " He came down from heaven, and was incarnate, and was made man." Hence we, following the Creed, say God was made man, and not as Berruyer says, man was made God; for this mode of expression would lead us to think that man, already subsisting, was united with God, and we should then, as Nestorius did, suppose two Persons in Christ; but Faith teaches us that God was made man by taking human flesh, and thus there is but one Person in Christ, who is both God and man. Neither is it lawful to say (as St. Thomas instructs us) (14), with Nestorius, that Christ was assumed by God as an instrument to work out man's salvation, since, as St. Cyril, quoted by St. Thomas, teaches, the Scripture will have us to believe that Jesus Christ is not an instrument of God, but God in reality, made man: " Christum non tanquam instrumenti officio assumptum dicit Scriptura, sed tanquam Deum vere humanatum."

31. We are bound to believe that there are in Christ two distinct natures, each of which has its own will and its own proper operations, in opposition to the Monothelites, who held that there was but one will and one operation in Christ. But, on the other hand, it is certain that the operations of the human nature of Jesus Christ were not mere human operations, but, in the language of the schools, *Theandric*, that is, Divine-human, and chiefly divine, for although, in every operation of Christ, human nature concurred, still all was subordinate to the Person of the Word, which was the chief and director of all the operations of the humanity. The Word, says Bossuet, presides in all; the Word governs all; and the Man, subject to the direction of the Word, has no other movements but Divine ones; whatever he wishes and does is guided by the Word (15). St. Augustin says that as in us the soul governs the body, so in Jesus Christ the Word governed his humanity: " Quid est homo?" says the Saint; "anima habens corpus. Quid est Christus? Verbum Dei habens hominem." St. Thomas says: " Ubicunque sunt plura agentia ordinata, inferius movetur a superiori......Sicut autem in homine puro corpus movetur ab animo......ita in Domino Jesu Christo humana natura movebatur et regebatur a Divina" (16). All, then, that Berruyer states on the subject is totally false: " Humanitas sola obedivit Patri, sola passa est, Jesu Christi oblatio, oratio, et mediato non sunt operationes a

(13) St. Cyr. Epist. ad Nestor. (14) St. Thom. 3 p. qu. 2, ar. 6, ad 4. (15) Bossuet, Diss. Histor. p. 2. (16) St. Thom. p. 3, q. 19, a. 1.

Verbo elicitæ tanquam a principio physico et efficiente. Ad complementum naturæ Christi humanæ in ratione principii producentis, et actiones suas sive physice sive supernaturaliter agentis, nihil omnino contulit unio hypostatica." If, as the Roman Censor says, it was the humanity alone of Christ that obeyed, prayed, and suffered; and if the oblation, prayers, and mediation of Jesus Christ were not operations elicited by the Word, but by his humanity alone, so that the hypostatic union had, in fact, added nothing to the humanity, for the completion of the principle of his operations, it follows that the humanity of our Redeemer operated by itself, and doing so must have had subsistence proper to itself, and a proper personality distinct from the Person of the Word, and thus we have, as Nestorius taught, two Persons in Christ.

32. Such, however, is not the fact. All that Jesus Christ did the Word did, which sustained both natures, and as God could not suffer and die for the salvation of mankind, he, as the Council of Lateran said, took human flesh, and thus became passible and mortal: " Qui cum secundum Divinitatem sit immortalis et impassibilis, idem ipse secundum humanitatem factus est mortalis et passibilis." It was thus that the Eternal Word, in the flesh he assumed, sacrificed to God his blood and his life itself, and being equal to God became a mediator with God, as St. Paul says, speaking of Jesus Christ: " In whom we have redemption through his blood, the remission of sins; who is the image of the invisible God..... for in him were all things created in heaven and on earth...... Because in him it has well pleased the Father that all fulness should dwell," &c. (Col. i. 13). According to St. Paul, then, it is Jesus Christ who created the world, and in whom the plentitude of the Divinity dwells.

33. One of Berruyer's apologists says, however, that when his master states, that the humanity alone of Christ obeyed, prayed, and suffered, that he then speaks of this humanity as the physical principle *Quo*, that is, the medium by which he operates, and this physical principle belonged to the humanity alone, and not to the Word, for it is through his humanity that he suffered and died. But we answer, that the humanity, as the principle, *Quo*, could not act of itself in Christ, unless put in motion by the principle, *Quod*—that is, the Word, which was the one only Person, which sustained the two natures. He it was who principally performed every action in the assumed humanity, although it was by means of that he suffered, prayed, and died. That being the case, how can Berruyer be defended, when he says that it was the humanity alone which prayed and suffered? How could he say that the oblations, prayers, and mediation of Christ were operations elicited by the Word? And, what is even of greater consequence, how could he say that the hypostatic union had no influence on the actions of Christ—Nihil omnino contulit unio hypostatica? I said already

that the Word was the principal agent in all operations. But, say those of the other side: Then, the humanity of Christ performed no operations? We answer that the Word did all; for, though the humanity might also act, still, as the Word was the sole Person sustaining and completing this humanity, he (the Word) performed every operation both of the soul and body, for both body and soul, by the unity of Person, became his own. Everything, then, which Jesus Christ did—his wishes, actions, and sufferings—all belonged to the Word, for it was he who determined everything, and his obedient humanity consented and executed it. Hence it is that every action of Christ was holy and of infinite value, and capable of procuring every grace, and we are, therefore, bound to praise him for all.

34. The reader, then, should totally banish from his mind the false idea which Berruyer (as the author of the "Essay" writes) wished to give us of Christ, that the humanity was a being, existing of itself, to whom God united one of his Sons by nature; for, as will be seen, by referring back to *N*. 11, there must have been, according to him, two natural Sons—one, generated by the Father from all eternity; the other, in time, by the whole Trinity; but, then, Jesus Christ, as he teaches, was not, properly speaking, the Word made incarnate, according to St. John—" The Word was made flesh"—but was the other Son of God, made in time. This, however, is not the doctrine of the Holy Fathers; they unanimously teach that it was the Word. St. Jerome writes: " Anima et Caro Christi cum Verbo Dei una Persona est, unus Christus" (17). Sr. Ambrose (18), showing that Jesus Christ spoke sometimes according to his Divine, and, at other times, according to his human nature, says: " Quasi Deus sequitur Divina, quia Verbum est, quasi homo dicit humana." Pope Leo says: " Idem est qui mortem subiit, et sempiternus esse non desiit"(19). St. Augustin says: " Jesus Christus Dei Filius est, et Deus, et homo. Deus ante omnia secula, homo in nostro seculo. Deus quia Dei Verbum, Deus enim erat Verbum: homo autem, quia in unitatem personæ accessit Verbo Anima, et Caro..... Non duo Filii, Deus, et homo, sed unus Dei Filius" (20). And, in another place (*cap*. 36): Ex quo homo esse cœpit, non aliud cœpit esse homo, quam Dei Filius, et hoc unicus, et propter Deum Verbum, quod illo suscepto caro factum est, utique Deus..... ut sit Christus una persona, Verbum et homo." The rest of the Fathers speak the same sentiments; but it would render the Work too diffuse to quote any more.

35. The Holy See, then, had very good reasons for so rigorously and so frequently condemning Berruyer's Book; for it not alone contains many errors, in opposition to the doctrines of the Church,

---

(17) St. Hieron. Tract. 49, in Joan. (18) St. Ambr. ap. St. Leon, in Ep. 134.
(19) St. Leo, Serm. 66.   (20) St. Augu. in Euchirid. *c*. 35.

but is, besides, most pernicious, because it makes us lose that proper idea we should have of Jesus Christ. The Church teaches that the Eternal Word—that is, the only natural Son of God (for he had but one natural Son, who is, therefore, called the only-begotten, born of the substance of God the Father, the first Person of the Trinity), was made man, and died for our salvation. Berruyer, on the contrary, would have us to believe that Jesus Christ is not the Word, the Son, born of the Father from all eternity, but another Son, which only he and Hardouin knew anything about, or, rather, dreamed of, who, if their ideas were founded in fact, would have the name alone, and the honour of being called the Son of God; for, in order that Jesus Christ should be the true natural Son of God, it was requisite that he should be born of the substance of the Father, but the Christ, according to Berruyer, was made in time by the whole Trinity. The whole idea, then, we had hitherto formed of our Redeemer is totally changed. We considered him to be God, who, for our salvation, humbled himself to take human flesh, in order to suffer and die for us; whereas Berruyer represents him to us, not as a God made man, but as a man made the Son of God, on account of the union established between the Word and his Humanity. Jesus Christ crucified is the greatest proof of God's love to us, and the strongest motive we have to induce, nay, as St. Paul says, to force us, to love him—" For the charity of Christ presseth us" (2 Cor. v. 14)—is to know that the Eternal Word, equal to the Father, and born of the Father, emptied himself, and humbled himself to take human flesh, and die on a cross for us; but, according to Berruyer's system, this proof of Divine love to us, and this most powerful motive for us to love him, falls to the ground. And, in fine, to show how different are Berruyer's errors from the truth taught by the Church: The Church tells us to believe that Jesus Christ is God, made man, who, for us, suffered and died, in the flesh he assumed, and who assumed it solely to enable him to die for our love. Berruyer tells us, on the contrary, that Jesus Christ is only a man, who, because he was united by God to one of the Divine Persons, was made by the Trinity the natural Son of God, and died for the salvation of mankind; but, according to Berruyer, he did not die as God, but as man, and could not be the Son of God at all, according to his ideas; for, in order to be the natural Son of God, he should have been born of the substance of the Father, but, according to Berruyer, he was a being *ad extra*, produced by the whole Trinity, and if he was thus an external product, he could not have been anything but a mere creature; consequently, he must admit two distinct Persons in Christ—one Divine, and one human. In fine, if we held this man's doctrine, we could not say that God " loved us, and delivered himself up for us" (Ephes. v. 2); for, according to him, it was not the Word " who delivered himself up for us," but the humanity of Christ, honoured, indeed, by the union with the Word, that alone it was which suffered, and was subjected to death. Let him keep these opinions to himself, however, for every faithful Catholic will say, with Saint Paul: "I live in the faith of the Son of God, who loved me, and delivered himself for me" (Gal. ii. 20). And we will praise and love with all our hearts that God who, being God, made himself man, to suffer and die for every one of us.

36. It is painful to witness the distortion of Scripture which Berruyer has recourse to in every part of his work, but more especially in his Dissertations, to accommodate it to his false system, that Jesus Christ was the Son of one God, subsisting in three Persons. We have already (*N.* 7) quoted that text of St. Paul (Phil. ii. 5, &c.): "Let this mind be in you which was also in Christ Jesus, who, being in the form of God, thought it not robbery to be equal with God, but emptied himself, taking the form of a servant," &c. Here is conclusive evidence to prove that the Word, equal to the Father, emptied himself, by taking the form of a servant, in becoming man. Berruyer says, on the contrary, that it was not the Word, not the Divine nature, which humbled itself, but the human, conjoined with the Divine nature: " Humiliat sese natura humana naturæ Divinæ physice conjuncta." To consider the Word humbled to become incarnate, and die on the cross, would, he says, be degrading the Divinity; it should, therefore, he says, be only understood according to the communication of the idioms, and, consequently, as referring to the actions of Christ after the hypostatic union, and, therefore, he says it was his humanity that was humbled. But in that case we may well remark, what is there wonderful in the humiliation of humanity before God? That prodigy of love and mercy which God exhibited in his Incarnation, and which astonished both heaven and earth, was when the Word, the only-begotten Son of God, equal to the Father, emptied himself (*exinanivit*), in becoming man, and, from God, became the servant of God, according to the flesh. It is thus all Fathers and Catholic Doctors understand it, with the exception of Berruyer and Hardouin; and it is thus the Council of Chalcedon, also (*Act.* V.), declared that the Son of God, born of the Father, before all ages, became incarnate in these latter days (*novissimis diebus*), and suffered for our salvation.

37. We will take a review of some other texts. St. Paul (Heb. i. 2) says, that God " in these days hath spoken to us by his Son ......by whom he also made the world." All the Fathers understand this, as referring to the Word, by whom all things were created, and who was afterwards made man; but Berruyer explains the passage, " By whom he also made the world," thus: In consideration of whom God made the world. He explains the text of St. John, " By him all things were made," in like manner, that in regard of him all things were made, so that he does not even admit

the Word to be the Creator. But hear St. Paul on the contrary. God, speaking to his Son, says: " Thy throne, O God, is for ever and ever...... In the beginning, O Lord, didst thou found the earth, and the works of thy hands are the heavens" (Heb. i. 8, 10). Here God does not say that he created the heavens and the earth in consideration or in regard of his Son, but that the Son himself created them; and hence St. Chrysostom remarks: " Nunquam profecto id asserturus, nisi conditorem Filium, non ministrum arbitraretur, ac Patri et Filio pares esse intelligeret dignitates."

38. David says: " The Lord hath said to me, thou art my Son; this day have I begotten thee" (Psalm, ii. 7). Berruyer says that the expression, " This day have I begotten thee," has no reference to the eternal generation, as all understand it, but to the generation in time, of which he is the inventor, when Jesus Christ was made in time the Son of one God, subsisting in three Persons. He thus explains the text, " This day have I begotten thee:" I will be your Father, and you will be my Son—that is, according to the second filiation, made by the one God in three Persons, as he imagines.

39. St. Luke says: " And, therefore, also the Holy which shall be born of thee shall be called the Son of God" (Luke, i. 35). Berruyer says that these words do not refer to Jesus Christ, as the Word, but as man; for the expression " Holy" is not adapted to the Word, but rather to humanity. All Doctors, however, understand by the Holy One, the Word, the Son of God, born before all ages. Bossuet sagaciously remarks, that the expression, " Holy," when it is only an adjective, properly speaking, is adapted to the creature; but when, as in the present case, it is a substantive, it means holiness essentially, which belongs to God alone.

40. St. Matthew (xxviii. 19) tells us that Christ said to his disciples: " Going, therefore, teach all nations, baptizing them in the name of the Father, and of the Son, and of the Holy Ghost." Berruyer says, then, that by the name of Father, the first Person of the Trinity is not meant, but the God of the Jews—that is, one God subsisting in three Persons; by the name of the Son, the Word is not understood, but Christ, as man, made the Son of God, by the act by which God united him to the Word. He says nothing at all about the Holy Ghost. Now, by this doctrine the sacrament of Baptism is not alone deranged, but totally abolished I may say; because, according to him, we would not be baptized at first in the name of the Father, but in the name of the Trinity, and Baptism, administered after this form, as all theologians hold, with St. Thomas, would be null and void (21). In the second place, we would not be baptized in the name of the real Son of God—that is, the Word who became incarnate, but in the name of that Son invented by Berruyer, made in time by the Trinity—a Son which never did nor

---

(21) St. Thomas, 3, *p. qu.* 60, *art.* 8.

ever can exist, because there never was, nor ever will be, any other natural Son of God, unless that only-begotten one, generated from all eternity from the substance of the Father, the principle, and first Person of the Trinity. The second generation, made in time, or, to speak more exactly, the Incarnation of the Word, did not make Christ the Son of God, but united him in one Person with the true Son of God; that did not give him a Father but merely a Mother, who begot him from her own substance. Rigorously speaking this cannot be called generation, for the generation of the Son of God is that alone which was from eternity. The humanity of Christ was not generated by God, but was created, and was begotten solely by the Virgin Mary. Berruyer says that the Blessed Virgin is the Mother of God by two titles—first, by begetting the Word, and secondly, by giving Christ his humanity, since, as he says, the union established between this humanity and the Word has caused Jesus Christ to be made the Son of God. Both reasons, however, are false, for first we cannot say that the Blessed Virgin begot the Word, for the Word had no Mother, but only a Father, that is God. Mary merely begot the Man, who was united in one Person with the Word, and it is on that account that she, the Mother of Man, is justly called the true Mother of God. His second reason is equally false, that the Blessed Virgin has contributed, with her substance, to make Jesus Christ become the Son of God, *one subsisting in three Persons*, for, as we have proved, this supposition is totally false, so that, by attributing thus two maternities to the Blessed Virgin, he does away with it altogether, for one destroys the other. Berruyer mangles several other texts, but I omit them not to weary the reader with such folly any longer.

SEC. IV.—THE MIRACLES WROUGHT BY JESUS CHRIST WERE NOT PERFORMED BY HIS OWN POWERS, BUT OBTAINED FROM HIS FATHER BY HIS PRAYERS.

41. BERRUYER says that Jesus Christ wrought his miracles in this sense alone, that he operated, with a beseeching power, by means of his prayers: " Miracula Christus efficit, non precatio.......prece tamen et postulatione........eo unice sensu dicitur Christus miraculorum effector." In another place he says that Christ, as the Son of God (but the Son in his sense—that is, of one God subsisting in three Persons), had a right, by his divinity, that his prayers should be heard. Remark the expression, " his prayers." Therefore, according to Berruyer, our Saviour did not work miracles by his own power, but obtained them from God by his prayers like any other holy man. This doctrine, however, once admitted, we should hold with Nestorius, that Christ was a mere human person, distinct from the Person of the Word, who, being God, equal to the Father, had no necessity of begging the Father to grant him power to work miracles, since he had all power himself. This error springs from

the former capital ones we have refuted—that is, that Christ is not the Word, but is that Son of God existing only in his imagination, his Son merely in name, made in time by God, *subsisting in three Persons*, and also that in Christ it was not the Word that operated, but his humanity alone: " Sola humanitas obedivit, sola passa est," &c.

42. He was just as much astray in this proposition that Christ wrought miracles merely by prayer and supplication as he was in his previous statements. St. Thomas, the prince of theologians, teaches " that Christ wrought miracles by his own power, and not by prayer, as others did" (1). And St. Cyril says that he proved, by the very miracles he wrought, that he was the true Son of God, since he performed them not by the power of another, but by his own: " Non accipiebat alienam virtutem." Only once, says St. Thomas (2), did he show that he obtained from his Father the power to work miracles, that was in the resurrection of Lazarus, when imploring the power of his Father, he said: " I know that thou hearest me always, but because of the people who stand about have I said it, that they may believe that thou hast sent me" (John, xi. 42). But, as the holy Doctor remarks, he did this for our instruction, to show us that in our necessities we should have recourse to God as he had. St. Ambrose then tells us not to imagine, from this fact of Lazarus, that our Saviour prayed to his Father for power to perform the miracle, as if he had not power to work it himself; that prayer, he says, was intended for our instruction: " Noli insidiatrices aperire aures, ut putes Filium, Dei quasi infirmum rogare, ut impetret quod implere non possit.......ad præcepta virtutis suæ nos informat exemplo" (3). St. Hilary says just the same; but he also assigns another reason: Christ, he says, did not require to pray, but he did so to make us believe that he was in reality the Son of God: "Non prece eguit, pro nobis, oravit, ne Filius ignoraretur" (4).

43. St. Ambrose (5) remarks, that when Jesus Christ wished, he did not pray, but commanded, and all creatures obeyed—the sea, the winds, and diseases. He commanded the sea to be at rest, and it obeyed: " Peace, be still" (Mark, iv. 39). He commanded that disease should leave the sick, and they were made whole: " Virtue went out from him, and healed all" (Luke, vi. 19). He himself tells us that he could do, and did, everything equal to his Divine Father: " For whatsoever things he (the Father) doth, these the Son also doth in like manner.......For as the Father raiseth up the dead, and giveth life, so the Son also giveth life to whom he will" (John, v. 19, 21). St. Thomas says (6) that the miracles alone which Christ wrought were sufficient to make manifest the Divine

(1) St. Thomas, 3, *p. q.* 44, *art.* 4.   (2) Idem, ibid. *qu.* 21, *art.* 1, ad. 1.   (3) St. Ambros. in Luc.   (4) St. Hilar. *l.* 10, de Trinit.   (5) St. Ambros. *l.* 3, de Fide, *c.* 4.   (6) St. Thom. 3, *p. q.* 43, *art.* 4.

power which he possessed: "Ex hoc ostendebatur, quod haberet virtutem coæqualem Deo Patri." This was what our Lord said to the Jews when they were about to stone him: "Many good works have I showed from my Father, for which of those works do you stone me?" The Jews answered him: "For a good work we stone thee not, but for blasphemy, and because that thou, being a man, maketh thyself God." Jesus answered them: "You say, thou blasphemest, because I said I am the Son of God. If I do not the works of my Father, believe me not; but if I do, though you will not believe me, believe the works," &c. (John, x. 32, &c.) We have said enough on this subject.

SEC. V.—THE HOLY GHOST WAS NOT SENT TO THE APOSTLES BY JESUS CHRIST, BUT BY THE FATHER ALONE, AT THE PRAYER OF CHRIST.

44. BERRUYER says that the Holy Ghost was not sent to the Apostles by Jesus Christ, but by the Father, at his prayer: "Ad orationem Jesu Christi, quæ voluntatis ejus efficacis signum erit, mittet Pater Spiritum Sanctum. Quæ quasi raptim delibavimus de Jesu Christo missuro Spiritum Sanctum, quatenus homo Deus est Patrem rogaturus."

45. This error is also a necessary consequence of the former ones; that is, Jesus Christ, the Word, did not operate, but the humanity alone, or the Man made the Son of one God subsisting in three Persons, by reason of the union of the Person of the Word with the humanity; and from this false supposition he deduces this present falsehood, that the Holy Ghost was not sent by Jesus Christ, but by the Father, at the prayer of Jesus Christ. If he said that the Holy Ghost does not proceed from the Word, but from the Father alone, he would fall into the Greek heresy already refuted (*Ref.* iv.); but he rather leans to the heresy of Nestorius, who, admitting two Persons in Christ, a Divine and a human Person, said, consequently, that the Divine Person dwelling in Jesus Christ, together with the Father, sent the Holy Ghost; and the human Person in Christ obtained from the Father, by his prayers, that the Holy Spirit should be sent. Berruyer does not expressly say this; but when he asserts that the Holy Ghost was not sent by Jesus Christ, only by his prayer alone, he appears to believe, either that there is no Divine Person in Christ at all, or that there are two Persons—one Divine, which sends, of himself, the Holy Ghost; the other human, which obtains, by his prayers, that he may be sent. He shows that that is his opinion, when he says that in Jesus Christ it was the humanity alone that acted and suffered, that is, the Man alone made in time the Son of God by the whole three Persons. This was not, certainly, the Word who was born of the Father alone before all ages. But the word, he says, was already united to the humanity of Christ in unity of Person; but then we should remember, that according to

2 R

his opinion the Word had nothing to do, for it was only the humanity that acted in Christ. That being the case, of what service was the union of the Word in unity of Person with the humanity? Merely, as he said, that by means of the hypostatic union Christ might be made the Son of God, of the three Divine Persons; and hence, he says, the operations of Christ were not elicited by the Word, but merely by his humanity, and the hypostatic union gave no value to his actions: " in ratione principii agentis..... unio hypostatica nihil omnino contulit."

46. With what face could Berruyer assert that the Holy Ghost was not sent by Jesus Christ, when he himself several times said he was, and promised his Apostles that he would send them the Paraclete: " But when the Paraclete cometh, whom I will send you from the Father, the Spirit of truth, who proceedeth from the Father" (John, xv. 26); " For if I go not, the Paraclete will not come to you; but if I go, I will send him to you" (John, xvi. 7). Listen to this! Christ says that he sent the Holy Ghost; and Berruyer says that the Holy Ghost was not sent by him, but only at his prayer. Perhaps he will argue that Christ himself said: " I will ask the Father, and he shall give you another Paraclete" (John, xiv. 16). But we answer with St. Augustin, that Christ then spoke as man; but when he spoke as God, he said not once, but several times, " whom I will send to you." And again he says: " The Paraclete, the Holy Ghost, whom the Father will send in my name, he will teach you all things" (John, xiv. 26). St. Cyril, explaining this text, says, " in my name," that is, by me, because he proceeds from me. It is certain the Holy Ghost could not be sent unless by the Divine Persons alone, who were his Principle, the Father and the Son. If, then, he was sent by Jesus Christ, there can be no doubt that he was sent by the Word, who operated in Jesus Christ, and the Word being equal to the Father, and with the Father, *co-principle* of the Holy Ghost, had no necessity to pray to the Father (as Berruyer says) that he might be sent; for as the Father sent him, so did he likewise.

SEC. VI —OTHER ERRORS OF BERRUYER ON DIFFERENT SUBJECTS.

47. Those writers who have refuted Berruyer's work remark several other errors which, though they may not be clearly opposed to Faith, still, in my opinion, are most extravagant, and totally opposed to the general opinion of Fathers and theologians. I will here refute some of the most strange and reprehensible.

48. In one place he says: " Revelatione deficiente, cum nempe Deus ob latentes causas eam nobis denegare vult, non est cur non teneamur saltem objecta credere, quibus religio naturalis fundatur." Speaking here of the revelation of the mysteries of the Faith, he says, that should no such revelation be made to us, we are, at all events,

obliged to believe those objects on which natural religion is based. And then he assigns the reasons subsequently: "Religio pure naturalis, si Deus ea sola contentus esse voluisset, propriam fidem, ac revelationem suo habuisset modo, quibus Deus ipse in fidelium cordibus, et animo inalienabilia jura sua exercuisset." Now the extravagance of this doctrine is only equalled by the confused manner in which it is stated. It would appear that he admits that true believers can be found professing mere natural religion alone, which, according to him, has, in a certain way, its own faith, and its own revelation. Then in mere natural religion there must be a faith and revelation with which God is satisfied. But, says Berruyer's friend, he intends this a mere hypothesis; but this does not render it less objectionable, for it would lead us to believe that God would be satisfied with a religion purely natural, without faith in the merits of Jesus Christ, and sufficient to save its professors. St. Paul answers this, however, for he says: "Then Christ died in vain" (Gal. ii. 21). If natural religion be sufficient to save those who neither believe nor hope in Jesus Christ, then he died in vain for man's salvation. St. Peter, on the contrary, says that salvation can only be obtained in Christ: "Neither is there salvation in any other. For there is no other name under heaven given to men whereby we must be saved" (Acts, iv. 12). If any infidels, either under the New or Old Law have been saved, it has only been because they knew the grace of the Redeemer, and hence St. Augustin says that it was granted to no person to live according to God, and save his soul, to whom Jesus Christ has not been revealed, either as promised or already come: "Divinitus autem provisum fuisse non dubito, ut ex hoc uno sciremus etiam per alias Gentes esse potuisse, qui secundum Deum vixerunt, eique placuerunt, pertinentes ad spiritualem Jerusalem: quod nemini concessum fuisse credendum est, nisi cui divinitus revelatus est unus Mediator Dei, et hominum homo Christus Jesus, qui venturus in carne sic antiquis Sanctis prænunciabatur, quemadmodum nobis venisse nuntiatus est" (1).

49. This is the faith required for the just man to live always united with God: "The just man liveth by faith;" says the Apostle: "But that in the law no man is justified with God it is manifest, because the just man liveth by faith" (Gal. iii. 11). No one, says St. Paul, can render himself just in the sight of God, by the law alone, which imposes commandments, but gives no strength to fulfil them. Neither can we, since the fall of Adam, fulfil them merely by the strength of our free will; the assistance of grace is requisite, which we should implore from God, and hope for through the mediation of our Redeemer. "Ea quippe fides," says St. Augustin (2), "justos sanavit antiquos, quæ sanat, et nos, idest

(1) St. Aug. l. 18 de C. D. c. 17.   (2) St. Aug. de Nat. et Grat. p. 149.

Jesu-Christi, fides mortis ejus." In another passage he tells us the reason of this (3): " Quia sicut credimus nos Christum venisse, sic illi venturum; sicut nos mortuum, ita illa moriturum." Where the Jews went astray was in presuming, without prayer, or faith in a Mediator to came, to be able to observe the law imposed on them. When God commanded Moses to ask them if they wished to perform all that he would reveal to them, they answered: "All that the Lord hath spoken, we will do" (Exod. xix. 8). But after this promise our Lord said to them: " Who shall give them to have such a mind to fear me, and to keep all my commandments at all times?" (Deut. vi. 29.) They say that they desire to fulfil the commandments, but who will give them power to do so? By this God means that if they had the presumption to hope to fulfil them, without praying for Divine assistance, they could never accomplish it. Hence it was that immediately after they forsook the Lord, and adored the golden calf.

50. The Gentiles, who, by power of their own wills alone expected to make themselves just, were even more blind than the Jews. What more has Jupiter, says Seneca, than other good men, only a longer life? " Jupiter quo antecedit virum bonum? diutius bonus est. Sapiens nihilo se minoris æstimat, quod virtutes ejus spatio breviore clauduntur" (4). And again he says Jupiter despises worldly things, because he can make no use of them, but the wise man depises them, because it is his will to do so: " Jupiter uti illis non potest, Sapiens non vult" (5). A wise man, he says, is like a God in everything, only that he is mortal: " Sapiens, excepta mortalitate, similis Deo" (6). Cicero said we could not glory in virtue, if it was given to us by God: " De virtute recte gloriamur, quod non contingeret, si id donum a Deo, non a nobis, haberemus" (7). And again he says: " Jovem optimum maximum appellant, non quod nos justos, sapientes efficiat, sed quod incolumes, opulentos," &c. See here the pride of those wise men of the world, who said that virtue and wisdom belonged to themselves, and did not come from God.

51. It was this presumption which blinded them more and more every day. The most learned among their sages, their philosophers, as they had a greater share of pride, were the most blind, and although the light of nature taught them to know that there was but one God, the Lord and Creator of all things, still, as the Apostle says, they did not avail themselves of it to thank and praise God as they ought: " Because that, when they knew God they have not glorified him as God, or given thanks: but became vain in their thoughts, and their foolish heart was darkened. For professing themselves to be wise they became fools" (Rom. i. 21). The

---

(3) St. Ang. de Nupt. et Concup. *l.* 2, *p* 113. (4) Seneca, Epist. 73. (5) Idem. de Constantia Sap. *c.* 8. (6) Idem. Epist. 53. (7) Cicero de Nat. Deor. *p.* 253.

presumption of their own wisdom increased their folly. Nay, so great was their blindness that they venerated as gods not only their fellow-mortals, but the beasts of the field: "And they changed the glory of the incorruptible God into the likeness of the image of a corruptible man, and of birds and four-footed beasts and of creeping things" (*ver.* 22.) Hence it was that God deservedly abandoned them to their own wicked desires, and they slavishly obeyed their most brutal and detestable passions: "Wherefore God gave them up to the desires of their heart, unto uncleanness," &c. (*ver.* 24.) The most celebrated among the ancient sages is Socrates, who, it is said, was persecuted by the idolaters, for teaching that there was but one supreme God, and still he called them who accused him of not adoring the gods of his country calumniators, and ordered his disciple Xenophon before his death to sacrifice a cock he had in his house, in honour of Esculapius. St. Augustin tells us (8) that Plato thought sacrifices ought to be offered to a multiplicity of gods. The most enlightened among the Gentiles, the great Cicero, though he knew there was only one supreme God, still wished that all the gods recognized in Rome should be adored. Such is the wisdom of the sages of Paganism, and such is the faith and natural religion of the Gentiles which Berruyer exalts so much that he says that it could, without the knowledge of Jesus Christ, make people good and innocent, and adopted children of God.

52. We now proceed to examine the other foolish opinions of this work. He says: "Relate ad cognitiones explicitis, aut media necessaria, quæ deficere possent, ut eveherentur ad adoptionem filiorum, dignique fierent cœlorum remuneratione, præsumere debemus, quod viarum ordinariarum defectu in animabus rectis ac innocentibus bonus Dominus cui deservimus, attenta Filii sui mediatione, opus suum perficeret quibusdam omnipotentiæ rationibus, quas liberum ipsi est nobis haud detegere" (9). He says, then, that when the means necessary for salvation are wanting, we ought to presume that God will save the souls of the upright and innocent by certain measures of his omnipotence, which he has not revealed to us. What an immensity of folly in few words! He calls those souls upright and innocent who have no knowledge of the means necessary for salvation, and consequently, know nothing of the mediation of the Redeemer—a knowledge of which, as we have seen, has been, at all times, necessary for the children of Adam. Perhaps, these upright and innocent souls were created before Adam himself, for, if they were born after his fall, they are undoubtedly children of wrath. How, then, can they be exalted up to the adoption of the children of God, and, without faith in Jesus Christ (out of whom there is no salvation), and without baptism, enter into heaven, and enjoy the beatific vision

(8) St. Aug. de Civit. Del. *l.* 8, *c.* 12.   (9) Berruyer, *t.* 1, *p.* 58.

of God? We have always believed, and do still, that there is no other way of obtaining salvation, but by the mediation of Christ. He himself says: "I am the way, the truth, and the life" (John, xiv. 6). And again: "I am the door; by me, if any man go in, he shall be saved" (John, x. 9). St. Paul says: "For by him we have access to the Father" (Ephes. ii. 18). Burruyer, however, tells us that there is another way—a hidden one, by which God saves those upright souls who live in the religion of nature—a way, of which neither Scripture, Fathers, nor Ecclesiastical Writers tell us anything. All grace and hope of salvation is promised to mankind, through the mediation of Jesus Christ. If you read Selvaggi, the annotator of Mosheim (10), you will see that all the prophecies of the Old Testament, and even the historical facts narrated, all speak of this in a prophetic sense, as St. Paul says: "These things were done in a figure" (1 Cor. x. 6). Our Saviour himself proved to the disciples, in the journey to Emmaus, that all the Scriptures of the Old Law spoke of him: "Beginning at Moses and all the prophets, he expounded to them in all the Scriptures the things that were concerning him" (Luke, xxiv. 27). And still Berruyer says, that souls, under the law of nature, were adopted as children of God, without any knowledge of the mediation of Jesus Christ.

33. How could those persons obtain the adoption of the children of God without Jesus Christ, when it is he who has given to the faithful the power "to become the children of God." Berruyer says: "Quod adoptio prima, eaque gratuito, cujus virtute ab Adamo usque ad Christum, intuitu Christi venturi fideles omnes sive ex Israel, sive ex Gentibus facti sunt filii Dei, non dederit Deo nisi filios minores semper et parvulos usque ad tempus præfinitum a Patre. Vetus hæc itaque adoptio præparabat aliam, et novam quasi parturiebat adoptionem superioris ordinis." He then admits two adoptions—the first and the second. The latter is that which exists in the New Law; the former, that by which all those who have received the Faith among the Jews or Gentiles, in regard to the promised Messiah, and these were only, as it were, younger children of God, minors. This ancient adoption, he said, prepared, and, we may say, brought forth, another one of a superior order; but those who were adopted under this ancient one scarcely deserved to be named among the faithful: "Vix filiorum nomen obtinerent." It would take volumes to examine all the extravagant opinions and extraordinary crotchets of this writer, which were never heard of by theologians before. The adoption of the children of God, as St. Thomas says (11), gives them a right to a share in his birthright—that is, eternal beatitude. Now, supposing Berruyer's system to be true, as the ancient adoption was of an

(10) Selvag. in Mosh. vol. i n 61. (11) St. Thom 3 p q. 32, a. 1.

inferior order, we ask, would it give a right to entire beatitude, or only to an inferior or partial sort, corresponding to the adoption? It is quite enough to state such paradoxical opinions, and the reader will perceive that they refute themselves. The truth of the matter is, that there never was but one true religion, which never had any other object but God, nor no way of approaching to God unless through Jesus Christ. It is the blood of Jesus Christ which has taken away all the sins of the world, and saved all those who are saved, and it is the grace of Jesus Christ that has given children to God. Berruyer says, that the natural law inspired faith, hope, and charity. What folly! These divine virtues are gifts infused by God; and how, then, could they be inspired by the law of nature? Why, Pelagius himself never went so far as that.

54. In another place, he says: " Per annos quatuor mille quotquot fuerunt primogeniti, et sibi successerunt in hereditate nominis illius, *Filius Hominis*, debitum nascendo contraxerunt." And again: " Per Adami hominum Parentis, et Primogeniti lapsum oneratum est nomen illud, sancto quidem, sed pœnali debito satisfaciendi Deo in rigore justitiæ, et peccata hominum expiandi." Berruyer then says that, for four thousand years, the first-born were obliged to make satisfaction for the sins of mankind. This opinion would bear rather heavy on me, as I have the misfortune to be the first-born of my family, and it would be too hard that I should make atonement, not only for my own manifold sins, but also for the crimes of others. But can he tell us where this obligation is laid down. He appears to think that the law of nature imposed it: " Erat præceptum illud quantum ad substantiam naturale." But no one with a grain of sense will admit this to be a precept of the law of nature, when neither the Scriptures nor the Canons of the Church make any allusion to it. It is not, then, imposed by the law of nature, nor by any positive command of God, for all children of Adam, as well as the first-born, are born with the guilt of original sin (with the exception of our Lord and his Immaculate Mother), and all are equally bound to have themselves cleaned from this stain.

55. Berruyer leaves the first-born alone, then, and applies this new doctrine of his to our Lord. All those, he says, from whom Jesus Christ sprung, were first-born down to Joseph, and hence, in the person of Christ, by the succession inherited from St. Joseph, all the rights, and all the debts of his first-born ancestors were united; but as none of these could satisfy the Divine justice, the Saviour, who alone could do so, was bound to make satisfaction for all, for he was the chief among the first-born, and on that account, he says, he was called the Son of Man. This title, however, St. Augustin says, was applied to our Lord as a title of humility, and not of majority or obligation. As the Son of Man, then, he says,

he was the first-born among men; and as the Son of God, he was bound, according to the rigour of justice, to sacrifice himself to God for his glory, and the salvation of mankind: " Debitum contraxerat in rigore justitiæ fundatum, qui natus erat Filius hominis, homo Primogenitus simul Dei Unigenitus, ut se Pontifex idem, et hostia ad gloriam Dei restituendam, salutemque hominum redimendam Deo Patri suo exhiberet." Hence, he says that Christ, by a natural precept, was bound, *ex condigno*, to satisfy the Divine Justice by his Passion: " Offerre Se tamen ad satisfaciendum Deo ex condigno, et ad expiandum hominis peccatum, quo satis erat passione sua, Jesus Christus Filius hominis, et Filius Dei præcepto naturali obligabatur." Christ, therefore, he says, as the Son of Man, and the first-born of man, contracted a debt, obliging him, in rigorous justice, to atone to God, by his Passion, for the sins of mankind. We answer, that our Saviour could not, either as the Son of Man, or first born of man, contract this strict obligation to make satisfaction for mankind. He could not be obliged, as the Son of Man, for it would be blasphemous to assert that he incurred original sin: " Accepit enim hominem," says St. Thomas (12), "absque peccato." Neither could he be obliged to it, as the first-born among men. It is true, St. Paul calls him the first-born among many brethren; but we must understand in what sense the Apostle applies this term. The text says: " For whom he foreknew he also predestinated to be made conformable to the image of his Son, that he might be the first-born among many brethren" (Rom. viii. 29). The Apostle here instructs us, that those whom God has foreseen will be saved, he has predestined to be made like unto Jesus Christ, in holiness and patience, poor, despised, and persecuted like him on earth.

56. Berruyer, however, asserts, that according to strict justice Christ could not be the mediator of all mankind, if he was not at the same time Man-God, and the Son of God, and thus make full satisfaction for the sins of man. But St. Thomas says (13) that God could be satisfied in two ways in regard to man's sin, perfectly and imperfectly—perfectly, by the satisfaction given him by a Divine Person, such as was given him by Jesus Christ; imperfectly, by accepting the satisfaction which man himself could make, and which would be sufficient, if God wished to accept it. St. Augustin says those are fools who teach that God could save mankind in no other manner, unless by becoming man himself, and suffering all he did. He could do so if he wished, says the Saint; but then their folly would not be satisfied: " Sunt stulti qui dicunt: ' Non poterat aliter sapientia Dei homines liberare, nisi susciperet hominem, et a peccatoribus omnia illa pateretur. Quibus

---

(12) St. Thom. 3 *p. q.* 14, *a.* 3.   (13) St. Thom. *p.* 3, *ar.* 1, *ad.* 2.

dicimus, poterat omnino; sed si aliter faceret, similiter vestræ stultitiæ displiceret' "(14).

57. Such being the case, it is insufferable to hear Berruyer assert that Christ, as the Son of Man, and first-born of man, had contracted, in rigorous justice, the obligation of sacrificing himself to God, by dying for the satisfaction of man's sins, and obtaining salvation for them. It is true in another place he says that the Incarnation of the Son of God was not a matter of necessity, but merely proceeded from God's goodness alone; but then he contradicts himself (see *n*. 55). No matter what his meaning was, one thing is certain—that Christ suffered for us, not because he was obliged to do so by necessity, but of his own free will, because he voluntarily offered himself up to suffer and die for the salvation of mankind: " He was offered because it was his own will" (Isaias, liii. 7). He says himself: " I lay down my life......no man taketh it away from me, I lay it down of myself" (John, x. 17, 18). In that, says St. John, he shows the extraordinary love he bore to mankind, when he sacrificed even his life for them: " In this we have known the charity of God, because he hath laid down his life for us. This sacrifice of love was called his decease by Moses and Elias on the Mount of Thabor: " They spoke of his decease, which he should accomplish in Jerusalem."

58. I think I have said enough about Berruyer's errors; the chief and most pernicious of all, the first and third, I have rather diffusely refuted. In these the fanatical author labours to throw into confusion all that the Scriptures and Councils teach regarding the great mystery of the Incarnation, the foundation of Christianity itself, and of our salvation.

In conclusion, I protest that all tnat 1 nave written in this Work, and especially in the Refutation of Heresies, I submit to the judgment of the Church. My only glory is, that I am her obedient child, and as such I hope to live and die.

(14) St. August. lib. de Agone Christiano, *c*. 11.

END OF THE REFUTATION.

EXHORTATION TO CATHOLICS.

DEAR READER—Leave heretics in their wilful blindness—I mean wilful when they wish to live deceived—and pay no attention to the fallacies by which they would deceive you. Hold on by the sure and firm anchor of the Catholic Church, through which God has promised to teach us the true faith. We should place all our hope of eternal salvation in the mercy of God and the merits of Jesus Christ our Saviour, but still we should co-operate ourselves, by the observance of the Divine Commandments, and the practice of virtue, and not follow the opinion of the innovators, who say that faith alone in the merits of Jesus Christ will save us, without works; that God is the author both of all the good and all the evil we do; that salvation or damnation has been decreed for us from all eternity, and, consequently, we can do nothing to obtain the one or avoid the other. God tells us that he wishes all to be saved, and gives to all grace to obtain eternal salvation; he has promised to listen to those who pray to him, so that if we are lost, it is solely through our own fault. He also tells us that if we are saved it must be by those means of salvation which he has given us, the fulfilment of his holy law, the sacraments by which the merits of Christ are communicated to us, prayer, by which we obtain the grace we stand in need of; and this is the order of the decree of God's predestination or reprobation, to give eternal life to those who correspond to his grace, and to punish those who despise it.

The devil always strives to deceive heretics, by suggesting to them that they can be saved in their belief. This was what Theodore Beza said to St. Francis de Sales, when hard pressed by him on the importance of salvation: "I hope to be saved in my own religion." Unhappy hope! which only keeps them in error here, and exposes them to eternal perdition hereafter, when the error cannot be remedied. I think the danger of eternal perdition, by dying separated from the Church, should be a sufficient motive to convert every heretic. It was this that made Henry IV. forsake Calvinism, and become a Catholic. He assembled a conference of Catholics and Calvinists, and after listening for a time to their arguments, he asked the Calvinistic doctors if it was possible a person could be saved in the Catholic faith; they answered that it was; "Then," said the King, "if the faith of the Roman Church secures salvation, and the Reformed faith is at least doubtful, I will take the safe side and become a Catholic."

All the misfortunes of unbelievers spring from too great an attachment to the things of this life. This sickness of heart weakens and darkens the understanding, and leads many to eternal ruin. If they would try to heal their hearts by purging them of their vices, they would soon receive light, which would show them the necessity of joining the Catholic Church, where alone is salvation. My dear Catholics, let us thank the Divine goodness, who, among so many infidels and heretics, has given us the grace to be born and live in the bosom of the Holy Roman Catholic Church, and let us take heed and not be ungrateful for so great a benefit. Let us take care and correspond to the Divine graee, for if we should be lost (which God forbid), this very benefit of grace conferred on us would be one of our greatest torments in hell.

GENERAL INDEX.

Abelard, Life of, 228.
——— Errors of, 228.
——— opposed by St. Bernard, 229.
Acacius, his Death, 165.
Acemetic Monks, 172.
Acephali, 168.
Admiral, Lord High, executed, 341.
Adoption, none without Christ, 630.
Aerius, 100.
Agnoites, 169.
Agricola, 281.
Albigenses, 234.
——— Doctrines and practices of, 235.
——— Crusade against, 238.
——— condemned by the Fourth Council of Lateran, 239.
Alexander, St., Death of, 71.
Alexandrian Synod condemns Arius, 57.
Alkoran, 178.
Alva, Duke of, 312.
Amalric, his Errors, 240.
Amboise, Conspiracy of, 304.
Amour de St. William, 241.
Anabaptists, Tenets of, 284.
Anastatius, Emperor, 166.
——— his Death, 168.
Anastatius, Patriarch, an Iconoclast, 190.
Anathematisms of St. Cyril, 123.
Andrew, St. Calabita, 195.
Angelicals, 50.
Anglo-Calvinists, 325.
Anna Boleyn executed, 325.
Antidicomarianites, 99.
Antinomians, 281.
Antropomorphites, 103.
Antwerp, Calvinistic outbreak at, 312.
Apollinaris, his Heresy, 98.
——— Dispute with St. Ephraim, 99.
Apostolicals, 232.
Arian Heresy, Refutation of, 400.
Arius, 55.
——— condemned in Alexandria, 57.
——— banished, 66.
——— recalled, and horrible Death of, 69.
Arles, Synod of, 72.

Armenians, 326.
——— at the Council of Florence, 222.
Armogasies, 89.
Arnauld, Death of, 371.
Arnold of Brescia, 230.
——— excites a sedition in Rome, and is burned, 231.
Athanasius, St., 64.
——— persecutions endured by, 66.
Audœans, 103.
Augsburg, Diet of, 267.
Augustin, St., opposes Pelagius, 112.
"Augustinus," the famous book, 365.
——— sensation caused by, 366.

Baius opposed by the Franciscans, and condemned by the Sorbonne, 363.
——— attends the Council of Trent, 363.
——— condemned by St. Pius V. and Gregory XIII. 364.
——— condemned Propositions of, refuted, 563.
Ball, Coadjutor of Wickliffe, 245.
Bands, Methodist, 385.
Bardesanes, 42.
Bardus put to death, 208.
Barefooted Heretics, 193.
Barnaveldt beheaded, 326.
Basilides, 36.
Basnage impugns the Virginity of the Blessed Virgin, 106.
——— defends Nestorianism, 133.
Beatific Vision, Decree of the Council of Florence concerning, 221.
Beghards and Beguines, Errors of, 243.
Berengarius, Heresy of, 224.
——— Refutation of, 487.
——— condemned by Pope Leo IX. 225.
——— dies repentant, 226.
Berruyer's Errors and Refutation of, 597.
Bessarion, Cardinal, unites the Greeks and Latins, 222.
Beza, Character of, 306.
——— Conference with St. Francis de Sales, and Death, 308.

GENERAL INDEX.

Blandrata, 353.
Bonomolists, 102.
Bread and Wine, quantity to be consecrated, 509.
Brenzius, 282.
Boetius the Philosopher put to death, 92.

Bucer, his Errors, 294.
Bulgarians, Legates sent to, 208.

Cainites, 38.
Caiphas, Council of, 556.
Calvin's birth, 296.
—— flies to Angouleme, 298.
—— fixes his residence in Geneva, 300.
—— his Writings, 302.
—— gets Servetus burned, 303.
—— his Character and Death, 305.
—— his numerous Errors, 317.
Calvinism refuted, 514.
Calvinistic Mission to Brazil, 303.
—— Doctrine on the Eucharist, 495.
Campeggio Legate in England, 330.
Campion, Martyrdom of, 346.
Canon of Scripture, 558.
Carlostad attacks the Real Presence, 288.
—— breaks with Luther, 288.
—— marries, and composes a Mass on the occasion, 289.
—— his Death, 289.
Carpocrates, 37.
Catholics, Exhortation to, 634.
Celestius, a disciple of Pelagius, 111.
Centuriators of Magdeburg, 280.
Cerdonius, 39.
Cerularius, Michael, an opponent of the Roman Church, 215.
Chalcedon, Council of, 150.
—— Decisions of, 152, 153.
Chemnitz, Martin, the Prince of Protestant Theologians, 283.
Christ Church Hospital, 338.
Cleves, Anne of, a Lutheran, 336.
Concupiscence, 575.
Condemnation, awful, of Pyrrhus, by Pope Theodore, 184.
Confession of Augsburg, 279.
Confession of Sins among Methodists, 385.
"Conscience, Case of," Jansenist, 370.
Constans, Death of, 185.
Constantine, Death of, 69.
—— divides the Empire, 70.
Constantinople, Sixth General Council held in, 186.
—————— Eighth General Council held in, 210.
—————— Canons of, 211.
Consubstantial, the Word, 60.
"Consultum," the, 375.
Contemplation, what, 591.
Cromwell, Oliver, 317.
Cyril, St., Anathematisms of, 123.

Darnley, Henry, Death of, 314.
Delectatio Victrix, 577.
Denmark becomes Lutheran, 272.
Dioscorus, his infamous character, 142.
Diospolis, Council of, 112.
Distinction of the three Divine Persons proved, 391.
Doceti, 39.
Dominick, St., his labours, 237.
—— Miracles, 237.
Dominis, Mark Anthony de, 359.
—— his return to the Church, and Death, 359.
Donatists, 50.
—— refuted by St. Augustin, 52.
Donatus, two of that name, 50.

Ebion, 35.
Ecolampadius, his explanation of the words of consecration, 293.
Ecthesis of Heraclius, 182.
Eleurus an Eutychian, 157.
—— his Death, 160.
Elizabeth crowned as a Catholic, 344.
—— gets Parliament to establish Protestantism, 345.
—— her Death, 348.
Elvidius, Errors of, 104.
—— a heretic, 104.
England, early religious state of, 327.
English Reformation, 327.
Ephesus, Council of, condemns Nestorius, 126, 462.
Epiphanes, 39.
Eranistes, an Apollinarist, 98.
Erasmus, 257.
—— doubtful doctrine of, 257.
—— his death, 258.
Ethiopian Ambassadors to the Council of Florence, 222.
Eucharist, Matter and Form of, 509.
Eusebius of Dorileum accuses Eutyches, 137.
Eusebius an Arian, 62.
Eutyches condemned, 140.
—— appeals to the Pope, 140.
—— Death of, 155.
Eutychian Heresy, 136.
—— Refutation of, 470.
Eutychians, objections of, answered, 477.
Evagrius, 172.
"Exurge Domini," Bull of, 264.

Faith alone not sufficient, 520.
Faith, commencement of, from God, 451.
Father and Son, Holy Ghost proceeds from, 433.
Faustus Socinus, distich on, 359.
Felix I. at first a schismatic, 78.
Felix and Elipandus, 132.
—————— Refutation of their Errors, 465.
Fenelon's Maxims of the Saints, 379.

GENERAL INDEX.

First-born, the curious opinion concerning, 631.
Fisher takes the Oath of Supremacy, conditionally, 332.
—— put to death, 334.
Five Propositions of Jansenius, 366.
Flagellants, history of, 242.
Flavian, St., held a Synod against Eutychianism, 137.
—— Martyrdom of, 146.
Florence, Council of, 219.
—— Proceedings of, 439.
Folmar, 232.
Formula signed by Gallican Clergy, 369.
Formula of Sirmium, signed by Liberius, 77.
Francis de Sales, St., visits Beza, 308.
Franciscan Friars, 200 imprisoned by Henry VIII., 333.
Frankfort, Council of, 200.
Fratricelli, 242.
—— condemned by John XXII., 243.
Frederic, Elector, protects Luther, 266.
—— his Death, 270.
Free Will denied by Calvin, 320.
—— existence of, proved, 514.
—— two sorts of, 514.

Geneva, establishment of Calvinism in, 326.
Genseric persecutes the Catholics, 87.
Gentilis, Valentine, 351.
—— his Doctrine, 352.
—— Punishment and Death, 353.
George, Duke of Saxony, his opinion of the Reformation, 282.
German Catholics, 389.
Germanus, St., 189.
Gilbert de la Poree, 231.
—— his Errors, 231.
Gnostics, 37.
Godeschalcus, his Errors and Death, 117, 118.
—— Opinions of Authors concerning his Doctrine, 118.
Gomarists, 326.
Grace and Free Will, Pelagian Doctrine of, 110.
—— necessity of, 443.
—— gratuity of, 446.
Greek Church, curious custom regarding the Eucharist, 508.
Greek Heresy refuted, 433.
Greeks, objections of, answered, 440.
Gregory III., Letter of, to Leo the Iconoclast, 192.
Grey, Lady Jane, 342.
Guion, Madam, 379.

Henoticon of Zeno, 163.
Henricians, 227.
Henry IV., his reasons for leaving the Calvinists, 635.

Henry VIII., his early days, 328.
—— becomes enamoured of Anna Boleyn, 329.
—— marries her, 330.
—— writes against Luther, 277.
—— Death of, 339.
Hermengild, St., 93.
Hernhutters, 381.
Holy Ghost, Descent of, Berruyer's Error regarding, 625.
—— Divinity of, proved, 421.
Honorius, Pope, not a Monothelite, 181.
Huguenots, 304, 310.
Human nature, three states of, according to Baius, 568.
Humanity of Christ, Berruyer's Errors regarding, 613.
Hunneric, 90.
—— his horrible Death, 91.
Huss, John, 250.
—— translates Wickliffe's works, 251.
—— his Errors, 251.
—— comes to the Council of Constance, 253.
—— dies at the stake, 254.
Hypsisteri, 100.

Iconoclasts, 188.
Ignatius, St., of Constantinople, 201.
—— dreadful persecution endured by, 204.
—— appeals to the Pope, 205.
—— forced to sign his own deposition, 206.
Ignorants, 169.
Incorruptibilists, 170.
"In eminenti," Bull of, 571.
Infidels, Doctrine of the Church concerning, 456.
Interim, the, of Charles V., 271.

Jacobites, 169.
James I., 316.
Jansenius, Bishop of Ghent, 365.
—— Bishop of Ipres, 365.
—— Errors of, refuted, 576.
Jarnac, Battle of, 311.
Jeane, Queen of Navarre, a Calvinist, 310.
Jerome of Prague, 255.
—— put to death, 255.
Joachim, Abbot, 232.
John, St., Pope, 92.
John, St., of Damascus, 193.
Jovian, Emperor, 84.
Jovinian, a Monk, his Heresy, 105.
—— denied the Virginity of the Blessed Virgin, 105.
—— this Error refuted, 106.
Julian the Apostate, 82.
—— his Death, 83.

Kant, his system of religion, 380.
Knox, John, 313.

GENERAL INDEX.

Knox, John, establishes Calvinism in Scotland, 313.

Lateran, Fourth Council of, 239.
—— Decrees of, 239.
—— condemns the Albigenses, 239.
Latrocinium Ephesinum, 142.
—— proceedings of, 143, 144.
Law, Divine, not impossible, 516.
Leo X. publishes the Bull against Luther, 264.
Leo the Isaurian an Iconoclast, 191.
Leyden, John of, Life and Death of, 286.
Liberius, Pope, banished, 73.
—— signs one of the Formulas of Sirmium, 77.
Liberius, his Death, 84.
Library of Constantinople burned, 191.
Lisosius, a Heretic, 224.
Lucifer of Cagliari, 82.
Luther, Martin, his Birth, 258.
—— becomes an Augustinian Friar, 259.
—— attacks Indulgences, 260.
—— interview with Cardinal Cajetan, 261.
—— burns the Pope's Bull and Decretals, 264.
—— marries a Nun, 267.
—— his Death, 270.
—— his Errors. Forty-one propositions condemned, 273.
—— threatens to recant, 563.
Lutherans invited to the Council of Trent, 270.
Lyons, Council of, 217.
—— Synodical Constitution of, 218.

Macedonians condemned, 97.
—— —— refuted, 421.
Macedonius, 95.
—— —— thousands put to death at his inauguration, 95.
—— —— persecutes the Catholics, 95.
—— —— his errors, 96.
Magus, Simon, 33.
Mahometanism, 177.
Manes, 44.
Manichean Heresy, 44.
Marcion, 40.
Marpurg, Conference of, 266.
Mary, Queen of England, 343.
Mary, Queen of Scots, forced to resign, 314.
—— puts herself under Elizabeth's protection, 315.
—— beheaded, 316.
Mass, Errors concerning condemned, 513.
Materialism, Refutation of, 408.
Matthias, Flaccus Illiricus, 280.
Maximus, St., refutes Pyrrhus, 184.
Mediation of Christ necessary, 630.
Meditation, what, 591.

Melancthon, character of, 279.
Melchites, 169.
Menander, 34.
Menandrinus, his errors, 244.
Mennonites, 287.
Mercy of God, 530.
Messalians, 100.
Messalian errors, 101.
Methodists, origin of, 382.
—— doctrine of, 383.
Michael Paleologus, excommunicated by Nicholas III., 219.
Milan, Council of, 72.
Ministers, Calvinistic, why so called, 299.
Miracles of Christ, Berruyer's errors concerning the, 623.
Miseries of human nature, 575.
Molinism refuted, 592.
Molinos, 377.
—— condemnation of, 378.
Mongus, 164.
Monophysites, 168.
Monothelite Heresy refuted, 199.
Monothelites, 179.
—— objections of, answered, 484.
Montanus, 40.
Montfort, Count, his glorious Death, 238.
Moravians, 381.
Mormon, book of, 387.
Mormonites, 387.
Mother of God, the Blessed Virgin, 466.
—— —— Objections to the doctrine, answered, 469.
Munzer, an Anabaptist, 285.
—— put to death, 286.
Musculus, Andrew, 282.

Natural Religion, Berruyer's opinion of, 627.
Negative Reprobation, 550.
Nestorius, his origin, 119.
—— made Bishop of Constantinople, 119.
—— promulgates his Heresy, 120.
—— his Death, 130.
New Jerusalemites, 381.
New Testament, Quesnel's, 371.
Nice, Council of, 58.
Nicene Canons, 63.
—— Profession of Faith, 61.
Nicholites, 36.
Nicholites, New, 224.
Noailles de, Cardinal, his Death, 375.
Novatian, 49.
—— first anti-Pope, 50.
Novatus, 49.

Ochino, an Antitrinitarian, 354.
—— his life as a Friar, 354.
—— his Death, 356.
Olaus Petri, 271.
Omousion, 60.
One Person in Christ, 458.

GENERAL INDEX.

Ophites, 38.
Opus Operatum, explanation of, 321.
Orebites, 256.
Origen, 45.
——— Editions of the Scriptures by, 46.
——— Errors of, 47.
Orphans, Hussites so called, 256.
Osiander, an Eutychian, 281.
Osius, fall of, 74.

Pattalorinchites, 41.
Paul of Samosata. 43.
Peasants, War of the, 285.
Pelagian Heresy, 109.
Pelagian objections answered, 449.
Pelagianism refuted, 443.
Pelagius, a Briton, 109.
People of God, History of, 597.
Peputians, 41.
Perieres, 359.
Peter Martyr, 295.
Peter the Fuller, 164.
Petrobrussians, Errors of, 226.
Phantasiasts, 170.
Philip the Landgrave marries two wives, 269.
Photius, 202.
——— condemned at Rome, 207.
——— excommunicates the Pope, 209.
Pietists, 381.
Pillar and Ground of Truth, the Church, 552.
Piscatorians, 325.
Pius V., St., excommunicates Elizabeth, 347.
Pneumatomachi, 26.
Pogonatus, Constantine, 186.
Poissy, Conference of, 304.
Pole, Cardinal, 336.
——————————— reconciles England to the Church, 343.
Polyglott, Origen's, 46.
Poor Men of Lyons, 233.
Postellus, 360.
——— his fanaticism, 360.
Praxeas, 42.
Preadamites, 359.
Predestinarians, 116.
Predestination, Calvinistic, 320.
——————— Catholic doctrine of, 544.
——————— to Hell, Calvin's doctrine, 543.
——————— secret of, 590.
Presbyterians, 324.
Priscillianists, 102.
Procession of the Holy Ghost, 433.
Prodicus, 39.
Proterius, St., Martyrdom of, 158.
Protestant, origin of the name, 266.
Protestants refuse to attend the Council of Trent, 560.
Ptolemy and Saturninus, 38.

Pulcheria, St., 149.
Pure Nature, state of, not impossible, 573.
Purgatory, denied by Calvin, 323.
——— Greek belief in, 221.
Puritans, 323.

Quakers 324.
Quesnel, 371.
——— escapes to Holland, 371.
——— his Death, 372.
Quesnelism, 375.

Ranters, 325.
Rationalism, 380.
Real Presence, Miracles in proof of, 248, 249.
——————— proved, 489.
——————— objections to, answered, 496.
Remonstrants, 326.
Rhetoricians and Theologians, disputation between, 257.
Richer, his doctrine, 376.
Rimini, Council of, 81.
Robe, Holy, of Treves, 889.
Roman people defend the Veneration of Images, 192
Sabellians, objections answered, 396.
Sabellianism refuted, 391.
Sabellius, 43.
Sacramentarians opposed by Luther, 278.
——————— origin of, 288.
——————— objections answered, 503.
Sacraments, the Calvinistic opinions on 321.
Salvation of all, Christ died for, 564.
——————— God wishes, 544.
Sardis, Council of, 71.
Saturninus, 35.
Scotland, Reformation established in, 313.
Scotus Erigena, 225.
Seekers, 343.
Semi-Pelagians, 115.
——————— Doctrine of, 116.
Sepulchre, Jesus Christ in the, 610.
Servetus, his History, 350.
——— his Errors, 350.
——— burned alive, 303.
Sethites, 38.
Severus, 39.
"Silence, Religious," Jansenistic, 370.
Sin, God not the author of, 539.
Sirmium, first Formula of, 75.
——— second Formula of, 76.
——— third Formula of, 76.
Six Articles of Henry VIII., 335.
Smalkalde, League of, 269.
Smith, Joe, 387.
Socinian Heresy, 357.
Socinus Lelius and Faustus, 356.
Somerset, Protector 340.
Sophronius, St., 180.
Southcott, Johanna, 386.
——— Delusion and Death. 387.

2 s

GENERAL INDEX.

Spinosa, 361.
────── his Atheistical Doctrine, 361.
────── his Death, 362.
Spire, Diet of 266.
"Spiritual Guide of Molinos," 378.
Stancaro, Francis, a Nestorian, 281.
Stephen and Lisosius, Heretics, 223.
Stephens', Robert, Edition of New Testament, 394.
Stilites, St. Simon, 160.
────── his Death, 162.
Storchius, Chief of the Anabaptists, 285.
Sudbury, Archbishop of Canterbury, killed, 246.
Supper, the Calvinistic, 299.
Supremacy, Oath of, 346.
Sweden, Lutheranism introduced into, 271.
────── becomes Lutheran, 271.
Swedenborg, extraordinary doctrine taught by, 381.

Tatian, 39.
Temptation, God does not lead us into, 539.
Tertullian, 45.
Tetzel preaches Indulgences, 260.
Thaborites, 256.
Theandric operations, 617.
Theodoret, account of, 147.
Theodoric, his extraordinary Death, 93.
Theodosius, the Eutychian, 155.
Theodotus, 42.
Three Chapters, the, 132.
─────────── condemnation of, 174.
Transubstantiation, doctrine of, 428.
─────────── objections to, answered, 501.
Trent, Council of, 269.
Tritheists, 170.
Type, the, of Constans, 183.
Tyre, Council of, 66.

Ubiquists, 282.
"Unigenitus," Bull of, 273.
────── Four Bishops appeal against, 374.

Unitarians, 356.
United Brethren, 381.
Ursacius and Valens, 79.

Valens, 79.
────── an Arian, 80.
────── Emperor, persecutes the Catholics, 85.
────── his horrible Death, 87.
Valentine, 38.
Vigilantius, 108.
────── opposed by St. Jerome, 108.
Vigilius, Pope, censured, 174.

Waldenses, 233.
────── Errors of, 239.
Waldo, Peter, 233.
Watch Night, 386.
Wesley goes to America, 383.
────── appoints a Bishop, 384.
────── his Death, 384.
Whitfield, a Calvinist, 384.
Wickliffe, 245.
────── doctrine condemned, 246.
────── his Death, 249.
Wills, two, in Christ, 481.
Wolsey, Cardinal, 329.
Word, the Divinity of, proved, 400.
"Work of Light," the Reformation, 311.
Works, good, necessary, 520.
Worms, Diet of, 265.

Zeno, Emperor, 160.
────── Henoticon of, 163.
Zinzendorf, 381.
Ziska, the Hussite, 256.
Zozymus, Pope, condemns Pelagius, 114.
Zuinglius, Heresy of, 290.
────── consecration, explanation of the words of, 291.
────── disputation with the Catholics, 292.
────── marries; is killed, 293.

THE END.

Printed by J. M. O'TOOLE, 13, Hawkins'-street, Dublin.

Other Books by St Athanasius Press

Religious Orders of Women in the U.S.
by Elinor Tong Dehey. Hardcover.
Unedited Reprint of the 1930 Revised Edition. 908 Pages.
Catholic. Retail $59.99

Terra Incognita or Convents of the United Kingdom
by John Nicholas Murphy. 757 pages. Unedited Reprint
of 1873 book. Catholic. Retail $59.99

*A Textual Concordance to the Holy Scriptures
Douay Rheims Version* by Thomas David Williams
HardCover. Unedited Reprint of the 1908 Original.
848 Pages. Catholic. Retail $49.99

*VESTIARIVM CHRISTIANVM: The Dress of Holy Ministry
in the Church-Christian Vestments.* **Unedited** *Reprint of the
1868 Original. 406 Pages, 62+ pages of Illustrations.
Hardcover. Anglican. Retail $49.99*

*Church Ornaments of our Manufacture. 1910 Benziger
Bros Catalog. Softcover. Unedited Reprint of Benziger's
1910 catalog. Fully Illustrated. Catholic. Retail $24.99*

Vera Sapentia Or True Wisdom by Thomas A Kempis.
Softcover. Unedited Reprint of 1904 book. Catholic
Retail $19.99

For Ordering info, please email wallmell@aol.com
*or call 1-800-230-1025
Or Write: St Athanasius Press/St Joan of Arc Books
133 Slazing Rd
Potosi, WI 53820*

Bookstore inquiries are welcome!

www.ingramcontent.com/pod-product-compliance
Lightning Source LLC
Chambersburg PA
CBHW020629230426
43665CB00008B/91